Historical Evolution of Strategic Management
Volume I

History of Management Thought
Series Editor: Derek S. Pugh

Titles in the Series:

Contingency Theory
Lex Donaldson

Management Science: An Anthology, Vols I, II and III
Samuel Eilon

Complex Organizations
Richard H. Hall

Managerial Decision Making
David J. Hickson

Market Research Theory
Dale Littler

Historical Evolution of Strategic Management, Vols I and II
Peter McKiernan

Administrative and Management Theory
John B. Miner

Human Relations: Theory and Developments
Lyman W. Porter & Gregory A. Bigley

Comparative Cross Cultural Management
Derek S. Pugh

Critical Perspectives on Organization and Management Theory
Linda Smircich & Marta B. Calás

Post-Modern Management Theory
Marta B. Calás & Linda Smircich

Early Management Thought
Daniel A. Wren

Historical Evolution of Strategic Management
Volume I

Edited by

Peter McKiernan

*Professor of Management, University of St Andrews,
and Visiting Professor of Strategic Management,
University of Warwick*

Dartmouth
Aldershot • Brookfield USA • Singapore • Sydney

© Peter McKiernan 1996. For copyright of individual articles please refer to Acknowledgements.

All rights reserved. No part of this publication may be reproduced, stored in a retrieval system, or transmitted in any form or by any means, electronic, mechanical, photocopying, recording, or otherwise without the prior permission of Dartmouth Publishing Company Limited.

Published by
Dartmouth Publishing Company Limited
Gower House
Croft Road
Aldershot
Hants GU11 3HR
England

Dartmouth Publishing Company
Old Post Road
Brookfield
Vermont 05036
USA

British Library Cataloguing in Publication Data
Historical evolution of strategic management. – (History of
  management thought)
 1. Strategic planning 2. Strategic planning – History
 I. McKiernan, Peter
 658.4'012

Library of Congress Cataloging-in-Publication Data
Historical evolution of strategic management / edited by Peter
  McKiernan.
          p. cm.— (History of management thought)
    Includes bibliographical references and index.
    ISBN 1-85521-797-X
    1. Strategic planning–History. I. McKiernan, Peter.
  II. Series: History of management thought (Aldershot, England)
  HD30.28.H575 1996
  658.4'012—dc20   96–984
                                                                  CIP

ISBN 1 85521 797 X

Printed in Great Britain at the University Press, Cambridge

Contents

Acknowledgements	vii
Editor's Note	ix
Series Preface	xi
Introduction	xiii

PART I   THE PLANNING AND PRACTICE SCHOOL

1   Chester I. Barnard (1956), 'Chapter XVIII: Conclusion', in *The Functions of the Executive*, Cambridge, MA: Harvard University Press, pp. 285–96.   3
2   Kenneth R. Andrews (1971), 'The Concept of Corporate Strategy', in *The Concept of Corporate Strategy*, Homewood, IL: Dow Jones-Irwin, pp. 18–46.   15
3   H. Igor Ansoff (1987), 'Concept of Strategy', in *Corporate Strategy*, London: Penguin Books, pp. 100–116.   45
4   George A. Steiner (1969), 'A Conceptual and Operational Model of Corporate Planning', in *Top Management Planning*, Toronto: Collier-Macmillan, pp. 31–61.   63
5   Sidney Schoeffler, Robert D. Buzzell and Donald F. Heany (1974), 'Impact of Strategic Planning on Profit Performance', *Harvard Business Review*, March-April, pp. 137–45.   95
6   The Boston Consulting Group, Inc. (1970), 'Costs and Experience', 'Price and Experience' and 'Experience and Competitive Interaction', in *Perspectives on Experience*, Boston: The Boston Consulting Group, Inc., pp. 12–26.   105
7   Pierre Wack (1985), 'Scenarios: Shooting the Rapids', *Harvard Business Review*, November-December, pp. 139–50.   121
8   Arie P. De Geus (1988), 'Planning as Learning', *Harvard Business Review*, March-April, pp. 70–74.   133

PART II   THE LEARNING SCHOOL

The Natural Selection View
9   Bill McKelvey and Howard Aldrich (1983), 'Populations, Natural Selection, and Applied Organizational Science', *Administrative Science Quarterly*, **28**, pp. 101–28.   143

The Incremental View

10 Charles E. Lindblom (1959), 'The Science of "Muddling Through"', *Public Administration Review*, **19**, pp. 79–88. — 173

11 Aaron Wildavsky (1973), 'If Planning is Everything, Maybe It's Nothing', *Policy Sciences*, **4**, pp. 127–53. — 183

12 James Brian Quinn (1978), 'Strategic Change: "Logical Incrementalism"', *Sloan Management Review*, Fall, pp. 7–21. — 211

13 Gerry Johnson (1988), 'Rethinking Incrementalism', *Strategic Management Journal*, **9**, pp. 75–91. — 227

The Cultural View

14 P.H. Grinyer and J.C. Spender (1979), 'Recipes, Crises, and Adaptation in Mature Businesses', *International Studies of Management and Organization*, **IX**, pp. 113–33. — 247

15 Alan Sheldon (1980), 'Organizational Paradigms: A Theory of Organizational Change', *Organizational Dynamics*, **8**, pp. 61–80. — 269

The Political View

16 D.J. Hickson, C.R. Hinings, C.A. Lee, R.E. Schneck and J.M. Pennings (1971), 'A Strategic Contingencies' Theory of Intraorganizational Power', *Administrative Science Quarterly*, **16**, pp. 216–29. — 291

17 Herbert A. Simon (1979), 'Rational Decision Making in Business Organizations', *American Economic Review*, **69**, pp. 493–513. — 305

18 John Child (1972), 'Organizational Structure, Environment and Performance: The Role of Strategic Choice', *Sociology*, **6**, pp. 1–22. — 327

19 Andrew M. Pettigrew (1977), 'Strategy Formulation as a Political Process', *International Studies of Management and Organization*, **VII**, pp. 78–87. — 349

20 Andrew M. Pettigrew (1992), 'On Studying Managerial Elites', *Strategic Management Journal*, **13**, pp. 163–82. — 359

The Visionary View

21 David K. Hurst, James C. Rush and Roderick E. White (1989), 'Top Management Teams and Organizational Renewal', *Strategic Management Journal*, **10**, pp. 87–105. — 381

Patterns of Strategy Development

22 Henry Mintzberg (1973), 'Strategy-Making in Three Modes', *California Management Review*, **XVI**, pp. 44–53. — 403

23 Henry Mintzberg and James A. Waters (1985), 'Of Strategies, Deliberate and Emergent', *Strategic Management Journal*, **6**, pp. 257–72. — 413

24 Ellen Earle Chaffee (1985), 'Three Models of Strategy', *Academy of Management Review*, **10**, pp. 89–98. — 429

Name Index — 439

Acknowledgements

The editor and publishers wish to thank the following for permission to use copyright material.

Academy of Management for the essay: Ellen Earle Chaffee (1985), 'Three Models of Strategy', *Academy of Management Review*, **10**, pp. 89–98.

Administrative Science Quarterly for the essays: Bill McKelvey and Howard Aldrich (1983), 'Populations, Natural Selection, and Applied Organizational Science', *Administrative Science Quarterly*, **28**, pp. 101–28. Copyright © 1983 by Cornell University. D.J. Hickson, C.R. Hinings, C.A. Lee, R.E. Schneck and J.M. Pennings (1971), 'A Strategic Contingencies' Theory of Intraorganizational Power', *Administrative Science Quarterly*, **16**, pp. 216–29.

American Economic Association for the essay: Herbert A. Simon (1979), 'Rational Decision Making in Business Organizations', *American Economic Review*, **69**, pp. 493–513.

American Management Association for the essay: Alan Sheldon (1980), 'Organizational Paradigms: A Theory of Organizational Change', *Organizational Dynamics*, **8**, pp. 61–80. Copyright © 1980 AMACOM, a division of American Management Association. All rights reserved.

American Society for Public Administration for the essay: Charles E. Lindblom (1959), 'The Science of "Muddling Through"', *Public Administration Review*, **19**, pp. 79–88.

H. Igor Ansoff, 'Concept of Strategy', in *Corporate Strategy*, pp. 100–116. Copyright © McGraw-Hill, 1965, 1968. Revised edition copyright © H. Igor Ansoff, 1987.

The Boston Consulting Group for the essay: 'Costs and Experience', 'Price and Experience' and 'Experience and Competitive Interaction', in *Perspectives on Experience*, pp. 12–26. Copyright © 1968, 1970 and 1972 by The Boston Consulting Group, Inc. All rights reserved.

B.S.A. Publications Ltd for the essay: John Child (1972), 'Organizational Structure, Environment and Performance: The Role of Strategic Choice', *Sociology*, **6**, pp. 1–22.

California Management Review for the essay: Henry Mintzberg (1973), 'Strategy-Making in Three Modes', *California Management Review*, **XVI**, pp. 44–53. Copyright © 1973 by The Regents of the University of California. Reprinted by permission of The Regents.

Harvard Business Review for the essays: Sidney Schoeffler, Robert D. Buzzell and Donald F. Heany (1974), 'Impact of Strategic Planning on Profit Performance', *Harvard Business Review*, March-April, pp. 137–45; Pierre Wack (1985), 'Scenarios: Shooting the Rapids', *Harvard Business Review*, November-December, pp. 139–50; Arie P. De Geus (1988), 'Planning as Learning', *Harvard Business Review*, March-April, pp. 70–74.

Harvard University Press for the essay: Chester I. Barnard (1956), 'Chapter XVIII: Conclusion', in *The Functions of the Executive*, pp. 285–96. Copyright © 1938 by the President and Fellows of Harvard College.

Kluwer Academic Publishers for the essay: Aaron Wildavsky (1973), 'If Planning is Everything, Maybe It's Nothing', *Policy Sciences*, **4**, pp. 127–53.

M.E. Sharpe Inc. for the essays: P.H. Grinyer and J.C. Spender (1979), 'Recipes, Crises, and Adaptation in Mature Businesses', *International Studies of Management and Organization*, **IX**, pp. 113–33; Andrew M. Pettigrew (1977), 'Strategy Formulation as a Political Process', *International Studies of Management and Organization*, **VII**, pp. 78–87.

Simon & Schuster for the essay: George A. Steiner (1969), 'A Conceptual and Operational Model of Corporate Planning' in *Top Management Planning*, Collier-Macmillan, pp. 31–60. Reprinted with permission of The Free Press, a division of Simon & Schuster. Copyright © 1969 by The Trustees of Columbia University in the City of New York.

John Wiley & Sons, Ltd for the essays: Gerry Johnson (1988), 'Rethinking Incrementalism', *Strategic Management Journal*, **9**, pp. 75–91. Copyright © 1988 by John Wiley & Sons, Ltd. Andrew M. Pettigrew (1992), 'On Studying Managerial Elites', *Strategic Management Journal*, **13**, pp. 163–82. Copyright © 1992 by John Wiley & Son, Ltd. David K. Hurst, James C. Rush and Roderick E. White (1989), 'Top Management Teams and Organizational Renewal', *Strategic Management Journal*, **10**, pp. 87–105. Copyright © 1989 by John Wiley & Sons, Ltd. Henry Mintzberg and James A. Waters (1985), 'Of Strategies, Deliberate and Emergent', *Strategic Management Journal*, **6**, pp. 257–72. Copyright © 1985 by John Wiley & Sons, Ltd.

Every effort has been made to trace all the copyright holders, but if any have been inadvertently overlooked, the publishers will be pleased to make the necessary arrangement at the first opportunity.

Editor's Note

I would like to express my gratitude to the following strategic management scholars for their generosity and guidance, both in conversation and correspondence, in preparation for this collection. The final choice of readings was entirely my own and so my colleagues duly escape any blame for errors in the construction of history as it appears here. They are:

David Asch	Charles Baden-Fuller
Richard Bettis	Roland Calori
Andrew Campbell	Eric Cassells
Balaji Chakravarthy	Derek Channon
Richard D'Aveni	Bob de Wit
Colin Eden	Colin Egan
David Faulkner	Arthur Francis
Luciano Fratocchi	Ari Ginsberg
Robert Grant	Peter Grinyer
John Hassard	Bo Hellgron
Gerry Johnson	Sammy Kristamulijana
Joseph Mahoney	John McGee
Geoff Mallory	Hugh Macmillan
Terry McNulty	Leif Melin
Ron Meyer	Henry Mintzberg
Gordon Murray	Rajendran Pandian
Derek Pugh	Andrew Pettigrew
Ken Starkey	Jason Spender
Bernard Taylor	John Stopford
Hans Thorelli	Howard Thomas
Richard Whittington	Robin Wensley
Richard Whipp	David Wilson

The St Andrews Management Institute[1] kindly donated funds to cover the survey overheads, travel and library research. Their generosity is gratefully appreciated.

---

[1] An Institute formed by Shell, Scottish Enterprise and the University of St Andrews (Scotland) to foster research and consultancy in strategic management.

Series Preface

The *History of Management Thought* is based on the assumption that a knowledge of the intellectual history of an academic field is vital for a present day understanding of it. In the past scholars of management as a discipline have tended to ignore or underrate the historical development of their subject. This ignorance has encouraged the 'reinventing the wheel' and 'old wine in new bottles' phenomena which have plagued the subject of management since its birth. The insight that those who ignore history are condemned to repeat it, is surely most true about the development of ideas.

This indifference now appears to be beginning to change, and the history of management and management thought is attracting greater interest. The *History of Management Thought* builds on this development by presenting a number of volumes which cover the intellectual history of the subject. It makes available to a wide range of academics contributions to management thought that have been influential over the years. The volume topics range across the whole field of management studies from early management thought through to post-modern management theory.

Each volume in the *History of Management Thought* is edited by a leading international scholar who gives an introductory analytical historical review of the development of the subject, and then presents a selection of key articles. Many of these articles have previously only been published in journals, often in early volumes which are not generally available. They are now conveniently presented in book form, with each chosen article reproduced in full. They offer an important resource for use by academics and advanced students in the field for increasing their knowledge and understanding of the historical development of the disciplines of management.

DEREK S. PUGH
General Editor
History of Management Thought
Visiting Research Professor of
International Management
Open University Business School, UK

Introduction

Overview

This collection of readings, representing the historical evolution of the subject of strategic management, covers two volumes. The first provides an introduction to the roots of modern thought and proceeds to classify more recent contributions into four schools. Discussion of the first two of these, the Planning and Practice school and the Learning school, are contained in this volume. Discussions of the latter two, the Positioning and the Resource-Based schools, are featured in Volume II. It is essential that the two volumes are read in conjunction as the study is continuous and the division made solely for practical printing purposes.

The Origins of Strategic Management

The construction of history is replete with dilemmas. Significant ones involve perception and time. Scholars' individual perceptions of seminal articles that have forged the study 'domain' are often formed from their own functional heritage. In a multi-disciplinary area like strategic management, any consensus on milestones is likely to be limited. Moreover, some key publications contain a time fuse whose impact can be delayed until ignited by an appropriate context. Only in retrospect is their importance realized.

As part of the preparations for this two-volume set, a survey was undertaken among a body of active international researchers in the area to establish what they considered to be the most significant journal articles in the development of the field. Scholars were kind; the response rate, quality and speed were all pleasing. But, *besides confirming the above assertions*, a number of patterns were observed. Firstly, given the many underlying disciplinary pathways to the present, the selection of salient contributions was both difficult and varied. Secondly, and expectedly, there was a distinct separation of choice between the content and process schools. One hopes that this will not develop into an unnecessary intellectual schism which could be damaging to the subject's integrative evolution. Thirdly, and understandably, all quoted articles were published in the last 30 years, with over 80 per cent of them in the last 10 years. This probably reflects the reality of a new area, with the few specialist journals and schools dominated by a handful of authors in each decade since the 1960s. This collection aims to unravel the origins of these seminal contributions.

However, Cummings (1993) suggests that most converts to corporate strategy have little knowledge of where the pathways to the present began. Two generic sources have current momentum. One is the biological route that knows that natural competition has been around forever, acknowledges the partial role of Darwinian selection, builds to encapsulate Gause's principle of competitive exclusion and adds the central gifts of imagination and logic to differentiate the strategist from the rest. Henderson (1989) argues that Darwin is probably a better guide to business competition than economists are. The other is the more traditional heritage by way of military analogy. In the East, China's oldest military classic, *The Art of*

War (*c*.500 BC) – with its claim that the highest form of leadership is to overcome the enemy by strategy – provides a succinct exposition of planning, organization, tactics and the seizure of opportunities. In the West, the parallel is with the ancient Athenian position of *strategos*, coined during the democratic reforms of Kleisthenes (508 BC) in reference to the leaders of the military and political sub-units that formed the Athenian war council. Salient *strategoi* included Pericles, Philip of Macedon, Aristotle and Alexander the Great; Aineias wrote the earliest surviving Western volume on military strategy (*c*.450 BC) and Frontinus provided the first specific definition of strategy (C1 AD), referring to a commander's achievements, which are characterized by foresight, advantage, enterprise and resolution. Certainly, contemporary terminology in strategic management has a military flavour and so this pathway cannot easily be denied. However, its assumption of a zero-sum game does not readily embrace the popular contemporary strategies of collaboration and renewal.

Fourthly, and significantly, the picture painted had a distinct North American hue. Clearly, important inputs to the subject's development have enjoyed that heritage. But it would be erroneous to accept, unquestioningly, that any single geographic source has monopolized the history of thought in the subject. For instance, the two major historic strands outlined above have very different origins. Moreover, much of the Greek-inspired military pathway can be traced through mediaeval Europe where it is pivotal in Machiavelli's *Prince*. Indeed, drawing on case material from the *strategoi*, Machiavelli warned several times that 'for intellectual training, the prince must read history, studying the actions of eminent men to see how they conducted themselves during war and to discover the reasons for their victories or their defeats, so he can avoid the latter and imitate the former'. From here, the threads can be discerned in the writings of the great French and German generals, Foch and von Clausewitz, in the 19th century.

Our construction of history must therefore be considered. The history of strategy is ancient, not modern; global and not entirely American. A perceived dominance by the latter must be tempered with broader views of replication and precedence. For instance, to mention the strategy-structure relationship is immediately to invoke the meritorious work of Chandler on large US businesses, but the 19th-century evolution of this relationship in America could easily have been identified 200 years earlier in the Japanese *Zaibatsu*. Research on latter-day *Keiretsu* as well as the *Chaebol* in Korea helps to prove the point. Similarly, the seminal work of Mintzberg (1979; read Canada) and Miller and Mintzberg (1984) on design parameters in organizational structures has long-established parallels in the UK stemming from the pioneering Aston studies of Pugh, Hickson et al. (1969).

This compilation is not immune from the editor's own ethnocentricity. However, it attempts, through the reading of history, to piece together the routes to our common stock of knowledge in strategic management and the flows to future stocks. It aims to provide a comprehensive collection of essays that can be readily accessed by academics, particularly where large collections of journals are not available in their institutions. Editorial policy limits the selection of extracts from the more expensive journals (e.g. *Harvard Business Review*) and from books (in such ways, history is massaged). Ironically, much of the material for modern frameworks in strategic management is sourced in books. This was especially so in the 1960s, when volumes by Ansoff, Chandler, Learned, Christensen, Andrews and Guth, and Steiner supplied the cornerstones of policy and planning. Guidelines also limit the number of papers chosen. To handle this, the collection deliberately closes around 1992.

Emergent patterns have unfortunately been omitted in order to concentrate on the main adopted routes. For instance, there is a pattern that can be traced back to Machiavelli (again) that emerged in the work of the industrial organization theorists from Schelling to Shapiro and Ghemawat by way of Cournot, Nash, Dixit and Baumol that dealt with the game theoretic approach. This technology has not transferred readily to mainstream strategic management. Its mathematical exposition may have been an entry barrier, preventing many scholars from mastering the language. But as Bronowski (1973) pointed out in the *Ascent of Man* when analysing the classic treatise on *Theory of Games* by von Neumann and Morgenstern (1943), 'what is running through the page is a clear intellectual line like a tune, and all the heavy weight of equations is simply the orchestration in the bass'. There is nothing too complex about this approach that should prevent its broader adoption in strategy formulation and choice, for instance in the area of acquisitions or conjectural variation. A further casualty is the networking pathway, in particular the link into international business activities endorsed by Swedish scholars like Johanson, Vahlne, Mattson, Hallen and Forsgren and reflected in the work of Prahalad, Hamel and Doz. One final and crucial area that does not receive sufficient treatment here is the managerial cognition research captured in the work of authors like Huff (1990) and Senge (1992) and important to our better understanding of decision making, alliances, competitive positioning and the development of the learning organization. Origins can be found in the work of Weick in the 1960s, and the pedigree remained strong in the 1970s and 1980s through the influence of Anderson and Paine (1975), Shrivastava and Schneider (1984) and Smircich and Stubbart (1985), among others. However, until the late 1980s, only a few scholars were fully conversant with the technical aspects of cognitive research methodology. Since then the field has broadened sufficiently to become a credible option. Game theoretic applications, networking and cognitive mapping should all become more central to the field, and future volumes on its history will no doubt specify their pathways.

For this collection, strategic management history has been divided into four main branches. These pertain to the Planning and Practice school and the Learning school (Volume I), and the Positioning school and the Resource-Based school (Volume II). Each has been fully incorporated into mainstream conceptual thinking and empirical testing. These represent the prominent influential disciplines that have forged the domain; they also help to provide a trans-Atlantic balance. Perhaps more important, they heed the advice of Machiavelli and look back before the 1960s for their historical roots. However, these four schools should not be seen as mutually exclusive avenues down which to travel. A better analogy is to see them as strands interwoven to form a strong rope. Authors appearing in one have also been influential in others. Andrews, whose work clearly shapes the Planning school, also contributed significantly to the Positioning school in the Harvard tradition of Porter. Equally, Rumelt has made important contributions to both the Resource-Based and the Positioning schools.

Part I: The Planning and Practice School

As a teaching subject, business policy had its origins at the beginning of the 20th century in the business schools. As a research subject, emphasis and systematic work did not begin until the 1960s, rather late in the study of organizations generally. The Industrial Revolution had produced Scottish and English pioneers in the evolution of modern management thought. From Steuart, Smith, Watt, Owen, Arkwright and others were received the principles of authority, specialization, control, standard operating procedures, planning, personnel policies, cost accounting and scientific management (such concepts were well known to the Sumerians, Egyptians, Hebrews and Chinese). Later, similar American contributions were consolidated in the Scientific Management school of Towne, Metcalfe, Halsey, Taylor and the Gilbreths. Thus, moving from 18th- and 19th-century Europe through to 20th-century America, the focus of thought was on internal organizational activities.

Early 20th-century writers such as Fayol, Church, Sheldon and Brech broadened this mechanistic approach to embrace the integration of these specialized activities within the organization. Porter (1991) recognizes this as the first concept of strategy. However, as Spender (1993) points out, 'prior to the 1930s, there seemed to be little difference between theories of organisations, their management and of their strategy'. As with the military analogy, strategy was essentially about large and long-term decisions, a view that still pervades the literature. But Barnard (1938) provided two crucial insights. First, he split organization theory from both management and strategy, with the latter dealing with executive leadership which was, he claimed, the most limiting factor in the organization: 'the functions of the executive ... are those of control, management, supervision and administration in formal organisations'. Secondly, where much of the science of management dealt with the creation of efficiency, Barnard suggested that other managerial work should focus on effectiveness which necessarily coupled the organization with its environment. This notion of organizational 'fit' formed the bedrock of modern analytical approaches to the subject and is, Porter (1991) claims, the second view of strategy. Chapter 13 of Barnard's book deals with this 'Environment of Decision'. His appendix is a marvellous treatise on the 'mind in everyday affairs' which should be the starting point for all scholars new to the cognitive mapping field. Chapter 1 in this volume is his concluding chapter which synthesizes his theory, providing inspiration for the development of SWOT analysis (SWOT = Strengths, Weaknesses, Opportunities and Threats) as well as an awareness of moral and ethical conduct.

Barnard's influence was extensive. His physical, personal, social and organizational systems were reflected in the key Harvard casebook authored by Learned, Christensen, Andrews and Guth in 1965. Andrews, who wrote the text material, was heavily influenced by Chandler's view of strategy. As Chandler's writing is widely available, it is not directly included here but its influence on shaping thinking in the genesis of a new research arena in the 1960s should never be underestimated. For instance, Andrews split strategy into formulation and implementation, dividing it neatly, after Chandler, into the four components of (a) market opportunity (what the firm *might* do), (b) corporate competence (what the firm *could* do), (c) personal aspirations (what the firm *wants* to do) and (d) social responsibility (what the firm *should* do). Strategy formulation thus dealt with external and internal influences and its decisions had to balance this 'fit'. Further, in recognizing the importance of the internal resources of the firm, Andrews had borrowed the notion of 'distinctive competence' from Selznick (1957). Porter (1991) claims this to be the third view of strategy, where firms gain competitive advantage through clever use of their heterogeneous resource set. Spender (1993) traces this to the evolutionary systems models utilized by Henderson and Follet. Whatever its origin, the resource-based view subsequently developed into a separate field of endeavour in the subject's evolution.

The work of Learned et al. emphasized the SWOT approach and became known as the Design school (Mintzberg, 1994) for its belief that strategy formation was a process of conception. Sadly, however, perhaps due to a naive interpretation of reality, it contributed to a schism in the subject – a division between research into strategy content (formulation) and process (implementation) that has left permanent and indelible scars. Chapter 2 is from Andrews's own 1971 book. It deals with definitions and concepts, the divorce between formulation and implementation and the limitations of strategy – none of which changed much from the 1965 text.

At the same time as the Harvard school was consolidating its case history in the Learned et al. text, a parallel development, which became known as the Planning school, emerged. Disillusioned both by scholars in decision theory and microeconomics and by the work of behaviouralists (e.g. Cyert and March) to deal satisfactorily with all classes of decisions in firms, Ansoff (1965) developed his own model of the *strategic* decision process. Concerned with the scope and direction of business growth, he showed how the evolving field of capital investment theory was inadequate in dealing with product-market decisions (1965, pp. 24–7). Though there was little difference between them in terms of model specification, the characteristics of Ansoff's approach were the opposite of the Design school's simplicity and informality. His was detailed and comprehensive; the planner was more significant than the chief executive; strategy output was generic rather than uniquely designed, and the terminology of *corporate* as opposed to *business* strategy was emphasized. Importantly, though these differences distinguish Ansoff's value added, similarities between these schools are germane to understanding the development of the modern domain. Environment, market positioning and internal resource capability were placed centre stage. Chapter 3 by Ansoff entitled 'Concept of Strategy' was generously described by the major Planning school critic, Mintzberg (1994), as 'among the best in the business literature'.

Planning school concepts of the 1960s were adapted for broad implementation and so popularized over the next decade on both sides of the Atlantic, by Ackoff (1970), Argenti (1974) and Steiner (1969) among others. Steiner's output was the most prolific. His original text (800 pages) drew upon his work experience in developing the corporate planning programme at the Lockheed Aircraft Company in the 1950s. Steiner believed that the formula for successful management was a first-rate planning system coupled with personal charisma and a sense of competitive urgency. He declared that 'during the last ten years the rapid expansion of comprehensive corporate planning has been matched only by the great dynamism with which new techniques, methods, and approaches have been injected into it' (1969). Though containing a framework similar to that of the Design school, his approach differed in its utter comprehensiveness across the organization, the prescriptive ordering of its stages, the precision and detail within them, and its universal applicability. Fundamentally, the model embraced the notion that such well-developed planning systems were indispensable to top management as well as a necessary, if not sufficient, condition for performance enhancement. This notion was later to be challenged conceptually by academic writers (see, for instance, Grinyer, 1973) and empirically by the innovative and flexible Japanese businesses. Chapter 4, from his 1969 text, illustrates the totality of the technique and its underlying philosophy.

Steiner's work linked planning theory with practice. The school had embraced the whole organization and given it a long-term horizon, but it was still mechanical and prescriptive and remained essentially corporate. Strategic planning, emphasizing the concept of strategy, did not appear until later in the 1970s. Academics (*pace* Chandler, Ansoff and Andrews) had originally raised the strategy concept issue and, as Schendel (1992) argues, there is little written today that cannot be traced back to their work. However, between the academics and practitioners were the management consultants who were a key influence in the shaping of strategic management. They wove a pattern between the two extremes, touching each with their observation and empirical experimentation. One of the earliest and most influential of these was the Boston Consulting Group (BCG), founded by Bruce Henderson in the early 1960s. His pragmatic observations on costs and prices gave rise to the study of the experience curve concept whereby all costs (capital, administrative, research and marketing) fell with increases in output and so, *ceteris paribus*, with increases in market share. This was a dynamic view of business strategy since first movers attained lowest cost and generated substantial cash flows to offset competitors' manoeuvres. The growth-share matrix evolved from this research and from directly confronting the contemporary problems of such diversified businesses as the Mead Paper Company. The fundamentals of the BCG's concept are included here as Chapter 6 in an excerpt from their own book *Perspectives on Experience* where the dynamics of costs, prices, competitive interaction and market share are articulated for the business executive.

About the same time (1972), independent research from the PIMS (Profitability Impact on Marketing Strategies) initiative provided some support for the positive association between market share and profitability. PIMS was organized by the Marketing Science Institute, affiliated to the Harvard Business School. It was another influence that linked an academic faculty with business planners. The original work began at the General Electric Company in 1960 and developed into a sharing of data and experience among major North American companies. Chapter 5 is the classic *HBR* essay from 1974 which addresses the crucial relationship between strategic planning and profit performance. It also includes an important caveat on the social justice of this type of research in capitalist economies.

Drawing on received history and experience, the Design and Planning schools – both influencers and practitioners – laid down many of the modern principles of strategic management in the 1960s, though they may not have invented the philosophy. They brought together the organization, its environment and resources in a multi-level framework. Analysis was provided by the comprehensive, yet qualitative, SWOT technique. Though well understood by practitioners, it was firm specific, ambiguous and not conducive to the rigorous appraisal of measurable categories. Hence, academic research into the complexity and specificity of the strategy problem was delayed. The onus was still upon the profession (or practice) at this juncture, rather than upon the development of a discipline. The impetus for the latter was to come mainly from other areas in the 1970s.

Besides the influential role of consultants, the corporate planning functions of large corporations were laboratories for the application and development of environmental analytical techniques. In particular, where the horizons were genuinely long term (for example in the oil sector), traditional forecasting methods proved futile for the prediction of raw material availability, oil prices and economic and political conditions over 25 years. Shell pioneered the construction of scenario models against which strategies could be evaluated. Scenarios represent a consistent and coherent view of the pattern of future variables and how these may interact. Shell had some early success in the anticipation of the quadrupling of the oil price in 1974 and again in 1978. Their approach was refined into a sophisticated analysis by the 1990s which drew upon the best multidisciplinary counsel available, including authors in these volumes, in creating scenarios over a two-year cycle. Chapter 7 by Pierre Wack, the main scenario instigator at Shell, is a comprehensive description of the process. His Shell colleague Arie De Geus, who directed the planning function, adds a complementary essay aptly entitled 'Planning as Learning' which helps to link this section with the next.

Part II: The Learning School

The Planning school preached that strategy could be formulated in a deliberate manner, with implementation following in a controlled sequence. Objectives were thereby achieved and the strategy realized. There was always a danger that this could become the unchallenged, entrenched view which it did. Ironically, it still is the preferred pedagogical layout for the major teaching texts. However, observations of both the process and effectiveness of strategy in practice jarred with this rational-analytic view. In reality, some intended strategies were not realized and many others emerged informally. It was clear that the Planning school was only one of many approaches to strategy development. For instance, organizational studies scholars challenged intentional choice and outcome, embraced notions of bounded rationality, context, politics, power and chance in choice processes and went on to study strategic change in implementation. There was an emphasis on organizational adaptability since the rational process was inherently constrained by both external and internal variables whose behaviour was unpredictable or simply unknown. This work, broadly grouped, became known as the Learning school (though Mintzberg, 1990, has a tighter definition). To gain a clear understanding, five views of the school are identified here.

The Natural Selection View

This view has a long tradition in the history of thought. At bottom, its arguments are based on change and difference. The variables in an organization's environment can be so powerful and unpredictable that no synoptic strategy can cope. The organization is constantly buffeted and has to react rather than plan; internally, organizations defy the neoclassical economic assumptions of homogeneity. They are different in terms of resources, culture, power centres, processes and systems. Since specific combinations will inevitably be more effective in certain environmental conditions than others, some organizations will survive and others will perish. Chapter 9 by McKelvey and Aldrich (1983) is a comprehensive introduction to the field of population ecology and the theory of natural selection. Its purposeful warnings on research method should be well heeded.

The Incremental View

Well before planning systems evolved into corporate and strategic variants, they were the focus of credible criticism. The argument was that organizations and their environments were so complex that the achievement of precise *ex ante*-derived objectives was impossible.

Strategists could not conceivably define any complete set of options from which to choose. Human capacity and behaviour muddied the precision of mathematical optimization, forcing organizations to satisfice by comparing available options for best output and possibility of implementation. In Chapter 10, Lindblom refers to such a process as strategy building by 'successive limited comparisons'. This was the reality of management, not the vacuum of planning. Despite this early warning and the lack of agreed definitions of the terms 'planning' and 'forecasting' among its adherents, the Planning school gained a hold in the 1960s and early 1970s.

From a background of political science, however, Wildavsky constantly echoed Lindblom's message. In his classic 1973 essay (Chapter 11), he argued that, in attempting to embrace the totality of organizational activity, planning had dissipated into nothing. The unfortunate planner could no longer discern its shape; it was beyond control, 'located everywhere in general and nowhere in particular'. Research into ten major American and European multinationals by Quinn (1978) confirmed the view that synoptic planning systems did not adequately characterize the empirical strategy process. He found that 'effective strategies tend to emerge from a series of strategic subsystems, each of which ... is blended incrementally and opportunistically into a cohesive pattern that becomes the company's strategy'. This approach was described as 'logical incrementalism' whereby top management forms a view of where it wants the organization to be in the future and attempts to get there by evolutionary adjustments to the core business and controlled venturing elsewhere. The latter becomes the responsibility of lower levels of management. As Quinn says in Chapter 12, such incrementalism is not 'muddling' but is purposeful and proactive, integrating the analytical and behavioural aspects of strategy formulation. Planning is not rejected but seen as one of many enablers of strategic change. Johnson (1988) extends this avenue by accepting incrementalism as preferable to planning, but takes issue with the 'logical' terminology. Logic suggests a degree of rationality which can be constrained in organizations by politics and paradigms. Strategy is frequently the result of a symbolic, cognitive and programmatic cocktail which can often appear illogical.

The Cultural View

Organizational culture is a complex web of individual assumptions and beliefs. These will have evolved through experiential learning in various management positions in the same or in different industries. As managers interact, a shared belief or 'organizational paradigm' is formed which can grow to dominate strategic decisions. New managers enter into the paradigm almost by osmosis as unconscious behavioural patterns are assumed. In this way, organizations deal with uncertainty. Key frames of reference that forge beliefs can come from the functional or professional background of managers, from organizations or the industry itself. Chapter 15 by Sheldon describes the 'cherished, ideal way of working' within the organization; this eventually creates the need for organizational change and shapes the effects of change. His supporting analogy comes from Kuhn's (1970) assertion that science advances through evolutionary and revolutionary periods, applicable here in terms of the impact of technological thrusts. Grinyer and Spender (1979) build upon work done by the latter in his doctoral thesis; they examine the prevalence of shared beliefs and assumptions across organizations that form 'recipes' for specific industries. Such recipes can constrain thinking and prevent change and adaptation, particularly when organizations face major crises. An understanding of the cultural view is therefore essential for any examination of the strategy process.

The Political View

The ownership of the organizational paradigm or 'way of doing business' is usually in the hands of a few top managers, thus yielding great power to a dominant coalition. Equally, the control of information or of some scarce but necessary resource gives owners power. Such power loci can be either inside the organization or outside (key stakeholders). This can create tension and conflict between different groups with different agendas. Hence, negotiation and bargaining become important features of what are essentially political organisms. The most powerful groups can effectively choose strategy options, not solely to obtain the neatest of fits with the environment, but because it is in their best fiscal or status interests. Power studies have a strong pedigree, stemming from the 1950s through the work of March, Etzioni, Cyert, Emerson, Hinings, Crozier, Lawrence and Lorsch, and Perrow among others. Chapter 16 by Hickson et al. (1971) was one of the first to treat power in organizations as a dependent variable and to attempt to explain it by examining its distribution through all the subunits and departments of the organization rather than merely in its vertical manifestations. However, this analysis falls short of full empirical testing.

Within this political body, decisions on strategy formulation and choice are far removed from the classical economic assumptions of perfect rationality and maximization. Simon's celebrated 1979 critique of economists' myopia (Chapter 17) articulates the behavioural theory of the firm in terms of managerial satisficing, alternative search, bounded rationality, learning and adaptation. Simon was greatly influenced by Barnard and, in attempting to explain the reality of decision making, uses evolutionary biology rather than economics or physics. Child (1972) is similarly critical of the economic constraints which contextual variables impose on organizational structure. In Chapter 18 he attacks contingency-derived theories that are removed from the underlying decision-making process. Structural variation emanates from the strategic decisions of power centres like the dominant coalition. Both Simon and Child argue for qualitative theories of choice and warn against the excessive rigidity of quantitative models.

Pettigrew (1977) looks deeper into the political process underlying decisions on strategy formulation, stressing the influential role of groups and individuals and the resolution of their conflicting demands (Chapter 19). He isolates the key roles of demand generation and how power is mobilized behind demands. This debate brings to the strategic management agenda the language of the organizational theorist – of legitimacy, symbolism, beliefs, myths and, above all, a sense of their linkage through an understanding of history. Pettigrew developed this arena through longitudinal and processual research programmes at the Centre for Corporate Strategy and Change at Warwick University. His second chapter (1992) helps to link political with visionary views by critically reviewing the various intellectual traditions in the study of managerial elites. These strategic decision makers at the top of organizations can form networks beyond the bounds of a single company through interlocking directorships. Thus the study of power relationships, of dominant paradigms and paradigm influencing is developed.

The Visionary View

Both the Planning and Incremental schools rely on rational analysis either to lead or to support the strategy process. The underlying notion is that some systems and techniques have utility in dealing with change to internal and external environments. Intuition and vision, frequently associated with the recalcitrant entrepreneur or Far Eastern management styles, were dismissed as important ingredients of Western top management decisions. But as external environments began to exhibit discontinuous change, greater attention was paid to the visionary executive, especially where more autocratic management styles were prevalent (e.g. recovery, MBOs). Such executives or executive teams rely on experience and intuitively seek out opportunities, thus driving their organizations forward with little help from formal systems. Some bring new recipes and paradigms from other industries or organizations, transplanting them into weary companies with great effect. The Hurst, Rush and White (1989) chapter deals cogently with this form of creative management, emphasizing its importance alongside synoptic systems.

Patterns of Strategy Development

The Learning school portrays strategy as a complex evolutionary, incremental, cultural, political and visionary process. The next three papers attempt to unravel this mix into patterns that are discernible in organizations. Besides reflecting the schism of rationality and incrementalism dominant in the early 1970s, Mintzberg's identification in Chapter 22 of three modes of strategy making – entrepreneurial, adaptive and planning – acknowledges the opportunistic leaps forward of the entrepreneur. These patterns are not mutually exclusive since a period of enterprise can revive an organization sleeping under an adaptive mode. His seminal essay with Waters (Chapter 23) develops the notion of strategy as an identifiable pattern in a stream of decisions. A decade of empirical observation confirmed what most suspected, i.e. that perfect deliberate and perfect emergent strategies are rare. The two form ends of a continuum along which real world strategies fall. It is the dominant characteristics of each which determine whether a strategy belongs to a particular school. Along the continuum lie many of the approaches detailed above. The first two of Chaffee's models capture the familiar planning and adaptive schema and Chapter 24 usefully traces their heritage. Her interpretative view draws on research into corporate culture and symbolism which, in the mid-1980s, were outside the strategy domain. This view is based on a social contract within organizations and thus assumes that reality is socially constructed rather than objective. Dealing with symbols, metaphors, frames of reference and paradigms, it is closely linked to the cultural view above. Much of the antecedent thought is contained in Chapter 19 by Pettigrew.

The second volume in this collection continues with the evolution of thought in the area of strategic management by examining the Positioning and Resource-Based schools.

References

Ackoff, R.L. (1970), *A Concept of Corporate Planning*, New York: Wiley.
Anderson, C.R. and Paine, F.T. (1975), 'Managerial Perceptions and Strategic Behaviour', *Academy of Management Journal*, **18**, pp. 811–23.
Andrews, K.R. (1971), *The Concept of Corporate Strategy*, Homewood, IL: Dow Jones-Irwin.
Ansoff, H.I. (1965), *Corporate Strategy*, New York: McGraw Hill.
Argenti, J. (1974), *Systematic Corporate Planning*, Sunbury-on-Thames, Middlesex: Thomas Nelson.
Barnard, C.I. (1938), *The Functions of the Executive*, Cambridge MA: Harvard University Press.
Bronowski, J. (1973), *The Ascent of Man*, London: BBC.
Chandler, A.D. (1962), *Strategy and Structure: Chapters in the History of the American Industrial Enterprise*, Cambridge, MA: MIT Press.
Cummings, S. (1993), 'Brief Case: The First Strategists', *Long Range Planning*, **26** (3), pp. 133–5.
Cyert, R.M. and March, J.G. (1963), *A Behavioural Theory of the Firm*, Englewood Cliffs, NJ: Prentice-Hall.
Grinyer, P.H. (1973), 'Some Dangerous Axioms of Corporate Planning', *Journal of Business Policy*, **3** (1), pp. 3–21.
Harrod, R.F. (1952), *Economic Essays*, London: Macmillan.
Henderson, B.D. (1989), 'The Origin of Strategy', *Harvard Business Review*, November/December, pp. 139–43.
Huff, A.S. (ed.) (1990), *Mapping Strategic Thought*, New York: Wiley.
Kuhn, T. (1970), *The Structure of Scientific Revolutions*, Vol.2, No.2, University of Chicago Press.
Learned, E.P., Christensen, C.R., Andrews, K.R. and Guth, W.D. (1965), *Business Policy: Text and Cases*, Homewood, IL: Irwin.
Machiavelli, N. (1961), *The Prince*, Harmondsworth: Penguin.
Marshall, A. (1913), *Elements of Economics of Industry*, London: Macmillan.
Miller, D. and Mintzberg, H. (1984), 'The Case for Configuration', in D. Miller and P.H. Friesen (eds), *Organizations: A Quantum View*, Englewood Cliffs, NJ: Prentice-Hall.
Mintzberg, H. (1979), *The Structuring of Organizations: A Synthesis of Research*, Englewood Cliffs, NJ: Prentice-Hall.
Mintzberg, H. (1990), 'The Design School: Reconsidering the Basic Premises of Strategic Management', *Strategic Management Journal*, **11**, pp. 171–95.
Mintzberg, H. (1994), *The Rise and Fall of Strategic Planning*, Hemel Hempstead: Prentice-Hall.
Neumann, J. von and Morgenstern, O. (1943), *Theory of Games and Economic Behavior*, Princeton: Princeton University Press.
Porter, M.E. (1980), *Competitive Strategy: Techniques for Analyzing Industries and Competitors*, New York: Free Press.
Porter, M.E. (1985), *Competitive Advantage*, New York: Free Press.
Pugh, D.S., Hickson, D.J., Hinings, C.R. and Turner, C. (1969), 'The Context of Organisational Structures', *Administrative Science Quarterly*, **14**, pp. 378–98.
Rumelt, R.P. (1974), *Strategy, Structure and Economic Performance*, Cambridge MA: Harvard University Press.
Schendel, D. (1992), 'Strategy Futures: What's Left to Worry About?', Working Paper, Krannert Graduate School of Management, Purdue University, Indiana.
Selznick, P. (1957), *Leadership in Administration: A Sociological Interpretation*, New York: Harper & Row.
Senge, P.M. (1992), 'Mental Models', *Planning Review*, **20**, pp. 4–10, 44.
Shrivastava, P. and Schneider, S. (1984), 'Organisational Frames of Reference', *Human Relations*, **37** (10), pp. 795–809.
Smircich, L. and Stubbart, C. (1985), 'Strategic Management in an Enacted World', *Academy of Management Review*, **10** (4), pp. 724–36.
Spender, J-C. (1993), 'Business Policy and Strategy: A View of the Field', Working Paper, Graduate School of Management, Rutgers University, New Jersey.

Steiner, G.A. (1969), *Top Management Planning*, New York: Macmillan.
Weick, K.E. (1967), *The Social Psychology of Organizing*, Reading MA: Addison-Wesley.
Williamson, O.E. (1975), *Markets and Hierarchies*, New York: Free Press.

Part I
The Planning and Practice School

CHAPTER XVIII

CONCLUSION

I

IN closing this study I shall first state what at the present time seem to me to be the more important general conclusions which may be drawn from it; and then offer certain more personal observations on its significance as a whole. The conclusions to which I would especially invite attention follow:

1. Physical and biological factors are basic in coöperation; if these factors permit, then social factors are essential to secure it. Coöperation, thus, may be called the process of synthesizing in action three quite different orders of factors.

2. From the point of view of organization, which is the chief instrument in economic development, all capital, whether of improvements, or machines, tools, and edifices, is always a part of the physical environment. The direct significance of capital is that it reduces the limitations imposed by the natural environment on coöperation. Its indirect result is the expansion of the incentives to coöperation.

3. All complex formal organizations grow from and consist of unit organizations, the inherent properties of which are the determining factors in the character of the complex.

4. The properties of unit formal organizations are determined by physical, biological, and social factors. The understanding of those factors and of the processes essential to conformation to them is the central method of the study of formal organizations.

5. The major structure of any society of substantial size is its complex of formal organizations, rather than its institutions,

286 FUNCTIONS OF ORGANIZATIONS

customs, etc., which are abstractions chiefly constructed on observed uniformities in the concrete acts, including the verbalizations, of such organizations as well as of individuals.

6. Informal organizations are found within all formal organizations, the latter being essential to order and consistency, the former to vitality. These are mutually reactive phases of coöperation, and they are mutually dependent.

7. Disturbances of the equilibrium of coöperative systems have come from false ideologies, particularly on the part of those who are leaders or executives in formal organizations. The effect of these false notions is to vitiate the sense of experience when consciously dealing with problems of the theory of organization, and to reinforce personal predilections, prejudices, and interests, as destructive factors, in the guidance of organization practice.

8. In this way arise four principal errors: an oversimplification of the economy of organization life; a disregard of the fact and of the necessity of informal organization; an inversion of emphasis upon the objective and the subjective aspects of authority; and a confusion of morality with responsibility.

9. The essential process of adaptation in organizations is decision, whereby the physical, biological, personal, and social factors of the situation are selected for specific combination by volitional action.

10. Error of decision must be large because of the unbalance due to the difference in the precision of perception as respects the physical, the biological, and the social environments. This is a general factor limiting successful coöperation.

11. Since any coöperative system contains physical, personal, and social factors, at least three secondary abstract systems of utilities, related to these factors respectively, are pertinent. To these must be added a primary system of utilities related to the whole organization. Each of these secondary systems comprises the phenomena or factors of the respective classes, together

CONCLUSION 287

with the utilities attached to them by the organization. The aggregate of these utilities in each system varies with the phenomena or factors and the utilities assigned to each factor. The primary system comprises the aggregate of these utilities and the phenomena and factors involved as a whole. These systems I have called economies. The respective economies are heterogeneous as between themselves, and widely variable as between the corresponding economies in other coöperative systems. They do not admit of quantitative comparison. These conceptions are on the whole new, and not now understood or adopted. They are theoretical and their use is limited at present to the analysis and description of coöperative systems. They are, however, intuitively taken into account in specific situations by those skilled in the executive arts and by others.

12. All scientific knowledge is expressed in languages and symbolic systems. These are socially developed with meanings that are socially determined; and all "finally" accepted observations of phenomena are coöperatively arrived at. Therefore, all sciences in the widest sense comprehend both social factors and others of different orders, depending upon their subject matter. Disregarding the social factors of science in the sense just stated, we find two kinds of abstract systems of knowledge other than those stated under 11, next above, as follows: (*a*) systems which relate exclusively, or substantially so, to one or the other order of factors (physical, biological, social), and (*b*) those which "cut across" or comprehend two or more orders of factors.

(*a*) Examples of systems of the first class are the systems of physical science, containing many sub-systems, including everyday or commercial classifications of materials; biological systems; and purely theoretical social systems.

(*b*) Examples of systems of the second class are: biochemical, architectural, engineering, and other technological systems;

FUNCTIONS OF ORGANIZATIONS

systems of psychology; economic systems; social, political, and ethical systems.

Abstract systems of the first class are basically scientific and are also practical. They do not attempt to explain coöperative phenomena. They involve few disadvantages except those of "misplaced concreteness" and an unbalanced approach to problems of coöperation. Abstract systems of the second class are often primarily practical and are also the subjects of scientific study. Some of these systems, especially those called "social," involve effects that often render them useless and even harmful through misstatement and false explanation of coöperative phenomena. In general they are developed without comprehension of the nature of coöperative systems, and accordingly their character and the limits of their usefulness are often misconceived.

13. An increasing degree of coöperation implies an increasing moral complexity. It is impossible for men to endure a high degree of moral complexity without commensurate technological proficiency.

14. The strategic factor in coöperation generally is leadership, which is the name for relatively high personal capacity for both technological attainments and moral complexity, combined with propensity for consistency in conformance to moral factors of the individual.

15. The strategic factor in the dynamic expression of leadership is moral creativeness, which precedes, but is in turn dependent upon, technological proficiency and the development of techniques in relation to it.

16. The strategic factor in social integration is the development and selection of leaders. The process is usually unbalanced by excessive emphasis either upon technological proficiency or upon moral status. In some ages moralities may have been cultivated in excess of the technological capacity to support them. In the present age the emphasis is upon technological profi-

CONCLUSION 289

ciency which is not adequately guided by the necessities of the coöperative system as a whole.

II

I estimate that in the United States not less than 5,000,000 individuals are engaged in the work of executives, of whom 100,000 occupy major executive positions. Concerning certain technical aspects of the various fields in which they work there is literature and instruction; but concerning the instrumentality with which they work — organization — and the techniques appropriate to it, there is little. More important is the lack of an accepted conceptual scheme with which to exchange their thought.

Important consequences of this state of affairs are unbalance and false emphases upon matters concerning which there is already much knowledge and appropriate language — for example, in the technologies like accounting and financial practice, in certain aspects of personnel work and measures — and concomitant disregard of equally important matters which heretofore have not been much discussed. Back of failure in personnel effort is often incompleteness of understanding of what I have called the "economy of incentives." Much abortive management arises from almost total disregard, in *thinking*, of the subjective aspects of authority. Despite its importance, *informal* organization in formal organizations is ignored as far as possible. The limits of the size of formal groups, although major considerations in the elaboration of organizations, are disregarded often for comparatively trivial reasons.[1] The moral fac-

---

[1] For example, as Director of the Emergency Relief organization in New Jersey I was in effect required *by law* to have not less than twenty-one immediate subordinates. Actually, I required twenty-five or twenty-six. Five should have been the maximum for this work and perhaps three would have been more effective and more efficient. There were some good reasons for the requirement; but I believed it impossible to convince enough legislators that it was such bad organization that the requirement should be changed.

tors upon which the vitality of organization depends are treated mostly as subjects for glowing generalities in inspirational addresses and there is woeful lack of appreciation of the interrelationships between personal character and ability.

Would a thoroughly scientific approach to the problems of coöperative systems and organization provide a useful tool for the executive arts? It is my belief that it ultimately would, and that the development of such a science is important in further progress in these arts and hence in coöperation generally. This belief is based upon reflection concerning the failure observed in many concrete instances to take into account all the elements of the situation as a whole. This failure is promoted by a specialization in *thinking* that arises in part from the specialization of the sciences. The action which is the essence of organization, or the coördination of action which is the function of the executive, relates to the synthesis of physical, biological, and social factors. The problems of mutual adjustment are outside these specific fields.

Neither the consideration of present experience nor that of the pertinent aspects of history permits escape from the suspicion that much sheer lack of good sense in human relations is to be explained by the history of the sciences. There is no science of organization or of coöperative systems; and the development of the sciences called social has clearly lagged far behind those called physical and mathematical. One reason for this appears to be a false emphasis upon intellectual and mental processes both as factors in human relations and as matters of study.

However, it is well to be quite clear as to the significance of a science in its relation to the arts. It is the function of the arts to accomplish concrete ends, effect results, produce situations, that would not come about without the deliberate effort to secure them. These arts must be mastered and applied by those who deal in the concrete and for the future. The func-

CONCLUSION

tion of the sciences, on the other hand, is to explain the phenomena, the events, the situations, of the past. Their aim is not to produce specific events, effects, or situations but explanations which we call knowledge. It has not been the aim of science to be a system of technology; and it could not be such a system. There is required in order to manipulate the concrete a vast amount of knowledge of a temporary, local, specific character, of no general value or interest, that it is not the function of a science to have or to present and only to explain to the extent that it is generally significant.

In the common-sense, everyday, practical knowledge necessary to the practice of the arts, there is much that is not susceptible of verbal statement — it is a matter of know-how. It may be called behavioral knowledge. It is necessary to doing things in concrete situations. It is nowhere more indispensable than in the executive arts. It is acquired by persistent habitual experience and is often called intuitive.

Nevertheless, the power of the arts and the arts themselves are capable of expansion when there is available scientific knowledge — explanations, concepts. Thus in the hands of those who apply themselves to the control of future events a developed science, even though it will be later superseded, *in conjunction with* local, temporary, specific, and behavioral knowledge and intuitional talents, is an additional means of great importance when properly used. This has been the case in recent years (and chiefly in recent years only) in the technological and medical fields. It has also been true in less degree in technical fields in which economic and political sciences have been used.

The present extent and success of coöperation is proof that the executive arts are already highly developed, but the restriction of coöperation in innumerable directions of which we are so unpleasantly aware shows that they are not sufficiently developed. The deficiency appears to be chiefly in lack of pro-

FUNCTIONS OF ORGANIZATIONS

portion. The executive arts are highly developed in the fields called technological; they are well developed in the technical commercial fields; they are least developed in the techniques of human interactions and organization. Relatively, this was not always so. The solidarity of small peoples, the long history of the Roman Republic and Empire, are examples of organization and control of human interrelations showing that the development of these arts in relation to the technological and economic arts was high.

Whether the present essay is a contribution to the science hoped for remains to be determined by others. What has been presented is a hypothetical scheme which at present explains roughly to me what I have observed in many years of practical work with organizations of various kinds and what I have constructed from the experience of others, supplemented, of course, by a little knowledge of the social sciences. It is not the work of a scientist or a scholar, but rather of an interested student of affairs.

For this reason perhaps its chief value, if presently it has any, will merely lie in its expression of one view of experience. By it I have at least submitted my mental processes in this field to inspection. If it has any further value it will lie in the suggestion it may give to more competent inquiry, which I hope can be undertaken. The test of it will come from its application to social phenomena as a whole, as they present themselves to others — many others.

Most persons of affairs will find much difficulty in applying that test, because the form of statement which seems to me necessary in work of this kind is so very different from that which they habitually employ. The administration of affairs proceeds on the basis of limited fictions, working hypotheses, practical assumptions, and highly symbolic expressions, which are local, special, or technical within a particular organization. Conventional attitudes must be modified to some extent at

CONCLUSION 293

least to test a scheme such as this; and many for this reason may think the treatment unrealistic and impatiently throw it aside.

I hope that the social scientist, on the other hand, may attempt a preliminary testing of it against the background of present knowledge. More concretely, I hope for a social anthropology, a sociology, a social psychology, an institutional economics, a treatise on management, etc., written with the concepts of a coöperative system and an organization which have been presented as a part of the working scheme. For what this kind of thinking requires at present is not so much the testing of details as the ascertainment of whether or not there is correspondence between it and general experience and social knowledge as a whole.

But we should not deceive ourselves by thinking that either a science of coöperation and organization or the further development of the executive arts will alone promote a greater integration of social forces, or even maintain the present status. The ethical ideal upon which coöperation depends requires the general diffusion of a willingness to subordinate immediate personal interest for both ultimate personal interest and the general good, together with a capacity of individual responsibility. The senses of what will be for the ultimate personal interest and of what will be for the general good both must come from outside the individual. They are social, ethical, and religious values. For their general diffusion they depend upon both intelligence and inspiration. Intelligence is necessary to the appreciation of the interdependence of peoples in a crowded world on their combined technological competence — an intelligence that perhaps will be derived from experience in coöperation rather than from anything suggestive of formal education. Inspiration is necessary to inculcate the sense of unity, and to create common ideals. Emotional rather than intellectual acceptance is required. No one who reads, or who observes the events of our times, but will recognize, it seems to me, the supreme importance of belief in ideals as indispensable to coöperation.

Men are now dismayed by the evidences of world disorganization, as if it represented a radical change from world integration; but their very discouragement is evidence of their belief in the need of greater integration which must precede its realization. Until that faith is universal and until the techniques of coöperation have been developed for much wider ranges than has as yet been possible, conflict may itself be the chief process toward ultimate integration. The possibilities of world coöperation might not be learned until half the world is organized against the other half. That would represent perhaps a greater integration than has yet occurred, but would make more evident than ever before the disorganization that remains.

However, the present questioning and discouragement do not come, it seems clear to me, merely from economic disturbances and international conflict. Much more do they arise from a deep conflict of beliefs concerning coöperation itself. There are two beliefs that are far apart, both struggling not only against each other but also against unrecognized limitations. One of them centers upon the freedom of the individual and makes him the center of the social universe. At the present time, on the whole, it is critical and pessimistic. It lays its emphasis upon failure of coöperation, upon wars and conflicts, confusion and disorganization, waste, hunger, disease and death, and yet it preaches uncritically an extreme liberty, an ideal individualism, a self-determination, that in their unrestricted dogmatism would prevent all formal coöperation beyond that imposed by the most obvious immediate opportunities and necessities.

The second extreme faith is adulatory and optimistic. It places its emphasis upon the order, the predictability, the consistency, the effectiveness, of untold myriads of concrete acts that are coöperatively determined, in systems so extensively interrelated that the effects have been enormously to expand the world's

CONCLUSION 295

population and to advance measurably the material and cultural state of many millions. Those who speak from this point of view are likely to advocate uncritically a vast regimentation, an endless subordination, a completeness of coördination, that in *their* unrestricted dogmatism would stifle all development of individuals beyond that found inescapable.

And so we find ourselves again with the very problem with which we began; for the issue between these faiths, I think, is unconsciously centered upon the old question of free will and determinism, or on sentiments from which this question takes its origin. Those who carry the banners of individualism are crying for the right of the individual to choose; and those who trumpet so loudly for the state and society proclaim the folly of individual choice and seek to prevent it. Thus what once was the center of philosophic and theological speculation, and more recently of the controversy of philosophically-minded scientists now becomes the battleground of nations fighting for social dogmas.

This issue I found, not in the philosophies or the theologies or the scientific papers or the polemics of Marxism, but in the behavior of men in coöperation, in the social limitations of organizations, in the essential burdens of the executive. I found it not as an abstract question unrelated to the daily lives of men, but as one evident in the collapse of actual coöperation and in the moral disintegration of living men and women. Scarcely a man, I think, who has felt the annihilation of his personality in some organized system, has not also felt that that same system belonged to him because of his own free will he chose to make it so. Many an executive, I believe, has seemed to himself at times to be merely the channel of imponderable universal forces, of all his associates the least free; and yet he has also believed that when men do not choose, do not will, do not regard themselves as responsible and are not so regarded by others, the very stuff of coöperation dissolves.

296   FUNCTIONS OF ORGANIZATIONS

This study, without the intent of the writer or perhaps the expectation of the reader, had at its heart this deep paradox and conflict of feelings in the lives of men. Free and unfree, controlling and controlled, choosing and being chosen, inducing and unable to resist inducement, the source of authority and unable to deny it, independent and dependent, nourishing their personalities, and yet depersonalized; forming purposes and being forced to change them, searching for limitations in order to make decisions, seeking the particular but concerned with the whole, finding leaders and denying their leadership, hoping to dominate the earth and being dominated by the unseen — this is the story of man in society told in these pages.

Such a story calls finally for a declaration of faith. I believe in the power of the coöperation of men of free will to make men free to coöperate; that only as they choose to work together can they achieve the fullness of personal development; that only as each accepts a responsibility for choice can they enter into that communion of men from which arise the higher purposes of individual and of coöperative behavior alike. I believe that the expansion of coöperation and the development of the individual are mutually dependent realities, and that a due proportion or balance between them is a necessary condition of human welfare. Because it is subjective with respect both to a society as a whole and to the individual, what this proportion is I believe science cannot say. It is a question for philosophy and religion.

[2]
The concept of corporate strategy

Kenneth R. Andrews

We come at last to the simple central concept called corporate strategy. Henceforth we will be concerned with deciding what it is as idea and management process and how in a company to formulate, evaluate, and implement it. In this chapter we will examine the comprehensive definition I propose as the most useful, the terms in which strategy should be stated to make sense, the forms different kinds of strategy take in different kinds of companies, and the tests of validity that may be applied to it.

WHAT STRATEGY IS

Corporate strategy is the pattern of decisions in a company that determines and reveals its objectives, purposes, or goals, produces the principal policies and plans for achieving those goals, and defines the range of business the company is to pursue, the kind of economic and human organization it is or intends to be, and the nature of the economic and noneconomic contribution it intends to make to its shareholders, employees, customers, and communities. In an organization of any size or diversity, "corporate strategy" usually applies to the whole enterprise, while "business strategy," less comprehensive, defines the choice of product or service and market of individual businesses within the firm. Business strategy, that is, is the determination of how a company will compete in a given business and position itself among its competitors. Corporate strategy defines the businesses in-which a company will compete, preferably in a way that focuses resources to convert distinctive competence into competitive advantage. Both are outcomes of a continuous process of strategic management that we will later analyze in detail.

The strategic decision contributing to this pattern is one that is effective over long periods of time, affects the company in many different ways, and focuses and commits a significant portion of its resources to the expected outcomes. The pattern resulting from a series of such decisions will probably define the central character and image of a company, the individuality it has for its members and various publics, and the position it will occupy in its industry and markets. It will permit the specification of particular objectives to be attained through a timed sequence of investment and implementation decisions and will govern directly the deployment or redeployment of resources to make these decisions effective.

Some aspects of such a pattern of decision may be in an established corporation unchanging over long periods of time, like a commitment to quality, or high technology, or certain raw materials, or good labor relations. Other aspects of a strategy must change as or before the world changes, such as product line, manufacturing process, or merchandising and styling practices. The basic determinants of company character, if purposefully institutionalized, are likely to persist through and shape the nature of substantial changes in product-market choices and allocation of resources.

It would be possible to extend the definition of strategy for a given company to separate a central character and the core of its special accomplishment from the manifestations of such characteristics in changing product lines, markets, and policies designed to make activities profitable from year to year. The New York Times, for example, after many years of being shaped by the values of its owners and staff, is now so self-conscious and respected an institution that its nature is likely to remain unchanged, even if the services it offers are altered drastically in the direction of other outlets for its news-processing capacity.

It is important, however, not to take the idea apart in another way, i.e. to separate goals from the policies designed to achieve those goals. The essence of the definition of strategy I have just recorded is *pattern*. The interdependence of purposes, policies, and organized action is crucial to the particularity of an individual strategy and its opportunity to identify competitive advantage. It is the unity, coherence, and internal consistency of a company's strategic decisions that position the company in its environment and give the firm its identity, its power to mobilize its strengths, and its likelihood of success in the marketplace. It is the interrelationship of a set of goals and policies that crystallizes from the formless reality of a company's environment a set of problems an organization can seize upon and solve.

What you are doing, in short, is never meaningful unless you can say or imply what you are doing it for: the quality of administrative action and the motivation lending it power cannot be appraised without knowing its relationship to purpose. Breaking up the system of corporate goals and the character-determining major policies for attainment leads to narrow and mechanical conceptions of strategic management and endless logic-chopping.

We should get on to understanding the need for strategic decision and for determining the most satisfactory pattern of goals in concrete instances. Refinement of definition can wait, for you will wish to develop definition in practice in directions useful to you.

SUMMARY STATEMENTS OF STRATEGY

Before we proceed to clarification of this concept by application, we should specify the terms in which strategy is usually expressed. A summary statement of strategy will characterize the product line and services offered or planned by the company, the markets and market segments for which products and services are now or will be designed, and the channels through which these markets will be reached. The means by which the operation is to be financed will be specified, as will the profit objectives and the emphasis to be placed on the safety of capital versus level of return. Major policy in central functions such as marketing, manufacturing, procurement, research and development, labor relations, and personnel, will be stated where they distinguish the company from others, and usually the intended size, form, and climate of the organization will be included.

Each company, if it were to construct a summary strategy from what it understands itself to be aiming at, would have a different statement with different categories of decision emphasized to indicate what it wanted to be or do.

To indicate the nature of such a statement, a student of a famous old policy case on the Heublein company deduced this statement from the account of the company when it was much smaller and less diversified than it is now and was about to make the mistake of acquiring Hamm's Brewery:

Heublein aims to market in the U.S. and via franchise overseas a wide variety of high margin, high quality consumer products concentrated in the liquor and food business, especially bottled cocktails, vodka, and other special-use and distinctive beverages and specialty convenience foods, addressed to a relatively prosperous, young-adult market and returning over 15 percent of equity after taxes. With emphasis on the techniques of consumer goods marketing [brand promotion, wide distribution, product representation in more than one price segment, and very substantial off-beat advertising directed closely to its growing audience] Heublein intends to make Smirnoff the number one liquor brand worldwide via internal growth [and franchise] or acquisitions or both. Its manufacturing policy rather than full integration is in liquor to redistill only to bring purchased spirits up to high quality standards. It aims to finance its internal growth through the use of debt and its considerable cash flow and to use its favorable price earnings ratio for acquisitions. Both its liquor and food distribution are intended to secure distributor support through advertising and concern for the distributor's profit.

Although it might be argued that the statement was not clearly in the chief executive's mind when he contemplated purchasing Hamm's Brewery and therefore did not help him refrain from that decision, it was in his experience and in the pattern of the company's past strategic decisions—at least as reported in the case. In many ways incomplete (no mention is made of organization or social responsibility sub-strategies) this statement does make possible a large question about the beer business as a compatible element in the company's marketing mix.

REASONS FOR NOT ARTICULATING STRATEGY

For a number of reasons companies seldom formulate and publish as complete a statement even as the one we have just illustrated. Conscious planning of the long-term development of companies has been until recently less common than individual executive responses to environmental pressure, competitive threat, or entrepreneurial opportunity. In the latter mode of development, the unity or coherence of corporate effort is unplanned, natural, intuitive, or even nonexistent. Incrementalism in practice sometimes gives the appearance of consciously formulated strategy, but may be the natural result of compromise among coalitions backing contrary policy proposals or skillful improvisatory adaptation to external forces. Practicing managers who prefer muddling through to the strategic process would never commit themselves to an articulate strategy.

Other reasons for the scarcity of concrete statements of strategy include the desirability of keeping strategic plans confidential for security reasons and ambiguous to avoid internal conflict or even final decision. Skillful incrementalists may have plans in their heads which they do not reveal, to avoid resistance and other trouble in their own organization. A company with a large division in an obsolescent business which it intends to drain of cash until operations are discontinued could not expect high morale and cooperation to follow publication of this intent. In a dynamic company, moreover, where strategy is continually evolving, the official statement of strategy, unless it was couched in very general terms, would be as hard to keep up to date as an organization chart. Finally, a firm that has internalized its strategy does not feel the need to keep saying what it is, valuable as that information might be to new members.

DEDUCING STRATEGY FROM BEHAVIOR

In your own company you can do what most managements have not done. In the absence of explicit statements and on the basis of your experience, you may deduce from decisions observed what the pattern is and what the company's goals and policies are, on the assumption that some perhaps unspoken consensus lies behind them. Careful examination of the behavior of competitors will reveal what their strategy must be. At the same time none of us should mistake apparent strategy visible in a pattern of past incremental decisions for conscious planning for the future. What will pass as the current strategy of a company may almost always be deduced from its behavior, but a strategy for a future of changed circumstance may not always be distinguishable from performance in the present. Strategists who do not look beyond present behavior to the future are vulnerable to surprise.

FORMULATION OF STRATEGY

Corporate strategy is an organization process, in many ways inseparable from the structure, behavior, and culture of the company in which it takes place. Nevertheless, we may abstract from the process two important aspects, interrelated in real life but separable for the purposes of analysis. The first of these we may call *formulation*, the second *implementation*. Deciding what strategy should be may be approached as a rational undertaking, even if in life emotional attachments (as to metal skis or investigative reporting) may complicate choice among future alternatives (for ski manufacturers or alternative newspapers). The principal subactivities of strategy formulation as a logical activity include identifying opportunities and threats in the company's environment and attaching some estimate or risk to the discernible alternatives. Before a choice can be made, the company's strengths and weaknesses should be appraised together with the resources on hand and available. Its actual or potential capacity to take advantage of perceived market needs or to cope with attendant risks should be estimated as objectively as possible. The strategic alternative which results from matching opportunity and corporate capability at an acceptable level of risk is what we may call an *economic strategy*.

The process described thus far assumes that strategists are analytically objective in estimating the relative capacity of their company and the opportunity they see or anticipate in developing markets. The extent to which they wish to undertake low or high risk presumably depends on their profit objectives. The higher they set the latter, the more willing they must be to assume a correspondingly high risk that the market opportunity they see will not develop or that the corporate competence required to excel competition will not be forthcoming.

So far we have described the intellectual processes of ascertaining what a company *might do* in terms of environmental opportunity, of deciding what it *can do* in terms of ability and power, and of bringing these two considerations together in optimal equilibrium. The determination of strategy also requires consideration of what alternatives are preferred by the chief executive and perhaps by his or her immediate associates as well, quite apart from economic considerations. Personal values, aspirations, and ideals do, and in our judgment quite properly should, influence the final choice of purposes. Thus what the executives of a company *want to do* must be brought into the strategic decision.

Finally strategic choice has an ethical aspect—a fact much more dramatically illustrated in some industries than in others. Just as alternatives may be ordered in terms of the degree of risk that they entail, so may they be examined against the standards of responsiveness to the expectations of society that the strategist elects. Some alternatives may seem to the executive considering them more attractive than others when the public good or service to society is considered. What a company *should do* thus appears as a fourth element of the strategic decision.

The ability to identify the four components of strategy—(1) market opportunity, (2) corporate competence and resources, (3) personal values and aspirations, and (4) acknowledged obligations to segments of society other than stockholders—is easier to exercise than the art of reconciling their implications in a final choice of purpose. Taken by itself each consideration might lead in a different direction.

If you put the various aspirations of individuals in your own organization against this statement you will see what I mean. Even in a single mind contradictory aspirations can survive a long time before the need to calculate trade-offs and integrate divergent inclinations becomes clear. Growth opportunity attracted many companies to the computer business after World War II. The decision to diversify out of typewriters and calculators was encouraged by growth opportunity and excitement which captivated the managements of RCA, General Electric, and

Xerox, among others. But the financial, technical, and marketing requirements of this business exceeded the capacity of most of the competitors of IBM. The magnet of opportunity and the incentive of desire obscured the calculations of what resources and competence were required to succeed. Most crucially, where coporate capability leads, executives do not always want to go. Of all the components of strategic choice, the combination of resources and competence is most crucial to success.

THE IMPLEMENTATION OF STRATEGY

Since effective implementation can make a sound strategic decision ineffective or a debatable choice successful, it is as important to examine the processes of implementation as to weigh the advantages of available strategic alternatives. The implementation of strategy is comprised of a series of subactivities which are primarily administrative. If purpose is determined, then the resources of a company can be mobilized to accomplish it. An organizational structure appropriate for the efficient performance of the required tasks must be made effective by information systems and relationships permitting coordination of subdivided activities. The organizational processes of performance measurement, compensation, management development—all of them enmeshed in systems of incentives and controls—must be directed toward the kind of behavior required by organizational purpose. The role of personal leadership is important and sometimes decisive in the accomplishment of strategy. Although we know that organization structure and processes of compensation, incentives, control, and management development influence and constrain the formulation of strategy, we should look first at the logical proposition that structure should follow strategy in order to cope later with the organizational reality that strategy also follows structure. When we have examined both tendencies, we will understand and to some extent be prepared to deal with the interdependence of the formulation and implementation of corporate purpose. Figure 1 may be useful in understanding the analysis of strategy as a pattern of interrelated decisions.

KINDS OF STRATEGIES

The most important characteristics of a corporate pattern of decision that may properly be called strategic is its uniqueness. A creative reconciliation of alternatives for future development is made unique by the special characteristics of an organization, its central competence, history, financial and technical resources, and the aspirations and sense of responsibility of its leaders. The environment—market opportunity and risk—is more

FIGURE 1

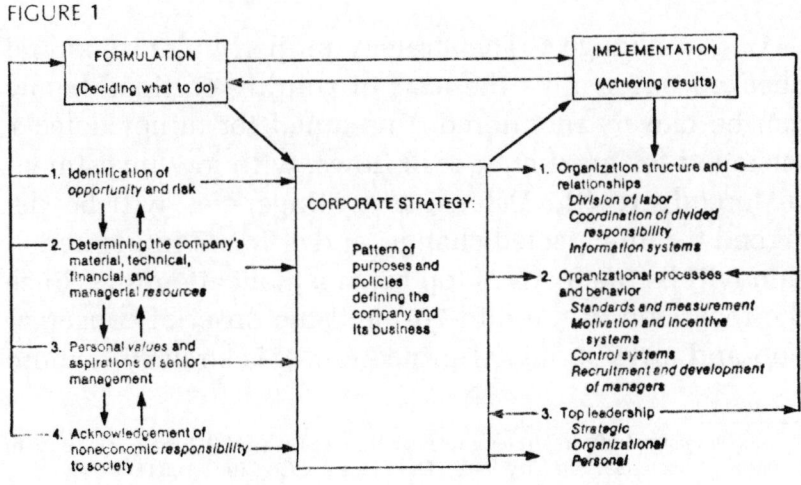

nearly the same for major companies operating in the same geographical regions than are the resources, values, and responsibility components of strategy. For the company unequipped to dominate the full range of opportunity, the quest for a profitable segment of, or niche in, a market is, if successful, also likely to distinguish one company from another. In fact in an industry where all companies seem to have the same strategy, we will find trouble for all but the leaders—as at various times American Motors, Chrysler, and Ford have had different degrees of difficulty following General Motors, which got where it is by *not* following the previous industry leader, Henry Ford.[1]

Nonetheless it is useful to have in mind the full range of possible strategies when the question is posed whether the present strategy is the best possible. When you begin to consider other possibilities, the generation of alternatives will take place within the following commonsense range of possibilities.

Low-growth strategies

1. *No change.* The strategy properly identified and checked out against the tests of validity outlined below can be closely monitored, fine-tuned for minor defects, managed for maximum cash flows, with low investment in forced growth. Defensive contingencies will be designed for unexpected change, and efficient implementation will be the focus of top management attention. Since the recession of the mid-70s, and the onset of conservation and environmental protection, this strategy is more

---

[1]For a basic study in strategy formulation, see Alfred P. Sloan, *My Years at General Motors* (Garden City, N.Y.: Doubleday & Co., Inc., 1964).

attractive than it was in the heyday of "more is better." The profit to be made from doing better what a company already knows how to do rather than investing heavily in growth is the attraction of this strategy, which can be protected by achievement of low costs. Its disadvantage is the possibility of being overtaken or displaced by new development and the restriction of opportunity for organization members.

2. *Retreat.* The possibility of liquidation is not to be sought out, but may for companies in deep trouble be a better choice than continuing the struggle. Less drastic alternatives than complete liquidation include discontinuance or divestment of marginal operations, or merging with a ceding of management control.

3. *Focus on limited special opportunity.* A more constructive course of contraction is concentration on a profitable specialty product or a limited but significant market niche. Success in a narrow line almost always tempts a company to broaden its line, but the McIlhenny strategy (Tabasco sauce only) may not be totally obsolete. If the proper focus is chosen, the limits may relax and growth may come in any case. Once the risk of limited life is accepted, the advantages of the no-change strategy can be sought.

Forced-growth strategies

1. *Acquisition of competitors.* In the early states of its development, a company with a successful strategy and proven record of successful execution can acquire small competitors in the same business to expand its market. Eventually antitrust regulation will put an end to this practice, unless the prospective acquisition is very

small or on the edge of bankruptcy. Such acquisitions are usually followed by an adaptation of strategy either by the parent or acquired company to keep the total company a single business or one dominated by its original product-market specialization.

2. *Vertical integration.* A conservative growth strategy, keeping a company close to its core competence and experience in its industry, consists of moving backward via acquisition or internal development to sources of supply and forward toward the ultimate customer. When a newspaper buys a pulp and paper mill and forest lands or news agencies for distribution, it is extending its strategy but not changing materially the nature of its business. Increasing the stages of integration provides a greater number of options to be developed or closed out as, for example, the making of fine paper and the distribution of magazines.

3. *Geographical expansion.* Enlargement of territory can be accomplished by building new plants and enlarging marketing organizations or by acquisition of competitors. For a sizeable company the opportunity to enlarge international operations by export, establishments of plants and marketing activities overseas, with or without foreign partners, may protect against contraction forced by domestic competition.

4. *Diversification.* The avenue to growth which presents the most difficult strategic choices is diversification. Diversification can range from minor additions to a company's basic product line to the acquisition of completely unrelated businesses. It can be sought through internal research and development, the purchase of new product ideas or technology, and the acquisition of companies.

KINDS OF COMPANIES

The process of strategic decision differs in complexity depending upon the diversity of the company in question. Just as having in mind the range of strategy from liquidation to multinational diversification will stimulate the generation of strategic alternatives, so a simple way of differentiating kinds of companies will help us see why different kinds of companies have different kinds of problems in making their activities coherent and effective and in setting a course for the future.

Bruce Scott of the Harvard Business School has developed a model of stages of corporate development in which each stage is characterized by the way a firm is managed and the scope of strategic choice available to it. *Stage I* is a single-product (or line of products) company with little or no formal structure run by the owner, who personally performs most of the managerial functions using subjective and unsystematic measures of performance and reward and control systems. The strategy of this firm is what the owner-manager wants it to be.

Stage II is the single-product firm grown so large that functional specialization has become imperative. A degree of integration has developed between raw materials, production processes, distribution, and sales. The search for product or process improvement is institutionalized in research and development, and performance management and control and compensation systems become systematic with the formulation of policy to guide delegation of operating decisions. The strategic choice is still under top control and centers upon the degree of integration, size of market share, and breadth of product line.

Stage III is a company with multiple product lines and channels of distribution, with an organization based on product-market relationships rather than function. Its businesses are not to a significant degree integrated; they have their own markets. Its research and development is oriented to new products rather than improvements, and its measurement and control systems are increasingly systematic and oriented to results. Strategic alternatives are phrased in terms of entry into and exit from industries, and allocation of resources by industry and rate of growth.

If a company grows it may pass from Stage I to Stage III, although it can be very large in Stage II. Its strategic decisions will grow in complexity. The stages of development model has proved productive in relating different kinds of strategies to kinds of companies and has led other researchers into productive classification. Leonard Wrigley and Richard P. Rumelt have carried Scott's work forward to develop suggestive ways of categorizing companies and comparing their strategies.[2]

First, of course, is the *single business* firm (Stages I and II firms) with 95 percent or more of its revenues arising from a single business—an oil, flour-milling, or metal container company, for example.

Second is the *dominant business* firm, diversified to some extent but still obtaining most of its revenues from a single business. The diversification may arise from end products of integration, with products stemming from strengths of the firm, or from minor unrelated activities. A large oil company in the petrochemical and fertilizer business would fall in this category.

---

[2]Leonard Wrigley, "Division Autonomy and Diversification" (unpublished doctoral dissertation, Harvard Business School, 1970) and Richard P. Rumelt, *Strategy Structure and Economic Performance* (Division of Research, Harvard Business School, 1974). Malcolm Salter has added a refinement to Stage III in "Stages of Corporate Development," *Journal of Business Policy*, vol. 1, no. 1 (1970), pp. 40–51.

Third is the *related business* firm in which the diversification has been principally accomplished by relating new activities to old—General Electric and Westinghouse, for example.

Fourth is the *unrelated business* firm. These firms have diversified primarily without regard to relationships between new businesses and current activities. The conglomerate companies fall in this category.

It is interesting to note that Rumelt has found significant superior performance in the related business firms, suggesting that the strategy of diversifying from the original business to a significant degree but staying within the sphere of established competence has been the most successful strategic pattern among the *Fortune 500* under conditions prevailing in recent years. Unfortunately, familiar problems in establishing causation prevent final conclusions.

The range of strategy and the kinds of company which different growth strategies have produced suggest, in short, that the process of defining the business of a company will vary greatly depending on the degree of diversification under way in the company. The product-market choices are crystal clear in a single business oil company; they could not even be listed for General Electric. That top management actually decides product-market questions in such a company, except in such instances as entry into nuclear energy, is conceivable only as an oversimplification.

As diversification increases, the definition of the total business turns away from literal description of products and markets (which becomes the business of the separate product divisions) toward general statements of financial results expected and corporate principle in other areas. A conglomerate firm made up of many different businesses

THE CONCEPT OF CORPORATE STRATEGY

will have many different business strategies, related or not depending upon the desire for synergy in the strategic direction of the total enterprise. The overall common strategy of a highly diversified firm may be only the total of its divisional strategies. That it should be more than that is a matter for argument. To make it so puts heavy demands on the ability to conceptualize corporate purpose.

The task of identifying the coherence and unity of a conglomerate is, of course, much greater than doing so for even a multidivision related business. You should be prepared, then, to adapt the beginning definition offered here to the complexity of the business you are examining. Since the trend over time is product diversity in growing firms and evolution from Stage I to Stage III, it is well to have this complication in mind now.

For as Norman Berg makes clear in "Strategic Planning in Conglomerate Companies," strategic choice is not merely the function of the chief executive office.[3] It is of necessity a multilevel activity, with each unit concerned with its own environment and its own objectives. The process will reflect the noneconomic goals of people at the level at which proposals are made. In a conglomerate of unrelated businesses the corporate staff is small, the division relatively autonomous, and the locus of strategic planning is in the divisions. This makes supervision of the strategic planning process and allocation of resources, depending upon the evaluation of strategies submitted, the strategic role of the corporate senior managers.

---

[3]Norman Berg, "Strategic Planning in Conglomerate Companies," *Harvard Business Review*, May–June 1965, pp. 79–92. See also his "What's Different about Conglomerate Management?" *Harvard Business Review*, November–December 1969)

The differences in the application of a concept of strategy to a modest single business on the one hand and to a multinational conglomerate on the other—although important—mean that the ability to conceive of a business in strategic terms must be distributed throughout the organization in a complex company. The problems of choosing among strategic alternatives and making the choice effective over time, together with the problems of ensuring that such organization processes as performance measurement do not impede the choice, must be a familiar part of the management tasks of many people besides the general managers. All those involved in the strategic process, it follows, are vitally concerned with how a strategy can be evaluated so that it may be continued, amended, or abandoned as appropriate. Operating level managers who make a strategic proposal should be able to test its validity against corporate norms if for no other reason than their own survival. Those who must approve and allocate funds to such proposals should have a criterion to evaluate their worth going beyond a general confidence (or lack of it) in the ability of the proponents.

CRITERIA FOR EVALUATION

How is the actual or proposed strategy to be judged? How are we to know that one strategy is better than another? A number of important questions can regularly be asked. As is already evident, no infallible indicators are available. With practice they will lead to reliable intuitive discriminations.

1. *Is the strategy identifiable and has it been made clear either in words or in practice?*

The degree to which attention has been given to the

strategic alternatives available to a company is likely to be basic to the soundness of its strategic decision. To cover in empty phrases ("Our policy is planned profitable growth in any market we can serve well") an absence of analysis of opportunity or actual determination of corporate strength is worse than to remain silent, for it conveys the illusion of a commitment when none has been made. The unstated strategy cannot be tested or contested and is likely therefore to be weak. If it is implicit in the intuition of a strong leader, the organization is likely to be weak and the demands the strategy makes upon it are likely to remain unmet. A strategy must be explicit to be effective and specific enough to require some actions and exclude others.

2. *Does the strategy exploit fully domestic and international environmental opportunity?*

An unqualified yes answer is likely to be rare even in the instance of such global giants as General Motors. But the present and future dimensions of markets can be analyzed without forgetting the limited resources of the company in order to outline the requirements of balanced growth and the need for environmental information. The relation between market opportunity and organizational development is a critical one in the design of future plans. Unless growth is incompatible with the resources of an organization or the aspirations of its management, it is likely that a strategy that does not purport to make full use of market opportunity will be weak also in other aspects. Vulnerability to competition is increased by lack of interest in market share.

3. *Is the strategy consistent with corporate competence and resources, both present and projected?*

Although additional resources, both financial and managerial, are available to companies with genuine opportunity, the availability of each must be finally determined and programmed along a practicable time scale. This may be the most difficult question in this series. The key factor which is usually left out is the availability of management for effective implementation or the opportunity cost implicit in the assignment of management to any task. It is also very difficult to assess distinctive competence, and few companies have done it to the satisfaction of more than one person.

4. *Are the major provisions of the strategy and the program of major policies of which it is comprised internally consistent?*

A foolish consistency, Emerson said, is the hobgoblin of little minds, and consistency of any kind is certainly not the first qualification of successful corporation presidents. Nonetheless, one advantage of making as specific a statement of strategy as is practicable is the resultant availability of a careful check on fit, unity, coherence, compatibility, and synergy—the state in which the whole of anything can be viewed as greater than the sum of its parts. For example, a manufacturer of chocolate candy who depends for two thirds of his business upon wholesalers should not follow a policy of ignoring them or of dropping all support of their activities and all attention to their complaints. Similarly, two engineers who found a new firm expressly to do development work should not follow a policy of accepting orders that, though highly profitable, in effect turn their company into a large job shop, with the result that unanticipated financial and production problems take all the time that might have gone into development. An examination of any substantial firm will reveal at least some details in which policies pursued by different departments tend to go in different directions. Where inconsistency threatens concerted effort to achieve budgeted results within a planned time period, then consistency becomes a vital rather than merely an esthetic problem.

5. *Is the chosen level of risk feasible in economic and personal terms?*

Strategies vary in the degree of risk willingly undertaken by their designers. For example, a small food company in pursuit of its marketing strategy deliberately courted disaster in production slowdowns and in erratic behavior of cocoa futures. But the choice was made knowingly and the return was likely to be correspondingly great. The president was temperamentally able to live under this pressure and presumably had recourse if disaster struck. At the other extreme, another company had such modest growth aspirations that the junior members of its management were unhappy. They would have preferred a more aggressive and ambitious company. Although risk cannot always be known for sure, the level at which it is estimated is, within limits, optional. The riskiness of any future plan should be compatible with the economic resources of the organization and the temperament of the managers concerned.

6. *Is the strategy appropriate to the personal values and aspirations of the key managers?*

Until we consider the relationship of personal values to the choice of strategy, it is not useful to dwell long upon this criterion. But, to cite an extreme case, the deliberate falsification of warehouse receipts to conceal the absence of soybean oil from the tanks which are supposed to contain it would not be an element of competitive strategy to which most of us would like to be committed. A strong personal attraction of leisure, to cite a less extreme example, is inconsistent with a strategy requiring all-out effort from the senior members of a company. Or if, for example, a new president abhors conflict and competition, then it can be predicted that the hard-driven firm of an earlier day will have to change its strategy when he takes over. Conflict between personal preferences, aspirations, and goals of the key members of an organization and the plan for its future is a sign of danger and a harbinger of mediocre performance or failure.

7. *Is the strategy appropriate to the desired level of contribution to society?*

Closely allied to the value is the ethical criterion. As the professional obligations of business are acknowledged by an increasing number of senior managers, it grows more and more appropriate to ask whether the current strategy of a firm is as socially responsible as it might be. Although it can be argued that filling any economic need contributes to the social good, it is clear that manufacturers of cigarettes might well consider diversification on grounds other than their fear of future legislation. That the strategy should not require violations of law or ethical practice to be effective has become abundantly clear with the revelation in the mid-70s of widespread bribery and questionable payments, particularly in overseas activities. Honesty and integrity may seem exclusively questions of implementation, but if the strategy is not distinctive, making it effective in competition may tempt managers to unethical practice. Thus a drug manufacturer who emphasizes the production of amphetamines at a level beyond total established medical need is inevitably compelling corruption. The meeting of sales quotas at the distribution level necessitates distribution of the drug as "speed" with or without the cooperation of prescribing physicians. To the extent that the chosen economic opportunity of the firm has social costs, such as air or water pollution, a statement of intention to deal with these is desirable and prudent. Ways to ask and answer this question will be considered in the section on the company and its responsibilities to society.

8. *Does the strategy constitute a clear stimulus to organizational effort and commitment?*

For organizations which aspire not merely to survive but to lead and to generate productive performance in a climate that will encourage the development of competence and the satisfaction of individual needs, the strategy selected should be examined for its inherent attractiveness to the organization. Some undertakings are inherently more likely to gain the commitment of able men of goodwill than others. Given the variety of human preferences, it is risky to illustrate this difference briefly. But currently a company that is vigorously expanding its overseas operations finds that several of its socially conscious young people exhibit more zeal in connection with its work in developing countries than in Europe. Generally speaking, the bolder the choice of goals and the wider range of human needs they reflect, the more successfully they will appeal to the capable membership of a healthy and energetic organization.

9. *Are there early indications of the responsiveness of markets and market segments to the strategy?*

Results, no matter how long postponed by necessary preparations, are, of course, the most telling indicators of soundness, so long as they are read correctly at the proper time. A strategy may pass with flying colors all the tests so far proposed, and may be in internal consistency and uniqueness an admirable work of art. But if within a time period made reasonable by the company's resources and the original plan the strategy does not work, then it must be weak in some way that has escaped attention. Bad luck, faulty implementation, and competitive counter-moves may be more to blame for unsatisfactory results than flaws in design, but the possibility of the latter should not be unduly discounted. Conceiving a strategy that will win the company a unique place in the business community, that will give it an enduring concept of itself, that will harmonize its diverse activities, and that will provide a fit between environmental opportunity and present or potential company strength is an extremely complicated task.

We cannot expect simple tests of soundness to tell the whole story. But an analytical examination of any company's strategy against the several criteria here suggested will nonetheless give anyone concerned with making, proving, or contributing to corporate planning a good deal to think about.

PROBLEMS IN EVALUATION

The evaluation of strategy is as much an act of judgment as is the original conception, and may be as subject to error. The most common source of difficulty is the misevaluation of current results. When results are unsatisfactory, as we have just pointed out, a reexamination of strategy is called for. At the same time, outstandingly good current results are not necessarily evidence that the strategy is sound. Abnormal upward surges in demand may deceive marginal producers that all is well within their current strategy, until expansion of more efficient competitors wipes out their market share. Extrapolation of present performance into the future, overoptimism and complacence, and underestimation of competitive response and of the time required to accommodate to changes in demand are often by-products of success. Unusually high profits may blind the unwary manager to impending environmental change. His concern for the future can under no circumstances be safely suspended. Conversely, a high-risk strategy that has failed was not necessarily a mistake, so long as the risk was anticipated and the consequences of failure carefully calculated. In fact, a planning problem confronting a number of diversified companies today is how to encourage their divisions to undertake projects where failure can be afforded but where success, if it comes, will be attended by high profits not available in run-of-the-mill, low-risk activities.

Although the possibility of misinterpreting results is by far the commonest obstacle to accurate evaluation of strategy, the criteria previously outlined suggest immediately some additional difficulties. It is as easy to misevaluate corporate resources and the financial requirements of a new move as to misread the environment for future opportunities. To be overresponsive to industry trends may be as dangerous as to ignore them. The correspondence of the company's strategy with current environmental developments and an overreadiness to adapt may obscure the opportunity for a larger share of a declining market or for growth in profits without a parallel growth in total sales. The decision of American Motors not to follow trends toward big cars in the middle 1950s was a strategic alternative running counter to massive current trends in demand.

The intrinsic difficulty of determining and choosing among strategic alternatives leads many companies to do what the rest of the industry is doing rather than to make an independent determination of opportunity and resources. Sometimes the companies of an industry run like sheep all in one direction. The similarity among the strategies, at least in some periods of history, of insurance companies, banks, railroads, and airplane manufacturers may lead one to ask whether strategic decisions were based upon industry convention or upon independent analysis. Whether the similarity of timing, decision, and reaction to competition constitutes independent appraisals of each company's situation, or whether imitation took the place of independent decision is the basis of some wonder. At any rate, the similarity of one company's strategy to that of its competitors does not constitute the assurance of soundness which it might at first suggest.

A strategy may manifest an all-too-clear correspondence with the personal values of the founder, owner, or chief executive. Like a correspondence with dominant trends and the strategic decisions of competitors, this may also be deceptive and unproductive. For example, a personal preference for growth beyond all reasonable expectations may be given undue weight. It should be only one factor among several in any balanced consideration of what is involved in designing strategy. Too little attention to a corporation's actual competence for growth or diversification is the commonest error of all.

It is entirely possible that a strategy may reflect in an exaggerated fashion the values rather than the reasoned decisions of the responsible manager or managers and that imbalance may go undetected. That this may be the case is a reflection of the fact that the entire business community may be dominated by certain beliefs of which one should be wary. A critic of strategy must be at heart enough of a nonconformist to raise questions about generally accepted modes of thought and the conventional thinking which serves as a substitute for original analysis. The timid may not find it prudent to challenge publicly some of the ritual of policy formulation. But even for them it will serve the purposes of criticism to inquire privately into such sacred propositions as the one proclaiming that a company must grow or die or that national planning for energy needs is anathema.

Another canon of management that may engender questionable strategies is the idea that cash funds in excess of reasonable dividend requirements should be reinvested whether in revitalization of a company's traditional activities or in mergers and acquisitions that will diversify products and services. Successful operations, a heretic might observe, sometimes bring riches to a company which lacks the capacity to reemploy them. Yet a decision to return to the owners substantial amounts of capital which the company does not have the competence or desire to put to work is an almost unheard-of development. It is therefore appropriate, particularly in the instance of very successful companies in older and stable industries, to inquire how far strategy reflects a simple desire to put all resources to work rather than a more valid appraisal of investment opportunity in relation to unique corporate strengths. We should not forget to consider an unfashionable, even if ultimately also an untenable, alternative—namely, that to keep an already large worldwide corporation within reasonable bounds, a portion of the assets might well be returned to stockholders for investment in other enterprises.

The identification of opportunity and choice of purpose are such challenging intellectual activities that we should not be surprised to find that persistent problems attend the proper evaluation of strategy. But just as the criteria for evaluation are useful, even if not precise, so the dangers of misevaluation are less menacing if they are recognized. We have noted some inexactness in the concept of strategy, the problems of making resolute determinations in the face of uncertainty, the necessity for judgment in the evaluation of soundness of strategy, and the misevaluation into which human error may lead us. None of these alters the fact that a business enterprise guided by a clear sense of purpose rationally arrived at and emotionally ratified by commitment is more likely to have a successful outcome, in terms of profit and social good, than a company whose future is left to guesswork and chance. Conscious strategy does not preclude brilliance of improvisation or the welcome consequences of good fortune. Its cost is principally thought and work for which it is hard but not impossible to find time.

[3]

Concept of Strategy

Strategy is when you are out of ammunition, but keep right on firing so that the enemy won't know.

AUTHOR UNKNOWN

The Problem

During the past twenty years the concept of strategy has become one of the everyday words of managers, and the practice of strategic planning is now widespread among large and medium-sized firms.

This interest in strategy was caused by growing realization that the firm's environment has become progressively changeable and discontinuous from the past and that, as a result, objectives alone are insufficient as decision rules for guiding the firm's strategic reorientation as it adapts to changing challenges, threats and opportunities.

The new decision rules and guidelines, which guide the process of development of an organization, have been defined as *strategy*. It will be recalled from discussion in Chapter 2 that capital investment theory makes no use of the concept of strategy. The need for it arises from characteristics which are peculiar to the strategic problem: the fact that a firm needs direction and focus in its search for and creation of new opportunities and the fact that it is to the firm's advantage to seek entries with strong synergistic potential.

The first two sections of this chapter develop the basic concept of strategy. The next three sections explore the usefulness of strategy and conditions under which explicit strategy formulation becomes necessary. The two following sections define two basic strategies used in modern practice: the portfolio and competitive strategies. The penultimate section then comments on the use of strategies in different types of firms, while the final section differentiates the concept of strategy from the concept of policy.

Concept of the Firm's Business and the Common Thread

Objectives set the performance levels which a firm seeks to achieve, but they do not describe the business of the firm, unless statements such as 'the firm is in 20 per cent ROI business' or in 'flexible position business' are constructed to provide the description.

In a pioneering article published in 1960, Theodore Levitt[1] suggested that a more definitive description of the firm's role in the environment is requisite for growth and success. Such a description should encompass a broad scope of natural extensions of the firm's product-market position, derived from some core characteristic of the present business. Thus railways would view themselves in the 'transportation business' and petroleum companies in the 'energy business'.

While plausible, such broad statements of 'the business we are in' are not sufficiently precise to guide the firm's strategic development. Does it follow from this concept that railways should be in the long-haul trucking industry? The answer would seem to be yes. But how about taxi-cab or rental-car business? These are also transportation industries, but at first glance would seem to have little in common with railways. It is hard to see where the skills, facilities, and experience of railway companies have anything to contribute to the latter areas. Consider the energy business for petroleum companies. Does it follow that they should diversify into fabrication of uranium fuel for atomic power plants, build the power plants, or retail electricity? The respective management, technical, production, and marketing skills are all different. Where is the common core capability?

The weakness with concepts such as 'transportation business' or 'energy business' is that they are too broad and do not provide a 'common thread' – a relationship between present and future product-markets which would enable outsiders to perceive where the firm is heading, and the inside management to give it guidance.

A separate question is how strong the common thread must be. Royal Little has built the first classic conglomerate company, the Textron Corp., composed of consumer electronics, textiles, helicopters, work shoes and satellite motors, etc. – all without a strongly apparent common thread. Many other firms have followed Little's example in creating numerous conglomerate firms. On the other hand many other firms followed the pioneering example of the Du Pont Company by closely following a very clearly defined common thread.

It is useful to review how firms usually identify the nature of their business. Some firms are identified by the characteristics of their product line. Thus there are 'transistor companies', 'machine-tool companies' and 'automobile companies'. Others are described by the technology which

102 · Strategy Formulation

underlies the product line. such as 'steel companies'. 'aluminium companies' and 'glass companies'. Each may sell a wide range of different products to different users. but a common thread is provided by a manufacturing and/or engineering technology.

Firms are also described in terms of their markets. Here it is useful to make a distinction between customers and missions. A *mission* is an existing product *need*; a *customer* is the actual *buyer* of the product: the economic unit (such as an individual, a family, a business firm) which possesses both the need and the money with which to satisfy it.

The usefulness of this distinction lies in the fact that sometimes the customer is erroneously identified as the common thread of a firm's business. In reality a given type of customer will frequently have a range of unrelated product missions or needs. He would not necessarily satisfy them through the same purchasing channels, nor use the same approach to buying.

Thus, the individual consumer fills his food needs at the supermarket and his entertainment needs at a television dealer's. Since the product technology, the distribution channels, and the customer motivation are different. no strong common thread is available to a firm which would attempt to sell both food and television sets. Similarly, a company which supplies weapon systems for the Army's combat missions would have a better common thread in supplying control systems to industry than in selling replacement parts for Army trucks.

In selecting a useful range of missions of a particular customer, a firm needs to find a common thread either in product characteristics, technology, or similarity of needs. Thus agricultural machinery firms supply a range of needs of the farmer. All of these are related parts of his overall mission of tilling and harvesting the soil. Similarly, a home-appliance manufacturer offers effort-saving products for the home which may range from washing machines to electronic irons.

In this perspective it is easy to see why the term 'transportation business' fails to supply the common thread. First, the range of possible missions is very broad: intra-urban, inter-urban, intra-continental, and inter-continental transportation; through the media of land, air, water, underwater; for moving passengers and/or cargo. Second, the range of customers is wide: the individual, family, business firm, or government office. Third, the 'product' varies: car, bus, train, ship, aeroplane, helicopter, taxi, truck. The number of practical combinations of the variables is large, and so is the number of common threads.

While such a concept of business is too broad to be useful, the traditional identification of a firm with a particular industry has become too narrow Today a great many firms find themselves in a number of different industries. Furthermore, the boundaries of industries are continually changing, and new ones are being born. For example, radio. television, transistor, home appliance and atomic energy are all industries which did not exist fifty years ago. The need is for a concept of business which on the one hand will give specific guidance for the firm and on the other hand will provide room for growth. We shall describe such a concept in the next section.

Concept of Strategy

Strategy is one of several sets of decision-making rules for guidance of organizational behaviour. For example:

1. Yardsticks by which the present and future performance of the firm is measured. The quality of these yardsticks is usually called *objectives* and the desired quantity *goals*.

2. Rules for developing the firm's relationship with its *external* environment: *what* products-technology the firm will develop, *where* and *to whom* the products are to be sold, and *how* will the firm gain advantage over competitors. This set of rules is called the product-market or *business strategy*.

3. Rules for establishing the internal relations and processes *within* the organization; this is frequently called the *administrative strategy*.

4. The rules by which the firm conducts its day-to-day business, called major *operating policies*.

A business strategy has several distinguishing characteristics:

1. The process of business-strategy formulation results in *no immediate action*. Rather, it sets the general directions in which the firm's position will grow and develop.

2. Therefore strategy must next be used to generate strategic projects through a *search process*. The role of strategy in search is first to *focus* it on areas defined by the strategy, and, second to *filter out* the uncovered possibilities which are inconsistent with the strategy.

3. Thus, *strategy becomes unnecessary whenever the historical dynamics of an organization will take it where it wants to go*. This is to say, when the search process is already focused on the preferred areas.

4. At the time of strategy formulation it is not possible to enumerate all

104 · Strategy Formulation

the project possibilities which will be uncovered. Therefore, strategy formulation must be based on *highly aggregated, incomplete* and *uncertain information* about classes of alternatives.

5. When the search uncovers specific alternatives, the more precise, less aggregated information which becomes available may cast doubts on the wisdom of the original strategy choice. Thus, successful use of strategy requires *strategic feedback*.

6. Since both strategy and objectives are used to filter projects, they appear similar. And yet they are distinct. *Objectives represent the ends* which the firm is seeking to attain, *while the strategy is the means to these ends*. The objectives are higher-level decision rules. A strategy which is valid under one set of objectives may lose its validity when the objectives of the organization are changed.

7. Finally, strategy and objectives are interchangeable; both at different points in time and at different levels of organization. Thus, some attributes of performance (such as, for example, market share) can be an objective of the firm at one time and its strategy at another. Further, as objectives and strategy are elaborated throughout an organization, a typical hierarchical relationship results: *elements of strategy at a higher managerial level become objectives at a lower one*.

In summary, strategy is an elusive and somewhat abstract concept. Its formulation typically produces no immediate concrete productive action in the firm. Above all, it is an expensive process both in terms of actual dollars and managerial time. Since management is pragmatic result-oriented activity, a question needs to be asked: whether an abstract concept, such as strategy, can usefully contribute to the firm's performance.

In the business firm, concern with explicit formulation of strategy is relatively recent. However, the history of business abounds with clear examples of deliberate and successful use of strategy. Du Pont's deliberate and successful move from explosives into chemicals in the 1920s is one example. Henry Ford's concentration on the Model T for the emerging mass market was another great success, but his strategy of vertical integration was a failure. As an alternative to Henry Ford's strategy, consider Durant's vision of a firm founded on a fully automotive product line, and Sloan's subsequent rationalization of this vision into a clear set of organizational guidelines.

A trained business observer can discern a unique strategy in a majority of successful firms. However, while discernible in most cases, frequently strategies are not made explicit. They are either a private concept shared only by the key management, or a diffuse, generally understood, but seldom verbalized sense of common purpose throughout the firm.

It has been argued by some managers, and with good reason, that this is a desirable state of things, that, because it represents a unique competitive advantage of the firm, strategy should not be made explicit and must be kept private.

Since the mid-1950s, American business literature has increasingly reflected an opposing view in favour of carefully and explicitly formulated strategy. This view favours not only making the strategy a matter of concern to many managers throughout the firm, but also to many of the relevant 'workers', particularly in marketing and R & D, since they are not only making important contributions to strategy formulation, but are also the principal agents of its implementation.

If the value of a concept is to be measured by its contribution to success, we would have to admit that somehow both of the above views are correct: a great many firms have succeeded and are succeeding without the benefit of an explicitly enumerated strategy, while a smaller and growing number have benefited from deliberate strategy formulation.

An explanation can be sought through resolution of another apparent paradox: strategy is a system concept which gives coherence and direction to growth of a complex organization. How is it possible, then, for a large and complex organization, such as a business firm, to attain coordination and coherence without making strategy explicit?

An answer is to be found in the nature of the firm's growth. If a firm is operating in growing markets, if the characteristics of demand change slowly, if the technology of products and processes is stable, if all these conditions exist, strategy needs to change slowly and incrementally. Coherence of behaviour and organizational coordination are attained through informal organizational learning and adaptation. New managers and workers are typically given long indoctrination periods into the nature of the business; their careers are shaped by gradual progression through the firm. In the process they acquire an experiential, almost intuitive, awareness of the firm's strategic guidelines. When environment, technology, or competition change in an orderly manner, these managers are able to adapt their responses incrementally, using their accumulated knowledge and experience. A manager in R & D can be expected to act coherently with managers in marketing and production. The result is reasonably coherent organizational growth. The strategy remains stable and implicit and the firm's products and market evolve in a logically incremental way.

106 · Strategy Formulation

It can be questioned whether such loosely coordinated behaviour produces the best possible growth, but it works demonstrably. Since the first half-century was a period of relatively stable continued growth, the absence of concern with strategy is not surprising.

The second half-century is a new 'ball game'. In many cases the historical organizational dynamics are a path to stagnation and/or decline. Therefore, strategy has emerged as a tool for reorienting the organizational thrust. Given this fact, several questions need to be asked concerning the utility of having a strategy.

The first is whether a systematic explicit strategy is a viable concept. Some writers (significantly, observers, not of the firm but of decision processes in the government) have argued that organizational complexity, uncertainties of information and limited human cognition make it impossible to approach strategy formulation in a systematic manner. Their argument is that strategy formulation must of necessity proceed in the adaptive, unsystematic, informal way observed in most organizations. The answer to this contention is that the proof of the pudding is in the eating. Numerous business firms, which in recent years formulated and announced their strategies, have put this argument to rest.

Given that systematic strategy formulation is feasible, the second question to be asked is whether it produces improvement in organizational performance, if used as an alternative to adaptive growth. Until quite recently we had no satisfactory answer to this question. However, within recent years, several pieces of evidence have been provided.

One of these comes from an extensive study of American mergers and acquisitions by this author and several colleagues. Among other significant results, we found that deliberate and systematic preplanning of acquisition strategy produces significantly better financial performance than an unplanned, opportunistic, adaptive approach. These results are valid under stringent tests of their statistic validity.[2]

Since this study, a number of subsequent research studies confirmed our findings, namely that explicit strategy formulation can improve performance.

When to Formulate Strategy

The third question we need to ask is when does recourse to strategy become essential. One condition is when rapid and discontinuous changes occur in the environment of the firm. This may be caused by saturation of traditional markets, technological discoveries inside or outside the firm, or sudden influx of new competitors.

Under these conditions, established organizational traditions and experience no longer suffice for coping with the new opportunities and new threats. Without the benefit of unifying strategy, the chances are high that different parts of the organization will develop different, contradictory and ineffective responses. Marketing will continue struggling to revive historical demand, production will make investments in automation of obsolete production lines, while R & D will develop new products based on an obsolete technology. Conflicts will result, and reorientation may come too late to guarantee survival of the firm.

When confronted with discontinuities, the firm is confronted with two very difficult problems:

1. How to choose the right directions for further growth from among many and imperfectly perceived alternatives; and
2. How to harness energies of a large number of people in the new chosen direction.

Answers to these questions are the essence of strategy formulation and implementation. At this point, strategy becomes an essential and badly needed managerial tool.

Such conditions were in fact the cause of interest in explicit strategy formulation in the United States during the mid-1950s, when pent-up wartime demand began to reach saturation; when technology began to make obsolete some industries and to proliferate new ones; and when restructuring of international markets presented both new threats and new opportunities for business firms.

An explicit new strategy also becomes necessary when the objectives of an organization change drastically as a result of new demands imposed on the organization by society. This is precisely what is happening today in many non-business purposive organizations: the church, the university, the government. And this was the reason for the efforts to introduce strategic planning into many of these institutions.

Difficulties Encountered in Implanting Strategy Formulation

One major source of difficulty comes from the fact that, in most organizations, the pre-strategy decision-making processes are heavily political in nature. Strategy introduces elements of rationality which are disruptive to the historical culture of the firm, and threatening to the political process.

108 · Strategy Formulation

A natural organizational reaction is to fight against the disruption of the historical culture and power structure, rather than confront the challenges posed by the environment. This reaction has been widely observed during introduction of strategic planning into business firms.

A no-less important difficulty is that introduction of strategic planning triggers conflicts between the historical profit making activities and the new innovative activities. Organizations typically do not have the capability, the capacity or the motivational systems to act and think strategically.

Finally, organizations generally lack the information about themselves and their environment which is needed for effective strategic planning; nor do they have the managerial talents capable of formulating and implementing strategy.

In Part 2 of this book we will be discussing approaches to anticipating and overcoming barriers to implanting strategy formulation in the firm.

Portfolio Strategy

In modern practice two related types of strategy are used to characterize the thrust of the firm's strategic development. We shall call the first the *strategic portfolio strategy* and the second the *competitive strategy*.

The portfolio strategy is the modern version of the 'business we are in' concept discussed in a previous section.

The firm can be conceived of as an assembly of distinctive *strategic business areas* (SBA's), each of which offers different future growth/profitability opportunities and/or will require different competitive approaches. (For a further discussion of the important concept of strategic business areas see Ansoff, *Implanting Strategic Management*.)

One way to state the portfolio strategy is by specifying the kinds of strategic business areas in which the firm intends to do business in the future, as well as the manner in which the SBA's will relate to one another.

There are four components of the portfolio strategy:

1. The first component is the *geographical growth vector* which specifies the scope and direction of the firm's future business.

The original edition of *Corporate Strategy* introduced the concept of the *growth vector* which specified the direction in which the firm intends to develop its strategic portfolio. This was illustrated by means of a matrix, shown in Figure 6.1. *Market penetration* denotes a growth direction through

Concept of Strategy · 109

Product Mission	Present	New
Present	Market penetration	Product development
New	Market development	Diversification

Figure 6.1. Growth Vector Components

the increase of market share for the present product-markets. In *market development* new missions are sought for the firm's products. *Product development* creates new products to replace current ones. Finally, *diversification* is distinctive in the fact that both products and missions are new to the firm. The common thread is clearly indicated, in the first three alternatives, to be either the marketing skills or product technology or both. In diversification, the common thread is less apparent and is certainly weaker.

Specification of the common thread through the growth vector is complementary to the product-market scope, since it gives the directions *within* an industry as well as *across* industry boundaries which the firm proposes to pursue.

With the perspective of twenty years' experience, a somewhat more complex description of the growth vector alternatives becomes apparent. Instead of the two dimensions of the original matrix (product and mission), it is more realistic to describe the geographical growth vector along the dimensions shown in Figure 6.2. The cube shows the three dimensions which the firm can use to define the thrust and the ultimate future scope of the business.

a. The dimension of *market need* (such as need for personal transportation or need for amplification of weak electrical signals).

b. The dimension of *product/service technology* (such as transistor technology, integrated circuit technology, or electro-optical technology).

110 · Strategy Formulation

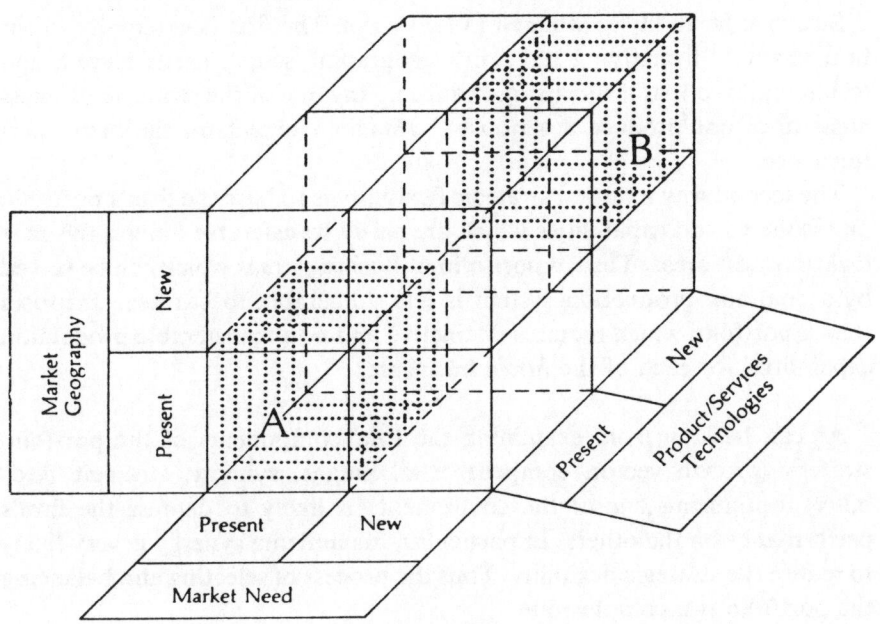

Figure 6.2. Dimensions of the Geographic Growth Vector

c. The *market geography* which defines the regions or nation states in which the firm intends to do business.

As the cube shows, the firm has a variety of combinations and directions in which it can modify its strategic portfolio. The extreme choices are: to continue serving its traditional need and geographical market with its traditional technology on the one hand (see the shaded cube labelled A in Figure 6.2), or to move vigorously to a new position on all three dimensions (see the shaded cube labelled B).

2. The second component of portfolio strategy is the *competitive advantage* which the firm will seek in its respective business areas. Thus the Du Pont Company has traditionally sought to succeed in all of its businesses through products based on patented advanced technology.

3. The third component of portfolio strategy is the *synergies* which the firm will seek among its businesses. In Du Pont's case the synergy was its advanced research and development capability in chemical technology.

4. The fourth component of portfolio strategy is the *strategic flexibility* of the strategic business portfolio.

Strategic flexibility is attained in two ways. The first is externally to the firm through diversifying the firm's geographic scope, needs served, and technologies so that a surprising change in any one of the strategic business areas does not produce a seriously damaging impact on the firm's performance.

The second way to attain strategic flexibility is to base the firm's portfolio on resources and capabilities which are easily transferable among the strategic business areas. Thus, a portfolio of business areas which can be served by a common production system is less vulnerable to strategic surprises than a portfolio which requires distinctive and non-transferable production capabilities for each of the firm's businesses.

As can be seen from examining the four components of the portfolio strategy (growth vector, competitive advantage, synergy, strategic flexibility), optimizing one of the components is likely to depress the firm's performance on the others. In particular, maximizing synergy is very likely to reduce the strategic flexibility. Thus the process of selecting and balancing the portfolio is a complex one.

Competitive Strategy

The portfolio strategy specifies the combinations of different strategic business areas in which the firm will seek to attain its objectives. The competitive strategy, on the other hand, specifies the distinctive approach which the firm intends to use in order to succeed in each of the strategic business areas.

According to micro-economic theory, success in a market-place is totally dependent on the price of the product or service. The logic is that the lowest price will enable the firm to capture a dominant market share. The resulting volume of sales will permit reduction of unit costs through economies of scale, thus making the firm the lowest cost producer in the industry. The firm will thus be able to maximize both its sales volume and its profits.

Two of the underlying assumptions of micro-economic theory are: (1) the products/services offered to the customers are undifferentiated, and (2) the customer seeks to minimize the cost of his purchases as the sole criterion in his decision.

These assumptions were valid in the developed nations during the first half of the twentieth century. Therefore, micro-economic theory offered a

Strategy Formulation

valid explanation of practice. As a result the optimal success strategy was simple: minimize the costs of the firm's products and sell at a price equal to or less than the competition. Since this behaviour resulted in optimization of the firm's market share, this strategy was frequently referred to as the *market share* or *market-position strategy*.

For reasons discussed earlier, significant changes occurred in the market-success factors during the second half of the century. Customers were no longer seeking a standard product at the lowest price. They demanded that products have a variety of features and performance characteristics that responded to their particular tastes, social status, buying power, etc. As a result, the ability to offer products responsive to the particular needs of a particular group of customers became a critical success factor and *product differentiation* became an important competitive strategy.

Micro-economic theory makes the implicit assumption that buyers have perfect information and are able to recognize not only price differences, but also differences in features and performance characteristics of the products/services offered to them. But experience has shown that their purchases were affected by the *image* of what products/services could do for them. Further, business firms discovered that customer tastes and preferences can be shaped, and new tastes and preferences can be created, through skilful advertising and promotion. As a result, *market (or image) differentiation* became another important competitive strategy.

Finally, success in the market-place against competitors no longer guaranteed satisfactory growth and profits, because an increasing number of industries were reaching the stage of demand saturation. If a firm had an aggressive growth objective it could no longer expect automatic growth from the market-place. To meet the growth objective the firm had to formulate and implement a growth thrust strategy, such as a geographic market expansion, market segmentation, stimulation of demand through artificial obsolescence, etc.

Thus, in a brief span of some twenty years new strategies critical to success in the market place were added to the traditional strategy of cost/price minimization.

To summarize, strategies which became important to success during the last quarter of the twentieth century are:

1. (The historical) *market-share maximization* strategy.
2. *Growth* strategy by which a firm assures its future growth.
3. *Market differentiation* (or market niche) strategy of creating a distinc-

tive image in the minds of potential customers for the firm's products/services.

4. *Product/service differentiation* (or product niche) strategy which differentiates the performance of the product/service from the competitors' products/services.

Need for Strategy in Different Types of Firms

In an earlier section we discussed the environmental conditions under which explicit strategy formulation becomes necessary. It remains to discuss the applicability of the components of the portfolio strategy to different types of firms:

1. A type of firm which needs the most comprehensive strategy is a fully integrated synergistic firm. Since its product-market decisions have long lead times, it needs guidance for R & D, and it must be able to anticipate change. Much of its investment is irreversible, since it goes into R & D, which cannot be recovered, and physical assets, which are difficult to sell. It must, therefore, minimize the chances of making bad decisions.

2. A conglomerate firm has less stringent strategy requirements. It does not seek synergy among its subsidiaries, nor does it use internal R & D as a primary source for diversification. Each subsidiary operates independently, and the common thread among them is primarily financial. The conglomerate does need objectives with threshold-goals type of provisions for partial ignorance. Its strategy would have no synergy component or growth vector component. A well-managed conglomerate would include the component of flexibility to protect the firm from strategic surprises. Such a firm may or may not have a well-defined growth vector to help focus search and develop local expert knowledge of some industries.

3. At the other extreme from a fully integrated, synergistic firm is a company which primarily buys and sells. This may be an investment trust, a pension fund or a real-estate syndicate. Its position differs from conglomerate in that the 'portfolio' of holdings is widely diversified and is highly negotiable, and the transfer costs are relatively low (sales tax, commission fees, etc.). Because portfolios are widely diversified, such firms seldom have the depth of knowledge of individual industries to enable them to seek a specific competitive advantage. Their planning is usually confined to objectives which are established on the basis of generally available industry data. Thus, for example, investment funds choose between the role of a 'growth fund' and that of a 'current earnings fund'.

114 · Strategy Formulation

Table 6.1. Strategy Requirements for Different Firms

Type of firm	P-M scope	Growth vector	Synergy	Competitive advantage	Objectives
Operating firm	√	√	√	√	√
Conglomerate firm	√(?)			√	√
Investment company					√

The three types of company above were described in what might be called their 'pure form'. In actuality there are various shadings of characteristics which make it difficult to place firms into one of the slots. There are different degrees of integration in synergistic companies, some companies act as conglomerates in some parts and are synergistic in others, and some investment firms *do* have industry experts and *do* specialize in certain industries. Therefore, each individual firm will have to determine its strategy requirement using the classification as a guide. Table 6.2 may be useful for this purpose.

It can easily be seen from the table that the synergistic firm requires the most complex strategy.* The remainder of our discussion will continue to deal with the more complex case.

Strategy, Policy, Programmes, and Operating Procedures

The origin of the term 'strategy' lies in the military art, where it is a broad, rather vaguely defined, 'grand' concept of a military campaign for *application* of large-scale forces against an enemy. Strategy is contrasted to *tactics*, which is a specific scheme for *employment* of allocated resources. In applications to business practice, the term *policy* has been often used interchangeably with strategy, thus creating unfortunate confusion between the two different concepts.

In the business vocabulary, long before the advent of strategy, the term policy was widely used in manuals of organization and procedures to denote a specific response to specific repetitive situations, e.g. 'overtime reimbursement policy', 'foul weather policy', 'educational refund policy'. 'policy for the evaluation of inventories'. A contingent event is recognized, such as a periodic need to work overtime, or a snowstorm. What needs to be done

---

* Investment funds which trade in listed securities have the additional advantage of knowing the full field of choice. There is no partial ignorance. This and low transfer costs permit an approach to the strategic problem which is much simpler than the present method.[3]

and the outcomes of such contingencies are *well known*; the contingencies are repetitive, but the time of specific occurrences cannot be specified in advance. In view of this, it is not worthwhile to require a new decision on what should be done each time overtime is needed or each time it snows. A better and more economical procedure is to prescribe, in advance, the response to be made whenever a specified contingency occurs. This is done through a written statement of the appropriate policy and of accompanying procedures for its implementation. Since the management decision is thus made in advance of the event, a rule for behaviour can be imposed on lower levels of supervision. Thus economies of management are realized, and consistency of action is assured.

When compared with our definition of strategy this meaning of policy is seen to be distinct and different. Policy is a *contingent decision*, whereas strategy is a *rule for making decisions*. Thus while implementation of policy can be delegated downward, implementation of strategy cannot, since last-minute executive judgement will be required. In technical terms, used by mathematical decision theorists, specification of strategy is forced under conditions of *partial ignorance*, when alternatives cannot be arranged and examined in advance, whereas under conditions of *risk* (alternatives are all known and so are their probabilities) or *uncertainty* (alternatives are known but not the probabilities), the consequences of different alternatives *can* be analysed in advance and decision made contingent on their occurrence. The lower-level executive merely needs to recognize the event and then act in accordance with his instructions.

As mentioned previously, condition of risk may mean assignment of probability either to the *occurrence* of an event or to its possible *outcomes*. When the occurrence is certain, but the outcome is either certain or uncertain, a different kind of decision, called a *programme*, is possible; this is a time-phased action sequence used to guide and coordinate operations. When the occurrence of an alternative is not only certain but also repetitive, the decision takes the form of a *standing operating procedure*.

Thus, the several types of decisions commonly made within a firm can be ranked in the order of increasing level of ignorance: standing operating procedures and programmes under conditions of certainty or partial risk, policies under conditions of risk and uncertainty, and strategies under conditions of partial ignorance.

There is an unfortunate coincidence in our definitions. We speak of 'strategic' decisions,* where 'strategic' means 'relating to firm's match to its environment', and of 'strategy', where the words means 'rules for decision

* Perhaps a better term would have been *entrepreneurial*

116 · Strategy Formulation

under partial ignorance'. This coincidence should not obscure the fact that all four basic types of decision described above – strategy, policy, programme, and standing operating procedure – occur in all three classes of problems: strategic, administrative, and operating.

It should further be made clear that all of the basic types of decisions may apply on organizational levels below the firm as a whole. Thus, for example, functional organizations, such as research, development, finance, and marketing, have a strong interface with the outside environment and will frequently be faced with conditions of partial ignorance. Under these conditions they will require appropriate strategies, such as R & D strategy, finance strategy, marketing strategy.

[4]

A Conceptual and Operational Model of Corporate Planning

INTRODUCTION

In this chapter are presented several basic conceptual and operational models of a comprehensive business planning structure and process. By a conceptual model is meant one that presents an idea of what a thing in general should be, or an image of a thing formed by generalizing from particulars. An operational model, in contrast, is one actually being used by an enterprise. An insightful conceptual model is a powerful tool because it provides proper guidance for practice.

A CONCEPTUAL MODEL FOR BUSINESS PLANNING

Chart 2-1 sets forth my conceptual model of the structure and process of effective and efficient business planning programs. This model was constructed after studying scores of planning systems. Consequently, it is not at all surprising that a large number of companies have planning systems in operation whose features correspond to it. This model records those plans needed in a typical business, their relationships with one another, and the sequence of actions necessary for proper planning and results. The model, therefore, is a logical expression of a required structure and process of planning and plans.

I have found the model to be flexible and adaptable to almost any size or type of business, style of management, or stage in the development of organized formal planning. These factors in a business can be counted on to cause great

32
A Conceptual and Operational Model of Corporate Planning

variations in the detailed planning practices of companies. But the strength of the model is revealed in the fact that when surface differences in planning are brushed aside, the model can be identified in most companies that have effectively organized comprehensive planning programs. So long as a manager is interested in undertaking coordinated corporate planning, this conceptual model can be made operational and adapted to most business environments.

It must be added, however, that although the model in Chart 2-1 is conceptually deceptively simple, it is also deceptively difficult to translate into a first-rate operational comprehensive planning program. We shall not in this chapter be concerned with the problems of putting the model into operation. That will be the subject of future chapters. Our intent here is to present as succinctly as possible the major features of the model and to compare it with other conceptual and operational models. A quick glance at Chart 2-1 and the table of contents of this book will show that various parts of the model will be the subject of future chapters. In these later discussions there will be presented detailed explanations and illustrations of each part of the model. The definitions and illustrations in the following presentation, therefore, can be brief.

BASIC FOUNDATIONS. To the left of Chart 2-1 are three underlying foundations of any company planning effort: fundamental organizational socio-economic purposes, values of top managers, and studies of the environment. Each has a profound and unique contribution to make in planning.

The socio-economic purposes refer to those underlying ends which society expects of its business institutions if they are to survive. At rock bottom this means that society demands that businesses utilize the resources at their disposal to satisfy the wants of society. If this is done, a business will profit and survive. If it is not done well, a business will make no profits and will die unless society wishes to subsidize it to assure its survival. It is useful for managers to keep in mind this underlying reason for the existence of business. It explains why, as businesses become larger and society becomes more complex, the things society wants from business, especially large business, become more numerous and sometimes contradictory.

The second fundamental set of foundations for planning are the values, ideas, and philosophies that managers hold. Each manager has a set of values, code of ethics, and moral standards which are unique to him. They are basic premises of planning. Those held by top managers are, of course, most influential in the overall planning program. Values are injected into all of the important elements of business planning. They may concern which objectives are to be sought. For instance, the decision to be the biggest and the technically best company in an industry, or both, depends upon a chief executive's values. The means chosen to achieve these ends are influenced by his values. How he wishes to treat employees, customers, competitors, or subcontractors also depends upon his values.

33

A Conceptual Model for Business Planning

Chart 2-1

Structure and Process of Business Planning

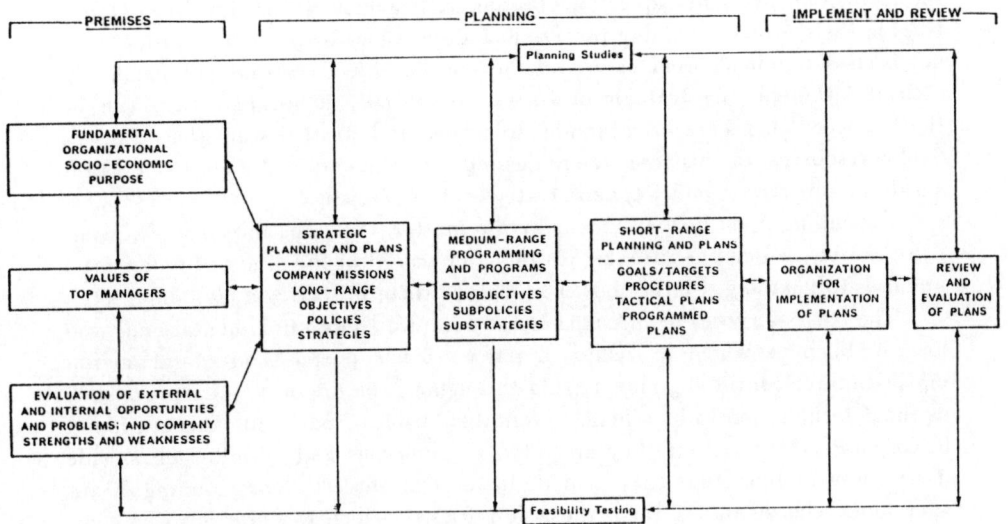

Similar to a diagram in "The Critical Role of Top Management in Long-Range Planning," *Arizona Review*, April 1966, also by George A. Steiner.

Some managers may demand that working conditions for employees be made pleasant; others may not think this important. Some may be ruthless competitors; others may seek to apply a rule of "do unto others as you would have others do unto you." Sometimes, as will be discussed in Chapter 6, the major values of top managers are expressed in written statements. Most values, however, are not. But whether written or not, they are of fundamental significance in the planning process.

A cardinal purpose of planning is to discover future opportunities and make plans to exploit them. Correspondingly, basic to long-range planning is the detection of obstructions that must be removed from the road ahead. The most effective plans are those which exploit opportunities and remove obstacles on the basis of an objective understanding of the strengths and weaknesses of the company. *The New York Times* several years ago saw an opportunity to exploit the Southern California market. The western version of its paper failed because it did not properly assess obstacles and weaknesses in entering this market. Among other things, it failed to see the impact of not having a residential house distribution system. As will be discussed in more detail in Chapter 8, the effort devoted to surveying the future is formidable in large companies, and the reasons are obvious—there is an enormous payoff to the skilled probing of a future and relating it to an unbiased study of a company's strengths and weaknesses.

34
A Conceptual and Operational Model of Corporate Planning

STRATEGIC PLANNING. The next major structural element in Chart 2-1 is strategic planning. Strategic planning is the process of determining the major objectives of an organization and the policies and strategies that will govern the acquisition, use, and disposition of resources to achieve those objectives. Objectives in the strategic planning process include missions or purposes, if they have not been determined previously, and the specific objectives that are sought by a firm. Although the strategic objectives are usually long-range, they can be short-range. Policies are broad guides to action, and strategies are the means to deploy resources. In this area we are dealing with the major, the most important and basic objectives, policies, and strategies of a company.

Depending upon how one looks at the matter, the basic missions of a company can be included in strategic planning, or placed in the area of fundamental premises to planning. I have chosen to include them in strategic planning.

The basic purposes or missions of the firm are those fundamental ends and lines of business which it wishes to pursue. Basic purposes are fundamental motivations or continuing aims lasting throughout the life of an enterprise, such as the determination to be a highly profitable business. Basic missions are found in corporate charters, but they are often so numerous and permit such a wide diversity of activity that they provide little or no direction for planning. Managers must choose among them those activities to which the firm is to be committed. A selection and statement of missions can make an enormous difference in planning. The Baldwin Locomotive Works might be a profitable company today if its mission had been changed from "making steam locomotives" to "providing motive power for railroads." In recent years more and more companies are coming to understand the power of a simple statement of basic company missions and are drafting such statements for general distribution. It is not necessary to express basic purposes and missions on paper, but as a starting point in planning it is desirable to do so.

The subject matter that may be covered in strategic planning includes every type of activity of concern to an enterprise. Among the areas are profits, capital expenditures, organization, pricing, labor relations, production, marketing, finance, personnel, public relations, advertising, technological capabilities, product improvement, research and development, legal matters, management selection and training, political activities, and so on.

The characteristics of strategic planning differ greatly from those of medium-range programming and short-range planning, differences which will be discussed later in the chapter. At this point it is pertinent to note that strategic planning covers different periods of time for different subjects. For example, a strategic plan may be made to merge with another company within a week. This is clearly short-range as compared with a plan to acquire a major company within a five-year period. Also, strategic plans are not always written; frequently they are found only in the head of the chief executive, who communicates them when he sees fit to do so.

35
A Conceptual Model for Business Planning

MEDIUM-RANGE PROGRAMMING. Medium-range programming is the process in which detailed, coordinated, and comprehensive plans are made for selected functions of a business to deploy resources to reach objectives by following policies and strategies laid down in the strategic planning process. All medium-range programs and plans for a company cover the same period of time, usually five years. Whatever the period covered, plans are worked out in considerable detail for each year of the planning period. For instance, if a major division of a decentralized company is working out medium-range programs on the basis of objectives, policies, and strategies developed by corporate headquarters in the strategic planning process, it will develop subobjectives, subpolicies, and substrategies for its own operations. It may have a separate set of objectives, policies, and strategies for each of its lines of business. It may develop sets of plans for each product. Or, it may develop only one set of plans for the entire division. But, whatever the breakdown, details are developed for all plans for each of the years included in the planning period.

Detailed plans are most often made in the medium-range programming process for such major functional areas as production, sales, profits, personnel, capital expenditures, finance, and research and development. Usually, *pro forma* balance sheets and profit-and-loss statements are also prepared for each year.

A major characteristic of medium-range programming is thorough coordination throughout the most important functions of the enterprise. At the strategic planning level there is an effort to assure broad general coordination among dominant parts of an enterprise. In the medium-range programming there is a specific and detailed meshing of the parts. For instance, details of research and development are closely related to products that the firm expects to produce and sell in the future, advertising plans are tied to the product, engineers work with production-line managers to design parts in conformance with efficient manufacturing practices, and employee hiring and transfer plans are related to anticipated production schedules. In this planning process an effort is made to have the most important parts of the business system mesh properly.

SHORT-TERM BUDGETS AND DETAILED FUNCTIONAL PLANS. Short-term budgets and detailed functional plans include such matters as short-range targets for salesmen, budgets for material purchases, short-term advertising plans, inventory replenishment, and employment schedules. If the medium-range programs are detailed and the timing of the overall planning cycle coincides with the required dates for budget-making, short-term plans may be the same as the first year of the medium-range programs. The detail of the medium-range programs is not usually deep enough for current operations, hence, a separate set of short-range plans is usually required. For instance, short-term plans may include details on schedules of specific raw materials going through production, into inventory, and out as finished products. Not only may the detail needed for current operations be much greater than required in the medium-range programming

A Conceptual and Operational Model of Corporate Planning

process, but it is usually needed on a short-time basis, such as weekly, monthly, or quarterly.

PLANNING STUDIES. At the top of Chart 2-1 recognition is given to planning studies. In mind are studies made especially for the planning process. They may include, for example, analyses of the future markets of a company upon which basis strategic planning proceeds. They may include studies of machinery replacement policy, as the basis for short-term equipment expenditures. These studies are usually basic premises which are of high significance in guiding the planning process. Chapter 8 will deal with them in some detail.

FEASIBILITY TESTING. At all stages in the planning process it is necessary to test the feasibility of aims and means to achieve them. Planning is not well done when ends and means are decided solely by seat-of-the-pants methods. All sorts of conflicts arise in planning which must be reconciled and balances struck. Feasibility tests differ among parts of the planning process, but in general they relate to such questions as the values that managers hold, available facilities, personnel capabilities, timing, cash flows, return on investment, and market penetration.

ORGANIZATION. Plans will not be carried out if suitable organizational arrangements are not made to do so. If plans are made to develop a new product, a suitable organization must be established to carry out those plans. In a company with many new products this may become rather complex. Or, if a set of plans is developed for a new integrated attack to penetrate a new market, there must be a careful organization of effort. These organizational arrangements, of course, should be considered in the planning process. Although they may be planned in the planning process, the organization *per se* assures the carrying out of the plans.

REVIEW AND EVALUATION. An effective planning program needs continuous surveillance as well as periodic review to assure that plans are being carried out and that new plans are devised as required. If events are not in conformance with plans, it then becomes management's responsibility to find out why. It may be that deviation from plans is quite appropriate in light of new considerations. In this event managers implement plans with flexibility and, we shall assume, to the net advantage of the firm. It may also be that plans are not being followed when they should be. In this event it is a function of management to see that plans are followed.

Conceptually, the entire comprehensive planning process should be recycled every year. Naturally, a review and evaluation of past experience should be a major ingredient in the new planning cycle.

FEEDBACK LOOPS. The process of planning is one in which complex feedback loops exist in each part and tie together the different parts. Although obvious, this fact is of high significance. By its coordination, feasibility, and balance, an over-all system optimization can be achieved at a minimum cost of effort and time.

CENTRALIZED VERSUS DECENTRALIZED COMPANIES. In a centralized company, such as Allstate Insurance, the entire process shown in Chart 2-1 is done in the central headquarters of the company. In a decentralized company, such as Celanese, the central headquarters prepares the strategic plans which are then transmitted to the divisions. There, medium-range programming and short-range plans are prepared and then transmitted to headquarters for review and approval. In some companies an over-all medium-range set of plans is prepared for the entire company from the divisional plans. Sometimes this step is omitted.

STRATEGIC VERSUS TACTICAL PLANNING

To comprehend corporate planning it is most important to understand the differences between strategic and tactical planning. At one extreme on a spectrum is strategic planning, as previously defined. At the other end is tactical planning or the detailed deployment of resources to achieve strategic plans. Our interest here is in drawing a line of demarcation between the two extremes to highlight the conceptual distinctions. The following elements are listed in no particular order of importance (Steiner and Cannon 1966, pp. 11-14; Anthony 1964, pp. 18-24; and Anthony 1965).

1. *Level of conduct.* Strategic planning is conducted at the highest levels of management (at headquarters and in major divisions) and relates exclusively to decisions in the province of these levels. Tactical planning is done at and relates to lower management levels.

2. *Regularity.* Strategic planning is both continuous and irregular. The process is continuous but the timing of decision is irregular for it depends upon and is triggered by the appearance of opportunities, new ideas, management initiative, crises, and other nonroutine stimuli. Tactical planning is done for the most part on a periodic cycle that is on a fixed time schedule.

3. *Subjective values.* Strategic planning is more heavily weighted with subjective values of managers than is tactical planning.

4. *Range of alternatives.* The total possible range of alternatives from which a management must choose is far greater, by definition, in strategic than in tactical planning.

5. *Uncertainty.* Again, uncertainty is usually much greater in strategic planning than in tactical planning. Not only is the time dimension much shorter

38
A Conceptual and Operational Model of Corporate Planning

in tactical than in strategic planning, but risks are much more difficult to assess and are considerably greater in strategic planning.

6. *Nature of problems.* Strategic planning problems are unstructured and tend to be one of a kind. Tactical planning problems are more structured and often repetitive in nature.

7. *Information needs.* Strategic planning requires large amounts of information derived from, and relating to, areas of knowledge outside the corporation. Most of the more relevant data needed relates to the future, is difficult to get with accuracy, and is tailored to each problem. In mind, for example, is information about competitors, future technology, social and political changes affecting corporate decisions, and economic developments altering markets. Tactical informational needs, in contrast, rely more heavily on internally generated data, particularly from accounting systems, and involve a higher proportionate use of historical information. For example, tactical plans to control production rest heavily upon internal historical records of past experience.

8. *Time horizons.* Strategic planning usually covers a long time spectrum but sometimes is very short, and varies from subject to subject. Tactical planning, in contrast, is of shorter duration and more uniform for all parts of the planning program.

9. *Completeness.* Strategic planning conceptually covers the entire scope of an organization. While at any one time only selected areas of business activity may be the subject of strategic planning, no corner of corporate activity is excluded from attention. Tactical planning covers the whole of a suborganizational unit responsible for executing parts of strategic plans. For example, tactical planning may include new product plans, construction, machine replacement, production, and so on, and coordinates these for the whole activity of a subunit.

10. *Reference.* Strategic planning is original in the sense that it is the source or origin for all other planning in an enterprise. In contrast, tactical planning is done within, and in pursuit of, strategic plans.

11. *Detail.* Strategic plans are usually broad and have many fewer details than tactical plans. The further out in time the strategic plans stretch, the fewer still are details. As Anthony (1964, p. 20) notes: "the concept of a master planner who constantly keeps all parts of the organization at some coordinated optimum is a nice concept but an unrealistic one. Life is too complicated for any human, or computer, to do this."

12. *Type of personnel mostly involved.* Strategic planning for the most part is done only by top management and its staff. Included in the concept of staff here would be line managers when acting as staff to top management. The numbers of people involved are comparatively few as contrasted with tactical planning where large numbers of managers and employees usually participate in the process.

13. *Ease of evaluation.* It is usually considerably easier to measure the effectiveness and efficiency of tactical plans than of strategic plans. Results of

Strategic versus Tactical Planning

strategic planning may become evident only after a number of years. Very frequently it is difficult to disentangle the forces which led to the results. In sharp contrast, tactical planning results are quickly evident and much more easily identified with specific actions.

14. *Development of objectives, policies, and strategies.* The objectives, policies, and strategies developed in strategic planning are new and generally debatable. Experience may be minimal in judging their correctness. At the other extreme, there usually is much experience to guide the development of tactical plans.

15. *Point of view.* Strategic planning is done from a corporate point of view, whereas tactical planning is done principally from a functional point of view.

BLURRING DIFFERENCES. Both conceptually and operationally, the lines of demarcation between strategic and tactical planning are blurred. At the extremes their differences are crystal clear, as in the above comparison. But these distinctions do not always hold. For example, both in theory and practice there is in planning an intricate ends-means chain. Strategy gives rise to tactics, and tactics may be considered a substrategy which in turn employs tactics for execution. What is one manager's strategy is another's tactics, what is one manager's tactics is another's strategy. For example, strategic planning is done at the headquarters of a company. Substrategic planning within this strategic plan may be done in the major divisions of the company. Concretely, the corporation may decide that its strategy is to penetrate the European market by divisional acquisitions of foreign companies. Part of the tactical plan might be for the electronics division to decide to buy a majority interest in a plant in Germany that produces a product similar to one of its own. But this may also be considered a substrategy giving rise to a tactical plan which might be to acquire a minority interest in a specific plant through stock exchange rather than cash.

Differentiation of types of plans within tactical plans is important. At one extreme are tactical plans that have a number of characteristics of strategic plans. At the other extreme are tactical plans that are rather automatic in operation. For example, tactical plans for product improvement involve difficult managerial decisions over design, markets, financing, and pricing. As noted above, such planning in a division of a large company may be said to encompass substrategic planning as well as tactical planning. All depends upon who is looking—top management in central headquarters, or lower management in a division. Also involved in tactical decisions over product improvement are inventory replenishment policy, raw material purchases, machine tool replacement, or handling of new orders. A basic characteristic of such plans is that they are often almost completely automatic. Once management decides on an inventory replacement policy, for example, it automatically operates until management reviews the process and modifies or retains it. Discretion in operation is rather small or nonexistent in this sort of planning.

40
A Conceptual and Operational Model of Corporate Planning

IMPORTANCE OF DISTINCTIONS. These distinctions are of consequence for many reasons. First of all, a methodology for assuring first-rate strategic planning may be completely inappropriate when applied to tactical planning. Permitting the looseness and intuitive problem-solving techniques to be applied to more or less automatically derived tactical decisions is unwise. On the other hand, a quantitative decision model applicable in tactical planning may not only be inappropriate in strategic planning but may be dangerous. Among the highest requirements for effective strategic planning are imagination, creativity, and a sense of proper timing. Attempts to optimize strategic planning decisions with inappropriate models can weaken rather than strengthen these talents. On the other hand, a proper use of quantitative methods can sharpen the intuition and judgment of managers. (This is an issue to which we shall return in a later chapter.)

Second, the difference between strategic and tactical planning may be the source of conflict in an enterprise. For example, top management may decide as a matter of strategy to grow in sales and profits by shifting its present technological know-how into new products which appear to be more promising than those now being made. This sort of shift will require tactical plans in the functional areas of the company. But, these shifts may serve to reduce the efficiency of the divisions because productivity may actually decline until the shift is made and the product fulfills its promise. The manager of the production division may see his earnings fall off as the transition is made. The head of sales may similarly find costs rising relative to sales as his training expenses mount. Of course, in such situations there may not be open opposition on the part of functional managers, but they can find subtle ways to resist. Resolving such problems demands an understanding of the differences between the two types of planning, how to blend them, and how to manage (Andersen, 1965).

Third, a failure to distinguish between the two types of planning can create problems between line and staff in large enterprises. For example, the staff of a chief executive who is concentrating on the priority strategic directions of his company can easily lose his ear if it gets too deeply enmeshed in tactical planning. In the other direction, a headquarters staff of a company with decentralized authority in division general managers may easily clash with the general managers. This can result, for example, if headquarters staff develops broad objectives and strategies without much clarity as to how the divisions can implement the strategies and achieve the objectives. This is frustrating to division managers especially if they do not readily see how the objectives can be achieved with the strategies devised. On the other hand, if staff develops tactical plans which the division managers do not like there is a tendency for them to say, "You made the plans, now carry them out."

Fourth, strategic planning is usually done at a more leisurely pace than tactical planning. If there is a conflict in schedules, the functional managers may grasp the nettle and do strategic planning. For example, prices may be set without waiting for a general company strategy. Salesmen may be moved about, distribution channels changed, or other major decisions made without waiting to hear from top management.

Finally, there is a tendency for strategic planning and tactical planning to be separated. Although it is important to understand the distinction between strategic and tactical planning, each must be developed with reference to the other.

DISTINCTIONS AMONG MAJOR TYPES OF PLANNING IN MODEL

These conceptual differences between strategic and tactical planning explain major distinctions among the strategic planning, medium-range programming, and short-range budgeting and detailed functional planning structures given in Chart 2-1. In a general sort of way, the strategic planning in the chart matches the concept in mind in the previous discussion. Although tactical planning is not quite the same thing as short-range planning, for our purposes they can be considered roughly synonymous. In between are the medium-range programs which obviously incorporate both strategic and tactical planning characteristics. So, again, while conceptually there are clear distinctions among these three major planning processes, the differences are blurred at the edges of each.

PLANNING VERSUS CONTROL

In most elementary textbooks on management there is a distinction drawn between the management function of planning and that of controlling. To oversimplify, the definition of control is usually given as the process of making sure that performance takes place in conformance with plans. This is in sharp contrast to plans which determine the objectives, means, and standards against which performance is measured. To be sure, the elementary texts underscore the fact that implementation of plans must be done with a flexibility that recognizes the changing circumstances which may make a deviation from the plans not only proper but essential. This sort of determination is a major managerial responsibility. The texts also usually assert that although the basic distinction between planning and control is sharp the two are inseparable. They are inseparable because planning is necessary before controlling can be meaningful, and each must be done in light of the other. I find nothing wrong with these definitions and distinctions except that they do not adequately explain the phenomena.

It is not the purpose of this book to examine management control in detail. But several important considerations are in order to relate the model of Chart

A Conceptual and Operational Model of Corporate Planning

2-1 with management control. First, control is a multidimensional term and should be defined in a manner similar to the treatment of planning in Chapter 1. Control, like planning, has different meanings for its different dimensions.

Second, there is no question about the fact that planning and control, both conceptually (in Chart 2-1) and operationally, are inextricably interwoven. Medium-range programming and short-range budgeting, for example, are a combination of planning and control activities. Each is done in light of the other and a manager mixes both in managing. For example, plans are set, activities then take place, corrections must be made, new plans are prepared to meet the needs for corrections, and so on, for we are dealing here with a continuum. Planning and control are interrelated in another way. In certain instances, people in an enterprise are encouraged and permitted to participate in setting goals and standards for their own achievement. If this is related to efforts to encourage self-control their performance is intermixed with their commitment.*

Third, despite this intermingling, planning and control must be distinguished both conceptually and operationally. Conceptually, for example, the development of plans without proper control of activities taken to carry them out may not only lead to poor results but to developments completely contrary to plans. Planned profits, for example, may turn out to be losses. Perhaps of more realistic consequence is the fact that managerial relationships with people are considerably different as between planning and controlling (McGregor 1967, Chapter 8). Furthermore, the philosophy, attitude, and pursuit of planning and control will differ very much depending on the center of attention. To illustrate, the way in which a manager may go about planning for a new automobile model will vary enormously from the way in which the production line is controlled when the manufacturing process begins. To fail to distinguish between planning and control conceptually and operationally may lead to a misunderstanding not only of the processes themselves but of the ways in which they interrelate. But simple definitions to mark the differences are not too helpful for better understanding.

ANTHONY'S CONCEPTUAL MODEL

In recent years a number of conceptual models of corporate planning have appeared. One that is similar to the model presented above is that of Robert N. Anthony (1965, p. 22).

Anthony's model distinguishes, as shown in Chart 2-2, among strategic

---

* For example, McGregor (1967, p. 127) says: "The principle is that human beings will direct their effort, exercise self-control and responsibility, use their creativity in the service of goals to which they are committed." The assumption, of course, is that performance is closely related to commitment.

43
Anthony's Conceptual Model

Chart 2-2
Planning and Control Processes in Organization

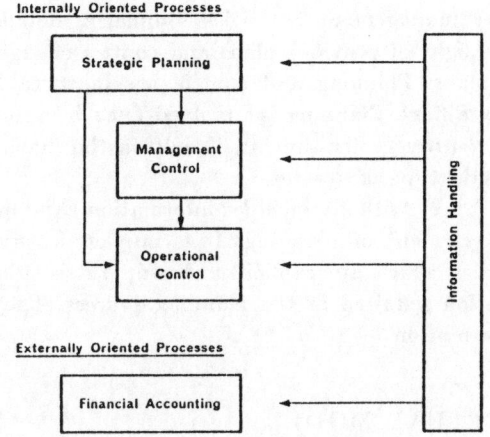

Source: Anthony, Robert N., *Planning and Control Systems: A Framework for Analysis* (Boston: Harvard Business School, Division of Research, 1965), p. 22.

planning, management control, and operational control. Strategic planning is defined as in my model. Management control, however, does not quite match my definition of medium-range programming. Anthony (1965, p. 27) defines management control as "the process by which managers assure that resources are obtained and used effectively and efficiently in the accomplishment of the organization's objectives." (Effectiveness and efficiency are defined by Anthony exactly as in Chapter 1.) Anthony draws a sharp distinction between management control and operational control. "Operational control," to him, "is the process of assuring that specific tasks are carried out effectively and efficiently" (1965, p. 69). What he has in mind are controls which are so programmed that rules prescribe actions, such as automated plants, production scheduling, order processing, check handling, and similar activities. His operational control is not synonymous with my short-range budgeting and detailed planning. Only a small part of this process in my model is synonymous with his operational control. Operational control is the same as that part of tactical planning, noted in my model, which is automatic in operation and requires no management attention other than to determine the automatic decision-making process or formula. As it turns out, Anthony's management control would encompass all of my medium-range programming plus a good bit of my short-range budgeting and detailed short-range functional planning.

There are merits in using Anthony's concept of management control because it embraces a combination of planning and control activities which managers

44
A Conceptual and Operational Model of Corporate Planning

actually employ. This is a useful insight, but it also applies to strategic planning at one extreme and to short-range planning at the other. A strategic plan cannot be conceived as being complete without some understanding of the control it exerts over management activities. Similarly, detailed short-range plans are made in the light of previous plans and control changes that may be required in existing plans. Planning and control are inextricably intermeshed in each; only the mix differs. Planning is involved even in automatic controls, such as automatic inventory replenishment, if only in the managerial planning decision to use a certain type of system.

As shown in Chart 2-2, Anthony includes information handling in his model. This is an important element of planning. It is implicit in my model except for the planning studies which are explicitly shown. These studies do not include all the information required in the planning process. They are only one type of planning information.

THE SRI CONCEPTUAL MODEL

Chart 2-3 shows the Stanford Research Institute model of plans. Fundamentally, the aggregations are similar to mine and Anthony's. The strategic plan "outlines in broad, general terms the characteristics and accomplishments that the firm can, and wants to, achieve" (Stewart 1963, p. 7). It includes basic company purpose, selected strategy to accomplish the purpose, specific goals of the strategy, the means for monitoring progress toward goals, and specific conditions (internal and external) which will permit the firm to attain its goals (Stewart, Allen, and Cavender 1963, p. 1). It would appear that this concept of strategic planning would embrace activity which includes all of my foundations for planning to the extreme left of Chart 2-1 plus some, but not all, of my strategic planning.

The SRI strategic plan then leads to a corporate development plan and an operations plan. These in turn lead to further detailed plans. The area covered by these plans presumably would include part of my strategic plan plus all of my medium-range programming plus all of my short-range planning.

THE GILMORE-BRANDENBERG MODEL

The Gilmore-Brandenberg concept was, to my knowledge, the first comprehensive formulation of a corporate planning model. This model breaks down the top-management planning job into four major phases. Furthermore, it identifies key decision or synergistic points in the planning process. These are defined as those where joint performance of several programs may be expected to be greater than the sum of the performance of individual programs before combination.

This model conceptually is quite comparable to the others discussed here.

45
Conceptual Steps in Planning

It is, however, much too detailed to be reproduced here (Gilmore and Brandenberg 1962).

CONCEPTUAL STEPS IN PLANNING

The conceptual steps in planning are essentially those basic problem-solving procedures which must be followed in decision-making. The simplest model includes these elementary steps: (1) determine and define the problem,

Chart 2-3

The System of Plans

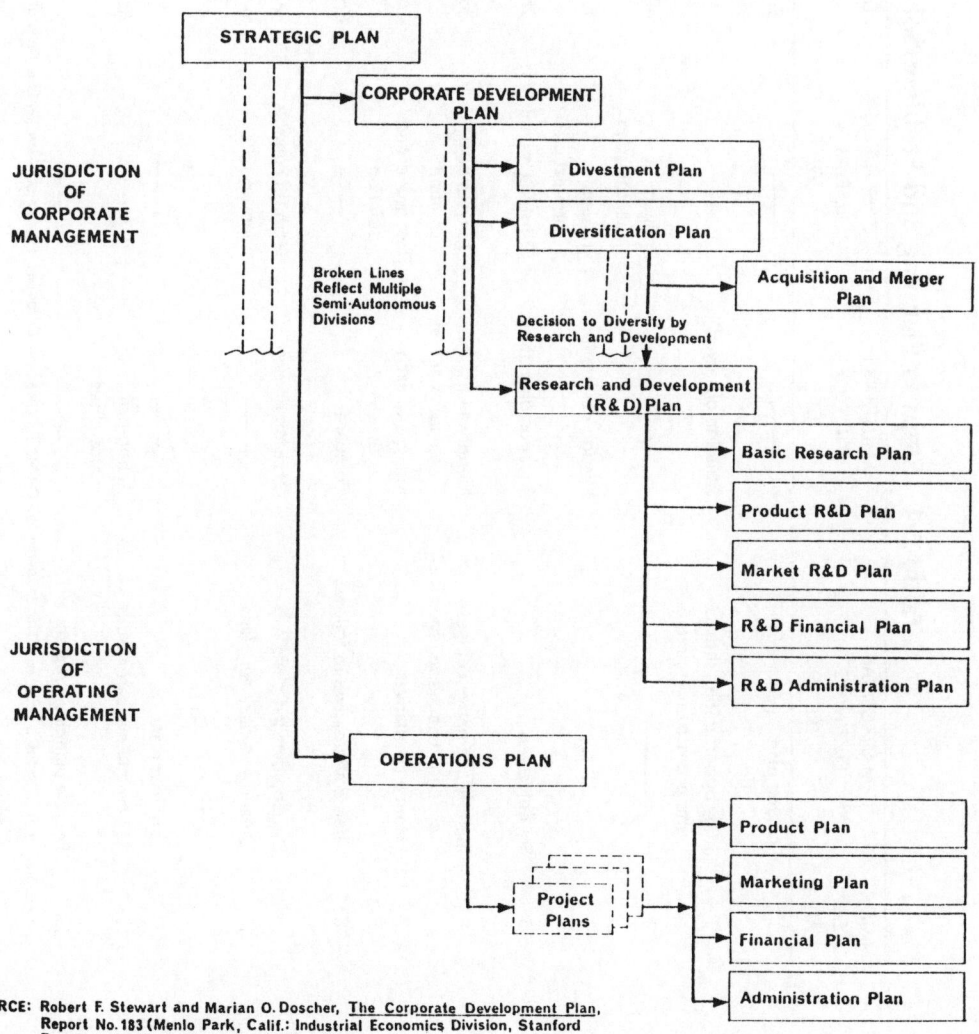

SOURCE: Robert F. Stewart and Marian O. Doscher, <u>The Corporate Development Plan</u>, Report No. 183 (Menlo Park, Calif.: Industrial Economics Division, Stanford Research Institute, September 1963), p. 21.

Table 2-1 Steps in Planning and Problem-Solving*

MAJOR STEPS (A)	MANAGERIAL PLANNING (B)	MILITARY STRATEGY (C)	OPERATIONS RESEARCH (D)	DOD WEAPONS SYSTEMS (E)	SYSTEMS ENGINEERING (F)
1	Plan the plan	—	—	(Strategy & Tactics Analysis)	—
2	Study opportunities, threats, and prepare other premises	Situation observed	—	—	Environmental/Needs Research
3	—	—	Problem identification	Military need identified	Unsatisfied need identified
4	—	Mission description	Problem formulation	Need specified	Problem definition
5	Set objectives	Situation objectives	Construct model	Objectives defined	Select objective criteria
6	Identify alternative courses of action to achieve objectives	Identify all feasible courses of action	Derive model solution	Concept proposals solicited	System synthesis alternatives
7	Examine alternatives	Analysis of each course	Test model and solution	Conceptual and feasibility studies	Systems analysis
8	Choose alternatives to follow	Compare	—	Cost/effectiveness comparison	Comparison
9	Develop detailed plans	Decision on best	Establish controls	Selection of best	Selection
10	Organize to carry out plans	—	Report results	System Package-Plan defined	Communicating results in prospectus
11	Carry out plans	—	—	—	—
12	Review and evaluate results	Action-plan assembled	—	Action-planning	Action-planning
13	Recycle planning program	—	—	—	—

*Adapted from Donald J. Smalter, "The Influence of D-O-D Practices on Corporate Planning," Management Technology, Vol. 4, No. 2, December 1964, pp. 131-2

Conceptual Steps in Planning

(2) collect all pertinent factors available to solve the problem, and (3) decide which actions to take to solve the problem.

Conceptual sequences for business planning build upon these basic analytical steps in problem-solving. As with conceptual models, there is not one single best series; there are a number of series each of which has its particular value. Fundamentally, however, they all contain the same basic elements.

Table 2-1 presents a comparison of different steps. The managerial planning steps follow the sequences which are found in elementary management textbooks. A little analysis will show that these steps compare with those related to military strategy, operations research, weapons systems analysis, and systems engineering. Each is different, yet each embraces the same fundamental elements. Although the actual step-by-step sequences vary, they show a basic movement from finding out what is to be done, through analysis of ways and means to do it, to laying detailed plans to do it.

A famous series of planning or problem-solving steps is the "Commander's Estimate of the Situation," familiar to military officers. Given in Table 2-2, it has wide applicability in military, business, as well as personal planning.

This by no means exhausts the list of useful conceptual steps in business planning. The steps mentioned apply to planning in a general sort of way. Two conceptual models more applicable to comprehensive corporate planning may be noted. The first is contained in Chart 2-1 and needs no further elaboration. A second is as follows:*

1. Planning the plan
2. Specifying objectives of the enterprise
   - forecasting future prospects
   - measuring the gaps between aspirations and projections
3. Developing strategies
   - to fill the major gaps
4. Developing derivative or detailed plans in major functional areas to fit the strategies
   - research and development
   - production
   - marketing and promotion
   - etc.
5. Carrying out plans
   - starting operations
   - introducing necessary controls
6. Review and recycling

* Adapted from George A. Steiner, 1962, p. 39. For a variety of other approaches specifically designed for small enterprises, see George A. Steiner 1967, pp. 3-16, which appears also as Chapter 7, in Pfeffer 1967.

48
A Conceptual and Operational Model of Corporate Planning

Table 2-2   Commander's Estimate of Situation

1. MISSION

   A statement of the task and its purpose. If the mission is general in nature, determine by analysis what task must be performed to insure that the mission is accomplished. State multiple tasks in the sequence in which they are to be accomplished.

2. THE SITUATION AND COURSES OF ACTION

   a. Determine all facts or in the absence of facts logical assumptions which have a bearing on the situation and which contribute to or influence the ultimate choice or a course of action. Analyze available facts and/or assumptions and arrive at deduction from these as to their favorable or adverse influence or effect on the accomplishment of the mission.

   b. Determine and list significant difficulties or difficulty patterns which are anticipated and which could adversely affect the accomplishment of the mission.

   c. Determine and list all feasible courses of action which will accomplish the mission if successful.

3. ANALYSIS OF OPPOSING COURSES OF ACTION

   Determine through analysis the probable outcome of each course of action listed in paragraph 2c when opposed by each significant difficulty enumerated in paragraph 2b. This may be done in two steps—

   a. Determine and state those anticipated difficulties or difficulty patterns which have an approximately equal effect on all courses of action.

   b. Analyze each course of action against each significant difficulty or difficulty pattern (except those stated in paragraph 3a above) to determine strength and weakness inherent in each course of action.

4. COMPARISON OF OWN COURSES OF ACTION

   Compare courses of action in terms of significant advantages and disadvantages which emerged during analysis (par. 3 above). Decide which course of action promises to be most successful in accomplishing the mission.

5. DECISION

   Translate the course of action selected into a complete statement, showing *who, what, when, where, how,* and *why* as appropriate.

Source: War Department, *Staff Officers' Field Manual*, FM 101-5, U.S. Department of Defense, Washington, U.S. Government Printing Office (1960 edition), page 142.

Operational Structures and Procedures

LENGTH OF PLANNING PERIODS

This subject was treated at some length in Chapter 1 and needs no elaboration here. Conceptually it can be said that statements of purposes and missions are made for all time, until changed. Strategic plans are both of short- and long-range and the timing depends upon subject matter. Medium-range programming should be from at least 2 to 10 years, depending upon the company, with the average company adopting a 5-year span. Short-range plans, of course, are generally for a year or less.

Most firms that have formal planning recycle their planning program once a year. Conceptually, this seems desirable.

OPERATIONAL STRUCTURES AND PROCEDURES

Variations from the above conceptual models in actual operating planning programs are wide. Many factors influence the way planning is done, as noted previously—styles of management, organization and size of the firm, and sophistication of its planning program, to name a few. Most managements also are interested in improving their planning program by changing older ways of doing things and by introducing into the system new techniques and methods. The result is that on the surface actual operating planning systems are not the same as the conceptual models, nor are they the same from one company to another or in the same company from time to time. In one fairly large corporation that I have observed over a long period of time the corporate planning procedures have been different in every year. The structure of plans has been more stable than procedures but it, too, has changed in major ways over a ten-year period.

Despite the detailed operational variations from the conceptual models, the more successful planning programs must reflect to an important degree the conceptual models. The reason is that a violation of the inherent logic in the conceptual models (both structurally and in the sequence of steps) sooner or later will bring about deficiencies in planning. Whatever the actual structural arrangement of plans and the steps in their development, an observer must see behind them the basic elements of the conceptual model structure and planning steps. If this is not possible trouble ahead can be predicted.

It is important to observe that planning should not be conceived as beginning, for example, at the left of Chart 2-1 and proceeding to the right in a sequence that completes one step before moving to the next. Similarly, planning does not conceptually proceed on the basis of the sequences of steps as presented, for example, in Table 2-1. Both conceptually and operationally, planning sequences are iterative. There is much retracing of steps, jumping around from step to step, and tentative trial-and-error decision-making in the process. Very typically, an objective may be set and after examining alternative courses of action to achieve it, or after considering competing objectives, the original mark

50
A Conceptual and Operational Model of Corporate Planning

may be modified. The process may then start all over again until finally an objective is set and current actions are actually taken to achieve it.

KAISER ALUMINUM AND CHEMICAL PLANNING

Chart 2-4 shows the major structural parts and sequential steps taken in the preparation of the comprehensive plans of the Kaiser Aluminum and Chemical Corporation. Comparison of this diagram with Chart 2-1 and column (b) of Table 2-1 shows fundamental similarities but great operational variations.

Chart 2-4
The Planning Process—Flow Chart
(A) Gathering Information

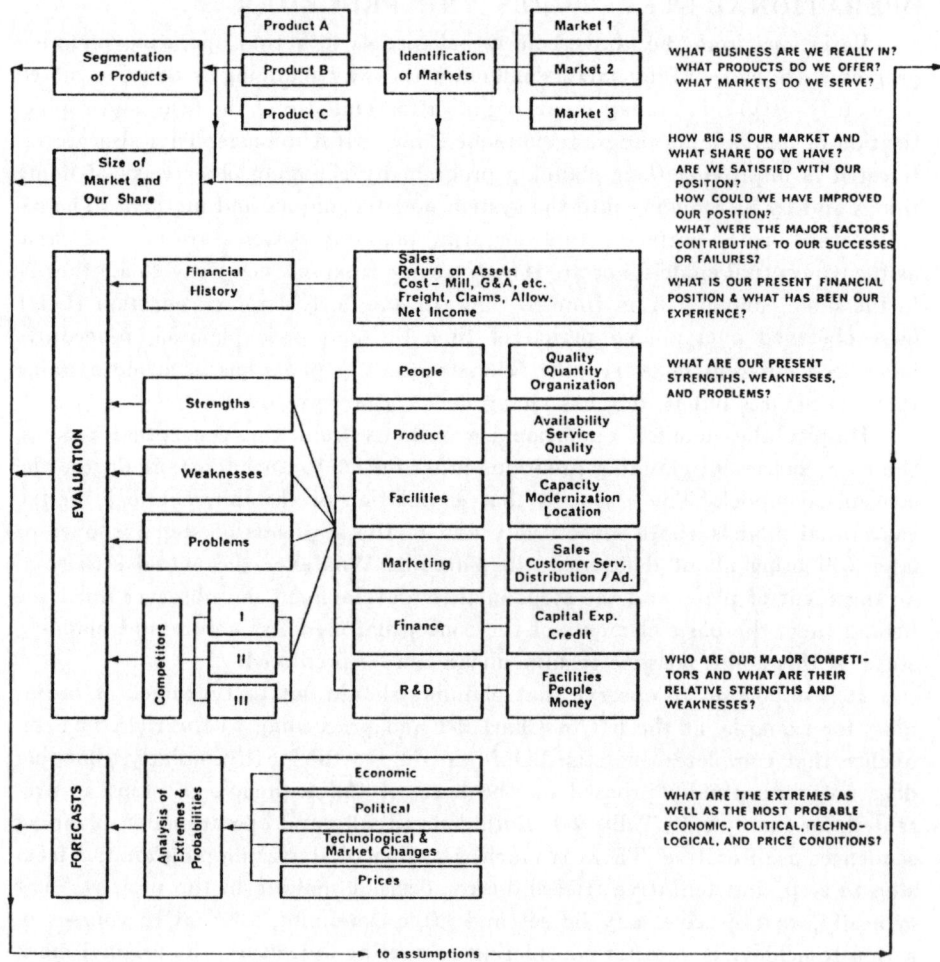

Kaiser Aluminum and Chemical Planning

Chart 2-4
The Planning Process—Flow Chart
(B) Assumptions—Establish the Framework
Within Which the Plan is Developed

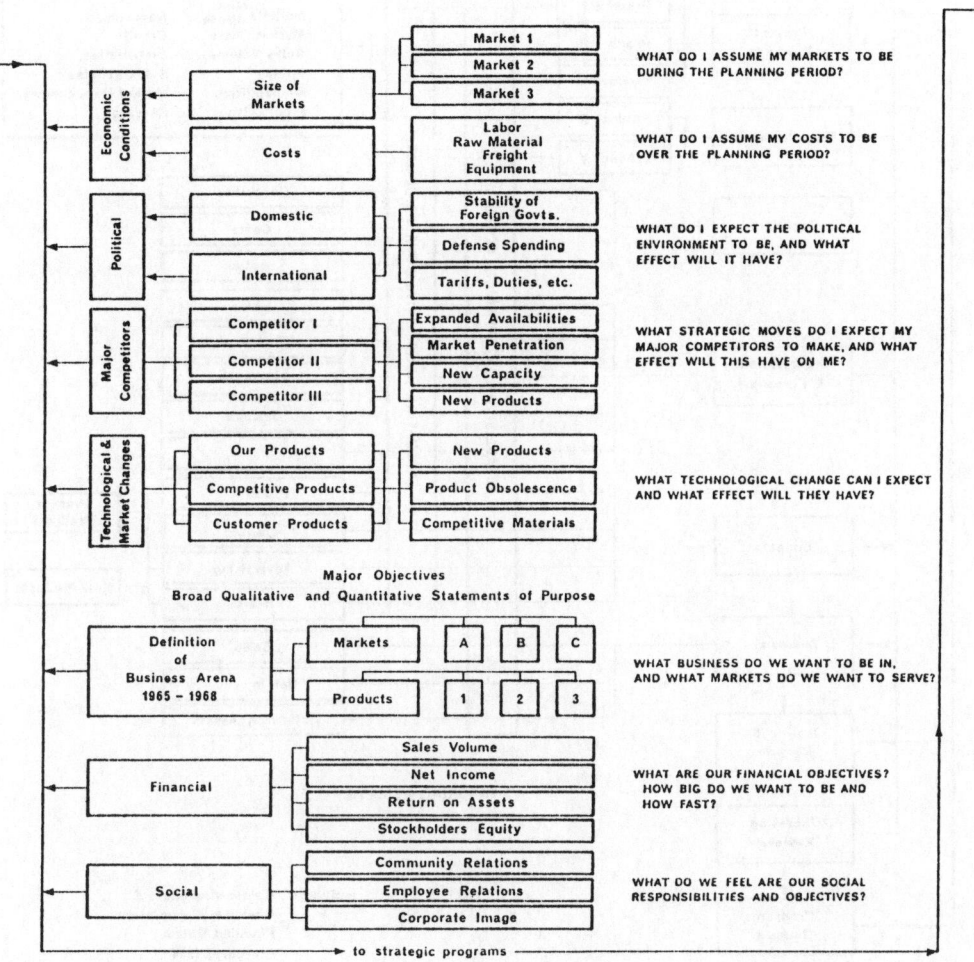

52
A Conceptual and Operational Model of Corporate Planning

Chart 2-4
The Planning Process—Flow Chart
(C) Strategic Programs

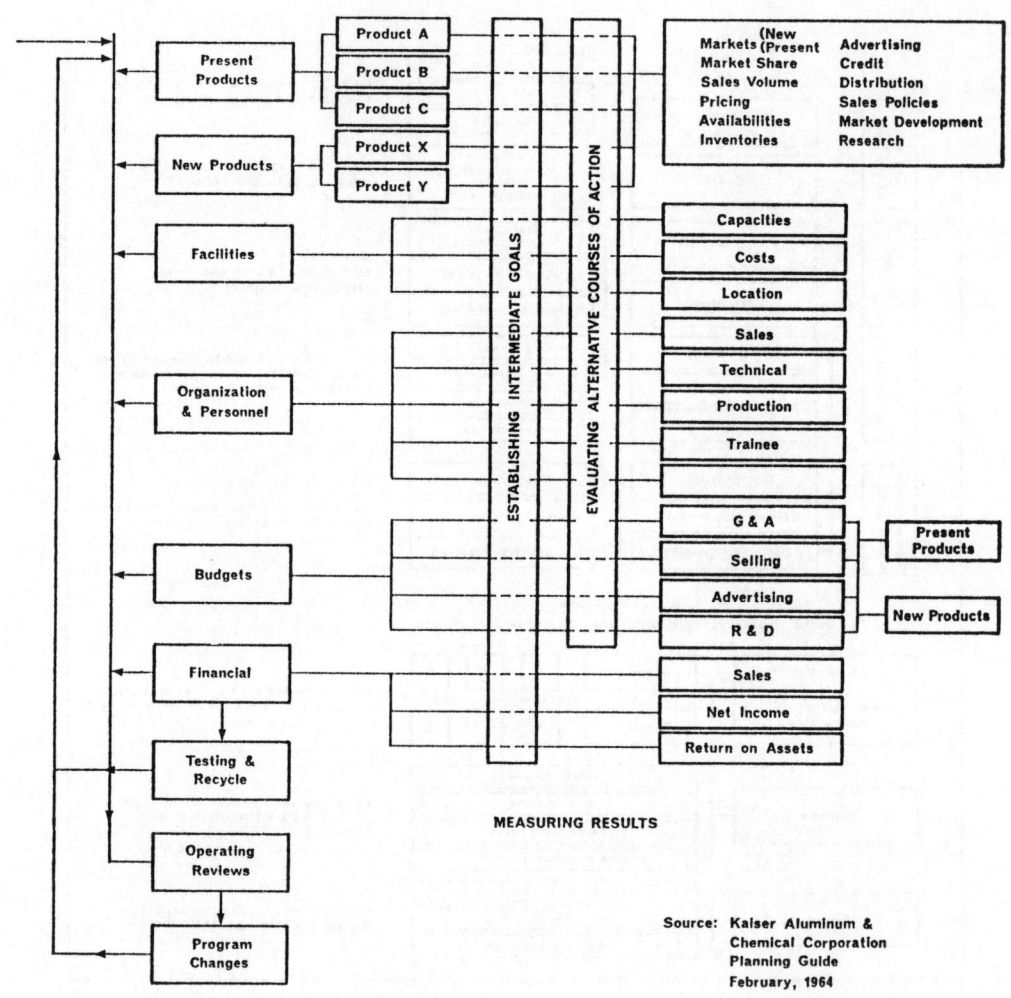

Source: Kaiser Aluminum &
Chemical Corporation
Planning Guide
February, 1964

Allstate Insurance Company Planning

Chart 2-5

Major Steps in Corporate Planning at Allstate Insurance

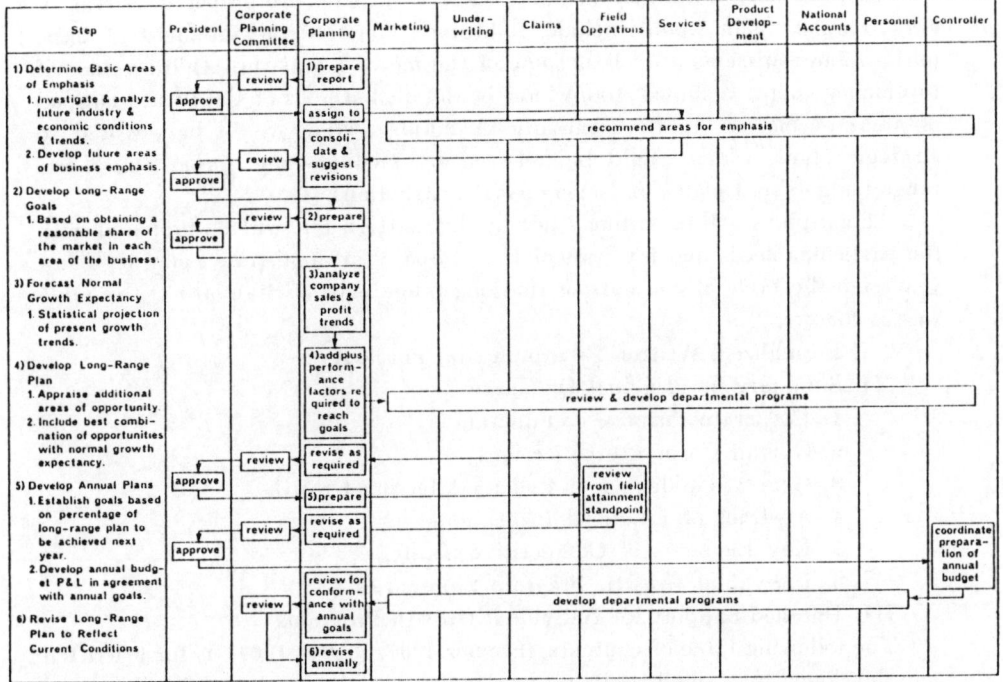

Source: From *Managerial Long-Range Planning*, edited by George A. Steiner. Copyright © 1963 by McGraw-Hill, Inc. Used by permission of McGraw-Hill Book Co.

ALLSTATE INSURANCE COMPANY PLANNING

Chart 2-5 gives the major steps in corporate planning at Allstate Insurance. In this chart there is added to types of plans and sequence of steps, the way in which decisions move among managers. A little of the iterative process of planning is evident in the chart although there is no doubt about the fact that the actual operational flows would show much more retracing of steps than is explicit in the diagram. Here, again, the actual operational model is much different from the conceptual models. But fundamentally their similarity is clear.*

* For descriptions of comprehensive corporate planning programs of many other companies see George A. Steiner 1963b, and Steiner and Cannon 1967.

A Conceptual and Operational Model of Corporate Planning

TABLE OF CONTENTS OF A CORPORATE PLAN

There is little uniformity in the ways written plans are prepared. A reasonably complete plan would include, following Chart 2-1, a statement of basic purposes and missions as well as some of the major moral and ethical values of top management. Included, too, would be detailed studies of the future outlook of areas of interest to the company. A major section would be devoted to strategic plans, which would be followed by medium-range programs, short-range budgets and plans, and operational instructions.

Actual plans will most likely not fit this pattern but will be prepared with the particular needs and interests of the company in mind. For example, a few years ago the table of contents of the long-range plan of Standard Oil of Ohio was as follows:

I. Formalized, Written Environmental Forecasts
II. Summary of Principal Objectives
    1. Corporate Purpose or Function
    2. Overall Corporate Objectives
    3. General Guidelines or Policies Affecting Growth
    4. Abstract of Financial Projections
    5. Key Elements of Competitive Strategy
    6. Individual Growth Program Summaries
III. Detailed Support for Individual Growth Programs

The following table of contents (Steiner 1967; Pfeffer 1967) is for a written plan developed by a small company having annual sales of about $2 million and 100 employees at the time the plan was drafted. The plan itself was developed by the company president and his four major department heads. Although parts of the plan stretch ahead for ten years, most of the detailed plans cover five years.*

A TABLE OF CONTENTS OF A CORPORATE PLAN
Corporate Long-Range Plan for Magnetic Design, Inc.

I. Corporate Purposes: the fundamental purposes of MDI. Two basic purposes are given, which is about standard. The four modifiers, however, are a little unusual.

    A. Two prime objectives of MDI are:
        • To improve earnings through productive effort primarily applied (but not limited) to the manufacture of magnetic devices and power supply equipment.

---

*For a detailed table of contents of a long-range plan for the Autonetics Division of North American Aviation, Inc., see George A. Steiner 1963b, pp. 151-157.

55
Table of Contents of a Corporate Plan

- To conduct the business in a manner that is constructive, honorable, and mutually profitable for stockholders, employees, customers, suppliers, and the general community.

B. These objectives are amplified further:
- To earn a reasonable return on investment with due regard to the interests of customers, employees, vendors.
- To expand sales while increasing profits.
- To support the military effort of the United States by producing top quality products.
- To grow at a steady rate.

C. Departmental purposes: Administration, marketing, production and engineering, and finance. It is a little unusual for departmental purposes to be specified at this point in a plan; they are usually blended into specific goals set for their operations. Following are the objectives of the production and engineering department:
- Manufacture and design quality products with cost and delivery schedules which will be attractive to prospective customers.
- Stay alert to developments that promise new and improved company products.

II. Basic Corporate Five- and Ten-Year Sales and Profit Objectives:

A. The five-year annual sales and profit objectives are:

	Sales	Pretax Profits	Pretax (%) Profit	Federal Tax	Posttax (%) Profit
First year					
Second year					
Third year		[Specified in dollars and percentages.]			
Fourth year					
Fifth year					

B. The ten-year sales and profit objectives are:
- After taxes, sales will be $5,000,000 and earnings will be $750,000.

III. Basic Premises: forecasts of future markets, technology, competition, and evaluations of internal strengths and weaknesses. A framework of premises, with illustrations from the MDI plan, follows:

A. External projections and forecasts:
- Survey of general business conditions, including Gross National Product forecast.
- Survey of the market for company products, based upon general

economic conditions for industrial products and estimates of government spending for company products.
- Forecast of company sales based on the above two forecasts. (MDI made forecasts for each of the next five years. Since the company is in the Midwest, government spending for its products in the Midwest was estimated. Included were the Department of Defense, the National Aeronautics and Space Administration, and the Federal Aviation Agency.)

B. Competition: Because competition is keen for most companies, objective estimates of its strength are important. After looking at what its major competition was likely to do, the firm looked at itself.
- Several advantages have placed MDI several years in advance of competition in the magnetic devices equipment field. These are cryogenic magnets for commercial applications and high reliability power supplies for long-endurance military application.
- However, in order to realize fully the growth commensurate with the above advantages, several weaknesses must be overcome by developing an ability to construct crystals as well as developing more sophisticated test procedures.

C. Internal examination of the past and projections: Analyses of various parts of the enterprise, e.g.
- Product line analysis:
  a. Product(s) performance (i.e., sales volume, profit margin, etc.).
  b. Customer class served.
  c. Comparison with major competitors' product(s).
  d. Comparison with substitutes and complementary performance.
  e. Possibilities for product improvement.
  f. Suggestions with regard to new products.
- Market analysis:
  a. Important factors in projected sales changes: product success; marketing organization; advertising; and competitive pressures.
  b. New markets to be penetrated (i.e., geographical areas and customer classes).
- Financial analysis:
  a. Profit position.
  b. Working capital.
  c. Cash position.
  d. Impact of financial policy on market price per share.
  e. Prospects for future financing.
- Production analysis:
  a. Plant and equipment (maintenance and depreciation).

57
Table of Contents of a Corporate Plan

- b. Productive capacity and productivity.
- c. Percent of capacity utilized.
- d. Suggestions for: productivity improvements; cost reduction; utilizing excess capacity; and planning expansion.
- Technical analysis:
  - a. Research and development performance.
  - b. Suggestions for improving research and development effectiveness.
- Employees:
  - a. Employment and future needs.
  - b. Technical manpower deficiencies.
  - c. Appraisal of employee attitudes.
- Facilities:
  - a. Evaluation of current facilities to meet new business.
  - b. Machine replacement policy and needs.

IV. Basic Objectives, Policies, and Strategies: This covers every important area of the business, but most companies concentrate on A through F of the following:

A. Profits.
B. Sales.
C. Finance.
D. Marketing.
E. Capital additions.
F. Production.
G. Research.
H. Engineering.
I. Personnel.
J. Acquisitions.
K. Organization.
L. Long-range planning.

This list can be expanded. As noted elsewhere, the more concrete the specification here can be, the easier it usually is to implement the plans. It is especially important for a business manager to know precisely what he is seeking and the method to be employed to get there. For example, MDI marketing objectives were set forth as follows:

- Increase sales of magnetic devices 100 percent in the next five years. Increase sales of power supply equipment 200 percent during the next five years.
- Increase the total volume of industrial sales from today's 25 percent to 50 per cent of total sales at the end of five years.
- Penetrate the western market to the point where the company will control 10 percent of it at the end of five years.
- Enter the foreign market within five years by a licensing agreement, a joint venture, or manufacturing facility.

For each of these objectives, the company prepared a detailed series of strategies ranging from a strategy to "sell custom designs directly to prime contractors in geographic regions where their main plants are located" to details such as special services to selected specified customers, training program for employees, and top management meetings with customers.

Further strategies which might be included in this section of the plan, with special regard to marketing, are organization, use of dealers, possibility of distributing products manufactured by others, salesmen's compensation plans, and pricing policy.

Drawing a proper line of demarcation between the strategic plans and the detailed operational plans is difficult. Ideally, the two blend together in a continuous line. This was the case with MDI, where those making the strategic plan also were the ones to implement it.

V. Detailed Medium-Range Plans: more detailed plans growing out of the above. For MDI these plans were developed for each of the succeeding five years:

A. *Pro forma* balance sheet, yearly.
B. Income statement, yearly.
C. Capital expenditure schedule, yearly.
D. Unit production schedule for major products, yearly.
E. Employment schedule, yearly.
F. Detailed schedule to acquire within three years a company with design capability in solid state magnetic devices.

VI. One-Year Plans: the next year's budgets. The first year's budgets for items A through F were, in the aggregate, the same for the first year of the five-year plan, but broken into quarterly time periods. In addition, MDI had other budgets, principally purchasing schedules for major components and raw materials and typical detailed administrative budgets covering such things as travel and telephone.

SOME CHARACTERISTICS OF CORPORATE PLANS

It will be readily recognized that for a much larger corporation than Magnetic Design, Inc., the documentation of the corporate plan will cover many more categories than noted above and be much more voluminous. For smaller companies the outline will be scantier. But the basic fundamental headings will remain the same for all.

A major problem of each company is to determine what areas shall be covered in a plan, how deeply they shall be studied, and how detailed plans shall be. No company can afford to study in great depth every facet of its business every year. Nor is this sort of examination required. Most companies concentrate their planning on profits, sales, distribution, finance, products, production, and personnel (Newell, Jr., 1963, pp. 100-101; Henry, 1965).

59
Summary and Conclusions

Very few companies prepare periodically or on a selected time basis a comprehensive and integrated strategic plan. Some companies give their divisions general guidance in the planning program upon which basis the divisions develop detailed plans. These are reviewed at the company's headquarters but not aggregated into a single corporate plan. This is the case at Litton Industries. On the other hand, there are companies that do aggregate these plans into a total integrated company plan. Managers are highly pragmatic people and tailor their efforts to fit need. As a result, parts of plans may be written, parts unwritten, and the mix may change from item to item, from time to time, and manager to manager.

Surveys of business plans, together with my empirical observations, lead me to conclude that most companies do not have a complete set of written plans approaching that presented above. The actual plans devised for most firms are a composite of both written and unwritten plans and documentation is made only for selected areas. For example, out of 822 companies recently surveyed (Stewart 1967) only about 40 percent had profit and loss statements and balance sheets extending beyond the current year. About the same percentage had long-range capital budgets. About the same percentage had written profit and sales objectives. When asked whether there were specific plans for future years, written or unwritten, the percentages responding affirmatively for different areas were as follows: between 40 and 49 percent said they had plans for accounting, sales, marketing, corporate management, and planning. Between 31 and 38 percent said they had plans for finance, manufacturing, acquisitions, and product research and development. Future purchasing and industrial relations plans existed for 25 percent, and 22 percent had future public relations plans. Since most companies that plan ahead do so for a 5-year period of time it is a fair presumption that most of these plans covered about the same length of time (Kaiden 1967; Newell, Jr., 1963).

SUMMARY AND CONCLUSIONS

This chapter presented and examined a number of conceptual and operational models of comprehensive corporate planning structures and steps, and compared them. Some of the major conclusions of the chapter are:

1. The author's conceptual model of the structure and process of corporate planning is flexible and adaptable to any size or type of business, style of management, or stage in the development of organized formal planning. Although there are differences with other conceptual models, all the models are fundamentally quite similar.

2. It is of major importance in the development and implementation of comprehensive corporate planning to understand the conceptual distinction be-

60
A Conceptual and Operational Model of Corporate Planning

tween strategic and tactical planning. The approaches to planning in these two areas differ importantly.

3. Once the distinction between strategic and tactical planning is understood, it is important to see that it is often impossible to draw a line of demarcation between them.

4. While actual operational planning structures and steps may on the surface appear to be rather different from the conceptual models given in this chapter, underneath the conceptual models should be discernible. If not, the planning process is missing some element which eventually will result in poor plans.

5. Planning steps are not sequential but iterative.

6. Planning and control, although considered as separate functions of management, are inextricably interwoven and each is developed and implemented in contemplation of the other. Nevertheless, it is important to distinguish conceptually between the two.

7. While it is desirable to have comprehensive corporate plans written, it is clear that a mass of plans of a company must remain unwritten simply because to record them would result in excessive bulk.

8. The major topics in the table of contents of an "ideal" as well as an acceptable operational plan are reasonably clear, but there is no standard which has received widespread acceptance. (A detailed table of contents of an operational plan was presented in the chapter.)

9. In making corporate plans, it is very important to know how deeply aspects of it should be studied and how detailed parts of it should be in relationship to other parts, and over time.

References

ANDERSEN, THEODORE A., "Coordinating Strategic and Operational Planning," *Business Horizons*, Vol. 8, Summer 1965, pp. 49-72.

ANTHONY, ROBERT N., "Framework for Analysis in Management Planning," *Management Services*, March-April 1964, pp. 18-24.

———, *Management Controls in Industrial Research Organizations* (Boston: Graduate School of Business, Harvard University, 1952).

———, *Planning and Control Systems: A Framework for Analysis* (Boston: Harvard University Press, 1965).

GILMORE, FRANK, and R. G. BRANDENBERG, "Anatomy of Corporate Planning," *Harvard Business Review*, Vol. 40, November-December 1962, pp. 61-69.

HENRY, HAROLD WILKINSON, *Long-Range Planning in Industrial Corporations: An Analysis of Formalized Practices* (Ann Arbor: The University of Michigan, doctoral dissertation, 1965).

KAIDEN, MARTIN R., *Planning for Tomorrow: How Large Industrial Companies Plan for the Future*, master's dissertation, mimeographed (New York: New York University, 1967).

NEWELL, WILLIAM T., JR., *Long-Range Planning, Policies and Practices: Selected Companies Operating in Texas*, Research Monograph No. 25 (Austin, Texas: Bureau of Business Research, The University of Texas, 1963).

PFEFFER, IRVING, ed., *The Financing of Small Business: A Current Assessment* (New York: Crowell-Collier, Macmillan, 1967).

STEINER, GEORGE A.,

———, "Approaches to Long-Range Planning For Small Business," in Irving Pfeffer, ed., *The Financing of Small Business: A Current Assessment* (New York: Columbia University Press, 1967).

STEWART, ROBERT F., "A Framework for Business Planning," Report No. 162, Long Range Planning Service (Menlo Park, California: Stanford Research Institute, February 1963).

———, "Summary Tabulation of Responses, 1966 Survey of Business Planning," (Menlo Park, California: Stanford Research Institute, March 1967, mimeographed).

———, J. KNIGHT ALLEN and J. MORSE CAVENDER, "The Strategic Plan," Report No. 168, Long Range Planning Service (Menlo Park, California: Stanford Research Institute, April 1963).

Impact of strategic planning on profit performance

Study of 57 corporations, with 620 diverse businesses, establishes relationship between strategic planning and profit performance

Sidney Schoeffler, Robert D. Buzzell, and Donald F. Heany

One of the most significant research projects undertaken by the Marketing Science Institute is the ongoing profit impact of market strategies (PIMS) study. The basic idea behind PIMS is to provide corporate top management, divisional management, marketing executives, and corporate planners with insights and information on expected profit performance of different kinds of businesses under different competitive conditions. Among the 37 factors investigated and analyzed are market share, total marketing expenditures, product quality, R&D expenditures, investment intensity, and so on. These factors account for more than 80% of the variation in profit in the more than 600 business units analyzed. In this article, the authors describe the highlights of their research findings.

Mr. Schoeffler, director of applications for the PIMS project, is a senior visiting research fellow at Harvard Business School; Mr. Buzzell, PIMS research director, is professor of business administration and chairman of marketing at HBS; Mr. Heany, manager-reports and liaison for the PIMS program, is a visiting research fellow at HBS.

What rate of return on investment (ROI) is "normal" in a given type of business, under given market and industry conditions? What factors explain differences in typical levels of ROI among various kinds of businesses?

How will ROI in a specific business be affected by a change in the strategy employed? By a change in competitive activity?

Many corporate presidents and planning directors wish they had more reliable answers to these kinds of questions, for they are at the heart of strategic planning in the modern corporation. Consider some of the ways in which these questions arise:

Forecasting profits: In a diversified company, the usual practice is for business plans to be prepared by each product division or other operating unit. These plans are then reviewed by corporate executives, often with the assistance of corporate staff specialists. Among the key elements of each unit's plan are, of course, estimates of investment requirements and profits for future periods.

Often these forecasts are simply projections of local experience. But when market conditions are expected to change, or when a change in strategy is

Authors' note: We wish to acknowledge the contributions to this article of our associates on the PIMS Project Team. Ralph Sultan, who is now chief economist, Royal Bank of Canada, served as project director of Phase I of PIMS during 1972 and was responsible for much of the basic design of the study. Bradley Gale, Thomas Wilson, Bernard Catry, James Conlin, and Robert McDowell also participated in various stages of the research and offered valuable suggestions on this presentation of the latest results.

contemplated, how reliable is the past as a guide to the future?

Allocating resources: A major purpose of reviewing divisional plans at the corporate level is to make effective allocations of capital, manpower, and other scarce resources among divisions. Often the capital appropriation requests of the divisions add up to more than headquarters can provide.

The problem, then, is one of emphasis: Which products and markets promise the greatest returns? Here, especially, the profit estimates supplied by divisional managers are likely to be of doubtful reliability, since each division is in the position of pleading its own case.

Measuring management performance: Closely related to the problem of forecasting profits is the need to evaluate actual profit results. Suppose Division A earns 30% on its investment (pretax), while Division B achieves an ROI of only 15%. Is A's management twice as effective as B's, and should it be rewarded accordingly?

Executives of Division B would no doubt object to this. They would attribute differences in ROI to differences in conditions such as market growth rate and strength of competition. Perhaps they are right. What corporate management would like, in this situation, is some way of determining what level of ROI is reasonable or "normal" for different operating units under given circumstances.

Appraising new business proposals: Still another common problem in strategic planning is that of estimating ROI in a prospective new business which is being considered for either internal development or acquisition. When the business is new to the company, actual experience, by definition, cannot be consulted. Even when entry is proposed via acquisition, the current performance of the existing business may be of doubtful reliability as a guide to its future.

The common thread running through the four types of strategic planning situations just described is the need for some means of estimating return on investment in a given business, under given industry and market conditions, following a given strategy. Every experienced business executive and corporate planner knows that ROI varies enormously from one business to another and from year to year in an individual division or product line. How can these variations be explained and predicted?

Some answers to these questions are beginning to emerge from a unique research project called PIMS —a study of actual experiences of hundreds of businesses which is aimed at measuring the profit impact of market strategies. Building on work that has been under way at the General Electric Company for more than 10 years (see accompanying ruled insert), the PIMS project is a sharing of experience among 57 major North American corporations.

PIMS was organized in early 1972 as a project of the Marketing Science Institute, a nonprofit research organization associated with the Harvard Business School. The project was established as a cooperative venture, with HBS faculty members and research assistants working alongside planning specialists from industry. (Industry personnel did not, of course, have access to any of the data supplied by other companies.) The project is now organizing its third yearlong phase.

This article is a progress report on Phases I and II of the PIMS project. In it, we shall describe how the study has been carried out and summarize some of the major findings of the first two years' work.

PIMS profit models

In Phase I of PIMS, 36 corporations supplied information on some 350 businesses. The information included descriptions of industry and market characteristics, as well as selected operating results and balance sheet figures for the years 1970 and 1971.

(All financial data were submitted to PIMS in "scaled" form—that is, actual dollar amounts were multiplied by a scaling factor, such as .5. This procedure served to ensure both the confidentiality of the original data and the relationships among the figures.)

GE's search for answers

The current effort to find better ways to explain and predict operating performance began back in 1960, as an internal project at the General Electric Company.

Fred J. Borch, then GE's vice president-marketing services, called in Jack McKitterick, his director of market research, and pointed out what today is generally accepted as an axiom: as the market share of a business goes up, so do operating economies. Borch asked McKitterick to survey any relevant published research and the experience of other businessmen with respect to this relationship. If the relationship were valid, executives might have an important clue as to how to improve operating results.

Equally important, Borch wanted to find a handle for GE's growing "manageability" problem. Sales were already at the $4 billion level. By 1970, they were likely to be $8 billion to $9 billion. How could corporate officers like himself stay in touch with so many diverse businesses, ranging all the way from turbine generators to toasters?

After months of exploration, McKitterick became convinced that the best way to address the question was to do some basic pioneering work on the apparent causes of GE's own successes and failures. Borch agreed and authorized a major research project to probe for "laws of the market place." Project PROM (profitability optimization model) was organized under the direction of coauthor Sidney Schoeffler.

After five years of intensive research and testing, Project PROM produced a computer-based model that captured the major factors which explain a great deal of the variability in return on investment. Since this model reflects data from diverse markets and industries, it is often referred to as a "cross-sectional" model—as contrasted to a time-series model based on data over a series of years for a single business.

With the help of this model, GE could estimate the "average" level of profit or investment or cash flow that went with various combinations of the success determinants. The model did not and could not predict the "precise" ROI of any one of GE's businesses in a given year.

When Borch became GE's chief executive officer in 1964, he found the PROM model to be (a) a tool for detecting high-risk strategic moves, (b) a rich source of questions for the review of strategies proposed by divisional managers, and (c) a means of computing the differential between the entire company's financial goals and the expected aggregate earnings of its components. (If the model predicted a shortfall, it could then be used to display the future implications of "belt tightening," component by component.)

In addition to making extensive use of the model himself, Borch also encouraged his group executives and division managers to use it. He supported follow-on research to improve the coverage and predictive powers of the early models.

Today, cross-sectional models are standard elements of GE's corporate planning system.

The primary purpose of Phase I was to establish the feasibility of obtaining reasonably comparable data from a large number of diverse companies. Although differences in accounting systems and terminology did pose problems, the project was successful: profit results were explained and predicted with considerable accuracy. Moreover, the principal results of GE's earlier work were confirmed. By and large, the same factors that influenced ROI in GE businesses also showed up in the analysis of profitability among the 36 diverse corporations.

Thus, in late 1972, MSI agreed to sponsor a second, enlarged phase of the PIMS project. This time, 57 companies enlisted in the study and supplied more extensive information, covering the years 1970-1972, for 620 businesses. Analysis of this data base over the past several months has led to the current set of PIMS profit models. For the composition of our sample of businesses, see Exhibit I.

Explaining ROI

The models we and our associates have developed are designed to answer two basic questions: What factors influence profitability in a business—and how much? How does ROI change in response to changes in strategy and in market conditions?

In building quantitative models to explain ROI and changes in ROI, we have drawn on economic theory and on the opinions and beliefs of experienced executives. Economic theory suggests, for example, that different "market structures"—i.e., the number and relative size of competitors—will lead to different

Exhibit I
PIMS sample of individual businesses

Number of companies	57
Number of businesses	620*
Type of company:	Percent of total:
Consumer product manufacturers	19.8%
Capital equipment manufacturers	15.6
Raw materials producers	11.9
Components manufacturers	24.1
Supplies manufacturers	16.5
Service and distribution	12.1
Total	100.0%

*The data presented in Exhibits III-X are based on analyses of 521 businesses. Since the time these analyses were made, information has been received on an additional 99 businesses.

Exhibit II
ROI and key profit influences

Return on investment (ROI):
The ratio of net, pretax operating income to average investment. Operating income is what is available after deduction of allocated corporate overhead expenses but before deduction of any financial charges on assets employed. "Investment" equals equity plus long-term debt, or, equivalently, total assets employed minus current liabilities attributed to the business.

Market share:
The ratio of dollar sales by a business, in a given time period, to total sales by all competitors in the same market. The "market" includes all of the products or services, customer types, and geographic areas that are directly related to the activities of the business. For example, it includes all products and services that are competitive with those sold by the business.

Product (service) quality:
The quality of each participating company's offerings, appraised in the following terms: What was the percentage of sales of products or services from each business in each year which were superior to those of competitors? What was the percentage of equivalent products? Inferior products? The measure used in Exhibit IV and Exhibit V is the percentage "superior" minus the percentage "inferior."

Marketing expenditures:
Total costs for sales force, advertising, sales promotion, marketing research, and marketing administration. The figures do not include costs of physical distribution.

R&D expenditures:
Total costs of product development and process improvement, including those costs incurred by corporate-level units which can be directly attributed to the individual business.

Investment intensity:
Ratio of total investment to sales.

Corporate diversity:
An index which reflects (1) the number of different 4-digit Standard Industrial Classification industries in which a corporation operates, (2) the percentage of total corporate employment in each industry, and (3) the degree of similarity or difference among the industries in which it participates.

profit levels. Business experience indicates that product quality—a factor that has received little attention from economists—is also related to ROI.

Whatever economic theory or businessmen's opinions may suggest, however, the ultimate test of whether and how a given factor is related to profitability is an empirical one. To make such a test, we have constructed an equation that explains more than 80% of the variation in profitability among the 620 businesses in the PIMS data base.

This profit level equation includes more than 60 terms composed of various combinations of 37 basic factors. As might be expected, profitability is related to many different factors. Some of the most important ones are listed and defined in Exhibit II.

The PIMS profit level equation and a separate equation which predicts changes in ROI have been used to construct separate reports for each business in the data pool. These reports "diagnose" the factors influencing ROI in a business, given all of its specific characteristics such as its market, competitive position, capital intensity, and so on.

Because every business is, in some respects, unique, these diagnostic reports vary enormously. But by comparing businesses that are similar in terms of one or more basic profit-influencing factors with businesses that have different characteristics, we can identify some general patterns or relationships.

For example, we can determine an average relationship between market share and profitability by comparing average levels of ROI for groups of businesses with different market shares. This is the approach we have used in subsequent sections of this article.

Profit determinants

As we mentioned a moment ago, our profit model includes 37 distinct factors which, in various combinations, are significantly related to profitability.

However, we shall limit our discussion to just 3 major determinants of return on investment revealed by our analysis of the PIMS data base—namely, market share, investment intensity, and company factors.

Market share

Our analyses give strong support to the proposition that market share is indeed a major influence on profitability. As shown in Exhibit III, ROI goes up steadily as market share increases. On the average, businesses with market shares above 36% earned more than three times as much, relative to investment, as businesses with less than 7% share of their respective markets. (Each of the five market share categories shown in this exhibit represents approximately one fifth of the sample.)

The relationship between market share and profitability has been widely discussed since the inception of Project PROM at General Electric, when the idea was relatively novel. But how and why market share affects profitability is not fully understood as yet.

Our findings suggest that businesses with relatively large market shares tend to have above-average rates of investment turnover, particularly working capital. Also, the ratio of marketing expense to sales is generally lower for high-share businesses than for those with small market shares. These differences are indications of economies of scale that may go along with strong market positions.

However, much remains to be done, both in exploring the connection between market share and ROI and in determining how the relationship varies for different types of businesses or for different market conditions.

Whatever the reasons, the data in Exhibit III clearly show that it is very profitable to have a high share of market. Beyond this, the PIMS profit model sheds some light on how market share and other factors work together to influence ROI.

Consider, for example, the impact of both market share and product quality on ROI, as shown in Exhibit IV. In this exhibit, and in several others that follow, we have divided the PIMS sample of businesses into three approximately equal groups on the basis of each of two factors. The percentages for

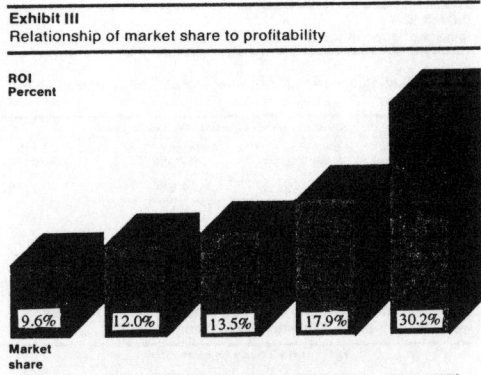

Exhibit III
Relationship of market share to profitability

ROI Percent

| 9.6% | 12.0% | 13.5% | 17.9% | 30.2% |

Market share
Under 7%   7%-14%   14%-22%   22%-36%   Over 36%

Exhibit IV
Effect of market share and product quality on ROI

Market share	Product quality		
	Inferior	Average	Superior
Under 12%	4.5%	10.4%	17.4%
12%-26%	11.0	18.1	18.1
Over 26%	19.5	21.9	28.3

each of the nine subgroups shown include between 40 and 70 businesses.

The best of all possible worlds is to have both high market share and superior quality: businesses in this category averaged 28.3% return on investment. But even when quality was relatively inferior, average ROI for high-share businesses was a respectable 19.5%. On the other hand, superior-quality producers with weak market positions earned an average 17.4% on investment, which suggests that quality can partially offset low share.

It should be noted that product quality and market share usually, but by no means always, go together. The percent distribution of the three market share groups, in terms of quality levels, was as follows:

Percent of businesses with:	Market share		
	Under 12%	12%-26%	Over 26%
Inferior quality	47%	33%	20%
Average quality	30	36	30
Superior quality	23	31	50
Number of businesses	169	176	176

Exhibit V
Impact of expenditures on product quality and market share

A
High marketing expenditures damage profitability when quality is low

Product quality	Ratio of marketing expenditures to sales		
	Low Under 6%	Average 6%-11%	High Over 11%
Inferior	15.4%	14.8%	2.7%
Average	17.8	16.9	14.2
Superior	25.2	25.5	19.8

B
High R&D spending hurts profitability when market position is weak but increases ROI when market share is high

Market share	Ratio of R&D costs to sales		
	Low Under 1.4%	Average 1.4%-3.0%	High Over 3.0%
Under 12%	11.4%	9.8%	4.9%
12%-26%	13.8	16.7	17.0
Over 26%	22.3	23.1	26.3

While it is not surprising that both market share and relative quality influence ROI, in the short term there may be relatively little that management can do to change these factors. Are some strategies more profitable than others, given the basic competitive position of a business? Analysis of the results achieved by the businesses in the PIMS sample suggests that some guidelines can, indeed, be formulated for businesses in different positions.

Consider, for example, the data in Part A of *Exhibit V*. Here, as in *Exhibit IV*, the sample has been divided into three roughly equal groups, this time in terms of (a) relative quality, and (b) the ratio of marketing expenditures to sales.

When quality is relatively low—exactly equivalent to competition or somewhat inferior—there is a strong negative relationship between marketing expenditures and ROI. In effect, these figures confirm the old adage that "it doesn't pay to promote a poor product."

ROI is somewhat diminished by a high level of marketing expenditure for businesses with "average" or "superior" relative product quality—but not nearly to the same extent as for competitors with lower-quality products. This might suggest, further, that sellers of higher-quality products or services could

1. For further thoughts on this topic, see Theodore Levitt, "Innovative Imitation," HBR September-October 1966, p. 63.

inflict severe short-term penalties on weaker competitors by escalating the level of marketing costs in an industry—and that lower-quality producers should avoid such confrontations like the plague.

Another clue to how profit influences vary, depending on competitive position, is given in Part B of *Exhibit V*. This shows, for businesses in the same market share categories as in *Exhibit IV*, the relationship of ROI to R&D spending levels. When market share is high, average ROI is highest when R&D spending is also high—above 3% of sales.

These figures do not, of course, show which is cause and which is effect; possibly businesses that are highly profitable—for whatever reason—are inclined to invest more of their earnings in research. Most likely, the positive relationship between ROI and R&D spending reflects both this kind of "reverse causation" and a positive impact, in the other direction, of R&D on profits.

When market share is low, the relationship between R&D and profitability is exactly the reverse of that experienced by those with strong positions. The higher the level of R&D spending, the lower profits were, on the average. Here, there appears to be little doubt about cause and effect: low profits would be very unlikely to lead to high R&D spending.

We should emphasize, however, that these data represent short-term effects. Since the PIMS participants supplied information only for a three-year period, it may well be that Part B of *Exhibit V* reflects a "transitional" cost of innovation. Some support can be given for this interpretation: among businesses with low market shares, ROI was higher (11.6%) when new products comprised a relatively high proportion of total sales than when new products represented only a small fraction of sales (average ROI, 5.3%).

Thus, when and if R&D spending is successfully converted into new products, it can pay off. But the most profitable course of all, for businesses with weak market positions, may be to seek new products without investing in research and development—via imitation, for instance.[1]

Investment intensity

Apart from market share and product quality, the most important determinant of return on investment that was revealed by our analysis of the PIMS data pool is investment intensity, which is simply the ratio of total investment to sales.

Exhibit VI shows the overall relationship between ROI and investment intensity: the higher the ratio of investment to sales, the lower ROI tends to be. Apparently businesses with high investment intensities are not able to achieve profit margins sufficient to offset the greater amounts of investment they require to sustain a given volume of sales. We suspect that a prime reason for this may be the heavy emphasis placed on achieving high volume, and thus high capacity utilization, in investment-intensive industries.

Since both market share and investment intensity are major determinants of profitability, it is not surprising that the combination of the two factors accounts for a substantial portion of total variation in ROI. As shown in Exhibit VII, average ROI for businesses that enjoyed both a high market share and a low degree of investment intensity was 34.6% — more than 17 times the average return earned by the unfortunate businesses with high investment intensity and small market share.

In most cases, the basic level of investment intensity required for a given business is probably not subject to much control by management. The amount of capital required to support a specified amount of sales is determined primarily by the technology of the business and by traditional terms of trade.

However, very often management does have some choices that affect investment intensity—such as the degree of mechanization or computer utilization. Our data indicate that these types of investments should be carefully controlled if market position is weak. Beyond this, what can managers do about investment intensity? Is a business that requires a high investment/sales ratio simply doomed to exist with low rates of return?

Comparison of various groups of businesses within the investment-intensive category shows that some strategies are likely to be more profitable than others. Consider, for example, the data in Exhibit VIII. Among businesses in the highest investment/sales group, ROI was strongly—and negatively—related to the level of marketing expenditures. For businesses with low investment intensity, the relationship of ROI to marketing expenditures was quite different: average profitability was actually higher when mar-

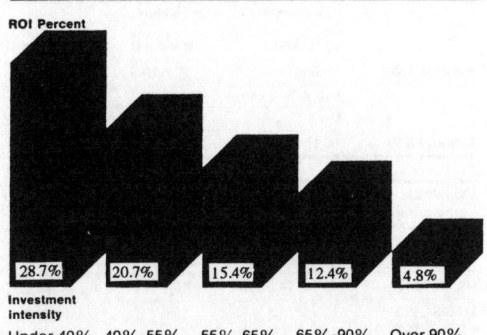

Exhibit VI
Relationship of investment intensity to profitability

Exhibit VII
Low market share plus high investment intensity equals disaster

Investment intensity	Market share		
	Under 12%	12%-26%	Over 26%
Under 45%	21.2%	26.9%	34.6%
45%-71%	8.6	13.1	26.2
Over 71%	2.0	6.7	15.7

Exhibit VIII
High marketing expenditures damage ROI in investment-intensive businesses

Investment intensity	Ratio of marketing expenditures to sales		
	Under 6%	6%-11%	Over 11%
Under 45%	29.3%	31.7%	22.0%
45%-71%	17.6	13.2	18.3
Over 71%	10.9	10.1	3.9

keting expenditures were "moderate" in relation to sales than when they were low.

Similar comparisons of subgroups within the PIMS sample show that when investment intensity is high (a) high levels of R&D spending depress earnings sharply, at least in the short run, and (b) high labor productivity is vital to profitability. (The average return for businesses with high investment intensity and low productivity—measured by sales per employee—was a negative 1% of investment.)

Company factors

A third category of profit determinants revealed by the PIMS project consists of characteristics of the

Exhibit IX
ROI varies with size and diversity of parent company

	Total company sales (in millions)		
	Low Under $750	Average $750–$1,500	High Over $1,500
Average ROI	15.8%	12.5%	21.7%
	Degree of diversity		
	Low	Average	High
Average ROI	16.1%	12.9%	22.1%

Exhibit X
Large companies benefit most from strong market positions

Company sales (in millions)	Market share		
	Under 12%	12%–26%	Over 26%
Under $750	14.5%	13.7%	19.6%
$750–$1,500	6.8	15.0	25.0
Over $1,500	12.0	17.8	29.4

company that owns a business. Even when all of the characteristics of two businesses are identical, our analysis suggests that their profit results may vary if they belong to corporations that differ in terms of size, diversity, and other factors.

Exhibit IX shows average ROI levels for businesses belonging to companies that are in "low," "average," and "high" sales categories, and that have different degrees of corporate diversity. The range of corporate size represented in the PIMS sample is, of course, limited: "small" companies are those with annual sales volume under $750 million. Within this range, ROI at the business level was highest for the largest companies and lowest for those in the "average" group.

The explanation for this, we believe, is that the large corporations benefit from economies of scale, while the smaller companies gain some advantages from greater flexibility. Those in the middle are neither fish nor fowl, and consequently they earn the lowest rates of return.

The relationship between business-level ROI and corporate diversity is similar to that based on company size. On the average, ROI was practically identical for businesses belonging to highly diversified corporations and for those operated by nondiversified companies. Presumably, the diversified corporations achieve good results through effectivenessness as "generalists."

At the other extreme, profitability reflects the advantages of corporate specialization. The lowest levels of ROI are for the middle group, which benefits from neither. (These and other observed relationships between ROI and company characteristics are tentative findings, of course, because of the limited number of companies included in our sample.)

Our final example of a relationship between ROI and a combination of factors serves to illustrate further how company characteristics affect profitability. In Exhibit X, we show average levels of ROI for businesses that have different market shares and that belong to different company size groups.

As in earlier exhibits, the positive impact of a high market share is apparent. But, in addition, the data indicate that larger companies derive greater advantages from strong market positions than smaller companies do. This probably reflects the ability of larger companies to provide adequate support for strong positions, in terms of management personnel and funds for marketing or R&D.

On the other hand, smaller companies do slightly better than large ones in businesses with low market shares. This lends support to the belief that the relatively small companies derive some advantages from flexibility.

Applying the findings

The corporate applications of the PIMS findings are many and varied. These include aid in profit forecasting for individual business units, measuring management performance, and appraising new business opportunities.

As part of the PIMS project, reports are prepared for each business, showing how its expected level of ROI is influenced by each of the 37 distinct factors included in the profit model. The result of this kind of analysis is what we call a "PAR" return on investment for a business, given its market and industry environment, its competitive position, its capital structure, and so on.

Some of the participating companies are beginning to put the findings to work by using the PAR reports as a standard of performance for individual divisions. For example, if actual ROI is substantially above the PAR level, this in an indication that divisional management is performing well. The excess of actual over PAR reflects gains made by current tactical superiority, since the factors considered in calculating PAR are largely aspects of the strategic position of the business.

Apart from management performance, special circumstances may cause actual ROI to fall above or below PAR. For instance, the effects of patents and trade secrets are not reflected in the profit model. Subject to this qualification, we believe that PAR or expected profit levels derived from the PIMS model —or from a similar analysis of actual experiences under different conditions—can serve as a meaningful standard for evaluating actual results. Certainly, this kind of standard is preferable to the simple interdivisional comparisons used to judge divisional profits in many large companies today.

Potentially, the most valuable application of the PIMS findings will come from using them to estimate the effects of strategic changes. Each participating corporation has recently received a second set of reports which show how ROI in a given business could be expected to change, both in the short and long term, if modifications were made in its strategic position.

It is too soon to tell how accurate those estimates will be. But it is clear already that many of the managers and planners have obtained valuable insights into the reasons for past performance and the most fruitful directions for change.

Summing up

The PIMS project has demonstrated the feasibility and the benefits to be realized when companies pool their experiences. Information on strategic actions, market and industry situations, and results achieved can be organized into a multipurpose data base, and analysis of this data base has yielded useful general findings. Executives of the participating companies are beginning to utilize these results in the development and appraisal of strategic plans for individual business units.

Beyond the current benefits, we can also speculate on the broader impact that the approach represented by PIMS may have on the functioning of the private enterprise economy.

Competition is at the heart of our economic system. Will the process of competition become more effective or less effective if PIMS-type information becomes increasingly available? Is the answer the same if we judge effectiveness by some index of "social benefit," rather than by the health and profitability of individual businesses?

It seems entirely probable that the answers are: *more effective* and *yes*.

While competition has been one of the mainsprings for the dynamic growth of the U.S. economy, the great wastage of competition is increasingly retarding our national productivity. Can we maintain the benefits while reducing the drag of the wastage?

Research on multicompany data may enable us to accomplish just that, by helping individual competitors to lessen the frequency and scale of their competitive mistakes. The pooled record of business successes and failures, analyzed in PIMS-type fashion, can identify the courses of action that simply have no plausible promise at all, whether for the company or the customer or anyone else. It can also identify the other courses of action that have a good probability of yielding viable results. Competitors can therefore concentrate their energies on the higher-yield actions, and not dissipate their resources on quixotic ventures and forlorn causes.

Business is not a zero-sum game, where one man's gain is inevitably another man's loss. Sometimes most everyone wins, and sometimes most everyone loses. The systematic comparative study of ongoing experience can help maximize the frequency of the first outcome and minimize the second.

1 costs and experience

Costs appear to go down on value added at about 20 to 30% every time total product experience doubles for the industry as a whole, as well as for individual producers.

A businessman can predict his normal costs far into the future if he understands their basic relationship to experience. Price and cost data show that *costs decline by some characteristic amount each time accumulated experience is doubled.*[1] Given this, it is clear that not only can one's own costs be projected, but costs relative to competitors can also be estimated, given some rather straightforward information about the market.

The characteristic decline is consistently 20 to 30% each time accumulated production is doubled. This decline goes on in time without limit (in constant dollars) regardless of the rate of growth of experience. The rate of decline is surprisingly consistent, even from industry to industry.

However, these observed or inferred reductions in costs as volume increases are not necessarily automatic. They depend crucially on a competent management that seeks ways to force costs down as volume expands. Production costs are most likely to decline under this internal pressure. Yet in the long run the average combined cost of all elements should decline under the pressure for the company to remain as profitable as possible. To this extent the relationship is of normal potential rather than one of certainty. However, competition characteristically produces survivors who achieve the full potential.

Variances in "costs" shown in plotting experience curves are probably best interpreted as indicating change in rates of expenditure, or cash flows. Such costs should include all of the cost elements which may have a trade-off against each other.[2] This therefore means all costs of every kind required to deliver the product to the ultimate user, including the cost of intangibles which affect perceived value. There is no question that R&D, sales expense, advertising, overhead, and everything else are included.

Any failure of the producer to relate any one of these cost elements properly to the other will have a degrading effect on the cost performance in serving the end user. This may be why the experience curve works, as it weeds out everyone who has not used the optimum combination of all cost elements compared to his competitors' combinations. This also distinguishes experience curves from the well-known learning curve, the latter relating only to labor and production inputs.

---

1. See Exhibit 1.
2. See "Application Considerations" for a more detailed discussion of the nature of "costs" as used with experience curves.

EXHIBIT 1

Representing Experience Relationships Graphically

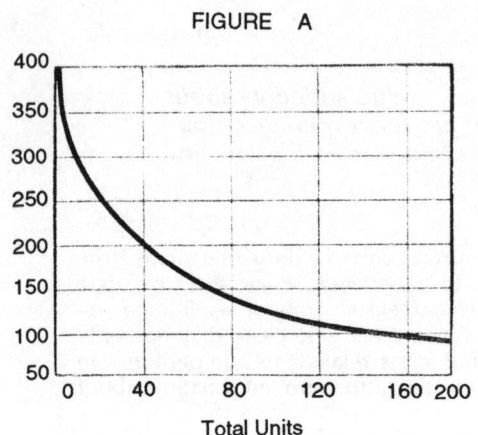

FIGURE A

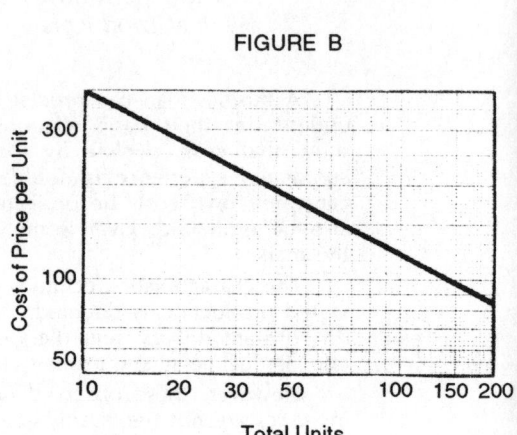

FIGURE B

When prices or costs are plotted against culmulative volume, the resulting graph characteristically takes the form of a curve on a linear scale (Figure A). Although the smoothness of the curve suggests the regularity of the relationship, some of the particular aspects are obscured. As a result, it is more useful to plot C/V or P/V slopes on double logarithmic scales (Figure B).

Plots on a log-log scale have the unique property of showing percentage change as a constant distance, along either axis at any position on the grid. A straight line on log-log paper means, then, that a given percentage change in one factor results in a corresponding percentage change in the other, the nature of that relationship corresponding to the slope of the line, which can be read right off a log-log grid.

In the case of cost-volume or price-volume slopes, the plotting of observed data about costs or prices and accumulated experience for a product on log-log paper has always produced straight lines reflecting a consistent relationship between experience and prices and experience and costs.

13

The growth rate of a product is an important factor in interpreting the experience curves. If the production of a product is not growing, then the rate of cost decline *per year* gradually slows down and approaches zero. This is easily demonstrated by inspection of Exhibit 2 where each dot on the line represents the successive years of production at a constant rate.

When accumulated units of a product are increasing annually at a constant percentage rate, then each year of product experience produces approximately the same percentage effect on cost. When plotted on log-log paper, the years eventually appear equally spaced. This is evident in Exhibit 3 and the accompanying table.

If competitors maintain the same relative market shares and have roughly equivalent histories of experience, then their costs will tend to move in parallel. This behavior is shown in Exhibit 4 where it is assumed that Company A has initially lower cost than that of Company B, i.e., a greater absolute market share.

EXHIBIT 2

The Effect of No Annual Growth in Physical Volume on the Rate of Increase in Accumulated Volume

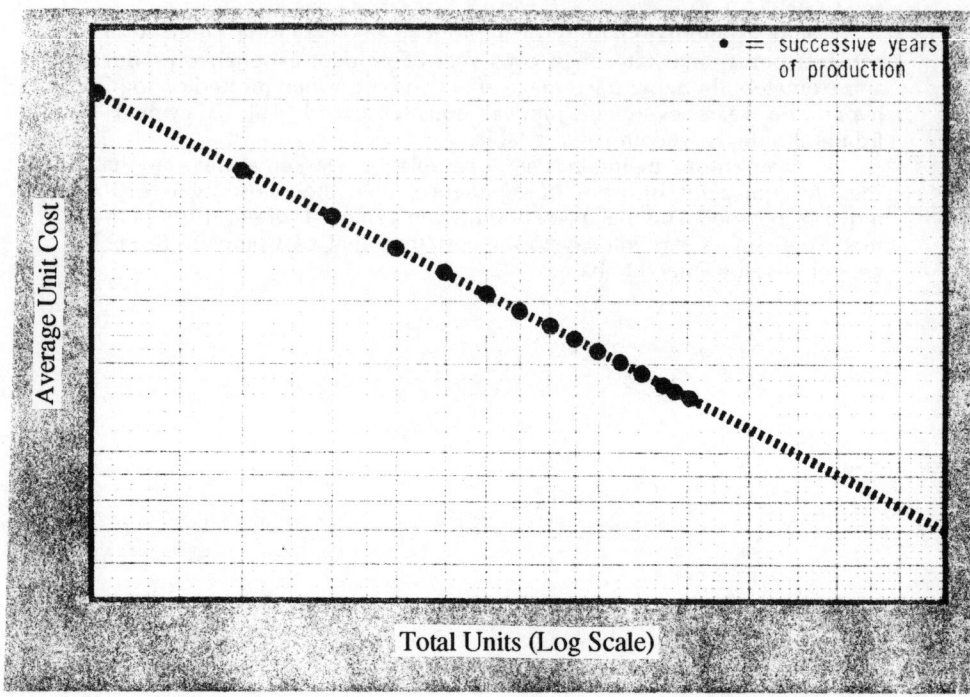

YEAR	PRODUCTION	ACCUMULATED EXPERIENCE	PERCENT INCREASE IN TOTAL EXPERIENCE
1	1	1	—
2	1	2	100%
3	1	3	50
4	1	4	33⅓
5	1	5	25
6	1	6	20
7	1	7	16½
8	1	8	14
9	1	9	12½
10	1	10	11
11	1	11	10
12	1	12	9
13	1	13	8½
14	1	14	7⅔
15	1	15	7

15

EXHIBIT 3

The Effect of Constant Rate of Growth in Physical Volume on Rate of Increase in Accumulated Experience

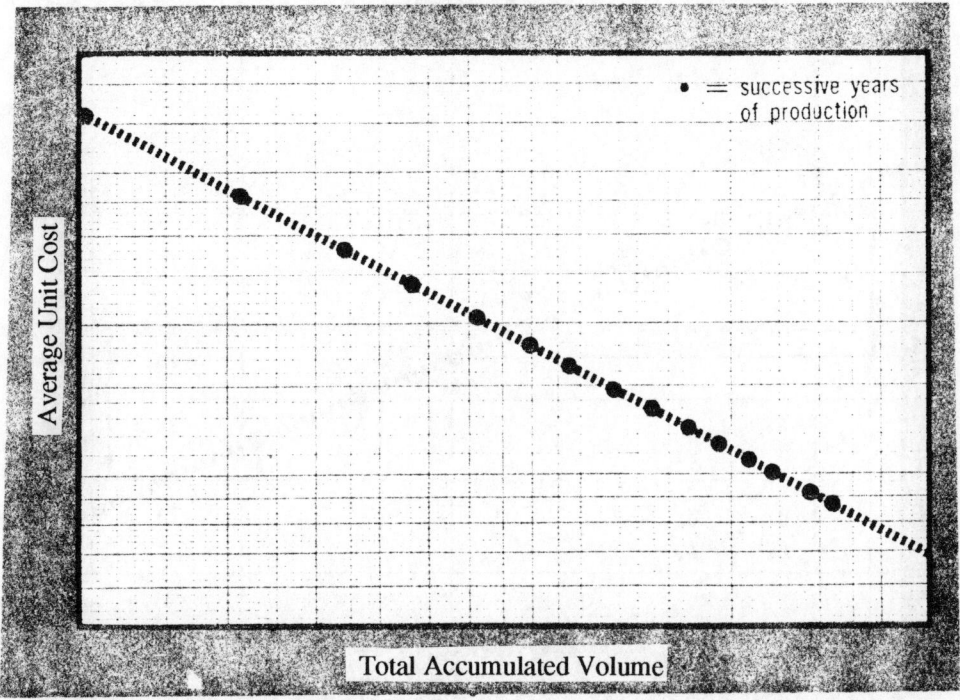

YEAR	PRODUCTION (10% GROWTH)	ACCUMULATED EXPERIENCE	PERCENT INCREASE IN TOTAL EXPERIENCE
1	1	1.00	
2	1.10	2.10	110.1%
3	1.21	3.31	57.6
4	1.33	4.64	40.2
5	1.46	6.11	31.5
6	1.61	7.81	26.4
7	1.77	9.58	22.7
8	1.95	11.53	20.4
9	2.14	13.67	18.6
10	2.35	16.02	17.2
11	2.59	18.61	16.2
12	2.85	21.46	15.3
13	3.14	24.60	14.6
14	3.45	28.05	14.0
15	3.80	31.85	13.5% (will approach 10%)

EXHIBIT 4

If Accumulated Experience Ratios (Market Share) Stay the Same, So Do Relative Costs Expressed in Percent.

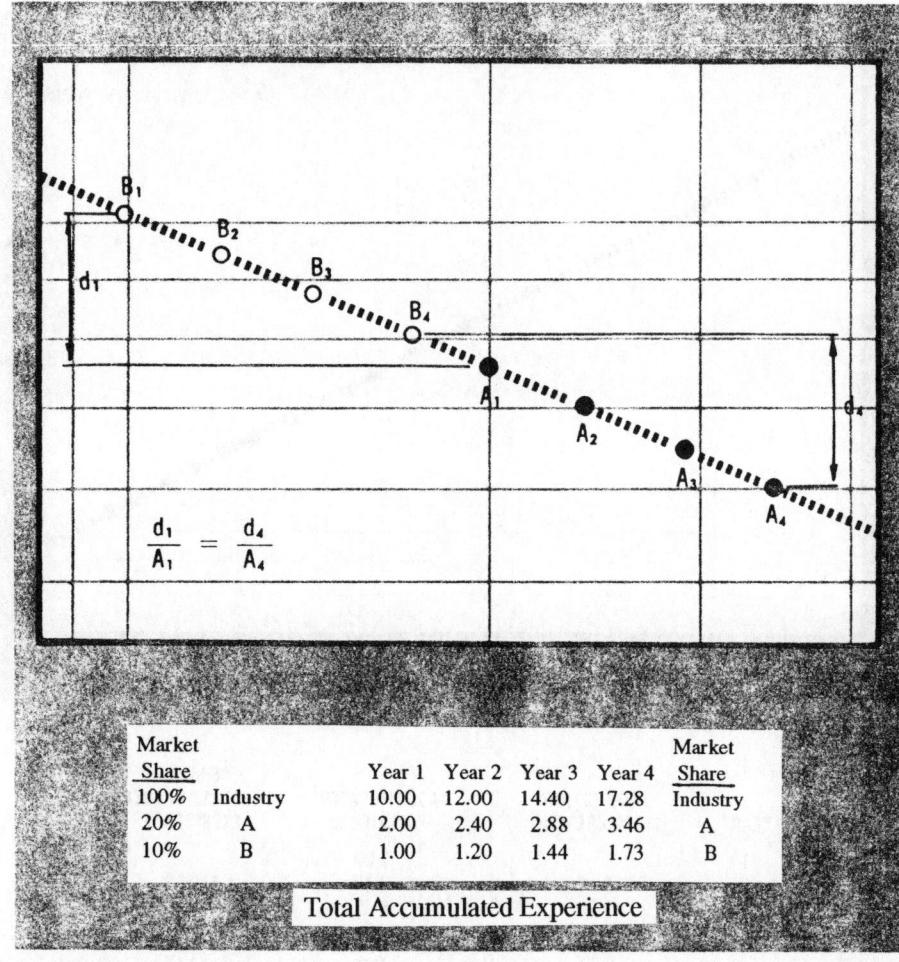

$$\frac{d_1}{A_1} = \frac{d_4}{A_4}$$

Market Share		Year 1	Year 2	Year 3	Year 4	Market Share
100%	Industry	10.00	12.00	14.40	17.28	Industry
20%	A	2.00	2.40	2.88	3.46	A
10%	B	1.00	1.20	1.44	1.73	B

Total Accumulated Experience

The accumulated volume of B and A, and Industry may be used simultaneously as coordinates of the chart above. As long as accumulated market share remains constant the cost relationships should also remain constant for A and B.

It is often difficult both to obtain and use cost data for comparative purposes. There are at least three reasons for this.
1. Internal cost data are closely guarded commercial secrets for most companies. For others, changes in cost accounting practices and aggregation conventions make such data effectively unavailable over sufficiently long periods of time.
2. Accounting practices with respect to depreciation, allocated costs, and capitalization can make comparative costs unreliable.
3. Costs for the individual product over short time spans often do not go down in a smooth curve but in a series of discrete steps which reflect specific changes in technique, method, process, design and facility utilization, as well as specific capacity additions.

In spite of this, data available from a number of representative companies among Boston Consulting Group clients provide remarkably consistent evidence that such cost-volume relationships as just described do in fact exist. Furthermore, their costs show a very high correlation with those that would have been forecast by inference from price trends.

It is reasonable to ask why these cost relationships should exist at all, let alone be so consistent. The answer lies in a combination of factors such as learning effects, scale effects, cost rationalization and technology.

- The cost consequences of scale are generally accepted. With scaled-up volume it is possible to use more efficient tools and spread their cost over enough units so that both labor and overhead costs are reduced. With increased scale it is usually possible to tailor facility-use factors more closely to capacity.
- Cost rationalization develops directly out of scale effect. With volume it is possible to consider alternative materials and alternative methods of manufacture and distribution which are uneconomic on a small scale.
- Redesign can usually reduce the unit cost of any product substantially, as long as the volume anticipated is adequate to spread the cost of redesign enough to produce a net overall reduction.
- Technology resulting from R&D can clearly reduce costs, but the cost of the R&D effort must be kept in proportion to the volume base to which it is to be applied. Therefore the potential application of R&D to cost reduction is a direct function of the volume to which its results can be applied.

2 price and experience

Prices follow the same pattern as costs if the relationship between competitors is stable. If they don't, the relationship between competitors becomes increasingly unstable.

Every businessman knows that predicting next year's prices better than the competition gives him a competitive edge. Predicting prices better for the next five or ten years can give him a major strategic advantage.

Not only does it appear possible to make long range price predictions, it appears possible to understand the competitive relationships which cause certain predictable patterns to exist. This is even more important to strategy development.

Data on price and industry experience are readily available for many products, and show, in general, that prices tend to decline by some characteristic amount each time accumulated experience is doubled. Plots of price tend to follow one of two characteristic forms. These may be identified in actual examples in Appendix A, as well as in Exhibits 5 and 6.

Where prices have paralleled costs over time, the price/experience slope is the straight line of Exhibit 5. Products following this pattern tend to be found in very competitive and rapid growth, technological industries. An example of such a product reflecting this straight-line trend relationship is integrated circuits.

EXHIBIT 5

A Typical Stable Pattern

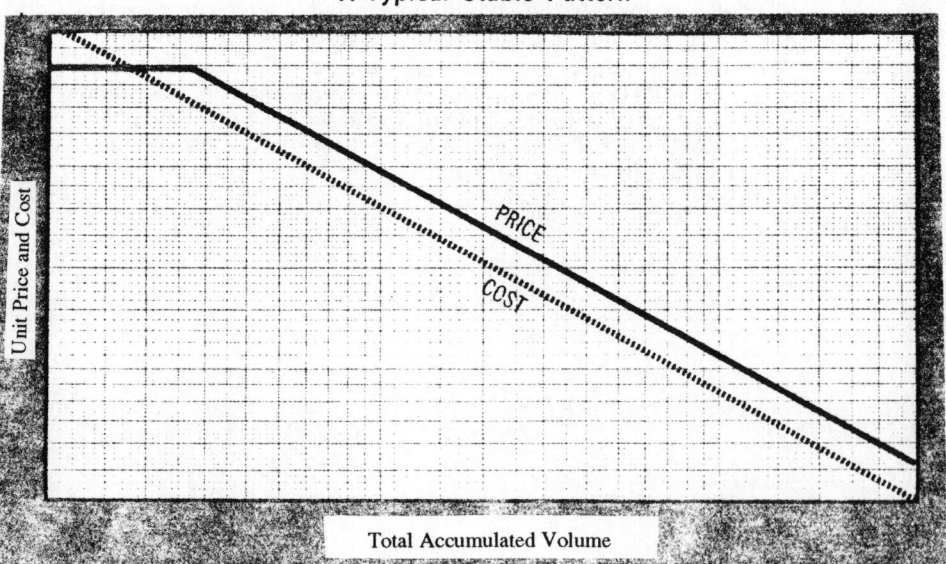

EXHIBIT 6

A Typical Unstable Pattern

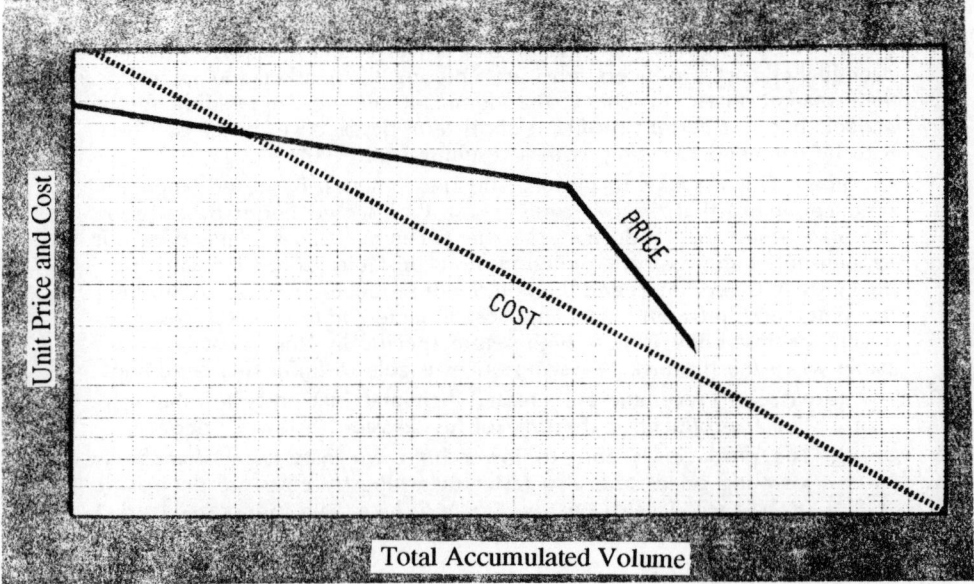

When prices do not decline as fast as cost in the early years, then a plot may show a definite knee such as that of Exhibit 6. The typical slope of the first portion of the plot is about 90%. That is to say, prices decline about 10% during the period in which industry experience doubles. The typical slope of the second portion of the plot is about 60%, i.e., prices decline 40% during the period in which industry experience doubles.

The classic case is shown in Exhibit 6. Prices are set below cost to establish an initial market. As volume and experience reduce cost, the prices are maintained, gradually converting the negative margin to a positive one. If prices do not decline as fast as costs, then competitors are attracted to enter. At some point prices *do* start to decline faster than costs. There are several examples of this in Appendix A. Characteristically this steep decline in prices eliminates many of the competitors.

Obviously prices cannot decline faster than costs indefinitely. At some point a reverse bend in the price curve reestablishes a characteristic relationship between costs and prices as in Phase D of Exhibit 7.

Exhibit 7 illustrates the various distinct stages of such price behavior. In Phase A costs typically exceed prices. This is always the case in the very early production stages of a new product. It covers an extensive period if the future potential is obvious and competition appears severe in the very early life of the product.

In Phase B the market leader is effectively holding a price umbrella over higher cost producers who are entering the market and increasing their market share. In effect, the dominant producer is trading future market share for current profits. A short term perspective can cause Phase B to be extended too long, with a resulting severe Phase C.

Phase C is a shakeout period. This phenomenon is caused when any producer thinks that his own interests will be served better by lowering the price faster than industry costs are declining. This, in fact, does not happen unless the cost-price relationship is unstable. Generally, when product growth is very rapid and the number of producers is large, and further, the difference between price and cost is large for the lowest cost producer, the instability is very high. More specifically, the situation is unstable when the producer lowering prices is able to fulfill two conditions.

1. Marginal revenues are greater than marginal costs for that particular producer at the time of his decision to lower price.
2. The producer is able to lower his own costs faster than he is lowering prices and also faster than industry costs are decreasing on balance. This can easily happen if he is able to increase market share fast enough.

EXHIBIT 7

A Characteristic Unstable Pattern After It Has Become Stable

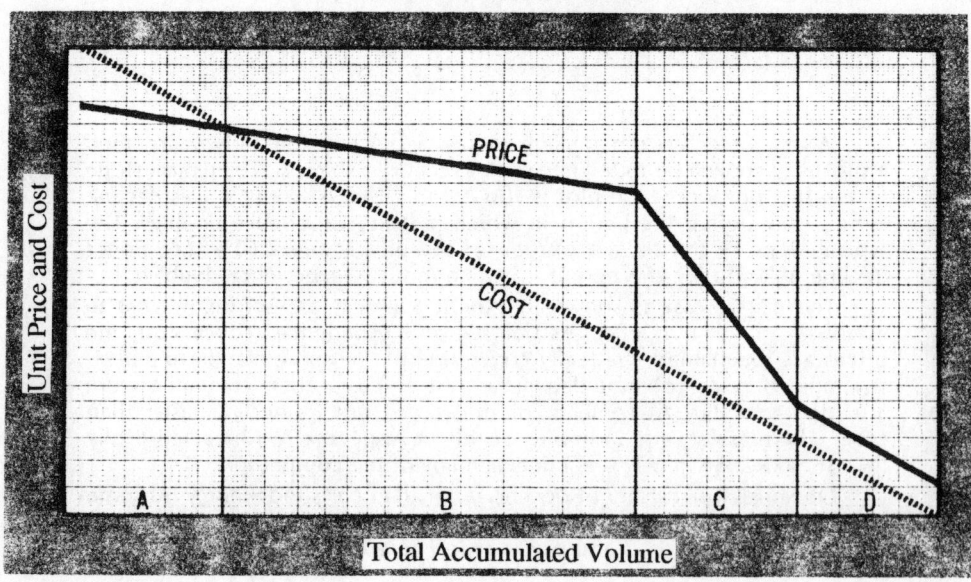

This instability becomes greater until almost any chance event can set off the shakeout. Actual breaks as shown in the plots seem to have been precipitated by one of several possibilities. One of these is a recession. For example, the mild recession year 1961 triggered such a break in several products in the semiconductor business. Apparently, 1958 did the same in some chemical products. Another source of price declines stems from the efforts of a major producer to buy into the market. Exactly the same result can occur if the dominant producer who has been holding up the price structure while steadily losing market share tries to regain his market position. Furthermore, if there is a high enough price level compared to achievable costs such that many producers are attracted to the market, then a shakeout will be produced by over-capacity eventually, when any one of the producers starts to gain market share rapidly for any reason.

At the end of the shakeout phase, the stability of the relationship of cost to price is fully established and Phase D emerges. If this did not occur, then prices, once started on a steep descent, would decline below costs and remain below costs indefinitely. This obviously cannot happen. If the prices began to decline again more slowly than costs, the whole process would be repeated, hence cost/price equilibrium.

Evidence of these price-experience relationships, as shown in Exhibits 5, 6 and 7, is clearest where the growth rate has been fast and the value added to the product is quite substantial. Where the growth rate is slow, many other factors come into play. The most important of these is a change in the general price level. For instance, inflation at 3% annually can completely offset the experience effect of approximately a 6% annual increase in volume if prices are declining with costs on a 70% slope.

Over any substantial period of time there are usually efforts by industry leaders to maintain prices. This produces temporary deferrals of the downward trend of prices but does not measurably affect the potential cost trend. As costs decline while prices do not, either substantial non-price, or price-equivalent, competition develops or an accelerated price decline occurs bringing costs and prices into their characteristic relationship again.[1]

These observations of price/experience curves suggest a number of important implications. One begins to see that many otherwise mysterious competitive relationships can be explained, and that some fundamental laws of competition can be derived.

---

1. It is important to note that price has many competitive equivalents, such as more advertising, more salesmen, more applications engineering, etc. Thus a "price reduction" as used throughout, can mean "a voluntary reduction in current net revenues in return for some future benefit in cost, volume, or competitive relationship".

3 experience and competitive interaction

If cost is a function of accumulated experience, then profit margin is a function of sustained market share.

Why does one competitor win while another loses? Even though a complete answer to this question may be complicated and appear to vary from case to case, the fundamental explanation is quite simple. If it is thoroughly understood, a whole new dimension is introduced into competitive strategy.

The interaction of competitors over time provides a guarantee that superior cost improvement on trend by one competitor will result eventually in the displacement of the less effective competitor. This must be true if there is no artificial barrier to competition. The costs of one competitor cannot decline indefinitely on a flatter cost/volume slope than another. Eventually prices will begin to parallel the most rapidly falling costs and the lagging competitor will be eliminated.

The net effect of competitive interaction over time is to produce one of two effects.

1. Either the least efficient competitor in terms of cost reducing effectiveness must continually increase his market share just to maintain his *relative* cost position;
2. or the relationship between competitors stabilizes at essentially constant market shares but at different profit margins. In this situation, the low cost producer would rather have his current profit margin than a larger market share. He therefore accepts the price level required for the highest cost producer to be able to grow fast enough to maintain his own share.

These cost-experience relationships can be demonstrated most vividly in graphic form. In Exhibit 8, if Company B, operating at breakeven at t_1 maintains market share but does not reduce costs as fast as a more efficient competitor, the cost advantage of A increases even at equal experience levels. Prices will trend with A's cost, since he will be inclined to adjust them in the hope of increased volume. Company B will be forced into an even less profitable position.

If Company B maintains the industry normal rate of cost decline but loses market share, the situation of Exhibit 9 prevails.

B is moving down the experience curve slower than the industry average.

A is moving down the experience curve *faster* than the industry average.

When A displaces B and becomes the dominant producer he then effectively *is* the industry average at that time. Under these conditions cost relationships will tend to stabilize.

EXHIBIT 8

There is a Minimum Rate of Cost Decline Required for Survival

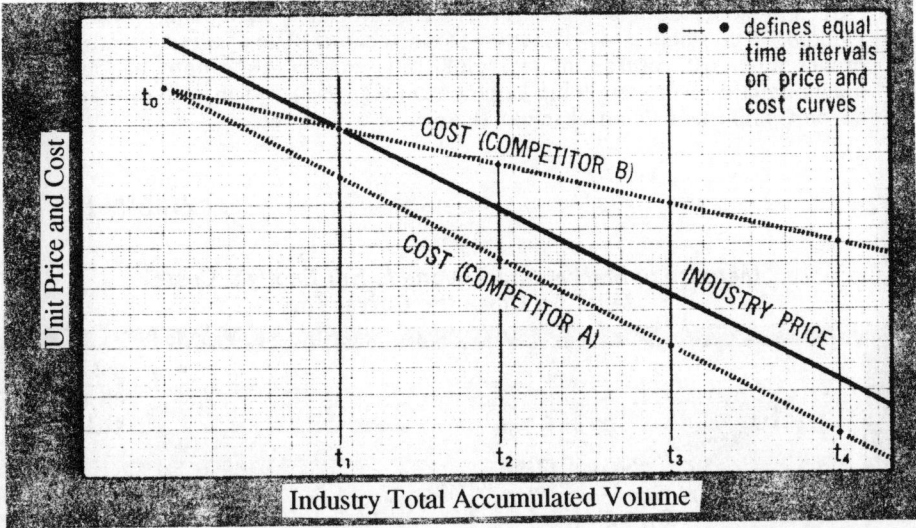

EXHIBIT 9

If Costs Decline at Normal Rates, Increased Market Share Results in Increased Cost Differentials

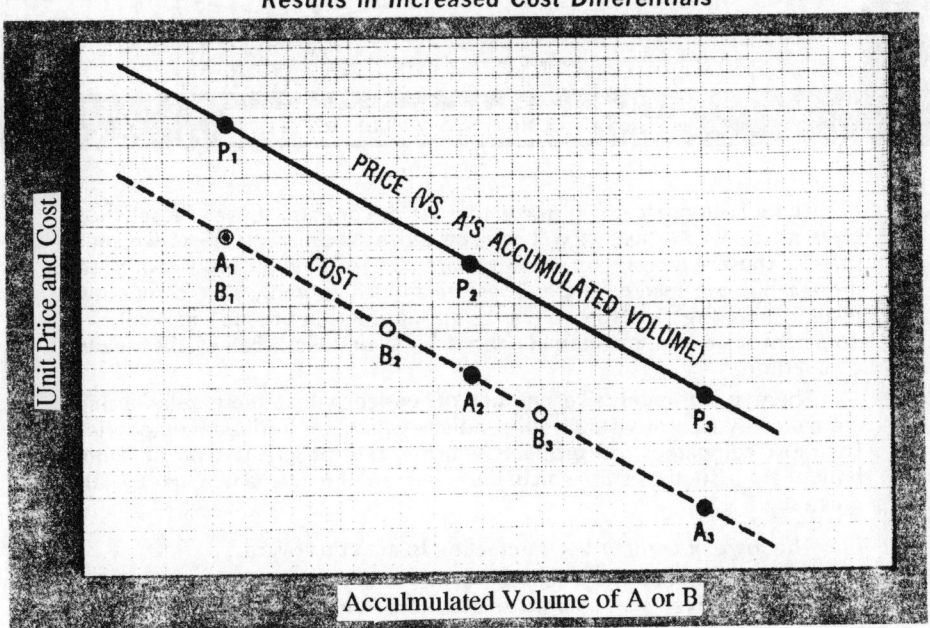

As shown in Exhibit 10, it is possible for a company to offset a below normal cost performance by a steady increase in market share, although obviously this would have severe limits when market share becomes very large. In this situation, while Company A moves down the industry-normal reduction slope, Company B offsets A's cost efficiency by moving down a *different*, less steep, cost reduction slope (characterizing a less effective program of cost control) more rapidly. Of course, this cannot happen indefinitely, or even very long. Large percentage variances in market share become important when absolute share is already large.

EXHIBIT 10

Increase in Market Share Alone Is Not Enough. Costs Must Go Down the Curve, Too.

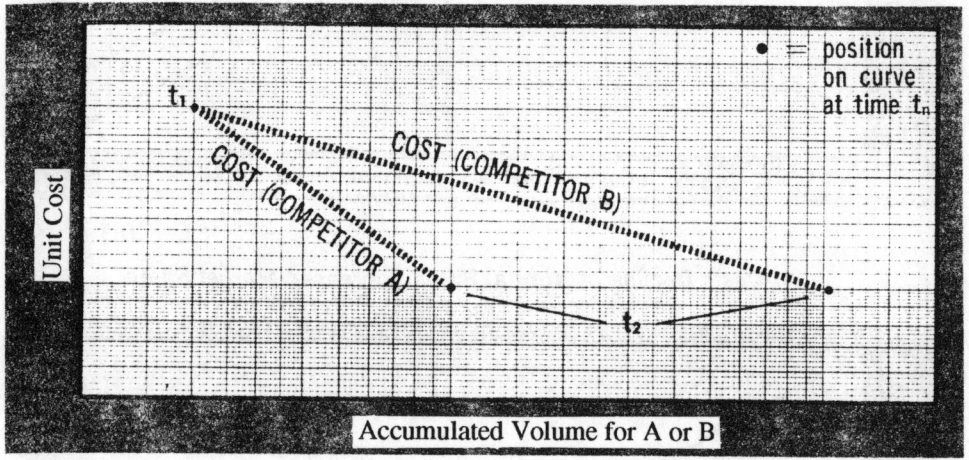

The whole relationship meets the test of common sense. Those whose costs go down the fastest will replace those whose costs go down more slowly. Those who gain in market share can lower their costs faster than those who lose market share. These relationships imply that competitive relationships are unstable on a given product until one maker has a dominant share of the market (about 50% or twice that of the nearest competitor).

There is an impressive amount of evidence that these relationships are generally true of virtually all products which are in direct competition. For most companies the products which make the greatest profit contribution are also those in which the share of the *relevant* market is the greatest.

The logic of competitive interaction is straightforward.
- If all competitors keep the same relative experience percentage, i.e., market share approximately the same, then cost differentials

should remain roughly constant.
- If any competitor fails to reduce his costs along the industry characteristic, he will steadily become less able to compete.
- Any competitor who gains market share should be able to convert this into an equivalent relative cost advantage.

[7]

Scenarios: shooting the rapids

How medium-term analysis illuminated the power of scenarios for Shell management

Pierre Wack

One of the most constant variables of today's management practices is the notion of change, adaptation, and innovation. Executives willingly embrace change when solutions can be found for and applied to particular problems. Losing sales? Improve product quality. Taking too long to get your product to the distributor? Shake up inventory. Threatened by a takeover? Make your management and corporation more lean, mean, and responsive to the shareholders.

In a way, such change is easy because it doesn't challenge the assumptions of good managers. Faced with a problem, they simply apply yet another formulaic solution. In the end, such easy change won't work against the kind of economic upheaval that has occurred in the last 15 years. Some fundamental modifications have been made in the way we do business. Shouldn't the corporate response be equally fundamental?

In the last issue of HBR, the author described how he and a group of strategic planners at Royal Dutch/Shell began to put in place a most innovative way to prepare managers to think more clearly about the future—scenario analysis. What was required was not the application of a new formula for planning but rather a new way of thinking. To show how difficult the transformation, the author described how the company came up with the idea and developed it in the early 1970s. In this sequel, he carries the story forward to describe the medium-term scenarios constructed in 1975. At a time when management's attention suddenly became fixed on the next quarter as opposed to the next decade, effective medium-term analysis proved vital in translating scenario theory into practice. The author patiently walks the reader through the development of the 1975 scenarios and then discusses the implications of scenario analysis on the practice of management.

Mr. Wack is retired head of the business environment division of the Royal Dutch/Shell Group planning department. Wack, an economist, developed with Edward Newland the Shell system of scenario planning. He now consults and participates in scenario development with management teams around the world. In 1983 and 1984, he was senior lecturer in scenario planning at the Harvard Business School.

I recently discussed scenario analysis with a well-known futurist. After I had listened to his presentation of a set of six scenarios, he asked me what I thought. "It was beautifully written, if complex," I replied. When pressed, I admitted that it was "impenetrable." I added, "The managers who hear it won't know what to do with it." To which the consultant responded, "That is not really my concern. I simply lay out the possibilities for them. It is up to the managers to know what they should do. I can't possibly tell them."

This small illustration points up the key problem with scenario planning: the interface of scenarios and decision makers is ignored or neglected. By interface, I mean the point at which the scenario really touches a chord in the manager's mind—the moment at which it has real meaning for him or her. The fact that those with the responsibility for preparing the scenario do not feel any responsibility for the interface is the main reason that—despite the logical appeal scenarios should have for managers disenchanted with forecasts—scenario planning has been scarcely developed.

Scenarios that merely quantify alternative outcomes of obvious uncertainties never inspire a management team's enthusiasm, even if all the alternatives are plausible. Most executives do not like to face such alternatives. They yearn for some kind of "definiteness" when dealing with the uncertainty that is the business environment, even if they have had their fingers burned for relying on past forecasts.

The same managers who can easily decide between different courses of action when they are in control often become unstuck when confronted with alternative futures they can't control and don't really understand. The reason is partly historical: many managers developed their skills in the 1950s and 1960s, an era characterized by an unusually high level of economic predictability. Being competent then meant knowing the right answer; it was considered incompetent or unprofessional to say, "Things could go this way —or that."

In truth, scenarios are often popular with middle managers who do not have to make awesome, final decisions. It is really top managers–who have ultimate responsibility for a company's long-term strategy–who find scenarios unhelpful. Most have risen to the top of large organizations based on their good judgment. They are proud of that judgment and trust it; their faith in it is one of their key motivations. The usual scenario analysis confronts them with raw uncertainties on which they cannot exercise their judgment. Because they cannot use what they consider to be their best quality, they often say, "Why bother with all that scenario stuff? We'll go on as before." Top management's desire for a framework in which to exercise good judgment is so strong that many executives continue to rely on forecasts, even though they know that forecasts often miss critical turning points in the business environment and even when they have been hurt by poor forecasts before.

What distinguishes Shell's decision scenarios from the first-generation analyses delineated in my earlier article is not primarily technical; it is a different philosophy, having to do with management perceptions and judgment.[1] The technicalities of decision scenarios derive from that philosophy. Almost by definition, scanning the business environment and crystallizing the findings in a set of scenarios means dealing with a world outside the corporation: for example, the evolution of demand, supply, prices, technology, competition, business cycle changes, and so forth. But this is only a half-truth and dangerous because there is another half. Because the raw materials of scenarios are made from this stuff of "outer space," it is not realized that more is needed: scenarios must come alive in "inner space," the manager's microcosm where choices are played out and judgment exercised.

Scenarios deal with two worlds: the world of facts and the world of perceptions. They explore for facts but they aim at perceptions inside the heads of decision makers. Their purpose is to gather and transform information of strategic significance into fresh perceptions. This transformation process is not trivial–more often than not it does not happen. When it works, it is a creative experience that generates a heartfelt "Aha!" from your managers and leads to strategic insights beyond the mind's previous reach.

I have found that getting to that management "Aha!" is the real challenge of scenario analysis. It does not simply leap at you when you've presented all the possible alternatives, no matter how eloquent your expression or how beautifully drawn your charts. It happens when your message reaches the microcosms of decision makers, obliges them to question their assumptions about how their business world works, and leads them to change and reorganize their inner models of reality.

Setting out

Scenario analysis demands first that managers understand the forces driving their business systems rather than rely on forecasts or alternatives (that is, someone else's understanding and judgment crystallized in a figure that then becomes a substitute for thinking). Using scenarios is as different from relying on forecasts as judo is from boxing: you want to use outside forces to your competitive advantage and make them work for you so that two plus two equals five or even more. You will find little or no power by merely accepting expert information about an outcome like the future price of oil or the future level of demand; power comes with an understanding of the forces behind the outcome. Scenarios must help decision makers develop their own feel for the nature of the system, the forces at work within it, the uncertainties that underlie the alternative scenarios, and the concepts useful for interpreting key data.

Scenarios structure the future into predetermined and uncertain elements (see *Exhibit I*). The foundation of decision scenarios lies in exploration and expansion of the predetermined elements: events already in the pipeline whose consequences have yet to unfold, interdependencies within the system (surprises often arise from interconnectedness), breaks in trends, or the "impossible." Decision scenarios rule out impossible developments; they deny much more than they affirm.

I will now take a risk and describe a ten-year-old scenario analysis. It is a risk because the scenario's subject is the business cycle, and no subject threatens to bore the reader in quite the same way as a business cycle that has passed. Even so, the discussion is important because:

1 We may be near the top of the business cycle, and a recession with serious implications could begin, given the fragility of the world economy. It troubles me that so few companies have analyzed the implications for them of economic developments outside the range of surprise-free possibility. Macroeconomists may discuss contingencies but managers do not.

2 The scenario analysis I presented in the first article was somewhat atypical. It dealt with an

---

[1] "Scenarios: Uncharted Waters Ahead," HBR September-October 1985, p. 72.

> The exhibits in Parts I and II are reprinted with the kind permission of Shell International Petroleum Company. I would like to acknowledge the original contributions of my former Shell colleagues and the members of Group Planning. G.A. Wagner, A. Bénard, K. Swart, and J.C. Davidson get special thanks because they were instrumental in launching the concept. My conceptualization of scenario analysis has benefited greatly from discussion with my former Harvard Business School colleagues, in particular Bruce Scott and David Bell. This article would not have been written without Norman Duncan and Peggy Evans. It expresses one or two things I have learned; it does not necessarily represent Shell's current planning views or practices.

economic disruption of a magnitude we do not often encounter. Moreover, we believed the disruption was a predetermined factor; uncertain were the reactions to it.

The following example deals with more typical cyclical fluctuations. We presented it in May 1975, when the world was nearly at the bottom of the worst recession since World War II.

Analyzing the predetermined elements

When the oil shock of 1973-1974 made the dreams – and nightmares – described in the scenarios discussed in my first article come true, managers at Shell (like managers everywhere) redirected their attention to the short term, focusing on economic growth, oil demand, inflation, interest rates, and their sensitive relationship with OPEC suppliers. In 1975, we addressed their concerns by developing medium-term scenarios for the rapids. The predetermined elements of these scenarios were:

The first wave – inflation. Like a large rock dropped in a lake, the 1973 oil price increase generated a series of waves, beginning with inflation, which was higher than simple cost-through-the-system arithmetic would indicate (on average, only 3% or 4%). Booming world economies were already out of balance prior to the oil shock and affected by high inflation. Furthermore, the enormous publicity surrounding the oil price increase (coming as it did with production cuts and selective embargoes) caused major economic actors – trade unions, entrepreneurs, and consumers – to overanticipate the actual inflationary impact. Such overreaction added fuel to the fire, accelerating the rate of inflation.

The second wave – deflation. From mid-1974, a contraction in demand to well below production capacity followed. The extra cash outflow to OPEC acted like an external excise tax on consumer demand of some $60 billion each year – or 2.5% of OECD economies. Government anti-inflation policies contributed toward pushing demand far below production potential. Economic dominoes fell one by one as:

☐ The automobile industry, always on the margin of discretionary spending and vulnerable to both the real increase in gasoline prices and the "oil link" in the consumer's mind, suffered an immediate decline, with extensive multiplier effects through the balance of the economy.

☐ Building and construction, also a powerful engine of economic activity, fell some six months later as government anti-inflation policies caused a credit crunch.

☐ The world iron and steel industry remained an island of continuing high activity for nine months after the oil shock. It was propped up by a backlog of orders (from shipyards, for instance) plus some stock building. Large orders from the communist world contributed toward keeping it buoyant longer than other sectors. Eventually, however, the decline in the automobile and construction industries had a domino effect on the iron and steel industry.

Two other actions deepened the recession. First, companies drastically ran down inventories. The imposition of credit controls in the face of shrinking demand and the expectation of a fall in prices guaranteed a drastic drop in inventories. When inventories are reduced by eight days, it is equivalent to forgoing six months of 5% economic growth; inventories in many segments were reduced by more than eight days. Next, consumer spending, long the stable engine of OECD economies, took a nosedive. For the first time since recovery started in the early 1950s, consumers stopped buying, increased savings, and began to worry about what the future might hold. The resulting recession was the most severe since World War II (see Exhibit II).

Electoral rendezvous. The governments of Japan, Germany, and the United States would each face the electorate in 1976. If the truism applies that people vote their pocketbooks, then presiding over a recession is an invitation to defeat at the polls. The incentives for incumbent governments to go for growth were thus overwhelming.

Reflation in the pipeline. Not only were politicians anticipating the 1976 elections, but they were also keenly aware that much of the hardship borne in 1975 was unnecessary and self-inflicted – the

Exhibit I   1975 global framework

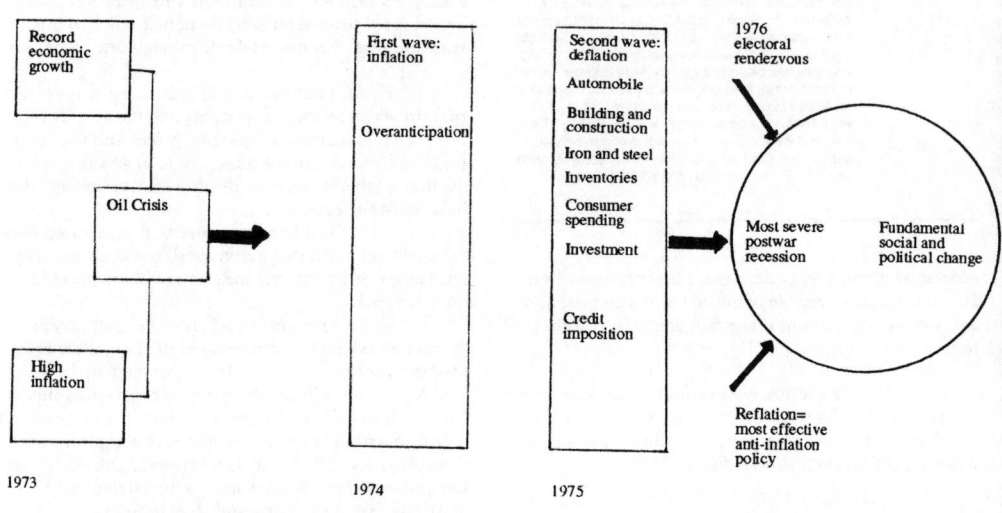

deflation was too harsh. With excess capacity so widespread, governments could safely reflate and expanding output could reduce unit prices and further curb inflation. Such reflation would largely be self-financing through taxation on increasing income, sales, and profits, and lowered costs for unemployment benefits.

Long-term unemployment was becoming evident as a social problem. Unemployment falls most heavily on the young. Few governments could afford to do nothing about the prospect of a third graduating class moving from the classroom to the welfare rolls.

All these predetermined elements combined to make it virtually certain that governments would attempt to reflate.

Reaching the rapids

We spent much time developing the predetermined elements and understanding the recent past. To recapitulate, managers will only accept scenarios when their common, predetermined elements enter and unfold in their minds. We call this process "rooting" because scenarios on their own – that is, as mere description of alternative courses of events – would be effective and alive in the minds of managers as long as a tree without roots. I have seen many scenarios suffer this fate.

That economies would reflate was largely predetermined. What was unknown in the spring of 1975 was the timing and nature of the recovery. To illuminate the forces driving the further development of the system and its critical uncertainties, we designed two scenarios of recovery:

> The "Boom and Bust" scenario foresaw a vigorous recovery that contained the seeds of its own destruction.

> The "Constrained Growth" scenario projected a kind of "muddling-through" recovery that would differ fundamentally from earlier business cycle recoveries.

We also considered the possibility that reflation would not happen; our "Depression Contingency" scenario seemed so improbable, however, that we did not think it relevant for planning. The three possibilities are arrayed in *Exhibit I*.

Scenario planning

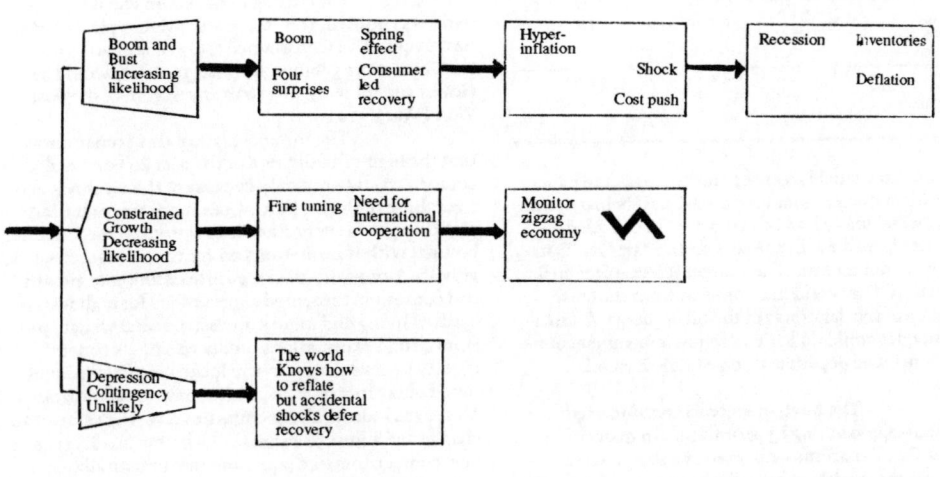

1976

Boom & Bust: a series of surprises

Boom and Bust described an economic world more characteristic of the 1950s than the 1960s. Cycles of greater amplitude and shorter duration would develop. We believed that the longer the recovery was deferred, the more likely this scenario – as governments turned to panic measures to reflate their economies.

First surprise – rapid recovery. Rather than tepid, the recovery would be swift, strong, and forceful, as some economies like that of the United States would grow by 11% or 12% in 18 months. Such growth would be as if an economy the size of Britain's were to appear all at once on the world map. Such a rebound would not imply spectacular achievements; it would only reflect the depth of the 1973-1975 dent in the economy – a coiled-spring effect.

Second surprise – oil-intensive recovery. Reports of OPEC's death, we believed, were premature. Even though news of energy savings might persuade governments that Western conservation measures could negate OPEC's negotiating strength, such a boast could not stand up to analysis. Reduced oil consumption resulted not from a fundamental change in behavior but mainly from the recession, which had cut both industrial and consumer demand. A boom in 1976 or 1977 would allow most consumers to revert to previous patterns of behavior and consumption. Economic growth in 1976-1977 would have to be fueled by a rise in energy demand, particularly for oil (see *Exhibit III*).

Third surprise – booming U.S. oil imports. The upsurge in U.S. oil imports would easily put to rest talk about "Project Independence," President Gerald Ford's import-reduction targets, and alternative energy projects. Our estimates indicated that in such a scenario U.S. imports would rise by 2.5 million barrels per day in 1976 (more than Britain's total imports or Kuwait's current exports), with a further increase of 2 million barrels per day in 1977 (in aggregate, more than Britain's total energy consumption).

Because we believed that a normal recovery would be equivalent to the sudden creation of a new economic nation, we could now add that the new nation would be almost totally dependent on Middle East oil. Consumer countries would once again be trapped.

Fourth surprise – stagnant alternative energies. Countries would find that alternative energy

Exhibit II	Decline in industrial production measured from previous cyclical peak		
	USA	Europe	Japan
Recession first quarter, 1975	−14%	−9%	−19%
Previous postwar recessions	−7%	−2%	−2%

programs consisted largely of empty words and paper tigers. Most nuclear plants operated well below design capacity, and many had been deferred or canceled. Little had been done in the coal sector. The OECD nations were not meeting their target forecasts for coal production. The world had come far from the crash programs of the dark days of the oil embargo. Alternative energies could do little to relieve consumer countries' continued dependence on Middle East oil.

The bust—a second recession. High inflation—approaching hyperinflation in many of the weaker OECD nations—threatened a sustained recovery. Rates that would exceed the highest levels of 1974-1975 by a further 5% would become politically and socially intolerable, signaling to governments that the boom was getting out of control. Their reaction would be to reapply deflationary measures, including credit restrictions, higher interest rates, oil import controls, and limits on oil consumption. Just as the recovery would be surprisingly rapid, so the downturn could be sharp. Inventories would play an important role: stock building, starting from the depths of the current recession, would promote growth in production during the upswing. But as liquidity disappeared in the face of strong deflationary measures, stocks would be run down rapidly, making the downturn that much sharper.

How probable was the Boom and Bust scenario? Because it held out dramatic implications for all sectors of the world economy and oil in particular, we found it hard to give equal attention to the other scenario. Even so, in 1975, we still considered it less probable than its alternative, Constrained Growth. While we made no forecasts about the start of a boom, we were willing to assume that the longer the recovery took to get under way, the more likely the Boom and Bust scenario would occur.

Constrained Growth: a new economic world

Everything in the Boom and Bust scenario was normal; the "surprises" were typical of business cycles. The Constrained Growth scenario was built on a more genuine surprise: recovery would be slower and more halting than any upturn of the post-World War II era.

The internal logic of this scenario was that the high-growth trend of the past 25 years had come to an end—not only because of the oil shock and the eclipse of the Bretton Woods monetary order, but also because the very success of the postwar economies brought with it limitations on continued vigorous growth. Along with unprecedented economic growth had come unprecedented expectations for higher standards of living and more impressive social welfare programs. High expectations produced a new economic rigidity as governments were locked into a continual round of tax increases to pay for these social programs. Moreover, industrialized countries now were slower to change and adjust to surprises—whether an oil crisis or new competitors like Japan and the industrializing countries of Southeast Asia.

Constrained growth would characterize the first years of this new economic world in which all the engines of growth—consumption, international trade, government spending, and investment—would work with less power.

Investment was emphasized as a change that we called a lasting "technological recession." From the end of World War II until the early 1970s, the best new technology in basic industries could, on its own merit, outcompete existing technology. A new steel plant, for example, was more economical than an existing one per ton of capacity; new cement and paper plants, new refineries and tankers, and new power generation plants were regularly more efficient than the previous technology. Beginning in the early 1970s, however, such technological progress could not beat rising costs. It was now cheaper to acquire existing capacity than it was to order new capacity.

For perhaps 10 to 15 years, the unit capital and operating costs of almost all new plants in basic industries would exceed the costs of existing equipment. That would obviously discourage new investment in industries that had been the engine of postwar economic growth and accentuate inflationary pressure. We analyzed the other engines of growth: government spending would result in budget deficits and more rigidity; consumer spending would be changed by the maturation in the life cycle of a large range of consumer durables; and international trade would be characterized by accumulating imbalances and frictions.

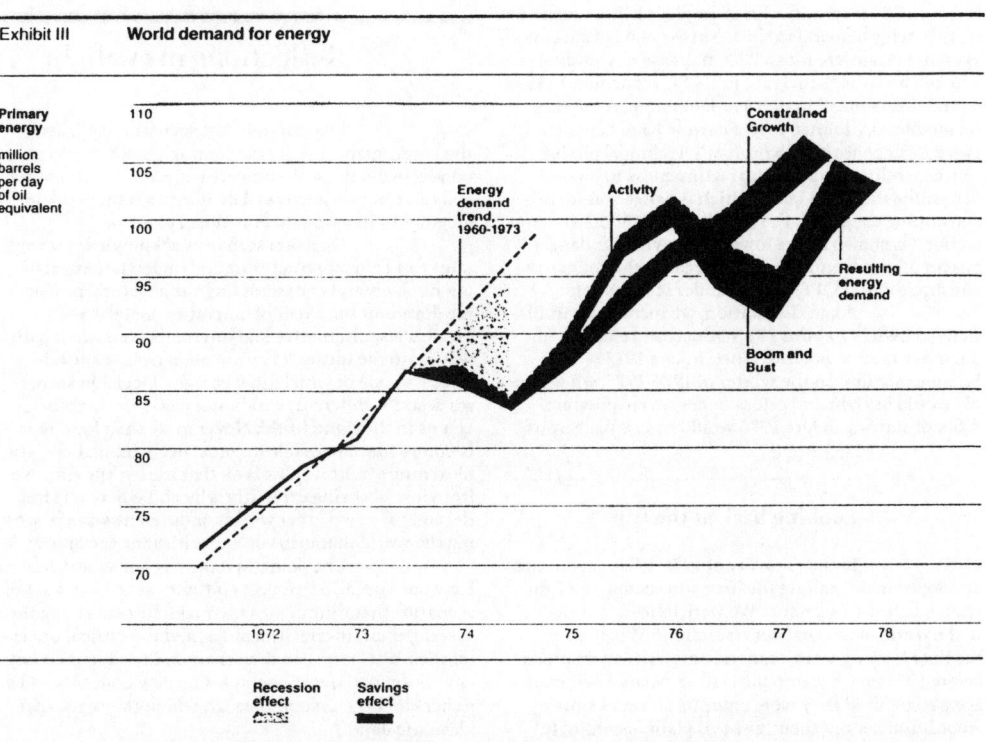

Exhibit III — World demand for energy

The overall conclusion was that the prospects for economic growth would be well below past achievements. This confirmed one of our long-term scenarios introduced in 1974: we would enter – by means of this constrained growth period – a completely new "world of internal contradictions": a world of low economic growth that would stand in stark contrast to the booming economies of the past 25 years.

Reaching shore

Let me give one final example of how global scenarios are used to bring focus to particular issues or projects. Scenarios are like cherry trees: their fruit grows neither on the trunk nor on the large boughs but rather on the small branches. The tree needs the trunk and boughs to grow the small branches.

The global scenarios I have described correspond to the tree's trunk; the country scenarios developed by the national Shell operating companies can be likened to boughs. They account for the predetermined and uncertain elements peculiar to their countries. The fruits are picked from the small branches. These are the scenarios that focus on a particular strategic issue, market, or investment.

One such set of focused scenarios has to do with the demand for OPEC oil – as opposed to oil received from other sources. Because OPEC oil is the balancing factor in the world energy system, its fluctuations reflect cyclical economic fluctuations – but amplified several times. A decline in economic activity translates into a larger decline in world oil consumption, which then translates into a much larger decline in OPEC oil demand. The reasons are: first, energy-intensive industries (like cement and steel) are more than proportionately affected in a recession; second, alternative energy sources are usually cheaper than oil; and third, OPEC oil, unlike domestic oil, has to be paid in foreign exhange.

In a recovery, a small rise in world energy demand would translate into larger rises in oil demand and even larger rises in OPEC oil demand. In the

Boom and Bust scenario, for example, a 13% increase in world energy demand in the first two years of a recovery would translate into a 23% increase in world oil demand and a 34% increase in OPEC oil demand. How would this demand match available supply? OPEC's oil production fluctuates in a narrow band between two danger zones (see *Exhibit IV*). Technical production capabilities and political willingness to produce determine the upper band, which is dangerous for oil-consuming countries; the threshold of "OPEC dissatisfaction" is shown in the lower band, which is dangerous for oil-producing countries because the solidarity and discipline of OPEC come under severe stress.

As an illustration, we made two simulations (shown in *Exhibit IV*). The demand changes implicit in a normal boom starting in late 1975 would become manifest in the winter of 1976-1977, when supply would be tight and prices under severe pressure. A boom starting in late 1976 would be less dangerous.

Looking back at the trip

In the recovery of 1976-1978, economies developed mainly along the lines foreseen in the Constrained Growth scenario. We were indeed introduced to the world of internal contradictions. What had been the floor for long-term economic growth expectations before 1973 now became the ceiling. Many Shell managers recognized they were entering an era of slower growth and hedged their business plans accordingly. When the 1980s demanded leanness and restructuring, Shell was ready because it had begun the regimen early. That Shell saw this new world earlier than most could be seen by comparing the various energy forecasts made at the time. Shell consistently projected one of the lowest energy growth paths for the 1980s.

Scenarios serve two main purposes. The first is protective: anticipating and understanding risk. The second is entrepreneurial: discovering strategic options of which you were previously unaware. This latter purpose is in the long run more important. But while the more dramatic and (for Shell) dangerous of the two scenarios—Boom and Bust—did not occur, the exercise proved useful enough to our managers that medium-term scenarios were prepared every year thereafter while in the rapids. As C.W. MacMahon of the Bank of England has succinctly observed: "No time is as usefully wasted as that spent guarding against disasters that do not in the event occur."

Reflections in twilight

I have found that scenarios can effectively organize a variety of seemingly unrelated economic, technological, competitive, political, and societal information and translate it into a framework for judgment—in a way that no model could do.

Decision scenarios acknowledge uncertainty and aim at structuring and understanding it—but not by merely crisscrossing variables and producing dozens or hundreds of outcomes. Instead, they create a few alternative and internally consistent pathways into the future. They are not a group of quasi-forecasts, one of which may be right. Decision scenarios describe different worlds, not just different outcomes in the same world. Never more than four (or it becomes unmanageable for most decision makers), the ideal number is one plus two; that is, first the surprise-free view (showing explicitly why and where it is fragile) and then two other worlds or different ways of seeing the world that focus on the critical uncertainties.

The point, to repeat, is not so much to have one scenario that "gets it right" as to have a set of scenarios that illuminates the major forces driving the system, their interrelationships, and the critical uncertainties. The users can then sharpen their focus on key environmental questions, aided by new concepts and a richer language system through which they exchange ideas and data.

A design that includes three scenarios describing alternative outcomes along a single dimension is dangerous because many managers cannot resist the temptation to identify the middle scenario as a baseline. A scheme based on two scenarios raises a similar risk if one is easily seen as optimistic and the other pessimistic. Managers then intuitively believe that reality must be somewhere in between. They "split the difference" to arrive at an answer not very different from a single-line forecast.

Experience shows that decision scenarios focus on critical uncertainties that are often very different from those that seemed obvious to managers at the beginning of the process. Despite this focus on uncertainty, decision scenarios do not paralyze managers. Rather, the deeper understanding of the risks that is gained often makes the decision maker capable of confronting apparently greater risk.

You can test the value of scenarios by asking two questions:

1   What do they leave out? In five to ten years, managers must not be able to say that the scenarios did not warn them of important events that subsequently happened.

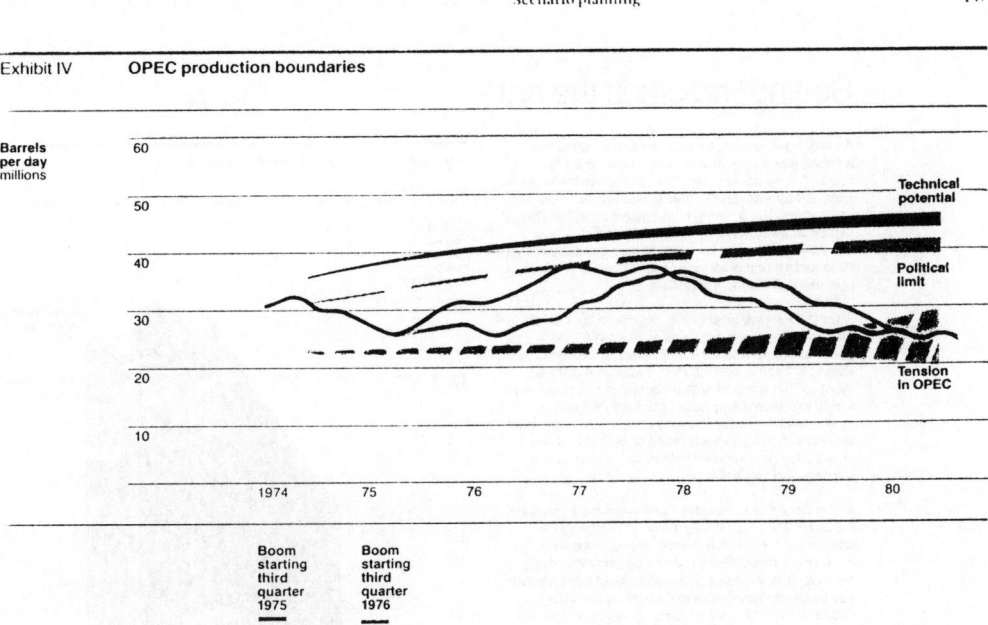

Exhibit IV OPEC production boundaries

2 Do they lead to action? If scenarios do not push managers to do something other than that indicated by past experience, they are nothing more than interesting speculation.

It is impossible to develop a set of decision scenarios without knowledge of managers' deepest concerns – something we did not fully appreciate when we developed our scenarios in the 1970s. We were lucky, however; our managers' concerns turned out to be precisely what we were studying. Later, we developed interview techniques to find out what was on their minds and to illuminate the existing decision framework. Today, the interview is one of the first steps taken when Shell starts a scenario exercise.

The decision scenarios I have described were global, or macroscenarios. To analyze particular aspects of a business, you develop focused scenarios that are custom tailored around a certain strategic issue, market, or investment. But you cannot start with a narrow focus because you will likely miss key things (or dimensions), or else you may cast the scenarios in the wrong way. You must wide-angle first to capture the big picture and then zoom in on the details.

We have found that scenarios are most effective when combined with:

Strategic vision. You should have a clear, structured view of what you want your company to be, which precedes your view of what you want your company to do (investing, divesting, penetrating new markets, and so forth).

Option planning. In most planning approaches, strategies are put forward on a single line and options – if there are any – are merely straw men. This is even more dangerous than single-line forecasting. Option planning, in which all options are put forward on a neutral mode, is practiced at both the business unit and corporate levels.

The purpose of a combined approach is option generation (see Exhibit V). If the scenario process does not bring out strategic options previously unconsidered by managers, then it has been sterile.

The gentle art of reperceiving

Companies differ greatly in their effectiveness and speed in transforming the potential of scientific research into new products and processes. In times of rapid change, their effectiveness and speed in identifying and transforming information of strategic significance into strategic initiatives differ just as much.

Today, however, such a capacity is critical. Unless companies are careful, novel information

Seeing "rabbits in the hat"

As any adult knows, a magician cannot produce a rabbit unless it is already in (or very near) his hat. In the same way, surprises in the business environment almost never emerge without warning. To understand the warnings, managers must be able to look at available evidence in alternative ways. Otherwise, they can be badly misled by apparently valid facts if that is all they see, or they do not interpret them in different ways.

After the second oil shock, a "scenario for the rapids" covering the medium term 1980-1985 introduced a notion at odds with prevailing wisdom. Called a "high savings case," it alerted management to "the possibility that consumers themselves would produce a surprise in the form of a much more rapid decrease in energy and oil intensity than that assumed for the reference case." This would mean a further drop of 6 million barrels per day in the demand for OPEC oil.

At the time, there was little hard evidence to support the case. There is always a lag in the impact on demand of a price rise. Furthermore, there was great uncertainty about the oil market and anxiety about further supplies. The outbreak of the Iran-Iraq war increased anxiety about supplies from the Middle East. Both oil consumers and oil companies tried to increase their stocks of oil; customers' orders were strong; and industry forecasts as well as the "feel of the market" all pointed toward sustained demand. The mood of the industry leaned toward expansion: 1980-1981 saw an enormous increase in drilling activity and feverish competition to secure term contracts for the supply of crude. The problems of the oil industry were obviously on the supply side, not on the demand side.

In March 1981, the new 1981-1985 scenarios for the rapids stated that "last year's conservation surprise can no longer be regarded merely as a contingency." We also introduced a new scenario, "Hard Times," that foresaw an economic recession deeper than most observers expected, an oil conservation surprise (drawn from the remarkable analysis by Aart Beijdorff), and societal change that would significantly affect both economic behavior and oil demand.

Under the Hard Times scenario, the combined effect of these three elements could lead to a totally different—and much lower—level of oil demand (see Figure A) than from the first oil shock—even though

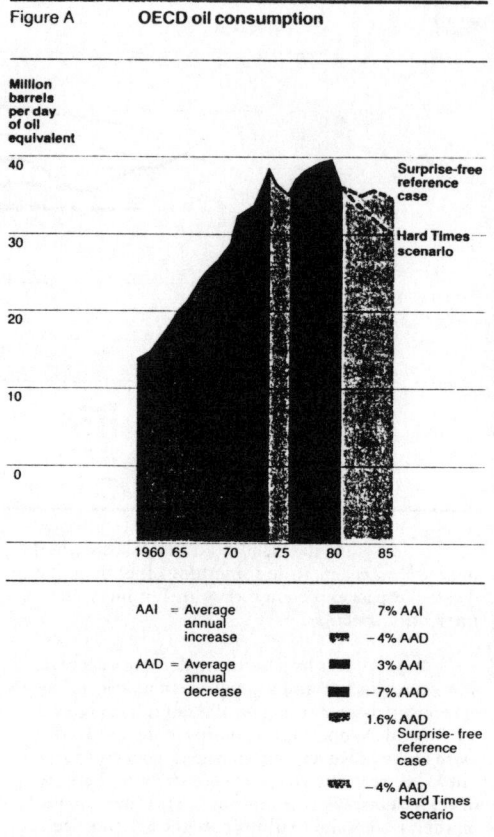

Figure A   OECD oil consumption

outside the span of managerial expectations may not penetrate the core of decision makers' minds, where possible futures are rehearsed and judgment exercised.

Historical examples abound. After concluding the nonaggression pact with Hitler in 1939, Stalin was so convinced the Germans would not attack as early as 1941—and certainly not without an ultimatum—that he ignored 84 warnings to the contrary. According to Barton Whaley, the warnings about Operation Barbarossa included communications from Richard Sorge, a Soviet spy in the German embassy in Tokyo, and Winston Churchill; the withdrawal of German merchant shipping from Soviet ports; and evacuation of German dependents from Moscow.[2]

Or consider the case of Pearl Harbor. "Noise," the massive volume of signals, impeded understanding of what was to come. As Roberta Wohlstetter points out, "To discriminate significant sounds the immediate impact on GNP, balance of payment of OECD, and so on was surprisingly similar.

We called the likelihood of there being a real conservation surprise a "rabbit in the hat." Moreover, we were increasingly convinced that at least the two ears of our particular "rabbit" were already visible. First, less than one-sixth of the 1973-1974 crude oil price increase had been passed on to final consumers because of the cushioning effect of refining and transport costs and of various taxes in the selling price of the total products barrel. This time, however, more than half of the crude price rise would be felt by final consumers, a change that suggested consumers' reactions would be nonlinear.

Second, a radical change in consumers' perceptions seemed likely to reinforce this growing price leverage. Few people had believed in the reality of an oil crisis after 1973-1974; now the popular consensus seemed to be that the upward price trend was irreversible. This change in attitude, combined with the normal effect of a large price increase, could reawaken previously dormant price elasticity from the first oil shock.

Finally, we believed that the oil industry and OPEC were being fooled by the demand statistics, which reflected not real demand or actual consumption but deliveries only. Stock building at the consumer level as well as at the oil company level was abnormally high (see Figure B).

It is now clear that much of the oil industry in 1980-1981 overestimated future demand. In such a context, a company can make a lot of money selling weeks of unnecessary stocks before prices erode. It may be just a coincidence, but Shell companies' reduction in oil stocks through 1981 was much greater and earlier than that for the commercial stocks of the industry as a whole, even though Shell stocks at the beginning of the year (in terms of days' supply of current demand) were already well below the average.

The Hard Times scenario used a new hypothesis to analyze demand behavior and thereby alerted decision makers to the possibility of a major discontinuity in future oil demand. We saw more than the conventional consensus view of the industry mainly because we had been looking for alternative ways of seeing our world. A new strategic option emerged that encouraged us to go against the mainstream of the oil industry.

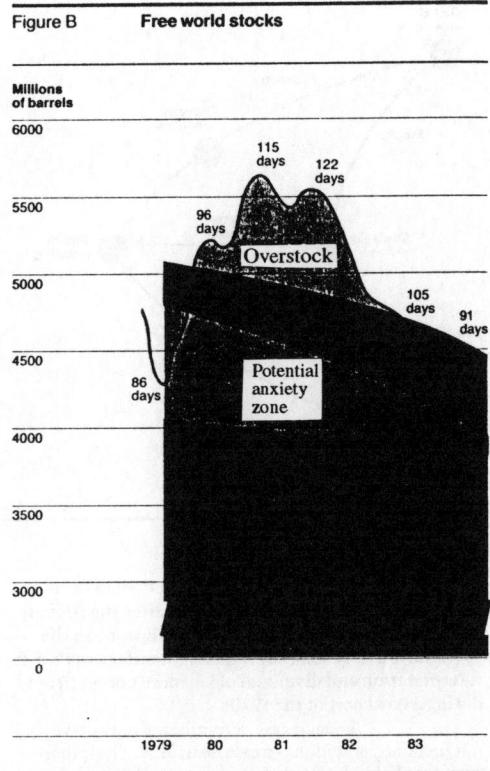

Figure B Free world stocks

against this background of noise, one has to be listening for something or for one of several things....One needs not only an ear but a *variety of hypotheses* that guide observation"[3] (emphasis added). Indeed, the Japanese commander of the Pearl Harbor attack, Mitsuo Fuchida, surprised at having achieved surprise, asked, "Had these Americans never heard of Port Arthur?" (the event preceding the Russo-Japanese War of 1904 – and famous in Japan – when the Japanese navy destroyed the Russian Pacific fleet at anchor in Port Arthur in a surprise attack).

Similar business cases are not as well documented. I have observed some: the French steel

[2] Barton Whaley, *Codeword Barbarossa* (Cambridge: MIT Press, 1973).

[3] Roberta Wohlstetter, *Pearl Harbor: Warning and Decision* (Stanford, Calif.: Stanford University Press, 1962).

Exhibit V   Generating management options

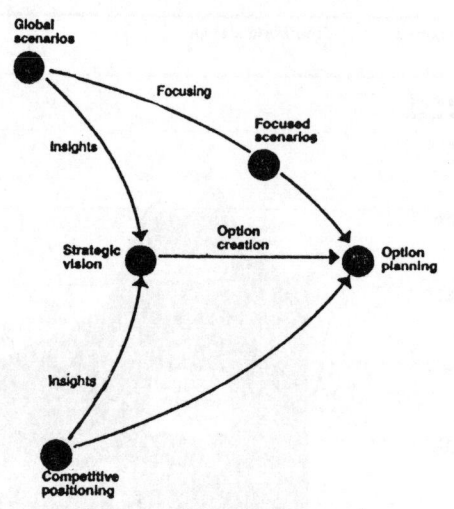

industry's handling of the "FOS project" near Marseilles; the tanker market before and after the first oil shock; petrochemical investments in Europe in the 1970s; and a large U.S. automobile manufacturer's misinterpretation and dismissal of Japanese competition during a good part of the 1970s.

In each case, a number of executives – not just one individual – made decisions. Their inappropriate behavior extended over several months or even years – it was not just a one-time error. Problems resulted from a crisis of perception rather than from poor strategic reasoning. These decision makers' strategies made sense and indeed were sometimes brilliant – within the context of their limited worldview.

In times of rapid change, a crisis of perception (that is, the inability to see an emerging novel reality by being locked inside obsolete assumptions) often causes strategic failure, particularly in large, well-run companies. Opportunities missed because managers did not recognize them in time are clearly more important than failures, which are visible to all. As Peter Drucker said, "The greatest danger in times of turbulence is not the turbulence; it is to act with yesterday's logic."

Central to decision scenarios – indeed the basis for their success or failure – is the microcosm of the decision makers: their inner model of reality, their set of assumptions that structure their understanding of the unfolding business environment and the factors critical to success. A manager's inner model never mirrors reality; it is always a construct. It deals with complexity by focusing on what really matters. It is a superior simplification of reality – the more so, the wider a manager's span of responsibility is.

During stable times, the mental model of a successful decision maker and unfolding reality match. Some adjustment and fine tuning will do. Decision scenarios have little or no leverage.

In times of rapid change and increased complexity, however, the manager's mental model becomes a dangerously mixed bag: rich detail and understanding can coexist with dubious assumptions, selective inattention to alternative ways of interpreting evidence, and illusory projections. In these times, the scenario approach has leverage and can make a difference.

In today's world, a management microcosm shaped by the past and sustained by the usual types of forecasts is inherently suspect and inadequate. Yet it is extremely difficult for managers to break out of their worldview while operating within it. When they are committed to a certain way of framing an issue, it is difficult for them to see solutions that lie outside this framework.

By presenting other ways of seeing the world, decision scenarios allow managers to break out of a one-eyed view. Scenarios give managers something very precious: the ability to reperceive reality. In a turbulent business environment, there is more to see than managers normally perceive. Highly relevant information goes unnoticed because, being locked into one way of looking, managers fail to see its significance (see the insert, "Seeing 'Rabbits in the Hat'").

It has been my repeated experience that the perceptions that emerge when the disciplined approach of scenario analysis is practiced are richer and often critically different from the previous implicit view. The scenario process of converting information into fresh perceptions has something of a "breeder effect": it generates energy, much more energy than has been consumed in time and effort during the process.

A mere high or low around a baseline can never achieve a conceptual reframing. The reperception of reality and the discovery of strategic openings that follow the breaking of the manager's assumptions (many of which are so taken for granted that the manager no longer is aware of them) are, after all, the essence of entrepreneurship. Scenario planning aims to rediscover the original entrepreneurial power of foresight in contexts of change, complexity, and uncertainty. It is precisely in these contexts – not in stable times – that the real opportunities lie to gain competitive advantage through strategy. ⊖

[8]

At Shell, planning means changing minds, not making plans.

Planning as Learning

by ARIE P. DE GEUS

Some years ago, the planning group at Shell surveyed 30 companies that had been in business for more than 75 years. What impressed us most was their ability to live in harmony with the business environment, to switch from a survival mode when times were turbulent to a self-development mode when the pace of change was slow. And this pattern rang a familiar bell because Shell's history is similarly replete with switches from expansion to self-preservation and back again to growth.

Early in our history, for example, there was a burst of prosperity in the Far East and we dominated the market for kerosene in tins and "oil for the lamps of China." Survival became the keynote, however, when Rockefeller's Standard Oil snatched market share by cutting price. In fact, it was the survival instinct that led in 1907 to the joining of Royal Dutch Petroleum and the Shell Transport and Trading Company – separate businesses until then and competitors in the Far East. This, in turn, paved the way for Shell's expansion into the United States in 1911 with a new product, Sumatran gasoline – also a reaction to Standard Oil's activities.

Outcomes like these don't happen automatically. On the contrary, they depend on the ability of a company's senior managers to absorb what is going on in the business environment and to act on that information with appropriate business moves. In other words, they depend on learning. Or, more precisely, on institutional learning, which is the process whereby management teams change their shared mental models of their company, their markets, and their competitors. For this reason, we think of planning as learning and of corporate planning as institutional learning.

Institutional learning is much more difficult than individual learning. The high level of thinking among individual managers in most companies is admirable. And yet, the level of thinking that goes on in the management teams of most companies is considerably below the individual managers' capacities. In institutional learning situations, the learning level of the team is often the lowest common denominator, especially with teams that think of themselves as machines with mechanistic, specialized parts: the production manager looks at production, the distribution manager looks at distribution, the marketing manager looks at marketing.

Because high-level, effective, and continuous institutional learning and ensuing corporate change are the prerequisites for corporate success, we at Shell* have asked ourselves two questions. How does a company learn and adapt? And, What is planning's role in corporate learning?

My answer to the first question, "how does a company learn and adapt," is that many do not or, at least, not very quickly. A full one-third of the *Fortune* "500" industrials listed in 1970 had vanished by 1983. And W. Stewart Howe has pointed out in his 1986 book *Corporate Strategy* that for every successful turnaround there are two ailing companies that fail to recover. Yet some companies obviously do learn and can adapt. In fact, our survey identified several that were still vigorous at 200, 300, and even 700 years of age. What made the difference? Why are some companies better able to adapt?

Sociologists and psychologists tell us it is pain that makes people and living systems change. And certainly corporations have their share of painful crises, the recent spate of takeovers and takeover threats conspicuously among them. But crisis management –pain management– is a dangerous way to manage for change.

---

*Author's note: I use the collective expression "Shell" for convenience when referring to the companies of the Royal Dutch/Shell Group in general, or when no purpose is served by identifying the particular Shell company or companies.

Arie P. de Geus is head of planning for the Royal Dutch/ Shell Group of companies. During more than 30 years with Shell, he has worked throughout the world, most recently as coordinator for Africa and South Asia and as the director of Shell's oil operations in Brazil.

Once in a crisis, everyone in the organization feels the pain. The need for change is clear. The problem is that you usually have little time and few options. The deeper into the crisis you are, the fewer options remain. Crisis management, by necessity, becomes autocratic management. The positive characteristic of a crisis is that the decisions are quick. The other side of that coin is that the implementation is rarely good; many companies fail to survive.

The challenge, therefore, is to recognize and react to environmental change before the pain of a crisis. Not surprisingly, this is what the long-lived companies in our study were so well able to do.

All these companies had a striking capacity to institutionalize change. They never stood still. Moreover, they seemed to recognize that they had internal strengths that could be developed as environmental conditions changed. Thus, Booker McConnell, founded in 1906 as a sugar company, developed shipping on the back of its primary resource. British American Tobacco recognized that marketing cigarettes was no different from marketing perfume. Mitsubishi, founded in 1870 as a marine and trading company, acquired coal mines to secure access to ships' bunkers, built shipyards to repair imported ships, and developed a bank from the exchange business it had begun to finance shippers.

Changes like these grow out of a company's knowledge of itself and its environment. All managers have such knowledge and they develop it further all the time, since every living person—and system—is continuously engaged in learning. In fact, the normal decision process in corporations is a learning process, because people change their own mental models and build up a joint model as they talk. The problem is that the speed of that process is slow—too slow for a world in which the ability to learn faster than competitors may be the only sustainable competitive advantage.

Some five years ago, we had a good example of the time it takes for a message to be heard. One way in which we in Shell trigger institutional learning is through scenarios.[1] A certain set of scenarios gave our planners a clear signal that the oil industry, which had always been highly integrated, was so no longer. That contradicted all our existing models. High integration means that you are more or less in control of all the facets of your industry, so you can start optimizing. Optimization was the driving managerial model in Shell. What these scenarios essentially were saying was that we had to look for other management methods.

The first reaction from the organization was at best polite. There were few questions and no discussion. Some managers reacted critically: the scenarios were "basic theory that everyone already knew"; they had "little relevance to the realities of today's business." The message had been listened to but it had not yet been heard.

After a hiatus of some three months, people began asking lots of questions; a discussion started. The intervening months had provided time for the message to settle and for management's mental models to develop a few new hooks. Absorption, phase one of the learning process, had taken place.

During the next nine months, we moved through the other phases of the learning process. Operating

> **The ability to learn faster than your competitors may be the only sustainable competitive advantage.**

executives at Shell incorporated this new information into their mental models of the business. They drew conclusions from the revised models and tested them against experience. Then, finally, they acted on the basis of the altered model. Hearing, digestion, confirmation, action: each step took time, its own sweet time.

In my experience this time span is typical. It will likely take 12 to 18 months from the moment a signal is received until it is acted on. The issue is not whether a company will learn, therefore, but whether it will learn fast and early. The critical question becomes, "Can we accelerate institutional learning?"

I am more and more persuaded that the answer to this question is yes. But before explaining why, I want to emphasize an important point about learning and the planner's role. The only relevant learning in a company is the learning done by those people who have the power to act (at Shell, the operating company management teams). So the real purpose of effective planning is not to make plans but to change the microcosm, the mental models that these decision makers carry in their heads. And this is what we at Shell and others elsewhere try to do.

In this role as facilitator, catalyst, and accelerator of the corporate learning process, planners are apt to fall into several traps. One is that we sometimes start with a mental model that is unrecognizable to our audience. Another is that we take too many steps at

---

1. Pierre Wack wrote about our system in "Scenarios: Uncharted Waters Ahead," HBR September-October 1985, p. 72 and in "Scenarios: Shooting the Rapids," HBR November-December 1985, p. 139.

once. The third, and most serious, is that too often we communicate our information by teaching. This is a natural trap to fall into because it's what we've been conditioned to all our lives. But teaching, as John Holt points out, is actually one of the least efficient ways to convey knowledge.[2] At best, 40% of what is taught is received; in most situations, it is only about 25%.

It was a shock to learn how inefficient teaching is. Yet some reflection on our own experience drove the point home. After all, we had spent nearly 15 man-years preparing a set of scenarios which we then transmitted in a condensed version in 2½ hours. Could we really have believed that our audience would understand all we were talking about?

Teaching has another disadvantage as well, especially in a business setting. Teachers must be given authority by their students based on the teachers' presumed superior understanding. When a planner presents the results of many man-years of looking at the environment to a management team, she is usually given the benefit of the doubt: the planner probably knows more about the environment than the management team she is talking to. But when the same planner walks into a boardroom to start teaching about the strategy of the company, her authority disappears. When you cannot be granted authority, you can no longer teach.

Fortified with this understanding of planning and its role, we looked for ways to accelerate institutional learning. Curiously enough, we learned in two cases that changing the rules, or suspending them, could be a spur to learning. Rules in a corporation are extremely important. Nobody likes them but everybody obeys them because they are recognized as the glue of the organization. And yet, we have all known extraordinary managers who got their organizations out of a rut by changing the rules. Intuitively they changed the organization and the way it looked at matters, and so, as a consequence, accelerated learning.

Several years ago one of our work groups introduced, out of the blue, a new rule into the corporate rain dance: "Thou shalt plan strategically in the first half of the calendar year." (We already had a so-called business planning cycle that dealt with capital budgets in the second half of the calendar year.)

The work group was wise enough not to be too specific about what it had in mind. Some operating companies called up and asked what was meant by "strategic planning." But the answer they got – that ideas were more important than numbers – was vague. Other companies just started to hold strategic planning meetings in the spring.

In the first year the results of this new game were scanty, mostly a rehash of the previous year's business plans. But in the second year the plans were fresher and each year the quality of thinking that went into strategic planning improved. So we asked ourselves whether, by having changed the rules of the game – because that's what the planning system is, one of the rules of the corporate game – we had accelerated institutional learning. And our answer was yes. We changed the rules and the corporation played by the new rules that evolved in the process.

A similar thing happened when we tried suspending the rules. In 1984 we had a scenario that talked about $15 a barrel oil. (Bear in mind that in 1984 the price of a barrel of oil was $28 and $15 was the end of the world to oil people.) We thought it important that, as early in 1985 as possible, senior managers throughout Shell start learning about a world of $15 oil. But the response to this scenario was essentially, "If you want us to think about this world, first tell us when the price is going to fall, how far it will fall, and how long the drop will last."

A deadlock ensued which we broke by writing a case study with a preface that was really a license to play. "We don't know the future," it said. "But neither do you. And though none of us knows whether the price is going to fall, we can agree that it would be

---

2. John Holt, *How Children Learn*, rev. ed. (New York: Delacorte, 1983) and John Holt, *How Children Fail*, rev. ed. (New York: Delacorte, 1982).

pretty serious if it did. So we have written a case showing one of many possible ways by which the price of oil could fall." We then described a case in which the price plummeted at the end of 1985 and concluded by saying: "And now it is April 1986 and you are staring at a price of $16 a barrel. Will you please meet and give your views on these three questions: What do you think your government will do? What do you think your competition will do? And what, if anything, will you do?"

Since at that point the price was still $28 and rising, the case was only a game. But that game started off serious work throughout Shell, not on answering the question "What will happen?" but rather exploring the question "What will we do if it happens?" The acceleration of the institutional learning process had been set in motion.

As it turned out, the price of oil was still $27 in early January of 1986. But on February 1 it was $17 and in April it was $10. The fact that Shell had already visited the world of $15 oil helped a great deal in that panicky spring of 1986.

By now, we knew we were on to something: games could significantly accelerate institutional learning. That's not so strange when you think of it. Some of the most difficult and complex tasks in our lives were learned by playing: cycling, tennis, playing an instrument. We did it, we experimented, we played. But how were we going to make it OK to play?

Few managers are able to say, "I don't mind a little mistake. Go ahead, experiment," especially with a crisis looming. We didn't feel we could go to executives who run some of the biggest companies in the world and say, "Come on, let's have a little game." And in any case, board meetings have agendas, are fixed to end at a certain time, and require certain action to be taken. Still, within these constraints, we have found ways to learn by playing.

One characteristic of play, as the Tavistock Institute in London has shown, is the presence of a transitional object. For the person playing, the transitional object is a representation of the real world. A child who is playing with a doll learns a great deal about the real world at a very fast pace.

Successful consultants let themselves be treated as transitional objects. The process begins when the consultant says something like this to a management team: "We know from experience that many good strategies are largely implicit. If you let us interview people at various levels in your organization, we'll see whether we can get your strategy out on paper. Then we'll come back and check whether we've understood it."

Some weeks later the consultant goes back to the team and says: "Well, we've looked at your strategy and we've played it through a number of likely possibilities, and here is what we think will be the outcome. Do you like it?" The management team will almost certainly say no. So the consultant will say: "All right, let's see how we can change it. Let's go back to your original model and see what was built in there that produced this result." This process is likely to go through a number of iterations, during which the team's original model will change considerably. Those changes constitute the learning that is taking place among the team's members.

Like consultants, computer models can be used to play back and forth management's view of its mar-

> To speed up learning, change the rules that managers live by.

ket, the environment, or the competition. The starting point, however, must be the mental model that the audience has at the moment. If a planner walks into the room with a model on his computer that he has made up himself, the chances are slim that his audience will recognize this particular microworld. If the target group is a management team, the starting model must be the sum of their individual models. How can this be done?

One way is to involve team members in the development of a new common model and leave their individual models implicit. Alternatively, one can bring the individual models out in the open through interviews and make them explicit. In both approaches, computers can serve as transitional objects in which to store the common models that get built.

To most planners, one all-important aspect of these microworlds is counterintuitive: the probability that they have little relation to the real world. God seems to have told model builders that a model should have predictive qualities and that therefore it should represent the real world. In building microworlds, however, this is totally irrelevant. What we want to capture are the models that exist in the minds of the audience. Almost certainly, these will not represent the real world. None of us has a model that actually captures the real world, because no complex reality can be represented analytically and a model is an analytical way of representing reality. Moreover, for the purpose of learning, it is not the reality that matters but the team's model of reality, which will change as members' understanding of their world improves.

But why go to all this trouble? Why not rely on the natural learning process that occurs whenever a management team meets? For us at Shell, there are three compelling reasons. First, although the models in the human mind are complex, most people can deal with only three or four variables at a time and do so through only one or two time iterations.

Look, for instance, at current discussions about the price of oil. Nine out of ten people draw on a price-elasticity model of the market: the price has come down, therefore demand will go up and supply will eventually fall. Ergo, they will conclude, at some time in the future the price of oil must rise. Now we all know that what goes up must come down. But our minds, in thinking through this complex model, work through too few iterations, and we stop at the point where the price goes up. If we computerize the model of the person who stops thinking at the moment the price rises, however, the model will almost certainly show the price falling after its rise. Yet this knowledge would be counterintuitive to the very person (or persons) who built the model.

The second reason for putting mental models into computers is that in working with dynamic models, people discover that in complex systems (like markets or companies) cause and effect are separated in time and place. To many people such insight is also counter-intuitive. Most of us, particularly if we are engaged in the process of planning, focus on the effect we want to create and then look for the most immediate cause to create that effect. The use of dynamic models helps us discover other trigger points, separated in time and place from the desired effect.

Lastly, by using computer models we learn what constitutes relevant information. For only when we start playing with these microworlds do we find out what information we really need to know.

When people play with models this way, they are actually creating a new language among themselves that expresses the knowledge they have acquired. And here we come to the most important aspect of institutional learning, whether it be achieved through teaching or through play as we have defined it: the institutional learning process is a process of language development. As the implicit knowledge of each learner becomes explicit, his or her mental model becomes a building block of the institutional model. How much and how fast this model changes will depend on the culture and structure of the organization. Teams that have to cope with rigid procedures and information systems will learn more slowly than those with flexible, open communication channels. Autocratic institutions will learn faster or not at all – the ability of one or a few leaders being a risky institutional bet.

Human beings aren't the only ones whose learning ability is directly related to their ability to convey information. As a species, birds have great potential to learn, but there are important differences among them. Titmice, for example, move in flocks and mix

> **Learning is not a luxury. It's how companies discover their future.**

freely, while robins live in well-defined parts of the garden and for the most part communicate antagonistically across the borders of their territories. Virtually all the titmice in the U.K. quickly learned how to pierce the seals of milk bottles left at doorsteps. But robins as a group will never learn to do this (though individual birds may) because their capacity for institutional learning is low; one bird's knowledge does not spread.[3] The same phenomenon occurs in management teams that work by mandate. The best learning takes place in teams that accept that the whole is larger than the sum of the parts, that there is a good that transcends the individual.

What about managers who find themselves in a robin culture? Clearly, their chances of accelerating institutional learning are reduced. Nevertheless, they can take a significant step toward opening up communication and thus the learning process by keeping one fact in mind: institutional learning begins with the calibration of existing mental models.

We are continuing to explore other ways to improve and speed up our institutional learning process. Our exploration into learning through play via a transitional object (a consultant or a computer) looks promising enough at this point to push on in that direction. And while we are navigating in poorly charted waters, we are not out there alone.[4]

Our exploration into this area is not a luxury. We understand that the only competitive advantage the company of the future will have is its managers' ability to learn faster than their competitors. So the companies that succeed will be those that continually nudge their managers towards revising their views of the world. The challenges for the planner are considerable. So are the rewards.

---

3. Jeff S. Wyles, Joseph G. Kunkel, and Allan C. Wilson, "Birds, Behavior and Anatomical Evolution," *Proceedings of the National Academy of Sciences, USA*, July 1983.
4. Through MIT's Program in Systems Thinking and the New Management Style, a group of senior executives are looking at this and other issues.

Reprint 88202

Part II
The Learning School

The Natural Selection View

[9]

Populations, Natural Selection, and Applied Organizational Science

Bill McKelvey and Howard Aldrich

This paper proposes that organizational science could be applied more widely if the field were more concerned with the conditions under which research findings are valid. Papers in the field generalize about organizations as if they were all alike, or refrain from generalizing at all, as if they were all unique. The population perspective presented de-emphasizes the all-alike and all-unique approaches, placing emphasis instead on research methods that improve the description and classification of organizational forms, define more homogeneous groupings, and specify the limited conditions under which predictions may be expected to hold true. The principles of the population perspective are reviewed, and an outline is presented for developing a classification of organizational forms. Suggestions are then made on how to use the perspective to increase and improve the application of organizational research.

A spirit of application pervades most sciences. The life sciences support medical practice, the hybridization of new plant strains, enhanced crop productivity, such as the "green revolution," and most recently, genetic engineering. Physics underlies aspects of our lives that are taken for granted such as electric power generation, electronics, and flight, and drugs, paints, and plastics reflect the innovation and productivity of chemistry. In the social sciences, economists are consulted daily in developing federal policy and budgeting, and many businesses depend on economic forecasts; psychologists apply psychology in psychotherapy, counseling, psychological and educational testing, and personnel selection; and sociologists have figured heavily in governmental policies on race and sex discrimination, welfare relief and family assistance, and international relations, and are affecting private sector developments in the emerging field of human resource management.

In organizational science (or, alternatively, macro-organizational behavior or organization studies) application is much less visible. The National Academy of Sciences, a body formed to advise the federal government, does not include organizational scientists. There is no president's council of organizational scientists, and they do not frequent congressional offices. At UCLA, 100 teams of M.B.A. students act as consultants to Los Angeles organizations each year and find numerous opportunities to apply their knowledge of accounting and finance, marketing, industrial and labor relations, and operations research, but they almost never find ways to apply ideas or findings from organizational science. In the twenty-five years since the founding of *ASQ*, Ouchi's (1981) *Theory Z* is the only book about organizational structure or form to reach the best-seller lists. Although some results of organizational science have proven useful, such as those from Lawrence and Lorsch's (1967) research on differentiation and integration and Likert's (1961) writings on effective work groups, organizational scientists lag behind their colleagues in the other social sciences in the utilization of their research.

Thompson (1956) wrote of "administrative science"; in the succeeding twenty-five years, it has come to include a macro- and a micro-component. We suspect that the component most utilized is the micro-component, which is rooted in psychology and social psychology — motivation, leadership, group dynamics, conflict resolution, and job design. Discovering how this subcomponent is utilized may require large-scale surveys or other methods, as proposed in the call for this special issue. The subcomponent we are interested in is one we term organizational science, one that others have called organizational sociology, organization theory, or more recently macro-organizational behavior. Organizational scientists in sociology departments do not seem to have emphasized utilization much, if at all, during the years they have been interested in the subject. Those in management schools who are more likely to be interested in applications have not established organizational science as a required course for the M.B.A. until very recently, and even now, the requirement is not widespread. Only in the last several years have professors of management published textbooks on the subject. We think that the organizational science component of administrative science is obviously not applied and that, although sophisticated studies of the obvious should not be discouraged, we should not wait for them to be completed. We therefore move directly toward a possible solution in this paper.

DEFICIENCIES OF EXISTING MODELS

Criteria of Scientific Method

An evaluation of the field in terms of three criteria of the scientific method — classifiability, generalizability, and predictability — reveals serious shortcomings. Samples of organizations are so poorly described that classifying them is impossible, generalizations can only be carelessly drawn, and the predictive power of most theories is extremely weak.

Classifiability. In biology, geology, physics, and chemistry much effort has been expended in analyzing naturally occurring mixtures of phenomena into pure groupings of their constituent specific substances — kinds of cells, minerals, subatomic particles, compounds, and elements. Only with research on pure substances did findings in these sciences become clear, consistent, and ultimately applicable. People who might use organizational science findings do not actually work in broad natural groups of mixed organizational forms — they work in specific kinds of organizations: paint shops, university departments, factories, job shops, or conglomerate headquarters. Most organizational research has been about organizations as legal entities, often large corporations, which are actually mixtures of different forms; broader forms like R&D, marketing, or production, and within production, the more specific forms like job shop, assembly line, or some other arrangement. Without adequate description and classification, users cannot be sure that such research findings are relevant to the specific organizational form they are actually responsible for or working in.

Generalizability. Much of the power of the physical and life sciences comes from the generalizability of their findings. These apply without exception in similar circumstances, and in different circumstances the conditional statements also apply without exception. Once mixtures were replaced with pure forms, it was found that species of white laboratory rats, gold, gamma rays, or whatever the form studied always behaved in

Populations, Natural Selection

the same way. One sample from the population of white rats, gold atoms, or gamma rays behaved just like other samples. Such populations have been very carefully described and consist of members that are very nearly the same in their distinctive aspects. Almost without exception, consumers of physical and life science findings have a very high expectation that findings about sampled members of the population will generalize to their member. We do not mean that members of biological, geological, or chemical populations are identical, only that they are similar enough to be distinguished from members of other populations.

In the field of organizational science, one is never really certain that findings about organizations actually sampled apply without exception to organizations *not* sampled. For example, Lawrence and Lorsch (1967) studied two plastics, two container, and two consumer organizations. As a vertically integrated producer of plastic containers of margarine, may I properly say my organization is like any of those sampled? All of them? None of them? Since the populations are not described and since the samples are only two out of x, how can I tell if my organization is in the same population and if the sample is representative of the population? May I safely use the results of this classic study? Or do I have to hire a researcher to perform the study again in my organization, whatever kind it is?

Predictability. To paraphrase Kurt Lewin's memorable statement, nothing is so practical as a good theory, nothing is so practical as predictable universal statements. Thrown objects always fall. Hot air always rises. Lithium always burns in water. Jet airplanes almost always take off and land safely. Almost? Even when statements are probabilistic, if they are close enough to universal statements, they can be used. Imagine an advertisement in *Scientific American,* announcing: "Transinternational Airline's latest study showed that on a sample of 1000 flights, the null hypothesis of no difference between the number of safe takeoffs and safe landings was not rejected at the $p < .01$ level." What sane person would still use the airline? Nevertheless, every issue of *ASQ* and other journals is full of predictive statements claiming certitude at the .05 or .01 level.

Thompson (1956: 103) said, "It is no longer a ridiculous idea that regularities can be found in human behavior." In the twenty-five years since then, many regularities have been found — at the .05 or .01 levels. But are patterns explaining less than 10 percent of the variance (a typical level) useful? Even in baseball, hitters are expected to do better than a 10 percent average. Is it reasonable to expect people to use findings that are correct only ten percent of the time — and one can't say when? Though living in a world where applications of physics, chemistry, biology, and geology are expected to be correct *all* the time, organizational scientists have satisfied themselves with finding faint patterns. These lack the strength or clarity users have come to expect from modern sciences.

Review of Research for Classifiability, Generalizability, and Predictability

A review of empirical, nonexperimental papers published in *ASQ* in 1979, 1980, and 1981 showed that very few investigators were concerned with the issues of classifiability or generalizability. In view of the uniformly low levels of explained variance, attention to predictability also appeared questionable. We examined 59 articles and evaluated the amount of information provided on the composition of the sample. Nine articles used samples of individuals drawn from other than an organization source, such as graduating M.B.A. classes, and thirteen articles (22 percent) were case studies of a single organization.

Of the 50 articles based on samples of organizations, 38 percent were based on fewer than 10 organizations, and 70 percent on fewer than 50 organizations. Descriptive information provided about the sampled organizations differed widely, but it was extremely brief in almost all cases. Only 15 articles provided enough information to allow an estimate of the size of the organization(s) studied, and even fewer provided information on size distributions. Only 9 articles provided information on organizational technologies, broadly defined.

With respect to generalizability, 68 percent were based on only one type of organization, where "type" is treated as a common-sense category (for example, banks, hospitals, or insurance companies). In some cases, descriptive information on the sampled organizations was so inadequate that we could not tell how many types were studied. Only four articles mentioned SIC codes as a basis for sampling or data collection. Of the 47 papers for which sufficient information on types was available, only 7 (15 percent) studied more than 10 types and therefore may presumably draw more broadly generalizable conclusions. We also examined articles in the *Academy of Management Journal* and other journals.

Our brief review of three years' of empirical articles in *ASQ* convinced us that few investigators are consciously attentive to differences between organizational types or forms. We recognize that many older studies (see March, 1965) or recent studies published in journals other than *ASQ* focus narrowly on institutions such as schools, prisons, hospitals, unions, or military organizations, and limit their generalizations to these kinds of organizations. A question unanswered by these studies is whether their results apply equally to intra-class kinds or to other types; for example, are general, teaching, chronic care, and proprietary hospitals all the same?

We explain these findings by the logic of the paradigm underlying the research design of these studies. The logic of research designs can be differentiated into reconstructed logic, which appears in articles as explicit statements about the philosophy of science and methodology, and logic-in-use, which may be extrapolated from the research reports (Kaplan, 1964). We think that investigators are using two broad approaches to describe organizations: (1) organizations are all alike, or (2) organizations are all unique, and that these approaches emerge at both the reconstructed logic and logic-in-use levels.

Organizations are all alike. Most studies are reported as if one organizational form characterized all larger, more complex organizations. Studies such as those by the Aston group (Pugh et al., 1968; Pugh, Hickson, and Hinings, 1969; and many subsequent ones), Child (1972), and Khandwalla (1977) sampled from broadly defined populations with the explicit objective of generalizing to all (or at least most) organizations. Other studies have sampled from a more narrowly defined population (Lawrence and Lorsch, 1967; Blau and Schoenherr, 1971;

Populations, Natural Selection

Meyer, 1979; Daft and Macintosh, 1981; Leatt and Schneck, 1981), but their results have been treated as probably applying more generally, as the following quote from Meyer and Brown (1977: 383–384) illustrates: "Several implications arise from these results. First, the patterns described here need not be peculiar to finance agencies or to the history of the civil service movement in the United States. Effects of origins and the environment and the discontinuous pattern of change should be evident for diverse institutional structures." What was actually studied was very specific — finance agencies in city governments — yet virtually no limitations were placed on the presumed generalizability of the results. Similarly, Leblebici and Salancik (1982: 239) noted in their case study that "Although only one setting, the Chicago Board of Trade, has been studied here, it is assumed that the phenomenon applies to all systems of exchange."

Blau and his associates worked on a research program that explicitly included organizations of more than one type (Blau, 1974: 18). Their objective was to formulate propositions that were true for all types studied. Major studies of employment security agencies, local branches of these agencies, city finance departments, department stores, and universities were compared, and deductive propositions applying to all organizations (not just these types) were proposed. They found that the amount of work performed, the amount of differentiation, and the number of employees were correlated in the organizations studied. A conservative conclusion would be that generalizations about these variables could be applied to these kinds of organizations. However, in research reports from this work, the implicit assumption is made that the results apply to *all* work organizations. We found no qualifying statements, or at least no obvious ones.

Since, for example, the organizations that Blau's group studied were *labor*-intensive, one might suspect that his fundamental proposition, "The larger the volume of work of a certain kind, the larger is the number of persons needed to perform it" (Blau, 1974: 346), does not apply with equal force to *capital*-intensive organizations. Some of the measured variables certainly do apply to kinds of organizations other than those studied, but the level in a hierarchical classification scheme where these kinds of organizations would all come together in the same class is so high, and consequently the relevant variables so abstract, that practical application of the findings is difficult.

In other studies, a small number of cases was chosen on which to build generalizations, with no attempt made to obtain a representative sample of the population. These case studies were then used to uncover models that were described as though they applied to unspecified broader populations (Biggart, 1977; Cafferata, 1979; Rosenbaum, 1979; Stern, 1979; Kimberly, 1980; Niv, 1980; Pfeffer and Moore, 1980; Roos and Hall, 1980; Hambrick, 1981; Ross and Ferris, 1981). Finally, in some studies, in perhaps the most straightforward expression of the all-alike approach, no attention was paid to organizational differences, representativeness, or populations (e.g., Oldham and Hackman, 1981).

The thrust of the all-alike approach is succinctly captured by the "fifth major proposition" in the lead article of *ASQ*'s first issue (Litchfield, 1956: 28): "Administration and the administrative process occur in substantially the same general form in industrial, commercial, civil, educational, military, and hospital organizations." If this proposition is accepted, investigators do not have to pay attention to different kinds of organizations and, thus, need not worry about methods for identifying subpopulations or describing them. If all x's are the same and all one is studying are x's, no detailed attention to description is necessary—all we have to do is differentiate x's from non x's. In the case of organizations, one can either point to them and say, "That's an organization" (March and Simon, 1958), or one can define them theoretically, as Parsons (1956) did in the same first issue of ASQ.

Organizations are all unique. Some studies are reported as if every organization possesses a unique form. Explicit statements of this logic-in-use are elusive. No one really writes something like: "This is an in-depth analysis of one organization. There is no reason to believe any other organizations like it exist, because its employees are unique, its history is unique, and its geographical location is unique. The findings here are clearly not generalizable to any other organization. However, this organization is important or interesting so let me tell you about it." Yet, the subjectivist reconstructed logic of phenomenology and humanistic psychology (Husserl, 1965; Schutz, 1967) and radical sociology (Horowitz, 1971) have pushed some theorists toward the position that organizations are unique entities. Grounded theory (Glaser and Strauss, 1967), ethnomethodology (Garfinkel, 1967), thick descriptions (Geertz, 1973), action research (Susman and Evered, 1978), Marxian praxis orientations (Benson, 1977; Frost, 1980), idiographic methods (Swidler, 1979), and qualitative methods (Van Maanen, 1979; Morgan and Smircich, 1980) all have the implication of organizational uniqueness when they are applied. We hasten to note that qualitative methods, if applied to a representative sample of organizations and properly coded, can be just as useful to the deductive nomological model as quantitative methods.

In specific studies that do not attempt to generalize in any way beyond the organization studied, it is very hard to find authors stating explicitly that their results are not generalizable. In a study of cause maps (Bougon, Weick, and Binkhorst, 1977), the authors say almost nothing about generalizability. Obviously they think cause maps exist in other organizations and that their method is applicable elsewhere, but they do not say or imply that any specific pattern in the Utrecht Jazz Orchestra's cause map has relevance for any other organization. Hall's (1976) paper on the *Saturday Evening Post*'s failure presented a wealth of detail on the magazine's operations and history, yet although Hall made some comparisons with other magazines, he carefully avoided generalizing his results to any population and limited his general remarks to methodological points. Miles (1979), in his account of the Project on Social Architecture in Education, documented a common tendency for case studies to be thought of as unique sites and as exceptions to general principles.

Studies under the all-unique approach may offer enough descriptive information to identify an organization in terms of a classification scheme, if one existed, but they do not meet the other criteria of generalizability and predictability. Are they

Populations, Natural Selection

scientific? Not according to the paradigm calling for generalizability and predictability. What is ironic about these studies is that the authors also sometimes appear to subscribe to the all-alike view. The papers usually end with a statement that, though the specific details of the study are unique, the model constructed appears to have broader application.

The progress of organizational science in satisfying the three criteria of classifiability, generalizability, and predictability, and thereby enhancing the utilization of findings, will not significantly improve until the prevailing reconstructed logic and logic-in-use are refocused. The orientation we propose is away from the all-alike and all-unique approaches and toward a view that places much more emphasis on research methods that improve the description and classification of organizational forms, defines more homogeneous groupings for purposes of improving generalization, and either improves the level of prediction or supplies a logic for de-emphasizing prediction as the only test of scientific understanding. A reorientation will not be easy, as reconstructed logic and logic-in-use are embedded in a scientific paradigm (Kuhn, 1970), i.e., a consensual system of beliefs, held by organizational scientists.

In his initial work, Kuhn (1970: 175) broadly defined a scientific paradigm as encompassing "the entire constellation of beliefs, values, techniques, and so on shared by members of a given community." Later, after much criticism, Kuhn considerably narrowed his definition. Still later, Ritzer (1975: 157) suggested a definition more like Kuhn's early one: "A paradigm is a fundamental image of the subject matter within a science. It serves to define what should be studied, what questions should be asked, how they should be asked, and what rules should be followed in interpreting the answer obtained. The paradigm is the broadest unit of consensus within a science and serves to differentiate one scientific community (or subcommunity) from another. It subsumes, defines and interrelates the exemplars, theories, methods, and instruments that exist within it."

We have described current organizational research as operating within two paradigms, the all-alike and the all-unique, and we expect that most papers for this special issue will fit one of them. We believe that the lack of utilization of organizational science results from fundamental paradigmatic assumptions, rather than from inadequate procedures within the paradigms. Rather than calling for modifications of procedures within the two approaches, we propose the basic outline of a new perspective. In our approach the findings underlying each established paradigm are placed in a complementary relation to each other, rather than being treated as antithetical. Because of space limitations, our discussion only outlines the new paradigm.

POPULATION PERSPECTIVE[1]

Definitions

To overcome barriers to the utilization of organizational science, we propose adoption of the population perspective, encompassing four related areas of investigation: taxonomy, classification, evolution, and population ecology. *Taxonomy* focuses on activities pertaining principally to developing a theory of

---

[1] In our discussion we use the term *organization* interchangeably with the term *organizational form*. These terms refer to any organizational unit having an identifiable form, (e.g., paint shop, assembly line, R&D section, university department, government agency, company, corporate headquarters). What the field comes to accept as organizational forms, we argue, is ultimately an empirical question.

organizational differences and a theory of classification. *Classification* procedures allow identification and description of organizational populations and their relation to other more or less similar populations. *Evolutionary* inquiry supports taxonomic and classificatory activities by providing an underlying theoretical framework explaining how different kinds of organizations come to be different, why they remain different, and what taxonomic characters might be evolutionarily significant. Evolutionarily significant characters are attributes that enhance an organization's ability to survive; they may persist even though the specific environmental condition for which they were favorable no longer exists. Ultimately they comprise the vast majority of attributes characterizing the population of which an organization is a member. *Population ecology* explains the relations of organizational forms to their niches and environments. We will not discuss the latter, since some work in that field has already been published and is continuing to be produced at a rapid pace (Hannan and Freeman, 1977; Brittain and Freeman, 1980; Hannan, 1980; Freeman, 1982). The basic work in the other three areas is developed in books by Aldrich (1979) and McKelvey (1982).

The population perspective is borrowed from biologists, who have developed it into an extensive, conceptually rich theory and method. The advantage of borrowing from another discipline is that much of the theoretical and methodological work has already been done; the disadvantage is that the perspective might not fit. Our view is that it has several clear advantages: (1), it offers a way to break the mental set of the existing models, as its theory and concepts sensitize us to see the organizational world in a new way; (2) it already has in place many essential concepts; and (3) the theoretical and methodological issues are already identified, so we have a map showing where all of the difficulties and points of interest are likely to be. Of course, while organizations in changing environments have many functional parallels to organisms in changing environments, there are differences. We are fully aware that alterations and new theoretical and conceptual inventions might have to be made for the perspective to be of use in the study of organizations. Our view is that the functional parallels are strong and that the approach has much of promise and ought not to be discarded until it has been thoroughly tried.

Population and Species

In biology, most populations are defined as sets of interbreeding members highly similar to each other (though it is recognized that some populations are asexual). The smallest of these are termed local populations. Species are composed of one or more local populations. The variance within local populations is low enough that they are formally recognized as classes (subspecies, varieties); however, they are isolated by geographic or other factors rather than by an inability to produce nonsterile, viable offspring, and thus they behave as one population with respect to the interbreeding criterion. The species rank is a bifurcating category in the hierarchical classification of biological organisms, because the lower ranked local populations are not sexually isolated, whereas the higher ranked groups are not interbreeding populations. Species are thus unique in that they are the only rank category in which the judgments of systematists, those who conduct taxonomic and

Populations, Natural Selection

classificatory research, may actually be empirically tested, that is, by testing for interbreeding capability (in sexual species, of course).

For organizations, a bifurcation in the classificatory hierarchy may not be so pronounced and thus the species label is somewhat more arbitrarily given to a particular category in a hierarchical ranking of categories. Warriner (1980: 11) defined a population as "similarly constituted organizations, occupying the same ecological niche, and sharing the same modeling or replication materials through interconnections among the organizations in that population." McKelvey (1982: 192) defined organizational species as "polythetic groups of competence-sharing populations isolated from each other because their dominant competencies are not easily learned or transmitted."[2] The key ideas embedded in these definitions are (1) the similarity of members, (2) the sharing of replication materials and competence within species or populations of organizations, and (3) the absence of sharing among species of organizations. Species differences materialize as different organizational forms that are discernable and measurable.

Organizational Form

Organizational scientists are beginning to believe that organizations come in so many varieties (populations) (Perrow, 1970; McKelvey, 1978; Aldrich, 1979; Lammers and Hickson, 1979; Scott, 1981; Hall, 1982) that it no longer makes sense to search for a few essential attributes captured in an all-encompassing definition of "organization." Traditional definitions are useful for separating organizations from other major social entities, such as families or societies. Aldrich (1979: 4) held that "organizations are goal-directed, boundary-maintaining, activity systems." Hall (1982: 32–33) offered a somewhat broader definition: "An organization is a collectivity with a relatively identifiable boundary, a normative order, ranks of authority, communications systems, and membership-coordinating systems; this collectivity exists on a relatively continuous basis in an environment and engages in activities that are usually related to a set of goals." Organizational scientists recognize that these definitions do not apply uniformly to all kinds of organizations. Scott (1981) recently suggested three definitions covering three kinds of organizations. The accumulating findings pointing to the diversity of organizations mean that these and other theoretical definitions do not offer investigators guidelines for defining groups of organizations homogeneous enough to ensure that the scope of a representative sample can be held to a manageable size.

We have defined populations as comprising highly similar organizations. The polythetic group idea underlying the definition of organizational form points to the expectation that even within populations, organizations are not identical on all significant attributes. We reject the idea of monothetic grouping that all members of a group must have the same attributes, and with it the essentialist classification theory that all members of classes must be identical with respect to the few essential attributes. Biologists (Mayr, 1969; Sneath and Sokal, 1973) and some organizational scientists (Bailey, 1973; McKelvey, 1978) now recognize that such a theory will not work for entities as complex as organisms and organizations because too many

---

[2] A polythetic group is one where (a) each member possesses many properties, p, of a set of properties P; (b) each p in P is possessed by many members; and (c) no p in P is possessed by all members. In a monothetic group, all members possess the same set of properties.

significant aspects of behavior are not accounted for by the few so-called essential attributes.

We believe the traditional approach of organizational scientists in defining organizations (an essentialist classification view), should be abandoned. A better approach is to describe different kinds of organizational forms empirically, letting thorough descriptions identify each kind of organizational form in some detail, thus providing the descriptive material that helps producers and users of scientific research set one form apart from another. Since an empirically valid taxonomy and classification of organizational forms is not yet available, we lean toward a definition of form that points inquiry toward any measurable attribute that is significant in discriminating one form from another and helps investigators understand why they have evolved to their present configuration. The definition at this time should be broad enough to avoid precluding any heretofore unrecognized element of organizational form. One such definition is given by McKelvey (1982: 458): Organizational form is composed of "the internal structure and process of an organization and the interrelation of its subunits which contribute to the unity of the whole of the organization and to the maintenance of its characteristic activities, function, or nature." Such an empirical approach calls for sophisticated classification methods.

The concept of organizational form is critical to the population perspective: organizations are neither all-alike nor all-unique, but rather appear to be a moderate number of different populations composed of similar forms. The complementary inclusion of findings underlying the two established paradigms by the population view materializes here in the sense that the all-alike approach is included as the within-population view, whereas the all-unique approach is used at the population level, at which differences among populations are posited. The latter approach is also used at the level of variations in human behavior within individual organizations.

Elements of a Concept of Organizational Species

Organizational scientists could frame an entirely new population theory, unique to organizations, or could, as we choose to do, take advantage of the biological one already developed, *changing it as necessary*. The central questions leading to an explanation of the existence of populations are: What forces create populations in the first place? How do organizations within a population come to be similar and remain similar? And do they remain different from organizations in other populations? We have adapted to an organizational context the three processes underlying the generation and persistence of forms suggested by Mayr (1969): ecological, generational, and isolating processes.

Ecological processes. Most theorists agree that environments influence individual organizations, but are there environmental forces that produce and shape populations of organizational forms? The actual number of discrete organizational forms is potentially nearly limitless. For example, for n generally accepted organizational attributes, each having two states, present or absent, $n!$ different forms are possible, if one assumes that the presence or absence of a single attribute signifies a recognizable difference. In reality, there could be more or less

Populations, Natural Selection

than *n* attributes; each could have more than two states; and it might take two or more state changes before one could discern a difference. Given the possibility of more or less than *n*! forms, why is the organizational world neither just one form nor a vast number of forms?

Constraints on population differentiation into endless variety are imposed by external forces that result in a limited number of homogeneous groups. Such forces are found mainly in the organizational-ecological community, rather than in the broader environment, which is the context for all social activities. An ecological community is a delimited association of interacting populations of organizational forms (Pianka, 1978: 271). The environment of one or more organizational forms is defined by the broader political, economic, legal, cultural, and technological forces prevailing (Hall, 1982).

One might conjecture that organizational environments are composed of discrete pockets of resources or conditions, which are well differentiated from one another. Under these conditions, organizations well adapted to their pockets would thus, ipso facto, be differentiated from organizations in other pockets. This approach strikes us as not very promising. Biologists considered the same possibility and concluded that the environment is not composed of niches that are "out there" waiting to be filled by some new form of organism (Pianka, 1978). Instead, niches are conceptualized as developing along with each species. A niche cannot be defined without considering a particular species (Lewontin, 1978). A niche is the activity space of an organization or population or community of organizational forms that reflects the sum total of both its adaptation *to* environmental forces that are not subject to its influence and adaptation *of* environmental forces that are subject to its influence (drawn from Pianka, 1978; and McKelvey, 1982). Organizational environments are not composed of pockets or niches, but rather are best seen as broad resource pools, which may be drawn upon in return for goods and services.

Population differentiation is best conceptualized at the level of the organizational ecological community, where the activities of one kind of organization create new resource possibilities for other organizations. For example, a large aerospace contractor in Southern California, tapping a large resource pool such as the federal government, generates product designs that create opportunities, in turn, for small subcontractors. Small entrepreneurial organizations, pioneering and developing new products, provide opportunities for the large conglomerates which try to survive by absorbing them. The actions of governments are often responsible for new resource opportunities, as when regulations of the Environmental Protection Agency forced utility companies to search for organizations manufacturing stack scrubbers.

Only resource opportunities, not niches, are created by an ecological community of organizations. It is possible that one large, flexible, diversified organizational form could emerge that would draw on all the available opportunities and thus prevent any other kind of organization from emerging. Alternatively, a large number of very small organizations might emerge. Our view is that it is possible for many kinds of organizational forms to evolve that tap a particular resource opportunity created by members of an ecological community.

Generational processes. Although ecological communities offer resource pools to organizational forms, elements within organizations explain why a particular population becomes associated with a particular pool and how the organizational form of a particular population persists over generations of employees and comes to be shared by other organizations in the population. The concept of competence elements (comps) (McKelvey, 1982), helps answer this question. Comps are defined as the elements of knowledge and skill that, in total, constitute the dominant competence of an organization. Dominant competence is defined as the combined workplace (technological) and organizational knowledge and skills (e.g., differentiation, coordination, control, measurement of effectiveness, and organizing processes) that together are most salient in determining the ability of an organization to survive. We view technical and organizational competence as human responses to environmentally imposed problems (Perrow, 1970); we do not posit a technological or environmental determinism.

If the technology of the workplace (the knowledge and skill involved in the way tasks are carried out) and the organizing processes surrounding the workplace can be disaggregated into relatively discrete elements (such as designing a work flow, scheduling, maintaining machines, hiring and training competent workers, measuring quality and productivity, or controlling deviations from intended goals), then each population has a population-wide set of comps that are held as knowledge and skill by employees of the organizations in the population. All such organizations have employees who hold a large proportion of the comps of the population. No organization holds all of them, and no single comp is held by all organizations. This is the definition of a polythetic group. Now, the key to answering the question, Why only one form per population?, is that comps seem to come in *highly probable combinations* under conditions of competition over resources. Some combinations are simply more effective and efficient than others. Some comps enhance effectiveness because they help an organization to produce goods or services especially likely to draw resources from a particular resource pool. Thus, an aircraft landing-gear subcontractor benefits more from holding comps about aluminum extruding, welding, and fabrication, hydraulic brakes, and bearings, than from holding comps about making oxygen, storing food, or educating handicapped children. Other comps help an organization in its competition against other members of the population by improving its efficiency. Hence the landing-gear subcontractor (if it survives) will drift toward technology and organizing processes aiding efficiency, perhaps adding items like automatic aluminum forging presses, sophisticated inventory control and production scheduling, better employee-training programs, or socio-technical systems design. Differentiation between populations is enhanced by the tendency of particular comps to cluster together. For example, once an organization decides to use an assembly-line competence, there is a constellation of other competences that are especially helpful, if not clearly necessary, such as: protection of the technical core from environmental change, management of sequential interdependence, coordination by planning (Thompson, 1967), focus on specialization (unless a socio-technical systems design is used), design of jobs to minimize

Populations, Natural Selection

training, not to mention the engineering competence to design an efficient work flow, select proper machines, and handle their maintenance. Needless to say, a rather different competence is apt to be associated with running an oil refinery, a foundry, a canning process, a film production workplace, a welfare office, or an elementary school.

Comps are held by the people in an organization. Presumably comps that are effective in enhancing survival are valued more highly than others. Of course this evaluation is not always timely, straightforward, or even correct in the short term, and their effectiveness in the longer run may be a better indication of appropriate comp selection. Effective comps are shared more widely within an organization than ineffective ones. Organizations having difficulty in surviving will probably try to hire people perceived as holding more effective comps away from more successful organizations. Hence the high salaries for members hired away from prestigious or effective organizations such as ARCO, Merrill Lynch, Hewlett-Packard, ABC, Dupont, or Stanford. People holding effective comps are often asked to speak at conferences, another way effective comps are spread around the population. This process of interchanging comps explains how organizational forms persist over time and how organizations within a population (all of which face the same constraints in tapping into the resource pool) come to share many of the same comps.

Isolating processes. If comps from all organizational populations were interchanged and adopted, there would cease to be differences among populations. A variety of isolating processes prevent this. Comps from one population are usually not thought to be very useful to another. Truckers usually do not hire restauranteurs to gain competence, nor do airlines usually look to universities. People at the workplace-technology level of an organization often do not understand the technology of organizations in another population and executives have been found to be generally unsuccessful when crossing industry boundaries (Shetty and Perry, 1976). Members of one population typically do not attend the professional meetings of interest to members of other populations.

Comps in many populations are complicated and difficult to learn. Many managers speak of the years it takes to "learn the business." Engineers, professors, lawyers, doctors, and many other professionals spend years being educated. Others in the building trades, police and fire protection, the military, and so on spend many years of apprenticeship or other experience-building time gaining knowledge "on the job." All of this makes learning the comps of a population difficult and so isolates the comps of one population from those of other populations. Finally, the tendency to resist learning of other comps, to be suspicious of new knowledge, to be suspicious of outsiders or of ideas "not invented here" (Kanter, 1983) also isolates the comps of different populations.

The Theory of Natural Selection

The elements of the species concept we have presented are embedded in the biological theory of natural selection, with key aspects of the theory expressed by four basic principles. We think these principles apply equally well to organizations. The species concept we present here is abstracted from Mayr's

(1969) "biological species concept," so named because its main elements make sense only in terms of the biological reproduction process. It explains speciation for the mainstream of biological organisms, though at least six other concepts (McKelvey, 1982) have been proposed to counter its deficiencies. Its advantage is that it has more explanatory power due to its basis in natural selection theory. We abstract from it rather than the others to gain the same explanatory leverage.

Principle of variation. The natural selection process begins with variations. Any kind of change is a variation. These may be purposeful or blind. Purposeful variations occur as an intentional response, when environmental pressures cause selection of adaptations. Blind variations are those that occur independent of environmental or selection pressures; they are not the result of an intentional response to adaptation pressures but rather occur by accident or chance. All the attention to organizational control by managers and management theorists is indirect evidence that variations occur. Corning (1974) argued that variations within organizations are purposeful; Campbell (1969), Aldrich (1979), and Weick (1979) believe they are blind; and McKelvey (1982) suggested that perhaps ninety percent of them are blind.

Principle of natural selection. Some variations in organizations prove more beneficial than others in acquiring resources from the environment. These variations contribute to the survival of an organization or subunit within it. Since subunits or organizations having useless or harmful variations are likely to have fewer resources and reduced chances of survival, it follows that, with the passage of time, the remaining organizations are likely to be characterized by the beneficial variations. In an ecological community, a population whose member organizations hold variations beneficial in acquiring resources against competition from other populations will have an increased likelihood of survival (Aldrich and Mueller, 1982).

Principle of retention and diffusion (heredity). This principle explains the retention of beneficial variations over generations of employees as well as the diffusion of beneficial variations throughout a population. Unlike biological organisms, organizations do not have offspring, though some have suggested that "spin-off" organizations may be analogous. Actually, thinking of physical bodies impedes clear thinking about the retention of favorable genes. Mayr (1969) wrote of bodies as temporary vessels holding parts of the gene pool of a population. The important thing is the preservation of the gene pool, not what actually happens in the passage of some genes from a parent to an offspring. So, for organizational scientists, the concern is rightly over the preservation of the pool of the comps of a population. Since comps are held by employees, the concern, then, is over how comps are passed through time, across successive generations of employees who belong to the organizations in an organizational population, and interchanged among organizations within a population.

An effective organization (i.e., one having enhanced chances of survival) will attempt to retain its beneficial variations by assuring that employees leaving have passed on the knowledge or skill to remaining employees. Competitors will attempt to hire people holding beneficial comps, or will attempt to learn of

Populations, Natural Selection

them and train their employees to use them, thus leading to the diffusion of comps throughout a population, and to the improvement, over time, of the pool of comps of the population. If the conditions in an organization were such that the comps held by a generation of employees were only randomly related to those held by the previous generation and only randomly related to the population's pool of comps, the theory of natural selection could not be applied to organizations. The present generation of an organization's employees has to hold comps more like those of the previous generation and more like those of the organization's population than like comps held by employees in members of other populations. A recent study by Zucker (1977) and a broader review of organizational persistence by Aldrich (1979) clearly show that the retention and diffusion principle holds for organizations.

Principle of the struggle for existence. The three foregoing principles explain the process of natural selection (Campbell, 1969), but Lewontin (1978) observed that a fourth principle is necessary, one clearly recognized by Darwin (1859: 61), the "struggle for life." The field of competitive strategy (Porter, 1980) is concerned with organizations competing within what Porter calls "industry structural groupings," roughly similar to what we call populations, as is the recent work of others (Hannan and Freeman, 1977; Pfeffer and Salancik, 1978; Brittain and Freeman, 1980; Carroll and Delacroix, 1982). This literature offers ample evidence of the competitive struggle among organizations.

Sometimes resources are so abundant that no selection takes place, as, for example, during the last five years in the population of solar energy organizations — tax credits and government subsidies meant that anyone could enter and survive. The Reagan administration's anti-solar-energy policies, however, have drastically increased the mortality rate of solar energy firms. Over the years the boom-and-bust business cycles characterizing the U.S. and other economies has assured that sometimes conditions made the struggle for existence intense (as it is right now).

One additional aspect of natural selection theory deserves attention. We build on Weick's (1979) idea that enactments by people in organizations are variations (mostly, if not all, blind). The form of populations and particular organizations takes shape over the years due to the selection of variations favorable to survival under competitive conditions. In this view environments determine "survival paths" (one or more per population), which effective organizations approach asymptotically (McKelvey, 1982). Continuing the metaphor, the resources of environments are located adjacent to survival paths. Organizations in a population approach the path as they evolve toward an effective form. Survival paths are usually only vaguely discernable in the complex mix of resources and competitors in environments.

Nothing *forces* organizations to choose a particular path. Organizations, through their dominant coalitions, can enact incorrectly, move slowly, copy other firms, innovate, avoid decisions, argue and fight over courses of action, and so forth. We call this "myopic purposefulness." People in organizations are intentional or purposeful, but conditions are such that it is highly unlikely that a successful organizational form can be attributed to any particular, identifiable, intentional act, or set of acts, especially so for a population form.

Since environments are diverse, uncertain, and imperfectly perceived, we think it improbable that a particular individual will *both* have the correct view *and* know it. Since organizations are composed of people limited by bounded rationality, suffering from limited or biased information and poor communication, and subject to processes of social influence and reconstructions of reality, we also think it improbable that a person with the "correct" variation will be in a position to implement it.

Classification

The population perspective would be nothing but arm-chair theorizing if taxonomy and classification methods were not available to identify populations and arrange them in a classification framework, usually termed a dendrogram or family tree. Classification methods have only recently been brought into the mainstream of the social sciences (Bailey, 1975; Mezzich and Solomon, 1980; Hudson and Associates, 1982). Although some empirical classifications of organizations have been made (Haas, Hall, and Johnson, 1966; Pugh et al., 1968; Dodder, 1969; Goronzy, 1969; Pugh, Hickson, and Hinings, 1969), McKelvey (1982) appears to be the first to provide an extended treatment of how classification theory and methods might be applied specifically to organizations. Of the several classification methods used in biology, numerical taxonomic and evolutionist methods seem most suitable for organizational systematics.

Actual numerical classification methods, such as factor analysis, multidimensional scaling, creation of numerical resemblance coefficients, structural clustering analysis, testing and comparison of resultant groupings by discriminant analysis, and methods of cophenetic correlation are reasonably well worked out, though hardly perfected. Two principal difficulties remaining for organizational scientists are the selection of taxonomic characters and the initial selection of organizations for study. In biology, a well-established evolutionist classification easily supplied numerical taxonomists with initial populations and taxonomic characters to be sampled as they began their studies in the late 1950s. Organizational scientists start without a classification, so that the risk of poor selection of either characters or organizations is high (McKelvey, 1975). The advantage of a combined evolutionist-numerical approach is that the evolutionary theory of classification provides a theoretical basis for selecting characters and cases.

Not all researchers will want to conduct elaborate taxonomic studies before getting to the substance of the problem that interests them. As progress is made in a theory of organizational differences, in the identification of various populations, and in the identification of evolutionarily significant characters, the number of organizations and characters needed to classify a broad initial grouping will decrease. The better the a priori understanding of populations and the better the theory of why they exist and are different from other populations, the easier the classification problem will be. Alternatively, those not trusting a priori theory may choose to base numerical taxonomic analysis on samplings of both organizations and characters

Populations, Natural Selection

without making initial delimitations, no matter how broad, as was suggested by McKelvey (1975). In that case, two guidelines to follow are: (1) draw organizations and characters from broadly defined sets of preliminary populations (really families of populations, such as the electronics group) and all known charcters; and (2) assume that closure on the definition of a particular population and appropriate, nontrivial characters will happen only after a number of studies. Modest taxonomic studies are better than nothing, but caution should be exercised until the population and sets of characters are confirmed in subsequent replications. Obviously this means a lot of work and funding. We expect that important, interesting, easily available populations will be studied first, and this seems appropriate.

USING THE POPULATION PERSPECTIVE

The population perspective is best seen as a fundamental reorientation of organizational science, and it cannot be judged at the start by how effective it is in offering practical advice to practicing managers. It may take some time before the implications of the new view are developed to the point where change in the application of findings is fully appreciated.

Explanation through Natural Selection Theory

Fundamental to the successful application of findings from organizational science is an understanding of why organizations succeed or fail. Except for the population ecology approach, explanations in the literature invariably attribute the behavior of organizations to individuals in organizations (e.g., see the review of the literature by Scott, 1981). Many analysts are reluctant to give up this view, as shown in their critiques of the population perspective (Miles, 1980; Van de Ven and Astley, 1981; Hall, 1982). Generally, the level of resistance and emotion about this issue is high. Perhaps the critics are correct in resisting a new, possibly very blind, variation; perhaps it is simply resistance to change; or perhaps it is a residue of the pre-Copernican need of people to see the earth as the center of the universe, now replaced by a need to attribute causality to a visible hand (Chandler, 1977).

Explanations of individual behaviors in organizations can be decoupled from explanations of why populations of organizations have the form that they do, how they came to have it, and why they are declining, remaining stable, or growing in size. Natural selection theory shifts the principle of inquiry guiding the formulation of specific research programs from reductionism — a focus on endogenous variables — to a focus on exogenous variables, termed rationalism by Schwab (1960). Our contention is that people cause variations in individual organizations, but that the process of natural selection leads to the form of those organizations that survive and characterize successful populations.

In our view *both* people and environments are causal agents that organizational scientists must pay attention to. We agree with the subjectivists that patterns of human behavior in individual organizations are idiosyncratic and not amenable to prediction and generalization as called for by the deductive nomological framework of the objectives (Hempel, 1965). Thus we incorporate as a basis of our perspective the findings underlying the subjectivist paradigm of substantial variation among individuals in organizations. Explaining these variations, or sometimes the relative absence of variations, is an important scientific activity and eventually may even result in more than the "faint patterns" alluded to by Thompson (1956). At the same time we suggest that findings pertaining to environmental causes of function and form will lead to explanations of organizational success or failure that are generalizable across all members of a population, and explanations of population growth or decline that are generalizable across populations. We see the role of predictive statements as limited, for the most part, to the behavior of a population of organizations during periods of environmental stability, a relatively infrequently occurring state of most environments, we suspect.

Population Research

The central point of this paper is to urge that researchers focus research and results around homogenous populations, which, we argue, will increase generalizability and level of explained variance. Such a reorganization puts considerable emphasis on methods of identifying populations and classifying them in relation to each other — highly similar ones, somewhat similar ones, and totally different ones.

Modern classification procedures, whether evolutionist or numerical, are complicated and contain many unresolved issues. It is possible, however, following the random selection methods outlined in McKelvey (1975), to develop an organizational classification scheme without, and in fact by very carefully avoiding, any theory whatsoever about how populations might form and what the significant characters might be. We recommend starting with a population easily identifiable by conventional wisdom or of interest to people outside the field, such as organizations in electronics, fiber optics, railroads, transportation, housing, or medicine. Research can begin on a population-by-population basis, checking, confirming, or rejecting common-sense ideas of populations and slowly developing definitions of populations that are based on classification research.

Previous attempts at empirical classification (Haas, Hall, and Johnson, 1966; Pugh et al., 1968; Goronzy, 1969; Pugh, Hickson, and Hinings, 1969) were not successful because they did not use random methods to carefully avoid poor theories of population speciation and evolution, nor did they develop any good theory that might point them toward selecting a useful set of initial groups or evolutionarily significant characters to study. Successful empirical classification must be based on a robust theory of organizational differences or on methods that are carefully atheoretical — there is no room in the middle.

To develop a theory of organizational differences, researchers beginning any kind of research on any substantive question about organizations should draw an initial grouping of organizations from some group of interest to the research or practitioner communities. Initial groups may be based on conventional wisdom and be of some public policy interest, may be available for public access, and ideally, associated with sources of funding. A broad industry group, such as the electronics industry studied by Ulrich (1982), is a good example. It was of considerable interest to U.S. policymakers, was part of a well-funded research project, and could be studied with pub-

Populations, Natural Selection

lished data available on all U.S. publicly held organizations. Ideally, selection of characters should be based on stratified sampling from all known categories of characters, such as formal structural, subunit characteristics, workplace conversion processes, or product distribution patterns. Several such lists are presented in McKelvey (1982: 355–365). These lists can be altered or improved as additional evolutionarily significant characters are found by an evolutionary analysis of the group being studied, its niche, and its broader environment. There is no such thing as a general list of all important characters for all populations. We expect that the list of characters most useful in discriminating among the populations will differ substantially across the populations. Various textbooks present methods and a great many clustering algorithms. Modern practice among systematists is to use combinations of methods, with many studies using all the methods mentioned above. A more detailed outline of the various steps one might follow in working up a classification study is given in McKelvey (1982: 430–431).

Not every analyst is interested in conducting a classification study as an end in itself. Most organizational scientists are probably not really interested in classification and do not want to take the time for such a digression. Not many biologists are systematists, either. The problem for the field of organizational science is that well-defined populations have not yet been described. Until they become available from the efforts of systematists, every investigator should expend some extra effort on at least a rudimentary classificatory analysis. The task is not onerous, as indicated by the following guidelines:

1. A clear, common-sense target group should be chosen and the results should be aimed at member populations of that group.

2. Within the target group, sampling should be narrow and intensive rather than broad, in the hope that the results will be broadly generalizable. It is preferable to study a series of specific populations within a larger group, rather than assorted organizations, scattering the research effort over a number of populations. For example, study populations within the electronics industry rather than a few organizations from each of a number of broad groups such as transportation, electronics, machine tools, mining, medical, unions, or education. Better to produce definite results about a specific population carefully studied than to produce vague results about many different kinds of organizations.

3. Enough of the environment and niche of the target group should be understood to identify at least a small set of environmental, niche, and form variables that might be useful in classificatory and later ecological analysis.

4. In the interim, imperfect and inadequate classificatory studies are better than none at all. Investigators should use whatever resources are available to define empirically the most homogeneous populations possible. One of the advantages of systematic studies is that once homogeneous populations are found, the size of the sample required to represent the population fully is greatly reduced. Investigators may thus pursue the scientific goal of generalizability while still putting considerable research effort into more intensive analyses of the form, function, and processes of organizations, as well as their ecological relations.

In our approach, the classification of the many populations across the organizational field progresses slowly on an incremental basis. The end result is a mosaic of narrow population studies. This will take some time, but if the most important or interesting populations are studied first, the delay will not be of great consequence. In the interim we would be offering more generalizable findings, within populations, to those working in or with the organizations studied. As classification studies progress, along with substantive analysis of the classified populations, it would be possible to begin to have a better understanding of how many of the findings about a particular population could be generalized to related or similar populations.

Population-Level Applications

One of the criticisms often made of the field of organizational studies is that investigators focus their research too narrowly on the concerns of top-level managers and owners of specific organizations, e.g., in studying organization design or strategy. Several value questions are raised by this narrowing of focus: Do we help managers at the expense of employees or outside constituents? Do we help a particular organization at the expense of more deserving organizations? Should we have a science oriented toward benefitting one particular social class?

One of the advantages of the population perspective is that it emphasizes population-level studies, of use to policymakers, rather than studies aimed at helping individual managers in particular organizations. Many policymakers are oriented toward a population of organizations rather than a single organization. Most government agencies, by law, focus national policy on populations of organizations in the public and private sector. Federal agencies set policy, regulate, and are concerned about the survival of populations of organizations in the health professions, transportation, education, aerospace, defense, and so on. Important policy questions right now are: Is the U.S. maintaining a strategically important capability in key defense industries? Is the trend toward large conglomerate corporations reducing the general level of innovation and productivity, which in the past has been associated with small business enterprise? Is the emphasis on the medical rights of adults, as reflected in the growth of populations of health-related organizations, cutting into the survival of populations of organizations devoted to educating young people? So far the field has offered little toward answering questions about the health, growth, or decline of populations of one or another kind of organization. Identifying populations is a prerequisite task, unless those studying populations of organizations, such as population ecologists, are going to settle for vague or common-sense definitions of populations.

Application of Population Studies

Providing extensive general guidelines on managing organizations would be contrary to the spirit of the population perspective, which places severe limits on cross-species generalizations. Applying population thinking to practical use should lead managers to exercise great caution in heeding the advice of consultants who offer the same solution to problems, no matter what the organizational form. Accordingly, we limit ourselves to general comments about the process of guiding organizational change.

Managers understand the significance of populations better than academics. Because of their academic training, M.B.A. graduates expect promotions to high levels of authority and responsibility fairly quickly, and this is a common complaint

Populations, Natural Selection

about them. Managers and executives of organizations often comment that it takes time "to learn the business" and that M.B.A.'s do not know much of specific use to a particular business when they leave graduate schools. Managers usually think the way of doing business in their industry group is different from everyone else's. We think academics will find the population perspective very welcome in practical circles, once managers find teachers, researchers, and consultants beginning to specialize in certain populations rather than claiming expertise about all kinds of organizations.

We expect the response to natural selection theory and its implications to be less enthusiastic. Current thinking about managerial versus environmental determination of form is expressed in the strategic-contingency theory approach (Child, 1972) and in related approaches stressing the central role of managers in guiding organizations toward effective strategies. Chamberlain (1968: 33–34) described how organizations adapt to, and manipulate, their environments:

Strategic decisions . . . express a firm's purpose, a future state of affairs which it expects to bring into being . . . . Strategic decisions imply a belief in power to control the future, to make it something *other* than predictable. A choice of objective is involved, and then a contrivance of means, and both of these involve an assertion of will rather than responses deterministically derived from what has gone on before, they are purposive thrusts into the future rather than decisions directed by testable logic or continuity of circumstance.

Thinking that one can control the future is heady stuff. Our view is that some conditions or effects, those that comprise the niche, *are* subject to manipulation by the organization, but that the broader environment is not open to influence. The environment of a particular population is best thought of as consisting of three components: (1) what has happened and is known; (2) what has happened and is not known; and (3) what has not happened. The first component is certain. The second component is also certain, though from a particular organization's point of view it is uncertain simply because it is not known yet. When organizations are slow to learn about such events, we can advise them to increase their intelligence- or information-processing capability (Galbraith, 1973). The third component may be predictable, lending itself to decision making under conditions of risk, or it may truly be uncertain and hence, unpredictable.

The first two components are reasonably well understood. Conventional approaches to decision making under risk when probabilities of future occurrence are high are also well known, and so also need no comment. Decision making under true uncertainty needs more explanation.

A common tendency under conditions of uncertainty is to impose probabilities, no matter how questionable, and then behave as if the condition were truly one of risk. Our question is, in searching for the survival path of an organization in an uncertain future environment, is it not better to design organizations to meet the uncertainty rather than to impose a specious probability and design as though that future had a real probability? McCaskey (1982) pointed out that the behavior required of executives under ambiguous conditions is substantially different from that required under conditions of certainty. Many of McCaskey's suggestions for managing change and ambiguity match those we offer below, and the case material he reviewed showed how difficult the task was for managers schooled in the traditional way of managing.

Application of Principles of Natural Selection

Many years ago, Ashby (1956) pointed out what he called the law of requisite variety, which held that in order to cope with an uncertainly varying environment, organizations had to have an equivalent amount of internal variety. Organizational scientists have not paid much attention to this law, and textbooks offer little advice on designing organizations to retain requisite variety. Following the four principles of natural selection, while not offering specific answers about surviving under uncertainty, reduces the problem to more manageable proportions.

Variations. Is it impossible for organizations to plan to have unplanned or blind variations? Fortunately, organizational control and planning methods are not so advanced as to preclude blind variations. The danger is that the more effective and adapted an organization becomes to present conditions, the more it will reduce its ability to maintain the requisite variety necessary to adapt to the future. Weick (1977) offered a useful plan for enhancing variations. The essence of his plan is his call for effective organizations to be garrulous, clumsy, superstitious, hypocritical, monstrous, octopoid, wandering, and grouchy. It is well to build in some clumsiness or "galumphing," defined as "patterned voluntary elaboration or complication of process" (Miller, 1973: 92) instead of designing organizational means that are streamlined, finely tuned, efficient, and inflexibly focused on a specified goal. Galumphing is a way of elaborating means and thereby introducing variations that may offer requisite variety, even though they may be inefficient in the short term. The good thing about superstition is that it is based on ignorance. Actions based on superstition are thus blind and not related to the present, and so result in blind variations. One of the dangers of well-informed, logical, analytical M.B.A.'s is that they are often trained to try to eliminate superstitious behavior in organizations and with it some of the ability to foster requisite variety. We leave the discovery of what octopoid, monstrous, grouchy organizations are like to the interested reader.

Another approach to enhancing variations in organizations is given in the following statement by a top-level corporate strategy expert with an internationally famous consulting organization (he must remain anonymous at this time, since the memo we quote from is an internal one not meant for public use):

So what do the great military strategists, like Patton or MacArthur, or the great business strategists, like Walter Wriston or Patrick Haggerty, really do? What are the excellent companies — who talk less, but do more about strategy — really up to? I think the answer is this: First they are experimenting far more than the rest — they are not more prescient than any others; they simply have lots and lots of experiments, trials, and miniature ventures going on at any one time. Second, they are better learners. Because their top managers have first-hand knowledge of all the trials going on in their companies (and perhaps those of competitors) they have first-hand knowledge of what works and what does not work. Third, they do not experiment expensively; they seem to have systems for quickly cutting off the failures and stepping up resources to the apparent successes. That's it. I submit

Populations, Natural Selection

that the real strategists are simply better *learners* who are *experimenting* more.

A footnote to the memo is obviously in the same line of thinking as Weick's clumsy organization: "Incidentally, what may be radically wrong with many clients' strategic processes is that they are *too* organized. By the time they have defined what they mean by mission, goal, strategy, objective, plan business unit, and the like, they may have so narrowly defined the boundaries as to proscribe experimentation."

Selection. In the population view, organizational forms develop because organizations generating and retaining beneficial variations survive more frequently than other organizations. While organizations, as variant forms, are selected for or against at the population level, variations also are selected for or against at the organizational level. Many variations are not beneficial to an organization and need to be selected out. Accordingly, selection processes abound in organizations; control systems are the primary place where variations are weeded out. Personnel evaluations and cost cutting programs are examples of other selection processes inside organizations. The risk is that beneficial variations may be selected out, along with the harmful ones, by overzealous control-oriented people. This has occurred in many industries. For example, Brittain and Freeman (1980), in their study of the semiconductor industry, described cases of successful "spin-off" organizations — variations that were not recognized or retained by the companies that spawned them. Informal organizational processes, such as norms against offering suggestions, against experimenting, or against taking initiative, may also select out beneficial variations.

People in organizations need to be continually aware of how internal selection processes are operating and what kinds of variations they are selecting for or against. Further, internal selection processes should be oriented toward population-level selection processes. External selection processes appear to be different for each population, as Ulrich's (1982) study of the electronics industry indicates, and the processes change over time. Under government regulation, airline costs of fuel, high union wages, and interest rates on loans to buy aircraft could be passed on to the customer by the industry, and thus they were not significant factors in determining which airline organizations survived or what the characteristics of the population form were. Under deregulation, these costs became extremely important almost immediately, and some airlines were slow in bringing them under control. It is possible that needed variations were not present in the failing airline organizations, but it is also possible that beneficial variations were selected against by resistant union, management, or owner constituencies. Survival paths do change, and sometimes quick and strong action is necessary to reorient internal selection processes toward favoring different kinds of variations, given a changed pattern of constraints in an environment. Depending on the environment and what appears to be working for other members of a population, beneficial variations might be of the cost-cutting, efficiency-oriented variety or might result in changed products or services. They might even lead to acquisitions, divestitures, mergers, or interlocking boards of directors.

Retention. The failure of organizations to retain people holding key comps is clearly illustrated in Brittain and Freeman's (1980) research on the evolution of the semiconductor industry. If resources, planning, executive talent, or experience counted for anything, one would expect that corporations like RCA, Sylvania, General Electric, Raytheon, and Westinghouse, the leading electronic (tube) component manufacturers in 1953, would still dominate the industry. Instead, by 1975 the leaders were Texas Instruments, Fairchild Semiconductor, National Semiconductor, Intel, and Motorola. We are not able, at this time, to offer extended guidelines on how to retain key people. We suspect the answer lies in tuning internal selection mechanisms to complement external selection mechanisms more and toward the ideas we have drawn from Weick and the anonymous quotation about fostering innovations or variations. Of course, many variations are retained through formalization, job-training programs and manuals, and equipment design, all of which persist after the innovators have left.

Struggle. Every management professor has a list of first-mover organizations that stagnated and lost their market share to competitors. The U.S. steel, automobile, and television industries are populations at the top of the list, as is the English motorcycle industry. Individual companies such as Ford Motor, Singer Sewing Machine, Everest and Jennings (wheelchairs), Baldwin-Lima (steam locomotives), Montgomery Ward, Leica (cameras), are just a few well-known examples of first-movers who, if they did not lose out altogether, never regained the position they once had.

Sudden increases in organizational mortality rates ("shake-outs") do not happen all the time — they are not continuous — but rather happen at uncertain intervals for many populations. Where shake-outs are frequent, organizations are more likely to show an ability to survive against considerable competitive pressure. Sometimes there is little struggle for existence, as in regulated industries, industries with vaguely measured outputs, such as educational institutions or hospitals, government agencies, or military organizations. Only wars bring shake-outs in military organizations, as Argentine military organizations have learned. Only broad-based political pressures seem to bring shake-outs in government agencies (e.g., Reagan's treatment of the energy and educational agencies). There is much to be said for business cycles because they do cause shake-outs. We suspect it is very hard to maintain a tough competitive edge when one is on top. The best practical message we have is to do anything possible to bring shake-out pressure to bear on organizational units and to place them in competitive postures against other organizational units, or against units outside the organization. One difficulty with a simple application of this strategy is that competitive pressures will drive people toward maximizing in the short term, and this is antithetical to what is necessary to generate variations.

Organizational science, as a field, has traditionally focused on control, decision making, and communication processes (March, 1965). This seems especially true of studies by investigators in management schools and in the design of training programs for professional managers. The intent of these studies and training has been to minimize unplanned variations by emphasizing tightening control systems, strengthening the

Populations, Natural Selection

logic of decision processes, and reducing breakdowns in the communication of goals, plans, and policies. These actions reinforce the application of the selection principle, since decisions are selections from among alternatives, and communication and control processes assure the implementation and retention of selections. It would appear, however, that human-enhanced internal selections, at the expense of variation, retention, and struggle, will probably not put organizations in a strong position for survival under conditions of uncertainty. We do not advocate becoming paralyzed by natural selection, all the while hoping for favorable selection. Managers should attempt a balanced emphasis on all four principles as the best way of increasing the chances of the survival of their organization. Such an even emphasis will not guarantee favorable selection, but at least it will keep a manager from inadvertently helping the organization more quickly toward failure. The theory of natural selection explains the effects of a force that cannot be anticipated or countered in its effect but that can be understood. Organizations have more ability to adapt than organisms, we think; they have more ability to alter their niche space than organisms; and they have the possibility of gaining a vision capable of steering them away from failure-enhancing mistakes.

CONCLUSIONS

If we take seriously an organizational level of analysis — assuming organizations are coherent units with integrity as units — then theories of organizations should reflect this assumption. The population perspective is then an extremely useful approach for studying the process of organizational change. A theoretically grounded empirical taxonomy would provide a conceptual framework for describing and understanding the diversity of organizational populations and would identify populations useful for research on other substantive concerns about organizations.

Adopting the population perspective would transform the field of organizational science. The distinction between macro- and micro-organizational behavior would be put on a solid theoretical footing. Organizational theorists now only partially recognize that it is as valuable to study organizations as social units as it is to study classes of their members, such as managers and decision makers. If theorists begin to take the integrity of organizations seriously, organizational forms and populations would become the fundamental units of analysis for the field. Generalizations and theories about organizations would no longer be acceptable unless they were qualified by the form(s) to which they applied.

Research on organizations would be guided by a clear conception of representative sampling, and investigators would become much more conscious of a priori choices of sampling frames. Many current studies are based on samples from probable populations, but they are not well defined, and investigators have moved too quickly in generalizing their results to other populations. With explicit recognition of the constraints on generalizability, much extant knowledge could be incorporated into the population perspective, particularly the many studies of specific institutions, such as hospitals, unions, and schools (March, 1965).

We believe adoption of the population perspective would have its most significant effect on the process of translating research findings into applications. Storage and retrieval of research results — and the accumulation, refinement, and critical analysis of results — would be greatly simplified by the availability of a dependable classification scheme. Consultants, managers, staff, and interested parties could make much more informed choices of tactics and strategies, were they guided by knowledge of where *their* organization fit in the larger class. Theory and practice would be in much closer harmony than they are now, and this, perhaps, would be the most salutary consequence of all.

REFERENCES

Aldrich, Howard E.
1979 Organizations and Environments. Englewood Cliffs, NJ: Prentice-Hall.

Aldrich, Howard E., and Susan Mueller
1982 "The evolution of organizational forms." In Barry M. Staw and Larry L. Cummings (eds.), Research in Organizational Behavior, 4: 33–87. Greenwich, CT: JAI Press.

Ashby, W. Ross
1956 An Introduction to Cybernetics. London: Chapman & Hall.

Bailey, Kenneth D.
1973 "Monothetic and polythetic typologies and their relation to conceptualization, measurement and scaling." American Sociological Review, 38: 18–33.
1975 "Cluster Analysis." In David R. Heise (ed.), Sociological Methodology: 59–128. San Francisco: Jossey-Bass.

Benson, J. Kenneth
1977 "Organizations: A dialectical view." Administrative Science Quarterly, 22: 1–21.

Biggart, Nicole Woolsey
1977 "The creative-destructive process of organizational change: The case of the Post Office." Administrative Science Quarterly, 22: 410–426.

Blau, Peter M.
1974 On the Nature of Organizations. New York: Wiley.

Blau, Peter M., and Richard A. Schoenherr
1971 The Structure of Organizations. New York: Basic Books.

Bougon, Michel, Karl Weick, and Din Binkhorst
1977 "Cognition in organizations: An analysis of the Utrecht Jazz Orchestra." Administrative Science Quarterly, 22: 606–639.

Brittain, Jack W., and John H. Freeman
1980 "Organizational proliferation and density-dependent selection: Organizational evolution in the semiconductor industry." In J. R. Kimberly and R. H. Miles and Associates, The Organizational Life Cycle: 291–338. San Francisco: Jossey-Bass.

Cafferata, Gail Lee
1979 "Member and leader satisfaction with a professional association: An exchange perspective." Administrative Science Quarterly, 24: 472–483.

Campbell, Donald T.
1969 "Variation and selective retention in sociocultural evolution." General Systems, 14: 69–85.

Carroll, Glenn R., and Jacques Delacroix
1982 "Organizational mortality in the newspaper industries of Argentina and Ireland: An ecological approach." Administrative Science Quarterly, 27: 169–198.

Chamberlain, Neil W.
1968 Enterprise and Environment: The Firm in Time and Place. New York: McGraw-Hill.

Chandler, Alfred
1977 The Visible Hand. Cambridge, MA: Belknap.

Child, John
1972 "Organization structure and strategies of control: A replication of the Aston study." Administrative Science Quarterly, 17: 163–177.

Corning, Peter A.
1974 "Politics and the evolutionary process." Evolutionary Biology, 7: 253–294.

Daft, Richard L., and Norman B. Macintosh
1981 "A tentative exploration into the amount and equivocality of information processing in organizational work units." Administrative Science Quarterly, 26: 207–226.

Darwin, Charles
1859 On the Origin of Species by Means of Natural Selection. London: Murry. (A Facsimile of the First Edition with an Introduction by Ernst Mayr. Cambridge, MA: Harvard University Press, 1964.)

Dodder, Richard A.
1969 "A numerical taxonomy of voluntary associations." Unpublished Ph.D. dissertation, University of Kansas.

Freeman, John H.
1982 "Organizational life cycles and natural selection processes." In Barry M. Staw and Larry L. Cummings (eds.), Research in Organizational Behavior, 4: 1–32. Greenwich, CT: JAI Press.

Frost, Peter
1980 "Toward a radical framework for practicing organization science." Academy of Management Review, 5: 501–507.

Galbraith, Jay R.
1973 Designing Complex Organizations. Reading, MA: Addison-Wesley.

Garfinkel, Harold
1967 Studies in Ethnomethodology. Englewood Cliffs, NJ: Prentice-Hall.

Geertz, Clifford
1973 The Interpretation of Culture. New York: Basic Books.

Glaser, Barney G., and Anselm L. Strauss
1967 The Discovery of Grounded Theory. Chicago: Aldine.

Goronzy, Friedhelm
1969 "A numerical taxonomy of business enterprise." In A. J. Cole (ed.), Numerical Taxonomy: 42–52. London: Academic Press.

Haas, J. Eugene, Richard H. Hall, and Norman J. Johnson
1966 "Toward an empirically derived taxonomy of organizations." In R. V. Bowers (ed.), Studies on Behavior in Organizations: 157–180. Athens, GA: University of Georgia Press.

Hall, Richard H.
1982 Organizations: Structure and Process, 3d ed. Englewood Cliffs, NJ: Prentice-Hall.

Hall, Roger I.
1976 "A system pathology of an organization: The rise and fall of the old *Saturday Evening Post.*" Administrative Science Quarterly, 21: 185–212.

Hambrick, Donald C.
1981 "Environment, strategy, and power within top management teams." Administrative Science Quarterly, 26: 253–275.

Hannan, Michael T.
1980 "Notes on the ecology of national labor unions." Mimeographed paper, Palo Alto, CA: Stanford University.

Hannan, Michael T., and John H. Freeman
1977 "The population ecology of organizations." American Journal of Sociology, 82: 929–964.

Hempel, Carl G. (ed.)
1965 Aspects of Scientific Explanation. New York: Free Press.

Horowitz, David
1971 Radical Sociology. San Francisco: Canfield Press.

Hudson, Herschel C., and Associates
1982 Classifying Social Data. San Francisco: Jossey-Bass.

Husserl, Edmund
1965 Phenomenology and the Crisis of Philosophy. New York: Harper Torchbooks.

Kanter, Rosabeth M.
1983 The Change Masters. New York: Simon & Schuster.

Kaplan, Abraham
1964 The Conduct of Inquiry. San Francisco: Chandler.

Khandwalla, Pradip N.
1977 The Design of Organizations. New York: Harcourt, Brace, Jovanovich.

Populations, Natural Selection

Kimberly, John R.
1980 "Initiation, innovation and institutionalization in the creation process." In John R. Kimberly, Robert H. Miles and Associates, The Organizational Life Cycle: 18–43. San Francisco: Jossey-Bass.

Kuhn, Thomas S.
1970 The Structure of Scientific Revolutions. Chicago: University of Chicago Press.

Lammers, Cornelis J., and David J. Hickson
1979 Organizations Alike and Unlike. London: Routledge & Kegan Paul.

Lawrence, Paul R., and Jay W. Lorsch
1967 "Differentiation and integration in complex organizations." Administrative Science Quarterly, 12: 1–47.

Leatt, Peggy, and Rodney Schneck
1981 "Nursing subunit technology: A replication." Administrative Science Quarterly, 26: 225–236.

Leblebici, Huseyin, and Gerald R. Salancik
1982 "Stability in interorganizational exchanges: Rulemaking processes of the Chicago Board of Trade." Administrative Science Quarterly, 26: 227–242.

Lewontin, R. C.
1978 "Adaptation." Scientific American, 239: 212–230.

Likert, Rensis
1961 New Patterns of Management. New York: McGraw-Hill.

Litchfield, Edward H.
1956 "Notes on a general theory of administration." Administrative Science Quarterly, 1: 3–29.

March, James G. (ed.)
1965 Handbook of Organizations. Chicago: Rand-McNally.

March, James G., and Herbert A. Simon
1958 Organizations. New York: Wiley.

Mayr, Ernst
1969 Principles of Systematic Zoology. New York: McGraw-Hill.

McCaskey, Michael B.
1982 The Executive Challenge: Managing Change and Ambiguity. Boston: Pittman.

McKelvey, Bill
1975 "Guidelines for the empirical classification of organizations." Administrative Science Quarterly, 20: 509–525.

1978 "Organizational systematics: Taxonomic lessons from biology." Management Science, 24: 1428–1440.
1982 Organizational Systematics: Taxonomy, Evolution, Classification. Berkeley and Los Angeles: University of California Press.

Meyer, Marshall W.
1979 Change in Public Bureaucracies. London: Cambridge University Press.

Meyer, Marshall W., and M. Craig Brown.
1977 "The process of bureaucratization." American Journal of Sociology, 83: 364–385.

Mezzich, Juan E., and Herbert Solomon
1980 Taxonomy and Behavioral Science. London: Academic Press.

Miles, Matthew B.
1979 "Qualitative data as an attractive nuisance: The problem of analysis." Administrative Science Quarterly, 24: 590–601.

Miles, Robert H.
1980 "Findings and implications of organizational life cycle research: A commencement." In J. R. Kimberley, R. H. Miles and Associates, The Organizational Life Cycle: 430–450. San Francisco: Jossey-Bass.

Miller, Stephen
1973 "Ends, means, and galumphing: Some leitmotifs of play." American Anthropologist, 75: 87–98.

Morgan, Gareth, and Linda Smircich
1980 "The case for qualitative research." Academy of Management Review, 5: 491–500.

Niv, Amittai
1980 "Organizational disintegration: Roots, processes, and types." In J. R. Kimberly, Robert H. Miles and Associates, The Organizational Life Cycle: 375–394. San Francisco: Jossey-Bass.

Oldham, Greg R., and J. Richard Hackman
1981 "Relationships between organizational structure and employee reactions: Comparing alternative frameworks." Administrative Science Quarterly, 26: 66–84.

Ouchi, William G.
1981 Theory Z: How American Business Can Meet the Japanese Challenge. Reading, MA: Addison-Wesley.

Parsons, Talcott
1956 "A sociological approach to the theory of organizations." Administrative Science Quarterly, 1: 63–85; 2: 225–239.

Perrow, Charles
1970 Organizational Analysis: A Sociological View. Belmont, CA: Brooks/Cole.

Pfeffer, Jeffrey, and William L. Moore
1980 "Average tenure of academic department heads: The effects of paradigm, size, and department demography." Administrative Science Quarterly, 25: 387–407.

Pfeffer, Jeffrey, and Gerald R. Salancik
1978 The External Control of Organizations. New York: Harper & Row.

Pianka, Eric R.
1978 Evolutionary Ecology, 2d ed. New York: Harper & Row.

Porter, Michael
1980 Competitive Strategy. New York: Free Press.

Pugh, D. S., D. J. Hickson, C. Hinings, and C. Turner
1968 "Dimensions of organizational structure." Administrative Science Quarterly, 13: 65–105.

Pugh, D. S., D. J. Hickson, and C. R. Hinings
1969 "An empirical taxonomy of structures of work organizations." Administrative Science Quarterly, 14: 115–126.

Ritzer, George
1975 "Sociology: A multiple paradigm science." The American Sociologist, 10: 156–167.

Roos, Leslie L., and Roger I. Hall
1980 "Influence diagrams and organizational power." Administrative Science Quarterly, 25: 57–71.

Rosenbaum, James E.
1979 "Tournament mobility: Career patterns in a corporation." Administrative Science Quarterly, 24: 220–242.

Ross, Jerry, and Kenneth R. Ferris
1981 "Interpersonal attraction and organizational outcomes: A field examination." Administrative Science Quarterly, 26: 617–632.

Schutz, Alfred
1967 The Phenomenology of the Social World. Evanston, IL: Northwestern University Press.

Schwab, Joseph J.
1960 "What do scientists do?" Behavioral Science, 5: 1–27.

Scott, W. Richard
1981 Organizations: Rational, Natural, and Open Systems. Englewood Cliffs, NJ: Prentice-Hall.

Shetty, Y. K., and Newman S. Perry, Jr.
1976 "Are top executives transferable across companies?" Business Horizons, 19: 23–28.

Sneath, Peter H. A., and Robert R. Sokal
1973 Numerical Taxonomy. San Francisco: Freeman.

Susman, Gerald I., and Roger D. Evered
1978 "An assessment of the scientific merits of action research." Administrative Science Quarterly, 23: 582–603.

Stern, Robert N.
1979 "The development of an interorganizational control network: The case of intercollegiate athletics." Administrative Science Quarterly, 24: 242–266.

Swidler, Ann
1979 Organization without Authority. Cambridge, MA: Harvard University Press.

Thompson, James D.
1956 "On building an administrative science." Administrative Science Quarterly, 1: 102–111.
1967 Organizations in Action. New York: McGraw-Hill.

Ulrich, David O.
1982 "United States and Japanese electronics industries: Description, taxonomy, and selection." Unpublished Ph.D. dissertation, University of California–Los Angeles.

Van Maanen, John (ed.)
1979 Special Issue on Qualitative Methodology. Administrative Science Quarterly, 24: 519–671.

Van de Ven, Andrew H., and W. Graham Astley
1981 "Mapping the field to create a dynamic perspective on organization design and behavior." In A. H. Van de Ven and W. F. Joyce (eds.), Perspectives on Organization Design and Behavior: 427–468. New York: Wiley.

Warriner, Charles K.
1980 "Organizational Types: Notes on the Organizational Species Concept." Mimeographed paper, Department of Sociology, University of Kansas, Lawrence.

Weick, Karl E.
1977 "Re-punctuating the problem." In P. S. Goodman, J. M. Pennings and Associates, New Perspectives on Organizational Effectiveness: 193–225. San Francisco: Jossey-Bass.
1979 The Social Psychology of Organizing, 2d ed. Reading, MA: Addison-Wesley.

Zucker, Lynn G.
1977 "The role of institutionalization in cultural persistence." American Sociological Review, 42: 726–743.

The Incremental View

[10]
The Science of "Muddling Through"

By CHARLES E. LINDBLOM
Associate Professor of Economics
Yale University

> ▶ Short courses, books, and articles exhort administrators to make decisions more methodically, but there has been little analysis of the decision-making process now used by public administrators. The usual process is investigated here—and generally defended against proposals for more "scientific" methods.
>
> Decisions of individual administrators, of course, must be integrated with decisions of others to form the mosaic of public policy. This integration of individual decisions has become the major concern of organization theory, and the way individuals make decisions necessarily affects the way those decisions are best meshed with others'. In addition, decision-making method relates to allocation of decision-making responsibility—who should make what decision.
>
> More "scientific" decision-making also is discussed in this issue: "Tools for Decision-Making in Resources Planning."

SUPPOSE an administrator is given responsibility for formulating policy with respect to inflation. He might start by trying to list all related values in order of importance, e.g., full employment, reasonable business profit, protection of small savings, prevention of a stock market crash. Then all possible policy outcomes could be rated as more or less efficient in attaining a maximum of these values. This would of course require a prodigious inquiry into values held by members of society and an equally prodigious set of calculations on how much of each value is equal to how much of each other value. He could then proceed to outline all possible policy alternatives. In a third step, he would undertake systematic comparison of his multitude of alternatives to determine which attains the greatest amount of values.

In comparing policies, he would take advantage of any theory available that generalized about classes of policies. In considering inflation, for example, he would compare all policies in the light of the theory of prices. Since no alternatives are beyond his investigation, he would consider strict central control and the abolition of all prices and markets on the one hand and elimination of all public controls with reliance completely on the free market on the other, both in the light of whatever theoretical generalizations he could find on such hypothetical economies.

Finally, he would try to make the choice that would in fact maximize his values.

An alternative line of attack would be to set as his principal objective, either explicitly or without conscious thought, the relatively simple goal of keeping prices level. This objective might be compromised or complicated by only a few other goals, such as full employment. He would in fact disregard most other social values as beyond his present interest, and he would for the moment not even attempt to rank the few values that he regarded as immediately relevant. Were he pressed, he would quickly admit that he was ignoring many related values and many possible important consequences of his policies.

As a second step, he would outline those relatively few policy alternatives that occurred to him. He would then compare them. In comparing his limited number of alternatives, most of them familiar from past controversies, he would not ordinarily find a body of theory precise enough to carry him through a comparison of their respective consequences. Instead he would rely heavily on the record of past experience with small policy steps to predict the consequences of similar steps extended into the future.

Moreover, he would find that the policy alternatives combined objectives or values in different ways. For example, one policy might offer price level stability at the cost of some risk of unemployment; another might offer less price stability but also less risk of unemployment. Hence, the next step in his approach—the final selection—would combine into one the choice among values and the choice among instruments for reaching values. It would not, as in the first method of policy-making, approximate a more mechanical process of choosing the means that best satisfied goals that were previously clarified and ranked. Because practitioners of the second approach expect to achieve their goals only partially, they would expect to repeat endlessly the sequence just described, as conditions and aspirations changed and as accuracy of prediction improved.

By Root or by Branch

For complex problems, the first of these two approaches is of course impossible. Although such an approach can be described, it cannot be practiced except for relatively simple problems and even then only in a somewhat modified form. It assumes intellectual capacities and sources of information that men simply do not possess, and it is even more absurd as an approach to policy when the time and money that can be allocated to a policy problem is limited, as is always the case. Of particular importance to public administrators is the fact that public agencies are in effect usually instructed not to practice the first method. That is to say, their prescribed functions and constraints—the politically or legally possible—restrict their attention to relatively few values and relatively few alternative policies among the countless alternatives that might be imagined. It is the second method that is practiced.

Curiously, however, the literatures of decision-making, policy formulation, planning, and public administration formalize the first approach rather than the second, leaving public administrators who handle complex decisions in the position of practicing what few preach. For emphasis I run some risk of overstatement. True enough, the literature is well aware of limits on man's capacities and of the inevitability that policies will be approached in some such style as the second. But attempts to formalize rational policy formulation—to lay out explicitly the necessary steps in the process—usually describe the first approach and not the second.[1]

The common tendency to describe policy formulation even for complex problems as though it followed the first approach has been strengthened by the attention given to, and successes enjoyed by, operations research, statistical decision theory, and systems analysis. The hallmarks of these procedures, typical of the first approach, are clarity of objective, explicitness of evaluation, a high degree of comprehensiveness of overview, and, wherever possible, quantification of values for mathematical analysis. But these advanced procedures remain largely the appropriate techniques of relatively small-scale problem-solving where the total number of variables to be considered is small and value problems restricted. Charles Hitch, head of the Economics Division of RAND Corporation, one of the leading centers for application of these techniques, has written:

I would make the empirical generalization from my experience at RAND and elsewhere that operations research is the art of sub-optimizing, i.e., of solving some lower-level problems, and that difficulties increase and our special competence diminishes by an order of magnitude with every level of decision making we attempt to ascend. The sort of simple explicit model which operations researchers are so proficient in using can certainly reflect most of the significant factors influencing traffic control on the George Washington Bridge, but the proportion of the relevant reality which we can represent by any such model or models in studying, say, a major foreign-policy decision, appears to be almost trivial.[2]

Accordingly, I propose in this paper to clarify and formalize the second method,

---

[1] James G. March and Herbert A. Simon similarly characterize the literature. They also take some important steps, as have Simon's recent articles, to describe a less heroic model of policy-making. See *Organizations* (John Wiley and Sons, 1958), p. 137.

[2] "Operations Research and National Planning—A Dissent," 5 *Operations Research* 718 (October, 1957). Hitch's dissent is from particular points made in the article to which his paper is a reply; his claim that operations research is for low-level problems is widely accepted.

For examples of the kind of problems to which operations research is applied, see C. W. Churchman, R. L. Ackoff and E. L. Arnoff, *Introduction to Operations Research* (John Wiley and Sons, 1957); and J. F. McCloskey and J. M. Coppinger (eds.), *Operations Research for Management*, Vol. II, (The Johns Hopkins Press, 1956).

much neglected in the literature. This might be described as the method of *successive limited comparisons*. I will contrast it with the first approach, which might be called the rational-comprehensive method.³ More impressionistically and briefly—and therefore generally used in this article—they could be characterized as the branch method and root method, the former continually building out from the current situation, step-by-step and by small degrees; the latter starting from fundamentals anew each time, building on the past only as experience is embodied in a theory, and always prepared to start completely from the ground up.

Let us put the characteristics of the two methods side by side in simplest terms.

Rational-Comprehensive (Root)

1a. Clarification of values or objectives distinct from and usually prerequisite to empirical analysis of alternative policies.

2a. Policy-formulation is therefore approached through means-end analysis: First the ends are isolated, then the means to achieve them are sought.

3a. The test of a "good" policy is that it can be shown to be the most appropriate means to desired ends.

4a. Analysis is comprehensive; every important relevant factor is taken into account.

5a. Theory is often heavily relied upon.

Successive Limited Comparisons (Branch)

1b. Selection of value goals and empirical analysis of the needed action are not distinct from one another but are closely intertwined.

2b. Since means and ends are not distinct, means-end analysis is often inappropriate or limited.

3b. The test of a "good" policy is typically that various analysts find themselves directly agreeing on a policy (without their agreeing that it is the most appropriate means to an agreed objective).

4b. Analysis is drastically limited:
   i) Important possible outcomes are neglected.
   ii) Important alternative potential policies are neglected.
   iii) Important affected values are neglected.

5b. A succession of comparisons greatly reduces or eliminates reliance on theory.

Assuming that the root method is familiar and understandable, we proceed directly to clarification of its alternative by contrast. In explaining the second, we shall be describing how most administrators do in fact approach complex questions, for the root method, the "best" way as a blueprint or model, is in fact not workable for complex policy questions, and administrators are forced to use the method of successive limited comparisons.

Intertwining Evaluation and Empirical Analysis (1b)

The quickest way to understand how values are handled in the method of successive limited comparisons is to see how the root method often breaks down in *its* handling of values or objectives. The idea that values should be clarified, and in advance of the examination of alternative policies, is appealing. But what happens when we attempt it for complex social problems? The first difficulty is that on many critical values or objectives, citizens disagree, congressmen disagree, and public administrators disagree. Even where a fairly specific objective is prescribed for the administrator, there remains considerable room for disagreement on sub-objectives. Consider, for example, the conflict with respect to locating public housing, described in Meyerson and Banfield's study of the Chicago Housing Authority[4]—disagreement which occurred despite the clear objective of providing a certain number of public housing units in the city. Similarly conflicting are objectives in highway location, traffic control, minimum wage administration, development of tourist facilities in national parks, or insect control.

Administrators cannot escape these conflicts by ascertaining the majority's preference, for preferences have not been registered on most issues; indeed, there often *are* no preferences in the absence of public discussion sufficient to bring an issue to the attention of the electorate. Furthermore, there is a question

---

[3] I am assuming that administrators often make policy and advise in the making of policy and am treating decision-making and policy-making as synonymous for purposes of this paper.

[4] Martin Meyerson and Edward C. Banfield, *Politics, Planning and the Public Interest* (The Free Press, 1955).

of whether intensity of feeling should be considered as well as the number of persons preferring each alternative. By the impossibility of doing otherwise, administrators often are reduced to deciding policy without clarifying objectives first.

Even when an administrator resolves to follow his own values as a criterion for decisions, he often will not know how to rank them when they conflict with one another, as they usually do. Suppose, for example, that an administrator must relocate tenants living in tenements scheduled for destruction. One objective is to empty the buildings fairly promptly, another is to find suitable accommodation for persons displaced, another is to avoid friction with residents in other areas in which a large influx would be unwelcome, another is to deal with all concerned through persuasion if possible, and so on.

How does one state even to himself the relative importance of these partially conflicting values? A simple ranking of them is not enough; one needs ideally to know how much of one value is worth sacrificing for some of another value. The answer is that typically the administrator chooses—and must choose—directly among policies in which these values are combined in different ways. He cannot first clarify his values and then choose among policies.

A more subtle third point underlies both the first two. Social objectives do not always have the same relative values. One objective may be highly prized in one circumstance, another in another circumstance. If, for example, an administrator values highly both the dispatch with which his agency can carry through its projects *and* good public relations, it matters little which of the two possibly conflicting values he favors in some abstract or general sense. Policy questions arise in forms which put to administrators such a question as: Given the degree to which we are or are not already achieving the values of dispatch and the values of good public relations, is it worth sacrificing a little speed for a happier clientele, or is it better to risk offending the clientele so that we can get on with our work? The answer to such a question varies with circumstances.

The value problem is, as the example shows, always a problem of adjustments at a margin. But there is no practicable way to state marginal objectives or values except in terms of particular policies. That one value is preferred to another in one decision situation does not mean that it will be preferred in another decision situation in which it can be had only at great sacrifice of another value. Attempts to rank or order values in general and abstract terms so that they do not shift from decision to decision end up by ignoring the relevant marginal preferences. The significance of this third point thus goes very far. Even if all administrators had at hand an agreed set of values, objectives, and constraints, and an agreed ranking of these values, objectives, and constraints, their marginal values in actual choice situations would be impossible to formulate.

Unable consequently to formulate the relevant values first and then choose among policies to achieve them, administrators must choose directly among alternative policies that offer different marginal combinations of values. Somewhat paradoxically, the only practicable way to disclose one's relevant marginal values even to oneself is to describe the policy one chooses to achieve them. Except roughly and vaguely, I know of no way to describe—or even to understand—what my relative evaluations are for, say, freedom and security, speed and accuracy in governmental decisions, or low taxes and better schools than to describe my preferences among specific policy choices that might be made between the alternatives in each of the pairs.

In summary, two aspects of the process by which values are actually handled can be distinguished. The first is clear: evaluation and empirical analysis are intertwined; that is, one chooses among values and among policies at one and the same time. Put a little more elaborately, one simultaneously chooses a policy to attain certain objectives and chooses the objectives themselves. The second aspect is related but distinct: the administrator focuses his attention on marginal or incremental values. Whether he is aware of it or not, he does not find general formulations of objectives very helpful and in fact makes specific marginal or incremental comparisons. Two policies, X and Y, confront him. Both promise the same degree of attainment of objectives a, b, c, d, and e. But X promises him somewhat more of f than does Y, while Y promises him somewhat more of g than does

THE SCIENCE OF "MUDDLING THROUGH"

X. In choosing between them, he is in fact offered the alternative of a marginal or incremental amount of f at the expense of a marginal or incremental amount of g. The only values that are relevant to his choice are these increments by which the two policies differ; and, when he finally chooses between the two marginal values, he does so by making a choice between policies.[5]

As to whether the attempt to clarify objectives in advance of policy selection is more or less rational than the close intertwining of marginal evaluation and empirical analysis, the principal difference established is that for complex problems the first is impossible and irrelevant, and the second is both possible and relevant. The second is possible because the administrator need not try to analyze any values except the values by which alternative policies differ and need not be concerned with them except as they differ marginally. His need for information on values or objectives is drastically reduced as compared with the root method; and his capacity for grasping, comprehending, and relating values to one another is not strained beyond the breaking point.

Relations Between Means and Ends (2b)

Decision-making is ordinarily formalized as a means-ends relationship: means are conceived to be evaluated and chosen in the light of ends finally selected independently of and prior to the choice of means. This is the means-ends relationship of the root method. But it follows from all that has just been said that such a means-ends relationship is possible only to the extent that values are agreed upon, are reconcilable, and are stable at the margin. Typically, therefore, such a means-ends relationship is absent from the branch method, where means and ends are simultaneously chosen.

Yet any departure from the means-ends relationship of the root method will strike some readers as inconceivable. For it will appear to them that only in such a relationship is it possible to determine whether one policy choice is better or worse than another. How can an administrator know whether he has made a wise or foolish decision if he is without prior values or objectives by which to judge his decisions? The answer to this question calls up the third distinctive difference between root and branch methods: how to decide the best policy.

The Test of "Good" Policy (3b)

In the root method, a decision is "correct," "good," or "rational" if it can be shown to attain some specified objective, where the objective can be specified without simply describing the decision itself. Where objectives are defined only through the marginal or incremental approach to values described above, it is still sometimes possible to test whether a policy does in fact attain the desired objectives; but a precise statement of the objectives takes the form of a description of the policy chosen or some alternative to it. To show that a policy is mistaken one cannot offer an abstract argument that important objectives are not achieved; one must instead argue that another policy is more to be preferred.

So far, the departure from customary ways of looking at problem-solving is not troublesome, for many administrators will be quick to agree that the most effective discussion of the correctness of policy does take the form of comparison with other policies that might have been chosen. But what of the situation in which administrators cannot agree on values or objectives, either abstractly or in marginal terms? What then is the test of "good" policy? For the root method, there is no test. Agreement on objectives failing, there is no standard of "correctness." For the method of successive limited comparisons, the test is agreement on policy itself, which remains possible even when agreement on values is not.

It has been suggested that continuing agreement in Congress on the desirability of extending old age insurance stems from liberal desires to strengthen the welfare programs of the federal government and from conservative desires to reduce union demands for private pension plans. If so, this is an excellent demonstration of the ease with which individuals of different ideologies often can agree on concrete policy. Labor mediators report a similar phenomenon: the contestants cannot agree on criteria for settling their disputes but can agree on specific proposals. Similarly, when

---

[5] The line of argument is, of course, an extension of the theory of market choice, especially the theory of consumer choice, to public policy choices.

one administrator's objective turns out to be another's means, they often can agree on policy.

Agreement on policy thus becomes the only practicable test of the policy's correctness. And for one administrator to seek to win the other over to agreement on ends as well would accomplish nothing and create quite unnecessary controversy.

If agreement directly on policy as a test for "best" policy seems a poor substitute for testing the policy against its objectives, it ought to be remembered that objectives themselves have no ultimate validity other than they are agreed upon. Hence agreement is the test of "best" policy in both methods. But where the root method requires agreement on what elements in the decision constitute objectives and on which of these objectives should be sought, the branch method falls back on agreement wherever it can be found.

In an important sense, therefore, it is not irrational for an administrator to defend a policy as good without being able to specify what it is good for.

Non-Comprehensive Analysis (4b)

Ideally, rational-comprehensive analysis leaves out nothing important. But it is impossible to take everything important into consideration unless "important" is so narrowly defined that analysis is in fact quite limited. Limits on human intellectual capacities and on available information set definite limits to man's capacity to be comprehensive. In actual fact, therefore, no one can practice the rational-comprehensive method for really complex problems, and every administrator faced with a sufficiently complex problem must find ways drastically to simplify.

An administrator assisting in the formulation of agricultural economic policy cannot in the first place be competent on all possible policies. He cannot even comprehend one policy entirely. In planning a soil bank program, he cannot successfully anticipate the impact of higher or lower farm income on, say, urbanization—the possible consequent loosening of family ties, possible consequent eventual need for revisions in social security and further implications for tax problems arising out of new federal responsibilities for social security and municipal responsibilities for urban services. Nor, to follow another line of repercussions, can he work through the soil bank program's effects on prices for agricultural products in foreign markets and consequent implications for foreign relations, including those arising out of economic rivalry between the United States and the U.S.S.R.

In the method of successive limited comparisons, simplification is systematically achieved in two principal ways. First, it is achieved through limitation of policy comparisons to those policies that differ in relatively small degree from policies presently in effect. Such a limitation immediately reduces the number of alternatives to be investigated and also drastically simplifies the character of the investigation of each. For it is not necessary to undertake fundamental inquiry into an alternative and its consequences; it is necessary only to study those respects in which the proposed alternative and its consequences differ from the status quo. The empirical comparison of marginal differences among alternative policies that differ only marginally is, of course, a counterpart to the incremental or marginal comparison of values discussed above.[6]

Relevance as Well as Realism

It is a matter of common observation that in Western democracies public administrators and policy analysts in general do largely limit their analyses to incremental or marginal differences in policies that are chosen to differ only incrementally. They do not do so, however, solely because they desperately need some way to simplify their problems; they also do so in order to be relevant. Democracies change their policies almost entirely through incremental adjustments. Policy does not move in leaps and bounds.

The incremental character of political change in the United States has often been remarked. The two major political parties agree on fundamentals; they offer alternative policies to the voters only on relatively small points of difference. Both parties favor full employment, but they define it somewhat differently; both favor the development of

---

[6] A more precise definition of incremental policies and a discussion of whether a change that appears "small" to one observer might be seen differently by another is to be found in my "Policy Analysis," 48 *American Economic Review* 298 (June, 1958).

THE SCIENCE OF "MUDDLING THROUGH"

water power resources, but in slightly different ways; and both favor unemployment compensation, but not the same level of benefits. Similarly, shifts of policy within a party take place largely through a series of relatively small changes, as can be seen in their only gradual acceptance of the idea of governmental responsibility for support of the unemployed, a change in party positions beginning in the early 30's and culminating in a sense in the Employment Act of 1946.

Party behavior is in turn rooted in public attitudes, and political theorists cannot conceive of democracy's surviving in the United States in the absence of fundamental agreement on potentially disruptive issues, with consequent limitation of policy debates to relatively small differences in policy.

Since the policies ignored by the administrator are politically impossible and so irrelevant, the simplification of analysis achieved by concentrating on policies that differ only incrementally is not a capricious kind of simplification. In addition, it can be argued that, given the limits on knowledge within which policy-makers are confined, simplifying by limiting the focus to small variations from present policy makes the most of available knowledge. Because policies being considered are like present and past policies, the administrator can obtain information and claim some insight. Non-incremental policy proposals are therefore typically not only politically irrelevant but also unpredictable in their consequences.

The second method of simplification of analysis is the practice of ignoring important possible consequences of possible policies, as well as the values attached to the neglected consequences. If this appears to disclose a shocking shortcoming of successive limited comparisons, it can be replied that, even if the exclusions are random, policies may nevertheless be more intelligently formulated than through futile attempts to achieve a comprehensiveness beyond human capacity. Actually, however, the exclusions, seeming arbitrary or random from one point of view, need be neither.

Achieving a Degree of Comprehensiveness

Suppose that each value neglected by one policy-making agency were a major concern of at least one other agency. In that case, a helpful division of labor would be achieved, and no agency need find its task beyond its capacities. The shortcomings of such a system would be that one agency might destroy a value either before another agency could be activated to safeguard it or in spite of another agency's efforts. But the possibility that important values may be lost is present in any form of organization, even where agencies attempt to comprehend in planning more than is humanly possible.

The virtue of such a hypothetical division of labor is that every important interest or value has its watchdog. And these watchdogs can protect the interests in their jurisdiction in two quite different ways: first, by redressing damages done by other agencies; and, second, by anticipating and heading off injury before it occurs.

In a society like that of the United States in which individuals are free to combine to pursue almost any possible common interest they might have and in which government agencies are sensitive to the pressures of these groups, the system described is approximated. Almost every interest has its watchdog. Without claiming that every interest has a sufficiently powerful watchdog, it can be argued that our system often can assure a more comprehensive regard for the values of the whole society than any attempt at intellectual comprehensiveness.

In the United States, for example, no part of government attempts a comprehensive overview of policy on income distribution. A policy nevertheless evolves, and one responding to a wide variety of interests. A process of mutual adjustment among farm groups, labor unions, municipalities and school boards, tax authorities, and government agencies with responsibilities in the fields of housing, health, highways, national parks, fire, and police accomplishes a distribution of income in which particular income problems neglected at one point in the decision processes become central at another point.

Mutual adjustment is more pervasive than the explicit forms it takes in negotiation between groups; it persists through the mutual impacts of groups upon each other even where they are not in communication. For all the imperfections and latent dangers in this ubiquitous process of mutual adjustment, it will often accomplish an adaptation of policies to a wider range of interests than could be done by one group centrally.

Note, too, how the incremental pattern of policy-making fits with the multiple pressure pattern. For when decisions are only incremental—closely related to known policies, it is easier for one group to anticipate the kind of moves another might make and easier too for it to make correction for injury already accomplished.[7]

Even partisanship and narrowness, to use pejorative terms, will sometimes be assets to rational decision-making, for they can doubly insure that what one agency neglects, another will not; they specialize personnel to distinct points of view. The claim is valid that effective rational coordination of the federal administration, if possible to achieve at all, would require an agreed set of values[8]—if "rational" is defined as the practice of the root method of decision-making. But a high degree of administrative coordination occurs as each agency adjusts its policies to the concerns of the other agencies in the process of fragmented decision-making I have just described.

For all the apparent shortcomings of the incremental approach to policy alternatives with its arbitrary exclusion coupled with fragmentation, when compared to the root method, the branch method often looks far superior. In the root method, the inevitable exclusion of factors is accidental, unsystematic, and not defensible by any argument so far developed, while in the branch method the exclusions are deliberate, systematic, and defensible. Ideally, of course, the root method does not exclude; in practice it must.

Nor does the branch method necessarily neglect long-run considerations and objectives. It is clear that important values must be omitted in considering policy, and sometimes the only way long-run objectives can be given adequate attention is through the neglect of short-run considerations. But the values omitted can be either long-run or short-run.

---

[7] The link between the practice of the method of successive limited comparisons and mutual adjustment of interests in a highly fragmented decision-making process adds a new facet to pluralist theories of government and administration.

[8] Herbert Simon, Donald W. Smithburg, and Victor A. Thompson, *Public Administration* (Alfred A. Knopf, 1950), p. 434.

Succession of Comparisons (5b)

The final distinctive element in the branch method is that the comparisons, together with the policy choice, proceed in a chronological series. Policy is not made once and for all; it is made and re-made endlessly. Policy-making is a process of successive approximation to some desired objectives in which what is desired itself continues to change under reconsideration.

Making policy is at best a very rough process. Neither social scientists, nor politicians, nor public administrators yet know enough about the social world to avoid repeated error in predicting the consequences of policy moves. A wise policy-maker consequently expects that his policies will achieve only part of what he hopes and at the same time will produce unanticipated consequences he would have preferred to avoid. If he proceeds through a *succession* of incremental changes, he avoids serious lasting mistakes in several ways.

In the first place, past sequences of policy steps have given him knowledge about the probable consequences of further similar steps. Second, he need not attempt big jumps toward his goals that would require predictions beyond his or anyone else's knowledge, because he never expects his policy to be a final resolution of a problem. His decision is only one step, one that if successful can quickly be followed by another. Third, he is in effect able to test his previous predictions as he moves on to each further step. Lastly, he often can remedy a past error fairly quickly—more quickly than if policy proceeded through more distinct steps widely spaced in time.

Compare this comparative analysis of incremental changes with the aspiration to employ theory in the root method. Man cannot think without classifying, without subsuming one experience under a more general category of experiences. The attempt to push categorization as far as possible and to find general propositions which can be applied to specific situations is what I refer to with the word "theory." Where root analysis often leans heavily on theory in this sense, the branch method does not.

The assumption of root analysts is that theory is the most systematic and economical way to bring relevant knowledge to bear on a specific problem. Granting the assumption, an unhappy fact is that we do not have adequate theory to apply to problems in any policy area, although theory is more adequate in some areas—monetary policy, for example—than in others. Comparative analysis, as in the branch method, is sometimes a systematic alternative to theory.

Suppose an administrator must choose among a small group of policies that differ only incrementally from each other and from present policy. He might aspire to "understand" each of the alternatives—for example, to know all the consequences of each aspect of each policy. If so, he would indeed require theory. In fact, however, he would usually decide that, *for policy-making purposes,* he need know, as explained above, only the consequences of each of those aspects of the policies in which they differed from one another. For this much more modest aspiration, he requires no theory (although it might be helpful, if available), for he can proceed to isolate probable differences by examing the differences in consequences associated with past differences in policies, a feasible program because he can take his observations from a long sequence of incremental changes.

For example, without a more comprehensive social theory about juvenile delinquency than scholars have yet produced, one cannot possibly understand the ways in which a variety of public policies—say on education, housing, recreation, employment, race relations, and policing—might encourage or discourage delinquency. And one needs such an understanding if he undertakes the comprehensive overview of the problem prescribed in the models of the root method. If, however, one merely wants to mobilize knowledge sufficient to assist in a choice among a small group of similar policies—alternative policies on juvenile court procedures, for example—he can do so by comparative analysis of the results of similar past policy moves.

Theorists and Practitioners

This difference explains—in some cases at least—why the administrator often feels that the outside expert or academic problem-solver is sometimes not helpful and why they in turn often urge more theory on him. And it explains why an administrator often feels more confident when "flying by the seat of his pants" than when following the advice of theorists. Theorists often ask the administrator to go the long way round to the solution of his problems, in effect ask him to follow the best canons of the scientific method, when the administrator knows that the best available theory will work less well than more modest incremental comparisons. Theorists do not realize that the administrator is often in fact practicing a systematic method. It would be foolish to push this explanation too far, for sometimes practical decision-makers are pursuing neither a theoretical approach nor successive comparisons, nor any other systematic method.

It may be worth emphasizing that theory is sometimes of extremely limited helpfulness in policy-making for at least two rather different reasons. It is greedy for facts; it can be constructed only through a great collection of observations. And it is typically insufficiently precise for application to a policy process that moves through small changes. In contrast, the comparative method both economizes on the need for facts and directs the analyst's attention to just those facts that are relevant to the fine choices faced by the decision-maker.

With respect to precision of theory, economic theory serves as an example. It predicts that an economy without money or prices would in certain specified ways misallocate resources, but this finding pertains to an alternative far removed from the kind of policies on which administrators need help. On the other hand, it is not precise enough to predict the consequences of policies restricting business mergers, and this is the kind of issue on which the administrators need help. Only in relatively restricted areas does economic theory achieve sufficient precision to go far in resolving policy questions; its helpfulness in policy-making is always so limited that it requires supplementation through comparative analysis.

Successive Comparison as a System

Successive limited comparisons is, then, indeed a method or system; it is not a failure of method for which administrators ought to apologize. None the less, its imperfections, which have not been explored in this paper, are many. For example, the method is without a built-in safeguard for all relevant values, and it also may lead the decision-maker to overlook excellent policies for no other reason than that they are not suggested by the chain of successive policy steps leading up to the present. Hence, it ought to be said that under this method, as well as under some of the most sophisticated variants of the root method—operations research, for example—policies will continue to be as foolish as they are wise.

Why then bother to describe the method in all the above detail? Because it is in fact a common method of policy formulation, and is, for complex problems, the principal reliance of administrators as well as of other policy analysts.[9] And because it will be superior to any other decision-making method available for complex problems in many circumstances, certainly superior to a futile attempt at superhuman comprehensiveness. The reaction of the public administrator to the exposition of method doubtless will be less a discovery of a new method than a better acquaintance with an old. But by becoming more conscious of their practice of this method, administrators might practice it with more skill and know when to extend or constrict its use. (That they sometimes practice it effectively and sometimes not may explain the extremes of opinion on "muddling through," which is both praised as a highly sophisticated form of problem-solving and denounced as no method at all. For I suspect that in so far as there is a system in what is known as "muddling through," this method is it.)

One of the noteworthy incidental consequences of clarification of the method is the light it throws on the suspicion an administrator sometimes entertains that a consultant or adviser is not speaking relevantly and responsibly when in fact by all ordinary objective evidence he is. The trouble lies in the fact that most of us approach policy problems within a framework given by our view of a chain of successive policy choices made up to the present. One's thinking about appropriate policies with respect, say, to urban traffic control is greatly influenced by one's knowledge of the incremental steps taken up to the present. An administrator enjoys an intimate knowledge of his past sequences that "outsiders" do not share, and his thinking and that of the "outsider" will consequently be different in ways that may puzzle both. Both may appear to be talking intelligently, yet each may find the other unsatisfactory. The relevance of the policy chain of succession is even more clear when an American tries to discuss, say, antitrust policy with a Swiss, for the chains of policy in the two countries are strikingly different and the two individuals consequently have organized their knowledge in quite different ways.

If this phenomenon is a barrier to communication, an understanding of it promises an enrichment of intellectual interaction in policy formulation. Once the source of difference is understood, it will sometimes be stimulating for an administrator to seek out a policy analyst whose recent experience is with a policy chain different from his own.

This raises again a question only briefly discussed above on the merits of like-mindedness among government administrators. While much of organization theory argues the virtues of common values and agreed organizational objectives, for complex problems in which the root method is inapplicable, agencies will want among their own personnel two types of diversification: administrators whose thinking is organized by reference to policy chains other than those familiar to most members of the organization and, even more commonly, administrators whose professional or personal values or interests create diversity of view (perhaps coming from different specialties, social classes, geographical areas) so that, even within a single agency, decision-making can be fragmented and parts of the agency can serve as watchdogs for other parts.

---

[9] Elsewhere I have explored this same method of policy formulation as practiced by academic analysts of policy ("Policy Analysis," 48 *American Economic Review* 298 [June, 1958]). Although it has been here presented as a method for public administrators, it is no less necessary to analysts more removed from immediate policy questions, despite their tendencies to describe their own analytical efforts as though they were the rational-comprehensive method with an especially heavy use of theory. Similarly, this same method is inevitably resorted to in personal problem-solving, where means and ends are sometimes impossible to separate, where aspirations or objectives undergo constant development, and where drastic simplification of the complexity of the real world is urgent if problems are to be solved in the time that can be given to them. To an economist accustomed to dealing with the marginal or incremental concept in market processes, the central idea in the method is that both evaluation and empirical analysis are incremental. Accordingly I have referred to the method elsewhere as "the incremental method."

If Planning is Everything, Maybe it's Nothing

AARON WILDAVSKY

Graduate School of Public Policy, University of California, Berkeley

ABSTRACT

Where planning does not measure up to expectations, which is almost everywhere, planners are handy targets. They have been too ambitious or they have not been ambitious enough. They have perverted their calling by entering into politics or they have been insensitive to the political dimensions of their task. They ignore national cultural mores at their peril or they capitulate to blind forces of irrationality. They pay too much attention to the relationship between one sector of the economy and another while ignoring analysis of individual projects, or they spend so much time on specific matters that they are unable to deal with movements of the economy as a whole. Planners can no longer define a role for themselves. From old American cities to British new towns, from the richest countries to the poorest, planners have difficulty in explaining who they are and what they should be expected to do. If they are supposed to doctor sick societies, the patient never seems to get well. Why can't the planners ever seem to do the right thing?

Introduction

The planner has become the victim of planning; his own creation has overwhelmed him. Planning has become so large that the planner cannot encompass its dimensions. Planning has become so complex planners cannot keep up with it. Planning protrudes in so many directions, the planner can no longer discern its shape. He may be economist, political scientist, sociologist, architect or scientist. Yet the essence of his calling—planning—escapes him. He finds it everywhere in general and nowhere in particular. Why is planning so elusive?

The concept of planning stands between actors and their societies. It conditions the way they perceive social problems and it guides their choice of solutions. Their understanding of planning helps them to choose the questions they ask and the answers they find. It leads them to evaluate their experience, including their attempt to plan, in certain ways rather than others. The difficulties they experience in society are related to their understanding of the mechanism—planning—they believe will help them solve its problems.

Men think through language. They can hardly conceive of phenomena their words cannot express. The ways in which men think about planning affect how they act just as their attempts to plan affect how they think about it. The problems they have with the word mirror their problems with the world.

Planners begin by attempting to transform their environment and end by being absorbed into it. This pattern of failure is most evident in the poor countries of the world where glittering promise has been replaced by discouraging performance.[1] Nor, despite the high economic growth, are the results different in rich countries; brief examination of two critical cases—France and Japan—will show they also do not follow their plans or make good on them when they do. Planning fails everywhere it has been tried.

How can this be? The reasonable man plans ahead. He seeks to avoid future evils by anticipating them. He tries to obtain a more desirable future by working toward it in the present. Nothing seems more reasonable than planning. And that is where the problem begins; for if planning is reason, then reasonable people must be for it. A reasonable author addressing a reasonable reader cannot be opposed to reason. Is it irrational to dissent from this position?

One good question deserves another: can it be rational to fail? Now anyone can do the best he can and still not succeed. Suppose, however, that the failures of planning are not peripheral or accidental but integral to its very nature. Suppose planning as presently constituted cannot work in the environment in which it is supposed to function. Is it irrational to entertain this hypothesis? If it is irrational to pursue any hypothesis that does not confirm the rational nature of planning, then you are about to read an irrational essay.

Planning as Future Control

Practitioners and students of planning have given the word countless interpretations. Every writer, it seems, feels compelled to redefine the concept. And I am no exception. For the confusion resulting from this semantic Tower of Babel impinges on the practice of planning. How does one evaluate a phenomenon when there is little agreement about what it is? How can one say that planning is good or bad or in between when there are no accepted criteria for determining degrees of success or failure? Judgement of the performance of planning rests upon the nature of the expectations it arouses; and these expectations naturally vary with the definition one adopts. If planning is designed to make goals consistent on paper, one would judge it quite differently than if its purpose is actually to achieve social goals in the future.

Planning is the attempt to control the consequences of our actions. The more consequences we control, the more we have succeeded in planning. To use somewhat different language, planning is the ability to control the future by current acts. Instead of discovering his fate in the future, man plans to make it in his own image. But the present may be reluctant to give birth to the future. Man can attempt to plan and he can fail. As St. Paul put it in his letter to the Romans, "I do not understand my own

---

[1] This essay is a revised and expanded version of material appearing in Naomi Caiden and Aaron Wildavsky. *A Constant Quantity of Tears: Planning and Budgeting in Poor Countries* (The Twentieth Century Fund, forthcoming).

actions. For I do not do what I want, but I do the very thing I hate. . . . I can will what is right, but I cannot do it. For I do not do the good I want, but the evil I do not want is what I do." While man has helped cause these unanticipated events, he has not consciously intended (that is, planned) to bring them about. We must distinguish, therefore, between attempts to plan and actual success in planning.

Attempts to plan are no more planning than the desire to be wise may be called wisdom or the wish to be rich entitles a man to be called wealthy. Promise must be dignified by performance. The determination of whether planning has taken place must rest on an assessment of whether and to what degree future control has been achieved.

Planning must not be confused with the existence of a formal plan, people called planners, or an institution (henceforth called the planning commission) with the word planning in its official title. Formal plans are only one possible manifestation of planning, since planning may take place outside of formal planning organizations. The distinction here is between a written and an unwritten plan. No one today would claim that the British do not have a constitution (rules specifying the procedures for exercising political power) merely because theirs is found in legislation and custom rather than in a single document like that of the United States. Perhaps the existence of a formal plan suggests a greater commitment to the objectives and the subordinate goals in the plan than one would expect in the absence of such a visible public document. This question should be resolved by observation rather than by definition. Certainly the absence of a Bill of Rights in the "unwritten" British constitution does not reveal a lesser commitment to due process or democratic procedure than America's formal statement in its Constitution. In like manner, it would be wrong to say that a government that consciously improved the conditions of its people and increased their ability to live productive lives was not planning because it lacked the formal apparatus, while another government whose people suffered in these respects was planning because it had a plan and planners.

It is tempting to identify planning with government ownership of industry. Then the government is directly making decisions for the entire economy, and that would appear to eliminate the difficulties of plan implementation caused by a recalcitrant private sector. The decisions that are made, however, may turn out to run counter to the plan. Planned decisions often have unplanned consequences. It would be more accurate to say that these governments attempt to plan but do not necessarily succeed, if success means controlling the future direction of their society through a predetermined series of actions. Achievement and not the plan must be the final arbiter of planning. Otherwise, planning exists because there is a plan, no matter what fate has in store for it.

We want a definition of planning that will enable us to compare the efficacy of different ways of achieving control over the future. We want to be able to say that one process or strategy or social structure is better or worse in enabling society to move in the direction it chooses in the most expeditious manner. Central direction of the economy, reliance on a price mechanism, devotion to traditional culture, emphasis on agriculture and small industry, any and all bases for action may be judged by their consequences so long as none are identified as planning itself.

A definition based on attempts to plan—planning as a goal-directed behavior—leaves open the question of whether the actions involved have resulted in the kind of future control envisaged. By defining planning according to its inputs (different modes of trying to control the future) rather than its outputs (extent of future control) the element of direction is removed from planning. Such a definition might be appropriate for those interested in different styles of decision for their own sake but not for people concerned with appraising purposeful social action.

For if a definition covers all attempts to plan, whether they succeed or not, planning encompasses whatever men intend to do in the world. Since practically all actions with future consequences are planned actions, planning is everything, and nonplanning can hardly be said to exist. Nonplanning only exists when people have no objectives, when their actions are random and not goal-directed. If everybody plans (well, almost) it is not possible to distinguish planned from unplanned actions.

A definition of planning based on formal position—planning is whatever planners do—is useful if one wishes to examine the activities of people who occupy these places. But a formal definition rules out on *a priori* grounds the likelihood that ability to control the consequences of current actions may be more widely diffused in society. The question becomes not "who in society succeeds in planning?" but "how successful are formal planners in planning?" The planners are the active element, their society the passive beneficiary of their efforts.

Planning is often used (though this definition is rarely made explicit) as if it were equivalent to rationality. Once norms associated with rational action are identified—efficiency, consistency, coordination—any process of decision may be appraised according to the degree to which it conforms to them. The assumption is that following these norms leads to better decisions. Defining planning as applied rationality focuses attention on adherence to universal norms rather than on the consequences of acting one way instead of another. Attention is directed to the internal qualities of the decisions and not to their external effects.

The confusions surrounding the meaning of planning may have a social explanation. Unable to control the future, planners have resisted any other definition that would brand them as failures. After all, no one else is forced to make public predictions that rarely turn out right. Planners want credit for their aspirations, for a noble effort, so they grope toward a definition that stresses the activities in which they engage or the processes through which they work. Exhibition displaces power. The focus of meaning can then shift from events in the world to their own exemplary behavior.

These definitions are not merely different ways of looking at the same thing. They are not just words. They imply different standards for planning and they direct our attention to different phenomena. To define planning as future control, for instance, does away with the distinction between drawing up plans and implementing them, setting goals and achieving them. The objective and its fulfillment are part of the same series of actions.[2] Separating goals from achievements, as most definitions do by emphasizing intention over accomplishment, blurs the distinction between planning

---

[2] See Jeffrey L. Pressman and Aaron Wildavsky, *Implementation* (University of California Press, 1973, forthcoming).

and other purposeful behavior. Hence planning becomes a self-protecting hypothesis; so long as planners try to plan, it cannot be falsified.

In order to understand the implications of these rival definitions, let us consider what is involved in the statements about planning made by practitioner and theorist alike. Virtually everyone would agree that planning requires: (1) A specification of future objectives and (2) a series of related actions over time designed to achieve them. We can now try to discover in general terms what is entailed by national planning.

Planning as Cause

We can say (beginning with the implementing actions) that the first requisite of national planning is causal knowledge: the existence of theory with at least some evidence to support it specifying causal relationships. If X and Y are done, then Z will result. If the consequences of contemplated actions cannot accurately be appraised, specified objectives will be achieved only by accident. The necessity for causal knowledge is made more stringent in long-range planning because the consequences of each action become the basis for the succeeding steps. Each error in prediction is magnified because of its impact on future decisions.

It will help if we specify the kinds of causal knowledge planning requires: a knowledge of the relationships in each of dozens of areas of policy from fisheries to foreign exchange. These relationships may be further subdivided: (1) interaction among the elements of the policy itself, (2) incentives for the people involved to carry out the policy or mechanisms for insuring compliance, (3) sufficient resources at the time required. In agriculture, for example, knowledge of the elements of the policy itself—the technology of production, the mechanisms of distribution, the availability of markets—must be right if the policy is to work. If the farmers will not plant the crops called for or if the prices do not bring them sufficient remuneration, they will sabotage the policy, either overtly or through passive resistance. If there is insufficient money for seeds or fertilizer or if the farmer lacks the education or the motivation to employ the necessary techniques, the policy will fail.

Even if good theory exists somewhere in the world, people in a particular society must be able to apply it in the specific context of their own country. Yet knowledge of how to apply theory is often as weak as the theory itself. Social circumstances may make a mockery of general principles. There may be few men who are capable of utilizing existing theory for practical purposes. Where causal theory is absent or imperfect, where applications are poor or nonexistent, where personnel to carry out policies is lacking or badly trained, the preconditions of formal planning cannot be met.

Yet we have not begun to exhaust the requirements of causal knowledge. Not only is it required in each important area of policy (actually it is also necessary to know which areas are important), but among areas of policy as well. Energy policy, for example, cannot be pursued apart from transportation, industrial and agricultural policy. The major consequences of each set of policy decisions for other areas of policy must be known; if they are not, some objectives will be achieved at the expense of others or none of the objectives will be achieved. Scarce as causal theory is within specific areas of policy, it is superabundant compared to the lack of knowledge of interaction effects. There are no useful models of economies as a whole; either they contain so few variables as to be too general, or they contain so many that one cannot understand what goes on inside them, let alone in the world to which they are supposed to refer. If economic theory is weak, theories of society involving human motivation and incentive are barely alive. The provision of information itself is dependent on cultural norms, political support and administrative practices that usually work in the opposite direction. Thus the lack of theory means that one often does not know what kind of information to collect, and, in any event, it would probably not be available.

Causal knowledge is also necessary to relate the policies of the nation over time to changes in the international economy and political systems. Low income countries are especially vulnerable to fluctuations in the price of imports and exports and in the willingness of previous donor nations to supply aid. Should the plan require a certain amount of foreign currency, it can easily disintegrate if commodity prices drop, imports rise, and foreign aid disappears. There are no good predictive models of international prices or of willingness to supply aid.

National planning provides a hard test of causal knowledge. Men, resources and institutions must be mobilized and related to one another at successive stages in time in order to obtain predicted results that lead to the achievement of objectives. Nothing less than control of the future is involved.

Any regime, whether it professes to love planning and enshrines *the plan* in its hall of fame, or whether it rejects formal planning entirely, plans to the extent that it can control its future. Planning takes place when people in a society are able to cause consequences they desire to occur. Planning is, therefore, a form of social causation. It requires causal knowledge and the ability to wield that knowledge effectively in society. Power and planning are different ways of looking at the same events.

Planning as Power

Power is the probability of changing the behavior of others against opposition.[3] As soon as the prevalence of disagreement over social goals or policies is admitted into the discussion, it becomes clear that there can be no planning without the ability to cause other people to act differently than they otherwise would. Planning assumes power. Planning is politics.

Power is a reciprocal relationship. It depends not only on what one actor can do but on how the other relevant actors respond in turn. A group may decide not to attempt to realize its intentions because doing so would use up resources that might be better employed elsewhere. Or its efforts may fail because others lack the ability to carry out their instructions. The wielders of power are restricted not only by the limits

---

[3] See Andrew McFarland, *Power and Leadership in Pluralist Systems* (Stanford, California: Stanford University Press, 1969); Herbert Simon, *Models of Man* (New York: Wiley, 1957); John Harsanyi, "Measurement of Social Power, Opportunity Costs, and the Theory of Two-Person Bargaining Games," *Behavioral Science*, Vol. VII (Jan. 1962), pp. 67–80; Robert Dahl, "Power," *International Encyclopedia of the Social Sciences* (New York: Macmillan and Free Press, 1968). Vol. XII, pp. 405–415; James March, "The Power of Power," in David Easton, ed., *Varieties of Political Theory* (Englewood Cliffs, N.J.: Prentice-Hall, 1966), pp. 39–70.

on their own resources but also by the capacities of the respondents. Power must be viewed in its social context.[4]

Planning requires the power to maintain the preeminence of future objectives in the present. The nation's rulers must be able to commit its existing resources to the accomplishment of future objectives. If new rulers arise who make drastic changes in objectives, the original plan is finished. The continuity of the regime, of course, is one of the more problematical features of the poor country. Its unity may crumble, its devotion to original objectives may be undermined from within, and its ability to command the nation's resources may be dissipated through disagreement. Either the rulers must stay in power long enough to accomplish their original purposes or their successors must be people who share the same commitments.

If planning is to be more than an academic exercise, it must actually guide the making of governmental decisions. Governmental actions (and the private activities they seek to influence) must in large measure conform to the plan if it is to have practical effect. Planning, then, at any point in time, involves governmental decisions on resource allocation. A theory of how planning should be done, therefore, would be a theory of governmental resource allocation over time. Planning theory becomes a theory of successive government budgets. If we substitute the words "what the government ought to do" for the words "ought to be in the plan," it becomes clear that a normative theory of planning would have to include a political theory detailing what the government's activities ought to be at a particular time.

To plan, therefore, is to govern. Planning thus becomes the process through which society makes its decisions. If one takes a narrow view of politics, only acts by official government bodies are planning acts. A broader view of politics would include all acts, whether ostensibly private or public, that have substantial future impact on society. To plan is to make decisions that affect others. Planners are presidents, ministers, bureaucrats, party leaders, scientists, entrepreneurs—anybody whose acts have large future consequences.

But the act of governing need not necessarily involve planning; intentions in actions may be unrealized. Political leaders, like planners, may find that they cannot control the future. All may try but none may succeed. Planners and politicians may compete for the right to attempt to plan but there may be no victor to claim the spoils.

Formal planners may be viewed as rivals for control of policy with other government agencies and private groups. Can planners dominate these competitors? They can be nothing if no one listens to them. They may be used by others but have no independent force of their own. Planners may also be everything. They may become the government and exert most of the public force in their nation. Although planning theory sometimes suggests that this is the position planners would need in order to carry out their purposes, and though planners in moments of frustration may wish they had this power, it would be fair to say they do not envisage total control. The vision they have of themselves is of a small but dedicated band that somehow enables the nation to meet goals by bringing it to its senses when necessary. They have in mind a regulator role of the type found in cybernetic systems: amidst a vast complex of machinery there is a small but sensitive device that returns the system to its true path whenever

---

[4] Harsanyi, *op. cit.*

it strays. By pushing in the right direction at critical times the sum of the corrections adds up to achievement of the original goals. France and Germany might well adopt this thermostatic view of planning. But poor countries require far more than occasional correction; they need large inputs of energy in order to build important components of their systems. Thus planners vacillate between the thermostatic view, which is more in accordance with their potential, and the assumption of total power, which is beyond their grasp, when the small changes they can cause are overwhelmed by the large ones over which they have little control.

The experience of formal planners has a universal tinge. Life is full of small corrections. Rarely is it possible to pursue objectives on a once-and-for-all basis. Relative success in meeting goals depends on new actions in response to changing circumstances. Learning, adjustment, adaptation are the keys to accomplishment. What happens to the original objectives when behavior changes in the light of new conditions?

Planning as Adaptation

Until now I have taken for granted the existence of future objectives, each one neatly labeled as if they came out of a great national sausage machine in the sky. They have been assumed to exist somehow "out there". The time has come to inquire into the setting of objectives.

One way to determine future objectives is to extrapolate present trends. The goal in the future is to go where the society was headed in any event. The very idea of planning, however, suggests that one is not letting things go any which way, but intervenes to make them move in a different direction or faster or slower in the same direction. You do not need a plan to get you where you were going to be. How, then, are new objectives created?

It turns out that there are no rules for determining objectives. The rules we do have for resource allocation—efficiency, productivity—assume that objectives are given. These rules specify: achieve a given objective at lowest cost or achieve as much of a given objective as possible from a fixed amount of resources. They posit relationships between inputs and outputs; they do not say what the outputs should be, other than getting the most out of the inputs related to them.

Suppose that governmental leaders simply pick any set that appeals to them. What validity should be accorded these objectives? The obvious answer is that they are authoritative if set out by leaders who will attempt to achieve them. This amounts to saying that they are valid because the government says so. Yet the idea of planning, with its connotations of reason and intelligence, resists the thought that objectives are just stuck out there. Presumably the planners must relate these objectives in some way to the capabilities of the nation as well as to the desires of its leaders.

An objective may be desirable but unobtainable. The result of seeking it may be a waste of resources. Fidel Castro publicly accepts blame for setting a quota of sugar cane so high that cutting went far past the time and use of resources that were economically justified.[5] But no one knows what the right level would be. If sights are

---

[5] *The New York Times*, January 25, 1971, p. 55.

set too low, less may be done than desirable. If too high, unnecessary effort may be devoted to the task. Like Goldilocks, the leaders would like to come out just right. But that is too complex a task. So they simplify by allowing experience to modify the goals they set.

The Soviet Union's response to this dilemma has been instructive. The goals stated in their plans are meant to be targets. If a particular sector of the economy achieves its production goal, the standard is raised next time. Should the goal remain unfulfilled, the people involved are driven harder. If they still cannot make it, the target is lowered through negotiation.[6] There may be an implicit Pavlovian theory of human behavior in this process, but there is nothing scientific about the setting of objectives. Essentially, an arbitrary objective goal is set and then is modified with experience or sometimes just abandoned.

Another approach is to think of objectives as distant rather than near targets. Leaders spell out their objectives and hope to achieve them sometime, even if not in the period specified in the plan. Some might call this utopian, but others would say it represents a society going in a predetermined direction, though the pace of that effort is subject to change. Although this approach may be reasonable, it subverts the basic element of control which is supposed to differentiate planning from just mucking about.

What is the point of saying that the seven-year plan has been achieved in 22 months or that a certain industry has exceeded its quota or that it will take $9\frac{1}{4}$ years to achieve some part of the five-year plan? Presumably the idea of planning is that you get where you are going when you say you will and in the manner specified. Can it mean that you get some other place faster or the same place slower and in a way you did not anticipate? This is not a quibble. It goes to the heart of the idea of planning.

What has happened is that the objectives and the means for obtaining them are no longer fixed but have become subject to modification. The original set of objectives and the plan that embodies them are considered merely starting points. They are altered on the basis of experience and necessity. A new regime, a change in commodity prices, discovery of a new theory, accumulation of changes in national cultural mores, may all signify the desirability of changing objectives and the policies to implement them. Adaptation to changing circumstances is certainly a virtue of the intelligent man. But it smacks of *ad hoc* decisionmaking.

When planning is placed in the context of continuous adjustment it becomes hard to distinguish from any other process of decision. By making planning reasonable it becomes inseparable from the processes of decision it was designed to supplant. One plans the way one governs; one does the best one can at the time and hopes that future information will enable one to do better as circumstances change. Some call this adaptive planning; others call it muddling through. Under the criteria of adaptation, almost any process for making decisions in a social context can be considered to be planning.

---

[6] Joseph Berliner, *Factory and Manager in the U.S.S.R.* (Cambridge: Harvard University Press, 1957); David Granick, *The Red Executive* (Garden City, N.Y.: Doubleday, 1961).

Planning as Process

One cannot, for instance, discuss democracy for long without using the terms—goals, alternatives, appraisals, objectives—which are at the heart of almost any contemporary definition of planning. This suggests that electoral democracy may be considered a mode of planning.

The United States does not seek to achieve goals stated in a national plan. Yet that does not mean that the United States has no goals its decisionmakers try to achieve. There are institutions—the Federal Reserve Board, the Council of Economic Advisers, the Office of Management and Budget, Congressional committees, and more —whose task is to find goals and policies that embody them. There are specific pieces of legislation that are dedicated to full employment, ending or mitigating the effects of pollution, building highways, expanding recreational opportunities, improving agricultural productivity, and on and on. When these goals conflict, new decisions must be made concerning how much of each to try to achieve. Even a single goal like full employment may not be capable of achievement because there is not enough knowledge to do it or because it entails other costs, such as inflation, that prohibit it. Moreover, these goals are related to ultimate objectives. The Preamble to the Constitution states national goals and the remainder presents an institutional plan for achieving them. The government of the United States seeks to achieve domestic prosperity and to protect its interests overseas. While these broad objectives remain constant the intermediate goals change in response to forces in society.

When he was a student in the City Planning Department of the University of California at Berkeley, Owen McShane wrote a paper making explicit the similarities between planning (as found in the model developed by West Churchman, in his book, *The Systems Approach*) and electoral democracy as a process of making decisions. Churchman postulates that planning is concerned with multi-stage decisionmaking and "hence it must study (1) a decisionmaker who (2) chooses among alternative courses of action in order to reach (3) certain first-stage goals, which lead to (4) other-stage objectives."[7] It is easy to parallel this model in terms of electoral democracy as the operation of (1) the electorate which (2) chooses from a group of candidates in order to reach (3) certain first-stage goals, which lead to (4) the implicit goals of the society at large.

Placing the steps in each system side by side, McShane found that the electoral process fitted Churchman's model with remarkable nicety. Every step has an operational equivalent in any electoral democracy.

Similar comparisons could be made between the process of planning and the process of legislation and administration. Consider, for instance, a recent description of how public policy is made: "Generically, one can identify at least six different steps in the process of making government policy—publicizing a problem, initiating a search for a solution, evaluating alternative solutions, choosing a solution or a combination of solutions, implementing the measures decided upon, and finally,

---

[7] West Churchman, *The Systems Approach* (New York: Delacorte Press, 1968), p. 150.

TABLE I

THE PLANNING SYSTEM	THE ELECTORAL DEMOCRATIC SYSTEM
Program 1: Legitimacy	**Program 1: Legitimacy**

Relationship between the planning system (P.S.) and the decisionmakers.
(a) Justification (why the P.S. should exist and its role).
(b) Staffing the P.S. and establishing responsibility and authority.
(c) The Communication Subsystem
    (i) Persuasion (selling the P.S.)
    (ii) Mutual education.
    (iii) Politics identifying and changing the power structure of the organization.
(d) Implementation (installing the plan).
	Relationship between the constitution, etc., and the electorate.
	(a) Justification (why democracy should exist and its role).
	(b) Designing the institutions of democracy and establishing responsibility and authority.
	(c) The Communication Subsystem
	    (i) Persuasion (e.g. the Federalist, etc.)
	    (ii) Public schools and media.
	    (iii) Politics (constitutional amendments, judiciary).
	(d) Implementation (setting up the institutions and operating them).

Program 2: Analysis	**Program 2: Analysis**
Measurement (Identification, classification, prediction, etc.) (a) Identifying the decisionmakers, and customers of the larger system. (b) Discovering and inventing the alternatives. (c) Identifying the first stage goals. (d) Identifying the ultimate objectives. (e) Measuring the effectiveness of each alternative for each first stage goal. (f) Measuring the effectiveness of each first stage goal for the ultimate objectives. (g) Estimating the optimal alternative.	Measurement (Identification, classification, prediction, etc.) (a) Identifying interest groups, setting the franchise, etc. (b) Selecting candidates for office. (c) Identifying and lobbying for first stage goals and policies. (d) Identifying the ultimate aims of society (e.g., Goal for Americans, Bill of Rights, etc.) (e) Assessing the candidate and his policy platform. (f) Assessing the effectiveness of policies for ultimate objectives (e.g. the Vietnam war as protecting democracy). (g) Voting for the candidates of one's choice.
Program 3: Testing (*Verifying the Plan*)	**Program 3: Testing** (*Does the democracy work?*)
(a) Simulation and parallel testing. (b) Controlling the plan once implemented.	(a) Comparison with other nations, self-appraisal by the citizenry. (b) Checks and balances, news media, public debate, the opposition.

evaluating the consequences of a measure."[8] At this level of description there appears to be no significant difference between the United States (and almost any other government, for that matter) and societies that engage in planning.

When planning is conceived of as goal-directed behavior, almost any decisionmaking process will be found to contain similar elements. How then can we evaluate planning? Asking what has been caused by goal-directed behavior is like requesting an explanation for all that has happened. If the process of planning cannot usefully be separated from other modes of choice, the observer will be unable to attribute consequences to

---

[8] Richard Rose, "The Variability of Party Government: A Theoretical and Empirical Critique," *Political Studies* (Dec. 1969) vol. XVII, no. 4, p. 415.

planning that do not also belong to other ways of making decisions; its merits cannot be challenged by future events because they all have their origin in someone's efforts to secure his aims.

If planning is to be judged by its consequences, by what it accomplishes, we must return to the problem of causality. What has planning caused? What has happened differently because of the presence of plans, planners and planning commissions than would have happened without them? What, in the economist's language, is the value added by planning?

Evaluation of planning is not possible so long as it refers to mere effort. The only sportsmanlike response to a runner who has given his all, is "good try," especially if he has fallen at the first turn. Only if planning is defined to mean completed action, achieving a set goal, can its relative degree of success be appraised.

If we are willing to equate national planning with a formal plan, it is possible to ask whether the interventions specified in it have been carried out, and whether they have come close to achieving the desired ends. Evaluation of formal planning depends on forging a valid link between intentions expressed in the plan and future performance of the nation.

Planning as Intention

I have grossly simplified the problem of deciding whether intentions have been carried out by placing them solely in the hands of planners and assuming that their intentions are manifested in the national plan. Judging plans and planners by their intentions nevertheless has strong attractions. The plan itself has the inestimable advantage of existing in time and space and being separable from other phenomena. The plan speaks of accomplishing certain things in specified ways and one can ask whether these future states of affairs have indeed come about. If the plan predicts a rate of economic growth, supported by the development of certain sectors of the economy, propelled by various key projects, one can ascertain whether that rate has been achieved, whether the sectors singled out for special attention have grown in the way specified and whether the projects have been built and are bringing in the returns that were claimed for them. To the extent that the planners are not impossibly vague about what they intend, and relevant information is available and accurate, the plan may be judged by the degree to which its intentions have been carried out.

Yet the criterion of intention may easily prove superficial. Let us suppose that a plan has failed the test of accomplishing the goals set down in it. How might one explain that failure? If the plan is viewed as a series of predictions, it is evident that they have not come true. Yet calling a bad prediction a failure in an uncertain world seems harsh. More to the point would be a statement that the planners were unable to move the nation in the directions they intended. The claim can still be made, however, that much progress occurred, even if it fell short of the initial aims. Imagine a situation in which under Plan I a 4% growth rate was postulated and only 3% achieved, while in Plan II a 10% rate was set out and one of 6% achieved. Plan I was more successful in the sense that the growth rate came closer to the target, but Plan II was more successful in that the overall rate of growth was greater. Assume for the moment that both levels of growth are attributable to the plan. Why should one set of planners be criticized because of their higher level of aspirations if their actual accomplishments are greater? When the intentions in plans are not realized it is difficult to know whether this failure is due to poor performance or unreasonable expectations. Did the nation try to do too little or too much? Were its planners over-ambitious or underachievers?

Planners are vulnerable. Unless they take the precaution of making their goals too vague to be tested, their failure is evident for all to see. They must spend their time not in explaining how they have succeeded but in arguing away their evident failures. A great deal can be learned about fulfilling intentions by noting what happens when early optimism is replaced by later rationalization.

When a venture runs into trouble there are a number of classic ways of justifying it without showing that its performance is actually better. The usual tactic is to claim that the venture has not been tried hard enough, that doing more of the same would bring the results originally envisaged. If the bombing of North Vietnam does not weaken the will of that government to resist, the answer is evidently not to stop but to do more of it. When the poverty programs in the United States lead to disappointing results, then the answer must be that not enough money has been poured into them. It is always difficult to know whether the theory behind the policy is mistaken, so that additional effort would mean throwing good money after bad, or whether greater input of resources would reach the critical mass presumed necessary to make it successful. The same argument is made in regard to formal planning: if only there were more effort, more dedication, more commitment, things would be better. This argument, however, presumes on behalf of formal planning precisely what it is supposed to prove. If things were as they were supposed to be, planning would not be necessary to correct them. The argument is reminiscent of a practitioner's comment about planning around the world: in Russia it is imperative, in France it is indicative, and in poor countries it is subjunctive.

The usual way of justifying formal planning in the absence of (or contrary to the evidence about) accomplishment is to shift the focus of discussion from goals to process. The critic of planning, it is said, has evidently mistaken the nature of the enterprise: by focusing in his simple-minded way on the intentions of the planners he has missed the beneficial effects of the processes through which the plan is made. A similar argument is heard about the United States space program: it is not merely reaching the moon but all the wonderful things learned on the way up and down (cf. technological fallout) that justify the cost of the effort. Planning is good, therefore, not so much for what it does but for how it goes about not doing it.

The process of planning presumably inculcates habits of mind leading to more rational choice. Officials are sensitized to the doctrine of opportunity costs, to what must be given up in order to pursue certain alternatives, and to the notion of enterprise as a productive force in the nation's economy. Time horizons are expanded because the future is made part of present decisions. Because of the existence of the plans and the planners, data may have been collected that otherwise would not have been; men with economic skills have been introduced into government. Those who come in contact with these new men are said to benefit from their new ways of looking at the world. To ask how these spinoff benefits are made tangible would be to retreat to the

139

fallacy—comparing the intentions of planners with their accomplishments—that the process argument was designed to subvert.

There is another way of getting around the problem of intention and its realization; instead of merely saying that the intentions specified in the plan are not the real ones, one can argue that the planners are not the people whose intentions count. An interest-group leader or a politician may have hidden agenda the plan is supposed to achieve. The plan thus becomes an instrument for the purposes of others; its provisions are to be judged by the degree to which it serves their needs. To determine whether planning was successful or not would, therefore, require specific knowledge of the real purposes for which it was used and no *a priori* judgements from afar would be appropriate.

Plans and planners in this context are simply one element in a repertoire of responses in the political arena that are available to those powerful and clever enough to use them. Plans may be weapons wielded by one political faction against another. The forces of logic, reason and rationality may be used by a president against a recalcitrant ministry or by one ministry or region versus another. The possibilities are endless. If national leaders wish to be thought modern, for instance, they have a document with which to dazzle their visitors. Charts, tables, graphs, regressions, are trotted out, but no one who matters attends to them. The plan need not be a means of surmounting the nation's difficulties, but rather may become a mode of covering them up.

By taking the argument one step further, the idea of plans as intentions can be dissolved entirely. One no longer asks whether the intentions in the plan are carried out, but which of many competing intentions is validated, if, indeed, any are. In this view there is no single set of intentions, any more than there is a general will that can be embodied in a single plan. There are different wills and various interests that compete for shares in planning. Some of these "wills" get adopted as government plans for a time and then are altered or revised. The great questions then become: whose intentions are realized? Are anyone's plans made good by the unfolding of events?

Once conflict over goals is admitted, intention evaporates as a useful criterion for judging the success of planning. The planners lose their hold over intention; it is no longer immutable but problematical, a subject for bargaining, a counter in the flux of events. The stage shifts from the intentions specified in the plan to a multitude of actors whose intentions are alleged to be the real ones. The success of planning depends entirely on whose plans one has in mind.

My discussion of intention may be rejected, not necessarily because it's misleading (though that may be the case), but because it's seen as irrelevant. Sophisticated people, critics might say, have long since abandoned both the idea of national planning and of national intentions. They may go along with it for its symbolic value but they know it does not work. "So why bother to spend all this time discussing it," one can hear them say. Planners have a much more modest conception—to reduce the scope of efforts by concentrating on individual sectors of the economy and move in the direction of dealing with relatively small and circumscribed problems. They seek to discover an actual opportunity for decision, to elaborate a few alternatives and to discuss their probable consequences in a limited way. They cut their costs of calculations by vastly reducing the magnitude of the tasks they set for themselves.

This approach is basically conservative. It takes for granted the existing distribution of wealth and power. It works with whatever price mechanism exists. It seeks not to influence many decisions at once but only a few. Now the ordinary men who would otherwise have made these decisions in the absence of planners also concentrate on a very narrow area of specialization; they also consider a few different ways of doing things; they also estimate the probable consequences in a limited way, and they also choose the alternative that seems best under the circumstances. By making planning manageable it appears we have made it indistinguishable from ordinary processes of decision. Planning has been rescued by diminishing, if not entirely obliterating, the difference between it and everyday decisionmaking. Of what, then, do the advantages of planning consist?

Maybe we have been looking at planning in the wrong way. The place to look for the virtues of planning, perhaps, is not in the world but in the word. Planning is good, it seems, because it is good to plan.

Planning is not really defended for what it does but for what it symbolizes. Planning, identified with reason, is conceived to be the way in which intelligence is applied to social problems. The efforts of planners are presumably better than other people's because they result in policy proposals that are systematic, efficient, coordinated, consistent, and rational. It is words like these that convey the superiority of planning. The virtue of planning is that it embodies universal norms of rational choice.

Planning as Rationality

Certain key terms appear over and over again: planning is good because it is *systematic* rather than random, *efficient* rather than wasteful, *coordinated* rather than helter-skelter, *consistent* rather than contradictory, and above all, *rational* rather than unreasonable. In the interest of achieving a deeper understanding of why planning is preferred, it will be helpful to consider these norms as instructions to decisionmakers. What would they do if they followed them?

Be systematic! What does it mean to say that decisions should be made in a systematic manner? A word like "careful" will not do because planners cannot be presumed to be more careful than other people. Perhaps "orderly" is better; it implies a checklist of items to be taken into account, but anyone can make a list. Being systematic implies further that one knows the right variables in the correct order to put into the list, and can specify the relationship among them. The essential meaning of systematic, therefore, is having qualities of a system, that is a series of variables whose interactions are known and whose outputs can be predicted from knowledge of their inputs. System, therefore, is another word for theory or model explaining and predicting events in the real world in a parsimonious way that permits manipulation.[9] To say that one is being systematic, consequently implies that one has causal knowledge.

Here we have part of the answer we have been seeking. Planning is good because inherent in the concept is the possession of knowledge that can be used to control the world. Knowledge is hard to obtain; the mind of man is small and simple while the

---

[9] See David J. Berlinski, "Systems Analysis", *Urban Affairs Quarterly*, September 1970, 7, no. 1, pp. 104–126.

world is large and complex. Hence the temptation to imply by a cover word possession of the very thing, causal knowledge, that is missing.

Be efficient! There is in modern man a deeply-rooted belief that objectives should be obtained at the least cost. Who can quarrel with that? But technical efficiency should never be considered by itself. It does not tell you where to go but only that you should arrive there (or part way) by the least effort.

The great questions are: efficiency for whom and for what? There are some goals (destroying other nations in nuclear war, decreasing the living standards of the poverty-stricken in order to benefit the wealthy) that one does not wish achieved at all, let alone efficiently. Efficiency, therefore, raises once more the prior question of objectives.

One of the most notable characteristics of national objectives is that they tend to be vague, multiple and contradictory. Increasing national income is rarely the only social objective. It has to be traded off against more immediate consumption objectives, such as raising the living standards of rural people. Cultural objectives such as encouraging the spread of native languages and crafts, may have to be undertaken at a sacrifice of income. Political objectives, such as the desire to improve racial harmony or assert national independence, may lead to distribution of investment funds to economically unprofitable regions and to rejection of certain kinds of foreign aid. A great deal depends on which objectives enter into national priorities first, because there is seldom room for emphasis on more than a few.

Stress on efficiency assumes that objectives are agreed upon. Conflict is banished. The very national unity to which the plan is supposed to contribute turns out to be one of its major assumptions.

Coordinate! Coordination is one of the golden words of our time. I cannot offhand think of any way in which the word is used that implies disapproval. Policies should be coordinated; they should not run every which-way. No one wishes their children to be described as uncoordinated. Many of the world's ills are attributed to lack of coordination in government. Yet, so far as we know, there has never been a serious effort to analyze the term. It requires and deserves full discussion. All that can be done here, however, is barely to open up the subject.

Policies should be mutually supportive rather than contradictory. People should not work at cross purposes. The participants in any particular activity should contribute to a common purpose at the right time and in the right amount to achieve coordination. A should facilitate B in order to achieve C. From this intuitive sense of coordination four important (and possibly contradictory) meanings can be derived.

If there is a common objective, then efficiency requires that it be achieved with the least input of resources. When these resources are supplied by a number of different actors, hence the need for coordination, they must all contribute their proper share at the correct time. If their actions are efficient, that means they contributed just what they should and no more or less.

Coordination, then, equals efficiency, which is highly prized because achieving it means avoiding bad things: duplication, overlapping and redundancy. These are bad because they result in unnecessary effort, thereby expending resources that might be used more effectively for other purposes. But now we shall complicate matters by introducing another criterion that is (for good reason) much less heard in discussion of planning. I refer to reliability, the probability that a particular function will be performed. Heretofore we have assumed that reliability was taken care of in the definition of efficiency. It has been discussed as if the policy in mind had only to work once. Yet we all know that major problems of designing policies can center on the need to have them work at a certain level of reliability. For this reason, as Martin Landau has so brilliantly demonstrated, redundancy is built-in to most human enterprises.[10] We ensure against failure by having adequate reserves and by creating several mechanisms to perform a single task in case one should fail.

Coordination of complex activities requires redundancy. Telling us to avoid duplication gives us no useful instruction at all; it is just a recipe for failure. What we need to know is how much and what kind of redundancy to build-in to our programs. The larger the number of participants in an enterprise, the more difficult the problem of coordination, the greater the need for redundancy.

Participants in a common enterprise may act in a contradictory fashion because of ignorance; when informed of their place in the scheme of things, they may obediently be expected to behave properly. If we relax the assumption that a common purpose is involved, however, and admit the possibility (indeed the likelihood) of conflict over goals, then coordination becomes another term for coercion. Since actors A and B disagree with goal C, they can only be coordinated by being told what to do and doing it. The German word, *Gleichschaltung*, used by the Nazis in the sense of enforcing a rigid conformity, can give us some insight into this particular usage of coordination. To coordinate one must be able to get others to do things they do not want to do. Coordination thus becomes a form of coercive power.

When one bureaucrat tells another to coordinate a policy, he means that it should be cleared with other official participants who have some stake in the matter. This is a way of sharing the blame in case things go wrong (each initial on the documents being another hostage against retribution). Since they cannot be coerced, their consent must be obtained. Bargaining must take place to reconcile the differences with the result that the policy may be modified, even at the cost of compromising its original purposes. Coordination in this sense is another word for consent.

Coordination means achieving efficiency and reliability, consent and coercion. Telling another person to achieve coordination, therefore, does not tell him what to do. He does not know whether to coerce or bargain or what mixture of efficiency and reliability to attempt. Here we have another example of an apparently desirable trait of planning that covers up the central problems—conflict versus cooperation, coercion versus consent—that its invocation is supposed to resolve. Planning suffers from the same disability that Herbert Simon illustrated for proverbial wisdom in administration:[11] each apparently desirable trait may be countered by its opposite—look before you leap, but he who hesitates is lost. An apt illustration is the use of "consistency".

Be consistent! Do not run in all directions at once. Consistency may be conceived

---

[10] Martin Landau, "Redundancy, Rationality, and the Problem of Duplication and Overlap", *Public Administration Review* (July 1969) vol. XXIX, pp. 346–358.

[11] Herbert Simon, "The Proverbs of Administration," *Public Administration Review* (Winter 1946) vol. VI, pp. 53–67.

as horizontal (at a moment in time) or vertical (over a series of time periods extending into the future). Vertical consistency requires that the same policy be pursued, horizontal consistency that it mesh with others existing at the same time. The former requires continuity of a powerful regime able to enforce its preferences, the latter tremendous knowledge of how policies affect one another. These are demanding prerequisites. One requires extraordinary rigidity to ensure continuity, the other unusual flexibility to achieve accommodation with other policies. Be firm, be pliant, are hard directions to follow at one and the same time.

The divergent directions implied in the term suggest that the virtues of consistency should not be taken for granted. It may well be desirable to pursue a single tack with energy and devotion but it may also prove valuable to hedge one's bets. Consistency secures a higher payoff for success but also imposes a steeper penalty for failure. If several divergent policies are being pursued in the same area they may interfere with each other but there also may be a greater chance that one will succeed. The admonition "Be consistent" may be opposed by the proverb, "Don't put all your eggs in the same basket."

Consistency is not wholly compatible with adaptation. While it may be desirable to pursue a steady course, it is also commonsensical to adapt to changing circumstances. There is the model of the unchanging objective pursued by numerous detours and tactical retreats but never abandoned and ultimately achieved. There is also the model of learning in which experience leads men to alter their objectives as well as the means of obtaining them. They may come to believe the cost is too high or they may learn they prefer a different objective. Apparent inconsistency may turn out to be a change in objectives. If both means and ends, policies and objectives, are changing simultaneously, consistency may turn out to be a will o' the wisp that eludes one's grasp whenever one tries to capture it.[12] The resulting inconsistency may not matter so much, however, as long as alternative courses of action are thoroughly examined at each point of decision.

Consider alternatives! Which ones? How many? Answers to these questions depend on the inventiveness of the planners; the acknowledged constraints; (such as limited funds, social values), and the cost in terms of time, talent, and money, that can be

---

[12] It is, by the way, often difficult to know when inconsistent actions are taking place. Leaving aside obtaining accurate information, there are serious conceptual problems. Policies are often stated in general terms that leave ample scope for varying interpretations of their intent. Ambiguity sometimes performs a political function by enabling people (who might otherwise disagree if everything was made clear) to get together. There cannot then be a firm criterion against which to judge consistency. There is also the question of conflicting perspectives among actors and observers. The observer may note an apparent commitment to a certain level and type of investment and see it vitiated by diversion of funds to wage increases. To the observer this means inconsistency. The actor, however, may feel consistent in pursuing his goal of political support. Given any two policies that lead to conflicts among two values one can always find a third value by which they are reconciled. Investment seemd to bring support when it was announced and so does spending for other purposes when its turn comes. The actors' values may be rephrased as "the highest possible investment so long as it does not seriously affect immediate political support." In view of the pressures to meet the needs of different people variously situated in society, most decisions are undoubtedly made on such a contingent basis. This is what it means to adapt to changing circumstance. As the goals of the actors shift with the times, consistency becomes a moving target, difficult to hit at the best of times, impossible to locate at the worst.

spent on each. While it used to be popular to say that all alternatives should be systematically compared, it has become evident that this won't work; knowledge is lacking and the cost is too high. The number of alternatives considered could easily be infinite if the dimensions of the problem (such as time, money, skill and size) are continuous.

Let us suppose that only a small number of alternatives will be considered. Which of the many conceivable ones should receive attention? Presumably those will be selected that are believed most compatible with existing values and to work most efficiently. But this presupposes that the planner knows at the beginning how the analysis will turn out; otherwise he must reject some alternatives to come up with the preferred set. At the same time there are other matters up for decision and choices must be made about whether they are to be given analytical time and attention. The planner needs rules telling him when to intervene in regard to which possible decisions and how much time to devote to each one. His estimate of the ultimate importance of the decision undoubtedly matters, but also it requires predictive ability he may not have. He is likely to resort to simple rules such as the amount of money involved in the decision and an estimate of his opportunities for influencing it.

We have gone a long way from the simple advice to consider alternatives. Now we know that this command does not tell anyone which decisions should concern him, how many alternatives he should consider, how much time and attention to devote to them or whether he knows enough to make the enterprise worthwhile. To say that alternatives should be considered is to suggest that something better must exist without being able to say what it is.

Be rational! If rationality means achieving one's goals in the optimal way, it refers here to technical efficiency, the principle of least effort. As Paul Diesing argues,[13] however, one can conceive of several levels of rationality for different aspects of society. There is the rationality of legal norms and of social structures as well as political rationality, which speaks to the maintenance of structures for decision, and economic rationality which is devoted to increasing national wealth.

What is good for the political system may not be good for the economy and *vice versa*. The overweening emphasis upon economic growth in Pakistan may have contributed to the relative neglect of the question of governmental legitimacy in the eastern regions. Any analysis of public policy that does not consider incompatibilities among the different realms of rationality is bound to be partial and misleading.

Strict economic rationality means getting the most national income out of a given investment. The end is to increase real GNP, no matter who receives it, and the means is an investment expenditure, no matter who pays for it. To be economically rational is to increase growth to its maximum. Speaking of economic rationality is a way of smuggling in identification with the goal of economic development without saying so.

Rationality is also used in the broader sense of reason. The rational man has goals that he tries to achieve by being systematic, efficient, consistent and so on. Since rationality in the sense of reason has no independent meaning of its own it

---

[13] Paul Diesing, *Reason in Society* (Urbana: University of Illinois Press, 1962).

can only have such validity as is imparted by the norms that tell us about what reasonable action is.

The injunction to plan (!!) is empty. The key terms associated with it are proverbs or platitudes. Pursue goals! Consider alternatives! Obtain knowledge! Exercise power! Obtain consent! Or be flexible but do not alter your course. Planning stands for unresolved conflicts.

Yet planning has acquired a reputation for success in some rich countries. Perhaps a certain level of affluence is required before planning becomes effective. Instead of stacking the deck against planning by asking whether it works in poor nations, let us play its best cards by looking at the record under the most propitious circumstances.

Planning in Rich Countries

Although I have geared my remarks to conditions existing in poor countries, they apply to rich ones as well. Formal planning aside, they are better able than poor nations to control their future. Governments in rich nations have more resources on which to draw, more adequate machinery for mobilizing them, and more trained people to make use of them. They can afford more failures as well as capitalize on their successes. Their prosperity is not guaranteed but their chances to do well for themselves are much higher than in the poor countries. It is possible that the failure of formal economic planning in rich countries actually has been hidden by their wealth. Confrontation with experience in formal planning has been avoided by casting the debate in terms that avoid the central question.

The debate over national economic planning in the past four decades has been conducted largely in terms of dichotomies: the individual versus the state; freedom versus dictatorship; private enterprise versus state control; price systems versus hierarchical command; rational economic choice versus irrational political interference. The great questions were: could state planning be reconciled with personal liberty? Was central administrative command a better or worse way to make decisions than dependence on prices determined in economic markets? Would rational modes of economic thought, designed to increase national income in the long run, be able to overcome irrational political forces seeking to accumulate power in the short run? All these questions assume that national economic planning—as distinct from mere arbitrary political intervention—is a real possibility. But—if it doesn't work—if the goals of the plan do not move from the paper on which they are written to the society to which they are supposed to refer, then why worry about it; it can neither crush nor liberate mankind.

Is there a single example of successful national economic planning? The Soviet Union has had central planning and has experienced economic growth. But the growth has not been exceptional and has not followed the plan. Is there a single country whose economic life over a period of years has been guided by an economic plan so that the targets set out in the plan bear a modest resemblance to events as they actually occur? No doubt each reader will be tempted to furnish the one he has heard about. Yet the very fact (as anyone can verify by posing the same query) that it is hard to name an example suggests that the record of planning has hardly been brilliant.

For all we know, the few apparent successes (if there are any) are no more than random occurrences.

When really pushed to show results, somewhere, some place, sometime, planning advocates are likely to cite the accomplishments of indicative planning on the French model as the modern success story of their trade. The French example is indeed a good one because it puts the least possible demands on the planning enterprise. Where many national plans are comprehensive, in the sense that they try to set targets for virtually all sectors of the economy, the French dealt only with the major ones. While planners in some countries have to set the entire range of prices, the modified market economy in France makes this burden unnecessary. France has not been afflicted by the rapid turnover of key personnel that has contributed to the discontinuities in planning elsewhere. France is rich in many ways besides money—information, personnel, communication—that should make it easier for her planners to guide future events. Where some plans hope to be authoritative, in that both government and private industry are required to follow the guidelines contained in them, the French plans have been indicative, that is, essentially voluntary. While efforts are made to reward those who cooperate, there are no sanctions for failure to comply. French plans indicate the directions wise and prudent men would take, if they were wise and prudent. If planning does not work in France, where conditions are so advantageous, it would be unlikely to do better in less favorable circumstances.[14]

But like it or not, formal planning in France is a failure. Economic growth has taken place but not according to instructions in the plan. Targets have not been met in the first four plans. Neither for individual sectors nor for the economy as a whole have growth rates been approximated. Governments have consistently ignored the plan or opposed it in order to meet immediate needs. In order to justify the idea of planning, Steven Cohen, author of the best book on the subject, *Modern Capitalist Planning: The French Experience*,[15] suggests that if there were a democratic majority agreed on its goals, if their purposes could be maintained over a period of years, if they had the knowledge and power necessary to make the world behave as they wish, if they could control the future, then central planning would work. If . . .!

What Cohen's book actually shows is that limited economic planning in a major industrial country with considerable financial resources and talent did not work. What hope would there be for poor nations whose accumulated wealth is definitely less, whose reservoir of human talent is so much smaller, whose whole life is surrounded by far greater uncertainties? How could planning help radically change Africa or Asia when it has failed to produce even limited changes in France?

Significant control of the future demands mobilizing knowledge, power, and resources throughout a society. It does no good to propose measures that require nonexistent information, missing resources, and unobtainable consent. The planner cannot create, at the moment he needs them, things his society does not possess. He can, however, assume them to be true in that artificial world created in the plan. But planning is not a policy. It is presumably a way to create policies related to one

---

[14] The following paragraphs on France are taken from Aaron Wildavsky, "Does Planning Work?" *Public Interest*, Summer 1971, no. 24, pp. 95–104.
[15] Harvard University Press, Cambridge, Mass., 1970.

another over time so as to achieve desired objectives. The immense presumption involved, the incredible demands, not merely on the financial, but on the intellectual resources of societal organization explain the most important thing about national planning—it does not work because no large and complex society can figure out what simple and unambiguous things it wants to do, or in what clear order of priority, or how to get them done.

Before admitting defeat the advocate of planning would at least gesture in the direction of Japan, whose extraordinary economic growth has taken place in a period during which "the government has established long-term economic plans as the guiding principle for economic policies."[16] Of the dozen or so economic plans formulated since the end of the Second World War, five were officially adopted by the government and four have advanced far enough to appraise the fit between intention and accomplishment. In his splendid account, Isamu Miyazaki notes that the Five-year Plan for Economic Self-Support for fiscal years 1955–60 called for a five per cent rate of growth in gross national product. But "the economic growth rate turned out to be twice as large as what had been projected in the plan, and the growth in mining and manufacturing production and exports proved far greater than that envisaged in the plan. Thus the targets in the plan were achieved in almost two years." A second effort, the New Long-Range Economic Plan for fiscal years 1958–62, set the desired growth rate at 6.5%. "However, in actual performance, the rate again exceeded the projection, reaching about 10% on the average during the plan period."[17] The Doubling National Income Plan for fiscal years 1961–70, the third effort, postulated a real growth rate of some 7 to 8%. Miyazaki states that "In actual performance, however, the rate reached 11% on the average from fiscal 1961–63. Particularly notable was the performance of private equipment investment, which grew by almost 40% in fiscal 1960, followed by an additional 29% increase in fiscal 1961. This meant that the level which was expected to be reached in the final year of the plan was achieved in the first year."[18] The fourth and last national economic effort for which the returns are in, the Economic and Social Development Plan for fiscal years 1967–71, resulted in even larger gaps between promise and fulfillment. According to Miyazaki, it was

> estimated that the real growth rate would reach nearly 13% on the average for fiscal 1967–70 against 8.2% in the plan. The rate of increase of private equipment investment (nominal) was twice as large as the 10.6% of the forecast. Since the economic growth rate and private equipment investment have gone far beyond the projection, the plan cannot any more fulfill the role of a guide to private economic activities.[19]

Evidently the economy has been growing faster than anyone thought. Yet the purpose of plans and planners must surely be to guide economic growth in the expected direction, not to gasp in amazement at how wonderfully the country has grown contrary to (or regardless of) what they indicated. If plans are not guides, they have lost any meaning they might have had.

Questioning the meaningfulness of planning is likely to lead to impatience on the grounds that it represents man's best hope. What have you got to offer in its place?

---
[16] Isamu Miyazaki, "Economic Planning in Postwar Japan", *The Journal of the Institute of Developing Economies* (December 1970), vol. VIII, no. 4, p. 369.
[17] *Ibid*, p. 373.   [18] *Ibid*, p. 374.   [19] *Ibid*, p. 378.

That is likely to be the response. Putting the question that way suggests that planning provides a solution to problems. But planning is not a solution to any problem. It is just a way of restating in other language the problems we do not know how to solve.

But where's the harm? If planning is not the epitome of reason, it appears innocuous enough. If some people feel better in the presence of formal planning why not let it go on?

Formal Planning: Costs and Benefits

Planning is like motherhood; everyone is for it because it seems so virtuous. Overpopulation on one side has not given birth to doubts on the other. If we leave out the old controversy over whether centrally directed economies are better or worse than reliance on the price mechanism, there has been virtually no discussion of possible adverse effects of formal planning. Although planners are often economists who profess to believe that there is a cost for everything, they have not applied this insight to their own activity. It may be instructive, therefore, to list a few of the possible costs of planning.

The plan may provide a substitute for action. Working on it may justify delay as the cry-word goes out, "Let's not act until the plan is ready." Delay may also be encouraged because the planning commission becomes another checkpoint in an already cumbersome administrative apparatus. If its consent or comments are required and its people overburdened, planners may discourage the speedy adaptation to emerging events that is so essential in the volatile environments of the poor countries.

Planning uses important human resources. In nations where talent is chronically scarce, men who might be contributing to important public and private decisions may be wading through huge bodies of data or constructing elaborate models whose applicability is doubtful at best. The planners not only take up their own time, they intrude on others. They call in people from the operating ministries who need to answer their questions and, if necessary, run around countering their advice. Time, attention and talent that might be spent improving the regular administration on which the nation depends, may have to be invested in internal hassling with the planners.

The direct financial cost of paying the planners and their consultants may be small, but the long-run financial costs to the nation may be high. Planners tend to be spenders. Their rationale is that they will help promote current investments that will lead to future increases in income. They, therefore, have a vested interest in increasing the total amount of investment. Frustrated at the efforts of the finance ministry to keep spending down, the planners have an incentive to get hold of their own sources of funds. They thereby contribute to one of the basic financial problems of poor countries—the fragmentation of national income. Then they become another independent entity able to resist whatever central authority exists.

Investments may come in large packages or small amounts, in humdrum improvement of human resources, or in spectacular projects. The tendency of planners is to seek the large and loud over the small and quiet. Their talents are better suited to the analysis of big projects that have a substantial impact on the economy and that, by their cost, justify expensive analytical attention. They have too few people to supervise the multitude of small projects whose total impact may nevertheless be more important to the nation than the few big projects. Their fame and fortune depend on identification with visible objects and these are not to be found in the rural classroom or the feeder road.

The stock in trade of the planner is the big model. Sometimes it appears the larger and more complex the model (though it may actually be nothing more than a long list of variables) the more important the planner. Only he can interpret it and he may gain a kind of status from being its guardian. Bad decisions may result because these models are taken beyond any merits they might have. A spurious specificity may ignore the fact that the data used is bad, that the relevant calculations cannot be performed or that the model does not apply to the case at hand. As bad decisions are dressed up in pseudo-analytical garb, ministerial officials may become unduly cynical about analysis. When the devil quotes scripture, holy writ becomes suspect.

The planner makes his way by talking about the need of considering the future in present decisions. Yet poor countries have great difficulty in knowing where they are (even where they have been) in terms of income, expenditure, manpower and the like. Retrodiction is as much their problem as prediction. Yet the planners may neglect efforts to bring knowledge up to date because they have little stake in the present. Indeed, they may work hard to create what turn out to be imaginary future problems, as a way of gaining additional influence over forthcoming decisions.

The optimism of the planners may be desirable in order to give the nation a sense of hope amidst crushing burdens. This optimism, however, may result in unreal expectations that cannot be met. Demands may be made in anticipation of future income that does not materialize. Subsequent disappointment may create political difficulty where none need have occurred.

Though their formal plans may be irrelevant, actions of planners as an interest group may have impact. There is no need for us to argue here that formal planners are necessarily wrong. It suffices to say that they have their own built-in biases, and that these sometimes lead to unfortunate consequences. Why, then, is the worth of formal planning so rarely questioned?

Despite intermittent disaffection with planning—the contrast between the plan and the nation mocked the planners—it was difficult for national elites to forgo sight of the promised land. They so wanted an easy way out of their troubles. Besides, they soon discovered that the nonoperational quality of planning could be helpful. If it did not commit them to anything, it might yet be made into a useful instrument.

Formal planning may be useful as an escape from the seemingly insurmountable problems of the day. If life is gloomy in the present then a plan can help offset that by creating a rosier vision of the future. If groups cannot be indulged in the present, they can be shown the larger places they occupy in future plans. Formal planning can also be a way of buying off the apostles of rationality by involving them in tasks that take them away from the real decisions.

The reputation of a nation's leaders may depend on their having a glowing plan. International elites may expect it as evidence of competence and dedication to determine control of the future rather than simply being overtaken by events. International prestige may rest to some degree on one of the few national products that are visible and transportable—a beautifully bound set of national plans.

A government may find uses for planners as a group apart from the regular bureaucratic apparatus. Planning machinery may be a way deliberately to introduce competitive elements into the administration, either as a means of provoking reform or of blocking departmental ambitions. Planners may be used as a source of ideas outside regular administrative channels (as a kind of general staff for the executive) bypassing the normal chain of command. All this, however, has little to do with their ostensible reason for being, namely, planning, but much to do with the fact that since planners do exist, they may as well serve the purposes of others.

Trivial functions aside, planning might have withered from disappointment and disuse had not new clients insisted on it. When the United States made foreign aid fashionable, a number of poor countries were in a position to secure sums of money that were large in comparison to their small budgets. This created a need for institutional mechanisms that could do two things: spend surpluses and obtain foreign aid. The United States would not, of course, do anything so simple as to give money just because a country said it needed it; capitalist America insisted upon a plan. Since an existing bureaucracy would have had no experience in putting together these documents, it was necessary to create a mechanism for preparing them. It did not matter whether the plan worked; what did count was the ability to produce a document which looked like a plan, and that meant using economists and other technical personnel. If these skills were not available within the country, they had to be imported in the form of planners and foreign aid advisors. A demand existed and an entirely new industry was created to fill the need. Thus national planning may be justified on a strict cash basis: planners may bring in more money from abroad than it costs to support them at home.

These uses for formal planning suggest that I have been looking at plans, planners and planning commissions in the wrong way. I have been assessing (in the language of the sociologist) their manifest functions, the purposes they are supposed to serve. Formal planning also has latent functions; it serves other purposes as well.

Planning as Faith

While there is every evidence that national plans are unsuccessful, there is virtually no evidence that they do good, however "good" might be described. Yet no one thinks of giving them up. When people continue to do things that do not help them the subject cries out for investigation. Neither the governments nor the people they rule are presumed to be masochists. Why, then, do they not change their behavior?

Planners are men of secular faith. The word "faith" is used advisedly because it is hardly possible to say that planning has been justified by works. Once the word is in them it leaps over the realm of experience. They are confirmed in their beliefs no matter what happens. Planning is good if it succeeds and society is bad if it fails. That is why planners so often fail to learn from experience. To learn one must make mistakes and planning cannot be one of them.

Planning concerns man's efforts to make the future in his own image. If he loses control of his own destiny, he fears being cast into the abyss. Alone and afraid, man is at the mercy of strange and unpredictable forces, so he takes whatever comfort he can by challenging the fates. He shouts his plans into the storm of life. Even if all he hears is the echo of his own voice, he is no longer alone. To abandon his faith in planning would unleash the terror locked in him. For if God is dead, only man can save himself.

The greater his need, the more man longs to believe in the reality of his vision. Since he can only create the future he desires on paper he transfers his loyalties to the plan. Since the end is never in sight he sanctifies the journey; the process of planning becomes holy. Since he is the end of his own striving, his reason becomes the object of his existence. Planning is reason and reason is embodied in the plan. Worshipping it, he glorifies himself. But a secular idolatry is no easier to maintain than a religious one.

Faith in planning has an intermittent hold on political leaders. Their ascension to power is full of everlasting hope. The end of despair, they tell their people, is within sight. The leaders too, are overwhelmed by the gap between the future they promise and the present they cannot change. Progress is slow and painful. By allying themselves with the forces of reason, by embracing the plan as a visible sign of salvation, they hope to overcome the past and create a new life for their nation. When plans fail governmental leaders are tempted to abandon the god of reason. Once they have lost faith in planning, it becomes difficult for them to believe that there is any place for reasoned analysis. So they manipulate the plan and its planners for tactical purposes. If planning is reason, then reason flees when planning is in flight. Misplaced faith in the norms of rationality is easily transmuted into normless use of power.

The task of relating processes of decision to the social conditions in which they must operate is hampered because rational planning is supposed to stand as universal truth not subject to alteration through experience. It thus becomes difficult to evaluate experience; departure from the norms of planning are suspect as contradicting reason. Discussion of what seems to work in a particular context is inhibited because it may be inconsistent with "good planning practice." Rather than face up to actual conditions, planners are tempted to wish them away. If planning is a universal tool, planners find it reasonable to ask why their countries cannot live up to the requirements of rational decisionmaking. If planning is valid, they feel, nations should adjust to its demands rather than the other way round.

To save planning, planners may actually accept the blame. For if better behavior on their part would make planning work, the solution is not to abandon plans but to hire more talented planners. Martyrdom may be appropriate to their profession, but I would argue against allowing them to make the ultimate sacrifice.

Planning requires the resources, knowledge, and power of an entire people. If commodity prices suddenly fall, leading to a precipitous drop in national income, the ensuing difficulties may be attributed to faulty predictions by planners, but the relationship of the nation to international markets would seem to be the proper realm in which to seek scapegoats. Should it turn out that political leadership is divided, that may be because the planners could not convince them all, but it is more likely the result of causes deeply rooted in the nation's political history. It seems odd to blame the planners because the political leaders who agreed on a particular set of priorities are suddenly replaced by another group of men with quite different preferences. If private citizens send their capital abroad rather than investing it at home, it is the values of economic elites rather than the investment plan that deserves priority investigation. When taxes are not collected because social mores prohibit direct personal confrontations, national culture, not the national plan, is the place to look. When planning is viewed as a function of the society's ability to control its future, we seem better able to explain difficulties than if we look at the alleged shortcomings of planners.

If formal planning fails not merely in one nation at one time but in virtually all nations most of the time, the defects are unlikely to be found in maladroit or untalented planners. Nor can a failure be argued successfully by saying that the countries in question are not prepared to behave rationally or to accept the advice of rational men called planners. That is only a way of saying that formal planning, after innumerable iterations, is still badly adapted to its surroundings. It cannot be rational to fail. To err is human; to sanctify the perpetuation of mistakes is something else. If governments perseverate in national planning, it must be because their will to believe triumphs over their experience. Planning is not so much a subject for the social scientist as for the theologian.

Strategic Change: "Logical Incrementalism"

James Brian Quinn   Dartmouth College

If you are a devotee of publications like the SMR, you may have come to believe that formal planning, replete with the latest analytical models, provides the ideal means by which corporate strategic goals should be established. Your faith may have been shaken, however, if you read this author's "Strategic Goals: Process and Politics" in the Fall 1977 SMR. This article, the second in what will be a three-part series, goes on to explain how "logical incrementalism" operates in several major corporations. The author further argues that such "muddling," far from being a "necessary evil," may provide the normative model for strategic decision making. Ed.

"When I was younger I always conceived of a room where all these [strategic] concepts were worked out for the whole company. Later I didn't find any such room. . . . The strategy [of the company] may not even exist in the mind of one man. I certainly don't know where it is written down. It is simply transmitted in the series of decisions made." Interview quote.

When well-managed major organizations make significant changes in strategy, the approaches they use frequently bear little resemblance to the rational-analytical systems so often touted in the planning literature. The full strategy is rarely written down in any one place. The processes used to arrive at the total strategy are typically fragmented, evolutionary, and largely intuitive. Although one can usually find embedded in these fragments some very refined pieces of formal strategic analysis, the real strategy tends to evolve as internal decisions and external events flow together to create a new, widely shared consensus for action among key members of the top management team. Far from being an abrogation of good management practice, the rationale behind this kind of strategy formulation is so powerful that it perhaps provides the normative model for strategic decision making — rather than the step-by-step "formal systems planning" approach so often espoused.

The Formal Systems Planning Approach
A strong normative literature states what factors should be included in a systematically planned strategy[1] and how to analyze and relate these factors step-by-step.[2] The main elements of this "formal planning approach" include: (1) analyzing one's own internal situation: strengths, weaknesses, competencies, problems; (2) projecting current product lines, profits, sales, investment needs into the future; (3) analyzing selected external environments and opponents' actions for opportunities and threats; (4) establishing broad goals as targets for subordinate groups' plans; (5) identifying the gap between expected and desired results; (6) communicating planning assumptions to the divisions; (7) requesting proposed plans from subordinate groups with more specific target goals, resource needs, and supporting action plans; (8) occasionally asking for special studies of alternatives, contingencies, or longer-term opportunities; (9) reviewing and approving divisional plans and summing these for corporate needs; (10) developing long-term budgets presumably related to plans; (11) implementing plans; and (12) monitoring and evaluating performance (presumably against plans, but usually against budgets).

While this approach is excellent for some purposes, it tends to focus unduly on measurable quantitative factors and to under-emphasize the vital qualitative, organizational, and power-behavioral factors which so often determine strategic success in one situation versus another. In practice, such planning is just one building block in a continuous stream of events that really determine corporate strategy.

The Power-Behavioral Approach
Other investigators have provided important insights on the crucial psychological, power, and behavioral relationships in strategy formulation. Among other things, these have enhanced understanding about: the multiple goal structures of organizations,[3] the politics of strategic decisions,[4] executive bargaining and negotiation processes,[5] satisficing (as opposed to maximizing) in decision making,[6] the role of coalitions in strategic man-

James Brian Quinn is the William and Josephine Buchanan Professor of Management at The Amos Tuck School of Business Administration, Dartmouth College. Dr. Quinn holds the B.S. degree in engineering from Yale University, the M.B.A. degree from the Harvard Business School, and the Ph.D. degree from Columbia University. As a renown lecturer and a special consultant to the U.S. Congress and the State Department, Dr. Quinn has served on a number of National Academy of Sciences panels and is currently a member on its Board on Science and Technology for International Development. Dr. Quinn has written widely on the topic of corporate and national policy questions.

agement,[7] and the practice of "*muddling*" in the public sphere.[8] Unfortunately, however, many power-behavioral studies have been conducted in settings far removed from the realities of strategy formulation. Others have concentrated solely on human dynamics, power relationships, and organizational processes and ignored the ways in which systematic data analysis shapes and often dominates crucial aspects of strategic decisions. Finally, few have offered much normative guidance for the strategist.

The Study

Recognizing the contributions and limitations of both approaches, I attempted to document the dynamics of actual strategic change processes in some ten major companies as perceived by those most knowledgeably and intimately involved in them. These companies varied with respect to products, markets, time horizons, technological complexities, and national versus international dimensions.[9] While the problems of this kind of research are well recognized,[10] many precautions were taken in order to insure accuracy.[11]

Summary Findings

Several important findings have begun to emerge from these investigations.

— Neither the "power-behavioral" nor the "formal systems planning" paradigm adequately characterizes the way successful strategic processes operate.

— Effective strategies tend to emerge from a series of "strategic subsystems," each of which attacks a specific class of strategic issue (e.g., acquisitions, divestitures, or major reorganizations) in a disciplined way, but which is blended incrementally and opportunistically into a cohesive pattern that becomes the company's strategy.

— The logic behind each "subsystem" is so powerful that, to some extent, it may serve as a normative approach for formulating these key elements of strategy in large companies.

— Because of cognitive and process limits, almost all of these subsystems — and the formal planning activity itself — must be managed and linked together by an approach best described as "logical incrementalism."

— Such incrementalism is not "muddling." It is a purposeful, effective, proactive management technique for improving and integrating *both* the analytical and behavioral aspects of strategy formulation.

This article will document these findings, suggest the logic behind several important "subsystems" for strategy formulation, and outline some of the management and thought processes executives in large organizations use to synthesize them into effective corporate strategies. Such strategies embrace those patterns of high leverage decisions (on major goals, policies, and action sequences) which affect the viability and direction of the entire enterprise or determine its competitive posture for an extended time period.

Critical Strategic Issues

Although certain "hard data" decisions (e.g., on product-market position or resource allocations) tend to dominate the analytical literature,[12] executives identified other "soft" changes that have at least as much importance in shaping their concern's strategic posture. Most often cited were changes in the company's:

1. Overall organizational structure or its basic management style;

2. Relationships with the government or other external interest groups;

3. Acquisition, divestiture, or divisional

control practices;

4. International posture and relationships;
5. Innovative capabilities or personnel motivations as affected by growth;
6. Worker and professional relationships reflecting changed social expectations and values;
7. Past or anticipated technological environments.

When executives were asked to "describe the processes through which their company arrived at its new posture" vis-à-vis each of these critical domains, several important points emerged. First, few of these issues lent themselves to quantitative modeling techniques or perhaps even formal financial analyses. Second, successful companies used a different "subsystem" to formulate strategy for each major class of strategic issues, yet these "subsystems" were quite similar among companies even in very different industries. Finally, no single formal analytical process could handle all strategic variables simultaneously on a planned basis. Why?

Precipitating Events
Often external or internal events, over which managements had essentially no control, would precipitate urgent, piecemeal, interim decisions which inexorably shaped the company's future strategic posture. One clearly observes this phenomenon in: the decisions forced on General Motors by the 1973-74 oil crisis,[13] the shift in posture pressed upon Exxon by sudden nationalizations, or the dramatic opportunities allowed for Haloid Corporation[14] and Pilkington Brothers, Ltd.[15] by the unexpected inventions of xerography and float glass.

In these cases, analyses from earlier formal planning cycles did contribute greatly, as long as the general nature of the contingency had been anticipated. They broadened the information base available (as in Exxon's case), extended the options considered (Haloid-Xerox), created shared values to guide decisions about precipitating events in consistent directions (Pilkington), or built up resource bases, management flexibilities, or active search routines for opportunities whose specific nature could not be defined in advance (General Mills, Pillsbury).[16] But no organization — no matter how brilliant, rational, or imaginative — could possibly foresee the timing, severity, or even the nature of all such precipitating events. Further, when these events did occur there might be neither time, resources, nor information enough to undertake a full formal strategic analysis of all possible options and their consequences. Yet early decisions made under stress conditions often meant new thrusts, precedents, or lost opportunities that were difficult to reverse later.

An Incremental Logic
Recognizing this, top executives usually consciously tried to deal with precipitating events in an incremental fashion. Early commitments were kept broadly formative, tentative, and subject to later review. In some cases neither the company nor the external players could understand the full implications of alternative actions. All parties wanted to test assumptions and have an opportunity to learn from and adapt to the others' responses. Such behavior clearly occurred during the 1973-74 oil crisis; the ensuing interactions improved the quality of decisions for all. It also recurred frequently in other widely different contexts. For example:

◊ Neither the potential producer nor user of a completely new product or process (like xerography or float glass) could fully conceptualize its ramifications without interactive testing. All parties benefited from procedures which purposely delayed decisions and allowed mutual feedback. Some companies, like IBM or Xerox, have formalized this concept into "phase program planning" systems. They make concrete decisions only on individual phases (or stages) of new product developments, establish interactive testing procedures with customers, and postpone final configuration commitments until the latest possible moment.

Similarly, even under pressure, most top executives were extremely sensitive to organizational and power relationships and consciously managed decision processes to improve these dynamics. They often purposely delayed initial decisions, or kept such decisions vague, in order to encourage lower-level participation, to gain more information from specialists, or to build commitment to solutions. Even when a crisis atmosphere tended to shorten time horizons and make decisions more goal oriented than political, perceptive executives consciously tried to keep their options open until they understood how the crisis would affect the power bases and needs of their key constituents. For example:

◊ General Motors's top management only incrementally restructured its various car lines as it understood, step-by-step, the way in which the oil crisis and environmental demands would affect the viability of each existing divisional and dealership structure. In the aggregate these amounted to the greatest shift in balance and positioning among GM's automobile lines since Alfred P. Sloan, and management was deeply concerned about the way its decisions would influence the power and prosperity of various groups.[17]

To improve both the informational content and the process aspects of decisions surrounding precipitating events, logic dictates and practice affirms that they should normally be handled on an incremental basis.

Incrementalism in Strategic Subsystems

One also finds that an incremental logic applies in attacking many of the critical subsystems of corporate strategy. Those subsystems for considering diversification moves, divestitures, major reorganizations, or government-external relations are typical and will be described here. In each case, conscious incrementalism helps to: (1) cope with both the cognitive and process limits on each major decision, (2) build the logical-analytical framework these decisions require, and (3) create the personal and organizational awareness, understanding, acceptance, and commitment needed to implement the strategies effectively.

The Diversification Subsystem

Strategies for diversification, either through R&D or acquisitions, provide excellent examples. The formal analytical steps needed for successful diversification are well documented.[18] However, the precise directions that R&D may project the company can only be understood step-by-step as scientists uncover new phenomena, make and amplify discoveries, build prototypes, reduce concepts to practice, and interact with users during product introductions. Similarly, only as each acquisition is sequentially identified, investigated, negotiated for, and integrated into the organization can one predict its ultimate impact on the total enterprise.

A step-by-step approach is clearly necessary to guide and assess the strategic fit of each internal or external diversification candidate. Incremental processes are also required to manage the crucial psychological and power shifts that ultimately determine the program's overall direction and consequences. These processes help unify both the analytical and behavioral aspects of diversification decisions. They create the broad conceptual consensus, the risk-taking attitudes, the organizational and resource flexibilities, and the adaptive dynamism that determine both the timing and direction of diversification strategies. Most important among these processes are:

— *Generating a genuine, top-level psychological commitment to diversification.* General Mills, Pillsbury,[19] and Xerox all started their major diversification programs with broad analytical studies and goal-setting exercises designed both to build top-level consensus around the need to diversify and to establish the general directions for diversification. Without such action, top-level bargaining for resources would have continued to support only more familiar (and hence apparently less risky) old lines, and this could delay or undermine the entire diversification endeavor.

— *Consciously preparing to move opportunistically.* Organizational and fiscal resources must be built up in advance to exploit candidates as they randomly appear. And a "credible activist" for ventures must be developed and backed by someone with commitment power. All successful acquirers created the potential for "profit centered" divisions within their organizational structures, strengthened their financial-controllership capabilities, took action to create low-cost capital access, and maintained the shortest possible communication lines from the "acquisitions activist" to the resource-committing authority. All these actions integrally determined which diversifications actually could be made, the timing of their accession, and the pace they could be absorbed.

— *Building a "comfort factor" for risk taking.* Perceived risk is largely a function of one's knowledge about a field. Hence well-conceived diversification programs should anticipate a trial-and-error period during which top managers reject early proposed fields or opportunities until they have analyzed enough trial candidates to "become comfortable" with an initial selection. Early successes tend to be "sure things" close to the companies' past (real or supposed) expertise. After a few successful diversifications, managements tend to become more confident and accept other candidates — farther from traditional lines — at a faster rate. Again the way this process is handled affects both the direction and pace of the actual program.

— *Developing a new ethos.* If new divisions are more successful than the old — as they should be — they attract relatively more resources and their political power grows. Their most effective line managers move into corporate positions, and slowly the company's special competency and ethos change. Finally, the concepts and products which once dominated the company's culture may decline in importance or even disappear. Acknowledging these ultimate consequences to the organization at the beginning of a diversification program would clearly be impolitic, even if the manager both desired and could predict the probable new ethos. These factors must be handled adaptively, as opportunities present themselves and as individual leaders and power centers develop.

Each of the above processes interacts with all others (and with the random appearance of diversification candidates) to affect action sequences, elapsed time, and ultimate results in unexpected ways. Complexities are so great that few diversification programs end up as initially envisioned. Consequently, wise managers recognize the limits to systematic analysis in diversification, and use formal planning to build the "comfort levels" executives need for risk taking and to guide the program's early directions and priorities. They then modify these flexibly, step-by-step, as new opportunities, power centers, and developed competencies merge to create new potentials.

The Divestiture Subsystem

Similar practices govern the handling of divestitures. Divisions often drag along in a less-than-desired condition for years before they can be strategically divested. In some cases, ailing divisions might have just enough yield or potential to offer hoped-for viability. In others, they might represent the company's vital core from earlier years, the creations of a powerful person nearing retirement, or the psychological touchstones of the company's past traditions.

Again, in designing divestiture strategies, top executives had to reinforce vaguely felt concerns with detailed data, build up managers' comfort levels about issues, achieve participation in and commitment to decisions, and move opportunistically to make actual changes. In many cases, the precise nature of the decision was not clear at the outset. Executives often made seemingly unrelated personnel shifts or appointments which changed the value set of critical groups, or started a series of staff studies which generated awareness or acceptance of a potential problem. They might then instigate goal assessment, business review, or "planning" programs to provide broader forums for discussion and a wider consensus for action. Even then they might wait for a crisis, a crucial retirement, or an attractive sale opportunity to determine the timing and conditions of divestiture. In some cases, decisions could be direct and analytical. But when divestitures involved the psychological centers of the organization, the process had to be much more oblique and carefully orchestrated. For example:

◇ When General Rawlings became president at General Mills, he had his newly developed Staff (Corporate Analysis) Department make informal presentations to top management on key issues. Later these were expanded to formal Management Operating Reviews (MORs) with all corporate and divisional top managers and controllers present. As problem operations were identified (many "generally known for a long time"), teams of corporate and divisional people were assigned to investigate them in depth. Once needed new data systems were built and studies came into place, they focused increasing attention on some hasty post-World War II acquisitions.

First to go was a highly cyclical — and unprofitable — formula feeds business for which "there was no real heavy philosophical commitment." Then followed some other small divisions and the low-profit electronics business "which the directors didn't feel very comfortable with because it was so different. . . ." At the time, this business was headed by a recently appointed former Finance Department man, "who had no strong attachments to electronics." Only then did the Annual Reports begin to refer to these conscious moves as ones designed "to concentrate on the company's major strengths." And only then, despite earlier concern, frustration, and discontent about its commodity aspects, could the traumatic divestiture of flour milling, the core of the company's traditions, be approached.

Careful incrementalism is essential in most divestitures to disguise intentions yet create the awareness, value changes, needed data, psychological acceptance, and managerial consensus required for such decisions. Early, openly acknowledged, formal plans would clearly be invitations to disaster.

The Major Reorganization Subsystem

It is well recognized that major organizational changes are an integral part of strategy.[20] Sometimes they constitute a strategy themselves, sometimes they precede and/or precipitate a new strategy, and sometimes they help to implement a strategy. However, like many other important strategic decisions, macro-organizational moves are typically handled incrementally and outside of formal planning processes. Their effects on personal or power relationships preclude discussion in the open forums and reports of such processes.

In addition, major organizational changes have timing imperatives (or "process limits") all their own. In making any significant shifts, the executive must think through the new roles, capabilities, and probable individual reactions of the many principals affected. He may have to wait for the promotion or retirement of a valued colleague before consummating any change. He then frequently has to bring in, train, or test new people for substantial periods before he can staff key posts with confidence. During this testing period he may substantially modify his original concept of the reorganization, as he evaluates individuals' potentials, their performance in specific roles, their personal drives, and their relationships with other team members.

Because this chain of decisions affects the career development, power, affluence, and self-image of so many, the executive tends to keep close counsel in his discussions, negotiates individually with key people, and makes final commitments as late as possible in order to obtain the best matches between people's capabilities, personalities, and aspirations and their new roles. Typically, all these events do not come together at one convenient time, particularly the moment annual plans are due. Instead the executive moves opportunistically, step-by-step, selectively moving people toward a broadly conceived organizational goal, which is constantly modified and rarely articulated in detail until the last pieces fit together.

Major organizational moves may also define entirely new strategies the guiding executive cannot fully foresee. For example:

◊ When Exxon began its regional decentralization on a worldwide basis, the Executive Committee placed a senior officer and board member with a very responsive management style in a vaguely defined "coordinative role" vis-à-vis its powerful and successful European units. Over a period of two years this man sensed problems and experimented with voluntary coordinative possibilities on a pan-European basis. Only later, with greater understanding by both corporate and divisional officers, did Exxon move to a more formal "line" relationship for what became Exxon Europe. Even then the move had to be coordinated step-by-step with similar experimental shifts to regionalized consolidations in other areas of the world. All of these changes together led to an entirely new internal power balance toward regional and non-U.S. concerns and to a more responsive worldwide posture for Exxon.

◊ At General Mills, General Rawlings and his team of outside professional managers actively redefined the company's problems and opportunities in ways the prior management could not have. Once the divestitures noted above were made, the funds released were used for acquisitions, thus automatically increasing the visibility and power of the Controllership-Financial group. Similarly, with fewer large divisions competing for funds, the Consumer-Food groups rapidly increased in their importance. This ultimately led to a choice between these two groups' leaders for the next chairmanship of the company — and hence for control over the corporation's future strategy.

In such situations, executives may be able to predict the broad direction, but not the precise nature, of the ultimate strategy which will result. In some cases, such as Exxon, the rebalance of power and information relationships becomes the strategy, or at least its central element. In others, such as General Mills, organizational shifts are primarily means of triggering or implementing new strategic concepts and philosophies. But in all cases, major organizational changes create unexpected new stresses, opportunities, power bases, information centers, and credibility relationships that can affect both previous plans and future strategies in unanticipated ways. Effective reorganization decisions, therefore, allow for testing, flexibility, and feedback. Hence, they should, and usually do, evolve incrementally.

The Government-External Relations Subsystem

Almost all companies cited government and other external activist groups as among the most important forces causing significant changes in their strategic postures during the periods examined. However, when asked "how did your company arrive at its own strategy vis-à-vis these forces?" it became clear that few companies had cohesive strategies (integrated sets of goals, policies, and programs) for government-external relations, other than lobbying for or against specific legislative actions. To the extent that other strategies did exist, they were piecemeal, ad hoc, and had been derived in a very evolutionary manner. Yet there seemed to be very good reasons for such incrementalism. The following are two of the best short explanations of the way these practices develop:

> We are a very large company, and we understand that any massive overt action on our part could easily create more public antagonism than support for our viewpoint. It is also hard to say in advance exactly what public response any particular action might create. So we tend to test a number of different approaches on a small scale with only limited or local company identification. If one approach works, we'll test it further and amplify its use. If another bombs, we try to keep it from being used again. Slowly we find a series of advertising, public relations, community relations actions that seem to help. Then along comes another issue and we start all over again. Gradually the successful approaches merge into a pattern of actions that becomes our strategy. We certainly don't have an overall strategy on this, and frankly I don't think we devote enough [organizational and fiscal] resources to it. This may be our most important strategic issue.

> I [the president] start conversations with a number of knowledgeable people.... I collect articles and talk to people about how things get done in Washington in this particular field. I collect data from any reasonable source. I begin wide-ranging discussions with people inside and outside the corporation. From these a pattern eventually emerges. It's like fitting together a jigsaw puzzle. At first the vague outline of an approach appears like the sail of a ship in a puzzle. Then suddenly the rest of the puzzle becomes quite clear. You wonder why you didn't see it all along. And once it's crystallized, it's not difficult to explain to others.

In this realm, uncontrollable forces dominate. Data are very soft, often can be only subjectively sensed, and may be costly to quantify. The possible responses of individuals and groups to different stimuli are difficult to determine in advance. The number of potential opponents with power is very high, and the diversity in their viewpoints and possible modes of attack is so substantial that it is physically impossible to lay out probabilistic decision diagrams that would have much meaning. Results are unpredictable and error costs extreme. Even the best intended and most rational-seeming strategies can be converted into disasters unless they are thoroughly and interactively tested. For example:

◇ In the 1960s General Motors found that technical discussions of cost vs. benefit tradeoffs were useless against demagogic slogans like "smog kills" or "GM is the worst polluter in the world." It publicly resisted some early attempts to impose pollution standards, stating that they were "beyond the state of the art." Then after successfully completing the costly and risky development of the catalytic converter, GM had its earlier concerns thrown in its face as "foot dragging" or "lying" about technical potentials. As one executive said, "You were damned if you did and damned if you didn't."

Only after prolonged interaction with regulators, legislators, and public interest groups did GM truly understand the needs and pressure potentials of its opponents. Area by area it learned to communicate better with various major interests. Only then could it identify effective *patterns* for dealing with all parties.

For such reasons, companies will probably always have to derive major portions of their government-external relations strategies in an experimental, iterative fashion. But such incrementalism could be much more proactive than it often has been in the past. Favorable public opinion and political action take a long time to mold. There is a body of knowledge about how to influence political action. There are also methods of informal and formal analyses which can help companies anticipate major political movements and adjust their goals or policies in a timely fashion. Once potential approaches are experimentally derived (without destroying needed flexibilities), more cohesive planning can ensure that the resources committed are sufficient to achieve the desired goals, that all important polities are included in plans, and that rigorous and adaptive internal controls maintain those high performance, attitude, service, and image qualities that lend credibility to the strategy. But again, one sees logical incrementalism as the essential thread linking together information gathering, analysis, testing, and the behavioral and power considerations in this strategic subsystem.

Formal Planning in Corporate Strategy

What role do classical formal planning techniques play in strategy formulation? All companies in the sample do have formal planning procedures embedded in their management direction and control systems. These serve certain essential functions. In a process sense, they:

— Provide a discipline forcing managers to take a careful look ahead periodically;
— Require rigorous communications about goals, strategic issues, and resource allocations;
— Stimulate longer-term analyses than would otherwise be made;
— Generate a basis for evaluating and integrating short-term plans;
— Lengthen time horizons and protect long-term investments such as R&D;
— Create a psychological backdrop and an information framework about the future against which managers can calibrate short-term or interim decisions.

In a decision-making sense, they:

— Fine tune annual commitments,
— Formalize cost reduction programs;
— Help implement strategic changes once decided on (for example, coordinating all elements of Exxon's decision to change its corporate name);

Finally, "special studies" had high impact at key junctures for specific decisions.

Formal Plans Also "Increment"

Although individual staff planners were often effective in identifying potential problems and bringing them to top management's attention, the annual planning process itself was rarely (if ever) the initiating source of really new key issues or radical departures into new product market realms. These almost always came from precipitating events, special studies, or conceptions implanted through the kinds of "logical incremental" processes described above.

In fact, formal planning practices actually institutionalize incrementalism. There are two reasons for this. First, in order to utilize specialized expertise and to obtain executive involvement and commitment, most planning occurs "from the bottom up" in response to broadly defined assumptions or goals, many of which are longstanding or negotiated well in advance. Of necessity, lower-level groups have only a partial view of the corporation's total strategy, and command only a fragment of its resources. Their power bases, identity, expertise, and rewards also usually depend on their existing products or processes. Hence, these products or processes, rather than entirely new departures, should and do receive their primary attention. Second, most managements purposely design their plans to be "living" or "ever green." They are intended only as "frameworks" to guide and provide consistency for future decisions made incrementally. To act otherwise would be to deny that further information could have a value. Thus, properly formulated formal plans are also a part of an incremental logic.

Special Studies

Formal planning was most successful in stimulating significant change when it was set up as a "special study" on some important aspect of corporate strategy. For example:

◊ In 1958, when it became apparent that Pilkington's new float glass process would work, the company formed a Directors Flat Glass Committee consisting of all internal directors associated with float glass "to consider the broad issues of flat glass [strategy] in both the present and the future." The Committee did not attempt detailed plans. Instead, it tried to deal in broad concepts, identify alternate routes, and think through the potential consequences of each route some ten years ahead. Of some of the key strategic decisions Sir Alastair later said, "It would be difficult to identify an exact moment when the decision was made.... Nevertheless, over a period of time a consensus crystallized with great clarity."

◇ In the late 1960s, after the extraordinary success of the 914 copier, Xerox's Chairman Wilson and President McColough began to worry about the positioning of their total product line. At their request the company's engineers worked with the product planning department to evaluate a series of experimental products (which were then in development) from which top management could choose. These groups developed a series of strategies (from A through Q) concerning these alternative products — where to concentrate and where to deploy lesser resources. Top management chose Strategy Q, which led to the development of the product lines on which the company concentrated in the 1970s. Yet many of the initial targets for product positioning, timing, and price were adjusted as cost and market realities became clearer.

In each case there were also important precursor events, analyses, and political interactions, and each was followed by organizational, power, and behavioral changes. But interestingly, such special strategic studies also represent a "subsystem" of strategy formulation distinct from both annual planning activities and the other subsystems exemplified above. Each of these develops some important aspect of strategy, incrementally blending its conclusions with those of other subsystems, and it would be virtually impossible to force all these together to crystallize a completely articulated corporate strategy at any one instant.

Total Posture Planning

Occasionally, however, managements do attempt very broad assessments of their companies' total posture. Two examples follow:

◇ Shortly after becoming CEO of General Mills, Mr. James McFarland decided that his job was "to take a very good company and move it to greatness," but that it was up to his management group, not himself alone, to decide what a great company was and how to get there. Consequently he took some thirty-five of the company's topmost managers away for a three day management retreat. On the first day, after agreeing to broad financial goals, the group broke up into units of six to eight people. Each unit was to answer the question, "what is a great company?" from the viewpoints of stockholders, employees, suppliers, the public, and society. Each unit reported back at the end of the day, and the whole group tried to reach a consensus through discussion.

On the second day the groups, in the same format, assessed the company's strengths and weaknesses relative to the defined posture of "greatness." The third day focused on how to overcome the company's weaknesses and move it toward a great company. This broad consensus led, over the next several years, to the surveys of fields for acquisition, the building of management's initial "comfort levels" with certain fields, and the acquisition-divestiture strategy that characterized the McFarland era at General Mills.

◇ Xerox Corporation used several such posture analyses between 1965 and 1974. The first of these was the Strategy Q analysis described above. In 1971, Mr. McColough formed another committee of top-line officers to define for the company how it should develop itself around a coalescing theme, "the architecture of information," which had seemed to catch the imagination of the company. This produced a plan defining some eight business areas for the company. This was flexibly implemented through acquisition and internal development.

In 1974, Mr. McColough asked another group, with the full support of internal staffs and external consultants, to help define for the company what its posture should be vis-à-vis many of the great issues of the times (food shortages, energy, ecology, materials supplies, the world's poor, etc.). They were to "discard every taboo written, stated, or believed objective of the company." They were to "write strategies and comment on strategies in a broad frame" and report to the chairman and president on these matters. The committee was to use a full array of all the available formal strategic analysis techniques in arriving at its conclusions. These resulted in a series of discussions with the CEO and president.

Yet even such major endeavors were only portions of a total strategic process. Values which had been built up over decades stimulated or constrained alternatives. Precipitating events, acquisitions, divestitures, external relations, and organizational changes developed important segments of each strategy incrementally. Even the strategies articulated left key elements to be defined as new information became available, polities permitted, or particular opportunities appeared (like Pilkington's Electro-float invention or Xerox's Daconics acquisition). Major product thrusts (like Pilkington's TV tubes or Xerox's computers) proved unsuccessful. Actual strategies therefore evolved as each company overextended, consolidated, made errors, and rebalanced various thrusts over time. And it was both logical and expected that this would be the case.

Logical Incrementalism

All of the above suggest that strategic decisions do not lend themselves to aggregation into a single massive decision matrix where all factors can be treated relatively simultaneously in order to arrive at a holistic optimum. Many have spoken of the "cognitive limits"[21] which prevent this. Of equal importance are the "process limits" — i.e., the timing and sequencing imperatives necessary to create awareness, build comfort levels, develop consensus, select and train people, etc. — which constrain the system, yet ultimately determine the decision itself. Unlike the preparation of a fine banquet, it is virtually impossible for the manager to orchestrate all internal decisions, external environmental events, behavioral and power relationships, technical and informational needs, and actions of intelligent opponents so that they come together at any precise moment.

Can the Process Be Managed?

Instead, the executive usually deals with the logic of each "subsystem" of strategy formulation largely on its own merits and usually with a different subset of people. He tries to develop or maintain in his own mind a consistent pattern among the decisions made in each subsystem. Knowing his own limitations and the unknowability of the events he faces, he consciously tries to tap the minds and psychic drives of others. He often purposely keeps questions broad and decisions vague in early stages to avoid creating undue rigidities and to stimulate others' creativity. Logic, of course, dictates that he make final commitments *as late as possible* consistent with the information he has.

Consequently, many a successful executive will initially set only broad goals and policies which can accommodate a variety of specific proposals from below, yet give a sense of guidance to the proposers.[22] As they come forward the proposals automatically and beneficially attract the support and identity of their sponsors. Being only proposals, the executive can treat these at less politically charged levels, as specific projects rather than as larger goal or policy precedents. Therefore, he can encourage, discourage, or kill alternatives with considerably less political exposure. As events and opportunities emerge, he can incrementally guide the pattern of escalated or accepted proposals to suit his own purposes without getting prematurely committed to any rigid solution set which unpredictable events might prove wrong or which opponents find sufficiently threatening to coalesce against.

A Strategy Emerges

Successful executives link together and bring order to a series of strategic processes and decisions spanning years. At the beginning of the process it is literally impossible to predict all the events and forces which will shape the future of the company. The best executives can do is to forecast the most likely forces which will impinge on the company's affairs and the ranges of their possible impact. They then attempt to build a resource base and a corporate posture that are so strong in selected areas that the enterprise can survive and prosper despite all but the most devastating events. They consciously select market/technological/product segments which the concern can "dominate" given its resource limits, and place some "side bets"[23] in order to decrease the risk of catastrophic failure or to increase the company's flexibility for future options.

They then proceed incrementally to handle urgent matters, start longer-term sequences whose specific future branches and consequences are perhaps murky, respond to unforeseen events as they occur, build on successes, and brace up or cut losses on failures. They constantly reassess the future, find new congruencies as events unfurl, and blend the organization's skills and resources into new balances of dominance and risk aversion as various forces intersect to suggest better — but never perfect — alignments. The process is dynamic, with neither a real beginning nor end. Pilkington Brothers Ltd. provides an excellent example:[24]

◇ After carefully formulating its broad float glass strategy in 1958, Pilkington Brothers Ltd. quickly developed a technical dominance in flat glass throughout the world. With its patents and established businesses it could control access to selected growth markets in specific countries. Float generated high growth and, after an initial investment period, high cash flows. These gave the company the resources to diversify geographically and into new product lines in order to decrease the risks inherent in the company's one product emphasis in a rapidly weakening British economy. It acquired, formed joint ventures, and expanded in selected product and geographical areas as opportunities became available. Meanwhile, socialism and modern communications combined to break down traditional dependencies among workers, employers, and communities. Growth and diversity required new professional managers and workers, and these executives created a new element in the lengthening gap between workers and owners. All these added to Pilkington's size and complexity.

By 1965, the company had become too complex to manage with its old centralized organization. When a key executive, Mr. Phelps, retired, this opened a chain of promotional possibilities, and after a number of formal and informal studies, the organization was decentralized. The process went too far, however, and the company had to be tightened up through further planning, reorganization, and new controls. Meanwhile, float technology led to entirely new product possibilities, even higher profits, and increased credibility for its successful (non-family) inventor, knighted as Sir Alastair Pilkington. All of these elements reinforced a decision made broadly in the early 1960s to go public near the end of the decade in order to help with the family owners' death duties and to provide a more flexible capital base for the company. In 1970, just before the company was to go public, a strike convinced the owners to ask Lord Pilkington, who was about to retire as chairman, to stay on for three more years before Sir Alastair became chairman. The strike also speeded moves away from Pilkington's paternalistic management style to a more professional one. In the mid-1970s, the company's strategy and posture were still being shaped by the key personalities and decisions of the 1950s.

When the original float strategy was formulated, no one could have forecast or foreseen the interaction of all these events. Any rigid posture would have been doomed. Logic, therefore, dictated the kind of constantly adjusted incrementalism one sees in this vignette. The history of all other companies studied would lead to similar conclusions. Strategy deals with the unknowable, not the uncertain. It involves forces of such great number, strength, and combinatory powers that one cannot predict events in a probabilistic sense. Hence logic dictates that one proceed flexibly and experimentally from broad concepts toward specific commitments, making the latter concrete as late as possible in order to narrow the bands of uncertainty and to benefit from the best available information. This is the process of "logical incrementalism."

Conclusion

"Logical incrementalism" is not "muddling," as most people use that word. It is conscious, purposeful, proactive, good management. Properly managed, it allows the executive to bind together the contributions of rational systematic analyses, political and power theories, and organizational behavior concepts. It helps the executive achieve cohesion and identity with new directions. It allows him to deal with power relationships and individual behavioral needs, and permits him to use the best possible informational and analytical inputs in choosing his major courses of action. This article discusses the rationale behind "logical incrementalism" in strategy formulation. A succeeding article is planned which will treat the management of this process in detail.

Funds for this project were provided by the Associates Program of Amos Tuck School, Dartmouth College, and by the author's chair, the William and Josephine Buchanan Professorship of Management. Sample data include Professor Mariann Jelinek's descriptions of strategic processes at Texas Instruments, Inc. The author gratefully acknowledges her contributions to the early sections of this paper and her insights on the intellectual and behavioral processes which helped interpret the data from this study.

References

1

M. L. Mace, "The President and Corporate Planning," *Harvard Business Review*, January-February 1965, pp. 49–62;
W. D. Guth, "Formulating Organizational Objectives and Strategy: A Systematic Approach," *Journal of Business Policy* (Fall 1971);
K. J. Cohen and R. M. Cyert, "Strategy: Formulation, Implementation, and Monitoring," *Journal of Business* (July 1973): 349–367;
G. J. Skibbins, "Top Management Goal Appraisal," *International Management* (1974);
F. Goronzy and E. Gray, "Factors in Corporate Growth," *Management International Review* (1974): 75–90;
W. E. Rothschild, *Putting It All Together: A Guide to Strategic Thinking* (New York: AMACOM, 1976).

2

J. T. Cannon, *Business Strategy and Policy* (New York: Harcourt, Brace & World, 1968);
G. A. Steiner, *Top Management Planning* (New York: Macmillan Co., 1969);
R. L. Katz, *Management of the Total Enterprise* (Englewood Cliffs, NJ: Prentice-Hall, 1970);
E. K. Warren, *Long-Range Planning: The Executive Viewpoint* (Englewood Cliffs, NJ: Prentice-Hall, 1970);
R. L. Ackoff, *A Concept of Corporate Planning* (New York: Wiley-Interscience, 1970);
H. I. Ansoff, "Managerial Problem Solving," *Journal of Business Policy* (1971): 3–20;
E. C. Miller, *Advanced Techniques for Strategic Planning* (New York: American Management Association, 1971);
R. F. Vancil and P. Lorange, "Strategic Planning in Diversified Companies," *Harvard Business Review*, January-February 1975, pp. 81–90;
R. F. Vancil, "Strategy Formulation in Complex Organizations," *Sloan Management Review*, Winter 1976, pp. 1–18.

3

H. A. Simon, "On the Concept of Organization Goal," *Administrative Science Quarterly* (June 1964): 1–22;
P. Diesing, "Noneconomic Decision-Making," *Organizational Decision Making*, by M. Alexis and C. Z. Wilson (Englewood Cliffs, NJ: Prentice-Hall, 1967), pp. 185–200;
C. Perrow, "The Analysis of Goals in Complex Organizations," *American Sociological Review* (February 1961): 854–866;
P. Georgiou, "The Goal Paradigm and Notes towards a Counter Paradigm," *Administrative Science Quarterly* 18, no. 2 (1973): 291–311.

4

R. M. Cyert, H. A. Simon, and D. B. Trow, "Observation of a Business Decision," *Journal of Business* (October 1956): 237–248;
J. M. Pfiffner, "Administrative Rationality," *Public Administration Review*, 1960, pp. 125–132;
W. J. Gore, *Administrative Decision-Making: A Heuristic Model* (New York: John Wiley & Sons, 1964);
J. L. Bower, "Planning within the Firm," *American Economic Review*, May 1970, pp. 186–194;
A. Zaleznik, "Power and Politics in Organizational Life," *Harvard Business Review*, May-June 1970, pp. 47–58;
R. A. Bauer and K. J. Gergen, eds., *The Study of Policy Formation* (New York: Free Press, 1968);
G. T. Allison, *Essence of Decision: Explaining the Cuban Missile Crisis* (Boston: Little, Brown & Co., 1971);
A. M. Pettigrew, "Information Control as a Power Resource," *Sociology*, May 1972, pp. 187–204.

5

R. M. Cyert and J. G. March, *A Behavioral Theory of the Firm* (Englewood Cliffs, NJ: Prentice-Hall, 1963);
L. R. Sayles, *Managerial Behavior: Administration in Complex Organizations* (New York: McGraw-Hill Book Co., 1964);
Bower (May 1970);
E. E. Carter, "The Behavioral Theory of the Firm and Top-Level Corporate Decisions," *Administrative Science Quarterly* (1971): 413–428;
H. Mintzberg, D. Raisinghani, and A. Théorêt, "The Structure of 'Unstructured' Decision Processes," *Administrative Science Quarterly* 21, no. 2 (June 1976): 246–275;
J. Pfeffer, G. R. Salancik, and H. Leblebici, "The Effect of Uncertainty on the Use of Social Influence in Organizational Decision Making," *Administrative Science Quarterly* 21, no. 2 (June 1976): 227–245;
R. E. Miles and C. C. Snow, *Organizational Strategy: Structure and Process* (New York: McGraw-Hill Book Co., 1978).

6

Simon (June 1964);
Cyert and March (1963).

7

W. H. Riker, *The Theory of Political Coalitions* (New Haven, CT: Yale University Press, 1962);
Cyert and March (1963);
W. D. Guth, "Toward a Social System Theory of Corporate Strategy," *Journal of Business* (July 1976): 374–388.

8

C. E. Lindblom, "The Science of Muddling Through," *Public Administration Review* (Spring 1959);
D. Braybrooke and C. E. Lindblom, *A Strategy of Decision: Policy Evaluation as a Social Process* (New York: Free Press, 1963);
H. E. Wrapp, "Good Managers Don't Make Policy Decisions," *Harvard Business Review*, September-October 1967, pp. 91–99;
J. B. Quinn, "Strategic Goals: Process and Politics,"

Sloan Management Review, Fall 1977, pp. 21-37.

9
Cooperating companies included: General Motors Corp., Chrysler Corp., Volvo (AB), General Mills, Pillsbury Co., Xerox Corp., Texas Instruments, Exxon, Continental Group, and Pilkington Brothers.

10
C. I. Barnard, *The Function of the Executive* (Cambridge, MA: Harvard University Press, 1968);
E. H. Bowman, "Epistemology, Corporate Strategy, and Academe," *Sloan Management Review,* Winter 1974, pp. 35-50;
Mintzberg, Raisinghani, and Théorêt (June 1976).

11
For each company the author has attempted to create a background of secondary source data; interview at least ten of the executives most intimately associated with the strategic change process; cross-check viewpoints wherever possible; compare internal references with published materials; seek internal documentation if available; draw up a case history describing the process; submit each quotation or paraphrase used to the executive who was its source; clear the entire case for accuracy with an appropriate corporate authority. All quotations in this article have been released by their sources or are derived from secondary sources as noted.

12
For example, H. I. Ansoff, *Corporate Strategy: An Analytic Approach to Business Policy for Growth and Expansion* (New York: McGraw-Hill Book Co., 1965);
R. L. Katz, *Cases and Concepts in Corporate Strategy* (Englewood Cliffs, NJ: Prentice-Hall, 1970);
S. Schoeffler, R. D. Buzzell, and D. F. Heany, "Impact of Strategic Planning on Profit Performance," *Harvard Business Review,* March-April 1974, pp. 137-145.

13
J. B. Quinn, "General Motors Corporation" (unpublished case, Amos Tuck School, 1978).

14
J. B. Quinn, "Xerox Corporation (A)" (secondary source case, Amos Tuck School, 1978).

15
J. B. Quinn, "Pilkington Brothers" (unpublished case, Amos Tuck School, 1977).

16
J. B. Quinn and M. Jelinek, manuscripts in preparation.

17
Quinn (General Motors case, 1978).

18
These include: (1) clarifying the overall objectives of the corporation, (2) setting forth broad goals for the diversification program within these overall objectives, (3) defining specific criteria which acquisitions or developments should meet, (4) systematically searching out new product or acquisition candidates, (5) setting priorities for pursuing these, (6) evaluating specific candidates in technical, operational, and financial terms, (7) pricing acquisition deals or controlling R&D projects for adequate returns, (8) planning the integration of the new division or line into the enterprise, (9) implementing its integration and following up to see that intended yields are realized;
M. L. Mace and G. G. Montgomery, *Management Problems of Corporate Acquisitions,* (Cambridge, MA: Harvard University Press, 1962);
J. B. Quinn and J. A. Mueller, "Transferring Research Results to Operations," *Harvard Business Review,* January-February 1963.

19
Quinn and Jelinek, manuscripts in preparation.

20
A. D. Chandler, *Strategy and Structure* (Cambridge, MA: MIT Press, 1962).

21
J. G. March and H. A. Simon, *Organizations* (New York: John Wiley & Sons, 1958).

22
For a more thorough explanation of goal-setting processes, see Quinn (Fall 1977).

23
Ansoff (1965) details the need for internal and external flexibilities.

24
Quinn (Pilkington Brothers case, 1977).

RETHINKING INCREMENTALISM

GERRY JOHNSON
Manchester Business School, University of Manchester, Manchester, U.K.

This paper discusses different notions of incremental strategic management and, on the basis of empirical data from a longitudinal study of strategic management, and existing research and theory, reconceives the subject within an 'organization action' framework. The paper also argues that such an approach raises important issues concerned with the management of strategic change in organizations.

INTRODUCTION

The notion of incrementalism as a descriptor of strategic management processes has become current in the 1980s and has taken on normative implications (Quinn, 1980). Incrementalism has been seen as a management learning process (Mintzberg, 1977), indeed as 'logical', purposive (Quinn, 1980) and 'unfolding rationality' (Pondy, 1983). It has also been accounted for as the outcome of the political and social processes in the organizations (Pettigrew, 1977, 1985); certainly research studies have shown the extent to which strategic decisisons are characterized by high degrees of bargaining, solicitation and political activity (Mintzberg, Raisinghani and Theoret, 1976; Lyles, 1981; Fahey, 1981). Moreover it has been argued that there exists a 'logic' in incremental strategy development insofar as by 'learning through doing' it facilitates decision-making and implementation within a political organizational context (Lindblom, 1959; Quinn, 1980; Pondy and Huff, 1983). The phenomenon of incrementalism has also been accounted for in terms of the routing of strategic decisions through the programmes and routines of the organization (Nelson and Winter, 1980), thus building on its prehistory and current modes of operation; or more proactively, in which organizational routines provide opportunities which amount to 'solutions looking for issues to which they might be the answer' (Cohen, March and Olsen, 1972: 2). Incrementalism has also been seen as a cognitive process (Hedberg and Jonsson, 1977; Grinyer and Spender, 1979a,b; Miller and Friesen, 1980) in which collective managerial cognition results in enactment, selection and retention processes (Weick, 1979) that take form in incremental processes of strategic change.

There are, then, various explanatory accounts of the phenomenon of incrementalism, but the underlying theme is that the strategic development of an organization needs to be seen as building on current practice and managerial beliefs about organizational competences within a political and historical context. Clearly the explanations for incremental processes of strategic change are complex: yet there are still few studies which have examined these processes *in context* and *over time* so as to identify how they come about.

This paper uses as an illustration the strategic development of one firm, which we shall call 'Coopers'. It begins with an outline of the major strategic changes within that firm from 1970 onwards and demonstrates that incremental pat-

Received 11 December 1985
Revised 21 January 1987

terns of strategic change were manifest in that organization. There follows a brief explanation of the research methods used. In the remainder of the paper a number of the key strategic decisions are examined in their historical context, and these are examined so as to provide explanatory models accounting for incremental processes of change which integrate some previous explanations and challenge others.

THE CONTEXT OF THE STUDY

The study on which this paper is based took place within three retail clothing companies operating mainly in the UK, and covered a time period of 1970 to 1985. Retailing was regarded as a useful basis for the study: first because the relative flexibility of retailing assets and short time horizons of decisions might point to a potential for incremental processess of strategic change; second because of a desire in this study to avoid highly diversified, conglomerate businesses—relatively uncommon amongst UK retail companies. The particular context of clothing retailing also provided some interesting phenomena. In the period under study all three companies faced a business environment which was characterized by low levels of growth in consumer expenditure in their traditional markets, particularly from 1978 to 1982. There was also a marked change in consumer tastes away from the traditional merchandise offered by the major retail companies and, in the early 1970s, a growth in the importing of merchandise. At different times during the period of the study all three companies went through periods of relative stability, of decline in performance, and all three achieved a measure of turnaround as a result of substantial strategic repositioning. Since the industry, prior to the 1960s, had been characterized by relatively little change, the study provided an interesting opportunity to examine how managers coped with a significantly changing business environment.

Fieldwork was undertaken within Coopers between the years 1980 and 1986 and, in particular, in the years 1980 and 1983. The company had experienced from 1970 to 1980 a decade of above-industry profitable growth, in which time it had concentrated on what the management saw as a defendable market niche—the working men's outerwear market—for which they provided relatively low-priced merchandise, a large percentage of which was imported from the Far East and sold through a national chain of specialist fairly small outlets. From 1970 onwards the company attempted to diversify into a number of other retail ventures, notably women's wear, children's wear and drugs and toiletries with varying degrees of success. The fieldwork of 1980 therefore provided an opportunity to reconstruct the strategic development of the business and some of the key strategic decisions during a period of undoubted success.

From 1981 to 1983 the company experienced a marked—and to the managers traumatic—decline in fortunes. Not only did the recession in the UK affect the spending on men's clothing, particularly the lower-income brackets, but other retailers, less successful in the 1970s, had significantly changd their strategies and were enjoying considerable success at Cooper's expense. During this time the management attempted first to rationalize and reduce costs and also shed some of the acquisitions of the late 1970s; and then substantially to reposition the business. The fieldwork of 1983 thus provided the opportunity to examine how managers coped with decline and attempts to turn the business around. In fact the attempts at turnaround were only partially successful from 1983 to 1985. In 1985 the company was taken over and a second round of strategic repositioning commenced.

This paper concentrates on the period from the early 1970s to 1983 and, in particular, on the incremental patterns of change evident during that time. An illustration of the strategies within Coopers during the period (see Figure 1) helps to show why the study provided a fertile basis of study. This 'map' of strategies not only summarizes their time scales and content but also provides a visual patterning of strategies as they developed between 1970 and 1983. In processual terms it supports the idea of an incremental pattern of strategy development, as for example observed by Mintzberg (1978). Whilst there are some relatively clear breaks in strategy, in the main strategic initiatives merge into each other, or grow out of one another. For example, before Coopers attempted to reposition their men's wear business in the early 1980s (8) the company had

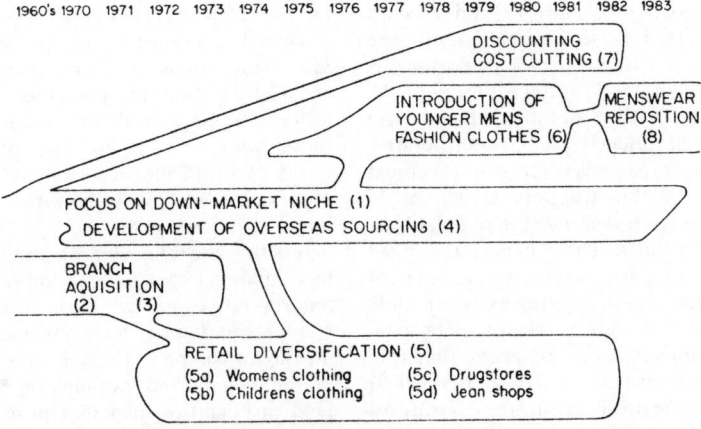

Figure 1. A pattern of strategy development

already embarked on a change in merchandise some years earlier (6). This attempted change, begun in the mid 1970s, was itself very gradual, and built on a long tradition of selling clothing items such as shirts, sweaters, jackets and trousers as 'separates' (1). The branch acquisition phase of development in the 1960s (2,3) also had its legacy: by the 1980s the company had many branches not suited to current forms of trading, or poorly sited, yet it was unwilling to dispose of them. Indeed it actively sought to develop business ventures such as jean shops (5d) in order to retain those branches or acquire businesses (5a) which could utilize available branches. The development of overseas sourcing (4) was a central plank of its strategy that persisted, became a central component of the move to younger fashions (6) and also in some of the diversified business operations (5a,b,d). The developing strategy of Coopers needs to be seen as substantially, explained by its history. The impact of the strategy of one period can be traced through to the strategy of another. What remains is to explain more precisely how this occurred.

RESEARCH METHOD

There have been few studies which have looked systematically at the processes of strategic change in context and over time. As Pettigrew has argued:

> There is still a dearth of studies which can make statements about the how and why of change, about the processual dynamics of change; in short which go beyond the *analysis of change* and begin to theorise about *changing* (Pettigrew, 1985: 15).

The research project sought to understand the complex processes of strategic change over time and within the cultural dimensions of organizations. With its focus on a limited number of companies (and on one in particular), the study is in the tradition of rich case research (Allison, 1971; Bower, 1972; Pettigrew, 1973, 1985; Biggart, 1977; Mintzberg and Waters, 1983; Pondy and Huff, 1983; Bartunek, 1984). In so doing it was possible to gain a depth of appreciation of the cultural, cognitive and political processes of mangement which form strategy, and thus achieve the 'application of conceptual knowledge about a phenomenon in a *specific and familiar* context' (Mintzberg, 1979: iv).

Data collection was primarily by means of tape-recorded non-scheduled standardized interviews (Richardson, Dohrenwand and Klein, 1965), the primary purpose of which was to allow managers to describe and discuss what they saw as key events in the companies' history and recount how they perceived these coming about. The interviews thus provided personal documents (Bogdan and Taylor, 1975) as a basis for analysis, an approach especially useful to those who are interested in understanding interpretative processes in their perceived historical context (Denzin, 1978). Within Coopers a total of 26 managers were interviewed, most of them at least twice at different times. These managers ranged from the chief executive through to members of the board, and senior executives to middle management levels. Care was taken to determine not only the subjects' views of events but also through triangulation (Denzin, 1978; Jick, 1979) to establish as objectively accurate a picture of events as possible. This was achieved through the cross-checking of personal documents against extensive secondary data, cross-checking personal documents against each other (Huber and Power, 1985) and by collecting data on the same periods from individuals at different times. The approach to data analysis was based on the approach of grounded theorists (Glaser and Strauss, 1967; Schatzman and Strauss, 1973; Turner, 1981) largely because they provide quite precise methods of analysis.

MODELS OF STRATEGIC MANAGEMENT

There exist a number of models to account for the process of strategic management. We can build on these to provide a framework by which to examine some of the decision processes in Coopers. One such framework is provided by Chaffee (1985), who proposes three generic categories. Her first is the 'linear' model corresponding to what others have called the 'planning' (Mintzberg, 1973), 'rational' (Peters and Waterman, 1982), 'rational comprehensive' or 'synoptic' (Fredrickson, 1983) approach. It is a model of strategy-making which assumes a progressive series of steps of goal-setting, analysis, evaluation, selection and the planning of implementation to achieve an optimal long-term direction for the organization.

Chaffee's second category is the 'adaptive' model of strategic management, a term also used by Mintzberg (1973). This model corresponds to the idea of incremental strategic change discussed previously and, as we have seen, the explanations for this phenomenon vary considerably from those who see incrementalism as essentially 'logical' or 'rational' through to those who account for the phenomenon in terms of satisficing behaviour in a political, or programmed, context or within the cognitive limits of management.

It is this cognitive view of strategy formulation that leads us to Chaffee's third category—the 'interpretative' model. Weick argues that there is a 'presumption of logic' (Weick, 1983: 223) in meeting a complex situation; this logic is rooted in the beliefs and assumptions that managers hold, a cognitive map that provides a view of the world, helps interpret the changes the organization faces and provide appropriate responses. These organizational sets of beliefs and assumptions have been variously referred to in management literature as 'paradigms' (Sheldon, 1980; Pfeffer, 1981; Johnson, 1987), 'interpretative schemes' (Bartunek, 1984) and 'ideational culture' (Schein, 1985; Sathe, 1985). The result of the application of such cognitive maps is well documented: the danger is of 'groupthink' as the application of 'collective cognitive resources to develop rationalisations in line with shared illusions about the invulnerability of . . . organizations' (Janis, 1985: 169). Other researchers have shown the extent to which symbolic aspects of the organization stories and myths (Schrank and Abelson, 1977; Wilkins, 1983), rituals and ceremonies (Meyer and Rowan, 1977; Trice and Beyer, 1984) and the language of the organization (Meyer, 1982)—act to legitimize and preserve such core beliefs and assumptions held within the organization. Indeed Abravanel (1983) argues that symbolic devices provide a mediating role between fundamental organizational beliefs and potentially conflicting exigencies the organization faces.

Arguably these three models more generally embrace two broad thrusts about views on strategy formulation. The one is that strategy formulation can be accounted for by logical, rational processes either through the planning mode or through the adaptive, logical incremental mode. In either event the manager is a proactive strategy formulator consciously seeking to understand a complex environment, so as to establish causal patterns and formulate strategy by configuring organizational resources to meet environmental needs. The other view is an 'organizational action' view of strategy formulation where strategy is seen as the product of political, programmatic, cognitive or symbolic aspects of management. In what follows we will take a closer look at Coopers in order to assess the extent to which these differing views explain the strategic development of the company.

EXPLAINING STRATEGIC MANAGEMENT PROCESSES

A rational view of strategy formulation

Referring back to Figure 1 it might appear that the notion of strategy as a logical response to environmental change is supported at least in so far as, over the period, the company did apparently try to make strategic changes in response to a changing business environment. For example, the introduction of more fashionable merchandise for a younger age group (6) can be associated with a growing customer demand for more fashionable men's wear. Discounting and cost-cutting (7) can be seen as a response to the negative pressures of recession on sales volume; the efforts to diversify into women's wear and children's clothing (5a,b) might be interpreted as a response to real decline in expenditure on men's clothing. However, the observation that strategies change given environmental change tells us little about the processes of strategic decision-making. If we were to account for such decisions in terms of 'linear, rational, planning' models, we would expect to find strong evidence and a significant impact of systematic environmental scanning, clear objective setting and evaluation of strategic options against such objectives, and probably a planning infrastructure through which this took place. In fact in Coopers throughout the period studied there was little evidence of any of this and, as will be seen, when such activity did take place, it had relatively little impact. We have to account for the observed strategic changes in other ways.

However, the managers themselves expressed views about the management of strategy which square well with rational but incremental models of strategic management—views which mirror closely Quinn's (1980) notion of logical incrementalism. These views included the following:

1. Small movements in strategy allow deliberate experimentation and sensing of the environment through action; if such small movements prove successful, then further development of strategy can take place.
2. Shareholders expect short-term returns; therefore it is not sensible to commit large sums of money or other resources to major shifts in strategy.
3. It is better to make continual adjustments to strategy so as to keep in line with market changes; if this is not done, then the company's strategy will become atrophied and over time will lead to the need for radical repositioning.
4. Opportunistic management are able to search for ways in which they can take advantage of the matching of an historic and developing strategy with a developing market.
5. The nature of retailing is particularly suited to incremental adjustment, since there are few really fixed costs and assets. It is much less of a commitment and risk to try out a new strategy, because it can be done by opening a few new shops, or adjusting merchandise in shops; if this does not work, then the shops can be disposed of, or the merchandise sold off with relatively little loss.
6. In a business in which there is high regard for people it is important not to 'rock the boat' too much; people will go along with change much more readily if it is gradual and they can become used to it.

If the espousal of the logic of incrementalism is examined in the context of the company's performance to 1980, it would be tempting to concur with the managers' view that such a process was, indeed, beneficial. Coopers had enjoyed a decade of virtually continuous profit growth and a 4-year period in which it had achieved record profits, whilst most large competitors could only generate book profits through the sale of properties. There are, however, two dangers in this interpretation. The first is a danger of dubious causality; it is one thing to recognize the phenomenon of incrementalism, even to note the espousal of 'logical incrementalism'; it is quite another to support that a good record of profit performance can be explained by it. Indeed the dramatic decline in performance between 1980 and 1983 was to show that the processes of management in the firm were not adequate to prevent it. The second danger is that of assuming that the logic of the processes described by the managers is necessarily a reasonable description of the processes which account for strategy formulation. This research was concerned to study strategic change as a longitudinal, contextual process, rather than as the espoused theory of managers. It will be shown that a somewhat different picture of the process of strategic management emerges if patterns of development of strategy in the business are examined in terms of the events, dramas and routines of organization life and the belief systems of managers.

An 'organizational action' view of strategy formulation and implementation

An 'organizational action' view of strategy formulation argues that strategy can best be seen as the product of the political, cognitive and cultural fabric of the organization. The expectation would be that strategic decisions could be explained better in terms of political processes than analytical procedures; that cognitive maps of managers are better explanations of their perceptions of the environment and their strategic responses than are analysed position statements and evaluative techniques; and that the legitimacy of these cognitive maps is likely to be reinforced through the myths and rituals of the organization.

Discernible from the analysis of the interviews with managers was a common set of beliefs and assumptions taken for granted by those managers; it was tacit knowledge, primarily about the modes of operation in the organization, typically in terms of trading procedures, organization and control, seen as bestowing beneficial competences and capabilities on the organization. For Coopers this set of beliefs and assumptions could be characterized and summarized thus:

> Low cost, good value, merchandise bought in bulk by experienced buyers, yielding high margins, linked to the tight centralised control of stock and distribution provides a secure position in our particular market niche. Moreover we can take decisions fast because of centralised 'entrepreneurial' top management and rely on speedy implementation by loyal staff with years of experience in the business.

This set of beliefs amounts to what other writers have referred to as a paradigm:

> those sets of assumptions, usually implicit, about what sort of things make up the world, how they act, how they hang together and how they may be known, . . . such paradigms function as a means of imposing control . . . (and) . . . provide roles to be enacted in particular ways, particular settings, and in particular relation to other roles' (Brown, 1978: 373).

In the case of Coopers this paradigm was closely related to the dominance of routines and programmes in the organization: it is essentially an operational view of the world built up over time through the experience of operating and encapsulating what the managers saw as the distinctive competences of their business. In particular we will see the extent to which the buying routines played a substantial part in shaping strategy in the business.

It was also clear that political processes and the exercise of power were important. In Coopers over most of the years under study the buyers in particular exercised high degrees of power in the business. The link between the paradigm and the power bases in the company is an observation made by many researchers: 'power accrued to those sub-units which could best deal with organisational uncertainty' (Pfeffer and Salancik, 1974: 137; also Crozier, 1964; Hickson et al., 1971; Hambrick, 1981). The merchandise strategy was perceived to have the effect of insulating the company from market threats; the price and margin advantages reduced the likelihood of competitive incursions and buffered them against downturns in demand. Changes in fashion were seen to be less important than for some other companies because they had elected to concentrate on 'commodity' mechandise policies. It was the merchandise strategy that became the mechanism through which company profits were to be guaranteed, and this became central within the set of assumptions about the basis upon which the business could compete in an uncertain world.

The dominance of buying and merchandise could be seen in the shop window displays of the 1970s, crowded with every item of merchandise the shop stocked with an emphasis given to that which the buyers had procured. The assumption of the dominant importance of merchandise and buying was also symbolized in the greater freedom and discretion enjoyed by buyers in an otherwise tightly controlled business. On the caring nature of management, managers told stories which emphasized the concern for staff and emphasized the difference between retailing and manufacturing because retailing was run on 'trust' and 'love'. Managers also emphasized the way in which they were given opportunity for career progression; promotion was always from within, and if someone was promoted beyond his competence, then he would still be 'looked after'. The emphasis on the importance of staff loyalty was also reflected in organizational stories; managers were proud to tell of how they and their staff would work extra hours or over the weekend to help with a store refit. The rituals of socialization ensured that everyone knew of the company way or retailing and acknowledged organizational features of loyalty, long service and deference to senior executives not only as proper but beneficial. The nature of top management in the firm, its perceived entrepreneurial flair, the speed of decision-making and the centrality of the chief executive, were enshrined in myths which showed how this had been so throughout the history of the company. In short the tenets of the paradigm were, indeed, legitimized symbolically.

Cases in the formulation and implementation of strategy

The extent to which these characteristics of organizational action help explain the formulation of strategy in the company, and in so doing the observed phenomenon of incremental strategic change, can best be shown by using some brief examples from the company's history (a fuller account is available in Johnson, 1987).

Younger fashions (6)—a process of lobbying and incremental adjustment

Prior to the mid-1970s the company had concentrated on what managers described as a 'pile it high and sell it cheap' approach to clothes for the working man. However there were managers in the business well aware of fashion changes in the market early in the 1970s; junior management, mainly from the relevatively lower power base of the retail side of the company, sensed the need to change and in some cases tried to put into effect such changes, if only locally, by the infiltration of merchandise into their shops. Moreover they were lobbying for merchandise changes, over a period of years, but their appeals for change were ignored or blocked by senior managers. It was these senior managers, and in particular senior merchandise executives, who were most wedded to, and arguably derived power from, the established and hitherto successful strategy. Moreover, those resisting change could draw on a whole raft of justifications for such resistance, usually embedded in organizational routines: lead times on high-volume purchasing were long; more fashionable items might jeopardize volume purchases and hence margins; it would be more difficult to control a widening merchandise range; in any case, profit growth was continuing, and there was no other serious competitor in their market sector. In short they could draw upon well-established bases of the strategic success of the business to defend the legitimacy of the approach upon which their power had been built.

However, it has to be noted that those from within the business who were advocating change were also conceiving of problems and solutions within much the same paradigm constraints. To them the customer was much the same as he always had been: he just wanted access to some more fashionable goods. Moreover it was seen as a merchandise problem which could be resolved through a change in merchandise by buyers whose ability was highly regarded. It was not, for example, seen as a problem to do with shop ambience, or requiring a change in definition of target market.

The picture emerges of two 'lobbies', one more powerful than the other, but both operating within much the same cognitive bounds. The divisions between the two groups appear to have lasted a number of years; yet the essential homogeneity of the management team was maintained. One of the mechanisms for its maintenance was undoubtedly the continued profitable growth of the business. Arguably another was the mediating role of the myths and rituals of the organization. The ritually elevated power base of merchandising, embedded in stories about the dominance of the merchandise director in decision-making on operational issues, legitimized his dominance and the relatively lower influence of the retail managers. Any potential schism was, however, overcome by the apparently benign and partriarchal role of the chairman, who embodied the caring nature of the firm: moreover managers could be ensured of a career of progression within a system known to look after its own.

The resolution of the problem was through the mechanism of what managers saw as logically incremental action. It can also be seen as a change in strategy which was defined in terms of the paradigm and implemented gradually so as not to interfere with what was 'known to work'. Although the aim was to 'become more fashionable', this was done in such a way that bulk buying could be retained from overseas, so each new range had to be tested to ensure volume sales. Fashion was defined as imitating what other fashionable retailers demonstrated they could sell in volume: buyers explained that 'we would take a garment to the Far East and ask them to make it for us; perhaps changing it a bit to meet the needs of our customers'. There was to be no loss of control on stocks: distribution was retained at the centre and shops had to 'qualify' for new stock on the evidence of past sales of the limited range of fashion merchandise available. The shops themselves were hardly changed; the range was introduced in most shops as a display area only, kept separate from the traditional merchandise and perhaps highlighted in a section of the window. Moreover such changes were moderately successful, and the effect of this success was to offer evidence that the changes which were taking place were sufficient and sensible.

Acquisition and diversification (5a,c)

Throughout the period of this study Coopers attempted on several occasions to launch women's wear chains; they also diversified through acquisition into drug stores. It was the avowed intent of the main board, at least, to move away from a reliance on men's wear; and on the face of it this would appear to indicate an intended break from traditional ways of operating. Yet if we look at the policies adopted on acquisition, again we find the interpretation of perceived opportunity in terms of the paradigm and the application of the current modes of operation.

The first women's wear venture in the early 1970s was by acquisition, and seen as particularly attractive because of the property portfolio it offered, at a time when property acquisition was seen as the primary basis of growth. That, combined with the opportunity to increase buying power overseas, and increase margins as a result, was sufficient to ensure the support of the powerful merchandise department. According to the managers who were party to the decision, there was little discussion about the market logic of the acquisition. With hindsight, the managers themselves explained the move in terms of a belief that the success of that time could be transposed into a women's wear operation. It was seen as compatible at the time with the logic of the existing business—'It was the body cover market: basically cheap awful crap. You could see the logic in the acquisition.'

The demise of this venture saw a second women's wear venture utilizing available branches. Coopers put in their control system and transferred managers from the men's wear operation to run the business. This too failed. Yet the same approach continued. In the late 1970s the company turned away from its search for women's wear chains and acquired two drug retailing operations. Coopers' control systems were introduced and their management were transferred to run the operation. Both operations failed and were disposed of. Again, some years later, managers could see the failings in their approach to acquisition and diversification:

We thought we knew enough about retailing to retail anything.

The centralised control at Coopers is not appropriate to acquisitions when there are small numbers of shops... there comes a time when you switch a small organization over and you try to put the system in but unless its over a certain size it won't do any better; in fact it will probably do a lot worse.

Jean shops 5(d)

Through the 1970s Coopers became one of the largest volume retailers of jeans and of its workwear merchandise base. However in the 1970s the growth of speciality jean shops eroded their share of that market. These developments coincided with the fact that there were shops within the men's wear company which were performing badly. There were two possibilities: one was to close them down and the other to develop them to return to profits.

In the late 1970s Coopers had tried to respond to the growing fashion consciousness of customers by rolling out the younger fashion initiative into more shops. But the chief executive believed that the experiments with the jeans shops provided another opportunity. It was not a view held by all but such opposition as did exist had relatively little impact. The recommendations of a 'retail committee' set up to examine the feasibility of such an operation were against its development. Their view was based on an evaluation of the suitability of available sites in terms of perceived market need. Similarly, a Group Board colleague of the CEO, taking an essentially analytical view of the venture, concluded that the likelihood of success was low. The problem for both his views, and the views of the committee, however, was that it raised the spectre of shop closures without providing an answer to declining sales. The alternative of developing a specialist jean operation, on the other hand, provided many organizational and political advantages.

Faced with declining performance in a number of shops thse whose status or reputation could be harmed by closure were seeking a solution which would reduce that threat; the possibility of using such branches for some other venture was attractive because it did precisely that. The accountants saw the possibility of increased productivity through low-performing branches. It also meant that the necessity to close branches and make staff redundant could be avoided; indeed the retail management could use it as a means of demonstrating still further their determination to look after the wellbeing of staff and provide them with new opportunities. The buyers, concerned that moves to introduce branded merchandise would reduce margins, were initially wary of an operation which might highlight branded goods; but this fear was reconciled by turning it on its head; the introduction of a limited quantity of branded merchandise would show just how comparatively good own-brand merchandise was. If there were reservations about the wisdom of the move, and the ability to make a success of it, then they were submerged within the general acceptance of rightness of developing shops and providing new opportunities for staff; and, in any case, it was known that the chairman was in favour of the idea.

The response to declining performance: 1980/81 (7)

In 1980 it was clear that growth was not being maintained. By the middle of 1981 the company was in a state of serious performance decline. The period provides some examples of a management team, faced with a problem it found difficult to understand, making sense of it through, and exerting greater efforts within, its paradigm, whilst seeking to preserve the legitimacy of that paradigm from the threats of growing contra-evidence.

The external events of that time were interpreted initially as remote from the strategy of the firms. Performance decline was to do with an economic downturn which was regarded as temporary. The chief executive commented in the financial press: 'As soon as the public returns to normal spending levels, upward growth in profits will resume'. The downturn was not seen as anything to do with what Coopers were doing; rather it was to do with what the customers were doing. In the meantime the paradigm offered a menu of response to the problems the business faced. This included tightening controls and cutting of controllable costs—for example, branch refurbishment costs. It also meant that managers sought to do better that which they had always done; to stack the merchandise higher, pack windows more fully and make sure staff were selling more aggressively. In addition there was the ability to manipulate price through the reduction of the normally healthy margin, and seek even better prices from suppliers.

When such measures failed to turn declining performance around, management opted to deal with that which it knew how to control best: the costs—this was achieved through major cuts in shop manning levels. For a company wedded to the belief that it was an efficient cost controller, the move was both a natural one and yet led to a significant contradiction of values. It was not easy for some managers to reconcile the ideal of more efficient cost control and redundancies with the notion that they had always been efficient anyway, and also the ideal of a caring management loyal to its staff.

Conflict and contradiction arose elsewhere too. If the initial response to downturn was to apply more vigorously those familiar aspects of management practice, embodied in the paradigm, by 1981 there was also growing dissonance. Whilst most managers may have accepted that the market would return, a newly arrived marketing director was convinced, through market research he had commissioned, of the dubious reliability of Coopers' traditional market. The research report not only questioned the validity of the management conception of the clothing market, but attacked their way of operating within it. The response to such questioning was much as Pfeffer (1981: 325) has indicated: 'Attacks on the dominant beliefs or paradigm of the organization are likely to be met with counter argument and efforts to reinforce the paradigm.' The report had the effect of being a major political threat to established senior management, and elicited heavy initial resistance. The resistance was concerned with more than the report itself; it was also addressed at the new director himself. There was raised the 'myth of retailing experience'. He was deemed not to have this retailing experience; and reasons for condemning the research were found, for example, in the obvious lack of retailing experience of those who presented it. For months the findings and conclusions that the research arrived at were disregarded.

It was a time of increasing conflict and contradiction. Managers throughout the operation found themselves facing evidence which conflicted with their taken-for-granted assumptions about sensible ways to operate, at the same time as they were having to take decisions to make staff redundant. Abravanel's (1983) argument about the mediatory role of myth in such circumstances is borne out. Such contradictions could not be explained logically; yet managers would tell stories about the flexibility of the company in crisis, the speed at which decisions could be taken, and the historical ability of successive chief executives to manage the business into growth through entrepreneurial decision-making.

FORMALIZING EXPLANATORY MODELS

Examination of the processes of strategic change in Coopers bears out many of the phenomena which characterize incremental strategic change explained in terms of an organizational action perspective. The patterns of change are indeed evolutionary; strategic decisions build upon history, and what managers at least perceive to be the core strength of the business. Decisions came about following long periods of incubation following identification of problems or opportunities through highly qualitative assessment. High levels of solicitation and bargaining characterize both problem definition and the selection of solutions. The primacy of cognitive maps in the interpretation of environmental stimuli, the configuration of responses and strategy implementation, is also evident; and it becomes clear that these belief sets are relatively commonly held within the organization and persistent, forming an organizational paradigm. Moreover the mediatory and legitimizing role of symbolic aspects of the organization is also borne out. Building on all this we can move towards more integrated explanatory models of strategic management which arguably help to provide assistance in understanding the complexity of strategic management.

The nature of the paradigm

The paradigm is the set of beliefs and assumptions, held relatively common through the organization, taken for granted, and discernible in the stories and explanations of the managers, which plays a central role in the interpretation of environmental stimuli and configuration of organizationally relevant strategic responses. Although this is a phenomenon observed in other studies, a number of points of explanation emerge from the examination of the impact of the paradigm on strategic decisions in Coopers. We need to start by distinguishing between what is meant by the paradigm and what is meant by 'strategy'. Following Mintzberg (1978) we can distinguish between intended and realized strategy. Realized strategy is taken to mean the observable output of an organization's activity in terms of its positioning over time. By intended strategy is

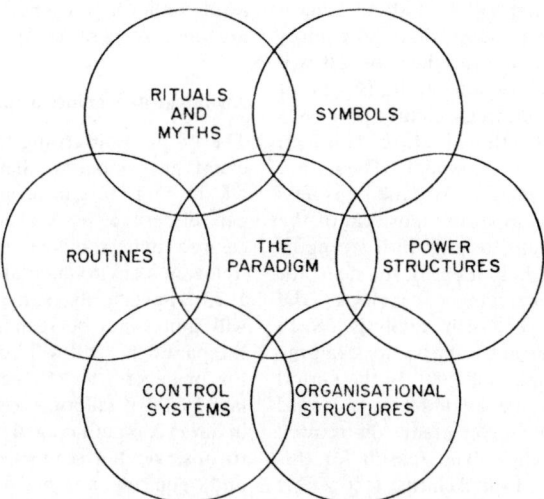

Figure 2. The cultural web of an organization

meant the strategy that managers espouse, perhaps in some sort of formal plan, public statement, or explanation. The paradigm, on the other hand, is a more generalized set of beliefs about the organization and the way it is or should be and, since it is taken for granted and not problematic, may be difficult to surface as a coherent statement. It is more likely to emerge in the explanations and stories of managers. The point is that both intended and realized strategy are likely to be configured within the parameters of the paradigm.

There were discernible reasons why the paradigm would be resistant to rapid change. First because the internal consistency of the paradigm as observed was self-preserving and self-legitimizing. For example the belief in Coopers in the efficacy of bulk buying was consistent with the accepted wisdom of centralized control of stocks and distribution; the belief that the company could be fast on its feet because of the entrepreneurial approach of top management and a loyal workforce helped account for how an apparently rigid and closed system could be regarded as capable of flexibility. It is not an easy matter to challenge or repudiate one construct of an internally supportive and consistent whole. Second, and particularly significant in terms of understanding management implications we need to understand the paradigm not just as a system of beliefs and assumptions; it is preserved and legitimized in a 'cultural web' of organizational action in terms of myths, rituals, symbols, control systems and formal and informal power structures which support and provide relevance to core beliefs (see Figure 2). In Coopers the assumptions about the approach to buying and merchandising, and the emphasis on centralized control of current costs and assets were not only linked themselves, but institutionalized, indeed capitalized, in the stock control and distribution systems. This is the inertia of technical organizational commitment, and is not likely ignored or overturned. The significance of many of the operational aspects of managing the business was, as has been seen, highlighted and arguably legitimized in the softer rituals, myths and symbols of the organization (Wilkins, 1983; Daft, 1983; Dandrige, Mitroff and Joyce, 1980).

Further, the constructs of the paradigm are closely linked to the power structures in the organization. In effect the paradigm represents the internally constructed belief set about 'uncertainty reduction' so it is likely that those most associated with operationalizing these beliefs will be most powerful in the organization. This point is of some significance. Strategic change processes traditionally advocated in the literature are linked to rational analytical planning models. The notion that it is through analysis of the business environment and the competitive position of the firm that managers yield insights into strengths and weaknesses which help identify the need for and opportunities for change, overlooks the political implications of such analysis. Such analysis was undertaken in Coopers—for example the market research report of 1980. In the period following the analysis the evidence it provided was either denied by management, discredited or led to minimal change. The reason for this was not that the analysis lacked clarity or cogency; quite the reverse: it pointedly questioned tenets of beliefs fundamental to the strategies being followed by the organization; in other words it raised explicit challenges to the paradigm and, as such, constituted not an intellectual analytical questioning of strategy, but a political threat to those whose power was most associated with it. Clarity of analysis is not, in itself, a sufficient basis to break the powerful momentum of the fundamental assumptions embraced within the paradigm, and indeed can actually increase resistance to change.

Such were the characteristics discernible in relation to the paradigm in Coopers. It is not suggested that such characteristics will necessarily obtain in all organizations, of course. For example, such homogeneity of beliefs and assumptions will not always exist. However other empirical studies (e.g. Grinyer and Spender, 1979a,b; Miles and Snow, 1979; Davis, 1984; Janis, 1972; Smircich, 1983 and Wilkins and Ouchi, 1983) do suggest there are many organizations in which just such homogeneity around a core set of beliefs is common. Also noticeable about the paradigm in Coopers was its operational orientation, and Spender (1980) and to some extent Pettigrew (1985) note similar phenomena. However, this may not necessarily be the case in all organizations. Indeed if the arguments of Peters and Waterman (1982), Quinn (1980), and Kanter (1983) are to be accepted, it is those organizations with core belief sets of a relatively high order (mission statements) and yet at other levels rather heterogeneous sets of beliefs, which are the 'excellent' companies.

An integrated model of process

The proposition arising from the analysis of the events in Coopers is that environmental signals will be reordered in terms of the paradigm. We can discern a pattern in this which allows a clearer understanding of what is meant by 'relevant environmental change' (Rhenman, 1973). Specifically, some environmental signals will simply not be seen as relevant in terms of the paradigm, and will be ignored. For example, for managers the strategic repositioning in the late 1970s of tailoring companies not historically in direct competition with Coopers was interesting to observe, but seen as of limited consequence and requiring no specific action. Coopers was perceived to be in a distinct market sector with a distinct way of operating. Other signals might be seen as 'consonant' with the paradigm, in so far as they were capable of interpretation and action within the bounds of that paradigm. For example, the apparent decline in consumer expenditure within the target market, in 1980, was seen as a matter which could be handled by more aggressive sales effort from loyal staff, price competition and even tighter cost control. The paradigm here provided a ready-made menu of responses to a set of circumstances.

There might also be signals from the environment seen as 'dissonant' with the paradigm; that is they might be actual or potential perceived threats to its basis, or not capable of being dealt with strictly within its bounds. For example, managers saw that there was a growing expectation of more fashionable merchandise within the 'C2D market', and youngsters in particular were increasingly shopping elsewhere for clothes. This was clearly relevant to the merchandise formula of the company but, as we saw in the mid-1970s, not capable of being handled by the 'pile it high and sell it cheap' approach of that time. It would, of course, theoretically be possible to see the same signals in quite different ways; analytically it might be argued that their notion of a defensible market sector had become groundless; or that changing fashion expectations could not be dealt with simply by adjusting merchandise but also required changes in retail shop ambience. This, however, is to take an

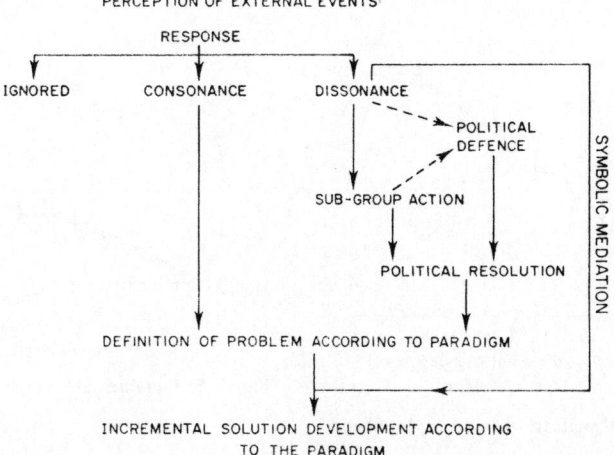

Figure 3. A pattern of problem resolution and strategy formulation

analytical perspective rather than a cognitive perspective. Market signals were not analysed in this sense but perceived in terms of organizationally and operationally relevant beliefs—what we have called the paradigm.

Given such perceived dissonance there appears to be a pattern of response. Dissonance with the paradigm is potentially threatening to its integrity. Given such a threat:

1. Dissonance will be mediated symbolically; that is the symbolic mechanisms within which the paradigm is embedded will perform the role of maintaining the legitimacy of the paradigm in the face of the apparent threat.
2. Since such a threat may take the form of a political challenge to those most associated with core constructs of the paradigm, such threats may well be strongly resisted.
3. The problem will be resolved by managers seeking for consonance within the paradigm. That is, managers will seek to resolve the extent to which elements of the environment and the paradigm are in a state of dissonance. It is here that the most significant acts of strategic adaptation take place. The evidence throughout the period under study here is that such consonance might be achieved by: (a) making sense of contra-stimuli in the terms of paradigm rather than questioning or reconstructing the paradigm—for example, defining changes in buying behaviour as relating to merchandise rather than indicating any fundamental change in the fundamental nature of the buyer; or (b) where necessary marginally adjusting the paradigm, but from within its own bounds, and whilst maintaining its essential form. For example, by shifting somewhat from a 'pile it high' conception of retailing to an admission of the relevance of 'fashionable' merchandise—providing it can meet buying and margin requirements of course. Action is then taken in line with the (adjusted) paradigm.

Figure 3 outlines this process schematically.

The notion of strategic drift

'Logical incrementalism' assumes a tension between identified environmental stimuli and 'the way we do things around here'. Indeed Quinn (1980) claims that such an approach explicitly recognizes the need for managing such ambiguity: in the terms of this paper, the process allows for the admission of threats to the paradigm. The argument here is that the very nature of the cultural context of the paradigm means that it is likely to militate against and stifle such tensions and such threats. The paradigm effectively

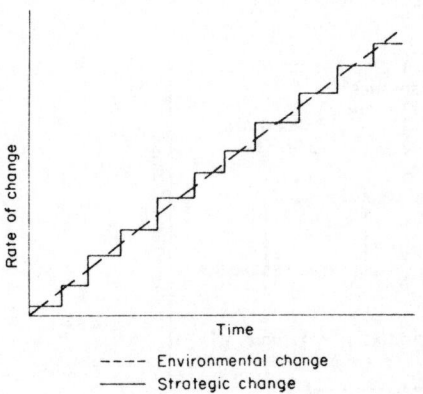

Figure 4. A national pattern of incremental change

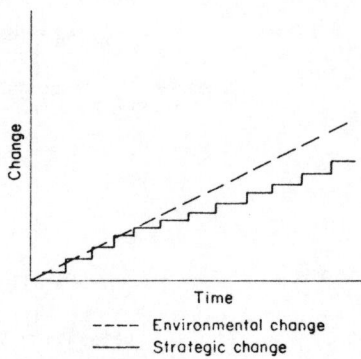

Figure 5. Incremental change and 'strategic drift'

defines environmental 'reality' and responses to environmental change. Quinn's logical notion is that strategic change, through environmental sensing by managers within subsystems and the interplay between subsystems and continual testing out of new strategies, results in a learning and readjustment process in organization by which the organization keeps itself in line with environmental changes. It is a notion which is summarized in Figure 4. The argument here is different: it is that managers may well see themselves as managing logically incrementally, but that such consciously managed incremental change does not necessarily succeed in keeping pace with environmental change. Indeed it is argued that there is a high risk that it will not. The situation in Coopers as it evolved through the 1970s was not as shown in Figure 4, but rather as shown in Figure 5. Gradually the incrementally adjusted strategic changes, and the environmental, particularly market changes, moved apart.

This phenomenon of 'strategic drift' was found in all three companies studies and can be accounted for thus:

1. Sensing of external stimuli is muted because the stimuli are not meaningful in themselves; they take on a relevance, and responses are operationalized in terms of the paradigm.
2. Managers believe they are adapting to a changing environment when in fact they are adapting to signals which coincide with the paradigm.
3. There is likely to be resistance to 'deviant' interpretations of the environment if they threaten the paradigm. This results in political pressure for conformity or marginal adjustments to strategy.
4. Strategic drift is not easily discerned by managers. However, in the event of its detection remedial action is likely to take the form of solutions constructed within the bounds of the paradigm anyway.
5. Moreover these adjustments may well be enough to demonstrate the efficacy of the action to the satisfaction of stakeholders since, given the application of the familiar, there is a good chance that there will be some signs of performance improvement, at least in the short term.

This notion of stategic drift, whilst accounted for differently, is similar to phenomena observed by other researchers. Mintzberg (1978) shows how organizations go through periods of strategy adjustment characterized by continuity, flux or incremental change, but infrequently require more global changes. Greiner (1972) charts periods of evolution and revolution in corporate development, and Chandler (1962) also noted the resilience of current strategies and structures, as more recently did Grinyer and Spender (1979); indeed, Miller and Friesen summarize their own research thus:

Managers demand a large potential benefit before they are willing to destroy the order and complementarity of elements inherent in the old gestalt and begin to construct a new one. The price paid for this sluggish responsiveness to the need for reversals in evolutionary trends, and occasional revolutionary periods with all of their turmoil, expense and confusion (Miller and Friesen, 1980: 612–13).

CONCLUSIONS AND NORMATIVE IMPLICATIONS

The main purpose of this paper has been to develop explanatory models relating to the phenomenon of incrementalism. It has not set out to be a normative management paper. However, there are implications which arise from the study which should be highlighted. The first is that the integrated model of strategic decision-making rooted in the organizational action approach does lend itself to the prediction of likely responses given certain circumstances. The prediction would be that in the context of organizations exhibiting dominant paradigms of the sort we see in Coopers, likely responses in line with Figure 3 may be expected, and represent a very different explanation of the phenomenon of incrementalism than is found in the arguments of the logical incrementalists. Indeed it is argued that managers are likely to espouse such 'logical incrementalism' but that such espousals may disguise a system of management rooted in the currency of the paradigm. The question therefore remains as to how it might be possible to achieve more nearly effective adaptive incremental strategic management and avoid 'strategic drift'.

If strategy is to be managed effectively adaptively there must exist a 'constructive tension' (Kanter, 1983) between that which is necessary to preserve and that which must be changed. A tension, for example, between the need for managers to question and challenge and the preservation of core values and organizational 'mission'; between the need for new ideas and directions and the need for continuity and preservation of the core business. This necessary tension is what Peters and Waterman (1982) call 'simultaneous loose–tight properties' or 'the co-existence of firm central direction and maximum individual autonomy' (p. 318). It is a view echoed elsewhere but, more specifically, at the cultural and cognitive levels. Meyer (1982) has argued that the reason an organization is more likely to adopt strategies more divergent from its previous strategies than other organization, is because it has a more heterogeneous organizational 'ideology', as manifested in terms of, for example, organizational images and symbols. It is a view supported by Friendlander (1983), who argues organizational learning in a 're-constructive' mode takes place more readily where there is such heterogeneity. A number of writers have argued that such ideological heterogeneity can be built into management systems in a variety of ways. For example through organic management styles with a removal or reduction of hierarchical lines of reporting and communication (Bartunek, 1984; Peters and Waterman, 1982; Pettigrew, 1985); through deliberate challenging and assumption surfacing devices, either formally promulgated (Mason and Mitroff, 1981) or as part of the organizational culture (Peters and Waterman, 1982; Kanter, 1983); through the active involvement of 'outsiders' with less adherence to organizational culture or the organizations paradigm (Mintzberg, 1978; Grinyer and Spender, 1979a; Schein, 1985) and through the avoidance of 'segmentalist' structures (Kanter, 1983).

Findings here also bear out those who argue the power of symbolic mechanisms for strategic management and change (Peters, 1978; Boje, Fedor and Rowland, 1982; Deal and Kennedy, 1982; Kotter, 1982; Martin and Powers, 1983; Sathe, 1985). The point that they argue is that strategic issues have, traditionally, been seen as linked to analytic, planning mechanisms of management, and as such run the risk of not being 'owned' by those within the organization. They point out that successful organizations are good at managing change, not by talking about it at an analytical level but by demonstrating it at a symbolic and therefore more meaningful level in terms of the interpretative models suggested here and as illustrated in Figure 2. Such organizations approach the management of change through the very artifacts (symbolic and political) that otherwise preserve the integrity of the paradigm and prevent change.

None of this is to say that the planning and analytical methods advocated in so much of the literature is of no relevance. It is rather to argue that planning and analysis are necessary but not sufficient, and need to be understood as mechanisms for problem and opportunity identification and strategy evaluation, rather than as a mechanism for strategic change. Indeed, the argument can be advanced that planning and anlytical mechanisms are likely to give rise to resistance to change unless they take place within a context where the mechanisms for managing strategic change through the social, cultural, political, cognitive and symbolic devices of the organization are already in place.

Overall the results of the study emphasize the importance of understanding strategic management processes essentially in terms of organization action perspectives, and argue for the continued development of models which more precisely explain both strategy formulation and implementation in these terms.

REFERENCES

Abravanel, H. 'Mediating myth in the service of organization ideology'. In Pondy, L. R. Frost, P. G., Morgan, G. and T. C. Danbridge (eds), *Organizational Symbolism*, JAI Press, Greenwich, CT, 1983

Allison, G. T. *The Essence of Decision*, Little, Brown, Boston, 1971.

Bartunek, J. M. 'Changing interpretive schemes and organizational restructuring: the examples of a religious order', *Administrative Science Quarterly* **29**, 1976, pp. 355–372.

Biggart, N. W. 'The creative-destructive process of organizational change: the case of the Post Office', *Administrative Science Quarterly*, **22**, 1977, pp. 410–426.

Bogdan, R. and J. S. Taylor. *Introduction to Qualitative Research Methods*, John Wiley and Sons, Chichester, 1975.

Boje, D. M., D. B. Fedor and K. M. Rowland. 'Myth Making: a Qualitative Step in O. D. interventions', *Journal of Applied Behavioural Science*, **18**(1), 1982, pp. 17–28.

Bower, J. L. *Managing the Resource Allocation Process: a Study of Corporate Planning and Investment*, Irwin, Homewood, IL. 1972.

Brown, R. H. 'Bureaucracy as praxis: toward a political phenomenology of formal organizations', *Administrative Science Quarterly*, **23**, 1978, pp. 365–382.

Chaffee, E. E. 'Three models of strategy', *Academy of Management Review*, **10**(1), 1985, pp. 89–98.

Chandler, A. D. *Strategy and Structure*, MIT Press, Cambridge, MA, 1962.

Cohen, M. D., J. C. March and J. P. Olsen. 'A garbage can model of organization choice, *Adminstrative Science Quarterly*, **17**, 1972, pp. 1–25.

Crozier, H. *The Bureaucratic Phenomenon*, University of Chicago Press, Chicago, 1964.

Daft, R. L. 'Symbols in organizations: a dual-content framework for analysis. In Pondy, L. R., P. J. Frost, G. Morgan and T. C. Danbridge (eds), *Organizational Symbolism*, JAI Press, Greenwich, CT, 1983.

Danbridge, T. C., I. Mitroff and W. F. Joyce. 'Organizational symbolism: a topic to expand organizational analysis', *Academy of Management Review*, **5**, 1980, pp. 77–82.

Davis, S. M. *Managing Corporate Culture*, Ballinger/ Harper & Row, Cambridge, MA, 1984.

Deal, T. and A. Kennedy. *Corporate Cultures: The Rites and Rituals of Corporate Life*, Addison Wesley, Reading, MA, 1982.

Denzin, N. K. *The Research Act*, McGraw-Hill, Maidenhead, Berkshire, 1978.

Fahey, L. 'On strategic management decision processes', *Strategic Management Journal*, **2**, 1981, pp. 43–60.

Fredrickson, J. W. 'Strategic process: questions and recommendations'. *Academy of Management Review*, **8**, 1983, pp. 565–575.

Friedlander, F. 'Patterns, of individual and organisational learning'. In Srivastva, (ed.). *The Executive Mind*, Jossey Bass, San Francisco, 1983.

Glaser, B. C. and A. L. Strauss. *The Discovery of Grounded Theory*, Aldine, Chicago, 1967.

Greiner, L. E. 'Evolution and revolution as organizations grow', *Harvard Business Review*, July/ August, 1972, pp. 37–46.

Grinyer, P. H. and J. C. Spender. 'Recipes, crises and adaptation in mature businesses'. *International Studies of Management and Organisations*, **IX**, 1979(a), pp. 113–123.

Grinyer, P. H. and J. C. Spender. *Turnaround: Managerial Recipes for Strategic Success: The Fall and Rise of the Newton Chambers Group*, Associated Business Press, London, 1979(b).

Hambrick, D. C. 'Environment, strategy and power within top management teams'. *Administrative Science Quarterly*, **26**, 1981, pp. 253–276.

Hedberg, B. and S. Jonsson, 'Strategy making as a discontinuous process', *International Studies of Management and Organisation*, **VII**, 1977, pp. 88–109.

Hickson, D. J., G. R. Hinings, C. A. Lee, R. E. Schneck and J. M. Dennings, 'A strategic contingencies theory of intraorganizational power', *Administrative Science Quarterly*, **16**(2), 1971, pp. 216–229.

Huber, G. P. and D. J. Power. 'Retrospective reports of strategic-level managers', *Strategic Management Journal*, **6**(2), 1985, pp. 171–180.

Janis, I. L. *Victims of Groupthink*, Houghton Mifflin, Boston, 1972.

Janis, I. L. 'Sources of error in strategic decision making'. In Pennings, J. M. (ed.) *Organizational Strategy and Change*, Jossey Bass, San Francisco, 1985, pp. 157–197.

Jick, T. D. 'Mixing qualitative and quantitative methods: triangulation in action, *Administrative Science Quarterly*, **24**, 1979, pp. 601–611.

Johnson, G. *Strategic Change and the Management Process*, Blackwell, Oxford, 1987.

Kanter, M. *The Change Masters: Innovation for*

Productivity in the American Corporation, Basic Books, New York, 1983.

Kotter, J. P. *The General Managers*, Free Press, 1982.

Lindblom, C. E. 'The science of muddling through', *Public Administration Review*, **19**, Spring 1959, pp. 79-88.

Lyles, M. A. 'Formulating strategic problems—empirical analysis and model development', *Strategic Management Journal*, **2**, 1981, pp. 61-75.

Martin, J. and M. E. Powers. 'Organizational stories: more vivid and persuasive than quantitative data'. In Staw, B. (ed.) *Psychological Foundations of Organizational Behavior*, Glenview, IL: Scott, Foresman, 1983, pp. 161-168.

Mason, R. O. and I. I. Mitroff. *Challenging Strategic Planning Assumptions*. Wiley, New York, 1981.

Meyer, A. D. 'How ideologies supplement formal structures and shape responses to environments', *Journal of Management Studies*, **19**(1), 1982, pp. 45-61.

Meyer, J. W. and B. Rowan. 'Institutional organizations: formal structures as myth and ceremony', *American Journal of Sociology*, **83**, 1977, pp. 340-363.

Miles, R. E. and C. C. Snow. *Organizational Strategy, Structure and Process*, McGraw-Hill, New York, 1978.

Miller, D. and P. Friesen. 'Momentum and revolution in organizational adaptation', *Academy of Management Journal*, **23**(4), 1980, pp. 591-614.

Mintzberg, H. 'Strategy making in three modes', *California Management Review*, Vol. **XVI**(2), Winter 1973

Mintzberg, H., O. Raisinghani and A. Theoret. 'The structure of unstructured decision processes', *Administrative Science Quarterly*, **21**, 1976, pp. 246-275.

Mintzberg, H. 'Strategy formulation as a historical process', *International Studies of Management and Organization*, **VII**(2), 1977, pp. 28-40.

Mintzberg, H. 'Patterns in strategy formation', *Management Science*, May, 1978, pp. 934-948.

Mintzberg, H. *The Structuring of Organizations*, Prentice Hall, Englewood Cliffs, 1979.

Mintzberg, H. and J. A. Waters. 'The mind of the strategist(s)'. In Srivastva, S. (ed.) *The Executive Mind*, Jossey Bass, San Francisco, 1983.

Nelson, R. R. and S. G. Winter. *An Evolutionary Theory of Economic Change*, Harvard University Press, Cambridge, MA, 1982.

Peters, T. 'Symbols, patterns and settings: an optimistic case for getting things done', *Organizational Dynamics*, Autumn 1978, pp. 2-23.

Peters, T. J. and R. H. Waterman, (Jr). *In Search of Excellence*, Harper & Row, New York, 1982.

Pettigrew, A. M. *The Politics of Organisational Decision Making*, Tavistock, London, 1973.

Pettigrew, A. M. 'Strategy formulation as a political process', *International Studies of Management and Organization*, **VII**(2), 1977, pp. 78-87.

Pettigrew, A. M. *The Awakening Giant*, Basil Blackwell, Oxford, 1985.

Pfeffer, J. 'Management as symbolic action: the creation and maintenance of organizational paradigms'. In Cummings, L. L. and B. M. Staw (eds). *Research in Organizational Behavior*, vol 3. JAI Press, Greenwich, CT, 1981, pp. 1-15.

Pfeffer, J. and G. R. Salancik. 'Organizational decision-making as a political process: the case of a university budget', *Administrative Science Quarterly*, **19**, 1974, pp. 135-151.

Pondy, L. R. 'Union of rationality and intuition in management action'. In Srivastva, S. (ed.). *The Executive Mind*, Jossey Bass, San Francisco, 1983.

Pondy, L. R. and A. S. Huff. 'Budget cutting in Riverside: emergent policy re-framing as a process of analytic discovery and conflict minimization'. Presented at a Symposium on 'The Management of Hard Times', at the National Academy of Management, Dallas, August 1983.

Quinn, J. B. *Strategies for Change*, Irwin, Homewood, IL, 1980.

Rhenman, E. *Organization Theory for Long Range Planning*, Wiley, New York, 1973.

Richardson, S. A., B. S. Dohrenwand and D. Klein. *Interviewing: Its Forms and Functions*. Basic Books, New York, 1965.

Sathe, V. *Culture and Related Corporate Realities*, Irwin, Homewood, IL, 1985.

Schatzman, L. and A. L. Strauss. *Field Research: Strategies for a Natural Sociology*, Prentice-Hall, Englewood Cliffs, NJ, 1973.

Schein, E. H. *Organizational Culture and Leadership*, Jossey Bass, San Francisco, 1985.

Schrank, R. and R. Abelson, *Scripts, Plans and Knowledge*, Hillsdale NJ: Erlabaum, 1977.

Sheldon, A. 'Organizational paradigms: a theory of organizational change', *Organizational Dynamics*, **8**(3), 1980, pp. 61-71.

Smircich, L. 'Organizations as shared meanings'. In Pondy, L. *et al*, (eds), *Organizational Symbolism*, JAI Press, Greenwich, CT, 1983, pp. 55-68.

Spender, J. C. 'Strategy making in business'. PhD thesis, School of Business, University of Manchester, 1980.

Trice, H. M. and J. M. Beyer. 'Studying organizational cultures through rites and ceremonials'. *Academy of Management Review*, **9**(4), 1984, pp. 653-669.

Turner, B. 'Some practical aspects of qualitative data analysis: one way of organising the cognitive process associated with the generation of grounded theory', *Quality and Quantity*, **15**, 1981, pp. 225-247.

Weick, K. E. *The Social Psychology of Organizing*, Addison Wesley, Reading, MA, 1979.

Weick, K. E. 'Managerial thought in the context of action'. In Srivastva, S. (ed.) *The Executive Mind*, Jossey Bass, San Francisco, 1983.

Wilkins, A. L. 'Organizational stories as symbols which control the organization'. In Pondy, L. R., P. J. Frost, G. Morgan and T. C. Dandridge (eds), *Organizational Symbolism*, JAI Press, Greenwich, CT, 1983.

Wilkins, A. L. and W. G. Ouchi. 'Effective cultures: exploring the relation between culture and organisational performance', *Administrative Science Quarterly*, **28**, 1983, pp. 468-481.

The Cultural View

RECIPES, CRISES, AND ADAPTATION
IN MATURE BUSINESSES

P. H. Grinyer (United Kingdom)
and J.-C. Spender (United Kingdom)

Management is a matter of making the organization effective; and part of this is the idea that most, if not all, of the organization's activity is directed toward the specific objectives established in the policy-setting processes. Such activity is then the enactment of management's overall plan to reach these objectives. This notion, which runs through contemporary management literature, creates a distinction between the lower-level management task of implementing the plan and the higher-level management task of creating the plan. The purpose of using terms such as strategy, tactic, plan, measurement, and controls is to draw attention to this distinction and to the special difficulties the higher-level manager must deal with.

Our hope in defining strategy or strategic decision-making is to help management cope with these special difficulties. Thus, Mintzberg's "intended strategy" as a "pattern in the stream of events" is evidence of a plan. (1) When there is no pattern, management may be assumed to have failed to direct the organization's activity effectively. However, this definition does not help managers identify the nature of the planning task.

Drs. Grinyer and Spender teach at the City University's Business School, London, England.

Bowman's (1976) definition, for instance, is more substantive and gets much closer to what managers must actually do. Strategy must guide the continuing stream of decisions, determining the organization's environmental domains — essentially its product-markets — the nature of its interactions with these domains, and the internal adjustments suggested by these choices.

Over the last twenty years, there has been a steady development of ideas about how this planning process may be done systematically — both rigorously, in an attempt to produce the best possible plan, and formally, so that the planning process conforms to carefully considered corporate procedures. It has seemed particularly important to fit the strategic planning process into a controlled cycle of evaluation and decision in order to anticipate strategic problems, rather than wait until crises arise (e.g., Ansoff, 1965; Bowman, 1976; Grinyer, 1971; Hussey, 1974; Steiner, 1969). At the same time, however, there has been a developing understanding that such rigor depends on certainty in management's information about the organizational environment, its internal processes, and the relationships among them, or at least a knowledge of the relevant probabilities. As writers such as Simon (1957), Lindblom (1958), and Normann (1976) have pointed out, management's information is invariably fragmentary, ambiguous, and riddled with uncertainty; and this proves to be a damning critique of the systematic approach. As a result, attention has been shifting from refinements in the purely systematic process of strategic planning to methods of dealing with the endemic uncertainties of management information (Cyert and March, 1963). Such uncertainty must be avoided or removed before the systematic process can begin, and this brings management's function in dealing with uncertainty into the center of the analysis (Thompson, 1967).

On the whole, this new thrust is empirical rather than theoretical, with researchers going back to managers and forming generalizations about the ways in which the readily evident uncertainties are being dealt with. This seems eminently sensible when one considers the difficulty in forming a theory of uncertainty, especially one that reflects Knight's (1965) classic

Recipes, Crises, and Adaptation

distinction between risk and uncertainty. But managers are brought back into the center of the analysis because it is the judgment they apply that resolves the uncertainties of the situation. If we argue that uncertainty is a generic term for shortcomings in the information that managers have available that make it less than certain (Shubik, 1954), then judgment is that which leaps beyond what can be legitimately justified by the evidence, making up for its deficiencies. In this way, our inquiry into strategic decision-making shifts from being an investigation of managerial rationality, whether prescriptive or descriptive, to an inquiry into the sources of managerial judgment.

Managers can justify their reasoning and those judgments that are not publicly justifiable only in terms of patterns of belief about their situation and its potentialities. Some of these beliefs may be highly personal, in the sense of being the idiosyncracies of a particular manager. They may also be private and beyond communication to others. But at the other end of the spectrum there are beliefs that are widely communicated and shared, such as those reflecting scientific knowledge and well-established commercial and industrial practices.

It is the empirically evident insufficiency of such purely scientific knowledge that makes the growing body of literature on management "styles," "mythologies," or "paradigms" so valuable. <u>Style</u> has generally been associated with tactical management, though recent researchers have begun to argue for a contingency approach in which the choice of an appropriate corporate style becomes an internal adjustment to the strategic choice of product-market (Burns and Stalker, 1961). <u>Myth</u> has more encompassing connotations, though it smacks of irrationality, the supernatural, or fantasy. But Hedberg and Johnsson's (1977) work is perfectly operational and down to earth. Similarly, Kuhn's (1962) work on the history of science has reestablished the term <u>paradigm</u> as an overall gestalt or coherent pattern of beliefs, despite the many unresolved arguments about the term's substantive meaning (Masterman, 1970). Notwithstanding these criticisms, the common thread is that the system of beliefs forming the basis of action is, on the one hand, complete enough to provide a rationality and, on the other, built up from widely shared knowledge together with less justifiable judgments. In this way, purely technical knowledge is supplemented by experience-based judgments about, for instance, the behavior of customers and suppliers, and about the outcome of productive activity.

The strength of the contingency approach is its implication that these less justifiable constituents of the managerial pattern of belief are derived from sharply limited domains of experience. An inquiry into the sources of managerial judgment thus becomes an inquiry into the corresponding domain of experience on which the judgments are based.

Normann (1976) uses the term "business-idea" to identify the pattern, and he puts his analysis at the level of the company, as do Argyris and Schon (1974). The "business-idea" is a distillation or summation of the company's unique history. Plainly, even without empirical support, the uniqueness of each company's pattern of beliefs is striking. Yet there are other possibilities and levels of analysis. There is an equally long tradition, deriving directly from the "great man" theory of history, that judgment is highly individual and that a company is, in essence, the articulation of one pivotal individual's pattern of belief (Sloan, 1965). (2) Similarly, emerging from the historicist approach, there is the view that similar patterns of environmental forces will generate similar patterns of beliefs as decision criteria.

Analyzing strategic decisions, therefore, begins with the selection of an appropriate level of analysis. Given an uncertain world, this is primarily an empirical matter. Following the older institutional or industrial economists' line (Andrews, 1949), Spender (3) gathered empirical evidence supporting the view that significant patterns of managerial belief exist at the industry level. This is illustrated, for instance, by the relative ease with which executives can move operations within an industry, but their greater difficulty in switching industries. Following Schutz's (1972) and Simon's (1962) typically insightful lead, the industry's pattern of managerial belief was called a "recipe." If this recipe for action can be made explicit, management has a way of evaluating its own judgments and beliefs against a wider pattern judged reasonable by others in the industry. Hatten's work (4) in the U.S. brewing industry is an example of the fruitfulness of such an industry-level analysis.

The notion of the recipe poses a question about the processes that transfer and diffuse knowledge and judgment among the industry's managers. Although most would accept the idea of the manager's becoming socialized into a particular company's pattern of beliefs, they would probably be less sanguine about a whole company's being socialized into an industrywide pattern of beliefs. Even without considering the changes taking place in the company, the process calls for extremely powerful patterns of interorganizational communication. Webster (1969) argues that such communications are infrequent and of little importance. Others, such as Allrine (1968) and Martilla (1971), come to opposite conclusions. A detailed empirical study by Czepiel (1975) found an interorganizational communication network to be active in diffusing knowledge of a major technological innovation within the U.S. steel industry. The evidence suggests a process of diffusion via informal contact occurring within some industries many levels below the chief executives. Likewise, Mintzberg (1973) found external contacts to be an important aspect of chief executives' work. Contact via trade associations and government bodies also reinforces interlocking directorships as means of strengthening the interpersonal communication network.

Once such interorganizational relations are treated as significant, the company may be regarded as under the influence of wider patterns of belief. Some will be at the level of the industry; some will be cultural or societywide. Each acts as a powerful orienting framework, filtering the buzzing, blooming confusion of the world to admit only that believed relevant. As such the framework acquires a specific character closely associated with Barnard's (1938) conception of "purpose" or Vicker's (1970) "appreciative system." Like Boulding's (1956) "image," the framework is the basis of predictive inferences about environmental behavior and the way in which the perceived action alternatives are delimited (Thomas and Bennis, 1972).

Although the individual manager is foolish if he habitually ignores all outside advice, it is obvious that the unique historical and environmental circumstances of each firm mean that though the recipe may be a major source of management's beliefs, it can never be the only source. The recipe has a generality that ensures that it can seldom be a prescription for action. The strategic decision process must remain at the level of the firm, reflecting its policy objectives, limited resources, and historical position. But the outcome is a plan whose fundamental rationality is shared within the industry, beyond the specific company. This has fundamental significance both for the reorientation of companies whose old approach to business is no longer viable and for problems of managing diversified organizations.

Dynamics of Reorientation

Models of fundamental managerial reorientation are found in much of the literature. Apart from Normann's (1976) model of "redefinition," the empirically based models have very similar features in that they involve cyclical patterns of commitment, elaboration of the recipe adopted by the firm, and its ultimate demise. As this is expressed concretely in successive strategies, the company learns; and the recipe becomes consolidated and adopted as a cognitive structure that permits both screening and interpretation of environmental events. It becomes embodied in procedures, programming and institutionalizing behavior, so that the growing obsolescence of the pattern of beliefs in the face of continuing environmental changes is not discerned. Ultimately, repeated failure of the strategies based on the recipe undermines management's faith in it, to the point at which it is replaced.

This process is well described by Hedberg, Nystrom, and Starbuck (1976), who provide an excellent review of the literature, and by Hedberg and Jonsson (1977). Argyris, too (5), provides a model of the impediments to learning present in a comprehensive system of beliefs, which he calls the "Model 1 the-

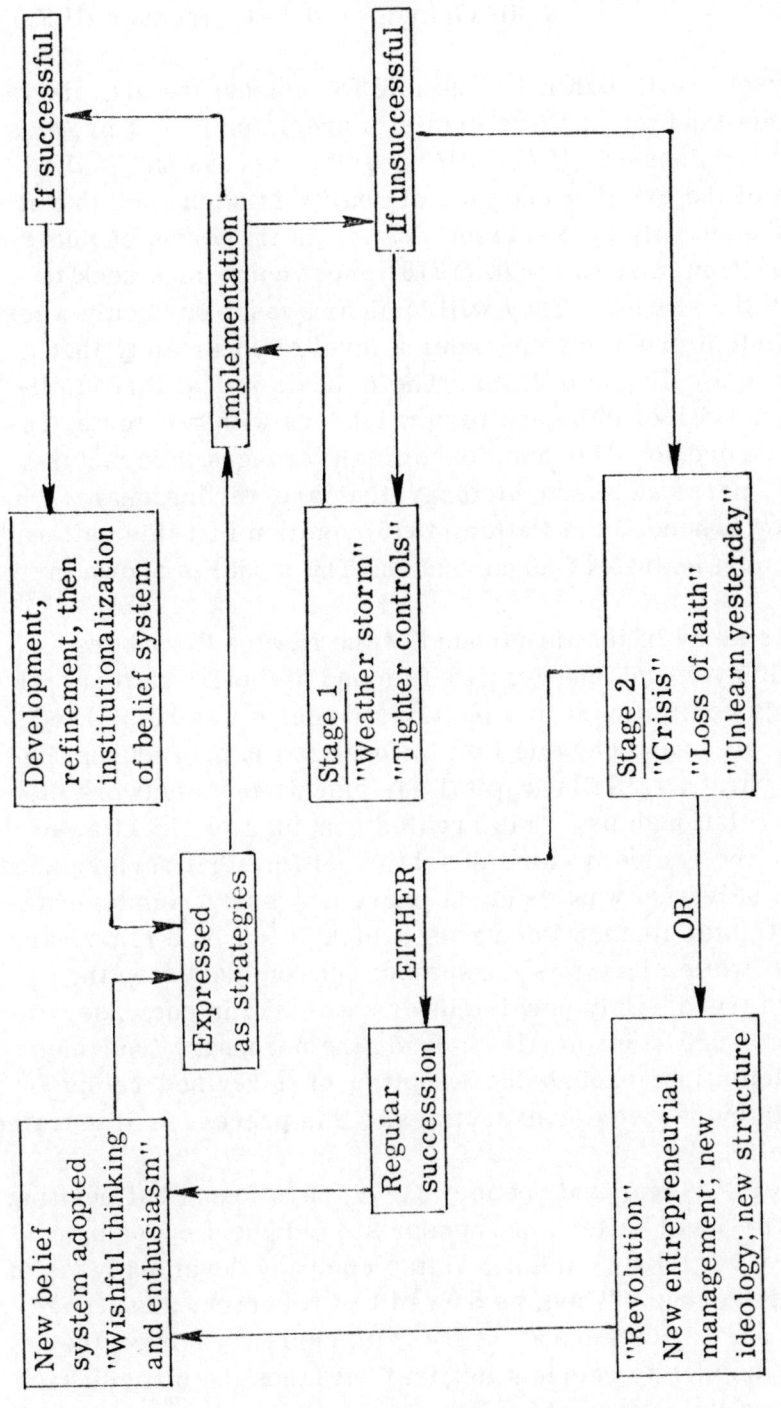

Figure 1

Source: Hedberg & Jonsson, and Hedberg, Nystrom, and Starbuck.

ory-in-use." Although it is possible to reorient the organization before this kind of cognitive crisis is precipitated — a process Hedberg and Jonsson (1977) call "regular succession" — the strength of the existing mapping of reality is often such that it can be shaken only by a serious crisis. In the terms of Hedberg, Nystrom, and Starbuck (1976), most companies seek to "weather the storm." They will "unlearn yesterday" only when the persistent problems engender a level of uncertainty that amounts to a collapse of faith. Their thesis is that this facilitates a transfer of influence to new leaders with greater entrepreneurial propensities and concomitant changes in structure, strategy, personnel, and ideology that are revolutionary. Studies by Schendel and Patton (1976) confirm that this pattern is a common feature of turnarounds. The model is shown in Figure 1.

In their study of the turnaround of the Newton Chambers Group, Grinyer and Spender (1979) found a similar pattern. The company's commitment to a particular recipe was reinforced by its success, and became institutionalized in procedures, behavioral patterns, skills, capital equipment, and a network of external relationships. This created considerable inertia, so that when the recipe became obsolete and financial performance declined, salvation was sought in more aggressive implementation and tighter financial controls, which produced a temporary recovery, while slack was consumed, but could not stop the downward trend. Only persistent crisis — and in one case, impending closure — eventually induced the necessary fundamental reorientation through the adoption of a revised recipe brought in by new senior executives. This process is illustrated in Figure 2.

However, Grinyer and Spender (1979) have found that positing an industry-level pattern of appropriate judgment opens up a possibility implicitly excluded in the company-level analyses of the Swedish group. When, as a result of recurrent dissatisfaction with strategies emanating from its current recipes, the company decides to reorientate itself, it faces the difficult task of adjusting its pattern of belief. To do this on its own, it must

Recipes, Crises, and Adaptation

innovate; this is both difficult and risky. If it is a member of an industry with a shared recipe, it can imitate. As Grinyer and Spender suggest, imitation is both quicker and safer than innovation. Indeed, the quickest way of imitating is the replacement of the chief executive by one who has already adopted an appropriate pattern of beliefs. Thus, the reorientation of the company frequently involves not a major innovation by entrepreneurial management, as in the models of Normann (1976) and Hedberg, Nystrom, and Starbuck (1976), but the introduction of a tried, tested, and currently successful recipe brought in by a chief executive with a track record of recent success within the industry.

Rather than the "wishful thinking" described by Hedberg and Jonsson (1977), these executives apply fully operationalized recipes, immediately and with considerable success. Their confidence, based on their past experience of applying their recipe, is an important factor in rallying the management and shop-floor work force previously demoralized by the persistent failures of the old method of operating. Quite spectacular turnarounds, reinforcing acceptance of the new recipe, were achieved that would not have been possible had a lengthy period of corporate learning been required.

In their study Grinyer and Spender found that the corporate senior management of Central & Sheerwood used this device to reconstruct the Newton Chambers's operating subsidiaries. The new chairman of Ransomes & Rapier, their principal operating unit, was already chairman of another engineering company when appointed, and retained both this position and nonexecutive directorships in other companies in the same industry. Similarly, the new managing director was active in interorganizational discussions as president of the Crane Makers Federation, was a member of the Construction Equipment Committee of the National Economic Development Office, and was thus fully socialized into an industry-related peer group. Moreover, most of the senior managers of the company, including the chief executive, had held important positions in other successful companies within the industry before joining the one under study.

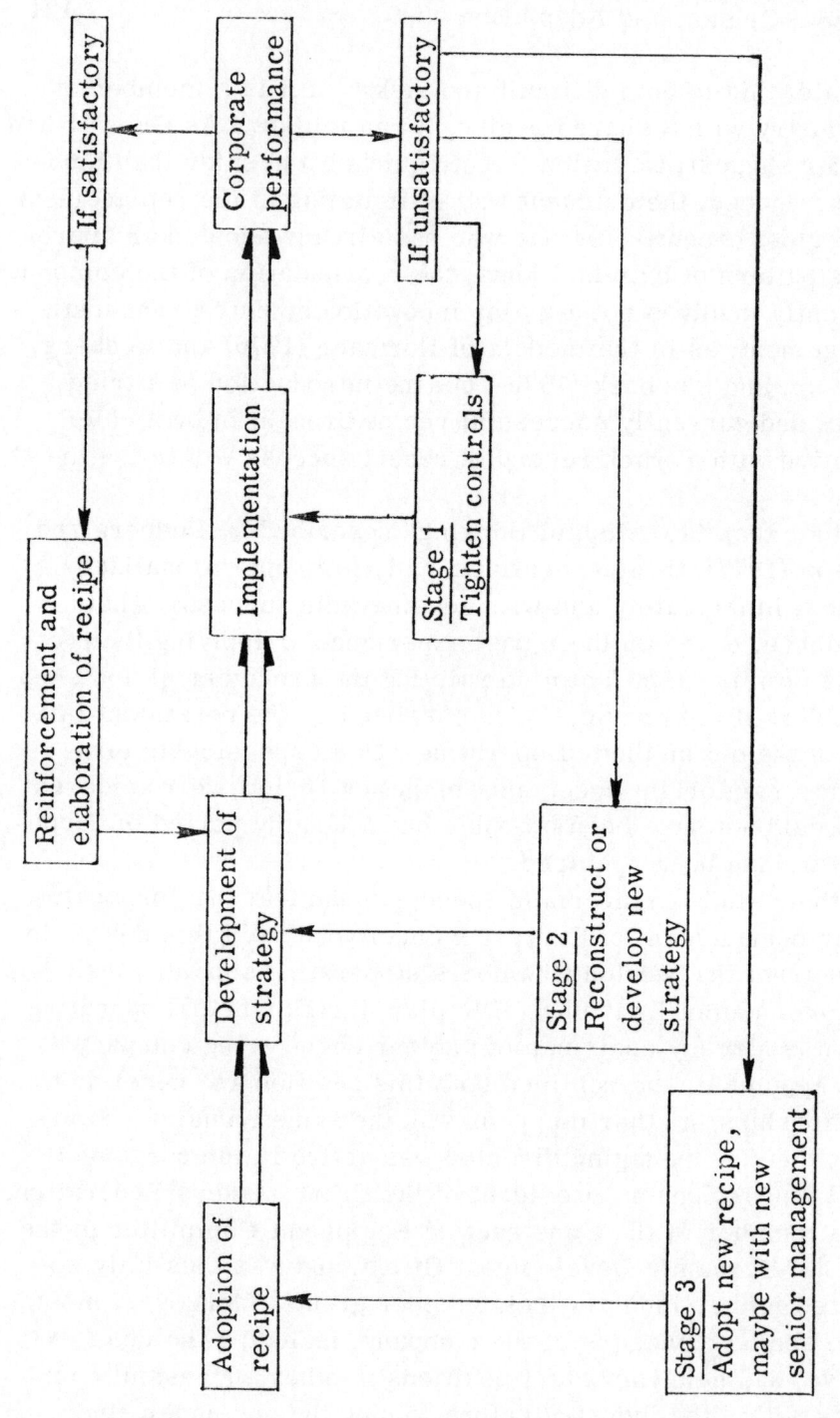

Figure 2

Recipes, Crises, and Adaptation

Obviously, they brought with them beliefs about ways of achieving success in the industry and retained many contacts with past colleagues.

An imitative approach to changing the orientation or recipe-in-use of the company is clearly inappropriate when the best recipe applied within the industry is no longer viable within new environmental conditions. Despite the frequency with which companies seem to do this, to adopt such a recipe is, apparently, to join the lemmings in their onward rush to the sea. Yet this is attractive; for although the performance of the company continues to deteriorate, it does so along with others, and management can appeal to comparatively good results in an industry suffering from adverse conditions beyond its control. Launching into a completely new recipe is, in contrast, a hazardous and lonely step that may lead to even greater disaster. Perhaps for this reason, companies tend to extend into a new pattern of operations by putting out "feelers" from their existing business (Rhenman, 1973) rather than leaping in the dark.

In general, a business is extended or given a new slant with a new synthesis of largely similar constituents. The new recipe's novel ingredients are often drawn directly from other recipes with which the senior management is familiar. For instance, Grinyer and Spender found that Newton Chambers's engineering subsidiary met a long-term decline in demand for general engineering within its market by, on the one hand, adding standardized products produced by the same processes and directed to the same major customers and, on the other, seeking to penetrate an entirely new market for project management services. Years of dealing with the project managers using its general engineering skills gave top management an insight into this related recipe, which they adopted to complement the company's existing ones. Were standardized products and project management to become the dominating and most profitable aspects of the company, resources, systems, and procedures would become increasingly oriented toward them, and the old jobbing engineering business might wither away. Till such time, however, the older type of business provides security while other recipes are explored and tested before adoption. Over time, this process may produce accumulated changes that are so great that the early adopters of the recipe may not even recognize it.

The Grinyer and Spender study differed from the others reported in the literature in a further respect, too. They studied individual businesses within the context of a diversified group and identified the interactions among the different corporate levels. They found that the change mechanisms differed among levels. Following a fairly familiar recipe for managing diverse industrial holdings, the Newton Chambers Group responded to persistent failure in a subsidiary by tightening its financial controls and putting heavy pressure on its chief executive to achieve sales and profit budgets. Continued failure resulted in the replacement of the chief executive. This happened with alarming frequency in one subsidiary: throughout the 1960s, its chief executives lasted, on average, little more than eighteen months. The group senior management, however, adapted and evolved, adopting a more appropriate recipe in response to the repeated financial crises. In any case, this reorientation seemed both too late and potentially too damaging to capture the shareholders' support. The management was finally displaced after a contested takeover.

Because it is so difficult to organize a shareholders' revolt, and because chief executives tend to control board composition, it is obviously important that group managements should be able to evolve new variants of old recipes or, indeed, entirely novel recipes if the corporate whole is to survive in a changing environment. This requires a broad field of vision, a questioning attitude toward the recipes adopted, a wide exposure to senior managers in industries with different recipes, and, ideally, breadth of experience among key executives. Given these, a holding company or conglomerate should be capable of evolving from recipe to recipe at a considerably faster pace than the industrial companies it owns, for the recipe it follows is less likely to be institutionalized in largely nontransferable skills, assets, procedures, and patterns of internal and external relationships. Companies can be sold as going concerns or closed and their assets stripped, or new business can be acquired quite quickly. The speed with which a holding company can successfully reorient itself, given appropriate senior executives, is illustrated by Central & Sheerwood's changing its recipe three times in five years and in the process growing from an insignificant operation into a major company.

Recipes and Diversification

The idea of an industry-level recipe greatly illuminated our study of the ways in which both Newton Chambers and Central & Sheerwood sought to maintain effective control of their operations. Chandler (1962) has shown how the divisional structure developed as a response to this problem, which is one of maintaining control over the increasing variety of recipes being employed by the operating units. He argues for a separation between group- and operating-level managements, so that the group-level management may be relieved of all responsibility for day-to-day affairs and can concentrate on the longer-term strategic issues. In this way the divisional structure is a solution to what March and Simon (1958) called "Gresham's Law of Planning"; for when burdened with both strategic and tactical responsibilities, managers tend to put off the less tractable strategic problems.

Given a divisional structure, group management can control the company by grouping the operating subsidiaries according to similarities of the recipes adopted and delegating a measure of their overall strategic responsibilities to the divisional general managers, who also control the group subsidiary interface. These divisional general managers are expected to understand the operating units and monitor and control them. Group management then controls the divisions by means of predominantly financial measures and targets, acting as a central capital market and owner. In this manner a conglomerate's management is able to manage a wide variety of operations; but because its only influence is financial and does not require an understanding of the recipes being applied, it actually makes little direct contribution to the operations' strategic thinking. Such management is also likely to find significant communication difficult, because of the narrowness of the purely financial discourse among its members. Even financial forecasts are located within patterns of operational beliefs; and without understanding these, the group management can scarcely hope to grasp the real operational meaning of the forecasts it receives. This could be one explanation of Rumelt's (1974) finding that "related product" companies, which diversified along paths closely linked through technology or market, tended to outperform "unrelated product" companies. Grinyer, Al-Bazzaz, and Yasai-Rardekani (6) produced similar findings for the United Kingdom.

Given an appropriate partitioning of subsidiaries into recipe-related divisions and an understanding of these recipes by the divisional manager, the divisional structure can effectively integrate the peripheral industrial or commercial operations with the separate, financially oriented corporate head office. The divisional general manager can communicate the needs of operating units to the corporate head office and, by interpreting their performance in other than purely financial terms, can protect them from sometimes inappropriately harsh application of financial controls, while representing and protecting the corporate interests. A firm grasp of the recipes of subsidiary operating units permits him to select their senior managers on the basis of context-related recipes currently successful within the industry and to influence their strategic decision-taking by talking in operationally significant terms.

The very separation of the corporate headquarters from the peripheral industrial operations that support it, at the base of the pyramid, may make this ideal difficult to achieve. Without a deep understanding of the recipes of its diverse industrial assets — an understanding that the divisional structure is designed to make unnecessary and must surely impede — the bases for both partitioning businesses into divisions and appointing their general managers are likely to be superficial and not fully adequate. For instance, a corporate chief executive who has not internalized the recipes of the businesses within a division is

Recipes, Crises, and Adaptation

unlikely to have means of telling whether a prospective general manager has experience-based beliefs and abilities that would make him eminently suitable to head it. Under the circumstances, he is likely to satisfy himself with someone judged to have "general management ability," which may amount to an apparent understanding of the corporate recipe for managing a conglomerate by largely financial logic and controls.

No doubt many divisional managers selected on this basis have acquired an adequate understanding of the recipes of at least the more important businesses in their divisions. But this requires a great capacity to socialize and learn, an underlying willingness to accept and internalize the beliefs of subordinates, and a narrow enough range of recipes within the division. It is not surprising, therefore, that many divisional managers, responding to largely financial demands from the corporate chief executive and his head office staff, put the business operations of the division's subsidiaries at arms' length. They embrace the recipe of the corporate head office, delegating strategic decision-taking to their subsidiaries' chief executives and controlling through primarily financial measures.

Consequently, even with the general manager of the division as an intermediary level, the integration of the separate corporate head offices and the subsidiary business operations may be almost purely financial. Yet this is tolerable only so long as the corporate (group) financial controls over the divisions, and theirs over the subsidiaries, remain effective. Once tight financial controls and personal pressure have failed to reverse an operating unit's declining performance, the next step is frequently to replace its chief executive in the hope of importing one who will implement a successful and appropriate recipe effectively. But where corporate and divisional general management lack a thorough understanding of the most appropriate recipes for their operating units, they can do little but hunt for someone with a recent track record of success in the general kind of business they believe to be involved, or select the person on the dangerous basis of "personal qualities" or other criteria unrelated to the context. Should successive chief executives fail to turn an ailing subsidiary around, as in Newton Chambers (see Grinyer and Spender), the final solution is to sell the company, either as a going concern or, more expensively, as assets after closure.

Ultimately, therefore, purely financial controls remain sensible only when the operating subsidiaries can be disposed of above or near the cost of acquiring and equipping them, should divisional management be unable to turn them around. Whether they can be disposed of depends on both their past and forecast profits, and on the state of the market for going concerns. Until the onset of the current recession, there was a good market in companies other groups felt they could not turn around. But once this market disappeared, the purely financial conglomerate recipe lost a crucial part of its viability. Central managements were forced to find alternative group recipes, ones that required group management to maintain a basic understanding of the recipes being applied by their subsidiaries. This would enable them to cut through the financial data to their operating significance, to evaluate management's performance and encourage it, to understand the consequences of the changing market, technology and skills, and, perhaps most important, to search out new management when the existing patterns of belief need changing. Of the five group recipes identified by Grinyer and Spender, all but two involve separating the corporate chief executive and head office from the operating units, and are exposed to the dangers inherent in the consequent reliance on mainly financial controls. The first exception is the "diversified major," i.e., a diversified firm dominated by a single line of business.

As Berg (7) has shown, the diversified major achieves this by concentrating on its major area of business, leaving its lesser diversified subsidiaries largely to their own devices. This amounts to a partial separation, but one that keeps the most important parts of the business under group management's immediate control. By contrast, the newer group recipe identified in the Grinyer and Spender study — the "participative diversifier" — attempts to keep close personal control of all of a restricted variety of operations. On the one hand, group management must grasp the outlines of all the recipes being applied; but on the other, they delegate part of their strategic burden selectively to divisional chairmen who know their operations' recipes. Instead of controlling through a net of financial measures and targets, the group focuses on managing these managers through a much broader and less formal pattern of communication and influence. The divisional chairmen are powerful enough to be able to educate group management about the realities of the operations, but they also operationalize the group's requirements at the subsidiary level. This protects the subsidiary from inappropriate demands while still giving group management considerable influence over the subsidiaries' strategies. It encourages a developmental approach in which group management endorses and reinforces subsidiary managements when their strategies seem sound and presses informally but forcibly when they no longer seem appropriate. It then acts as both owner and banker, but also as an information center, drawing the subsidiaries' attention to facts that they are not privy to, or that might have been treated as irrelevant, given the short-term view of subsidiary management.

Further Points

The concept of the industry recipe combines several features that seem to highlight managers' own attitudes toward their work. It is dynamic, and consistent with a cyclical pattern of growth and decay; it captures the managements' experience and learning; and it allows reorientation through both innovation and imitation. At the same time, it opens up the possibility of cross-sectional research into patterns of management beliefs and judgments within an industry. Once made explicit, these patterns can form the basis of theories of the firm as a member of a specific industry, applying the inductive methodology outlined, for instance, by Christenson (1976).

Such recipes enable management to identify the significant technological, financial, and social dimensions of its concrete situations without demanding their articulation within a coherent theory of the firm. The pattern of diverse beliefs can be visualized as a multiplicity of constraints defining a feasible solution space within which the firm's strategy must be located. Spender illustrates this in his identification of the principle components of managerial thought, implying these are only synthesized in the context of a specific set of operations. (8) Thus, as Normann (1976) also argues, the business idea or recipe-based strategy can only, in the final analysis, be expressed as a pattern of tangible activity.

Notes

1) H. Mintzberg (1977) "Patterns in Strategy Formation." Working paper, McGill University.

2) Mintzberg (1977) ibid.

3) J.-C. Spender (1979) "Strategy-making in Business." Ph.D. thesis, Manchester Business School, Manchester, England.

4) K. Hatten (1975) "Strategy, Beer and Profits." Working paper 75-14, Harvard Business School; K. Hatten and D. Schendel (1976) "Heterogeneity within an Industry; US Brewing 1952-71." Working paper 76-27, Harvard Business School.

5) C. Argyris (1976) "Organizational Learning and Effective Management Information Systems: A Prospectus for Research." Working paper 76-4, Harvard University.

6) P. H. Grinyer, S. Al-Bazzaz, and M. Yasai-Rardekani (1978) Strategy, Structure, the Environment, and Financial Performance in 48 U.K. Companies. Unpublished manuscript, City University Business School, London.

7) N. Berg (1971) "Corporate Role and Diversified Companies." Working paper HBS 71-72, Harvard University, Graduate School of Business Administration.

8) J.-C. Spender (1976) "Analysis, Dialectic and Praxis in Business Policy Teaching." Internal working paper of the City University Business School, London.

References

Allrine, F. C. (1968) "Diffusion of Competitive Innovation." In R. L. Ring (Ed.), Marketing and the New Science of Planning (Proceedings of the American Marketing Association's National Conference). Pp. 341-51. Quoted by Czepiel (1975).

Andrews, P. W. S. (1949) Manufacturing Business. New York: Macmillan.

Ansoff, H. I. (1965) Corporate Strategy. New York: McGraw-Hill.

Argyris, E., and Schon, D. (1974) Theory in Practice. San Francisco: Jossey-Bass.

Barnard, C. (1938) The Functions of the Executive. Cambridge, Mass.: Harvard University Press.

Boulding, K. E. (1956) The Image. Ann Arbor: University of Michigan Press.

Bowman, E. H. (1976) "Strategy and the Weather." Sloan Management Review, 17(2), 49-58.

Burns, T., and Stalker, G. M. (1961) The Management of Innovation. London: Tavistock.

Chandler, A. D. (1962) Strategy and Structure: Chapters on the History of American Industrial Enterprise. Cambridge, Mass.: MIT Press.

Christenson, C. "Concepts, Theory and Techniques: Proposals for a Program of Empirical Research into the Properties of Triangles." Decision Sciences, 7(4), 631-48.

Cyert, R. M., and March, J. G. (1963) A Behavioral Theory of the Firm. Englewood Cliffs, N.J.: Prentice-Hall.

Czepiel, J. A. (1975) "Patterns of Interorganizational Communications and the Diffusion of a Major Technological Innovation in a Competitive Industrial Community." Academy of Management Journal, 18(1), 6-24.

Grinyer, P. H. (1971) "The Anatomy of Business Strategy Planning Reconsidered." The Journal of Management Studies, 8(3), 199-212.

Grinyer, P. H., and Spender, J.-C. (1979) "Turnaround: Managerial Recipes for Strategic Success. London: Associated Business Publications.

Hedberg, B. L. T., and Jonsson, S. A. (1977) "Strategy Formulation as a Discontinuous Process." International Studies of Management & Organization, VII(2), 88-109.

Hedberg, B. L. T., Nystrom, P. C., and Starbuck, W. H. (1976) "Camping on Seesaws: Prescriptions for a Self-designing Organization." Administrative Science Quarterly, 21(1), 41-65.

Hussey, D. (1974) Corporate Planning: Theory and Practice. New York: Pergamon Press.

Knight, F. (1965) Risk, Uncertainty and Profit. London.

Kuhn, T. S. (1962) The Structure of Scientific Revolutions. Chicago: University of Chicago Press.

Lindblom, C. E. (1959) "The Science of 'Muddling Through.'" Public Administration Review, 19, 79-88.

March, J. G., and Simon, H. A. (1958) Organizations. New York: Wiley.

Martilla, J. A. (1971) "Word-of-Mouth Communication in the Industrial Adoption Process." Journal of Marketing Research, 8, 173-78.

Masterman, M. (1970) "The Nature of a Paradigm." In I. Lakatos and A. E. Musgrave (Eds.), Criticism and the Growth of Knowledge. Cambridge: Cambridge University Press.

Mintzberg, H. (1973) The Nature of Managerial Work. New York: Harper and Row.

Normann, R. (1976) Management and Statesmanship. Stockholm: Scandinavian Institutes for Administrative Research. [See also his paper on the same topic in International Studies of Management & Organization, VII(3-4) (Fall-Winter 1977), 20-36.]

Rhenman, E. (1973) Organization Theory for Long Range Planning. New York: Wiley.

Rumelt, R. P. (1974) Strategy, Structure and Economic Performance. Cambridge, Mass.: Harvard University Press.

Schendel, D., and Patton, G. R. (1976) "Corporate Turnaround Strategies: A Study of Profit Decline and Recovery." Journal of General Management, 3(3), 3-11.

Schutz, A. (1972) The Phenomenology of the Social World. London: Heinemann.

Shubik, M. (1954) "Information, Risk, Ignorance and Indeterminacy." Quarterly Journal of Economics, 68(3), 629-39.

Simon, H. A. (1957) Administrative Behavior. New York: Macmillan.

Simon, H. A. (1962) "The Architecture of Complexity." In Proceedings of the American Philosophical Society, 106(6), 479.

Sloan, A. P. (1964) My Years with General Motors. New York: Doubleday.

Steiner, G. A. (1969) Top Management Planning. New York: Macmillan.

Thomas, J. H., and Bennis, W. G. (1972) Management of Change and Conflict. Harmondsworth: Penguin Books.

Thompson, J. (1967) Organizations in Action. New York: McGraw-Hill.

Vickers, G. (1970) Value Systems and the Social Process. Harmondsworth: Penguin Books.

Webster, F. E. (1969) "New Product Adoption in Industrial Markets: A Framework for Analysis." Journal of Marketing, 33, 35-39.

Scientific theory helps explain the forces that both create the need for massive organizational change and shape its effects.

Organizational Paradigms: A Theory of Organizational Change

Alan Sheldon

An organization is a "world" with a particular view that colors what its members see and let in from the world outside. An organizational world consists of people practicing their technologies, organized by their tasks, and structured into relationships kept dynamic by the way they are measured and controlled. Inevitably, these people are to some degree self-selected, inadvertently or deliberately, and share values and attitudes. All this is directed toward some end—sometimes explicit, sometimes implicit.

Contingency theory posits that any organization not actually failing must have a high degree of fit not only with the environment, but also between the dimensions of technology, structure, motivations of organizational members, and the control system. Since such fit is rarely perfect, organizations are constantly tinkering with one dimension or another—and this is what may be called normal change. Normal change is often needed when the environment (broadly, the market or the availability of resources) shifts in some unstabilizing fashion—and, since such change is experienced as a need to tune up, it is rarely resisted strenuously.

All organizations tend toward a paradigm—toward some perfect fit reflecting some idealized way of working that is cherished. (See the box on page 64.) Normal change does not threaten that paradigm. But when, on occasion, a near-perfect fit is achieved, with all dimensions harmoniously directed toward some cherished end, the organization becomes ultrastable—an end in itself—and any change in any dimension now threatens the paradigm. The world will dissolve if any part of it should change; if anything is lost, all is lost. Western Psychiatric Hospital reached that point. (See case history 1, beginning on page 67.) It is at such a point that people feel they would rather fight—or die—than switch.

Applicability of Paradigmatic Theory To Organizational Change

When an organization senses a disadvantageous change—either in itself or in its environment—it may modify one or the other to regain at least some of its lost efficiency. If the change that occurs is evolutionary and circumscribed in scope, it triggers a normal process of organizational change called adaptation. The process might also be labeled organizational learning, for as the organization gets information about what is less than adaptive, it acts accordingly. Such a reaction typifies the normal organization which, since it is open to learning, functions as an "open" system.

Sometimes, however, discontinuous changes occur in an organization's environment, or the process of organizational adaptation may involve a number of significant organizational dimensions. When changes of this kind occur, adaptation of the normal kind may not be sufficient to ensure the organization's survival. In such cases, paradigmatic shifts may be necessary.

Paradigmatic shifts may also be required in organizations that have had a near-perfect fit to their environment. Such organizations are in an ultrastable state, unable to adapt or to learn. Because changing any dimension is threatening, they change none. These organizations function as closed systems, rejecting any information they receive that implies their failure, in whole or in part, because acceptance would destroy their stability. Such organizations begin to act as though the paradigm were an end rather than a means to their organizational mission. In this state, keeping constant who they are and what they do is more important than any consideration of the value of this activity in and to the outside world.

Change under these circumstances can only be discontinuous, not relatively continuous as normal change is. The organization changes not at all for awhile and then, if the fit between organization and environment is poor enough, the old paradigm must be renounced and a new one adopted; there is a lurch to a new, relatively steady state. Such organizations are somewhat like a crystal that, having reached a stable state, shifts radically under changes of pressure to a new stable state. Whether any organization can in fact learn continuously is questionable, since the tendency toward stability is profound.

Paradigmatic resistance

What are some of the characteristics of adherence to paradigms that produce resistance and what root causes must be tackled in order to effect change?

The closed paradigmatic state is

Dr. Alan Sheldon is *associate professor at Harvard University's School of Public Health and director of executive programs, in which he teaches organizational issues and is faculty chairman at several programs. He trained as a physician and psychiatrist at Cambridge University and Westminster Hospital in England before becoming involved in management education at Harvard Business School, where he headed the first-year organizational behavior course in the M.B.A. program. His research interests are in leadership and in the management of planning and collaboration. He consults widely in both the private and the public sector, specializing in the health field and public broadcasting, and has published over 12 books and 70 articles.*

not unlike the state of group-think described by Irving Janis. Members of the organization collude to avoid any questioning of their ideology or what they do. They seem to experience "doublethink," a state in which they simultaneously acknowledge and deny aspects of the organization that do not work. Thus at South Clinic (see case history 2, beginning on page 71), doctors said they felt that the role of department chairman was perfectly viable, yet acknowledged that the chairman had no power to affect anything. An illusion of unanimity is created—one in which people repeatedly make statements they believe are shared by others, yet without checking this belief. Finally, any deviance from the norm is regarded as betrayal or desertion. One reason that organizations in such a state are hard to change lies in the "bundling" of organizational dimensions—a process in which all of them are regarded as crucial to one another and any threatened change in one threatens the whole. Normal change techniques, which involve a large measure of rationality, cannot work under these circumstances. Kuhn points out, and these studies echo his, that paradigmatic change is only partly rational.

Paradigmatic Change

As already mentioned, the need for a paradigmatic change arises under two circumstances. One, if an organization enters a paradigmatic state, it becomes closed and stops adapting. At some point it will get out of fit with its environment—and when this misfit becomes significant enough, a paradigmatic shift must occur.

More commonly, however, the need for paradigmatic shift occurs when a single changing factor that has been triggering normal adaptive response reaches a size or intensity that requires multidimensional adaptation by the organization. Normal change, in other words, is a change in one dimension, whereas paradigmatic change involves several or all dimensions at once. All too often, an organization continues to behave as though normal adaptation will suffice when, in fact, a paradigmatic shift is needed. To avoid such a radical shift, organizations may begin squirming, trying to change this dimension or that—yet finding no significant and effective result. By tinkering with structure or fiddling with job definitions, organizations hope to ignore what they dread yet need: a change of the whole.

Obviously, techniques appropriate in dealing with normal change are not at all appropriate in dealing with paradigmatic change. When worlds are not being shattered and resistance is not enormous, it is

63

Kuhn's Paradigmatic Theory

A decade ago Thomas Kuhn first put forward an analysis of the development of scientific theory in which he suggested that science advances through evolutionary and revolutionary periods. Most science, what he calls normal science, works within an accepted set of rules and spends its time exploring their nooks and crannies. Occasionally, however, there erupts a kind of science that changes the rules, and this he calls paradigmatic science. A paradigm is a scientific theory, yet more than that. It is what the members of a scientific community share; conversely, a scientific community consists of people who share a paradigm. It is both a way of going about the business of science and what it is the scientist sees. Thus paradigms are, in a way, worlds as well as world views. Moreover, since people can agree on identifying a paradigm without being able to agree on exactly what it is, the term may be employed in a usefully vague way.

Nevertheless, paradigms guide science and scientific research by providing models in addition to the rules already in place. Actually, normal science can get along without much recourse to rules as long as scientists accept the way things are done. Rules become important, however, when paradigms or models are felt to be in question—so the period just before a paradigm changes is marked by intense argument over whether models and rules are proper or not. Such debates further intensify with the appearance of a new paradigm—a new and alternative world and world view.

Crises are prerequisites for the emergence of new theories. When scientists find that old theories do not altogether work anymore, they may begin to consider alternatives, but they do not yet give up on the old theories. In fact, they will discard a scientific theory only if an alternative theory is available to take its place. So the decision to reject one paradigm simultaneously marks the decision to accept another. Crises help facilitate a fundamental paradigm shift; simply by occurring, they throw into disrepute the stereotypes that aren't adequate to deal with them and forcefully point up the need for a different model.

Not everyone may be impressed by this need, however; there are always those who cling tenaciously to the old paradigm, claiming that it is entirely adequate. The problem with arguing about paradigms is that each group uses its own to argue in that paradigm's defense. Since, as noted earlier, paradigms represent totally different worlds and world views, they do not offer a base for logical argument—in other words, the basic assumptions of the two parties are so different that those involved cannot even compare and contrast them. Indeed, the values of each are so different that the proponents of competing paradigms are always at least slightly at cross-purposes and are bound partly to talk past each other. Though each may hope to convert the other to his way of seeing and sharing his paradigm, neither may hope to prove the case. Nor is the competition between paradigms the sort of battle that can be resolved by proofs, for the proponents of competing paradigms will often disagree even about the list of problems that any paradigm candidate must resolve. In other words, the opposing proponents not only live in different worlds, they see different worlds out there even though the objects viewed are the same.

reasonable and appropriate to be open, confronting, and involving. Paradigmatic change, on the other hand, requires a radical change in world and world view—often accompanied by mourning because the old world is felt to be dying. If a new paradigm exists, it may be abhorred (the case at Western Psychiatric Hospital); if none exists, a known

After adopting a new paradigm, scientists use its new instruments to see new things. In other words, they see a different world with their own new internal world. It is as though the people sharing the new paradigm were suddenly transported to another planet where familiar objects are seen in a different light and are joined by unfamiliar ones as well.

When a new paradigm is born from an old one, the old terms, concepts, and approaches fall into new relationships with those of the new paradigm. This inevitably leads to some kind of misunderstanding between the two competing schools of thought, for the proponents of each practice their trades in different worlds and see different things when they look from the same point in the same direction. Obviously, before they can hope to communicate fully, one group or the other must experience a conversion, or paradigm shift. Because this shift is a transition between different worlds, it cannot be made a step at a time but must occur all at once, although not necessarily instantaneously. How can such a radical transition be made? Being only human, scientists cannot always admit their errors even when confronted with strict proof, and the shift from an old to a new paradigm is not one based totally on logic. Nor is it a conversion that can be forced. In fact, lifelong resistance to such a change is all too often the case, particularly from those whose productive careers have been committed to an older tradition of normal science. Such an investment may produce not only intense allegiance to tradition, but intense antipathy to any threatened change.

Strengthening such resistance is a feeling of assurance that the older paradigm will ultimately solve all its problems, that nature can be shoved into the box the paradigm provides. At times of revolution that assurance seems stubborn and pigheaded, as indeed it sometimes becomes. But the older model should not be viewed as worthless; after all, it was the process of exploring the value of the older paradigm and discovering its shortcomings that, paradoxically, revealed the need for a new one.

To say that resistance is inevitable and legitimate and that the need for change cannot be justified by proof is not to say that no arguments are relevant, or that scientists cannot be persuaded to change their minds. A generation may be required to effect change, but scientific communities have, again and again, been converted to new paradigms. These conversions occur in spite of indefinite resistance on the part of older and more experienced scientists. They occur a few at a time until, after the last holdouts have died, the whole profession once again practices under a single, different paradigm. How does such conversion occur—conversion in terms not of an individual, but of a group? We know that initial arguments for change are based on the proposition that the new paradigm can solve the problems that led the old one into crisis. If these arguments are not compelling, the new paradigms may be advanced as being neater or simpler than the old—and such esthetic considerations can sometimes be decisive. Finally, there are two related elements that hold persuasive power. These are the beliefs and values of the paradigm's proponents. Belief in a particular model helps shape the values of the group as a whole and thus helps determine what the group will accept and what it will not. The particular importance of widely shared values emerges at crisis times when choices have to be made.

old world, however fallible, is to be replaced by the fearful unknown. It is hardly surprising that such a major upheaval requires special handling. But even before dealing with the emotional turbulence involved, it's important to establish the death of the old paradigm—for as long as it lingers, the new one will have little hope for survival.

Paradigmatic Change: Approaches

Anyone or any group contemplating paradigmatic change must recognize that, on the one hand, paradigmatic shifts involve multidimensional changes and yet, on the other, that people have to be anchored in stability and security in order to entertain change of such magnitude without becoming unhinged. Obviously, those in charge of effecting it must sequence and modulate the process for those who must change along with it.

It should start, like any, with a diagnosis—one aimed at questioning not only the effectiveness of the existing ways of doing things, but also the "world" and beliefs of the members of the organization. As in the South Clinic example, it may be possible to identify the existing paradigm and raise questions about its shortcomings. Only if there is sufficient concern over the shortcomings of the existing paradigm will an exploration of alternative new ones become possible. This questioning process, in which the organization is confronted with whether it wants to change or stay the same and face the consequences, must also tackle the bundling phenomenon and aim at unlinking the elements involved—thus weakening irrational connections. A second crucial process is the identification of values and beliefs—especially those that, on the one hand, contribute to the problem or hamper efforts to solve it, and those that, on the other, facilitate movement toward a solution. As Kuhn points out, the three keys to a paradigm death and rebirth are the sterility of the old paradigm, the efficacy of the new one, and the values and beliefs of organizational members.

Structurally, there are three kinds of paradigmatic shift—those involving: (1) A side-by-side overlap in the existence of the old and the new paradigm; (2) a transformation in which the old paradigm is dying or dead before the new one is born; and (3) a supraparadigm, or the superimposition of the new above the old. The two case studies represent, in microcosm, the first and second types of paradigmatic shift. In each of these, the shift occurs because of the old paradigm's failure. In the third type, the new paradigm is a positive force impelled by a vision of some new world. To wit:

1. In Western Psychiatric Hospital, the new paradigm emerges alongside the old, which continues to exist. If change is to be successful, the two must be buffered from

". . . paradigmatic shifts involve multidimensional changes and . . . people have to be anchored in stability and security in order to entertain change of such magnitude without becoming unhinged."

each other—physically, organizationally, and fiscally. Failure to do this inevitably leads to adverse consequences.

2. The South Clinic illustrates the second type of shift—and elements of the third. Transformation is lengthy; before any structural changes can occur, values and beliefs must change and the old paradigm must be repudiated. The new cannot be entertained until the old is moribund, if not defunct. This requires:

• Condemnation, through a careful process of confronting consequences, of the old paradigm. Problems must reach a critical point before a shift is entertained—so normal change should be neglected, or people will cling to the old paradigm.

• Attitude change through presentation of data on the new and the old and, if necessary, replacement of key people.

• A mourning process for what is gone.

• The creation of a transitional organization in which the old paradigm is condemned and attitudes—particularly those of key people—are swung over to favoring the new. The fact that this organization replaces the old one before the new one is in place serves to stabilize as well as educate if the process involved has the trust of all.

3. The supraparadigm, as exemplified by Monnet's Council of Europe, is a long-standing idea that has never proved enormously stable because the old paradigm(s) remain in place for a long period. The essential element is that the original parts do not change initially, and therefore the binding works only as long as the vision has force, or there is some need for mutuality. For example, if there is some superordinate goal or, say, a "common enemy" that is clearly defined, the original parts will stay together. Otherwise, what persistence remains is usually a function of moral rather than economic pressure. The United Nations has never worked very well, but has continued to exist because it was harder to get out of it than stay in it. Europe, however, is moving slowly toward those necessary irreversible shifts that may give it some permanency if they do not precipitate collapse. A single monetary system is an instance in point.

This example of supraparadigmatic change is well known.

CASE HISTORY 1: WESTERN PSYCHIATRIC HOSPITAL

In the late 1950s, an instructor of psychiatry at a western medical school started an experimental psychotherapy program for acute psychotics at a California hospital. Initially a four-bed unit with four doctors and eight patients, in four or five years it grew to half the size of the hospital, with 25 doctors and 70 patients—losing, along the way, the founding father. The last year or so was characterized by administrative conflict with the hospital that had given them a great deal of autonomy and later regretted it.

In this period, the present medical director had been joined by three colleagues: one of his residents, a charismatic and talented clinician who later became clinical director; the then medical director; and a fourth clinician. After adding three more investor colleagues, they set up business as a for-profit private hospital—Western Psychiatric Hospital (WPH). Then they sold off half their investment to a for-profit hospital company, realizing both a substantial return to the investors and a salary satisfactory to the clinicians who retained control through their seats on the board and were employed in their clinical roles via management contracts. Thus the clinicians were not only board members, owners, and investors, but also administrators and clinicians, for each had a private practice in the hospital and each ran a clinical unit. They saw themselves as a sort of clan in which the tribal chieftains were equal, with the clinical director more equal than the others—not as members of a hospital bureaucracy.

The hospital specialized in the treatment of severe psychotics, borderline character disorders, and sociopaths. Essentially it dealt in tertiary care, referrals from other psychiatric hospitals, and the failures of other psychiatrists. In other words, it dealt in the hardest type of patient to treat. The therapeutic technology consisted essentially of intensive psychotherapy without the aid of drugs, except on rare occasions, and without electric shock therapy. However, restraints were necessary because of the therapeutic technique used—a technique intended to break down maladaptive defense by fostering regression. The typical hospital stay for these patients lasted from 18 months to two years, since a long period was required to break down their defenses and then to build them up.

The hospital was relatively light on administrative staff and procedures, and heavy on nurses and therapeutic support staff. Under the guidance of the clinical director, it had innovated the development of a new administrative-therapeutic role, the unit leader. To some degree this role has arisen in the absence of strong nursing leadership, and to some degree was a function of the particular therapy involved. There was a wide diversity of background among unit leaders; some, for example, had been active in nursing or psychology, and some had simply been attendants. They were promoted irrespective of background on the basis of their therapeutic effectiveness, and the most senior had a great deal of power in the hospital.

The hospital was originally divided into four long-term clinical wards plus an adolescent ward and an admission and evaluation ward. Three of the clinic owners each ran a ward. The 20 or so medical staff were assigned in about equal numbers to each of the major wards, and in addition could admit to the adolescent ward. No one really ran a ward, however, since most of the decision making was delegated and made at the unit or group level, and the senior unit leaders, of whom there were ten, had a major say over what went on at the unit level.

Thus a unique choice of patient and an innovative form of therapy had led to the development of innovative roles and a very informal, decentralized form of administration. It was clear, moreover, that there was some self-selection for the kinds of people who found this work interesting and were good at it. Medical staff, for example, normally never had more than two to four patients, each of whom they might see for half an hour a day, five days a week. Staff tended to be somewhat compliant and, with but a few exceptions, busied themselves with clinical rather than administrative matters. Perhaps it was a combination of the innovative excitement and enthusiasm and the self-selected passivity that led to the suppression or nonrecognition of so many potential administrative and interpersonal conflicts.

Success was unabated through 1975, but 1975 to 1978 proved to be a checkered and turbulent time. A private hospital, it was still heavily dependent on reimbursement of charges through insurance and Blue Cross, and the insurance organizations leaned heavily on long-term patient coverage to a situation that led to a drop in referrals and therefore in patient census. Although this was a common effect across the United States, the specialized nature of this particular hospital made the blow an especially hard one. The census dropped from a maximum of 100 or so to 87 in 1976, 77 in 1977, and 70 in 1978—but the hospital is currently licensed for 100 beds and has 90 available. Even though the hospital was able to cut back from a high of 1.9 employees per patient to 1.6, it became clear that its unique approach was no longer economically viable. Coincident with these economic pressures was what appeared to be some burning out of some of the original protagonists. The then medical director withdrew entirely, although he maintained his financial interests, and the charismatic clinical director withdrew much of his energy and interest. The staff remaining after census pressures increased turnover and reduced staff became overburdened—especially since some 18 months to two years were required to train the relatively inexperienced newer staff members in the specialized techniques required. In response to these pressures, the hospital began to change its approach and its organization.

In 1976, in response to the economic pressures, one of the long-term wards was converted into a general psychiatry program for shorter-stay patients. This new, general psychiatry program had fewer acute patients—but they were still quite sick, and there were more of them moving more rapidly through it. The three long-term wards—which had had approximately 17 beds each, although the wards were often only two-thirds full—were transformed into 18-bed wards. (The adolescent ward was kept essentially unchanged, although moved physically.) The change was a difficult one, and since the clinician/owners had both clinical and administrative roles on the wards, choices and methods were both questioned. Even worse, favoritism was implied and suspicions expressed as to whether clinical decisions might be financially based. Medical staff worried about whether there would be enough beds for their patients—despite the fact that none of them had any fewer beds than previously. Of course, some of these feelings and concerns might have arisen because management was perceived as being amateur—that is, the kind of management that moves from crisis to crisis without any long-term plans.

The success of the previous approach was being brought into question. Conflicts (whether real or imagined) that had been ignored or suppressed began to preoccupy the staff, which identified the clinical director with the original, "pure" approach, and viewed the medical director as being largely responsible for the evolving new approach with its heavier emphasis on administration. Actually, it is not surprising that staff ambivalence over new methods that might be required but were unwelcome would get played out upon these two characters. The medical director failed to diminish their concern when he began to tighten up administrative procedures and appointed a new, managerially oriented nursing director. To make matters worse, she had a background in reality therapy rather than long-term therapy.

Reaction was not long forthcoming. It was felt at all levels that an organization characterized by excitement, intuition, and caring for one another was being replaced by one in which dollar signs and administrative procedures were paramount. An overall reduction in the number of beds and the lack of success of an ill-conceived outpatient clinic turned off the medical staff, who themselves referred fewer patients when they had any to refer. Although unit leaders felt threatened by the shift to formal structures, they despaired over what they might do since they perceived themselves, not incorrectly, to be uniquely adapted to their existing situation with little hope of transferring to a job elsewhere. The general feeling was one of moving from a family to a business, and many things that once had passed without comment now raised hostilities. Money interests on the part of the once-revered clinician/owners were felt to be suspect. The pay inequity between unit leaders and psychiatrists was felt to be intolerable in view of the relatively heavy load taken on by unit leaders. Staff involvement diminished, morale dropped, and turnover exacerbated the problem for those that remained. More extreme symptoms developed, too: Some staff members themselves succumbed to psychiatric disorders, and a number of discharged patients, largely from the new program, committed suicide—a first in the history of the hospital. Perhaps despair is contagious.

It was in this context that the final blow fell. After one social worker resigned for personal reasons, the remaining three tried to renegotiate their relationship with the hospital. This point marked the culmination of a year-long conflict that started with a proposal that one social worker see a patient alone—without the supervision of a physician. The social workers had always done therapy under the supervision of a physician—and, whether the physicians viewed the issue as economic or territorial, they responded sharply, banning the solo procedure. Believing, not incorrectly, that the hospital was making a lot of money on them, and fed up with working a 50-hour week for a 40-hour salary with additional hours if they wanted to see their private patients, the social workers asked for a better split of the clinical fee plus higher payment for their administrative services. As an alternative, they asked for a relationship with the hospital like that of the medical staff—meaning that they work on contract, using the hospital premises when appropriate. The social workers knew pretty much what they wanted. But both sides were inexperienced in negotiating, so when the clinician/owners responded in what the social workers felt was a totally inadequate way topped off with condescension, all three social workers resigned.

It was at this point that the medical director began to wonder whether the institution was dying and what he could do about his organization. But the picture, while bleak, was not in fact as desperate as many felt. Taking an overall perspective revealed two worlds in conflict. The first had evolved with near-perfect fit between its parts, but then had begun to find diminishing success in the larger world. Perhaps because of the neat fit between its parts, it was unwilling or unable to make the adjustments that might have alleviated its economic distress. The clinical director had once said that the owners never wanted a hospital, but rather a clan or cult. As such, its members preferred to fight rather than switch. Entrapped by their own world view, they were unable to make changes that could have kept them afloat (because making them would have been to betray their ideal)—worse, they could not even let others in the organization do it for them. As the medical director began to be identified with the development of an alternative world, he and it were undercut in two disastrous ways. Old-timers on the staff denigrated the new approach as being unsuitable for use with the old patients. That is, short-term therapy for less sick people could not be approached with the same techniques and staff that had been appropriate in long-term therapy for very sick people. The shorter-term approach of necessity had to be defense-enhancing, not defense-reducing, because there was no time to break down and rebuild defenses—a process requiring aftercare support. The war between these two worlds is what Thomas Kuhn calls paradigmatic conflict.

Suffice it to say that simply understanding that two totally different worlds were engaged in a brutal and bruising fight led to the beginning of an appreciation of how to approach the solution. Remedy lay at a number of levels, but first and most important was separation of the two warring paradigms. To accomplish this, it was proposed that the hospital be divided into two divisions—physically, organizationally, and fiscally. Different people were to be in charge of each, and there were even to be two nursing directors. Different staff would work in each, with the newly recruited staff assigned to the general psychiatry program. Administrative rules, procedures, and organizations would be more structured and formal in the general psychiatry program, and traditional and informal in the long-term program.

The basic problem for the staff at Western Psychiatric Hospital lay in not recognizing that what they were engaged in was paradigmatic change. Failing to recognize this, they had simply tried to change only one organizational dimension—the kind of patients they were treating—without seeing that they actually needed to change many dimensions simultaneously. Apparently, the model solution arrived at helped, and in ensuing months the divisional concept was implemented and even symbolized by the uniforms worn by staff in the general psychiatry program to signal their greater formality. Turnover dropped, morale rose, and what had seemed terminal become, phoenixlike, a new beginning.

CASE HISTORY 2: SOUTH CLINIC

South Clinic is a medical group practice organized as a partnership of physicians with 85 partners; it is run by a board of management of seven doctors. The administration includes a medical director, associate and assistant medical directors, and a sizable administrative staff. The clinic employs many doctors in addition to the partners, and has a total of 650 employees. The partnership rents the clinic building from the South Medical Foundation and its partners use the Foundation Hospital. A nonprofit corporation, South Medical Foundation has several operating divisions, major ones including the Foundation Hospital with

1,869 employees, the graduate medical education division, the school of allied health sciences, and the research institute. The president of the foundation is also chief executive officer of the hospital (a recent innovation) and there is a board of trustees of 51 members and an executive committee of 15 members, seven of whom are physicians; each of the latter is a partner in the clinic. The foundation has 107 employees working outside of the hospital in such additional foundation divisions as finance, employee relations, planning and development, and public affairs. There is also a service corporation whose stock is held solely by people who work at the medical institutions; this corporation owns and operates a hotel and affiliated services.

South Clinic started in 1940 when five professors at a southern university school of medicine decided that a well-organized group practice would meet a great medical need in the area. Advice was sought from such existing clinics as Lahey, Mayo, Minnesota, and Cleveland. Although initial attempts to get financial assistance from philanthropists failed, a patient of one of the founders just happened to run a bank and proffered its support should plans be forthcoming. An office building was found and a first public announcement mentioned "plans for establishment of a 'little Mayo Clinic' where people from all over the South and from South and Central American countries could come for diagnostic check-ups by groups of the most skilled medical specialists in the city. . . ." It is noteworthy that the market for the clinic has not changed in four decades.

Notice that the first building was to be purchased started many rumors among local physicians, most of whom were bitterly opposed to group practice because they considered it unfair competition. On Holy Thursday night, April 13, 1941, unknown persons sent to each of the five founders a small leather bag containing 30 silver dimes and a typewritten note which read, "to help pay for your clinic—from the local physicians, surgeons, and dentists." The implication that the founders were Judases did not change their plans.

South Clinic opened its doors to patients on January 2, 1942. To begin with, patients who came represented primarily the consolidated clientele of the founders. Appointments were arranged through a central appointment office, records were filed in a central record room, and the clinical X-ray labs and pharmacy were centralized with reports filed in patient records. Bookkeeping and accounting were also centralized, and patients received a single statement for all services rendered. Hospitalization was at a local infirmary, and those hospitalized were under the care of the clinic staff. Soon patients were being referred for complete clinic service—that is, for a diagnostic survey or clinic check—rather than for care by an individual physician.

Early on, the foundation considered changing the partnership into an association similar to Mayo or a foundation like Cleveland or Ford, but state law prohibited such practice by a nonprofit corporation or foundation, so the partnership was retained. In 1944, however, the Medical Foundation was created by dissolving the property-holding corporation and giving its assets to the nonprofit corporation. Thereafter, the clinic leased its buildings, grounds, furnishings, and equipment from the foundation, which applied the rentals to its declared purposes of education, research, and charity. This set-up, which was similar to that of the Mayo Foundation, ensured the continued success of the clinic after the founders died. The foundation today continues this tradition. An early step was the addition of lay members to the board of trustees—competent businessmen who could help in the handling of affairs.

The critical shortage of beds in the city soon forced the clinic to consider either developing its own hospital or joining the university. Raising the necessary capital delayed matters and it was not until 1951 that a site, consisting of 21 acres between a major highway and a river, was bought from the local railroad. It was on this site that first the hotel—dedicated to patients, families, and visitors—and then the hospital (1954) and the clinic were built. In 1957, much of the clinic moved to some floors of the hotel and in 1959, the research building was completed. The new clinic building was started in 1961 and completed in 1963.

The South Medical Institutions went through three organizational phases:

1. *The Founders' Era (1941 to late 1950s)*. This era was characterized by placement of decision making in the hands of the five founders at a multiple levels.

• *South Clinic:* During this period, the clinic was a partnership composed solely of the five founders, who also headed the major departments. The other physicians were employees of the partnership. South Clinic's board of management, formed at the behest of the employed physicians, was composed of the five founders plus two senior employed physicians, the chief of medicine, and the associate chief of surgery. The first two medical directors were recruited from academia but proved unsatisfactory, so one founder agreed to lend stability to the group practice by becoming medical director. In addition, a less-than-satisfactory business manager was replaced early in the history of the organization by a strong director who remains in this position today.

• *The Foundation:* The foundation's board of trustees was composed of the five founders plus two strong lay trustees. The original founder served as president of the foundation, but his role was largely titular. The post of hospital director was at first filled by relatively undistinguished individuals.

2. *The Successors' Era (late 1950s to early 1970s)*. This era was characterized by replacement of the founders in all of their multiple roles by a group of hand-picked successors.

• *South Clinic:* The partnership was broadened in 1957 by the formation of a new partnership. Half of the ownership remained in the hands of the five founders, the remaining half belonging to a new group of physicians eligible on the basis of five years of service. There was a provision for a phase-out of the original founding partners over a number of years.

The five founders on the board of management were gradually replaced by senior physicians, usually department heads. Members of the board served ten-year terms and were eligible to succeed themselves and to serve until age 65. Any vacancy would be filled by the board of management, and the partnership could reject the proposed candidate only by a vote of 75 percent. In general, the board of management was composed of heads of major departments or divisions. One of the founders, in his 70s, stepped down from the medical director position. He was succeeded by a physician who had served as the associate medical director and who had headed the department of colon and rectal surgery. There was a subtle change in the role of the medical director during this period of time. While the former medical director had been one of five founders, his successor became the *primum inter pares*. He headed the board of management, the finance committee, and other important decision-making bodies. And he took on the additional role of administrative director of the South Medical Foundation.

• *The Foundation:* The two laymen on the original board of trustees of the foundation were succeeded by another two executives from the business community. And during this period, the founders were gradually replaced on the board by the members of the board of management. The new medical director succeeded the original founder as president of the South Medical Foundation and also became chief executive officer of the South Medical Center. A largely titular and honorary board of governors for the South Foundation Hospital had been formed after the current hospital was constructed, serving largely in recognition of their role as donors to the foundation and to the hospital.They were gradually replaced by an energetic group of young businessmen who felt isolated from the decision-making process since this role was filled by the board of trustees.

3. *Current Era (early 1970s to present).*

• *South Clinic:* The eligibility for election to the partnership was reduced to three years' service—there are now 85 partners. The value of the partnership, which was approximately $2,500 when the expanded partnership was formed in 1957, now exceeds $100,000. And there is an undercurrent of feeling that entry into the partnership should be restricted to avoid diluting the holdings of the current partners.

The partnership agreement was rewritten in the early 1970s to provide popular election to the board of management. Annually, the partnership has two candidates presented to it and majority vote determines the winner. Members elected to the board of management serve seven-year terms and cannot succeed themselves. The initial phases of popular election brought a subtle change in board character: The most visible and most vocal anti-establishment candidates tended to be elected. Only one department head is on the board of management at the present time. In general, as the major department heads have relinquished administrative roles, they have not been replaced by members of the board of management. In recent years, outside recruiting plus a tendency to identify talent early has resulted in a situation in which anywhere from four to six major departments have been headed by physicians who are not yet partners in the group practice. The second medical director was succeeded in 1975 by a younger physician and gave up his role with the South Medical Foundation.

• *The Foundation:* Largely to address concerns of the board of governors of the hospital as to their role, a drastic change in the board of trustees was effected in the early 1970s. A board of trustees with over 40 members was created, incorporating members of the previous board of trustees, the board governors, others from the region and community, and physicians from the South Clinic. An executive committee of the board of trustees composed of eight laymen and seven physicians was elected to serve as the decision-making body of the foundation. The seven physicians were those who had served on the board of trustees in the previous era. As these physicians reached 60 years of age they were phased out of their administrative roles, and a change in the election rules removed them from the board of management of the clinic. The physicians who replaced them on the executive committee are former department heads and former members of the board of management.

In the early 1970s, the hospital administrator died. The lay members on the committee seeking his replacement became convinced that they would be unable to recruit a man of stature without making him head of the foundation as well. In autumn of 1974, the new administrator and president and chief executive officer of South Medical Foundation was hired. The medical director, who until that time had been president of South Medical Foundation, medical director of South Clinic, and chief executive officer of South Medical Center, became the chairman of the board of trustees.

Thus the situation in the mid-1970s, entirely aside from the personalities involved, was fraught with the potential for miscommunication and polarization. There were three identifiable groups of physicians in the power structure: (1) the board of management and the medical director, (2) the major department heads, who carry line responsibility for running the departments, carrying out the mandates of the board of management, and (3) the physician members of the executive committee of the South Medical Foundation. Although in the past all three groups consisted of the same group of physicians, practically no overlap now existed between the three groups.

There was a legacy of mistrust between the physicians of the clinic and the foundation. The clinic had given the local medical school a large donation at a time when a merger seemed possible and continued to give the foundation money, even in lean years. On the other hand, the foundation, as the clinic's landlord, increased its rent threefold during this same period.

Starting in 1976, the new foundation CEO proposed a variety of hospital affiliations, takeovers, or amalgamations. These involved an ear, nose, and throat hospital in suburban Atlanta, which was having a trying time; a proposed private hospital and group practice in Costa Rica; another hospital in New Orleans, which was having census problems; and a children's hospital, a specialty hospital that had not only census problems, but cash-flow and managerial problems as well. For a variety of reasons, none of these latter hospital acquisitions came to fruition—but with each succeeding venture, there seemed to be a flood of publicity and community reaction, some of it adverse. A local periodical ran an extensive story under the title "The South Octopus." At the same time, negotiations were undertaken, and have continued, with the state for supplying house staff to a state hospital, the newest member of the state's charity hospital system. The *quid pro quo* involved in serving the hospital for house staff training is the responsibility for providing senior staffing for that institution as well.

During the discussion about several of these hospital affiliations, it appeared that the aspirations and desires of clinic management and foundation management, particularly the new CEO, were not congruent. Management of the group practice tended to view such ventures as desirable to the extent that they furthered the success of the group practice in some areas, while foundation management has tended to view all acquisitions as desirable, whether they would involve group practice or not. Often the acquisition meant adding an entirely new group of nonclinic physicians who would relate to the foundation.

By early 1978, there appeared to be progressive polarization between (1) the board of management and the partnership of the South Clinic and (2) the management and, to a lesser extent, the board of trustees of the South Medical Foundation. The clinic medical director attempted to serve as a buffer between these two groups, but it became apparent that further severe deterioration left serious questions as to whether the board of management of the clinic would be willing to engage in any joint projects with the South Medical Foundation. It was at this point that the foundation CEO was confronted with the fact that physician confidence in him had eroded to a point of no return and he resigned.

At the same time that relationships

between clinic and foundation were deteriorating, the rationale for keeping them separate seemed to be diminishing. As there was strengthening of the management of the foundation and its hospital, there seemed to be less and less point in duplicating many of the administrative departments. Strengthening the board of lay trustees had led, paradoxically, to an increase in their frustration as they found themselves unable to have much effective influence over the somewhat mysterious and paramount workings of the doctor-dominated clinic.

In summary, the clinic's 50-year history has been characterized by continued growth and success. This has come despite a decision-making process that has been largely one of reacting to events rather than being proactive.

The institution is now in the third generation of its "family"—leaning toward professional management for the first time, as indicated by the hiring of the new CEO. In the first generation, the clinic was run essentially by the founders and then by their successors. The third generation seems to recognize the need to share the running of the institution with the professional managers, or to become managers themselves. However, the CEO's evident skills and energy have been mitigated by his failure to involve in his decision making the physicians who dominate the power structure and who regarded his actions as opportunistic rather than strategic.

Finally, for the first five decades of its existence, South Clinic was essentially the only institution in the city, and perhaps in the region, where a first-rate physician who did not wish to go into private practice would care to practice. Now a first-rate physician has many alternatives, including better opportunities today for private practice as well as teaching hospitals, medical schools, and community hospitals where he may feel that he can get a larger salary, greater freedom, or more organizational support for his ambitions than the South Clinic offers.

Symptoms of Frustration

The level of conflict had obviously risen to an abrasive and dysfunctional level. In addition, concern was being expressed over the present or future likelihood of some erosion of the market—as well as an increase in the turnover of physicians. And it was noted that there were fewer leaders in their field in South Clinic than there used to be.

Some felt that many of the recent problems and breakdowns in communica-

---

"Traditional physician ambivalence about management in particular and leadership in general . . . had created their reluctance either to take on managerial responsibilities or to delegate them fully to others."

tion were attributable to personalities and would be remedied by the CEO's departure. Others felt that although personalities may have contributed, more fundamental problems were affecting the clinic and the hospital. Doing nothing was possible but risked having others preempt the institutions' future options. What really was wrong and what really needed to be done?

Some Questions: The Two Paradigms Elucidated

The institution's environment had changed markedly in recent years. It had become more complex and more competitive—and in addition, of course, the organization had grown to a size where it could not be managed easily or in the informal fashion of earlier days. Attitudes and values, however, had not changed as sharply, and the old remained intermixed with the new.

Traditional physician ambivalence about management in particular and leadership in general, which has often led doctors to find it easier to say no than yes—especially by default—had created their reluctance either to take on managerial responsibilities or to delegate them fully to others. Certainly, physicians exercised power—but the institution had not been managed in the usual sense of the word. This ambivalence was now leading lay trustees to feel frustrated and their tolerance was becoming limited. It also discouraged excellence in lay administration. This ambivalence resulted in some feeling that the role of department chief was the most important role for the organization's future—yet despite this responsibility, department chiefs were given negligible power. The board of management, representing the partnership, made policy (to the extent that it was made) and managed—including hiring, firing, setting salaries, appointing department and section chiefs, and deciding on budgets. The question was whether the doctors wanted to manage the institution themselves or have others manage it for them.

There was clearly some consensus that the clinic was an organizational setting in which physicians could participate free of many of the constraints they believed they would experience in other settings. It was more supportive than private practice, and less constraining than a medical school. However, there were many different views on what additional constraints would be acceptable, if required, and in what direction such constraints should go. Thus the identity was inchoate. This had some value since possibly disruptive differences could be contained in an illusion of unanimity. However, the institution was not proceeding in any defined direction with a set of clear-cut actions and decisions. The cost of establishing a clearer identity might be to lose some people or support; the cost of not making an identity clear would be a diminished institution. The question was whether the partnership and the boards wanted to clarify identity—and therefore strategy, decision, and action.

In the governance of the institution there had been a blurring of the distinctions between influencing, policy making, and managing. The board of management made policy, and certainly it managed. The partnership, however, felt entitled not only to exert influence, but also to make policy. The managers (the medical director and the department heads, for example) felt that they were not being allowed to manage. As a result, neither policy making nor managing was being done as effectively as it might have been. In an era that allowed for slippage, this was perhaps not crucial. The question was whether these three important functions should be clearly identified and separated.

77

In any organization, there is always a question of what information to share with whom. People always want more information, often meaning more influence—but when they get it, they resent the time it takes, whether in reading memoranda or attending meetings. Power in any organization can to some degree be exercised by sharing or withholding information. This point in the life of South Clinic was marked by many rumors, fantasies, and misapprehensions caused by a lack of information, especially between the foundation and the clinic. The question was whether the institution wished to disclose information about relevant matters more fully or not.

The increase in turnover among physicians had been noted. It has been pointed out that there were attractive options both in private practice, which offered higher incomes, and in teaching institutions, which offered organizational support. Some felt that it was important to stabilize the physician population. But was South Clinic prepared to accept a higher degree of turnover as a fact of life, or did it want to alter its organizational environment—making it more attractive for young physicians to come and stay?

For historical and tax-related reasons, the clinic and the foundation were created as separate entities. Although once essentially governed as a single entity, the distance between them had grown. This had led to communication and governance problems, as well as inefficiencies. The question was whether the two institutions at some future point should be joined in such a way that they could be better managed, or should remain as essentially separate entities.

The failure to confront some of the above questions had led to a mild condition of doublethink. On the one hand, some said that the department chiefs were all-important and had sufficient power—when in fact they had little, if any. People believed that there was a unanimous view of their institutional identity, yet it was anything but unanimous. The advantage of doublethink is that it maintains the illusion of oneness; the disadvantage is that it results in potentially difficult consequences when decisions are not followed through. The question was whether the institution wanted to confront its differences and the consequences of its desires, or to maintain its illusions.

The institution is typical of many physician-dominated institutions in its somewhat short-run and piecemeal approach to problems. This is inevitable to some degree because the tasks of most physicians are relatively short run. However, the organizational problems that faced the institution could be dealt with only in a long-run and fundamental fashion, not piecemeal. The question was whether the institution wished to deal with fundamental and long-run issues, or to continue to essentially muddle through on a short-run and piecemeal basis.

These questions or dilemmas could be summarized as a conflict between (1) personal values and philosophies and (2) organizational imperatives and realities. The issue was whether a traditional approach of muddling through, which had certainly been successful in the past, should become more deliberative, and whether the variety of views and concomitant differences that characterize any vital organization should be clouded or should be confronted to produce clear-cut choices.

The two paradigms thus elucidated were *physician muddling through* versus *deliberative management*. The latter required not only attitude and value changes, but a different kind of person in the managerial role (especially if a physician), and a different structure for housing organizational power and decision making—probably a structure cutting across the institutions in some fashion. The ultimate organizational form might well be a matrix in which there would be some functions totally centralized for both institutions and some departments decentralized within each institution, but reporting both to the institutions (for responsiveness) and to a central department head (for efficiency). In turn, this structural change in the organization would require some shift in clinic ownership, perhaps from a partnership to a corporation. These changes represent a transformation of paradigm, as well as the emergence of a true supraparadigm in a single central identity for the organization transcending, but containing, the separate existing identities. These changes contrast with the side-by-side emergence of a new paradigm in the example of Western Psychiatric Hospital. Given the need to change a total way of operating, the first and hardest change is one of attitude. This process requires much time and some changing of people who cannot themselves change. It requires also a transitional process in which existing members of the organization have confidence. Thus it was proposed that before any major structural changes were to be considered, some preliminary steps would be implemented. These were felt to be realistic, given the existing circumstances and the goal of transforming attitudes and facilitating rapid movement into further fundamental consideration of future strategy and organization.

Two new and cross-institutional bodies to deliberate policy and enact action concerning the total institution were created. The first, a joint policy committee, consisted of the board of management together with the executive committee of the board of trustees. The second, a joint operating committee, brought together the clinic medical director and his associate and the major department and division heads in the clinic, the hospital, and the foundation.

The reasons for the interim and possibly lengthy bridging process are that the ultimate new arrangements being proposed represent a paradigmatic shift that would be totally unacceptable to the existing clinic organization. Time must pass, attitudes change, information shared, and educational programs completed for the movement toward the different state of being to occur.

A Final Word

The essential importance of the concept of paradigm change is that it allows a sharp distinction to be made between the techniques suitable for managing the more common "normal change" and the different approaches required in the more revolutionary changes associated with paradigm shift. This recognition allows appropriate courses of action to be taken for each.

Selected Bibliography

Russell L. Ackoff and Fred E. Emery's book *On Purposeful Systems* (Aldine Press, 1972) is a highly theoretical but stimulating work based, not unexpectedly, on the authors' broad experience with a very wide variety of organizations and taking a cybernetic and general systems point of view. Paul R. Lawrence and Jay W. Lorsch's

Organization and Environment (Division of Research, Graduate School of Business Administration, Harvard University, 1967) is an early presentation of contingency theory, which states that organization is a matter of context rather than prescription. Irving Janis's *Victims of Groupthink* (Houghton Mifflin Company, 1972) describes a number of famous and infamous political decisions in which executive groups made decisions with widely differing outcomes. He concludes that the more disastrous had certain common features, which he describes, and he prescribes certain steps that groups could take to minimize the pitfalls that he had found.

Finally, Thomas Kuhn wrote his highly controversial study *The Structure of Scientific Revolutions* (Volume 2, No. 2, University of Chicago Press, 1970) nearly a decade ago, and while he has modified his thesis somewhat in the interim, it remains compelling and provocative.

The Political View

[16]

D. J. Hickson, C. R. Hinings, C. A. Lee, R. E. Schneck,
and J. M. Pennings

A Strategic Contingencies' Theory of Intraorganizational Power

> *A strategic contingencies' theory of intraorganizational power is presented in which it is hypothesized that organizations, being systems of interdependent subunits, have a power distribution with its sources in the division of labor. The focus is shifted from the vertical-personalized concept of power in the literature to subunits as the units of analysis. The theory relates the power of a subunit to its coping with uncertainty, substitutability, and centrality, through the control of strategic contingencies for other dependent activities, the control resulting from a combination of these variables. Possible measures for these variables are suggested.*

Typically, research designs have treated power as the independent variable. Power has been used in community studies to explain decisions on community programs, on resource allocation, and on voting behavior; in small groups it has been used to explain decision making; and it has been used in studies of work organizations to explain morale and alienation. But within work organizations, power itself has not been explained. This paper sets forth a theoretical explanation of power as the dependent variable with the aim of developing empirically testable hypotheses that will explain differential power among subunits in complex work organizations.[1]

The problems of studying power are well known from the cogent reviews by March (1955, 1966) and Wrong (1968). These problems led March (1966: 70) to ask if power was just a term used to mask our ignorance, and to conclude pessimistically that the power of the concept of power "depends on the kind of system we are confronting."

Part of March's (1966) pessimism can be attributed to the problems inherent in community studies. When the unit of analysis is the community, the governmental, political, economic, recreational, and other units which make up the community do not necessarily interact and may even be oriented outside the supposed boundaries of the community. However, the subunits of a work organization are mutually related in the interdependent activities of a single identifiable social system. The perspective of the present paper is due in particular to the encouraging studies of subunits by Lawrence and Lorsch (1967a, 1967b), and begins with their (1967a: 3) definition of an organization as "a system of interrelated behaviors of people who are performing a task that has been differentiated into several distinct subsystems."

Previous studies of power in work organizations have tended to focus on the individual and to neglect subunit or departmental power. This neglect led Perrow (1970: 84) to state: "Part of the problem, I suspect, stems from the persistent attempt to define power in terms of individuals and as a social-psychological phenomenon. . . . Even sociological studies tend to measure

---

[1] This research was carried out at the Organizational Behavior Research Unit, Faculty of Business Administration and Commerce, University of Alberta, with the support of Canada Council Grants numbers 67-0253 and 69-0714.

power by asking about an individual. . . . I am not at all clear about the matter, but I think the term takes on different meanings when the unit, or power-holder, is a *formal group* in an *open system* with *multiple goals*, and the system is assumed to reflect a political-domination model of organization, rather than only a cooperative model. . . . The fact that after a cursory search I can find only a single study that asks survey questions regarding the power of functional *groups* strikes me as odd. Have we conceptualized power in such a way as to exclude this well-known phenomenon?"

The concept of power used here follows Emerson (1962) and takes power as a property of the social relationship, not of the actor. Since the context of the relationship is a formal organization, this approach moves away from an overpersonalized conceptualization and operationalization of power toward structural sources. Such an approach has been taken only briefly by Dubin (1963) in his discussion of power, and incidentally by Lawrence and Lorsch (1967b) when reporting power data. Most research has focused on the vertical superior-subordinate relationship, as in a multitude of leadership studies. This approach is exemplified by the extensive work of Tannenbaum (1968) and his colleagues, in which the distribution of perceived power was displayed on control graphs. The focus was on the vertical differentiation of perceived power, that is, the exercise of power by managers who by changing their behavior could vary the distribution and the total amount of perceived power.

By contrast, when organizations are conceived as interdepartmental systems, the division of labor becomes the ultimate source of intraorganizational power, and power is explained by variables that are elements of each subunit's task, its functioning, and its links with the activities of other subunits. Insofar as this approach differs from previous studies by treating power as the dependent variable, by taking subunits of work organizations as the subjects of analysis, and by attempting a multivariate explanation, it may avoid some of the previous pitfalls.

ELEMENTS OF A THEORY

Thompson (1967: 13) took from Cyert and March (1963) a viewpoint which he hailed as a newer tradition: "A newer tradition enables us to conceive of the organization as an open system, indeterminate and faced with uncertainty, but subject to criteria of rationality and hence needing certainty . . . we suggest that organizations cope with uncertainty by creating certain parts specifically to deal with it, specializing other parts in operating under conditions of certainty, or near certainty."

Thus organizations are conceived of as interdepartmental systems in which a major task element is coping with uncertainty. The task is divided and allotted to the subsystems, the division of labor creating an interdependency among them. Imbalance of this reciprocal interdependence (Thompson, 1967) among the parts gives rise to power relations. The essence of an organization is limitation of the autonomy of all its members or parts, since all are subject to power from the others; for subunits, unlike individuals, are not free to make a decision to participate, as March and Simon (1958) put it, nor to decide whether or not to come together in political relationships. They must. They exist to do so. Crozier (1964: 47) stressed in his discussion of power "the necessity for the members of the different groups to live together; the fact that each group's privileges depend to quite a large extent on the existence of other group's privileges." The groups use differential power to function within the system rather than to destroy it.

If dependency in a social relation is the reverse of power (Emerson, 1962), then the crucial unanswered question in organizations is: what factors function to vary dependency, and so to vary power? Emerson (1962: 32) proposed that "the dependence of actor A upon actor B is (*1*) directly proportional to A's motivational investment in goals mediated by B, and (*2*) inversely proportional to the availability of those goals to A outside of the A–B relation." In organizations, subunit B will have more power than other subunits to the extent that (*1*) B has the capacity to fulfill the requirements of the other subunits and (*2*) B monopolizes this ability. If a central problem facing modern organizations is uncertainty, then B's power in the organization will be partially determined by the extent to which B copes with uncertainties for other subunits, and by the extent to which B's coping activities are available elsewhere.

Thus, intraorganizational dependency can be associated with two contributing variables: (1) the degree to which a subunit copes with uncertainty for other subunits, and (2) the extent to which a subunit's coping activities are substitutable. But if coping with uncertainty, and substitutability, are to be in some way related to power, there is a necessary assumption of some degree of task interconnection among subunits. By definition, organization requires a minimum link. Therefore, a third variable, centrality, refers to the varying degree above such a minimum with which the activities of a subunit are linked with those of other subunits.

Before these three variables can be combined in a theory of power, it is necessary to examine their definition and possible operationalization, and to define power in this context.

Power

Hinings et al. (1967: 62) compared power to concepts such as bureaucracy or alienation or social class, which are difficult to understand because they tend to be treated as "large-scale unitary concepts." Their many meanings need disentangling. With the concept of power, this has not yet been accomplished (Cartwright, 1965), but two conceptualizations are commonly employed: (1) power as coercion, and (2) power as determination of behavior.

Power as coercive force was a comparatively early conceptualization among sociologists (Weber, 1947; Bierstedt, 1950). Later, Blau (1964) emphasized the imposition of will despite resistance.

However, coercion is only one among the several bases of power listed by French and Raven (1959) and applied across organizations by Etzioni (1961); that is, coercion is a means of power, but is not an adequate definition of power. If the direction of dependence in a relationship is determined by an imbalance of power bases, power itself has to be defined separately from these bases. Adopting Dahl's (1957) concept of power, as many others have done (March, 1955; Bennis et al., 1958; Emerson, 1962; Harsanyi, 1962; Van Doorn, 1962; Dahlstrom, 1966; Wrong, 1968; Tannenbaum, 1968; Luhmann, 1969), power is defined as the determination of the behavior of one social unit by another.

If power is the determination of A's behavior by B, irrespective of whether one, any, or all the types of bases are involved, then authority will here be regarded as that part of power which is legitimate or normatively expected by some selection of role definers. Authority may be either more or less than power. For subunits it might be represented by the formally specified range of activities they are officially required to undertake and, therefore, to decide upon.

Discrepancies between authority and power may reflect time lag. Perrow (1970) explored the discrepancy between respondent's perceptions of power and of what power should be. Perhaps views on a preferred power distribution precede changes in the exercise of power, which in turn precede changes in expectations of power, that is in its legitimate authority content. Perhaps today's authority hierarchy is partly a fossilized impression of yesterday's power ranking. However this may be, it is certainly desirable to include in any research not only data on perceived power and on preferred power, but also on positional power, or authority, and on participation, or exercised power (Clark [ed.], 1968).

Kaplan (1964) succinctly described three dimensions of power. The weight of power is defined in terms of the degree to which B affects the probability of A behaving in a certain way, that is, determination of behavior in the sense adopted here. The other dimensions are domain and scope. Domain is the number of A's, persons or collectivities, whose behavior is determined; scope is the range of behaviors of each A that are determined. For subunit power within an organization, domain might be the number of other subunits affected by the issues, scope the range of decision issues affected, and weight the degree to which a given subunit affects the decision process on the issues. In published research such distinctions are rarely made. Power consists of the sweeping undifferentiated perceptions of respondents when asked to rank individuals or classes of persons, such as supervisors, on influence. Yet at the same time the complexity of power in organizations is recognized. If it is taken for granted that, say, marketing has most to do with sales matters, that accounting has most to do with finance matters, supervisors with supervisory matters, and so on, then the validity of forcing respondents to generalize single opinions across an unstated range of possibilities is questionable.

To avoid these generalized opinions, data collected over a range of decision topics or issues are desirable. Such issues should in principle include all recognized problem areas in the organization, in each of which more than one subunit is involved. Examples might be marketing strategies, obtaining equipment, personnel training, and capital budgeting.

Some suggested subvariables and indicators of power and of the independent variables are summarized in Table 1. These are

TABLE 1. VARIABLES AND OPERATIONALIZABLE SUBVARIABLES

Power (weight, domain, scope)
Positional power (authority)
Participation power
Perceived power
Preferred power

Uncertainty
Variability of organizational inputs
Feedback on subunit performance;
　Speed
　Specificity
Structuring of subunit activities

Coping with uncertainty, classified as:
By prevention (forestalling uncertainty)
By information (forecasting)
By absorption (action after the event)

Substitutability
Availability of alternatives
Replaceability of personnel

Centrality
Pervasiveness of workflows
Immediacy of workflows

intended to include both individual perceptions of power in the form of questionnaire responses and data of a somewhat less subjective kind on participation in decision processes and on formal position in the organization.

It is now possible to examine coping with uncertainty, substitutability and centrality.

Uncertainty and Coping with Uncertainty

Uncertainty may be defined as a lack of information about future events, so that alternatives and their outcomes are unpredictable. Organizations deal with environmentally derived uncertainties in the sources and composition of inputs, with uncertainties in the processing of throughputs, and again with environmental uncertainties in the disposal of outputs. They must have means to deal with these uncertainties for adequate task performance. Such ability is here called coping.

In his study of the French tobacco manufacturing industry, Crozier (1964: 164) suggested that power is related to "the kind of uncertainty upon which depends the life of the organization." March and Simon (1958) had earlier made the same point, and Perrow (1961) had discussed the shifting domination of different groups in organizations following the shifting uncertainties of resources and the routinization of skills. From studies of industrial firms, Perrow (1970) tentatively thought that power might be due to uncertainty absorption, as March and Simon (1958) call it. Lawrence and Lorsch (1967b) found that marketing had more influence than production in both container-manufacturing and food-processing firms, apparently because of its involvement in (uncertain) innovation and with customers.

Crozier (1964) proposed a strategic model of organizations as systems in which groups strive for power, but his discussion did not clarify how uncertainty could relate positively to power. Uncertainty itself does not give power: coping gives power. If organizations allocate to their various subunits task areas that vary in uncertainty, then those subunits that cope most effectively with the most uncertainty should have most power within the organization, since coping by a subunit reduces the impact of uncertainty on other activities in the organization, a shock absorber function. Coping may be by prevention, for example, a subunit prevents sales fluctuations by securing firm orders; or by information, for example, a subunit forecasts sales fluctuations; or by absorption, for example, a drop in sales is swiftly countered by novel selling methods (Table 1). By coping, the subunit provides pseudo certainty for the other subunits by controlling what are otherwise contingencies for other activities. This coping confers power through the dependencies created.

Thus organizations do not necessarily aim to avoid uncertainty nor to reduce its absolute level, as Cyert and March (1963) appear to have assumed, but to cope with it. If a subunit can cope, the level of uncertainty encountered can be increased by moving into fresh sectors of the environment, attempting fresh outputs, or utilizing fresh technologies.

Operationally, raw uncertainty and coping will be difficult to disentangle, though theoretically the distinctions are clear. For all units, uncertainty is in the raw situation which would exist without the activities of the other relevant subunits, for example, the uncertainty that would face production units if the sales subunit were not there to forecast and/or to obtain a smooth flow of orders. Uncertainty might be indicated by the variability of those inputs to the organization which are taken by the subunit. For instance, a production subunit may face variability in raw materials and engineering may face variability in equipment performance. Lawrence and Lorsch (1967a) attempted categorizations of this kind. In addition, they (1967a: 14) gave a lead with "the time span of definitive feedback from the environment." This time span might be treated as a secondary indicator of uncertainty, making the assumption that the less the feedback to a subunit on the results of what it is doing, and the less specific the feedback, the more likely the subunit is to be working in a vague, unknown, unpredictable task area. Both speed and specificity of feedback are suggested variables in Table 1.

Furthermore, the copious literature on bureaucratic or mechanistic structures versus more organic and less defined structures could be taken to imply that routinized or highly structured subunits, for example, as conceptualized and measured by Pugh et al. (1968), will have stable homogeneous activities and be less likely to face uncertainty. This assumption would require empirical testing before structuring of activities could be used as an indicator of uncertainty, but it is tentatively included in Table 1.

In principle, coping with uncertainty might be directly measured by the difference between the uncertainty of those inputs taken by a subunit and the certainty with which it performs its activities nonetheless. This would indicate the degree of shock absorption.

The relation of coping with uncertainty to power can be expressed by the following hypothesis:

Hypothesis 1. The more a subunit copes with uncertainty, the greater its power within the organization.

The hypothesis is in a form which ignores any effects of centrality and substitutability.

Substitutability

Concepts relating to the availability of alternatives pervade the literature on power. In economics theory the degree of competition is taken as a measure of the extent to which alternatives are available from other organizations, it being implied that the power of an organization over other organizations and customers is a function of the amount of competition present. The same point was the second part of Emerson's (1962) power-dependency scheme in social relations, and the second requirement or determinant in Blau's (1964) model of a power relationship.

Yet only Mechanic (1962) and Dubin (1957, 1963) have discussed such concepts as explanations of organizational power. Mechanic's (1962: 358) hypothesis 4 stated: "Other factors remaining constant, a person difficult to replace will have greater power than a person easily replaceable." Dubin (1957) stressed the very similar notion of exclusiveness, which as developed later (Dubin, 1963: 21), means that: "For any given level of functional importance in an organization, the power residing in a functionary is inversely proportional to the number of other functionaries in the organization capable of performing the function." Supporting this empirically, Lipset et al. (1956) suggested that oligarchy may occur in trade unions because of the official's monopoly of political and negotiating skills.

The concept being used is represented here by the term substitutability, which can, for subunits, be defined as the ability of the organization to obtain alternative performance for the activities of a subunit, and can be stated as a hypothesis for predicting the power of a subunit as follows:

Hypothesis 2. The lower the substitutability of the activities of a subunit, the greater its power within the organization.

Thus a purchasing department would have its power reduced if all of its activities could be done by hired materials agents, as would a personnel department if it were partially substituted by selection consultants, or by line managers finding their staff themselves. Similarly, a department may hold on to power by retaining information the release of which would enable others to do what it does.

The obvious problem in operationalization is establishing that alternative means of performing activities exist, and if they do, whether they could feasibly be used. Even if agents or consultants exist locally, or if corporation headquarters could provide services, would it really be practicable for the organization to dispense with its own subunit? Much easier to obtain are data on replaceability of subunit personnel such as length of training required for new recruits and ease of hiring, which can be regarded as secondary indicators of the substitutability of a subunit, as indicated in Table 1.

Centrality

Given a view of organizations as systems of interdependent roles and activities, then the centrality of a subunit is the degree to which its activities are interlinked into the system. By definition, no subunit of an organization can score zero centrality. Without a minimum of centrality, coping with uncertainty and substitutability cannot affect power; above the minimum, additional increments of centrality further differentiate subunit power. It is the degree to which the subunit is an interdependent component, as Thompson (1967: 54) put it, distinguishing between pooled, sequential, and reciprocal interdependence patterns. Blau and Scott (1962) made an analogous distinction between parallel and interdependent specialization. Woodward (1965: 126) also introduced a concept of this kind into her discussion of the critical function in each of unit, large batch and mass, and process production: "there seemed to be one function that was central and critical in that it had the greatest effect on success and survival."

Within the overall concept of centrality, there are inconsistencies which indicate that more than one constitutive concept is being used. At the present stage of conceptualization their identification must be very tentative. First, there is the idea that the activities of a subunit are central if they are connected with many other activities in the organization. This workflow pervasiveness may be defined as the degree to which the workflows of a subunit connect with the workflows of other subunits. It describes the extent of task interactions between subunits, and for all subunits in an organization it would be operationalized as the flowchart of a complete systems analysis. For example, the integrative subsystems studied by Lawrence and Lorsch (1967a: 30), "whose members had the function of integrating the sales-research and the production-research subsystems" and which had structural and cultural characteristics intermediate between them, were presumably high on workflow pervasiveness because everything they did connected with the workflows of these several other subsystems. Research subsystems, however, may have been low on this variable if they fed work only to a single integrative, or production, subsystem.

Secondly, the activities of a subunit are central if they are essential in the sense that their cessation would quickly and substantially impede the primary workflow of the organization. This workflow immediacy is defined as the speed and severity with which the workflows of a subunit affect the final outputs of the organization. Zald (1962) and Clark (1956) used a similar idea when they explained differential power among institution staff and education faculty by the close relation of their activities to organization goals.

The pervasiveness and immediacy of the workflows of a subunit are not necessarily closely related, and may empirically show a low correlation. A finance department may well have pervasive connections with all other subunits through the budgeting system, but if its activities ceased it would be some time before the effects were felt in, say, the production output of a factory; a production department controlling a stage midway in the sequence of an automated process, however, could have high workflow immediacy though not high pervasiveness.

The two main centrality hypotheses can therefore be stated as follows:

Hypothesis 3a. The higher the pervasiveness of the workflows of a subunit, the greater its power within the organization.

Hypothesis 3b. The higher the immediacy of the workflows of a subunit, the greater its power within the organization.

CONTROL OF CONTINGENCIES

Hypotheses relating power to coping with uncertainty, substitutability, and the subvariables of centrality have been stated in a simple single-variable form. Yet it follows from the view of subunits as interdependent parts of organizational systems that the hypotheses in this form are misleading. While each hypothesis may be empirically upheld, it is also hypothesized that this cannot be so without some values of both the other main independent variables. For example, when a marketing department copes with a volatile market by forecasting and by switching sales staff around to ensure stable orders, it acquires power only because the forecast and the orders are linked to the workflow of production, which depends on them. But even then power would be limited by the availability of a successful local marketing agency which could be hired by the organization, and the fact that salesmen were low skilled and easily replaceable.

To explain this interrelationship, the concept of control of contingencies is introduced. It represents organizational interdependence; subunits control contingencies for one another's activities and draw power from the dependencies thereby created. As a hypothesis:

Hypothesis 4. The more contingencies are controlled by a subunit, the greater its power within the organization.

A contingency is a requirement of the activities of one subunit which is affected by the activities of another subunit. What makes such a contingency strategic, in the sense that it is related to power, can be deduced from the preceding hypotheses. The independent variables are each necessary but not sufficient conditions for control of strategic contingencies, but together they determine the variation in interdependence between subunits. Thus contingencies controlled by a subunit as a consequence of its coping with uncertainty do not become strategic, that is, affect power, in the organization without some (unknown) values of substitutability and centrality. A strategic contingencies theory of power is therefore proposed and is illustrated by the diagram in Figure 1.

In terms of exchange theory, as developed by Blau (1964), subunits can be seen to be exchanging control of strategic contingencies one for the other under the normative regulation of an encompassing social system, and acquiring power in the system through the exchange. The research task is to elucidate what combinations of values of the independent variables summarized in hypotheses 1–3 allow hypothesis 4 to hold. Ultimately and ideally the aim would be to discover not merely the weightings of each in the total effect upon power, but how these variables should be operationally interrelated to obtain the best predictions. More of one and less of another may leave the resulting power unchanged. Suppose an engineering subunit has power because it quickly absorbs uncertainty by repairing breakdowns which interfere with the different workflows for each of several organization outputs. It is moderately central and non-

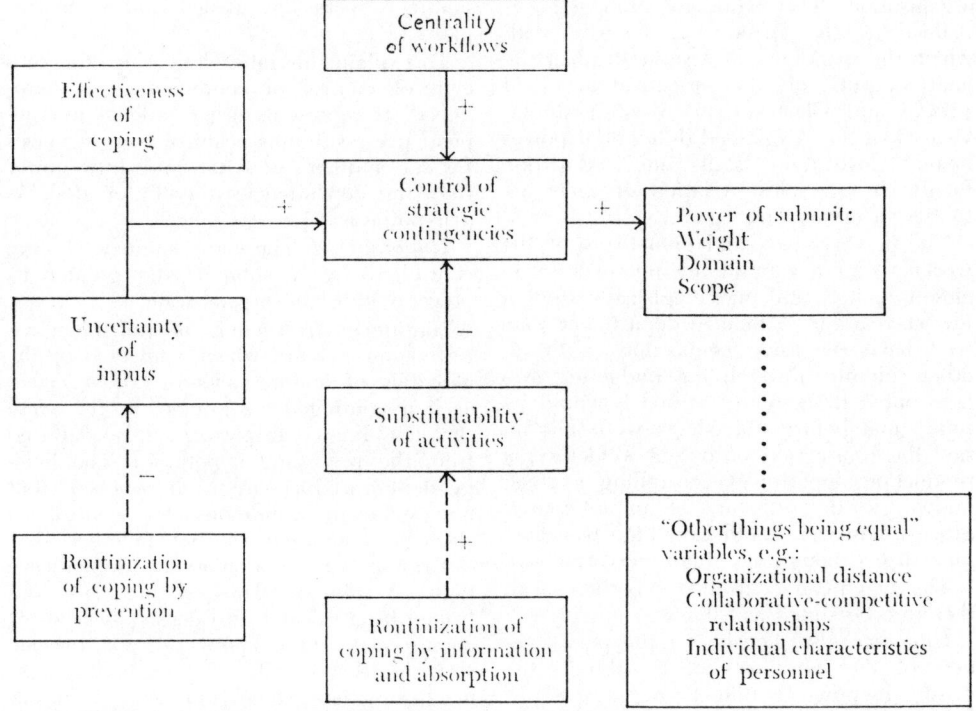

Figure 1. The strategic contingencies theory and routinization

substitutable. A change in organization policy bringing in a new technology with a single workflow leading to a single output would raise engineering's centrality, since a single breakdown would immediately stop everything, but simultaneously the uncertainty might be reduced by a maintenance program which all but eliminates the possibility of such an occurrence.

Though three main factors are hypothesized, which must change if power is to change, it is not assumed that all subunits will act in accord with the theory to increase their power. This has to be demonstrated. There is the obvious possibility of a cumulative reaction in which a subunit's power is used to preserve or increase the uncertainty it can cope with, or its centrality, or to prevent substitution, thereby increasing its power, and so on. Nor is it argued that power or authority are intentionally allocated in terms of the theory, although the theory is open to such an inference.

Routinization

Most studies that refer to uncertainty contrast is with routinization, the prior prescription of recurrent task activities. Crozier (1964) held that the power of the maintenance personnel in the tobacco plants was due to all other tasks being routinized. A relative decline in the power of general medical personnel in hospitals during this century is thought to be due to the routinization of some tasks, which previously presented uncertainties which could be coped with only by a physician, and the transfer of these tasks to relatively routinized subunits, such as inoculation programs, mass X-ray facilities, and so on (Perrow, 1965; Gordon and Becker, 1964). Crozier (1964: 165) crystallized the presumed effects of routinization: "But the expert's success is constantly self-defeating. The rationalization process gives him power, but the end results of rationalization curtail his power. As soon as a field is well covered, as soon as the first intuitions and innovations can be translated into rules and programs, the expert's power disappears."

The strategic contingencies' theory as developed in Figure 1 clarifies this. It suggests that research has been hampered by a confusion of two kinds of routinization, both of which are negatively related to power but in different ways. Routinization may be (*a*) of coping by prevention, which prevents the occurrence of uncertainty; and (*b*) of coping by information or absorption which define how the uncertainty which does occur shall be coped with.

Preventive routinization reduces or removes the uncertainty itself, for example, planned maintenance, which maintenance in Crozier's (1964) tobacco factories would have resisted; inoculation or X-ray programs; and long-term supply contracts, so that the sales staff no longer have to contend with unstable demand. Such routinization removes the opportunity for power, and it is this which is self-defeating (Crozier, 1964: 165) if the expert takes his techniques to a point when they begin not only to cope but to routinely diminish the uncertainty coped with. Thus reducing the uncertainty is not the same as reducing the impact of uncertainty. According to the hypothesis, a sales department which transmits steady orders despite a volatile market has high power; a sales department which reduces the uncertainty itself by long-term tied contracts has low power.

Routinization of coping by information and absorption is embodied in job descriptions and task instructions prescribing how to obtain information and to respond to uncertainty. For maintenance personnel, it lays down how to repair the machine; for physicians, it lays down a standard procedure for examining patients and sequences of remedies for each diagnosis. How does this affect power, since it does not eliminate the uncertainty itself, as preventive routinization does? What it does is increase substitutability. The means of coping become more visible and possible substitutes more obvious, even if those substitutes are unskilled personnel from another subunit who can follow a standard procedure but could not have acquired the previously unexpressed skills.

There is probably some link between the two kinds of routinization. Once preventive routinization is accomplished, other coping routinization more easily follows, as indeed it follows any reduction of uncertainty.

STUDIES OF SUBUNIT POWER

Testing of Hypotheses on Earlier Work

The utility of the strategic contingencies theory should be tested on published work, but it is difficult to do this adequately, since most studies stress only one possibility. For example, Crozier (1964) and Thompson (1967) stressed uncertainty, Dubin (1963) stressed exclusiveness of function, and Woodward (1965) spoke of the critical function.

The difficulty is also due to the lack of data. For example, among several studies in which inferences about environmental uncertainty are drawn, only Lawrence and Lorsch (1967b) presented data. They combine executive's questionnaire responses on departmental clarity of job requirements, time span of definitive feedback on departmental success in performance, and uncertainty of cause and effect in the department's functional area.

Lawrence and Lorsch (1967b: 127) found that in two food-processing organizations, research was most influential, then marketing, excluding the field selling unit, and then production. However, influence, or perceived power as it is called here, was rated on the single issue of product innovation and not across a range of issues as suggested earlier in this paper; validity therefore rests on the assumption of equal potential involvement of each function in this one issue. Would research still be most influential if the issues included equipment purchase, or capital budgeting, or personnel training? Even so, on influence over product innovation, an uncertainty hypothesis could be said to fit neatly, since the subunits were ordered on perceived uncertainty of sub-environment exactly as they were on influence.

But uncertainty alone would not explain power in the other firms studied. Although in six plastics firms, coordinating sections or integrating units were perceived as having more influence than functional subunits because "integration itself was the most problematic job" (Lawrence and Lorsch 1967b: 62), it was also a central job in terms of workflow pervasiveness.

Furthermore, in two container manufacturing organizations, although the market subenvironment was seen as the least uncertain, the sales subunit was perceived as the most influential (Lawrence and Lorsch 1967b: 111). An explanation must be sought in the contingencies that the sales subunit controls for production and for research. In this industry, outputs must fit varying customer requirements for containers. Scheduling for production departments and design problems for research departments are therefore completely subject to the contingencies of orders brought in by the sales department. Sales has not only the opportunity to cope with such uncertainty as may exist over customer requirements, it is highly central; for its activities connect it directly to both the other departments—workflow pervasiveness—and if it ceased work production of containers would stop—workflow immediacy. The effects of centrality are probably bolstered by nonsubstitutability, since the sales subunit develops a necessary particularized knowledge of customer requirements. Production and research are, therefore, comparatively powerless in face of the strategic contingencies controlled by the sales subunit.

In short, only a sensitive balancing of all three factors can explain the patterns of contingencies from which power strategically flows.

This is plain also in Crozier's (1964) insightful study of small French tobacco-manufacturing plants. Crozier (1964: 109) had the impression that the maintenance engineers were powerful because "machine stoppages are the only major happenings that cannot be predicted"; therefore the engineers had (Crozier, 1964: 154) "control over the last source of uncertainty remaining in a completely routinized organizational system." But this is not enough for power. Had it been possible to contract maintenance work to consulting engineers, for example, then programs of preventive maintenance might have been introduced, and preventive routinization would have removed much of the uncertainty. However, it is likely that union agreements ensured that the plant engineers were nonsubstitutable. In addition, in these small organizations without specialist control and service departments, the maintenance section's work linked it to all production subunits, that is, to almost every other subunit in the plant. So workflow pervasiveness was high, as was workflow immediacy, since cessation of maintenance activities would quickly have stopped tobacco outputs. The control of strategic contingencies which gave power to the engineers has to be explained on all counts and not by uncertainty alone.

Crozier's (1964) study is a warning against the facile inference that a power distribution fitting the strategic contingencies theory is necessarily efficient, or rational, or functional for an organization; for the power of the engineers to thwart the introduction of programmed maintenance was presumably neither efficient, rational, nor functional.

A challenge to the analysis made is presented by Goldner's (1970) description of a case where there was programmed maintenance and yet the maintenance section held power over production. Goldner (1970) attributed the power of the maintenance subunit to knowing how to install and operate such programs, to coping with breakdowns as in the Crozier (1964) cases, and to knowing how to cope with a critical problem of parts supplies. The strategic contingencies theory accords with his interpretation so long as knowing how to install a program takes effect as coping with uncertainty and not yet as preventive routinization which stops breakdowns. This is where an unknown time element enters to allow for changes in the variables specified and in any associated variables not yet defined. For a time, knowing the answer to an uncertainty does confer power, but the analyses of routinization derived from the theory, as shown in Figure 1, suggests that if this becomes successful preventive routinization, it takes a negative effect upon power. The net result for power in Goldner's (1970) case would then be from the interplay of the opposed effects of activities some of which are preventively routinized, thus decreasing power, and some of which continue to be nonroutine, thus increasing power.

On the other hand, Goldner's (1970) description of the powerful industrial relations subunit in the same plant clearly supports the strategic contingencies theory by showing that coping with uncertainty, centrality, and substitutability had the effect predicted here. The industrial relations subunit exploited uncertainty over the supply and cost of personnel, which arose from possible strikes and pay increases, by (Goldner, 1970: 104) "use of the union as an outside threat." It coped effectively by its nonroutinized knowledge of union officials and of contract interpretation; and its activities were centrally linked to those of other subunits by the necessity for uniform practice on wages and employment. Industrial relations staff developed nonsubstitutable interpersonal and bargaining skills.

There are no means of assessing whether the univariate stress on uncertainty in the handful of other relevant studies is justified. Perrow (1970) explained the greater perceived power of sales as against production, finance, and research, in most of 12 industrial firms, by the concept of uncertainty absorption (March and Simon, 1958). Sales was strategic with respect to the environment. Is the one case where it came second to production the only case where it was also substitutable? Or not central?

White (1961) and Landsberger (1961) both suggested that power shifts over periods of time to follow the locus of uncertainty. Both studied engineering factories. From the histories of three firms, Landsberger (1961) deduced that when money was scarce and uncertain, accounting was powerful; when raw materials were short, purchasing was powerful; and, conversely, when demand was insatiable sales were weakened. In the Tennessee Valley Authority, a nonmanufacturing organization, Selznick (1949) attributed the eventual power of the agricultural relations department to its ability to cope with the uncertain environmental threat represented by the Farm Bureau.

Yet while these earlier studies emphasized uncertainty in one way or another, others called attention to substitutability and probably also to centrality. Again the implication is that contingencies are not strategically controlled without some combination of all three basic variables. For example, the engineers described by Strauss (1962, 1964) appeared to have more power than purchasing agents because the latter were substitutable, that is, the engineers can set specifications for what was to be bought even though the purchasing agents considered this their own responsibility. Thompson (1956: 300) attributed variations in perceived power within and between two U.S. Air Force wings to the changing "technical requirements of operations," which may have indicated changing centralities and substitutabilities.

In the absence of data, consideration of further different kinds of organization must remain pure speculation, for example, the power of surgical units in hospitals, the power of buyers in stores, the power of science faculties in universities.

Other Variables Affecting Power

In order that it can be testable, the strategic contingencies theory errs on the side of simplicity. Any theory must start with a finite number of variables and presume continual development by their alteration or deletion, or by the addition of new variables. As stated, the theory uses only those variables hypothesized to affect power by their contribution to the control of contingencies exercised by a subunit. Other possible explanations of power are not considered. This in itself is an assumption of the greater explanatory force of the theory. Blalock (1961: 8) put the problem clearly: "The dilemma of the scientist is to select models that are at the same time simple enough to permit him to think with the aid of the model but also sufficiently realistic that the simplifications required do not lead to predictions that are highly inaccurate."

In recognition of this, Figure 1 includes several "other things being equal" variables as they are called, that may affect power, but are assumed to do so in other ways than by control of contingencies. One such range of possible relevant variables is qualities of interdepartmental relationships, such as competitiveness versus collaborativeness (Dutton and Walton, 1966). Does the power exercised relate to the style of the relationship through which the power runs? Another possibility is pinpointed by Stymne (1968: 88): "A unit's influence has its roots partly in its strategical importance to the company and partly in nonfunctional circumstances such as tradition, or control over someone in top management through, for example, family relationship." The tradition is the status which may accrue to a particular function because chief executives have typically reached the top through it. Many case studies highlight the personal links of subunits with top personnel (Dalton, 1959; Gouldner, 1955). The notion might be entitled the organizational distance of the subunit, a variant of social distance.

Finally, but perhaps most important, individual differences must be accepted, that is, differences in the intelligence, skills, ages, sexes, or personality factors such as dominance, assertiveness, and risk-taking propensity, of personnel in the various subunits.

CONCLUSION

The concept of work organizations as interdepartmental systems leads to a strategic contingencies theory explaining differential subunit power by dependence on contingencies ensuing from varying combinations of coping with uncertainty, substitutability, and centrality. It should be stressed that the theory is not in any sense static. As the goals, outputs, technologies, and markets of organizations change so, for each subunit, the values of the independent variables change, and patterns of power change.

Many problems are unresolved. For example, does the theory implicitly assume perfect knowledge by each subunit of the contingencies inherent for it in the activities of the others? Does a workflow of information affect power differently to a workflow of things? But with the encouragement of the improved analysis given of the few existing studies, data can be collected and analyzed, hopefully in ways which will afford a direct test.

David J. Hickson is Ralph Yablon professor of behavioural studies, organizational analysis research unit, University of Bradford Management Centre, England; Christopher R. Hinings is a senior lecturer in sociology, industrial administration research unit, University of Aston-in-Birmingham, England; Charles A. Lee and Rodney E. Schneck are professors in the faculty of business administration and commerce, University of Alberta, Canada; and Johannes M. Pennings is an instructor and doctoral student at the institute for social research, University of Michigan.

REFERENCES

Bennis, Warren G., N. Berkowitz, M. Affinito, and M. Malone
1958 "Authority, power and the ability to influence." Human Relations, 11: 143–156.

Bierstedt, Robert
1950 "An analysis of social power." American Sociological Review, 15: 730–736.

Blalock, Hubert M.
1961 Causal Inferences in Nonexperimental Research. Chapel Hill: University of North Carolina Press.

Blau, Peter
1964 Exchange and Power in Social Life. New York: Wiley.

Blau, Peter, and W. Richard Scott
1962 Formal Organizations: A Comparative Approach. London: Routledge and Kegan Paul.

Cartwright, Darwin
1965 "Influence, leadership, control." In James G. March (ed.), Handbook of Organizations: 1–47. Chicago: Rand McNally.

Clark, Burton R.
1956 "Organizational adaptation and precarious values: a case study." American Sociological Review, 21: 327–336.

Clark, Terry N. (ed.)
1968 Community Structure and Decision-Making: Comparative Analyses. San Francisco: Chandler.

Crozier, Michel
1964 The Bureaucratic Phenomenon. London: Tavistock.

Cyert, Richard M., and James G. March
1963 A Behavioral Theory of the Firm. Englewood Cliffs, N.J.: Prentice-Hall.

Dahl, Robert A.
1957 "The concept of power." Behavioral Science, 2: 201–215.

Dahlstrom, E.
1966 "Exchange, influence, and power." Acta Sociologica, 9: 237–284.

Dalton, Melville
1959 Men Who Manage. New York: Wiley.

Dubin, Robert
1957 "Power and union-management relations." Administrative Science Quarterly, 2: 60–81.
1963 "Power, function, and organization." Pacific Sociological Review, 6: 16–24.

Dutton, John M., and Richard E. Walton
1966 "Interdepartmental conflict and cooperation: two contrasting studies." Human Organization, 25: 207–220.

Emerson, R. E.
1962 "Power-dependence relations." American Sociological Review, 27: 31–41.

Etzioni, Amitai
1961 A Comparative Analysis of Complex Organizations. New York: Free Press.

French, John R. P., and Bertram Raven
1959 "The bases of social power." In D. Cartwright (ed.), Studies in Social Power: 150–167. Ann Arbor: University of Michigan.

Goldner, Fred H.
1970 "The division of labor: process and power." In Mayer N. Zald (ed.), Power in Organizations: 97–143. Nashville: Vanderbilt University Press.

Gordon, Gerald, and Selwyn Becker
1964 "Changes in medical practice bring shifts in the patterns of power." The Modern Hospital (February): 89–91, 154–156.

Gouldner, Alvin W.
1955 Wildcat Strike. London: Routledge.

Harsanyi, John C.
1962 "Measurement of social power, opportunity costs, and the theory of two-person bargaining games." Behavioral Science, 7: 67–80.

Hinings, Christopher R., Derek S. Pugh, David J. Hickson, and Christopher Turner
1967 "An approach to the study of bureaucracy." Sociology, 1: 61–72.

Kaplan, Abraham
1964 "Power in perspective." In Robert L. Kahn and Elise Boulding (eds.), Power and Conflict in Organizations: 11–32. London: Tavistock.

Landsberger, Henry A.
1961 "The horizontal dimension in bureaucracy." Administrative Science Quarterly, 6: 299–332.

Lawrence, Paul R., and Jay W. Lorsch
1967a "Differentiation and integration in complex organizations." Administrative Science Quarterly, 12: 1–47.
1967b Organization and Environment. Cambridge: Division of Research, Graduate School of Business Administration, Harvard University.

Lipset, Seymour M., Martin A. Trow, and James A. Coleman
1956 Union Democracy. Glencoe, Ill.: Free Press.

Luhmann, Niklaus
1969 "Klassische theorie der macht." Zeitschrift fur Politik, 16: 149–170.

March, James G.
1955 "An introduction to the theory and measurement of influence." American Political Science Review, 49: 431–450.
1966 "The power of power." In David Easton (ed.), Varieties of Political Theory: 39–70. Englewood Cliffs, N.J.: Prentice-Hall.

March, James G., and Herbert A. Simon
1958 Organizations. New York: Wiley.

Mechanic, David
1962 "Sources of power of lower participants in complex organizations." Administrative Science Quarterly, 7: 349–364.

Perrow, Charles
1961 "The analysis of goals in complex organizations." American Sociological Review, 26: 854–866.
1965 "Hospitals: technology, structure, and goals." In James G. March (ed.), Handbook of Organizations: 910–971. Chicago: Rand McNally.
1970 "Departmental power and perspectives in industrial firms." In Mayer N. Zald (ed.), Power in Organizations: 59–89. Nashville: Vanderbilt University Press.

Pugh, Derek S., David J. Hickson, Christopher R. Hinings, and Christopher Turner
1968 "Dimensions of organization structure." Administrative Science Quarterly, 13: 65–105.

Selznick, Philip
1949 T.V.A. and the Grass Roots. Berkeley: University of California Press.

Strauss, George
- 1962 "Tactics of lateral relationship: the purchasing agent." Administrative Science Quarterly, 7: 161–186.
- 1964 "Work-flow frictions, interfunctional rivalry, and professionalism." Human Organization, 23: 137–150.

Stymne, Bengt
- 1968 "Interdepartmental communication and intraorganizational strain." Acta Sociologica, 11: 82–100.

Tannenbaum, Arnold S.
- 1968 Control in Organizations. New York: McGraw-Hill.

Thompson, James D.
- 1956 "Authority and power in 'identical' organizations." American Journal of Sociology, 62: 290–301.
- 1967 Organizations in Action. New York: McGraw-Hill.

Van Doorn, Jaques A. A.
- 1962 "Sociology and the problem of power." Sociologica Neerlandica, 1: 3–47.

Weber, Max
- 1947 The Theory of Social and Economic Organization. Glencoe, Ill.: Free Press.

White, Harrison
- 1961 "Management conflict and sociometric structure." American Journal of Sociology, 67: 185–199.

Woodward, Joan
- 1965 Industrial Organization: Theory and Practice. London: Oxford University Press.

Wrong, Dennis H.
- 1968 "Some problems in defining social power." American Journal of Sociology, 73, 673–681.

Zald, Mayer N.
- 1962 "Organizational control structures in five correctional institutions." American Journal of Sociology, 68: 335–345.

[17]
Rational Decision Making in Business Organizations

By HERBERT A. SIMON*

In the opening words of his *Principles*, Alfred Marshall proclaimed economics to be a psychological science:

> Political Economy or Economics is a study of mankind in the ordinary business of life; it examines that part of individual and social action which is most closely connected with the attainment and with the use of the material requisites of wellbeing.
>
> Thus it is on the one side a study of wealth; and on the other, and more important side, a part of the study of man. For man's character has been moulded by his every-day work, and the material resources which he thereby procures, more than by any other influence unless it be that of his religious ideals.

In its actual development, however, economic science has focused on just one aspect of man's character, his reason, and particularly on the application of that reason to problems of allocation in the face of scarcity. Still, modern definitions of the economic sciences, whether phrased in terms of allocating scarce resources or in terms of rational decision making, mark out a vast domain for conquest and settlement. In recent years there has been considerable exploration by economists even of parts of this domain that were thought traditionally to belong to the disciplines of political science, sociology, and psychology.

---

*Carnegie-Mellon University. This article is the lecture Herbert Simon delivered in Stockholm, Sweden, December 8, 1978, when he received the Nobel Prize in Economic Science. The article is copyright © the Nobel Foundation 1978. It is published here with the permission of the Nobel Foundation.

The author is indebted to Albert Ando, Otto A. Davis, and Benjamin M. Friedman for valuable comments on an earlier draft of this paper.

I. Decision Theory as Economic Science

The density of settlement of economists over the whole empire of economic science is very uneven, with a few areas of modest size holding the bulk of the population. The economic Heartland is the normative study of the international and national economies and their markets, with its triple main concerns of full employment of resources, the efficient allocation of resources, and equity in distribution of the economic product. Instead of the ambiguous and over-general term "economics," I will use "political economy" to designate this Heartland, and "economic sciences" to denote the whole empire, including its most remote colonies. Our principal concern in this paper will be with the important colonial territory known as decision theory. I will have something to say about its normative and descriptive aspects, and particularly about its applications to the theory of the firm. It is through the latter topic that the discussion will be linked back to the Heartland of political economy.

Underpinning the corpus of policy-oriented normative economics, there is, of course, an impressive body of descriptive or "positive" theory which rivals in its mathematical beauty and elegance some of the finest theories in the physical sciences. As examples I need only remind you of Walrasian general equilibrium theories and their modern descendants in the works of Henry Schultz, Samuelson, Hicks, and others; or the subtle and impressive body of theory created by Arrow, Hurwicz, Debreu, Malinvaud, and their colleagues showing the equivalence, under certain conditions, of competitive equilibrium with Pareto optimality.

The relevance of some of the more refined parts of this work to the real world can be, and has been, questioned. Perhaps some of these intellectual mountains have been climbed simply because they were there—because of the sheer challenge and joy of scaling them. That is as it should be in any human scientific or artistic effort. But regardless of the motives of the climbers, regardless of real world veridicality, there is no question but that positive political economy has been strongly shaped by the demands of economic policy for advice on basic public issues.

This too is as it should be. It is a vulgar fallacy to suppose that scientific inquiry cannot be fundamental if it threatens to become useful, or if it arises in response to problems posed by the everyday world. The real world, in fact, is perhaps the most fertile of all sources of good research questions calling for basic scientific inquiry.

A. Decision Theory in the Service of Political Economy

There is, however, a converse fallacy that deserves equal condemnation: the fallacy of supposing that fundamental inquiry is worth pursuing only if its relevance to questions of policy is immediate and obvious. In the contemporary world, this fallacy is perhaps not widely accepted, at least as far as the natural sciences are concerned. We have now lived through three centuries or more of vigorous and highly successful inquiry into the laws of nature. Much of that inquiry has been driven by the simple urge to understand, to find the beauty of order hidden in complexity. Time and again, we have found the "idle" truths arrived at through the process of inquiry to be of the greatest moment for practical human affairs. I need not take time here to argue the point. Scientists know it, engineers and physicians know it, congressmen and members of parliaments know it, the man on the street knows it.

But I am not sure that this truth is as widely known in economics as it ought to be. I cannot otherwise explain the rather weak and backward development of the descriptive theory of decision making including the theory of the firm, the sparse and scattered settlement of its terrain, and the fact that many, if not most, of its investigators are drawn from outside economics—from sociology, from psychology, and from political science. Respected and distinguished figures in economics—Edward Mason, Fritz Machlup, and Milton Friedman, for example—have placed it outside the Pale (more accurately, have placed economics outside *its* Pale), and have offered it full autonomy provided that it did not claim close kinship with genuine economic inquiry.

Thus, Mason, commenting on Papandreou's 1952 survey of research on the behavioral theory of the firm, mused aloud:

> ... has the contribution of this literature to economic analysis really been a large one? ... The writer of this critique must confess a lack of confidence in the marked superiority, *for purposes of economic analysis*, of this newer concept of the firm, over the older conception of the entrepreneur. [pp. 221–22]

And, in a similar vein, Friedman sums up his celebrated polemic against realism in theory:

> Complete "realism" is clearly unattainable, and the question whether a theory is realistic "enough" can be settled only by seeing whether it yields predictions that are good enough *for the purpose in hand* or that are better than predictions from alternative theories.
> [p. 41, emphasis added]

The "purpose in hand" that is implicit in both of these quotations is providing decision-theoretic foundations for positive, and then for normative, political economy. In the views of Mason and Friedman, fundamental inquiry into rational human behavior in the context of business organizations is simply not (by definition) economics—that is to say, political economy—unless it contributes in a major way to that purpose. This is sometimes even interpreted to mean that economic theories of decision making are not falsified in any interesting or relevant sense when their empirical predictions of *microphenomena* are found to be grossly incompatible with the observed data. Such theories, we are told, are still realistic "enough" provided that they do not contradict aggregate observations of concern to political economy. Thus economists who are zealous in insisting that economic actors maximize turn around and become satisficers when the evaluation of their own theories is concerned. They believe that businessmen maximize, but they know that economic theorists satisfice.

The application of the principle of satisficing to theories is sometimes defended as an application of Occam's Razor: accept the simplest theory that works.[1] But Occam's Razor has a double edge. Succinctness of statement is not the only measure of a theory's simplicity. Occam understood his rule as recommending theories that make no more assumptions than necessary to account for the phenomena (*Essentia non sunt multiplicanda praeter necessitatem*). A theory of profit or utility maximization can be stated more briefly than a satisficing theory of the sort I shall discuss later. But the former makes much stronger assumptions than the latter about the human cognitive system. Hence, in the case before us, the two edges of the razor cut in opposite directions.

In whichever way we interpret Occam's principle, parsimony can be only a secondary consideration in choosing between theories, unless those theories make identical predictions. Hence, we must come back to a consideration of the phenomena that positive decision theory is supposed to handle. These may include both phenomena at the microscopic level of the decision-making agents, or aggregative phenomena of concern to political economy.

B. Decision Theory Pursued for its Intrinsic Interest

Of course the definition of the word "economics" is not important. Like Humpty Dumpty, we can make words mean anything we want them to mean. But the professional training and range of concern of economists does have importance. Acceptance of the narrow view that economics is concerned only with the aggregative phenomena of political economy defines away a whole rich domain of rational human behavior as inappropriate for economic research.

I do not wish to appear to be admitting that the behavioral theory of the firm *has been* irrelevant to the construction of political economy. I will have more to say about its relevance in a moment. My present argument is counterfactual in form: *even if* there were no present evidence of such relevance, human behavior in business firms constitutes a highly interesting body of empirical phenomena that calls out for explanation as do all bodies of phenomena. And if we may extrapolate from the history of the other sciences, there is every reason to expect that as explanations emerge, relevance for important areas of practical application will not be long delayed.

It has sometimes been implied (Friedman, p. 14) that the correctness of the assumptions of rational behavior underlying the classical theory of the firm is not merely irrelevant, but is not even empirically testable in any direct way, the only valid test being whether these assumptions lead to tolerably correct predictions at the macroscopic level. That would be true, of course, if we had no microscopes, so that the micro-level behavior was not directly observable. But we do have microscopes. There are many techniques for observing decision-making behavior, even at second-by-second intervals if that is wanted. In testing our economic theories, we do not have to depend on the rough aggregate time-series that are the main grist for the econometric mill, or even upon company financial statements.

The classical theories of economic decision making and of the business firm make very specific testable predictions about the con-

---

[1] The phrase "that works" refutes, out of hand, Friedman's celebrated paean of praise for lack of realism in assumptions. Consider his example of falling bodies (pp. 16–19). His valid point is that it is advantageous to use the simple law, ignoring air resistance, when it gives a "good enough" approximation. But of course the conditions under which it gives a good approximation are not at all the conditions under which it is unrealistic or a "wildly inaccurate descriptive representation of reality." We can use it to predict the path of a body falling in a vacuum, but not the path of one falling through the Earth's atmosphere. I cannot in this brief space mention, much less discuss, all of the numerous logical fallacies that can be found in Friedman's 40-page essay. For additional criticism, see Simon (1963) and Samuelson (1963).

crete behavior of decision-making agents. Behavioral theories make quite different predictions. Since these predictions can be tested directly by observation, either theory (or both) may be falsified as readily when such predictions fail as when predictions about aggregate phenomena are in error.

C. *Aggregative Tests of Decision Theory: Marginalism*

If some economists have erroneously supposed that micro-economic theory can only be tested by its predictions of aggregate phenomena, we should avoid the converse error of supposing that aggregate phenomena are irrelevant to testing decision theory. In particular, are there important, *empirically verified,* aggregate predictions that follow from the theory of perfect rationality but that do not follow from behavioral theories of rationality?

The classical theory of omniscient rationality is strikingly simple and beautiful. Moreover, it allows us to predict (correctly or not) human behavior without stirring out of our armchairs to observe what such behavior is like. All the predictive power comes from characterizing the shape of the environment in which the behavior takes place. The environment, combined with the assumptions of perfect rationality, fully determines the behavior. Behavioral theories of rational choice—theories of bounded rationality—do not have this kind of simplicity. But, by way of compensation, their assumptions about human capabilities are far weaker than those of the classical theory. Thus, they make modest and realistic demands on the knowledge and computational abilities of the human agents, but they also fail to predict that those agents will equate costs and returns at the margin.

D. *Have the Marginalist Predictions Been Tested?*

A number of empirical phenomena have been cited as providing more or less conclusive support for the classical theory of the firm as against its behavioral competitors (see Dale Jorgensen and Calvin Siebert). But there are no direct observations that individuals or firms do actually equate marginal costs and revenues. The empirically verified consequences of the classical theory are almost always weaker than this. Let us look at four of the most important of them: the fact that demand curves generally have negative slopes; the fact that fitted Cobb-Douglas functions are approximately homogeneous of the first degree; the fact of decreasing returns to scale; and the fact that executive salaries vary with the logarithm of company size. Are these indeed facts? And does the evidence support a maximizing theory against a satisficing theory?

Negatively Sloping Demand Curves. Evidence that consumers actually distribute their purchases in such a way as to maximize their utilities, and hence to equate marginal utilities, is nonexistent. What the empirical data do confirm is that demand curves generally have negative slopes. (Even this "obvious" fact is tricky to verify, as Henry Schultz showed long years ago.) But negatively sloping demand curves could result from a wide range of behaviors satisfying the assumptions of bounded rationality rather than those of utility maximization. Gary Becker, who can scarcely be regarded as a hostile witness for the classical theory, states the case very well:

> Economists have long been aware that some changes in the feasible or opportunity sets of households would lead to the same response *regardless of the decision rule used.* For example, a decrease in real income necessarily decreases the amount spent on at least one commodity... It has seldom been realized, however, that the change in opportunities resulting from a change in relative prices also tends to produce a systematic response, regardless of the decision rule. In particular, the fundamental theorem of traditional theory—that demand curves are negatively inclined—largely results from the change in opportunities alone and is largely independent of the decision rule. [p. 4]

Later, Becker is even more explicit, saying, "Not only utility maximization but also many other decision rules, incorporating a wide variety of irrational behavior, lead to negatively inclined demand curves because of the effect of a change in prices on opportunities" (p. 5).[2]

First-Degree Homogeneity of Production Functions. Another example of an observed phenomenon for which the classical assumptions provide sufficient, but not necessary, conditions is the equality between labor's share of product and the exponent of the labor factor in fitted Cobb-Douglas production functions (see Simon and Ferdinand Levy). Fitted Cobb-Douglas functions are homogeneous, generally of degree close to unity and with a labor exponent of about the right magnitude. These findings, however, cannot be taken as strong evidence for the classical theory, for the identical results can readily be produced by mistakenly fitting a Cobb-Douglas function to data that were in fact generated by a linear accounting identity (value of goods equals labor cost plus capital cost), (see E. H. Phelps-Brown). The same comment applies to the SMAC production function (see Richard Cyert and Simon). Hence, the empirical findings do not allow us to draw any particular conclusions about the relative plausibility of classical and behavioral theories, both of which are equally compatible with the data.

The Long-Run Cost Curve. Somewhat different is the case of the firm's long-run cost curve, which classical theory requires to be U shaped if competitive equilibrium is to be stable. Theories of bounded rationality do not predict this—fortunately, for the observed data make it exceedingly doubtful that the cost curves are in fact generally U shaped. The evidence for many industries shows costs at the high-scale ends of the curves to be essentially constant or even declining (see Alan Walters). This finding is compatible with stochastic models of business firm growth and size (see Y. Ijiri and Simon), but not with the static equilibrium model of classical theory.

Executive Salaries. Average salaries of top corporate executives grow with the logarithm of corporate size (see David Roberts). This finding has been derived from the assumptions of the classical theory of profit maximization only with the help of very particular *ad hoc* assumptions about the distribution of managerial ability (see Robert Lucas, 1978). The observed relation is implied by a simple behavioral theory that assumes only that there is a single, culturally determined, parameter which fixes the average ratio of the salaries of managers to the salaries of their immediate subordinates (see Simon, 1957). In the case of the executive salary data, the behavioral model that explains the observations is substantially more parsimonious (in terms of assumptions about exogenous variables) than the classical model that explains the same observations.

Summary: Phenomena that Fail to Discriminate. It would take a much more extensive review than is provided here to establish the point conclusively, but I believe it is the case that specific phenomena requiring a theory of utility or profit maximization for their explanation rather than a theory of bounded rationality simply have not been observed in aggregate data. In fact, as my last two examples indicate, it is the classical rather than the behavioral form of the theory that faces real difficulties in handling some of the empirical observations.

Failures of Classical Theory. It may well be that classical theory can be patched up sufficiently to handle a wide range of situations where uncertainty and outguessing phenomena do not play a central role—that is, to handle the behavior of economies that are relatively stable and not too distant from a competitive equilibrium. However, a strong positive case for replacing the classical theory by a model of bounded rationality begins to emerge when we examine situations involving decision making under uncertainty and imperfect competition. These situations the classical theory was never designed to handle, and has never handled satisfactorily. Statistical decision theory employing the idea of subjective expected utility, on the one hand, and game theory, on the other, have contributed enormous conceptual clarification to these kinds of situations without providing

---

[2]In a footnote, Becker indicates that he denotes as irrational "[A]ny deviation from utility maximization." Thus, what I have called "bounded rationality" is "irrationality" in Becker's terminology.

satisfactory descriptions of actual human behavior, or even, for most cases, normative theories that are actually usable in the face of the limited computational powers of men and computers.

I shall have more to say later about the positive case for a descriptive theory of bounded rationality, but I would like to turn first to another territory within economic science that has gained rapidly in population since World War II, the domain of normative decision theory.

E. *Normative Decision Theory*

Decision theory can be pursued not only for the purposes of building foundations for political economy, or of understanding and explaining phenomena that are in themselves intrinsically interesting, but also for the purpose of offering direct advice to business and governmental decision makers. For reasons not clear to me, this territory was very sparsely settled prior to World War II. Such inhabitants as it had were mainly industrial engineers, students of public administration, and specialists in business functions, none of whom especially identified themselves with the economic sciences. Prominent pioneers included the mathematician, Charles Babbage, inventor of the digital computer, the engineer, Frederick Taylor, and the administrator, Henri Fayol.

During World War II, this territory, almost abandoned, was rediscovered by scientists, mathematicians, and statisticians concerned with military management and logistics, and was renamed "operations research" or "operations analysis." So remote were the operations researchers from the social science community that economists wishing to enter the territory had to establish their own colony, which they called "management science." The two professional organizations thus engendered still retain their separate identities, though they are now amicably federated in a number of common endeavors.

Optimization techniques were transported into management science from economics, and new optimization techniques, notably linear programming, were invented and developed, the names of Dantzig, Kantorovich, and Koopmans being prominent in the early development of that tool.

Now the salient characteristic of the decision tools employed in management science is that they have to be capable of actually making or recommending decisions, taking as their inputs the kinds of empirical data that are available in the real world, and performing only such computations as can reasonably be performed by existing desk calculators or, a little later, electronic computers. For these domains, idealized models of optimizing entrepreneurs, equipped with complete certainty about the world—or, at worst, having full probability distributions for uncertain events—are of little use. Models have to be fashioned with an eye to practical computability, no matter how severe the approximations and simplifications that are thereby imposed on them.

Model construction under these stringent conditions has taken two directions. The first is to retain optimization, but to simplify sufficiently so that the optimum (in the simplified world!) is computable. The second is to construct satisficing models that provide good enough decisions with reasonable costs of computation. By giving up optimization, a richer set of properties of the real world can be retained in the models. Stated otherwise, decision makers can satisfice either by finding optimum solutions for a simplified world, or by finding satisfactory solutions for a more realistic world. Neither approach, in general, dominates the other, and both have continued to co-exist in the world of management science.

Thus, the body of theory that has developed in management science shares with the body of theory in descriptive decision theory a central concern with the *ways* in which decisions are made, and not just with the decision outcomes. As I have suggested elsewhere (1978b), these are theories of *how* to decide rather than theories of *what* to decide.

Let me cite one example, from work in which I participated, of how model building in normative economics is shaped by computational considerations (see Charles Holt, Franco Modigliani, John Muth, and Simon).

In face of uncertain and fluctuating production demands, a company can smooth and stabilize its production and employment levels at the cost of holding buffer inventories. What kind of decision rule will secure a reasonable balance of costs? Formally, we are faced with a dynamic programming problem, and these generally pose formidable and often intolerable computational burdens for their solution.

One way out of this difficulty is to seek a special case of the problem that will be computationally tractable. If we assume the cost functions facing the company all to be quadratic in form, the optimal decision rule will then be a linear function of the decision variables, which can readily be computed in terms of the cost parameters. Equally important, under uncertainty about future sales, only the expected values, and not the higher moments, of the probability distributions enter into the decision rule (Simon, 1956b). Hence the assumption of quadratic costs reduces the original problem to one that is readily solved. Of course the solution, though it provides optimal decisions for the simplified world of our assumptions, provides, at best, satisfactory solutions for the real-world decision problem that the quadratic function approximates. In-principle, unattainable optimization is sacrificed for in-practice, attainable satisfaction.

If human decision makers are as rational as their limited computational capabilities and their incomplete information permit them to be, then there will be a close relation between normative and descriptive decision theory. Both areas of inquiry are concerned primarily with procedural rather than substantive rationality (Simon, 1978a). As new mathematical tools for computing optimal and satisfactory decisions are discovered, and as computers become more and more powerful, the recommendations of normative decision theory will change. But as the new recommendations are diffused, the actual, observed, practice of decision making in business firms will change also. And these changes may have macro-economic consequences. For example, there is some agreement that average inventory holdings of American firms have been reduced significantly by the introduction of formal procedures for calculating reorder points and quantities.

II. Characterizing Bounded Rationality

The principal forerunner of a behavioral theory of the firm is the tradition usually called Institutionalism. It is not clear that all of the writings, European and American, usually lumped under this rubric have much in common, or that their authors would agree with each other's views. At best, they share a conviction that economic theory must be reformulated to take account of the social and legal structures amidst which market transactions are carried out. Today, we even find a vigorous development within economics that seeks to achieve institutionalist goals within the context of neoclassical price theory. I will have more to say about that a little later.

The name of John R. Commons is prominent—perhaps the most prominent—among American Institutionalists. Commons' difficult writings (for example, *Institutional Economics*) borrow their language heavily from the law, and seek to use the *transaction* as their basic unit of behavior. I will not undertake to review Commons' ideas here, but simply remark that they provided me with many insights in my initial studies of organizational decision making (see my *Administrative Behavior*, p. 136).

Commons also had a substantial influence on the thinking of Chester I. Barnard, an intellectually curious business executive who distilled from his experience as president of the New Jersey Bell Telephone Company, and as executive of other business, governmental, and nonprofit organizations, a profound book on decision making titled *The Functions of the Executive*. Barnard proposed original theories, which have stood up well under empirical scrutiny, of the nature of the authority mechanism in organizations, and of the motivational bases for employee acceptance of organizational goals (the so-called "inducements-contributions" theory); and he provided a realistic description of organizational decision making, which he characterized as "opportunistic." The numerous references to Barnard's work in *Administrative Behavior* attest, though inadequately, to the impact he had on my own thinking about organizations.

A. *In Search of a Descriptive Theory*

In 1934–35, in the course of a field study of the administration of public recreational facilities in Milwaukee, which were managed jointly by the school board and the city public works department, I encountered a puzzling phenomenon. Although the heads of the two agencies appeared to agree as to the objectives of the recreation program, and did not appear to be competing for empire, there was continual disagreement and tension between them with respect to the allocation of funds between physical maintenance, on the one hand, and play supervision on the other. Why did they not, as my economics books suggested, simply balance off the marginal return of the one activity against that of the other?

Further exploration made it apparent that they didn't equate expenditures at the margin because, intellectually, they couldn't. There was no measurable production function from which quantitative inferences about marginal productivities could be drawn; and such qualitative notions of a production function as the two managers possessed were mutually incompatible. To the public works administrator, a playground was a physical facility, serving as a green oasis in the crowded gray city. To the recreation administrator, a playground was a social facility, where children could play together with adult help and guidance.

How can human beings make rational decisions in circumstances like these? How are they to apply the marginal calculus? Or, if it does not apply, what do they substitute for it?

The phenomenon observed in Milwaukee is ubiquitous in human decision making. In organization theory it is usually referred to as *subgoal identification*. When the goals of an organization cannot be connected operationally with actions (when the production function can't be formulated in concrete terms), then decisions will be judged against subordinate goals that can be so connected. There is no unique determination of these subordinate goals. Their formulation will depend on the knowledge, experience, and organizational environment of the decision maker. In the face of this ambiguity, the formulation can also be influenced in subtle, and not so subtle, ways by his self-interest and power drives.

The phenomenon arises as frequently in individual as in social decision making and problem solving. Today, under the rubric of *problem representation*, it is a central research interest of cognitive psychology. Given a particular environment of stimuli, and a particular background of previous knowledge, how will a person organize this complex mass of information into a problem formulation that will facilitate his solution efforts? How did Newton's experience of the apple, if he had one, get represented as an instance of attraction of apple by Earth?

Phenomena like these provided the central theme for *Administrative Behavior*. That study represented "an attempt to construct tools useful in my own research in the field of public administration." The product was actually not so much a theory as prolegomena to a theory, stemming from the conviction "that decision making is the heart of administration, and that the vocabulary of administrative theory must be derived from the logic and psychology of human choice." It was, if you please, an exercise in problem representation.

On examination, the phenomenon of subgoal identification proved to be the visible tip of a very large iceberg. The shape of the iceberg is best appreciated by contrasting it with classical models of rational choice. The classical model calls for knowledge of all the alternatives that are open to choice. It calls for complete knowledge of, or ability to compute, the consequences that will follow on each of the alternatives. It calls for certainty in the decision maker's present and future evaluation of these consequences. It calls for the ability to compare consequences, no matter how diverse and heterogeneous, in terms of some consistent measure of utility. The task, then, was to replace the classical model with one that would describe how decisions could be (and probably actually were) made when the alternatives of search had to be sought out, the consequences of choosing particular alternatives were only very imperfectly known both because of limited computational power and because of uncertainty in the external world, and the decision maker did not possess a general and consistent utility function for comparing heterogeneous alternatives.

Several procedures of rather general applicability and wide use have been discovered that transform intractable decision problems into tractable ones. One procedure already mentioned is to look for satisfactory choices instead of optimal ones. Another is to replace abstract, global goals with tangible subgoals, whose achievement can be observed and measured. A third is to divide up the decision-making task among many specialists, coordinating their work by means of a structure of communications and authority relations. All of these, and others, fit the general rubric of "bounded rationality," and it is now clear that the elaborate organizations that human beings have constructed in the modern world to carry out the work of production and government can only be understood as machinery for coping with the limits of man's abilities to comprehend and compute in the face of complexity and uncertainty.

This rather vague and general initial formulation of the idea of bounded rationality called for elaboration in two directions: greater formalization of the theory, and empirical verification of its main claims. During the decade that followed the publication of *Administrative Behavior*, substantial progress was made in both directions, some of it through the efforts of my colleagues and myself, much of it by other research groups that shared the same Zeitgeist.

B. *Empirical Studies*

The principal source of empirical data about organizational decision making has been straightforward "anthropological" field study, eliciting descriptions of decision-making procedures and observing the course of specific decision-making episodes. Examples are my study, with Guetzkow, Kozmetsky, and Tyndall (1954), of the ways in which accounting data were used in decision making in large corporations; and a series of studies, with Richard Cyert, James March, and others, of specific nonprogrammed policy decisions in a number of different companies (see Cyert, Simon, and Donald Trow). The latter line of work was greatly developed and expanded by Cyert and March and its theoretical implications for economics explored in their important work, *A Behavioral Theory of the Firm*.

At about the same time, the fortuitous availability of some data on businessmen's perceptions of a problem situation described in a business policy casebook enabled DeWitt Dearborn and me to demonstrate empirically the cognitive basis for identification with subgoals, the phenomenon that had so impressed me in the Milwaukee recreation study. The businessmen's perceptions of the principal problems facing the company described in the case were mostly determined by their own business experiences—sales and accounting executives identified a sales problem, manufacturing executives, a problem of internal organization.

Of course there is vastly more to be learned and tested about organizational decision making than can be dealt with in a handful of studies. Although many subsequent studies have been carried out in Europe and the United States, this domain is still grossly undercultivated (for references, see March, 1965; E. Johnsen, 1968; G. Eliasson, 1976). Among the reasons for the relative neglect of such studies, as contrasted, say, with laboratory experiments in social psychology, is that they are extremely costly and time consuming, with a high grist-to-grain ratio, the methodology for carrying them out is primitive, and satisfactory access to decision-making behavior is hard to secure. This part of economics has not yet acquired the habits of patience and persistence in the pursuit of facts that is exemplified in other domains by the work, say, of Simon Kuznets or of the architects of the MIT-SSRC-Penn econometric models.

C. Theoretical Inquiries

On the theoretical side, three questions seemed especially to call for clarification: what are the circumstances under which an employment relation will be preferred to some other form of contract as the arrangement for securing the performance of work; what is the relation between the classical theory of the firm and theories of organizational equilibrium first proposed by Chester Barnard; and what are the main characteristics of human rational choice in situations where complexity precludes omniscience?

The Employment Relation. A fundamental characteristic of modern industrial society is that most work is performed, not by individuals who produce products for sale, nor by individual contractors, but by persons who have accepted employment in a business firm and the authority relation with the employer that employment entails. Acceptance of authority means willingness to permit one's behavior to be determined by the employer, at least within some zone of indifference or acceptance. What is the advantage of this arrangement over a contract for specified goods or services? Why is so much of the world's work performed in large, hierarchic organizations?

Analysis showed (Simon, 1951) that a combination of two factors could account for preference for the employment contract over other forms of contracts: uncertainty as to which future behaviors would be advantageous to the employer, and a greater indifference of the employee as compared with the employer (within the former's area of acceptance) as to which of these behaviors he carried out. When the secretary is hired, the employer does not know what letters he will want her to type, and the secretary has no great preference for typing one letter rather than another. The employment contract permits the choice to be postponed until the uncertainty is resolved, with little cost to the employee and great advantage to the employer. The explanation is closely analogous to one Jacob Marschak had proposed for liquidity preference. Under conditions of uncertainty it is advantageous to hold resources in liquid, flexible form.

Organizational Equilibrium. Barnard had described the survival of organizations in terms of the motivations that make their participants (employees, investors, customers, suppliers) willing to remain in the system. In *Administrative Behavior*, I had developed this notion further into a motivational theory of the balance between the inducements that were provided by organizations to their participants, and the contributions those participants made to the organizations' resources.

A formalization of this theory (Simon, 1952; 1953) showed its close affinity to the classical theory of the firm, but with an important and instructive difference. In comparing the two theories, each inducement-contribution relation became a supply schedule for the firm. The survival conditions became the conditions for positive profit. But while the classical theory of the firm assumes that all profits accrue to a particular set of participants, the owners, the organization theory treats the surplus more symmetrically, and does not predict how it will be distributed. Hence the latter theory leaves room, under conditions of monopoly and imperfect competition, for bargaining among the participants (for example, between labor and owners) for the surplus. The survival conditions—positive profits rather than maximum profits—also permit a departure from the assumptions of perfect rationality.

Mechanisms of Bounded Rationality. In *Administrative Behavior*, bounded rationality is largely characterized as a residual category—rationality is bounded when it falls short of omniscience. And the failures of omniscience are largely failures of knowing all the alternatives, uncertainty about relevant exogenous events, and inability to calculate consequences. There was needed a more positive and formal characterization of the mechanisms of choice under conditions of bounded rationality. Two papers (Simon, 1955; 1956a) undertook first steps in that direction.

Two concepts are central to the characterization: *search* and *satisficing*. If the alternatives for choice are not given initially to the decision maker, then he must search for them. Hence, a theory of bounded rationality must incorporate a theory of search. This idea was later developed independently by George Stigler in a very influential paper that took as its example of a decision situation the purchase of a second-hand automobile. Stigler poured the search theory back into the old bottle of classical utility maximization, the cost of search being equated with its marginal return. In my 1956 paper, I had demonstrated the same formal equivalence, using as my example a dynamic programming formulation of the process of selling a house.

But utility maximization, as I showed, was not essential to the search scheme—fortunately, for it would have required the decision maker to be able to estimate the marginal costs and returns of search in a decision situation that was already too complex for the exercise of global rationality. As an alternative, one could postulate that the decision maker had formed some *aspiration* as to how good an alternative he should find. As soon as he discovered an alternative for choice meeting his level of aspiration, he would terminate the search and choose that alternative. I called this mode of selection *satisficing*. It had its roots in the empirically based psychological theories, due to Lewin and others, of aspiration levels. As psychological inquiry had shown, aspiration levels are not static, but tend to rise and fall in consonance with changing experiences. In a benign environment that provides many good alternatives, aspirations rise; in a harsher enviornment, they fall.

In long-run equilibrium it might even be the case that choice with dynamically adapting aspiration levels would be equivalent to optimal choice, taking the costs of search into account. But the important thing about the search and satisficing theory is that it showed how choice could actually be made with reasonable amounts of calculation, and using very incomplete information, without the need of performing the impossible—of carrying out this optimizing procedure.

D. *Summary*

Thus, by the middle 1950's, a theory of bounded rationality had been proposed as an alternative to classical omniscient rationality, a significant number of empirical studies had been carried out that showed actual business decision making to conform reasonably well with the assumptions of bounded rationality but not with the assumptions of perfect rationality, and key components of the theory—the nature of the authority and employment relations, organizational equilibrium, and the mechanisms of search and satisficing—had been elucidated formally. In the remaining parts of this paper, I should like to trace subsequent developments of decision-making theory, including developments competitive with the theory of bounded rationality, and then to comment on the implications (and potential implications) of the new descriptive theory of decision for political economy.

III. The Neoclassical Revival

Peering forward from the late 1950's, it would not have been unreasonable to predict that theories of bounded rationality would soon find a large place in the mainstream of economic thought. Substantial progress had been made in providing the theories with some formal structure, and an increasing body of empirical evidence showed them to provide a far more veridical picture of decision making in business organizations than did the classical concepts of perfect rationality.

History has not followed any such simple course, even though many aspects of the Zeitgeist were favorable to movement in this direction. During and after World War II, a large number of academic economists were exposed directly to business life, and had more or less extensive opportunities to observe how decisions were actually made in business organizations. Moreover, those who became active in the development of the new management science were faced with the necessity of developing decision-making procedures that could actually be applied in practical situations. Surely these trends would be conducive to moving the basic assumptions of economic rationality in the direction of greater realism.

But these were not the only things that were happening in economics in the postwar period. First, there was a vigorous reaction that sought to defend classical theory from behavioralism on methodological grounds. I have already commented on these methodological arguments in the first part of my talk. However deeply one may disagree with them, they were stated persuasively and are still influential among academic economists.

Second, the rapid spread of mathematical knowledge and competence in the economics profession permitted the classical theory, especially when combined with statistical decision theory and the theory of games due to von Neumann and Morgenstern, to develop to new heights of sophistication and elegance, and to expand to embrace, albeit in highly stylized form, some of the phenomena of uncertainty and imperfect information. The flowering of mathematical economics and econometrics has provided two generations of economic theorists with a vast garden of formal and technical problems that have absorbed their energies and postponed encounters with the inelegancies of the real world.

If I sound mildly critical of these developments, I should confess that I have also been a part of them, admire them, and would be decidedly unhappy to return to the premathematical world they have replaced. My concern is that the economics profession has exhibited some of the serial one-thing-at-a-time character of human rationality, and has seemed sometimes to be unable to distribute its attention in a balanced fashion among neoclassical theory, macroeconometrics, and descriptive decision theory. As a result, not as much professional effort has been devoted to the latter two, and especially the third, as one might have hoped and expected. The Heartland is more overpopulated than ever, while rich lands in other parts of the empire go untilled.

A. *Search and Information Transfer*

Let me allude to just three of the ways in which classical theory has sought to cope with some of its traditional limitations, and has even sought to make the development of a behavioral theory, incorporating psychological assumptions, unnecessary. The first was to introduce search and information transfer explicitly as economic activities, with associated costs and outputs, that could be inserted into the classical production function. I have already referred to Stigler's 1961 paper on the economics of information, and my own venture in the same direction in the 1956 essay cited earlier.

In theory of this genre, the decision maker is still an individual. A very important new direction, in which decisions are made by groups of individuals, in teams or organizations, is the economic theory of teams developed by Jacob Marschak and Roy Radner. Here we see genuine organizational phenomena—specialization of decision making as a consequence of the costs of transmitting information—emerge from the rational calculus. Because the mathematical difficulties are formidable, the theory remains largely illustrative and limited to very simple situations in miniature organizations. Nevertheless, it has greatly broadened our understanding of the economics of information.

In none of these theories—any more than in statistical decision theory or the theory of games—is the assumption of perfect maximization abandoned. Limits and costs of information are introduced, not as psychological characteristics of the decision maker, but as part of his technological environment. Hence, the new theories do nothing to alleviate the computational complexities facing the decision maker—do not see him coping with them by heroic approximation, simplifying and satisficing, but simply magnify and multiply them. Now he needs to compute not merely the shapes of his supply and demand curves, but, in addition, the costs and benefits of computing those shapes to greater accuracy as well. Hence, to some extent, the impression that these new theories deal with the hitherto ignored phenomena of uncertainty and information transmission is illusory. For many economists, however, the illusion has been persuasive.

B. *Rational Expectations Theory*

A second development in neoclassical theory on which I wish to comment is the so-called "rational expectations" theory.

There is a bit of historical irony surrounding its origins. I have already described the management science inquiry of Holt, Modigliani, Muth, and myself that developed a dynamic programming algorithm for the special (and easily computed) case of quadratic cost functions. In this case, the decision rules are linear, and the probability distributions of future events can be replaced by their expected values, which serve as certainty equivalents (see Simon, 1956; Henri Theil, 1957).

Muth imaginatively saw in this special case a paradigm for rational behavior under uncertainty. What to some of us in the HMMS research team was an approximating, satisficing simplification, served for him as a major line of defense for perfect rationality. He said in his seminal 1961 *Econometrica* article, "It is sometimes argued that the assumption of rationality in economics leads to theories inconsistent with, or inadequate to explain, observed phenomena, especially changes over time... Our hypothesis is based on exactly the opposite point of view: that dynamic economic models do not assume enough rationality" (p. 316).

The new increment of rationality that Muth proposed was that "expectations, since they are informed predictions of future events, are essentially the same as the predictions of the relevant economic theory" (p. 316). He would cut the Gordian knot. Instead of dealing with uncertainty by elaborating the model of the decision process, he would once and for all—if his hypothesis were correct—make process irrelevant. The subsequent vigorous development of rational expectations theory, in the hands of Sargent, Lucas, Prescott, and others, is well known to most readers (see, for example, Lucas, 1975).

It is too early to render a final verdict on the rational expectations theory. The issue will ultimately be decided, as all scientific debates should be, by a gradual winnowing of the empirical evidence, and that winnowing process has just begun. Meanwhile, certain grave theoretical difficulties have already been noticed. As Muth himself has pointed out, it is rational (i.e., profit maximizing) to use the "rational expectations" decision rule if the relevant cost equations are in fact quadratic. I have suggested elsewhere (1978a) that it might therefore be less misleading to call the rule a "consistent expectations" rule.

Perhaps even more important, Albert Ando and Benjamin Friedman (1978, 1979) have shown that the policy implications of the rational expectations rule are quite different under conditions where new information continually becomes available to the system, structural changes occur, and the decision maker learns, than they are under steady-state conditions. For example, under the more dynamic conditions, monetary neutrality—which in general holds for the static consistent expectations models—is no longer guaranteed for any finite time horizon.

In the recent "revisionist" versions of consistent expectations theory, moreover, where account is taken of a changing environment of information, various behavioral assumptions reappear to explain how expectations are formed—what information decision makers will consider, and what they will ignore. But unless these assumptions are to be made on a wholly *ad hoc* and arbitrary basis, they create again the need for an explicit and valid theory of the decision-making *process* (see Simon, 1958a; B. Friedman, 1979).

C. *Statistical Decision Theory and Game Theory*

Statistical decision theory and game theory are two other important components of the neoclassical revival. The former addresses itself to the question of incorporating uncertainty (or more properly, risk) into the decision-making models. It requires heroic assumptions about the information the decision maker has concerning the probability distributions of the relevant variables, and simply increases by orders of magnitude the computational problems he faces.

Game theory addresses itself to the "outguessing" problem that arises whenever an economic actor takes into account the possible reactions to his own decisions of the other actors. To my mind, the main product of the very elegant apparatus of game theory has been to demonstrate quite clearly that it is virtually impossible to define an unambiguous criterion of rationality for this class of situations (or, what amounts to the same thing, a definitive definition of the "solution" of a game). Hence, game theory has not brought to the theories of oligopoly and imperfect competition the relief from their contradictions and complexities that was originally hoped for it. Rather, it has shown that these difficulties are ineradicable. We may be able to reach consensus that a certain criterion of rationality is appropriate to a particular game, but if someone challenges the consensus, preferring a different criterion, we will have no logical basis for persuading him that he is wrong.

D. Conclusion

Perhaps I have said enough about the neoclassical revival to suggest why it has been a highly attractive commodity in competition with the behavioral theories. To some economists at least, it has held open the possibility and hope that important questions that had been troublesome for classical economics could now be addressed without sacrifice of the central assumption of perfect rationality, and hence also with a maximum of a priori inference and a minimum of tiresome grubbing with empirical data. I have perhaps said enough also with respect to the limitations of these new constructs to indicate why I do not believe that they solve the problems that motivated their development.

IV. Advances in the Behavioral Theory

Although they have played a muted role in the total economic research activity during the past two decades, theories of bounded rationality and the behavioral theory of the business firm have undergone steady development during that period. Since surveying the whole body of work would be a major undertaking, I shall have to be satisfied here with suggesting the flavor of the whole by citing a few samples of different kinds of important research falling in this domain. Where surveys on particular topics have been published, I will limit myself to references to them.

First, there has been work in the psychological laboratory and the field to test whether people in relatively simple choice situations behave as statistical decision theory (maximization of expected utilities) say they do. Second, there has been extensive psychological research, in which Allen Newell and I have been heavily involved, to discover the actual microprocesses of human decision making and problem solving. Third, there have been numerous empirical observations—most of them in the form of "case studies"—of the actual processes of decision making in organizational and business contexts. Fourth, there have been reformulations and extensions of the theory of the firm replacing classical maximization with behavioral decision postulates.

A. *Utility Theory and Human Choice*

The axiomatization of utility and probability after World War II and the revival of Bayesian statistics opened the way to testing empirically whether people behaved in choice situations so as to maximize subjective expected utility (SEU). In early studies, using extremely simple choice situations, it appeared that perhaps they did. When even small complications were introduced into the situations, wide departures of behavior from the predictions of SEU theory soon became evident. Some of the most dramatic and convincing empirical refutations of the theory have been reported by D. Kahneman and A. Tversky, who showed that under one set of circumstances, decision makers gave far too little weight to prior knowledge and based their choices almost entirely on new evidence, while in other circumstances new evidence had little influence on opinions already formed. Equally large and striking departures from the behavior predicted by the SEU theories were found by Howard Kunreuther and his colleagues in their studies of individual decisions to purchase or not to purchase flood insurance. On the basis of these and other pieces of evidence, the conclusion seems unavoidable that the SEU theory does not provide a good prediction—not even a good approximation—of actual behavior.

Notice that the refutation of the theory has to do with the *substance* of the decisions, and not just the process by which they are reached. It is not that people do not go through the calculations that would be required to reach the *SEU* decision—neoclassical thought has never claimed that they did. What has been shown is that they do not even behave *as if* they had carried out those calculations, and that result is a direct refutation of the neoclassical assumptions.

B. *Psychology of Problem Solving*

The evidence on rational decision making is largely negative evidence, evidence of what people do *not* do. In the past twenty years a large body of positive evidence has also accumulated about the processes that people use to make difficult decisions and solve complex problems. The body of theory that has been built up around this evidence is called information processing psychology, and is usually expressed formally in computer programming languages. Newell and I have summed up our own version of this theory in our book, *Human Problem Solving*, which is part of a large and rapidly growing literature that assumes an information processing framework and makes use of computer simulation as a central tool for expressing and testing theories.

Information processing theories envisage problem solving as involving very selective search through problem spaces that are often immense. Selectivity, based on rules of thumb or "heuristics," tends to guide the search into promising regions, so that solutions will generally be found after search of only a tiny part of the total space. Satisficing criteria terminate search when satisfactory problem solutions have been found. Thus, these theories of problem solving clearly fit within the framework of bounded rationality that I have been expounding here.

By now the empirical evidence for this general picture of the problem solving process is extensive. Most of the evidence pertains to relatively simple, puzzle-like situations of the sort that can be brought into the psychological laboratory for controlled study, but a great deal has been learned, also, about professional level human tasks like making medical diagnoses, investing in portfolios of stocks and bonds, and playing chess. In tasks of these kinds, the general search mechanisms operate in a rich context of information stored in human long-term memory, but the general organization of the process is substantially the same as for the simpler, more specific tasks.

At the present time, research in information processing psychology is proceeding in several directions. Exploration of professional level skills continues. A good deal of effort is now being devoted also to determining how initial representations for new problems are acquired. Even in simple problem domains, the problem solver has much latitude in the way he formulates the problem space in which he will search, a finding that underlines again how far the actual process is from a search for a uniquely determined optimum (see J. R. Hayes and Simon).

The main import for economic theory of the research in information processing psychology is to provide rather conclusive empirical evidence that the decision-making process in problem situations conforms closely to the models of bounded rationality described earlier. This finding implies, in turn, that choice is not determined uniquely by the objective characteristics of the problem situation, but depends also on the particular heuristic process that is used to reach the decision. It would appear, therefore, that a model of process is an essential component in any positive theory of decision making that purports to describe the real world, and that the neoclassical ambition of avoiding the necessity for such a model is unrealizable (Simon, 1978a).

C. *Organizational Decision Making*

It would be desirable to have, in addition to the evidence from the psychological research just described, empirical studies of the process of decision making in organizational contexts. The studies of individual problem solving and decision making do not touch on the many social-psychological factors that enter into the decision process in organizations. A substantial number of investigations have been carried out in the past twenty years of the decision-making process in organizations, but they are not easily summarized. The difficulty is that most of these investigations have taken the form of case studies of specific decisions or particular classes of decisions in individual organizations. To the best of my knowledge, no good review of this literature has been published, so that it is difficult even to locate and identify the studies that have been carried out.[3] Nor have any systematic methods been developed and tested for distilling out from these individual case studies their implications for the general theory of the decision-making process.

The case studies of organizational decision making, therefore, represent the natural history stage of scientific inquiry. They provide us with a multitude of facts about the decision-making process—facts that are almost uniformly consistent with the kind of behavioral model that has been proposed here. But we do not yet know how to use these facts to test the model in any formal way. Nor do we quite know what to do with the observation that the specific decision-making procedures used by organizations differ from one organization to another, and within each organization, even from one situation to another. We must not expect from these data generalizations as neat and precise as those incorporated in neoclassical theory.

Perhaps the closest approach to a method for extracting theoretically relevant information from case studies is computer simulation. By converting empirical evidence about a decision-making process into a computer program, a path is opened both for testing the adequacy of the program mechanisms for explaining the data, and for discovering the key features of the program that account, qualitatively, for the interesting and important characteristics of its behavior. Examples

[3]For leads into the literature, see March and Simon; March; Johnsen; J. M. Dutton and W. H. Starbuck. However, there are large numbers of specific case studies, some of them carried out as thesis projects, some concerned with particular fields of business application, which have never been recorded in these reference sources (for example, Eliasson, 1976).

of the use of this technique are G.P.E. Clarkson's simulation of the decision making of an investment trust officer, Cyert, E. A. Feigenbaum, and March's simulation of the history of a duopoly, and C. P. Bonini's model of the effects of accounting information and supervisory pressures in altering employee motivations in a business firm. The simulation methodology is discussed from a variety of viewpoints in Dutton and Starbuck.[4]

D. *Theories of the Business Firm*

The general features of bounded rationality—selective search, satisficing, and so on—have been taken as the starting points for a number of attempts to build theories of the business firm incorporating behavioral assumptions. Examples of such theories would include the theory of Cyert and March, already mentioned; William Baumol's theory of sales maximization subject to minimum profit constraints; Robin Marris' models of firms whose goals are stated in terms of rates of growth; Harvey Leibenstein's theory of "X-inefficiency" that depresses production below the theoretically attainable; Janos Kornai's dichotomy between supply-driven and demand-driven management; Oliver Williamson's theory of transactional costs; the evolutionary models of Richard Nelson and Sidney Winter (1973); Cyert and Morris DeGroot's (1974) models incorporating adaptive learning; Radner's (1975a,b) explicit satisficing models; and others.

Characterized in this way, there seems to be little commonality among all of these theories and models, except that they depart in one way or another from the classical assumption of perfect rationality in firm decision making. A closer look, however, and a more abstract description of their assumptions, shows that they share several basic characteristics. Most of them depart from the assumption of profit maximization in the short run, and replace it with an assumption

[4]In addition to simulations of the firm, there are very interesting and potentially important efforts to use simulation to build bridges directly from decision theory to political economy. See G. Orcutt and R. Caldwell-Wertheimer, and Eliasson (1978).

of goals defined in terms of targets—that is, they are to greater or lesser degree satisficing theories. If they do retain maximizing assumptions, they contain some kind of mechanism that prevents the maximum from being attained, at least in the short run. In the Cyert-March theory, and that of Leibenstein, this mechanism can be viewed as producing "organizational slack," the magnitude of which may itself be a function of motivational and environmental variables.

Finally, a number of these theories assume that organizational learning takes place, so that if the environment were stationary for a sufficient length of time, the system equilibrium would approach closer and closer to the classical profit-maximizing equilibrium. Of course they generally also assume that the environmental disturbances will generally be large enough to prevent the classical solution from being an adequate approximation to the actual behavior.

The presence of something like organizational slack in a model of the business firm introduces complexity in the firm's behavior in the short run. Since the firm may operate very far from any optimum, the slack serves as a buffer between the environment and the firm's decisions. Responses to environmental events can no longer be predicted simply by analyzing the "requirements of the situation," but depend on the specific decision processes that the firm employs. However well this characteristic of a business firm model corresponds to reality, it reduces the attractiveness of the model for many economists, who are reluctant to give up the process-independent predictions of classical theory, and who do not feel at home with the kind of empirical investigation that is required for disclosing actual real world decision processes.

But there is another side to the matter. If, in the face of identical environmental conditions, different decision mechanisms can produce different firm behaviors, this sensitivity of outcomes to process can have important consequences for analysis at the level of markets and the economy. Political economy, whether descriptive or normative, cannot remain indifferent to this source of variability in response. At the very least it demands that—before we draw policy conclusions from our theories, and particularly before we act on those policy conclusions—we carry out sensitivity analyses to test how far our conclusions would be changed if we made different assumptions about the decision mechanisms at the micro level.

If our conclusions are robust—if they are not changed materially by substituting one or another variant of the behavioral model for the classical model—we will gain confidence in our predictions and recommendations; if the conclusions are sensitive to such substitutions, we will use them warily until we can determine which micro theory is the correct one.

As reference to the literature cited earlier in this section will verify, our predictions of the operations of markets and of the economy *are* sensitive to our assumptions about mechanisms at the level of decision processes. Moreover, the assumptions of the behavioral theories are almost certainly closer to reality than those of the classical theory. These two facts, in combination, constitute a direct refutation of the argument that the unrealism of the assumptions of the classical theory is harmless. We cannot use the *in vacua* version of the law of falling bodies to predict the sinking of a heavy body in molasses. The predictions of the classical and neoclassical theories and the policy recommendations derived from them must be treated with the greatest caution.

V. Conclusion

There is a saying in politics that "you can't beat something with nothing." You can't defeat a measure or a candidate simply by pointing to defects and inadequacies. You must offer an alternative.

The same principle applies to scientific theory. Once a theory is well entrenched, it will survive many assaults of empirical evidence that purports to refute it unless an alternative theory, consistent with the evidence, stands ready to replace it. Such conservative protectiveness of established beliefs is, indeed, not unreasonable. In the first place, in empirical science we aspire only to approximate truths; we are under no illusion that we can find a single formula, or even a moderately complex one, that captures the whole truth and nothing else. We are committed to a strategy of successive approximations, and when we find discrepancies between theory and data, our first impulse is to patch rather than to rebuild from the foundations.

In the second place, when discrepancies appear, it is seldom immediately obvious where the trouble lies. It may be located in the fundamental assumptions of the theory, but it may as well be merely a defect in the auxiliary hypotheses and measurement postulates we have had to assume in order to connect theory with observations. Revisions in these latter parts of the structure may be sufficient to save the remainder.

What then is the present status of the classical theory of the firm? There can no longer be any doubt that the micro assumptions of the theory—the assumptions of perfect rationality—are contrary to fact. It is not a question of approximation; they do not even remotely describe the processes that human beings use for making decisions in complex situations.

Moreover, there is an alternative. If anything, there is an embarrassing richness of alternatives. Today, we have a large mass of descriptive data, from both laboratory and field, that show how human problem solving and decision making actually take place in a wide variety of situations. A number of theories have been constructed to account for these data, and while these theories certainly do not yet constitute a single coherent whole, there is much in common among them. In one way or another, they incorporate the notions of bounded rationality: the need to search for decision alternatives, the replacement of optimization by targets and satisficing goals, and mechanisms of learning and adaptation. If our interest lies in descriptive decision theory (or even normative decision theory), it is now entirely clear that the classical and neoclassical theories have been replaced by a superior alternative that provides us with a much closer approximation to what is actually going on.

But what if our interest lies primarily in normative political economy rather than in the more remote regions of the economic sciences? Is there then any reason why we should give up the familiar theories? Have the newer concepts of decision making and the firm shown their superiority "for purposes of economic analysis"?

If the classical and neoclassical theories were, as is sometimes argued, simply powerful tools for deriving aggregative consequences that held alike for both perfect and bounded rationality, we would have every reason to retain them for this purpose. But we have seen, on the contrary, that neoclassical theory does not always lead to the same conclusions at the level of aggregate phenomena and policy as are implied by the postulate of bounded rationality, in any of its variants. Hence, we cannot defend an uncritical use of these contrary-to-fact assumptions by the argument that their veridicality is unimportant. In many cases, in fact, this veridicality may be crucial to reaching correct conclusions about the central questions of political economy. Only a comparison of predictions can tell us whether a case before us is one of these.

The social sciences have been accustomed to look for models in the most spectacular successes of the natural sciences. There is no harm in that, provided that it is not done in a spirit of slavish imitation. In economics, it has been common enough to admire Newtonian mechanics (or, as we have seen, the Law of Falling Bodies), and to search for the economic equivalent of the laws of motion. But this is not the only model for a science, and it seems, indeed, not to be the right one for our purposes.

Human behavior, even rational human behavior, is not to be accounted for by a handful of invariants. It is certainly not to be accounted for by assuming perfect adaptation to the environment. Its basic mechanisms may be relatively simple, and I believe they are, but that simplicity operates in interaction with extremely complex boundary conditions imposed by the environment and by the very facts of human long-term memory and of the capacity of human beings, individually and collectively, to learn.

If we wish to be guided by a natural science metaphor, I suggest one drawn from biology rather than physics (see Newell and Simon, 1976). Obvious lessons are to be learned from evolutionary biology, and rather less obvious ones from molecular biology. From molecular biology, in particular, we can glimpse a picture of how a few basic mechanisms—the DNA of the Double Helix, for example, or the energy transfer mechanisms elucidated so elegantly by Peter Mitchell—can account for a wide range of complex phenomena. We can see the role in science of laws of qualitative structure, and the power of qualitative as well as quantitative explanation.

I am always reluctant to end a talk about the sciences of man in the future tense. It conveys too much the impression that these are potential sciences which may some day be actualized, but that do not really exist at the present time. Of course that is not the case at all. However much our knowledge of human behavior falls short of our need for such knowledge, still it is enormous. Sometimes we tend to discount it because so many of the phenomena are accessible to us in the very activity of living as human beings among human beings that it seems commonplace to us. Moreover, it does not always answer the questions for which we need answers. We cannot predict very well the course of the business cycle nor manage the employment rate. (We cannot, it might be added, predict very well the time of the next thunderstorm in Stockholm, or manage the earth's climates.)

With all these qualifications and reservations, we do understand today many of the mechanisms of human rational choice. We do know how the information processing system called Man, faced with complexity beyond his ken, uses his information processing capacities to seek out alternatives, to calculate consequences, to resolve uncertainties, and thereby—sometimes, not always—to find ways of action that are sufficient unto the day, that satisfice.

REFERENCES

A. A. Alchian, "Uncertainty, Evolution, and Economic Theory," *J. Polit. Econ.*, June 1950, 58, 211-21.
A. Ando, "On a Theoretical and Empirical Basis of Macroeconometric Models," paper presented to the NSF-NBER Conference on Macroeconomic Modeling, Ann Arbor, Oct. 1978.
Chester I. Barnard, *The Functions of the Executive*, Cambridge, Mass. 1938.
William Baumol, *Business Behavior, Value and Growth*, New York 1959.
G. S. Becker, "Irrational Behavior and Economic Theory," *J. Polit. Econ.*, Feb. 1962, 70, 1-13.
Charles P. Bonini, *Simulation of Information and Decision Systems in the Firm*, Englewood Cliffs 1963.
Alfred Chandler, *Strategy and Structure*, Cambridge, Mass. 1962.
N. C. Churchill, W. W. Cooper, and T. Sainsbury, "Laboratory and Field Studies of the Behavioral Effects of Audits," in C. P. Bonini et al., eds., *Management Controls*, New York 1964.
G. P. E. Clarkson, "A Model of the Trust Investment Process," in E. A. Feigenbaum and J. Feldman, eds., *Computers and Thought*, New York 1963.
John R. Commons, *Institutional Economics*, Madison 1934.
R. M. Cyert, E. A. Feigenbaum, and J. G. March, "Models in a Behavioral Theory of the Firm," *Behav. Sci.*, Apr. 1959, 4, 81-95.
⎯⎯⎯ and M. H. DeGroot, "Rational Expectations and Bayesian Analysis," *J. Polit. Econ.*, May/June 1974, 82, 521-36.
⎯⎯⎯ and ⎯⎯⎯ "Adaptive Utility," in R. H. Day and T. Groves, eds., *Adaptive Economic Models*, New York 1975, 233-46.
⎯⎯⎯ and James G. March, *A Behavioral Theory of the Firm*, Englewood Cliffs 1963.
⎯⎯⎯ and H. A. Simon, "Theory of the Firm: Behavioralism and Marginalism," unpublished work. paper, Carnegie-Mellon Univ. 1971.
⎯⎯⎯, ⎯⎯⎯, and D. B. Trow, "Observation of a Business Decision," *J. Bus., Univ. Chicago*, Oct. 1956, 29, 237-48.
D. C. Dearborn and H. A. Simon, "Selective Perception: The Identifications of Executives," *Sociometry*, 1958, 21, 140-144; reprinted in *Administrative Behavior*, ch. 15, 3d ed., New York 1976.

J. M. Dutton and W. H. Starbuck, *Computer Simulation of Human Behavior*, New York 1971.

G. Eliasson, *Business Economic Planning*, New York 1976.

——, *A Micro-to-Macro Model of the Swedish Economy*, Stockholm 1978.

B. M. Friedman, "Optimal Expectations and the Extreme Information Assumptions of 'Rational Expectations' Macromodels," *J. Monet. Econ.*, Jan. 1979 5, 23–41.

——, "A Discussion of the Methodological Premises of Professors Lucas and Sargent," in *After the Phillips Curve: The Persistence of High Inflation and High Unemployment*, Boston 1978.

Milton Friedman, *Essays in Positive Economics*, Chicago 1953.

J. R. Hayes and H. A. Simon, "Understanding Written Problem Instructions," in W. Gregg, ed., *Knowledge and Cognition*, Potomac 1974, 167–200.

A. O. Hirschman, *Exit, Voice and Loyalty*, Cambridge, Mass. 1970.

Charles C. Holt, Franco Modigliani, John F. Muth, and Herbert A. Simon, *Planning Production, Inventories and Work Force*, Englewood Cliffs 1960.

Y. Ijiri and H. A. Simon, *Skew Distributions and the Sizes of Business Firms*, Amsterdam 1977.

E. Johnsen, *Studies in Multiobjective Decision Models*, Lund 1968.

D. W. Jorgenson and C. D. Siebert, "A Comparison of Alternative Theories of Corporate Investment Behavior," *Amer. Econ. Rev.*, Sept. 1968, 58, 681–712.

D. Kahneman and A. Tversky, "On the Psychology of Prediction," *Psychol. Rev.*, July 1973, 80, 237–51.

Janos Kornai, *Anti-Equilibrium*, Amsterdam 1971.

Howard Kunreuther et al., *Disaster Insurance Protection: Public Policy Lessons*, New York 1978.

Harvey Leibenstein, *Beyond Economic Man*, Cambridge, Mass. 1976.

J. Lesourne, *A Theory of the Individual for Economic Analysis*, Vol. 1, Amsterdam 1977.

R. E. Lucas, Jr., "An Equilibrium Model of the Business Cycle," *J. Polit. Econ.*, Dec. 1975, 83, 1113–44.

——, "On the Size Distribution of Business Firms," *Bell J. Econ.*, Autumn 1978, 9, 508–23.

James G. March, *Handbook of Organizations*, Chicago 1965.

—— and H. A. Simon, *Organizations*, New York 1958.

Robin Marris, *The Economic Theory of "Managerial" Capitalism*, London 1964.

Jacob Marschak, "Role of Liquidity under Complete and Incomplete Information," *Amer. Econ. Rev. Proc.*, May 1949, 39, 182–95.

—— and Roy Radner, *Economic Theory of Teams*, New Haven 1972.

Alfred Marshall, *Principles of Economics*, 8th ed., New York 1920.

E. S. Mason, "Comment," in Bernard T. Haley, ed., *A Survey of Contemporary Economics*, Vol. II, Homewood 1952, 221–22.

J. M. Montias, *The Structure of Economic Systems*, New Haven 1976.

J. F. Muth, "Rational Expectations and the Theory of Price Movements," *Econometrica*, July 1961, 29, 315–53.

——, "Optimal Properties of Exponentially Weighted Forecasts," *J. Amer. Statist. Assn.*, June 1960, 55, 299–306.

R. R. Nelson, and S. Winter, "Toward an Evolutionary Theory of Economic Capabilities," *Amer. Econ. Rev. Proc.*, May 1973, 63, 440–49.

—— and ——, "Neoclassical vs. Evolutionary Theories of Economic Growth," *Econ. J.*, Dec. 1974, 84, 886–905.

Allen Newell and Herbert A. Simon, *Human Problem Solving*, Englewood Cliffs, 1972.

—— and ——, "Computer Science as Empirical Inquiry: Symbols and Search," *Communications of the ACM*, Mar. 1976, 19,113–26.

G. Orcutt, and R. Caldwells-Wertheimer II, *Policy Exploration through Microanalytic Simulation*, Washington 1976.

A. Papandreou, "Some Basic Problems in the Theory of the Firm," in Bernard F. Haley, ed., *A Survey of Contemporary Economics*, Vol. II, Homewood 1952.

E. H. Phelps-Brown, "The Meaning of the Fitted Cobb-Douglas Function," *Quart. J. Econ.*, Nov. 1957, *71*, 546–60.

R. Radner, (1975a) "A Behavioral Model of Cost Reduction," *Bell J. Econ.*, Spring 1975, *6*, 196–215.

_____, (1975b) "Satisficing," *J. Math. Econ.*, June–Sept. 1975, *2*, 253–62.

David R. Roberts, *Executive Compensation*, Glencoe 1959.

P. A. Samuelson, "Discussion: Problems of Methodology," *Amer. Econ. Rev. Proc.*, May 1963, *53*, 231–36.

Henry Schultz, *The Theory and Measurement of Demand*, Chicago 1938.

Herbert A. Simon, *Administrative Behavior*, New York 1947; 3d ed. 1976.

_____, "A Formal Theory of the Employment Relation," *Econometrica*, July 1951, *19*, 293–305

_____, "A Comparison of Organization Theories," *Rev. Econ. Stud.*, No. 1, 1952, *20*, 40–48.

_____, "A Behavioral Model of Rational Choice," *Quart. J. Econ.*, Feb. 1955, *69*, 99–118.

_____, "Rational Choice and the Structure of the Environment," *Psychol. Rev.*, Mar. 1956, *63*, 129–38.

_____, "Dynamic Programming under Uncertainty with a Quadratic Criterion Function," *Econometrica*, Jan. 1956, *24*, 74–81.

_____, *Models of Man*, New York 1957.

_____, "The Compensation of Executives," *Sociometry*, 1957, *20*, 32–35.

_____, "Theories of Decision Making in Economics and Behavioral Science," *Amer. Econ. Rev.*, June 1959, *49*, 223–83.

_____, "Discussion: Problems of Methodology," *Amer. Econ. Rev. Proc.*, May 1963, *53*, 229–31.

_____, "From Substantive to Procedural Rationality," in Spiro J. Latsis, ed., *Methodological Appraisal in Economics*, Cambridge 1976.

_____, (1978a) "Rationality as Process and as Product of Thought," *Amer. Econ. Rev. Proc.*, May 1978, *68*, 1–16.

_____, (1978b) "On How to Decide What to Do," *Bell J. Econ.*, Autumn 1978, *9*, 494–507.

_____, G. Kozmetsky, H. Guetzkow, and G. Tyndall, *Centralization vs. Decentralization in Organizing the Controller's Department*, New York 1954; reprinted Houston 1978.

_____ and F. K. Levy, "A Note on the Cobb-Douglas Function," *Rev. Econ. Stud.*, June 1963, *30*, 93–94.

G. J. Stigler, "The Economics of Information," *J. Polit. Econ.*, June 1961, *69*, 213–15.

H. Theil, "A Note on Certainty Equivalence in Dynamic Planning," *Econometrica*, Apr. 1957, *25*, 346–49.

John von Neumann and Oscar Morgenstern, *Theory of Games and Economic Behavior*, Princeton 1944.

A. A. Walters, "Production and Cost Functions: An Econometric Survey," *Econometrica*, Jan.–Apr. 1963, *31*, 1–66.

Oliver Williamson, *Markets and Hierarchies: Analysis and Antitrust Implications*, New York 1975.

S. Winter, "Satisficing, Selection, and the Innovating Remnant," *Quart. J. Econ.*, May 1971, *85*, 237–61.

[18]
ORGANIZATIONAL STRUCTURE, ENVIRONMENT AND PERFORMANCE: THE ROLE OF STRATEGIC CHOICE

JOHN CHILD

Abstract This paper critically examines available theoretical models which have been derived from statistically established patterns of association between contextual and organizational variables. These models offer an interpretation of organizational structure as a product of primarily economic constraints which contextual variables are assumed to impose. It is argued that available models in fact attempt to explain organization at one remove by ignoring the essentially political process, whereby power-holders within organizations decide upon courses of strategic action. This 'strategic choice' typically includes not only the establishment of structural forms but also the manipulation of environmental features and the choice of relevant performance standards. A theoretical re-orientation of this kind away from functional imperatives and towards a recognition of political action is developed and illustrated in the main body of the paper.

SYSTEMATIC comparative investigation of the relationships between organizational structure and situational variables has been the guiding principle for major research programmes both in the United States, under Blau, Hage and Aiken, Hall, Lawrence and Lorsch, and in Britain under Pugh and Woodward. In their work, referenced at the close of this paper, these researchers have attempted to discover the degree of empirical variation in organizational structures and to establish the conditions of such variation. Their findings, together with those from other less extensive studies, provide the material from which models of structural determination have been constructed. This procedure is regarded as essential to the development of organization theory; as Blau has put it, 'only systematic comparisons of many organizations can establish relationships between characteristics of organizations and stipulate the conditions under which these relationships hold, thereby providing the material that needs to be explained by theoretical principles and important guides for deriving these principles'. (1965: 338)

However, research designed to establish statistically the presence of associations between organizational characteristics usually leaves underlying processes to be inferred. An example is the attempt by Pugh and his colleagues to construct from factorial data a causal sequence of organization development (Pugh *et al.* 1969b). The difficulty here is that adequate explanation derives from an understanding of process, and in this regard the 'fact' of a statistically established relationship does not 'speak for itself'. At the very least, it may mask a more complex set of direct and indirect relationships as Blalock (1969) points out. In addition, little understanding is afforded as to how the relationship was established and whether it is a necessary condition for the presence of other, perhaps desirable, phenomena. For these reasons, not only is research into organization of a processual and change-oriented type still required but so equally is an attempt to offer more adequate theoretical schemes in step with the advance of empirical research. At the present time, some of the most influential models of organization explicate little more than positively established associations between dimensions of organizational structure and 'contextual' (i.e. situational) factors such as environment, technology or scale of operation. These models proceed to the simplest theoretical solution which is that the contextual factors determine structural variables because of certain, primarily economic, constraints the former are assumed to impose.

It is the purpose of this paper to argue that this simple theory is inadequate, primarily because it fails to give due attention to the agency of choice by whoever have the power to direct the organization. We shall argue that this 'strategic choice' extends to the context within which the organization is operating, to the standards of performance against which the pressure of economic constraints has to be evaluated, and to the design of the organization's structure itself. Incorporation of the process whereby strategic decisions are made directs attention onto the degree of choice which can be exercised in respect of organizational design, whereas many available models direct attention exclusively onto the constraints involved. They imply in this way that organizational behaviour can be understood by reference to functional imperatives rather than to political action.

Our concern will be with work organizations, which are seen as operating within particular environments to certain performance objectives. 'Work organizations' are defined as those within which work is carried out on a regular basis by paid employees, and which have been deliberately established for explicit purposes. The category includes organizations with formal objectives as diverse as business enterprises, hospitals, educational institutions, government departments and the administrative offices of trade unions. An assumption underlying much available research, as well as the present discussion, is that the engagement in systematic work and exchange which characterizes all these types, provides a basis for comparison within a common theoretical framework. 'Organizational structure' is defined as the formal allocation of work roles and the administrative mechanisms to control and integrate work activities including those which cross formal organizational boundaries. The concept of 'strategic choice' is discussed later in the paper, where its full meaning should emerge.

Available Theoretical Models

There are three particularly influential arguments relevent to an explanation of variation in organizational structure. Each postulates the effects of a major contextual factor. The first argument is from environment, in which environmental conditions are posited as critical constraints upon the choice of effective structural forms. The second and third arguments single out the influence on structure of two physical organizational attributes: technology and size. These three arguments highlight constraints upon structural design because contextual factors are regarded as important determinants of structural patterns. The need to secure a certain level of organizational performance is seen to lend contextual factors an exigent character.

1. The Argument from Environment

This argument starts from the observation that the maintenance of organizations depends upon some degree of exchange with outside parties. This dependency upon the environment is seen to impose a degree of constraint upon those directing an organization. As Sadler and Barry put it (1970: 58) 'an organisation cannot evolve or develop in ways which merely reflect the goals, motives or needs of its members or of its leadership, since it must always bow to the constraints imposed on it by the nature of its relationship with the environment'. Different environmental conditions and different types of relationship with outside parties will, it is argued, require different types of organizational structural accommodation for a high level of performance to be achieved.

Three environmental conditions have been singled out as of particular importance. *Environmental variability* has attracted most attention as the major factor contributing to uncertainty among organizational decision-makers. The concept refers to the degree of change which characterizes environmental activities relevant to an organization's operations. Degree of change may in turn be seen as a function of three variables:

(1) the frequency of changes in relevant environmental activities
(2) the degree of difference involved at each change
(3) the degree of irregularity in the overall pattern of change—in a sense the 'variability of change'.

A number of writers have arrived at the same broad conclusion: that the higher the environmental variability and the uncertainty consequently experienced, the more the prevailing structure of organization should be adaptive, with roles open to continual redefinition and with co-ordination being achieved by frequent meetings and considerable lateral communication (cf. Stinchcombe 1959; Burns and Stalker 1961; Hage and Aiken 1967; Lawrence and Lorsch 1967).

Environmental complexity refers to the heterogeneity and range of environmental activities which are relevant to an organization's operations. The greater the degree of complexity, the more a profusion of relevant environmental information is likely to be experienced by organizational decision-makers. The monitoring of diversified information, it is argued, establishes a requirement for greater role specialization in areas of the organization dealing directly with the environment, and problems of co-ordination between specialists may correspondingly increase

(Lawrence and Lorsch 1967). The causal interconnectedness between environmental segments which Emery and Trist (1965) have identified, together with many economists before them, could be regarded as contributing towards complexity. But environmental complexity does not of itself necessarily give rise to uncertainty if little environmental variability is present, and if sufficient organizational resources are devoted to monitoring all the facets of the complex environment. Thus, while Emery and Trist tend to link causal interconnectedness with uncertainty, the latter would not necessarily be high if the nature of environmental sectors is changing slowly and if the order of connectedness between them is not variable.

Thirdly, the concept of *environmental illiberality* refers to the degree of threat that faces organizational decision-makers in the achievement of their goals from external competition, hostility or even indifference. Khandwalla (1970: 12–13) has called this environmental stress, though strictly speaking this is the way in which organizational decision-makers are likely to experience an illiberal environment rather than a feature of the environment *per se*. Khandwalla suggests several consequences of increasing environmental illiberality associated with the reduction of 'organizational slack' which is likely. For instance, the achievement of pluralistic group goals becomes more difficult and an overriding goal for the whole organization becomes accentuated—that of survival. The associated structural consequence is an attempt to centralize decision-making and to exercise tighter controls, a proposition which Hage (1965) has also discussed.

The argument from environment is one of the more persuasive accompaniments of the growing use of open system theory in the study of organizations. However, in its present form it fails to allow sufficiently for several manifestations of strategic choice. First, organizational decision-makers may have certain opportunities to select the types of environment in which they will operate. Thus businessmen may have a choice between new markets to enter, educators may exclude certain subjects from their institutions' courses, trade union officers may decide on the bounds of their recruitment policy. Secondly, the directors of at least large organizations may command sufficient power to influence the conditions prevailing within environments where they are already operating. The debate surrounding Galbraith's thesis (1967) that the large business corporation in modern industrial societies is able very considerably to manipulate and even create the demand for its products centres on this very point. Some degree of environmental selection is open to most organizations, and some degree of environmental manipulation is open to most larger organizations. These considerations form an important qualification to suggestions of environmental determinism.

The exercise of choice implies a prior evaluation of the situation. The argument from environment has frequently blurred the distinction between characteristics of the environment as such and their perception and evaluation by those within an organization: the distinction between variability and an experience of uncertainty, between complexity and an experience of cognitive profusion, between illiberality

ORGANIZATIONAL STRUCTURE, ENVIRONMENT AND PERFORMANCE 5

and an experience of stress. Lawrence and Lorsch (1967: 28–29), for example, imply that uncertainty is a quality of the environment, while we have already noted how Khandwalla regards stress as an environmental characteristic. It is important not to overlook these fine distinctions between 'reality' and its evaluation because they can explain why organizational decision-makers in practice may not react to observable environmental changes. Thus if an environment becomes less liberal, little change will be made to the structure of an organization if the development is considered only to be temporary or if it is preferred to expend reserves on carrying the organization through the lean period. In other words, the predictive power of the argument from environment is further qualified by the fact that decisions about organizational structure depend upon the prior processes of perception and evaluation and that the evaluation may well have other important referents apart from those of a purely economic nature.

2. The Argument from Technology

There are several distinct variants of the argument from technology. These reflect the different definitions of technology at the organizational level of analysis which theorists and researchers have employed (Hickson et al. 1969: 380). The two most developed approaches are probably found in Woodward's studies of the 'operations technology' of manufacturing organizations (1965; 1970), and in Perrow's more generalizable analysis of 'materials technology' (1967; 1970). Operations technology refers to the equipping and sequencing of activities in an organization's workflow, while materials technology refers to characteristics of the physical and informational materials used. Both Woodward and Perrow consider that the nature of technological variables presents important implications for the design of effective organizational structure. Woodward has recently concentrated her attention upon problems of production control and administrative rationality which tend to arise with the middle range of complexity in operations technology—large-batch and mass production. Perrow argues that the degree of stability in the nature of materials used and the extent to which routine codifiable techniques ('analyzable search') can be applied to them, influence the way in which work roles can effectively be defined. Their arguments, taken together, imply that a high structuring of activities (task specialization and high role definition by rules and paperwork) is likely to be most effective under conditions of standardized mass production.

Although there is considerable confusion in the literature as to what technology is and as to what aspects of organizational structure it may influence, a more fundamental problem is whether it is even a useful theoretical strategy to direct attention on to this concept in the first place. Rather than concentrating upon the technological adjuncts of executing tasks, and on the technical logic whereby such tasks are linked, there would seem to be a good case for focusing upon the work itself. The planning and ordering of work, together with its meaning to those involved, is likely to be more contingent with observed behaviour within organizations, with the structural manifestation of managerial control, and with factors such as uncertainty about the environment. Thus, Woodward herself has recently come to consider production control systems as more direct behavioural 'determinants' (1970), while Hage and Aiken (1969) have operationalized technology in terms of 'routineness of work'. Harvey (1968) regarded the frequency of 'major product changes' as a necessary extension of Woodward's earlier conceptualization which, he argued, took account of technological form but not of changes in work within that form.

A theoretical reorientation towards work and workplans makes the association between environmental conditions and organizational operations far more intelligible. The prevailing technology is now seen as a product of decisions on workplans, resources, and equipment which were made in the light of certain evaluations of the organization's position in its environment. A given technological configuration (equipment, knowledge of techniques, etc.) may exhibit certain short-term rigidities and perhaps indivisibilities, and will to that extent act as a constraint upon the adoption of new workplans. However, rather than the technology possessing 'implications' for effective modes of organizational structure, any association between the two may be more accurately viewed as a derivative of decisions made by those in control of the organization regarding the tasks to be carried out in relation to the resources available to perform them. Indeed, this may render any association between technology and structure quite tenuous. The work of the Tavistock Institute suggests the scope for considerable structural choice to suit the preferences of human 'resources' at the work group level within the given overall technological rationale of a particular production process (Trist *et al.* 1963; Miller and Rice 1967). The 'job enrichment' approach equally entails a manipulation of structure to suit human capabilities within a given technology (Paul and Robertson 1970).

3. *The Argument from Size*

The argument from size has a long history within organizational theory. Weber (1947) in his classic analysis of bureaucracy, did not believe that bureaucratic characteristics would be present within small organizations. More recent research evidence appears to lend strong support to this view. For example, Pugh and his colleagues (1969a) found larger size to be the most powerful predictor of higher values on their main structural factor which related to the bureaucratic dimensions of specialization, use of procedures, and reliance on paperwork. Blau (1970) has produced data suggesting that increased size generates structural differentiation within organizations, and that structural differentiation in turn enlarges the absolute (though not the relative) size of an organization's administrative component.

If we draw together the strands of the argument from size, two main causal processes appear to be suggested, both having similar ultimate implications for effective structural design. The first argues that increasing size offers more opportunities to reap the benefits of increased specialization. Increased specialization is likely to manifest itself in the form of greater structural differentiation which exhibits higher heterogeneity among a larger number of organizational sub-units, but which may exhibit a greater homogeneity of role within each sub-unit. This increasing complexity will render the managerial co-ordination of sub-unit activities more difficult, especially as strains towards functional autonomy may well appear, and for this reason pressure will be placed upon senior management to impose a system of impersonal controls through the use of formal procedures, the recording of information in writing and the like. The second argument reaches much the same conclusion by pointing out how the problem of directing larger numbers of people makes it impossible to continue employing a personalized, centralized style of management. Instead, a more decentralized system, using impersonal mechanisms of control, has to be adopted. The operation of such a system requires higher numbers of administrative and clerical personnel.

However, the relationship of size to organizational structure cannot, any more than that of technology, be regarded as deterministic. The need to cope administratively with a large number of organizational members and their activities may well impose constraints upon certain structural choices, especially in respect of functions such as, say, accounting which service the membership as a whole. Nonetheless, at least two important avenues of choice remain open. First, the size factor may be modified directly by breaking down a large unit into smaller quasi-independent ones, a common enough adaptation among large business and governmental organizations. Secondly, the nature of the functional activities may be modified through the application of different techniques or technologies in order that a different administrative system can be adopted—the computerization of accounting systems provides an example.

There is in fact considerable debate as to the type of constraints which size and technology may each and both imply for organizational structure. Indeed, apparently rival explanations are offered by exponents of the arguments from these two contextual factors (cf. Hickson et al. 1970). Some of the disagreement may be understood in the light of several probabilities: (1) that size of plant or operating unit is often associated with the nature of operations technology because of the presence of indivisibilities; (2) that total organizational size, for instance company size, is far less likely to be associated with technology, because it is not necessarily associated with plant size; (3) that no association is likely to exist between total size and materials technology; and (4) that the relative degree of constraint imposed by the size and technology factors will vary between different areas of organizational activity. Only a few organization theorists have taken account of such detailed differentiations with respect to size, technology or area of activity (e.g. Hickson et al. 1969; Child 1970).

Illustrating the need to distinguish between areas of activity, it is arguable that any implications which size has for organizational designers are likely to be tempered by considerations of technological economics most particularly in the central areas of activity directly concerned with the production of goods or services. This is the area which Thompson (1967) has appropriately called the 'Technological Core' of an organization. In this core area, the prevailing technological logic may militate against a high degree of functional and role complexity even in a large organization, while under conditions where uncertainty is experienced about the environment, the consequent desire to preserve a measure of flexibility may operate to the same structural effect. In contrast, the nature of work within certain supporting functions is not likely to vary greatly, even with rapid changes in core activities. Such functions include accounting, legal, personnel and welfare. In their case increasing scale may well be reflected in a progressive functional complexity: first with such activities being differentiated away from central workflow functions, and secondly with a progressive differentiation between specialized support units carrying out different tasks. Wasmuth (1970) has illustrated how this process can affect the personnel function. It would appear that 'technology theorists' such as Thompson (1967: 74) and Woodward (1965: 31) have given little weight to the argument from size because their attention was concentrated on core activities, while investigators such as Pugh et al. (1969a) have been led to stress the argument because their attention was concentrated on the organization of non-core roles.

Sources of Structural Variation

The three preceding arguments attempt to explain observable patterns of organizational structure by reference to constraints imposed by contextual factors. These constraints are assumed to have force because work organizations must achieve certain levels of performance in order to survive. If organizational structure is not adapted to its context, then opportunities are lost, costs rise, and the maintenance of the organization is threatened.[1]

Certain objections to this theory have already been raised in passing, and these require amplification, particularly with respect to the role of environment and of performance. The environment has normally been regarded as the primary source of constraint upon organizational design, while assumptions about performance requirements underlie the whole notion of constraint itself. It is hoped that a re-examination of these two issues will demonstrate the need for a revised analysis of variation in organizational structure.

Organization and Environment

The environment of an organization cannot be satisfactorily defined without reference to what Levine and White have called 'organizational domain' (1961: 597). This consists of the specific goals which organizational decision-makers wish

ORGANIZATIONAL STRUCTURE, ENVIRONMENT AND PERFORMANCE 9

to pursue and the functions which they cause an organization to undertake in order to implement those goals.

With this in mind, writers such as Thompson (1967) and Normann (1969a) have distinguished different segments of the environment in terms of their immediacy for the goals and functions ascribed to an organization. Organizational decision-makers normally perceive themselves as operating only incerta in 'markets' and utilizing selected sources of inputs; they regard success in these areas as particularly vital for the organization's survival. The organization may also have transactions in other areas, but these are regarded as less central to the main purpose. Finally, there are yet further sectors of the environment with which the organization normally enters into little or no direct contact.

This distinction of several environmental boundaries proceeding 'outwards' from the organization implies that organizational decision-makers do take positive steps to define and manipulate their own corners of the environment. Such action is in fact commonly found. Thus trade unions distinguish their own particular environments with respect to categories of membership, as do hospitals regarding types of patient, and business organizations where this takes the familiar form of creating and manipulating product differentiation (Bain 1959). Cyert and March have suggested that the posture towards the environment which those in control of organizations attempt to adopt will reflect their perception of environmental conditions in relation to their desire to attain with some certainty the goals they have set for the organization (1963: 118–120). In regard to organizational structure, these goals may reflect a preference for an ordered existence and a 'quiet life', or for a distribution of power and status which those in control are determined not to upset. In such circumstances, they may choose either to ignore or restrain certain developments within the environment, a positive response to which would entail a modification to the organizational *status quo*. If the organization is seen to have a secure grip upon its immediate operating environment, its decision-makers may well attach little economic cost to this policy. Again it is possible to find examples of this hypothetical case in real life. For instance, Norman (1969b) found in thirteen case studies of new product development in Swedish companies that the existing values and power structure of an organization played a critical role in predicting reaction to new ideas and information.

Similarly, the distinction between environment and the organization itself (the 'inner' boundary of the environment) is relative to the goals and actions of organizational decision-makers. As Kronenberg points out (1969: Chapter III), traditionally an organization has been said to comprise all the positions or roles bound together by the same authority system. Yet within its immediate environment, which Normann has called its 'territory' (1969a: 3), those in control of an organization may in practice be able to exercise a degree of authority (influence that is accepted as legitimate by those over which it is held) over other organizations or individuals which are nominally independent. A similar problem of boundary definition arises in the case of an organization which forms part of a wider unit, such as the subsidiary of a multi-national firm, where both share the same authority system.[2]

These examples suggest that the relationships between organization and environment are variable, a notion expressed in the concept of inter-dependence which refers to the closeness of relationships between organizations (Pugh *et al.* 1963: 312). Moreover, the most important aspect of these relationships concerns the degree of influence which the controllers of one organization can exert over their counterparts in other organizations, and *vice versa*. Thompson and McEwen (1958) have identified the various procedures which may be chosen in order to assert this influence in support of organizational goals. The value of adopting this perspective lies in its rejection of any notion that environmental circumstances determine intra-organizational features directly or inevitably. On the other hand, it still allows that under certain conditions the actions taken by environmental parties may exert considerable pressures for change.

To summarize, we have argued that the analysis of organization and environment must recognize the exercise of choice by organizational decision-makers. They may well have some power to 'enact' their organization's environment, as Weick has put it (1969: 63 ff). Thus to an important extent, their decisions as to where the organization's operations shall be located, the clientele it shall serve, or the types of employees it shall recruit determine the limits to its environment—that is, to the environment significant for the functions which the organization performs. The boundaries between an organization and its environment are similarly defined in large degree by the kinds of relationships which its decision-makers choose to enter upon with their equivalents in other organizations, or by the constraints which more dominant counterparts impose upon them. In view of these essentially strategic and political factors, environmental conditions cannot be regarded as a direct source of variation in organizational structure, as open system theorists often imply. The critical link lies in the decision-makers' evaluation of the organization's position in the environmental areas they regard as important, and in the action they may consequently take about its internal structure.

Organization and Performance

The available theoretical models reviewed earlier assume at least implicitly that the sanctions which would be invoked against organizational decision-makers in the event of not achieving a certain level of organizational performance act as a severe limitation on the degree of indeterminateness that exists in the relationships between contextual factors and organizational structure.

A theory of organizational structure has, therefore, to take account of performance dimensions. Most research and discussion on organizational performance within the social sciences has been devoted to a study of the conditions under which organizations achieve different levels of effectiveness (cf. Price 1968). From this

ORGANIZATIONAL STRUCTURE, ENVIRONMENT AND PERFORMANCE 11

perspective structural and other variables have normally been treated as independent, with some measure of effectiveness constituting the dependent variable. Performance has been treated as an outcome. In contrast, a theory of organizational structure would posit structural variables as depending upon decisions which were made with reference to some standard of required performance as well as to some prediction of the effects of structural alternatives upon the performance achieved. Performance is treated as an input to this model, as well as an outcome.[3] Thus two questions which are of some moment for a theory of organizational structure are, first, how performance standards and their degree of achievement may act as a stimulus to structural variation, and, secondly, how far structural variation is likely to affect performance levels. Both questions bear on the issue of how far the choice of organizational structure is subject to economic constraints.

There is little research evidence on the effect that performance standards and their degree of achievement will have upon structural variation. A primary condition here would seem to be that the operation of any particular structural arrangement depends upon a sufficient supply of resources. A declining level of performance, or even a level that fails to meet expectations, may therefore lead to decisions aimed at effecting administrative economies, probably in the direction of simplified procedural and paperwork systems together with a proportionately lower administrative staff component. Allowing for the possibility that alternative structural designs are available and that they represent rather similar overhead costs, then a further condition for performance considerations to influence structural choice must be that those making the choice believe that structural arrangements do have some influence on the level of organizational effectiveness achieved. If they do not believe this, then the level of performance actually reached will only affect structural choice in terms of straight administrative costs.

However, it is likely that in most cases organizational decision-makers do believe that structural design has some consequences for performance. In this event, the level of performance actually achieved will probably influence decisions on structural design, subject to an important proviso. This is that the performance attained does not exceed any target which the decision-makers may have decided is adequate. If performance exceeds this 'satisficing' level (and one is assuming that this level represents a degree of return that is at least sufficient to secure resources required for the fulfilment of present and future plans), then the decision-making group *may* take the view that the margin of surplus permits them to adopt structural arrangements which accord the better with their own preferences, even at some extra administrative cost to the organization. In such circumstances the dominant organizational power-holders may also permit other interest groups to make or retain their own preferred structural adaptations, a kind of 'organizational slack' (cf. Cyert and March, 1963: 36–38). Given the widespread prevalence of imperfections in the economics of resource allocation and competition, especially for non-business organizations, considerable organizational slack may often be present. The conclusion reached once again is therefore that organizational decision-makers may well perceive that they have a substantial element of choice in the planning of organizational structure. This consideration is of immediate theoretical relevance, even though it represents a speculation that remains eventually to be investigated empirically.

The second question concerns the extent to which structural variation is likely to affect the levels of organizational performance actually achieved. Is there any reason to believe that other strategic choices, such as the choice of environment, of market strategies or of operating scale and technology, could significantly influence performance outcomes quite apart from the structural design which is adopted? The results of economic research into business organizations suggest that other strategic considerations may have considerable influence. For instance, the choice of markets to be served can considerably affect the performance of an enterprise because the return available from different markets and industries varies considerably and because some markets are expanding while others are not—a poor choice here leads to 'market inefficiency'. A business firm may suffer from 'technical inefficiency' if it operates plants that are too small to gain the advantages attainable through economics of scale, and if it utilizes an operations technology that does not allow full advantage to be taken of standardization and long production runs. Thirdly, the failure to seize opportunities for profitable investment either in production facilities or in research and development will cause performance to suffer through a 'lack of progressiveness'. This classification of strategic choices has been utilized by Caves in his review of performance in British industry (Caves 1968), but it is by no means exhaustive. However, it is sufficient to demonstrate that structural design is likely to have only a limited effect upon the level of organizational performance achieved, even though the type of structure utilized may affect the quality of other strategic decisions because of the way it influences the communication of necessary information and so on.

The conclusion that the design of organizational structure may have a restricted influence upon performance levels, and that performance standards may themselves allow for some 'slack', weakens the general proposition that contextual factors will exert a high degree of constraint upon the choice of structural design. In practice, there does appear to be some variation in the structures of otherwise comparable organizations, a variation which is sustained over periods of time without much apparent effect on success or failure. This is frequently remarked upon by the senior personnel within such organizations, and it is not refuted by the fact that multivariate predictions of particular structural dimensions still leave large proportions (40 per cent upwards) of the structural variance unaccounted for (cf. Pugh et al. 1969a).[4] In addition, a review of research and discussion on business organizations led the present writer to conclude that while there may be limits within which their size, technology and rate of adjustment to the environment should fall if they are to to obtain a high level of economic performance, these limits do not as yet seem capable of precise definition (Child 1969: 95–98). In so far as a choice may be exercised in respect of these contextual factors without incurring significant net performance penalties, the possibilities of structural choice would seem to be further strengthened.

Strategic Choice and Organization Theory

The considerations so far raised direct our attention towards those who possess the power to decide upon an organization's structural rationale, towards the limits upon that power imposed by the operational context, and towards the process of assessing constraints and opportunities against values in deciding organizational strategies. Up to this point, there has been implicit in our analysis an assumption that in work organizations the actions of all members are not usually of equal weight in identifying the source of variation in major organization-wide features such as the formal structure of work roles, procedures and communications. The term 'decision-makers' has been employed to refer to the power-holding group on the basis that it is normally possible within work organizations to identify inequalities of power which are reflected in a differential access to decision-making on structural design, and even in a differential ability to raise questions on the subject in the first place. While it has often been suggested that the advancing level of technical expertise required to operate large, sophisticated organizations is in effect taking many decisions out of the hands of senior administrators or officials, there is little evidence to show that the latter do not retain control over policy initiation and implementation (Burns 1966a). This conclusion speaks for the relevance of the 'dominant coalition' concept which was formulated by Cyert and March (1963) and has been employed extensively by Thompson (1967).

The notion of a dominant coalition is advantageous in the way it highlights the immediate source of major structural variation in organizations, but it is an abstraction and could be misleading if not used cautiously. Certain qualifications are therefore apposite. First, the term dominant coalition does not necessarily identify the formally designated holders of authority in an organization; rather it refers to those who collectively happen to hold most power over a particular period of time. Indeed, one may find situations where there is more than one dominant coalition, where one group is constrained or challenged by another. Some British trade unions illustrate this possibility, in which a degree of polarization has developed between those elected to national offices and those occupying elected positions at the local or regional level.

Secondly, use of the concept need not imply that other members of an organization do not have some power to modify plans and decisions which have been formulated; indeed, the modification may be substantial when it is the result of collective action. Information reaching the dominant coalition is open to reinterpretation at the hands of the people who have to pass it on, such as those in boundary roles with respect to information coming in from the environment and those in roles lower down in the hierarchy with respect to information passing up from operating levels. Similarly, the implementation of decisions reached depends on securing the co-operation of other parties to the organization; this political process accounts for the considerable length of time taken to reach many major organizational decisions (cf. Dubin 1962).

The purpose of employing a concept such as the dominant coalition is primarily to distinguish those who normally have the power to take the initiative on matters such as the design of organizational structure from others who are in a position of having to respond to such decisions. The concept is tenable if one regards the norm within work organizations to be what Mann (1970) in another context has called a 'pragmatic acceptance' by lower level participants of power-holding roles and of the decisions emanating from these. Needless to say, a use of the concept does not imply that the student of organization should internalize the perspective of organizational power-holders, as has often been the case in the past. However, it does require him to incorporate this perspective and the action to which it gives rise as major variables in his theory.

The dominant coalition concept opens up a view of organizational structures in relation to the distribution of power and the process of strategic decision-making which these reflect.[5] If, as we have argued, there is some freedom of manoeuvre with respect to contextual factors, standards of performance and structural design, then some choice is implied as to how the organization as an on-going system will be maintained. The dominant coalition concept draws attention to the question of who is making the choice. It thus provides a useful antidote to the sociologically unsatisfactory notion that a given organizational structure can be understood in relation to the functional imperative of 'system needs' which somehow transcend the objectives of any group of organizational members. In this way the analytical contribution of a functional interpretation of organizational behaviour referring to system maintenance in response to contextual constraints, is supplemented by a political interpretation which does not regard such constraints as necessarily acute or immutable, and which highlights the role of choice. In shifting attention towards the role of choice, we are led to account for organizational variation directly through reference to its sources rather than indirectly through reference to its supposed consequences. This shift of emphasis meets one of the major criticisms that Silverman (1970) has raised against much contemporary organization theory.

In the course of his historical study of American industrial enterprise, Chandler (1962) developed the concept of strategy in referring to the exercise of choice by a dominant coalition as the major source of organizational variation. Chandler's insight lies at the heart of the argument being developed in this paper. 'Strategy', he writes (p. 13), 'can be defined as the determination of the basic long-term goals and objectives of an enterprise, and the adoption of courses of action and the allocation of resources necessary for carrying out these goals. Decisions to expand the volume of activities, to set up distant plants and offices, to move into new economic functions, or become diversified along many lines of business, involve the defining of new basic goals'.

In Chandler's view, the modification of organizational goals is, therefore, a major source of changes in size, technology and location. In regard to structure, his general thesis (which he supports with comparative historical data) is that 'a new strategy required a new or at least refashioned structure if the enlarged enterprise was to be operated efficiently'. (p. 15). The process of strategy formulation in this way constitutes a major interface between what Burns (1966b) has called the 'working organization' and the 'political system' within organizations.

Chandler's analysis, and that presented in this paper, leads to the conclusion that strategic choice is the critical variable in a theory of organizations. Other variables which have often been regarded as independent determinants of organizational structures are, within this perspective, seen to be linked together as multiple points of reference for the process of strategic decision-making. Woodward's recent research (1970) has, for example, illustrated how the degree of uncertainty about the environment together with the underlying technological rationale of the product both enter into decisions on the operating plans that are adopted in manufacturing firms. These operating plans in turn were found to possess implications for both formal and informal structures in the organization. To take another example involving environment and technology, Khandwalla has suggested that if the dominant coalition in a manufacturing firm experiences greater stress from the environment, it is likely to increase the attention it gives to cost reduction (1970: 39–45). The technological manifestation of this will probably be a move towards more standardized and larger batch production. Both the environmental and the technological change are likely to enter as points of reference into any subsequent decisions to standardize working procedures, define work roles more closely, increase centralized decision-making and other structural changes.

In a similar way, it is likely that environmental conditions and organizational size will *together* impinge upon the framework of organizational decision-making. For instance, the extent to which high environmental complexity will be considered by the dominant coalition to establish requirements for greater specialization in boundary roles will probably depend also on how it assesses the implications of its organization's size. This helps to explain why small organizations generally have a low degree of specialization in boundary-spanning activities even though, as in the case of trade union administrations, they face relatively complex environments. The role of size and technology in relation to organizational structure requires a similar theoretical development, as we suggested when reviewing the 'argument from size'.

These simple examples with pairs of contextual referents should not obscure the full complexity of strategic choice in which numerous referents may be involved— the multinational enterprise illustrates this complexity to an extreme degree (Brooke and Remmers 1970). There is also a further important complication to which we have already alluded: that as referents in organizational decision-making, contextual and structural variables may be brought into a reciprocal relationship. Thus if one takes the variable of size, the high value placed by a dominant coalition on the retention or attainment of a given structure may well lead to an attempt to control or change the organization's scale of operations. We have argued that this action may be economically feasible in some circumstances. Size, many organization theorists assume, leads to structure; but considered in its relation to other referents of organizational strategic action, such an assumption is naive, for the reverse could also apply.

In short, when incorporating strategic choice in a theory of organization, one is recognizing the operation of an essentially political process in which constraints and opportunities are functions of the power exercised by decision-makers in the light of ideological values. A consideration of these values has been outside the scope of this paper, but their existence implies that the degree of association which different contextual factors have with structural variables will not conform to any stable mathematical function. Only when these political factors can be adequately measured is greater predictive certainty likely to be achieved.

Conclusion

Our contention in this paper has been that many available contributions to a theory of organizational structure do not incorporate the direct source of variation in formal structural arrangements, namely the strategic decisions of those who have the power of structural initiation—the dominant coalition. In this respect, the theoretical models we reviewed attempt to explain organizational structure at one remove. They draw attention to possible constraints upon the choice of effective structures, but fail to consider the process of choice itself in which economic and administrative exigencies are weighed by the actors concerned against the opportunities to operate a structure of their own and/or other organizational members' preferences. A theoretical incorporation of the structural decision-making process has suggested that constraints upon structural choice are weakened in their effect to the extent that:

1. The design of organizational structure only has a limited effect on performance levels achieved, and this is perceived to be the case by a dominant coalition.
2. Because of this, contextual variables only represent limited exigencies bearing upon structural design, and this is perceived to be the case.
3. Even though they perceive structural design to have some effect upon performance levels because of contextual pressures, organization decision-makers may be in a position to institute modifications to the context (through, for instance, a revised environmental strategy) in order to retain a preferred structure without serious detriment to performance.
4. If they perceive structure as possessing performance implications, organizational decision-makers may prefer to satisfice: to 'trade off' some potential gain in

ORGANIZATIONAL STRUCTURE, ENVIRONMENT AND PERFORMANCE 17

performance for a congenially structured mode of operation. In other words, they may be able and willing to exercise some choice over performance standards.
5. Organizational decision-makers perceive that the nature of contextual constraints pose conflicting implications for structural design—this could, for example, be the case with a combination of large size and location within a variable environment. Conflicting implications derived from contextual combinations of this kind themselves impose some degree of structural choice.

The type of theoretical development suggested by these considerations centres upon the concept of strategic choice exercised by an organization's 'dominant coalition'. While in this paper we have merely been concerned to speak for a revised theoretical perspective rather than to propose a series of considered propositions in any detail, clearly some overall conception has been underlying our argument. This is represented in outline by Figure 1, which summarizes the major postulated relationships emerging from the foregoing discussion.

In this theoretical model, the exercise of strategic choice by the dominant coalition refers to a process the first stage of which is the coalition members' evaluation of their organization's position—what expectations are presented by resource providers such as business shareholders, what is the trend of events in the environment, what has been the organization's recent performance, the congeniality of its present internal configuration, and so on. Their prior ideology is assumed to colour this evaluation in some degree. The choice of goals or objectives for the organization is seen to follow on from this evaluation, and to be reflected in the strategic action which is decided upon. With respect to external variables, strategic action may include a move into or out of given markets or areas of activity in order to try and secure a favourable demand or response that will be expressed by a high valuation of the organization's products or services.

With respect to internal variables, strategic action will involve an attempt, within the limits of availabilities and indivisibilities, to establish a configuration of manpower, technology, and structural arrangements which is both internally consistent and consistent with the scale and nature of operations planned. The 'goodness of fit' that is in the event achieved is seen to determine the level of efficiency secured which is expressed by output in relation to costs. The conjunction of efficiency with demand will determine the organization's overall level of performance. Performance achieved is in turn regarded as an informational input to the dominant coalition. It is within this scheme of organizational processes that our analysis of organizational structure, environment, and performance has been located, and the writer is currently subjecting important parts of this framework to empirical investigation.

A final comment places our argument in its wider context. We have been concerned with the role of strategic choice as a necessary element in any adequate

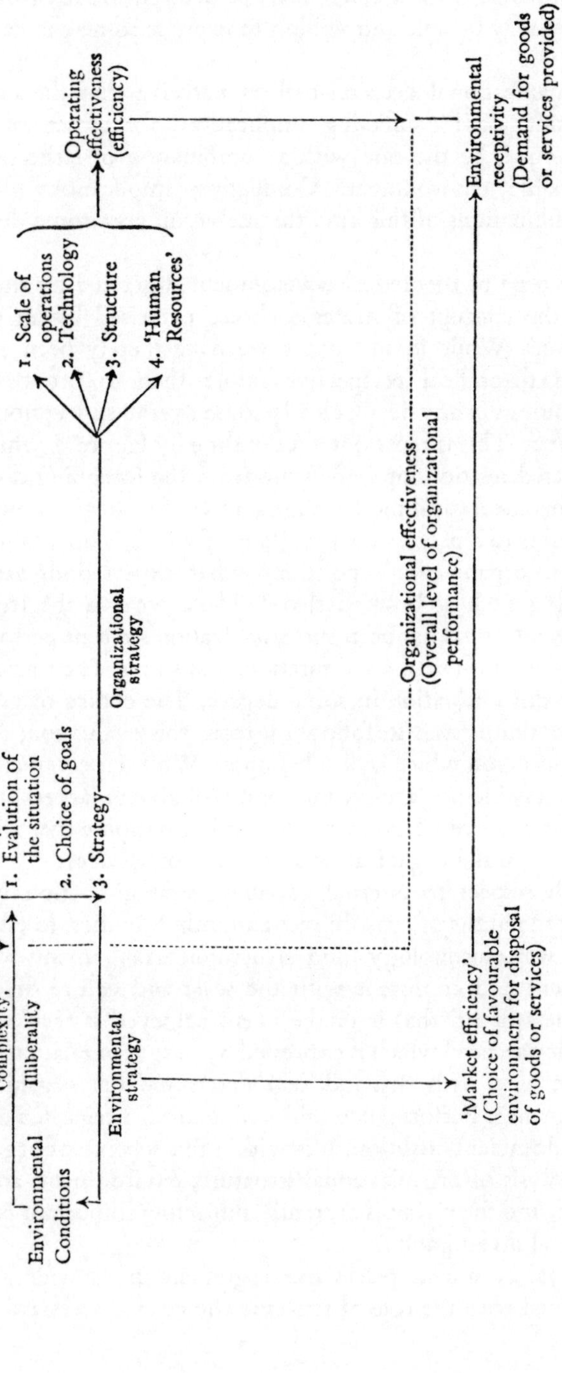

FIG. 1. The Role of Strategic Choice in a Theory of Organization.

ORGANIZATIONAL STRUCTURE, ENVIRONMENT AND PERFORMANCE 19

theory of organizational structure, and have suggested that many available explanations over-emphasize constraints upon that choice. In so doing they draw our attention away from the possibilities first of choosing structural arrangements that will better satisfy the priorities of those in charge of organizations, or indeed of any interested party; and secondly away from the exploration of organizational design as a means of reconciling more successfully economic and social criteria of performance. Until we revise these theoretical perspectives, we shall fail to shake off 'the metaphysical pathos of much of the modern theory of group organization ... that of pessimism and fatalism' which Gouldner noted fifteen years ago (1955: 498).

Notes

I am grateful to Professors H. Aldrich, W. F. Glueck, J. Hage, D. S. Pugh, and colleagues in the London Graduate School of Business Studies for helpful comments on a draft of this paper.

1. A further important contribution to this theory of constraint has not been reviewed because, unlike the other arguments, it is not necessarily relevant for the structural rationale of an organization as a whole. This is the 'argument from motivation' which draws primarily upon contributions from psychological need theory. In a nutshell, this maintains that if the structuring of work roles does not allow for the individual's needs to be met adequately, his level of motivation to satisfy organizational performance requirements is likely to be low—perhaps so low that he leaves the organization. Thus the type of needs individuals or groups bring to the work situation is regarded as a further constraint upon structural choice. Problems with this argument include (1) the continuing dispute over the validity of available need theories (e.g. House and Wigdor 1967), and (2) evidence suggesting that employees with a primarily 'extrinsic' orientation to work may be relatively indifferent to structural manipulations not affecting extrinsic rewards (cf. Goldthorpe et al. 1968; Ingham 1970).
2. Brooke and Remmers (1970) provide an insightful analysis of this very case.
3. In whatever perspective organizational performance is placed, an adequate definition is problematic. If the point of reference is the determination of organization-wide structural forms, then a definition which is consistent with an organization-level referent is appropriate. Yuchtman and Seashore have proposed 'that organizational effectiveness be defined as the ability of the organization, in either absolute or relative terms, to exploit its environment in the acquisition of scarce and valued resources'. (1967: 898). This definition is consonant with organizational maintenance and growth which are likely to represent major concerns for decision-makers, and it also recognizes that organizational performance is a function of interdependence with the environment.
4. However, as Professor Aldrich has reminded the writer, a large part of the unaccounted variance could be due to error variance.
5. We are here concerned with power and decision-making as the source of structural variation. Hickson et al. (1971) have developed an analysis in which structural forms are in turn seen to contribute towards the prediction of the power held by different sections of the organization.

Bibliography

BAIN, J. S. 1959. *Industrial Organization*, New York: Wiley.
BLALOCK, H. 1969. *Theory Construction: From Verbal to Mathematical Formulations*, Englewood Cliffs, N.J.: Prentice-Hall.
BLAU, P. M. 1965. 'The Comparative Study of Organizations', *Industrial and Labor Relations Review*, 18, April: 323–338.

BLAU, P. M. et al. 1966. 'The Structure of Small Bureaucracies', *American Sociological Review*, 31, April: 179–191.
BLAU, P. M. 1970. 'The Formal Theory of Differentiation in Organizations', *American Sociological Review*, 35, April: 201–218.
BROOKE, M. Z. and REMMERS, H. L. 1970. *The Strategy of Multinational Enterprise*, London: Longmans.
BURNS, T. 1966a. Preface to second edition of Burns and Stalker (1961).
BURNS, T. 1966b. 'On the Plurality of Social Systems', in J. R. Lawrence (ed), *Operational Research and the Social Sciences*, London: Tavistock, 165–177.
BURNS, T. and STALKER, G. M. 1961. *The Management of Innovation*, London: Tavistock.
CAVES, R. E. et al. 1968. *Britain's Economic Prospects*, London: Allen and Unwin.
CHANDLER, A. 1962. *Strategy and Structure: Chapters in the History of the Industrial Enterprise*, Cambridge: M.I.T. Press.
CHILD, J. 1969. *The Business Enterprise in Modern Industrial Society*, London: Collier-Macmillan.
CHILD, J. 1970. 'More Myths of Management Organization?' *Journal of Management Studies*, 7: 376–390.
CYERT, R. M. and MARCH, J. G. 1963. *A Behavioural Theory of the Firm*, Englewood Cliffs, N.J: Prentice-Hall.
DUBIN, R. 1962. 'Business Behaviour *Behaviourally* Viewed', in G. B. Strother (ed). *Social Science Approaches to Business Behaviour*, London: Tavistock, 11–55.
EMERY, F. E. and TRIST, E. L. 1965. 'The Causal Texture of Organizational Environments', *Human Relations*, 18: 21–32.
GALBRAITH, J. K. 1967. *The New Industrial State*, London: Hamish Hamilton.
GOLDTHORPE, J. H., LOCKWOOD, D., BECHHOFER, F., and PLATT, J. 1968. *The Affluent Worker: Industrial Attitudes and Behaviour*, Cambridge: The University Press.
GOULDNER, A. W. 1955. 'Metaphysical Pathos and the Theory of Bureaucracy'. *American Political Science Review*, XLIX: 496–507.
HAGE, J. 1965. 'An Axiomatic Theory of Organizations', *Administrative Science Quarterly*, 10: 289–320.
HAGE, J. and AIKEN, M. 1967. 'Program Change and Organizational Properties—A Comparative Analysis', *American Journal of Sociology*, 72: 503–19.
HAGE, J. and AIKEN, M. 1969. 'Routine Technology, Social Structure and Organizational Goals', *Administrative Science Quarterly*, 14: 366–376.
HAGE, J. and AIKEN, M. 1970. *Social Change in Complex Organizations*, New York: Random House.
HALL, R. H. 1962. 'Intraorganizational Structural Variation: Application of the Bureaucratic Model', *Administrative Science Quarterly*, 7:295–308.
HALL, R. H. 1963. 'The Concept of Bureaucracy: An Empirical Assessment', *American Journal of Sociology*, 69:32–40.
HALL, R. H., HAAS, J. E., and JOHNSON, J. N. 1967. 'Organizational Size, Complexity and Formalization', *American Sociological Review*, 32:903–12.
HALL, R. H. and TITTLE, C. R. 1966. 'A Note on Bureaucracy and its "Correlates" ', *American Journal of Sociology*, 72:267–72.
HARVEY, E. 1968. 'Technology and the Structure of Organizations', *American Sociological Review*, 33, 2:247–59.
HICKSON, D. J. et al. 1969. 'Operations Technology and Organization Structure: An Empirical Reappraisal', *Administrative Science Quarterly*, 14:378–397.
HICKSON, D. J. et al. 1970. 'Organization: Is Technology the Key?'. *Personnel Management*: 21–26.

HICKSON, D. J. et al. 1971. 'A Strategic Contingencies Theory of Intra-Organizational Power', *Administrative Science Quarterly*. (forthcoming)
HOUSE, R. J. and WIGDOR, L. A. 1967. 'Herzberg's Dual-Factor Theory of Job Satisfaction and Motivation: A Review of the Evidence and a Criticism', *Personnel Psychology*, 20:369–89.
INGHAM, G. K. 1970. *Work and Behaviour in Industrial Organization*, Cambridge: The University Press.
KHANDWALLA, P. N. 1970. *Environment and the Organization Structure of Firms*, Montreal: McGill University Faculty of Management Working Paper.
KRONENBERG, P. S. 1969, *Micropolitics and Public Planning*, Chapter 3 on 'Interorganizational Behavior', pre-publication manuscript.
LAWRENCE, P. R. and LORSCH J. W. 1967. *Organization and Environment*, Boston: Harvard Business School.
LEVINE, S. and WHITE P. E. 1961. 'Exchange as a Conceptual Framework for the Study of Interorganizational Relationships', *Administrative Science Quarterly*, 5:583–601.
MANN, M. 1970. 'The Social Cohesion of Liberal Democracy', *American Sociological Review*, 35:423–39.
MILLER, E. J. and RICE, A. K. 1967. *Systems of Organization*, London: Tavistock.
NORMANN, R. 1969a. 'Organization, Mediation, and Environment', *S.I.A.R. Report*, No. UPM-RN-91, Stockholm.
NORMANN, R. 1969b. 'Some Conclusions from 13 Case Studies of New Product Development', *S.I.A.R. Report*, No. UPM-RN-100, Stockholm.
PAUL, W. J. and ROBERTSON, K. B. 1970. *Job Enrichment and Employee Motivation*, London: Gower Press.
PERROW, C. 1967. 'A Framework for the Comparative Analysis of Organizations,' *American Sociological Review*, 32:194–208.
PERROW, C. 1970. *Organizational Analysis: A Sociological View*, London: Tavistock.
PRICE, J. L. 1968. *Organizational Effectiveness: An Inventory of Propositions*, Homewood, Ill.: Irwin.
PUGH, D. S., et al. 1963. 'A Conceptual Scheme for Organizational Analysis', *Administrative Science Quarterly*, 8: 289–315.
PUGH, D. S., et al. 1968. 'Dimensions of Organization Structure', *Administrative Science Quarterly*, 13:65–105.
PUGH, D. S. et al. 1969a. 'The Context of Organization Structures', *Administrative Science Quarterly*, 14:91–114.
PUGH, D. S. et al. 1969b. 'An Empirical Taxonomy of Structures of Work Organizations', *Administrative Science Quarterly*, 14:115–126.
SADLER, P. J. and BARRY, B. A. 1970. *Organisational Development*, London: Longmans.
SILVERMAN, D. 1970. *The Theory of Organisations*, London: Heinemann.
STINCHCOMBE, A. L. 1959. 'Bureaucratic and Craft Administration of Production: A Comparative Study', *Administrative Science Quarterly*, 4:168–187.
THOMPSON, J. D. 1967. *Organizations in Action*, New York: McGraw-Hill.
THOMPSON, J. D. and McEWEN, W. J. 1958. 'Organizational Goals and Environment: Goal-Setting as an Interaction Process', *American Sociological Review*, 23:23–31.
TRIST, E. L. et al. 1963. *Organizational Choice*, London: Tavistock.
WASMUTH, W. J. et al. 1970. *Human Resources Administration*, Boston: Houghton Mifflin.
WEICK, K. E. 1969. *The Social Psychology of Organizing*, Reading, Mass.: Addison-Wesley.
WOODWARD, J. 1965. *Industrial Organization: Theory and Practice*, London: Oxford University Press.

WOODWARD, J. 1970. editor, *Industrial Organization: Behaviour and Control*, London: Oxford University Press.
YUCHTMAN, E. and SEASHORE, S. E. 1967. 'A System Resource Approach to Organizational Effectiveness'. *American Sociological Review* 32: 891–903.

Biographical note: JOHN CHILD, born 1940, Manchester. University of Cambridge M.A. 1965, Ph.D. 1967. Employed in Rolls-Royce Ltd., 1965–66, Research Fellow, Industrial Administration Research Unit, University of Aston in Birmingham 1966–68. Senior Research Officer, London Graduate School of Business Studies 1968-. Author of *British Management Thought* (1969), *The Business Enterprise in Modern Industrial Society* (1969), Co-author of *The Sociology of Industry* (1968).

STRATEGY FORMULATION AS A POLITICAL PROCESS

Andrew M. Pettigrew (United Kingdom)

The formation of strategy in organizations is a continuous process. Specific dilemmas within the firm, or in the firm's environment, may raise the organization members' consciousness of strategy and allow us, as analysts, to think of strategy formulation as an intentional process built around certain discrete decisions; but strategy is being formed implicitly all the time. Choices are made and acted upon in processes involving individuals and subgroupings, at various organizational levels, that develop into the pattern of thinking about the world, evaluating that world, and acting upon that world that we call strategy. Study of the process of strategy formulation therefore involves analyses of both discrete and identifiable decision events and of the pathways to and outcomes of those decision events, together with the connections between successive decisions over time. (1)

Andrew Pettigrew is Professor of Organizational Behavior in the School of Industrial and Business Studies, University of Warwick, Coventry, England.

Author's note: In line with the Saint-Maximin conference objectives, this paper has been written with theory development in mind. It is also very much a personal statement, although the discerning reader will see that I have been influenced by Bachrach and Baratz (1970), Cohen, March, and Olsen (1972), and Easton (1965).

Strategy formulation is <u>contextually</u> based. Strategy may be understood as a flow of events, values, and actions running through a context. Part of the context is the location of strategy in time. Yesterday's strategies will provide some of the pathways to and inputs for today's strategies; and today's strategies will have a concept of the future built into them. The consequences of the implementation of today's strategies will provide part of the context for tomorrow's strategies. But time is but a segment of the context: context also includes the culture of the organization; its environment and the rate of change or stability thereof; the organization's task, structure, and technology; and the leadership and internal political system of the organization. (<u>2</u>) At any point in time, the focus for strategic choices will be environmental and intra-organizational <u>dilemmas</u>; and the process of resolving those dilemmas will be influenced by organizational, cultural, task, leadership, and internal political factors.

This context affects the process of strategy formulation. The implementation of any outcomes of the strategy-formulation process in turn become the new contextual background for resolving future strategic dilemmas. The existing context can provide the enabling conditions for new strategies or the dynamic conservatism to sustain existing definitions of what the organization's core dilemmas are, and therefore to maintain the existing strategies for resolving those dilemmas. Out of the context come the dilemmas or issues that do or do not receive organizational attention. Out of the partial resolution of those dilemmas evolves <u>strategy</u>.

The subject matter and analysis of the process of strategy formulation include the following:

(1) identification of the set of dilemmas faced by an organization over time;

(2) analysis of the dilemmas that become a focus for organizational interest <u>and</u> of those that are suppressed;

(3) specification of the individuals or subgroupings that seek to define alternative dilemmas as worthy of organizational attention;

(4) study of the demand by those individuals and subgroupings that certain dilemmas be discussed, and of the attempts to mobilize power in support of those demands;

(5) specification of the outcomes of these processes of demand-generation and power-mobilization and their implementation as the patterns of thinking about, evaluating, and acting upon the world, i.e., as strategy;

(6) finally, consideration of the relationship between strategy formulation and strategy implementation (3) and of the impact of the implementation of strategy on the formulation of future strategy.

Strategy Formulation as a Political Decision-making Process

The present assumption is that strategy formulation can be understood as a process of political decision-making. This process will include debate about which dilemmas should receive organizational attention and the choice of which alternative courses of action should be adopted to resolve those dilemmas. Strategies emanate from the decision processes about which dilemmas and which modes of resolution will be selected. In these processes of bringing new dilemmas to the organization's attention or holding existing dilemmas at the forefront of attention, certain demands are made by various parties in the organization. The demands may be precisely that certain dilemmas move from the strategic wings to the strategic stage, or that the old dilemmas stay on stage. But the analytical issue is not just what demands are made but how the parties making the demands mobilize power around their various demands.

A demand is politically feasible only if sufficient power can be mobilized and committed to it. The study of the "political" in the process of strategy formulation therefore involves the isolation of two analytically separate but empirically interdependent processes. The first concerns the demand-generation process, including the sources of the disparate demands in the

Strategy Formulation as a Political Process

strategy-formulation process; the second deals with the processes of power mobilization in association with each demand. In what follows I shall briefly delineate the theoretical language system, in order to unravel the above two processes; but first let us consider the issue of why one expects political behavior to occur in the process of strategy formulation.

Political processes in organizations evolve at the <u>group</u> level from the division of work in the firm, and at the <u>individual</u> level from associated career, reward, and status systems. Subgroupings develop interests on the basis of specialized functions and responsibilities, whereas individual careers are bound up with the maintenance or dissolution of certain types of organizational activity and with the distribution of organizational resources.

Political behavior is defined as behavior by individuals or — in collective terms — subgroupings within an organization that makes a claim against the resource-sharing system of the organization. Decisions about the formulation of new strategy or the maintenance of the old are, to a greater or less degree, likely to threaten the existing distribution of organizational resources as represented in salaries, in promotion opportunities, and in control of tasks, people, information, and new areas of a business.

Bringing a new dilemma to attention and having that dilemma at least partially resolved may induce sufficient organizational change to unscramble current distributions of resources. Additional resources may be created and appear to fall within the jurisdiction of a department or individual who previously had not been a claimant in a particular area. This department or its principal representative may see this as an opportunity to increase its/his power, status, and rewards in the organization. Others may see their interests threatened by the focus on the new dilemma and its resolution, and needs for security or the maintenance of power may provide the impetus for the release of political energy. It should be clear, then, that the release of political energy during the strategy-formulation process is concerned not just with aggrandizement or the acquisition of power but also with security and thus the maintenance of power.

Politics as the Generation of Disparate Demands

In this view of strategy formulation as a process of political decision-making, the choices will focus on which dilemmas receive attention and how those dilemmas are resolved in further choice behavior. The political decision process can be understood in part as the resolution of conflicting demands from various interested individuals and groups. The analytical question therefore centers on why there is a disparity in demand. Why is individual A or subgrouping B demanding that a certain dilemma be brought to the decision-making table and other demands, made by other individuals or groups, removed?

At the stage at which dilemmas are or are not discussed, the disparities may come from the functional responsibilities and intra-organizational and environmental search behavior of different functional units. Different parts of an organization, because of their interaction patterns and modes of problem solving and information processing, may see the problems and opportunities of the organization differently. Indeed, it may be the explicit task of certain development and planning groups to bring emerging organizational dilemmas to debate. Whether the existing power structure screens out such attempts at strategic influence is likely to be a key question. Dilemmas are likely to be pushed forward for discussion and decision on the basis of firmly held value positions about the organization's future direction or in the belief that the debate and resolution of those dilemmas will have a consequential effect on individual or subgroup distributions of activities, roles, and power.

Once a dilemma receives organizational attention, the process of its partial resolution may also stimulate disparate demands from various individuals and groupings. The extent of the disparities will be conditional on:

1. The structure of the decision unit dealing with the dilemma, whether, for example, the structure was relatively complex.

Strategy Formulation as a Political Process

One would expect greater disparities in a decision unit that was both vertically and horizontally differentiated than in one that was structurally simple, i.e., composed of people from one vertical level or one horizontal unit.

2. The complexity and uncertainty of the dilemma. On simple-complex and static-dynamic dimensions, one would expect the greatest room for disparities in the complex-dynamic case, the situation in which the dilemma was both a complex and ever-changing problem.

3. The level of salience of the dilemma for various parties and the system repercussions of the dilemma will also affect the propensity of individuals or groups to intervene in the process with demands.

4. The existence of specific and publicly stated value positions and of exclusive styles of language use and problem-solving style will also add to the disparities in the demand-generating process.

5. Additional fuel may be added to the conflicts about demands by the selective and/or sporadic intervention of external pressure on the decision unit.

6. Finally, the history of relationships, and thus of personal likes and dislikes, among individuals in the decision process will affect the extent of the disparities in demands. (4) It may be a case of "If he's for it, I'm against it!"

Politics as the Mobilization of Power Around Demands

If one key aspect of strategy formulation as a political decision process is the process of demand generation, the other linked process concerns the mobilization of power around those demands. Demands are generated and processed in the context of social structures in which individuals are differentially located and have, by implication, access to varying amounts of the resources that are the bases of power. A demand is politically feasible only if sufficient power can be mobilized and committed to its support. Decisional outcomes evolve from the processes of power mobilization attempted by each party in support of its demand. But in the context of strategy formulation, what is power?

A power relation is a causal relation between the preferences of an actor regarding an outcome and the outcome itself. Power involves the ability of an actor to produce outcomes consonant with his perceived interests. From this viewpoint, the analysis of organizational power in the context of processes of strategy formulation requires some attempt to map out the distribution and use of certain power resources and the ability of individuals or groups to produce outcomes consonant with their interests. The assumption is that in a competitive demand-generating process, the decisional outcome will not necessarily be a product of the greater worthiness or weight of the issues ranged to uphold one or other demand in the dispute, but may result from the differential awareness of, possession of, control over, and tactical skill in using certain power resources.

The analysis of power therefore does not just entail specifying that because of structural position, an individual or group possesses certain power resources. Individuals may indeed possess certain power resources, but not be aware they have them. Without awareness, such resources can hardly be marshaled, controlled, and put to use. This view of the resource theory of power suggests that the analysis include data on individual or group: (1) awareness of power resources, (2) possession of power resources, (3) control of power resources, (4) tactical use of power resources — assuming the individual or group possesses the resource and is aware of that possession and can control it.

In previous research (Pettigrew, 1972, 1973, 1975), I have indicated the kinds of power resources that may be crucial in having one's demands met. These include (5): system-relevant expertise, political access and sensitivity, control over information, assessed stature, and group support.

Politics as the Management of Meaning

Earlier in this paper I suggested that one way to analyze

Strategy Formulation as a Political Process

strategy formulation as a political decision-making process was to focus on processes of demand-generation and power-mobilization. The bare outlines of such analyses have been presented above. But there is also the issue of the connections between the demands people make in the strategy-formulation process and their capacity to mobilize power for those demands. In presenting a demand that a dilemma be considered for discussion or that it be resolved in a certain way, one usually encounters a question about that demand's legitimacy in its particular institutional context. There is clearly a point at which any particular demand may be unsupportable, and the issue becomes not one of mobilizing power for the preexisting demand, but determining how the existing demand can be modified so that its power requirement can be assembled.

In considering <u>what</u> demand is presented and <u>how</u> it is presented and later modified, issues of <u>legitimacy</u> are likely to be crucial. Legitimacy is a highly diffuse and movable resource, but one whose significance and unequal distribution can structure decisional outcomes. Politics concerns the creation of legitimacy for certain ideas, values, and demands — not just action performed as a result of previously acquired legitimacy. The management of meaning refers to a process of symbol construction and value use designed both to create legitimacy for one's own demands and to "delegitimize" the demands of opponents in a political decision-making process. Therefore, a fundamental factor in the life history of a demand in a strategy-formulation process will be the answer to the question "What does that demand <u>symbolize</u>, what does it <u>mean</u> to the various interested parties in the process?"

Key concepts for analyzing this process of the management of meaning are symbolism, language, belief, and myth. (6) Language is not just a means of expressing thoughts, categories, and concepts: it is also a vehicle for achieving practical effects. Language is a carrier not only of information but also of meanings. Presentation of a demand involves the choice of language to describe it and the stylistics of language use. Stylistics may include the use of dialectic forms of presentation and the use of metaphors and myths — the latter being devices for simplifying and giving meaning to complex issues that evoke concern. Myths serve as ways of legitimizing the present (demands) in terms of a perhaps glorious past, of reconciling apparent dilemmas, and of explaining away the discrepancies that may exist between what is happening and what ought to be happening. As such, myths provide part of the social cement that links old strategies with new strategies and that justifies the very existence of the new strategy.

But the temporal connecting role of language, beliefs, and myths in linking old strategy and new strategy takes us back to the opening statement that strategy formulation is a continuous process. Part of politics as the management of meaning is to legitimize after the fact a strategy that has been implicitly formulated through action yet never placed before the organization as a dilemma for consideration. Much of what is known in organizations as strategy is the reconstruction and relabeling of old ways of thinking about, evaluating, and acting upon the world. In this way, through time, organizations deal with their members' and their environment's needs for both continuity and change.

Notes

1) See A. Pettigrew (1973) for such a time-based analysis.

2) Culture includes the language and other symbolic systems of the organization, including the organization's ideology, beliefs, rituals, and myths. See A. Pettigrew (1976) "The Creation of Organisational Cultures," paper presented to the Joint EIASM-Dansk Management Center research seminar "Entrepreneurs and the Process of Institution-Building." Copenhagen, May 18-20, 1976.

3) One treatment of the issue of implementation of strategy is provided by Mumford and Pettigrew (1975).

4) See Pettigrew (1973) for detailed empirical examples from a research study of these six factors.

5) See Pettigrew (1973) for detailed definitions of these concepts and empirical examples.

6) See Pettigrew (1976) (note 2 above) for a more extended theoretical discussion of these concepts and their relevance to entrepreneur-follower relationships in organizations.

References

Bachrach, P., and Baratz, M. S. (1970) Power and Poverty: Theory and Practice. New York: Oxford University Press.

Cohen, M. D., March, J. G., and Olsen, J. P. (1972) "A Garbage-can Model of Organizational Choice," Administrative Science Quarterly, 17, 1-25.

Easton, D. (1965) A Systems Analysis of Political Life. New York: Wiley.

Mumford, E., and Pettigrew, A. (1975) Implementing Strategic Decisions. London: Longman.

Pettigrew, A. (1972) "Information Control as a Power Resource," Sociology, 6(2), 187-204.

Pettigrew, A. (1973) The Politics of Organisational Decision-Making. London: Tavistock.

Pettigrew, A. (1975) "Towards a Political Theory of Organisational Intervention," Human Relations, 28(3), 191-208.

ON STUDYING MANAGERIAL ELITES
ANDREW M. PETTIGREW
Centre for Corporate Strategy and Change, Warwick Business School, Warwick University, Coventry, U.K.

> The study of managerial elites is one of the most important, yet neglected areas of social science research. This paper synthesizes and critically reviews three intellectual traditions in the study of managerial elites. These are: interlocking directorates and the study of institutional and societal power, the study of boards and directors, and the composition and correlates of top management teams. The paper concludes by arguing for the development of a complementary research tradition which combines a contextual and processual analysis of managerial elites.

The purpose of this paper is to synthesize and critically review elements of the research literatures on managerial elites. The paper assesses a number of intellectual traditions and studies of managerial elites, and then offers a research agenda for future scholarly work in this most important but difficult area of social science research.

The phrase managerial elite is certainly not neutral, indeed many scholars have articulated the long tradition of value laden debate around the term elite (Giddens, 1974; Field and Higley, 1980). But if the term elite is emotive and analytically value laden for some, it also has the virtue of inclusiveness in the social sciences. This is important for the aims of this paper, since it is being written partly to draw together aspects of the sociological, organizational and managerial literature, which in the past have not talked to one another. So who are we to embrace in this inclusive term managerial elite? Broadly the interest is in those who occupy formally defined positions of authority, those at the head of, or who could be said to be in strategic positions in private and public organizations of various sizes. Institutionally the interest, in the first instance, is in position holders who carry labels such as Chairman, President, Chief Executive Officer, Managing Director, or inside or outside Director. However, the focus goes beyond the individual position holder to consider the behavior of groups of actors as they operate as boards of directors, executive committees or top management teams. No assumption is made by starting with position holders or formal groupings of individuals, that power lies with those at the strategic apex of the organization. There is now ample empirical evidence from organizations of many different kinds, in many societies, that the power and influence of senior position holders is constrained by the countervailing influence of others inside and outside their own organizations, as well as by rules, traditions, and other institutional arrangements (Mechanic, 1964; Pettigrew, 1973; Herman, 1981). The question of the relative power of managerial elites and others is a crucial empirical issue.

Sociologists and political scientists will quickly remind us that the study of managerial elites has to include not only the leaders of business and

Key words: Studying managerial elites, process research

0143–2095/92/100163–20$15.00
© 1992 by John Wiley & Sons, Ltd.

political institutions, but also 'members of the media, trade unions, educational, cultural, and religious institutions, and voluntary associations', (Mizruchi, 1992: 18). Thus the focus of analysis is not just power and control within the business institution, or indeed within a broader range of institutions, but whether, and to what extent, and under what conditions, there may be an inner circle of business leaders 'who define and promote the shared needs of large corporations .... and give coherence and direction to the politics of business' (Useem, 1984: 3).

Whilst the purposes and activities of managerial elites are a source of fascination in everyday conversation and in journalistic accounts of the fate of large enterprises (Auletta, 1991), the study of elites within institutions and societies by social scientists remain few and far between. Access difficulties have been and remain a source of constraint on studies of elites. As long ago as 1957, Kahl was arguing 'those who sit amongst the mighty do not invite sociologists to watch them make the decisions about how to control the behavior of others' (Kahl, 1957: 10). Pahl and Winkler (1974), Norburn (1989) and many others have reported the real practical difficulties of getting close to the top of large institutions. But access problems are not insurmountable. The early and clever use of publicly available data by Wilson and Lupton (1959) to reveal the interconnecting networks in the City of London, and the astute use of archival data more recently by Kosnik (1987) and Davis (1991), all show what can be done from public sources. Equally well, the Harvard Business School tradition of work on boards of directors and chief executives (Mace, 1971; Gabarro, 1987; Vancil, 1987, and Lorsch and MacIver, 1989) demonstrates that direct access to key figures and important processes is negotiable. The developing tradition of research on top level strategic change processes in the U.K. by, for example, Pettigrew (1985a), Johnson (1987), Smith, Child and Rowlinson (1991) and Pettigrew and Whipp (1991) should provide further optimistic signals that substantial access to managerial elites is possible even in a society with perhaps even stronger norms of privacy than is customary in the U.S.A. I remain sanguine that access difficulties alone need not be an impediment to the extended development of managerial elites as a field of empirical study.

Progression in the study of managerial elites can be characterized under six themes:

1. Interlocking directorates and the study of institutional and societal power.
2. The study of boards and directors.
3. The composition and correlates of top management teams.
4. Studies of strategic leadership, decision making and change.
5. Chief executive compensation.
6. Chief executive selection and succession.

It is beyond the scope of this paper to review all six of these often quite separated areas of intellectual enquiry. The choice of the first three offers a number of analytical possibilities. First of all there are strong and distinctive intellectual traditions in two of the three areas. The study of interlocking directorates has a clear focus on the structural analysis of business in its societal context and a distinctive methodological approach in its use of the quantitative techniques of network analysis. Important representative studies in this tradition include Burt (1983), Clawson, Neustadtl, and Scott (1992), Galaskiewicz (1985), Mintz and Schwartz (1985), Mizruchi (1992), Palmer (1983), Pfeffer and Salancik (1978), Stokman, Scott and Ziegler (1985); Useem (1984) and Whitt (1982).

Research on top management teams was given a fresh lead in 1984 by the Hambrick and Mason paper setting out a research agenda for the study of the 'upper echelons' of business. Since then a noteworthy pattern of work has emerged linking the demographic characteristics of top management teams to a variety of organizational outcomes such as performance, innovativeness, and strategic change. Illustrative studies in this tradition include D'Aveni (1990), Finkelstein and Hambrick (1990), Hambrick and D'Aveni (1991), Keck and Tushman (1991), Norburn and Birley (1988), O'Reilly, Snyder and Boothe (1992) and Wiersema and Bantel (1992). With the notable exception of D'Aveni, this research has neither sought nor made any connections with the sociological research on elites and interlocking directorates. Like the interlocks research, the top management team research is held together by a common methodological approach, but this time the use of demographic data and multivariate analysis, rather than network based multivariate analysis.

Without doubt the weakest of these three areas of research is the work on the composition and operation of boards and the activities of inside and outside directors. A good deal of the literature in this area 'is non-academic, even nonanalytical, and relies heavily on unquestioned assumptions as a basis of prescription' (Pettigrew, 1992). Nevertheless, there are some scholarly pillars to stand on to develop this intellectual approach exemplified, for example, in the empirical work of Bradshaw, Murray and Wolpin (1992), Goodstein and Boeker (1991), Herman (1981), Kosnik (1987), Lorsch and MacIver (1989), Mace (1971), Norburn (1989), Pahl and Winkler (1974), Pearce and Zahra (1991), Stewart (1991), and Zajac (1990). As yet, this research has developed neither a coherent methodological approach or a sound set of conceptual categories and findings. Links with research on interlocking directorates and top management teams remain undeveloped. The whole field of research on boards and directors awaits energetic intellectual leadership.

This paper has four sections. The first three characterize the underlying assumptions and main findings of research on interlocking directorates, boards, and top management teams. Each section identifies the strengths and weaknesses of the three areas of research and suggests some profitable themes and questions for future enquiry.

Because three research areas are being considered for critical review, the paper has had to trade-off a certain amount of depth of presentation for breadth. Nevertheless the central tendencies of each research tradition are considered and in the fourth and final section the beginnings of a new research tradition is articulated for all three areas of research which combines a contextual and processual analysis of managerial elites (Pettigrew, 1990, 1992).

INTERLOCKING DIRECTORATES AND THE STUDY OF INSTITUTIONAL AND SOCIETAL POWER

Research in this tradition is avowedly sociological. The focus is on the analysis of business power and the corporate elite rooted in the quantitative techniques of network analysis. The concern is less with the structure of power relations within individual organizations than the social relations between enterprises. Thus Scott (1991: 182) characterizes work in this area as focusing 'on the social networks in which enterprises are embedded and the importance of viewing these networks as arenas of power.' The deeper sociological assumption in this work picks up on the Granovetter (1985) embeddedness thesis reinterpreted by Mizruchi (1992: X) as 'the ability of business to accomplish its goals must ultimately be studied in the context of the actions of other segments of society.' United more by method than theory, a strong tradition of work has developed over the past 20 years suggesting that structures of interorganizational relations are consequential for managing resource dependencies, Pfeffer and Salancik (1978); class action, Zeitlin (1974); the formation of inner circles of corporate power in society, Useem (1984); the political activities of business, Mizruchi (1992); Clawson, et al. (1992); and corporate charitable donations in regional, Galaskiewicz (1985), and national settings, Useem (1991). This research has been comprehensively reviewed by Glasberg and Schwartz (1983), Scott (1991), Mizruchi and Schwartz (1987), and Davis and Powell (1992). Although this stream of research has had its descriptive reviewers and commentators, it is only very recently that stronger critical attention has been given to assessing the additive outcomes of such work. Recent notable critical reviewers include Zajac (1988, 1992), Stinchcombe (1990), Davis (1992), and Davis and Powell (1992).

Central to the network approach is the view that interlocking boards of directors represent political and social as well as business ties. An interlocking directorship is said to exist when a particular individual sits on two or more corporate boards. Direct as well as indirect linkages may be included in the analysis. Indirect linkages exist where directors of firms A and B do not sit on each other's board, but are linked through joint membership of a third board. Zajac (1992: 13) argues that while the study of indirect links increases the number of ties that can be uncovered, this further aggregation of the network analysis merely adds to the systemic problems of assessing the significance of the wider set.

As Davis and Powell (1992) and others have argued, it is method rather than theory which unites the interlock research. Sonquist and Koenig (1975) describe the developments in graph theory and associated computational algorithms and programs which have allowed the network researchers to isolate and identify linkages between corporations and other interest groups. Aside from this common methodological approach, one or two data bases have been crucial in harnessing interest in the study of interlocking directorates. A notable driving force has been the data base developed by Schwartz of the State University of New York, Stony Brook. Indeed the Stony Brook group of scholars, (Schwartz, Mintz, Glasberg, Mizruchi, and Palmer) have themselves formed a crucial part of the academic network which has launched and perpetuated the interlocking directorates tradition of research.

But what are the consistent empirical findings to evolve from the network researchers? After very careful reading of nearly all the original studies and personal conversations with a few of the key scholars, this writer finds it remarkably difficult to summarize the key patterns from these studies of interlocking directorates. Part of the reason for the difficulty in identifying unequivocal findings lies in the challenge made to earlier apparently conclusive results. For example, Zajac (1988) has used the 1969 Schwartz data base to successfully question previous conclusions about collusive relationships between competing firms in the chemicals, primary metals, and transportation equipment industries. Reanalyzing the same data set, but this time using a control group comparison, Zajac (1988: 436) is able to query earlier work by Dooley (1969) and Burt (1980) and contend that 'interlocking directorates among competing firms are not significant in number and probably not significant in meaning.' However, an even bigger obstacle to pattern recognition in the findings derives from the widely different theoretical interpretations made from the interlock results.

Mizruchi's (1992) successful attempt to describe the natural history of development of the different theoretical interpretations and frameworks used to expose network findings leads him to attempt a synthesis of the interorganizational and class theorists in what he describes as an interorganizational model of class cohesion. But this Herculean effort of intellectual synthesis cannot paper over the cracks of the different intellectual traditions, or the inconsistent empirical findings.

The two most easily isolatable theoretical interpretations of interlocks data are the resource dependency and class theorists. Resource dependency approaches, for example, by Pfeffer and Salancik (1978), argue that interlocks are mechanisms designed to reduce the uncertainties created by the dependency relationships which develop between firms. Such links, although widespread, are normally seen as particular instrumental acts by one firm in relation to another and do not represent class-wide based entities. The purpose of interlocks in this tradition may be to reduce uncertainty, effect cooptation, or diffuse information.

Class based theorists interpret interlocking directorates as evidence of linking between powerful elites into elite class networks, (Zeitlin, 1974). Within this approach, bank control and financial hegemony theorists have studied the development of ties between industry and financial institutions and see the allocation of capital through regional and national networks as evidence of class based financial hegemony (Mintz and Schwartz, 1985). Useem (1984) takes this argument a stage further and uses a U.K.-U.S. comparison to propose that the individuals who form the interlocks are an inner circle of the corporate elite who can represent that elite in societal wide political processes. Later work summarized by Stokman, et al. (1985) and Scott (1991) uses international comparative data to note the striking variations in patterns of interlocks between different countries, and in particular how the centrality of banks differs from country to country. Thus British networks stood out for the low level of interlocking and a much less dense and weakly tied network than, for example, the United States. The Stokman et al. (1985) 10-country comparison also found a positive relationship between the profitability of firms and interlocking with banks, a finding not replicated from the U.S. data. Correspondingly, highly indebted companies in Belgium and The Netherlands seemed less able to attract bankers, or network specialists (1985: 282). Some general tendencies found across all 10 countries were for the largest firms to be most interlocked, for regionally based and foreign owned firms to be less central in national networks, and for family owned companies generally speaking to be poorly interlocked compared with publicly owned enterprises.

Mizruchi and Schwartz (1987) conclude their review of resource dependency and class theorists by contending that the empirical predictions made by both approaches are often similar, since the dependency theorists acknowledge the existence of leadership discretion and to varying degrees the class theorists admit the possibility of the autonomous dynamics of corporate processes. 'As a result much of the dispute between proponents of the two perspectives centers around divergent interpretations of the same data,' Mizruchi and Schwartz (1987: 9).

A more recent stream of work on network ties seeks to go beyond the descriptive codification of interlocks and tries to link the effects of networks on organizational structure, ideology, and action. (See the Davis and Powell review, 1992). Thus Palmer, Jennings and Zhou (1989) found a link between the adoption of the multidivisional form by firms and their ties with previous adopters. The relationship between ties and innovation was also studied in a quite different domain by Davis (1991). He reports findings that larger firms were quicker to adopt a poison pill takeover defence to the extent that they were tied to prior adopters. These studies, along with research by Galaskiewicz and his colleagues on the impact of networks on charitable giving (Atkinson and Galaskiewicz, 1988), and by Clawson et al. (1992) on the consequences of business networks for political party contributions, represent attempts to redirect this analysis of interlocking directorates away from the description and interpretation of structural anatomy to examine the more fundamental question of the consequences and effects of network relationships.

Interlocking directorates research: A brief critique

Three broad areas of criticism can be directed towards the interlocking directorates research. The criticisms are themselves interlinked, but they can be disentangled and labeled as, the so what problem, what do interlocks really mean; the methodological problem of aggregation and randomness; and problems of inference and proof.

Of these three areas of criticism of interlock research the most fundamentally disabling is 'that nobody really knows what they mean' (Mizruchi, 1984: 142). As Stinchcombe (1990: 380) penetratingly argues, this area of research is driven more by the allure of network methods and the ready availability of data than by substantive issues. . .'using a method that starts with a dichotomy of present or absence as a descriptor of a link between corporations condemns us to the sterility of structural theory and irrelevance of the data. . .the result is theoretical floundering in tables of data that seem to be mostly random numbers.'

This strident criticism is echoed and amplified by Zajac (1992), Davis (1992) and Davis and Powell (1992). In Zajac's (1992) view the very term interlocking directorate prejudges the issue of linkage. He would prefer to use the phrase multiple-board membership than interlocking directorate, since the former stops short at describing the phenomenon, whilst the more customary phrase is already interpreting it. Zajac (1992) wants to start with the basic question, does dual board membership actually serve a linkage function, and if so what function? The related criticism from Davis (1992) and Davis and Powell (1992) starts from the proposition that the network analysts' preoccupation with describing the structural anatomy of networks has not allowed them to adequately explore the consequences and effects of ties. Whilst interlocks research serves a crucial theoretical function in countering atomistic approaches to the corporation, a vexing problem remains, 'there is virtually no empirical evidence that particular interlock ties serve any discernible corporate purpose, or that the interlock network has any substantive impact on what corporations do' (Davis, 1992: 8).

Of course, doubts about the real purposes of interlocks are very much a function of the highly aggregated data sets used by the network scholars. As Zajac (1988) has argued, there is a need to disaggregate network data to examine precisely who is linked with whom. Adding indirect to direct links merely adds to problems of aggregation and ultimately creates further problems of inference and proof. Hirsch (1982) has been equally scathing of interlock studies iterating around competing models for which critical tests are not provided. The interlocks tradition illustrates 'the costs entailed by allowing accessible data to serve as proxies and indicators for theoretical positions whose substantive likelihood and plausibility is increasingly ambiguous and difficult to articulate' (Hirsch, 1982: 3). A good example of the shifting and ambiguous character of the interpretation process in empirical research on interlocking directorates is provided by Useem's otherwise notable book on *The Inner Circle*. Thus Useem wobbles between the view that the inner circle 'can impose a class-wide logic on corporate decisions, and they often do' (1984: 116), to the view that 'most corporate decisions are, of course, still largely a product of the internal logic of the firm' (1984: 146).

The above sharp criticisms invite a corresponding search for positive suggestions to redirect research on interlocking directorates and the structure of corporate power. Clearly one important way forward is to move away from an exclusive concern with the structural analysis of networks and begin to analyze the purposes of networks and how and why key actors in the networks use links to achieve corporate, political, or class wide interests. In this approach, studies of networks in action, and of links between actions and processes and the achievement of outcomes, would take center stage in the analysis. So the content of ties, their development and use, would become critical for analysis and not just the structure of ties in the network. As Stinchcombe (1990: 381) has so eloquently put it 'we need to know what flows across the links, who decides on those flows in the light of what interests, and what collective or corporate action flows from the organization of the links, in order to make sense of intercorporate relations.

In a soundly argued paper, Zajac (1992) argues that the label interlocking directorates has itself historically led researchers to assume that multiple board membership is a linkage mechanism. He contends that the study of multiple board membership should begin with the study of individual board membership motives, rather than the study of interlocks. Rather than asking as a lead question what does multiple board membership represent, the starting questions should be, what does single and then multiple board membership represent? Such an approach might complement interorganizational and intraclass views of network ties with 'a personal advancement pespective' on multiple board representation. In Zajac's view (1992: 21) 'personal prestige, monetary rewards, and friendship would be posited as significant factors in the decision to accept *and* extend offers of dual board membership.'

But any redirection of interlocking directorates research surely needs to go beyond questions of personal motive. Central to any development should be the exploration of how, why and when networks of intercorporate relations affect corporate behavior and outcomes. How are variations in the structure and conduct of elites decisive for major commercial, political, and social outcomes? How are actual relationships of control, coordination, and power mobilized around concrete issues and events which are of importance to individual organizations, or sets of organizations in the same or different markets and sectors? It is studies of the actual exercise of corporate and societal power which are needed and not just distant and highly aggregated analyses of the attribution of power.

Recent reviews of research patterns by Stokman *et al.* (1985) and Scott (1991) indicate the analytical and empirical promise of the comparative analysis of intercorporate relations and interlocking directorates. As Scott (1991) argues, much U.S. research has focused on the organization of business activity in relatively homogeneous economic, cultural and political terms. However, European and Asian businesses show important differences in the pattern of intercorporate relations. Revealing such empirical differences has now stimulated a search for explanations of those variations. This in turn is drawing scholars to offer more contextualist explanations of the origins and trajectory of development of interlocking directorates across a variety of societies. An important benefit of this process is that historical and cultural factors, the structure of the state, kinship systems, and processes of industrialization are now more explicitly being used to explain the fashioning of intercorporate relations both within and between societies (Fligstein, 1990; Hamilton and Biggart, 1988; Stokman *et al.*, 1985).

None of the above conceptual and empirical developments are possible, however without progress in complementing existing network research methods with other styles of research and other forms of data. All the studies mentioned above on the motives for joining and extending offers to join boards; on the analysis of networks in action; and the varying trajectories of development of corporate relations and elites in different societies, require first hand data much closer to the phenomenon than was envisaged by the structural analysts of network relations. Perhaps as Davis and Powell (1992) assert, the primacy of method over substance in the study of interlocking directorates is now nearing its end and the close observation and analysis of actual relationships can begin to inform traditional social science concerns with interlocking directorates and the study of institutional and societal power.

THE STUDY OF BOARDS AND DIRECTORS

Whilst the 1980s has witnessed a burgeoning of popular and scholarly interest in the contribution of top leaders to the fate of organizations, (see Bryman, 1992, for a recent review) this preoccupation with charisma, vision, and transformation has not been complemented by equivalent scholarly concern with the study of boards and directors. Policy interest in boards is, of course, now very evident in the U.K. and U.S. as boards have been placed at the center of a number of financial scandals involving major public companies and corporations. (See Cadbury Report (1992) and Lorsch and MacIver (1989) for recent policy discussions of corporate governance matters). This policy interest, buttressed by the legal and financial requirements expected of boards, and the assumption that board effectiveness can contribute to corporate performance, has produced a constant stream of prescriptive writing about alternative ways of harnessing the productive potential of boards (Charkham, 1986; Loose and Yelland, 1987). Statements about the importance of boards in the business process are normally underpinned by a list of the critical board functions. Thus Cadbury (1990) summarizes board functions in these terms:

- to define the company's purpose
- to agree the strategies and plans for achieving that purpose
- to establish the company's policies
- to appoint the chief executive and to review his performance and that of top executives

- in all this to be the driving force of the company.

Other writers (Pearce and Zahra, 1991) suggest that powerful boards provide useful business contacts, thus strengthening the link between corporations and their environments; that powerful boards are necessary to ensure the protection of shareholder interest; and finally, that powerful boards play a crucial role in creating corporate identity, especially in the establishment and maintenance of a code of ethics.

Such apparently sensible statements of business intention and practice conceal the dearth of basic descriptive information on the composition, conduct, and performance of boards and their directors. Tricker's 1978 observation that 'the work of the director, in and out of the boardroom, is rated as the most under-researched management topic' is still ringingly true in 1992. The study of boards and their directors must rank near the top of any management scholar's list of priority areas for the 1990s.

Because research on boards and directors is still in its infancy, there are few theoretical, empirical, or methodological guideposts to assist the optimistic yet wary researcher through the prescriptive minefield. What has been written from a descriptive and analytical viewpoint is fragmented and largely nonadditive. Methodological difficulties in gaining access for behavioral or interview based studies, or poor response rates from questionnaire based studies, have also contributed to the patchy and often inconclusive findings on boards. The interlocks research tradition, reviewed in the previous section of this paper, still comprises a large proportion of the scholarly literature on boards.

Perhaps the most clearly stated theme in the prescriptive and descriptive writing about boards has to do with board composition. Typically boards are composed of a combination of executive (inside) directors (who are also senior managers and include the chief executive) and nonexecutive (outside) directors who are external to the day-to-day operation of the firm. From either of these two groups a chairperson of the board will also be chosen. Thus although a board is composed of individuals, analysis and prescription tends to assume that boards can be subdivided into homogeneous, interest sharing groups. The ready availability of demographic data at least on gender, age, present functional or business responsibility, and, of course, number and proportion of inside to outside directors, has contributed to the range of studies linking board size and composition to variables such as performance (Pfeffer, 1972; Baysinger and Butler, 1985; Hermalin and Weisbach, 1991). However, inherent difficulties in separating out the multitude of endogenous and exogenous factors that influence company performance, make the assumed effects of board demographic characteristics on board effectiveness very difficult indeed to establish. The recently published work by Hermalin and Weisbach (1991), which could find no relationship between board composition and performance, provides a good instance of this general problem.

The issue of CEO duality, where the positions of chairperson and CEO are occupied by the same individual, has also attracted prescriptive and descriptive writing and research. Rechner and Dalton (1991) examined the financial implications of CEO duality (as opposed to the position of an independent chairperson) in terms of investment returns, equity returns and profitability over a 6-year period. Their study concluded that firms opting for independent leadership consistently outperformed those relying on CEO duality.

Pearce and Zahra (1991) examined the relative power of CEOs and boards of directors and their association with board performance. Their study suggested that powerful, independent boards were associated with superior corporate financial performance. The study also provided loose support for the author's typology of four board types with different emphases on the power relationship between CEO and board member. One of their most interesting findings was that more powerful board types were viewed by the CEOs as being more progressive and more encouraging and supportive of CEO efforts, which in turn raised a question about the widespread belief that CEOs desired weaker boards that rubber stamp their decisions. Promising as this line of enquiry is, replication of the findings using different populations and measures is certainly necessary to give confidence to the stated results. Behavioral evidence of board processes is also necessary in this kind of study to counter the possible self-reporting biases of CEOs.

Stewart (1991) focused not on this duality problem but on how a separate chairperson and chief executive interact. Her study of 20 general managers and their chairmen in the National Health Service (NHS) revealed the extent to which such senior roles are open to wide operational interpretation, and how different individuals come to different conclusions about their precise duties, and their relationship with the other. Perhaps because of the particular political and accountability issues in the NHS, the two roles were often seen as interdependent, complementary, indeed as a partnership. This kind of detailed, longitudinal field based study, examining from first hand reports the balance of activities, interdependencies, and choices between key figures in and around the board, is a very necessary complement to the more quantitative, correlational, and empirically distant studies which suggest board composition, power, and performance linkages.

Another tradition of research and writing on boards debates and analyzes the Berle and Means (1932) thesis that although shareholders have legal ownership and control of large corporations, they no longer effectively control them. Although this area of research has been bedevilled by conceptual disagreements about the term control (see Mizruchi, 1983 and Herman, 1981) there is now a body of analytical work in this tradition. Mace (1971) in an oft quoted study concludes that the powers of control rest with the president—not the board. Herman (1981) in an extended and subtle analysis argues that management (the CEO and inside directors) control the firm, but always in the context of the varying sets of constraints and latent powers of stakeholders such as the outside members of the board, shareholders, and at certain moments, creditors. Different studies using what Kosnik (1987) describes as the managerial hegemony theory, offer different explanations of management's control over the board. The mixture often includes the management's control over the selection of outside board members and the latter's subsequent co-optation; the limited time outsiders have to devote to their duties; the superior expertise, information, and advice available to management; and norms of board conduct which restrict the outsiders abilities to operate as strident independent voices (Mace, 1971; Herman, 1981; Lorsch and MacIver, 1989).

As we have seen, there are a host of difficulties in the research attempting to link board composition to the overall financial performance of the firm. However, recently scholars within the managerial hegemony tradition have been attempting to study the slightly more confined link between board composition and board as distinct from company financial performance. Thus Kosnik (1987), using board decisions to pay greenmail (the repurchasing of its stock at a premium above market price), and Kesner and Johnson (1990) who focused on shareholder suits rather than greenmail as an indicator of board performance, have both attempted to link board composition to board performance.

In the Kosnik (1987) study, green-mail was assumed to be universally defined as against the interests of shareholders and thus indicative of board failure to fulfill its principal function of representing shareholder interests. It was further assumed that green-mail payments allowed poor company management to consolidate its control position when faced with a challenging raider. The study found that the board's effectiveness in preventing green-mail was increased when it was composed of relatively more outside directors, more outside directors with executive experience, and more outside directors with contractual interests in the company. Thus, according to the structure of Kosnik's investigation, board composition did have an effect on board performance.

The Kesner and Johnson (1990) research operated under the assumption that the more times shareholders pressed legal charges against their board, the less effective was the board at reflecting or representing shareholder interests. In this way they hoped to evaluate the effect that a predominance of outside directors had in representing shareholder interest. Their results indicated that boards sued tended to have a greater percentage of inside directors than those not sued, a relationship that was even stronger when the CEO also had the position of chairperson. Crucial also to their findings was the apparent fact that in actual rulings against the boards there was no difference in outcome for the differently composed boards. Thus the proportion of outside to inside director was not related to the company's 'guilt' and therefore composition did not affect the degree to which shareholder's interests were represented by the board.

The use of archival data to derive indicators or surrogate measures of board composition and control is also evident in research on CEO 'golden parachutes' and board 'poison pill' (a form of takeover defence) adoption. Thus research by Cochran, Wood, and Jones (1985) and Singh and Harianto (1989) has found that greater outsider representation on the board is associated with a higher likelihood of having a golden parachute. However, contrary to hypothesis, Davis (1991) found that boards with more insiders were no more likely to adopt a poison pills takeover defence.

Methodologically adroit as the Kosnik (1987), Kesner and Johnson (1990) and Davis (1991) studies are in their clever use of surrogate measure from archival data, they cannot represent the only way forward for studies of boards of directors. All three studies utilize the crisis situations of takeover or litigation to study the performance of boards, when we perhaps also need data on the performance of boards in situations of relative normality. But these studies also suffer from their distance from the phenomenon they are addressing. As a result great inferential leaps are made from input variables such as board composition to output variables such as board performance with no direct evidence on the processes and mechanisms which presumably link the inputs to the outputs. The celebrated studies by Donaldson and Lorsch (1983) and Lorsch and MacIver (1989) get much closer to the actual operation of the strategic apex of the enterprise.

The Donaldson and Lorsch (1983) study draws on the analysis of 12 'mature successful industrial companies' from the upper half of the *Fortune* 500 list to explore the decision making behavior of corporate management (defined as the CEO and those who report directly to him). The corporate decision makers are portrayed as pursuers of corporate survival rather than shareholder wealth. The decision making process is characterized as one of great complexity and uncertainty, with beliefs and experience performing crucial roles in filtering out ambiguity in the choice process. 'Beliefs serve as uncertainty reducers and to provide continuity and stability when change threatens to undermine the lessons of experience' (1983: 80). Like Herman (1981), Donaldson and Lorsch (1983) capture the constraints on top-management choice. There is no pretense of the 'senior corporate executive as a man who moves mountains with a memo,' (1983: 172). Rather top level decision making is constrained by a combination of industry sector pathways and standards, capital market restrictions, the need to attract and retain personnel to achieve rates of growth, and by the implicit belief systems of the executives themselves.

The Donaldson and Lorsch (1983) book provided fresh direct evidence on decision making at the top without dealing specifically with the structure and dynamics of board operation. The study published in 1989 by Lorsch and MacIver responds to that gap. The Lorsch and MacIver research is exceptional not only in terms of the methodology employed, but also the nature and quality of the empirical findings. The investigation covered the period 1986–89 and involved a combination of large scale questionnaire survey, interviewing, and case study analysis. Although the response rate from the questionnaire survey of outside directors was a disappointing 32 percent, the authors claim the respondents are representative of the underlying population from which they self-selected in terms of age, primary occupation, number of directorships held and the size of companies whose boards they are on.

If this had been the sole aspect of the method employed it would have been open to serious objection from what Mace (1971: 3) had earlier described as a director's 'self serving and conscience-solving descriptive phrases of his own perception of his role as a responsible director.' Consequently the second dimension of the Lorsch and MacIver methodology, the random selection of 100 directors to be interviewed for an hour or more, is significant. In all 80 were actually spoken to (roughly the same number as in the 1971 Mace study). The interviews were conducted throughout the U.S. and in several European countries. The third and final element of the methodology involved interviews with 35 directors and other corporate officers relating to the book's four case studies of boards in crisis.

The Lorsch and MacIver (1989) book confirms the stream of work in the managerial hegemony tradition (exemplified by Mace, 1971 and Herman, 1981) that real power lies with the governed, that is the top management team, and the success or failure of individual companies normally rests with them. The problem for the outside directors on the board is to translate their legal mandate into effective power over the top managers, especially the CEO. The Lorsch and MacIver case studies illustrate how this can be achievable in crisis situations such as takeover attempts, the death or incapacity or succession of CEOs, or legal, environmental or performance threats, but control relations are quite different in normal times. Lorsch and MacIver argue that gradual declines are a tremendous challenge to directors. Their study also suggests a need for future work on boards to examine processes of problem sensing, choice, and change over longish periods of time.

The other strong feature of the Lorsch and MacIver (1989) study is their attempt to characterize directors and boards in operation. Although the Harvard study is still one stage removed from the direct observation of boards in action (for an example of this rare species of work see Alderfer, 1986) the findings of the Lorsch study do add to the little that is known about how and why the norms of conduct on boards influence power relationships between outside and inside directors and the CEO.

The study of boards and directors: A brief critique

The above brief attempts to characterize existing research on boards and directors has emphasized its limited scale and scope. It is remarkably difficult to offer a thorough going critique of a body of work which hardly exists. Indeed one might argue that the issue at present is not one of critical reflection on what exists, but the open positive encouragement of any serious social science research on the conduct and performance of boards and their directors.

At the early phases of the development of any field of research there is a requirement for certain basic descriptive information. Even given the apparent preoccupation with publicly available demographic data on board composition, and the useful contribution made by surveys conducted by, for example, the Bank of England (1985, 1988) and consultancy firms such as Korn/Ferry International (1992), there is still a need for further surveys of board member characteristics and boards structure, culture, and process, linked to theoretical traditions such as managerial hegemony and agency theory (Kosnik, 1987; Fama and Jensen, 1983; Jensen and Meckling, 1976; Davis, 1991).

Studies of the locus of power in and around the boardroom are of crucial importance not only for theorists of intraorganizational power, but also to bridge with the interlocking directorate tradition, with its interest in the structure of elite power in different industrial societies. We still know remarkably little about the behavior patterns and consequences of the CEO duality situation (where the roles of chairperson and CEO are held by the same person); or of any of the other crucial areas of relational dynamics in and around the board, for example between chairperson and CEO, CEO and outside and inside director, and inside and outside director. Indeed as Stewart (1991) and others have reminded us, we still have limited knowledge of the similarities and differences in what chairpersons, CEOs and directors actually do, and what motivates individuals to be invited, or to join boards.

Recent work by Murray, Bradshaw, and Wolpin (1992) trying to establish typologies of patterns of board power and linking those patterns to board and organizational performance, illustrates the analytical value of typologies and classificatory systems at the early development of new research fields. But again, before tenuous links can be made between independent variables and dependent variables, perhaps we need to know more about the substance we are seeking to link with other phenomena. Alongside an interest in different patterns of board power, we need to know much more about the general conduct of board affairs and how and why board processes impact on empirical patterns and theories of choice and change (Pettigrew and Whipp, 1991; Fennell and Alexander, 1989; Goodstein and Boecker, 1991).

The Pettigrew and Whipp (1991) study reminds us that the examination of choice and change processes cannot stop with the analysis of the strategic apex of the firm. Boardroom and other top influences are shaped not only by the activities of actors at other levels in and outside the firm, but also a much broader range of contextual forces and processes emanating from economic, political, and industry sector conditions. When and if the ground breaking work is done on board patterns of behavior, including questions of control, choice, and change; there will be a need in parallel or in sequence to link such analyses to the different settings and contexts in which boards operate, and ultimately to board level and firm level performance.

THE COMPOSITION AND CORRELATES OF TOP MANAGEMENT TEAMS

The Social Science literature on leadership is immense as reviews by Stogdill (1974), Bass (1990), and others can testify. However, research on leadership in bureaucratic contexts is much less developed, and still contains a number of controversies, chief amongst which is whether, and to what extent, leaders make a difference to various kinds of organizational outcomes. Recent writing by, for example, Thomas (1988), Meindl (1990), House, Spangler, and Woycke (1991), and Pettigrew and Whipp (1991) illustrate that the leadership impact debate is still very much alive. In 1984, partly as a response to the controversies around leadership studies, Hambrick and Mason published an important research agenda paper arguing that the strategic apex of firms contained more than individual leaders, and was it not time that scholars began to give more attention to top management teams. In so doing, Hambrick and Mason (1984) can justifiably argue to have created a relatively coherent stream of research with its own distinctive set of empirical findings. In this section of the paper, the aim is to describe this body of work, its assumptions and findings, strengths and weaknesses, and then suggest some complementary research themes and questions on the characteristics, conduct, and performance of top management teams.

Hambrick and Mason (1984) describe their approach as the upper echelons perspective in macro-organizational research. The target group for study is the dominant coalition of the firm and their starting general proposition was that 'organizational outcomes—both strategies and effectiveness—are viewed as reflections of the values and cognitive bases of powerful actors in the organization' (1984: 193). Eschewing 'some important but complex psychological issues,' Hambrick and Mason (1984: 196) recommend that the primary emphasis is placed on observable managerial characteristics as indicators of the givens that a manager brings to an administrative situation. 'These observable managerial givens are demographic factors such as age, tenure in the organization, functional background, education, socioeconomic roots, and financial position.'

Although the 1984 paper by Hambrick and Mason was already sensitive to problems of causality, disentangling intercorrelations and needs for time series data, and there was a special plea for clinical and statistical studies, in fact, the tradition that has emanated from the paper has largely been driven by cross-sectional studies using demographic data. Within this tradition, Hambrick and his students and colleagues have explored links between top-team characteristics, managerial discretion and corporate strategies (Finkelstein and Hambrick, 1990; Michel and Hambrick, 1992); and top-team characteristics and organizational bankruptcy (D'Aveni, 1990; Hambrick and D'Aveni, 1991). The Hambrick stimulus has also encouraged a stream of research suggesting that the integration and functioning of the top management team is at least partly affected by the demographic composition of the team (O'Reilly et al., 1993). This demographic research is now also broadening to include studies linking team characteristics to firm innovation (Bantel and Jackson, 1989), and the nature and extent of corporate strategic change, such as diversification level (Wiersema and Bantel, 1992). Another group of scholars seek to link director and top-team characteristics to firm performance (Norburn, 1986; Norburn and Birley, 1988; Keck, 1991). Inconsistent findings, particularly in linking group demography to firm performance, and whether homogeneous or heterogeneous teams contribute to team and organizational success, have forced some rethinking of the theoretical interpretations given to findings, but not yet the wholescale questioning of this style of research.

Faced with inconsistent and contradictory findings about the homogeneity/heterogeneity top team and firm performance link, Priem (1990) in a conceptual paper, argues for a curvilinear relationship between the two. In Priem's view, performance is likely to suffer with extreme levels of homogeneity or heterogeneity. The appropriate degree of homogeneity and heterogeneity is predicted on how much variation exists in the firm's environment. In stable environments, more consensus is productive, while in dynamic conditions, more heterogeneity may be required. This attempt to contextualize theory development has led to a study by Keck (1991) which found that open teams lead to higher performance in turbulent contexts and stable teams lead to higher performance in nonturbulent contexts. More importantly perhaps, as the former rather acontextual theorizing in this area is discarded, so scholars are beginning to examine the relationships, if any, between executive team context and executive team characteristics. In an important new study, Keck and Tushman (1991) are able to conclude from time series data from the United States Cement Industry from 1900–86, that within the firm, reorientation and CEO succession were both associated with significant changes into and out of the executive team, decreased team tenure and increased executive team heterogeneity. Interestingly, this study was also able to link different kinds of changes, internal and external to the firm to different forms and degrees of impact on the top team. Thus, for example, technological jolts and non-retirement successions of the CEO, were more associated with significant changes in the senior team, decreased executive team tenure and increased team heterogeneity than either changes driven by legal and/or regulatory shifts.

The above brief characterization of the Hambrick inspired research on top management teams can only give a flavor of what can be achieved by setting out an ambitious research agenda and then following through with a sustained set of empirical enquiries. Progress has been tied to a narrow focus and the rather singular use of demographic data, but the pattern of development has also been to add conceptual and analytical complexity. Control variables are now used more extensively than in the earlier input–output based work. Time series data is helping somewhat with problems of causal attribution. Early universalistic theorizing is being sharpened by the exploration of contextual variation, and notably in D'Aveni's work, there is an explicit attempt to link the top management team tradition both to the interlocking directorates research, (D'Aveni, 1990) and to agency theory (D'Aveni and Kesner, 1991). However, if the top management team tradition is not to end up as another triumph of method over substance, new questions and methods need to emerge in order to complement and redirect this research.

Top management teams: A brief critique and some suggestions

So dominated is the upper echelons perspective by demographic analysis that any assessment of its strengths and weaknesses must start there. It is probably no coincidence that a year before the Hambrick and Mason (1984) article appeared, an important review article on organizational demography was published by Pfeffer (1983). In this article Pfeffer defines what he means by organizational demography, outlines his view of the structure of demographic hypotheses and explanations, and uses a range of examples to explore the largely untested and unfulfilled promise of demographic approaches. Thus 'demography refers to the composition, in terms of basic attributes such as age, sex, educational level, length of service or residence, race and so forth of a social entity under study' Pfeffer (1983: 303). Demographic distributions are described as having a theoretical and empirical reality distinct from the aggregation of responses of individual members, and crucially, are 'readily measured and reasonably objective,' certainly as compared with a range of 'hypothetical unobservable constructs such as commitment, arousal, conflict, aspiration level, and so forth' (Pfeffer, 1983: 352). Demography is portrayed as an important causal variable that affects a number of intervening variables and processes and, through them, a number of organizational outcomes. Pfeffer illustrates the demographic characteristic (independent variable), intervening variable, and outcome variable linear-link by, for example, research on the length of service distribution of an organization, assumed intraorganizational conflict, and rates of turnover.

Pfeffer (1983) suggests the promise in such an approach will be dependent on resolving a number of empirical and philosophy of science issues. Thus empirically, to what extent does demography predict and explain variation in either the intervening construct (conflict) or the dependent variable (turnover)? But the bigger issue Pfeffer (1983: 351) describes as a matter of taste and philosophy of scientific explanation. 'To what extent is it incumbent on the research to trace through a demographic effect on the various intervening constructs; or, to what extent can the postulating effect of demographic effect and a plausible mechanism be examined simply by investigating the empirical relationship between demography and what demography affects?' (Pfeffer, 1983: 351). Pfeffer answers his own question. 'As soon as you say it is necessary to understand the intervening constructs or process, one inevitably embarks on an infinite regress of reductionism from which there is no logical escape' (Pfeffer, 1983: 352). In a carefully researched, and soundly argued article, Lawrence (1991) draws on a good deal of the organizational demography research since the Pfeffer article to present a contrary point of view.

The title of Lawrence's (1991) article, 'The Black Box of Organizational Demography' makes clear her debate with Pfeffer and also the Achilles heel of the top management team research. Basically, Lawrence challenges the demographers' assumption that the use of demographic variables as surrogates for intervening processes negates the need to study the intervening process and thereby actually tests the links between the independent variable, intervening process, and predicted outcome. Lawrence (1991) goes on to put forward a competing case that the black box (between the input and output variable) is populated by weak relationships between dependent variables and intervening constructs, by many intervening social psychological processes besides those assumed, and that perhaps the links between input and output variables are not linear and unidirectional, but dynamic and recursive. Demographic forms of analysis alone 'move researchers further and further away, both empirically and theoretically, from the actual mechanisms underlying observed relationships' (Lawrence, 1991: 21), and without the direct, concrete analysis of the intervening mechanisms and processes, how indeed can the reasons for any empirical link between input and output variable be explained?

The more damning indictment of the demography-based top management team research is that no-one has ever been anywhere near a top team in an organizational setting, either to directly observe a team in action, or to interview the members about the links between their characteristics and structure, processes of communication and decision making and their impact and performance. Recent studies, for example, by O'Reilly et al. (1993) which have tried to go beyond archival data and demographic analysis have relied upon CEO reports of top-team characteristics, structure, and dynamics. Thus enormous interpretative leaps are made from distant demographic surrogates of team characteristics such as homogeneity and heterogeneity, through unobserved and remote intervening processes such as information processing, conflict resolution, and problem solving, to outcome variables such as team effectiveness or organizational performance. The result is a series of inconsistent and inconclusive findings, for example, about the relationship between homogeneity and heterogeneity and team effectiveness (see Keck, 1991 and O'Reilly *et al.*, 1993, for reviews) and continuous problems of disentangling cause and effect. Examples of the reverse causality problem include, do long tenure top teams lead to the persistence of business strategies or are the existence of persistent strategies a cause of long tenure teams? (Finkelstein and Hambrick, 1990) And do top teams embark on diversification strategies because of their team composition, or does the pursuit of diversification lead to the creation of certain kinds of top team competences and characteristics? (Michel and Hambrick, 1992).

A further difficulty with the top management team literature is the inconsistency in defining who the top team is. Flatt (1992) is absolutely right in arguing that this issue may be crucially determining the results and in so doing contributing to inconsistency in the empirical findings. Current variants of who is in the top team include, those executives on the board, (Finkelstein and Hambrick, 1990), the CEO and direct reports, (O'Reilly *et al.*, 1992), or the two highest executive levels (Wiersema and Bantel, 1992). But this issue cannot be resolved just by the arbitrary choice of titles or levels of management. Keck (1991) has argued that some players without titles may have a role in the team, and others with titles may be marginalized. There is also the deeper issue which warrants investigation, do all executives interact as teams? Such questions can only be answered by some combination of observation and interviewing of top teams in action as has been demonstrated, for example, by Eisenhardt and Bourgeois (1988), and Eisenhardt (1989).

Some of the lines of future research on top management teams have been signaled above. Within the top team demography tradition there is a need to treat team characteristics as a dependent variable—why do teams look the way they do? With this approach can emerge more refined theoretical and empirical work contextualizing the demographic characteristic, intervening process, outcome variable, linkages. But surely the real pay-off in future work will come from a parallel research stream on top teams which examines the structure, process, and performance of top teams in action. How and why do teams emerge? How do particular constellations of complementary team assets build up, develop and dissolve in certain firms and industries at certain points in the firms trajectory of development? What cliques and cabals emerge and how is power won and lost within the team as certain key issues are resolved? How do team interpretations of leadership behavior match against previous assumptions about the heroic roles of CEOs? How do the task interdependencies within top teams and associated features of intrateam culture and power affect the control relationships between team members, the CEO, and the board? Does the character and quality of the group process impact the capacity of the team to learn and change, and if so in what way, and why does team process affect team effectiveness and ultimately the competitive performance of the firm?

CONCLUSION

All three research areas reviewed in this article have their strengths and weaknesses. In different ways, using contrasting methods and levels of analysis, they have each contributed to the little we know about managerial elites. The distinctive methodological approach in the interlocks and top management team work has given those traditions greater intellectual coherence and impact than work on boards and directors. The more scattered, limited, and prescriptive character of the boards work, has produced a less easily identifiable set of theoretical and empirical achievements. By and large all three areas of research have developed in isolation from one another. A case can certainly be made that incremental developments are possible within the logic and methods of all three areas of research. Progress is also possible, as D'Aveni (1990), Goodstein and Boeker (1991) and others have suggested, by linking some of the questions posed by the three approaches into more broadly based studies.

However, the conclusions of this paper go beyond suggestions of incremental development within each of the traditions. With a few noteworthy exceptions, all three areas of research share the common limitation of studying managerial elites several paces from the actors, processes, and issues facing those elites. Rarely can we see interlocking networks in action. We know little at first hand why directors form ties across the boundaries of their own organization, to what purposes such ties are put, and what issues are created or resolved through such behavior. Power relationships are attributed. Control relationships within and between social classes are inferred. The mobilization and use of power to achieve outcomes in line with perceived interests remain unobserved. In the top management team research, easily measurable demographic characteristics are used as surrogates for unobserved intervening processes and inferential leaps are then made to a range of organizational outcomes. The existence of a top management team is assumed. No-one sits close enough to the phenomenon to identify whether and to what extent the top team exists and through what processes the team fashions its impact. Tilting research on managerial elites towards processual studies of interlocking networks, boards, and top management teams in action is surely no longer a nice to have, but now an essential.

In making the argument for process studies of managerial elites, there is no concomitant assumption being made that the three traditions reviewed here be replaced by this alternative one. Quite the contrary, the intellectual purpose is to complement, not replace. By tilting the study of managerial elites in a process direction, new answers may be possible to previous baffling questions, new questions will emerge not posed by prevailing approaches, and new forms of knowledge can arise to inform existing empirical patterns. Of course, it is beyond the ambitions of this paper to specify in detail a range of detailed processual hypotheses on interlocking directorates and networks, boards, and top management teams. In conclusion, this paper suggests some broad areas and questions for empirical enquiry guided by a processual and contextual analysis of managerial elites.

Elsewhere this author has described a range of analytical requirements for studying processes in a contextualist manner (Pettigrew, 1985a, 1985b, 1990, 1992). In summary, six requirements call for attention. These are in turn:

1. Embeddedness, the study of processes across a number of levels of analysis;
2. Temporal interconnectedness—studying the processes in past, present, and future time;
3. A role in explanation for context and action;
4. A search for holistic rather than linear explanations of process;
5. A need to link process analysis to the location and explanation of outcomes; and,
6. A need for the researcher to balance involvement and distance with actors in the research process.

Set against these requirements, existing research in the interlocking directorates and top management team traditions, has little to offer the process analyst. Indeed the logic of both approaches eschews any real concern for process questions. In each case inputs are measured, the structure of interlocking networks or the demographic characteristics of teams and then inferences are made about the causal role of these independent variables on some dependent or outcome variables. The processes in between the input and outputs have a role in explanation but are not directly analyzed or observed. Thus the interlocks tradition is strong on describing the structural anatomy of director ties, but is largely silent on the observation of the emergence, use, and impact of such linkages. It is not surprising that doubts remain about the meaning and significance of interlocking directorates.

Any attempt to redress this imbalance between structural and process analysis would entail the following lines of questioning. Why and how do interlocking ties emerge, consolidate and dissolve? What mixed motives are behind the offering and acceptance of multiboard membership? What flows across the interlinkages, shapes those flows and with what purpose and interests in mind? How are influence processes conducted in the network and is it possible to unravel the place of influence processes from coordination, information giving and control? What indeed are the purposes of linkages and do those purposes alter over time in the context of broad changes in the political, social, economic and commercial context of the firm? Are there network stars in any set of sectoral or national patterns of interlinkage? Who are these network stars? Do they share any common social class, educational, gender, or professional characteristics? Are there common threads in the career of network stars, and how and why are they able to exert power in certain kinds of spheres of activity but not others? If as Bauer and Bertin-Mourot (1992) and Hamilton and Biggart (1988) have shown there are differences in the structure and demographic characteristics of business elites in different societies, what explains these differences and what consequences do they have for the conduct of corporate affairs within and between societies? Empirical enquiry guided by the above broad questions (and many others capable of development) will rapidly take the interlocks tradition on from the distant description of the structure of networks, to examine the substance, processes, consequences, and impact of interorganizational ties.

The black box in the top management team research contains the assumed but unobserved mediating process which are purported to link demographic characteristics with organizational outcomes. More fundamentally, however, the black box also contains the essence of enquiry for the process scholar, the emergence, developments, conduct, impact, and performance of the team itself. The actual close analysis and observation of the top team will at least help to clear up some of the intractable definitional problems of who the top team is, and whether and to what extent managers operate in groups or teams in processing strategic issues (Jackson, 1992). Rather than assuming titles and positions as indicators of involvement in choice and change processes, the first task for the process scholar is to identify which players are involved, and why. We still know little about why and how top teams and other groupings look the way they do, the processes by which top teams go about their tasks, how CEOs engage with their immediate subordinates, and how, why, and when the upper echelons engage in fundamental processes of problem sensing, decision making, learning, and change. The pessimists who consider access is never forthcoming for such research might gain some confidence from progress made in recent studies by Eisenhardt (1989), Eisenhardt and Schoonhoven (1990), and Pettigrew and Whipp (1991).

Progress in our third area of research, the study of boards and their directors, has not been helped by over-ambitious attempts to link independent variables such as board composition to outcome variables such as board and firm performance. The research agenda here need not be guided just by studies testing the relative explanatory power of agency theory or theories of managerial hegemony. The task is perhaps a simpler one, to redress the overwhelmingly prescriptive bias in this literature, and begin to provide some basic descriptive findings about boards and their directors. We need to know more about the structure and functioning of boards beyond customary preoccupations with size and composition. There are still few surveys of who external directors are, what motivates them to join boards and what they, CEOs and internal directors do. Very little is known of the relational dynamics in and around the boardroom. How relationships are formed and developed between the CEO and a separate chairman if one exists. How CEOs engage with their internal director colleagues on matters of substance, and how and why patterns of relationships between internal directors impact on their relations with external board members.

For the process scholar, however, the real fascination is with the actual operation of the board in and outside the boardroom. What is the extent of the involvement of the board in the strategy process, how and why are they involved in different kinds of issues at various time periods in the organization's development, and with what consequences? The exploration of board functioning and performance needs in the first instance to be linked to the specific concrete issues normally thought to be within the board's sphere of interest and influence. How are boards involved in processes of CEO and director selection and compensation? Who assesses the performance of the CEO, when and how?

What board committees are created for what purposes, and how does information flow in and around these committees, the board, the CEO, and individual directors? How are complementary assets of human resources on the board defined, created, and dissolved around different eras of organization development when crises of performance and succession shake the credibility of cadres of external and internal directors? How does the mobilization and use of power in and around the board impact on the major choices and changes faced by the organization? And how and why are the powerful bolstered by linkages outside the firm and checked by nonelites inside the firm? Sustained attention to these empirical questions, informed by existing theoretical advances in decision making, change, and power in and between firms, will advance our knowledge of the conduct of managerial elites in organizations.

ACKNOWLEDGEMENT

I am grateful to Matthew Pettigrew for his assistance in compiling elements of the literature for this paper.

REFERENCES

Alderfer, C. P. (November–December 1986). 'The invisible director on corporate boards', *Harvard Business Review*, pp. 2–8.
Atkinson, L. and J. Galaskiewicz (1988). 'Stock ownership and company contributions to charity', *Administrative Science Quarterly*, **30**, pp. 224–241.
Auletta, K. (1991). *Three Blind Mice: How the TV Networks Lost Their Way*. Random House, New York.
Bank of England (June 1985). 'The boards of quoted companies', *Bank of England Quarterly Bulletin*, pp. 233–236.
Bank of England (May 1988). 'Composition of company boards', *Bank of England Quarterly Bulletin*, p. 242.
Bantel, J. A. and S. E. Jackson (1989). 'Top management and innovation in banking: Does the composition of the top team make a difference?', *Strategic Management Journal*, **10**, pp. 107–124.
Bass, M. M. (1990). *Bass and Stogdill's Handbook of Leadership: Theory, Research and Managerial Applications* (3rd ed). Free Press, New York.
Bauer, M. and B. Bertin-Mourot (1992). *Les 200 en France en Allemagne*. C.N.R.S. and Heidrich and Struggles, Paris.
Baysinger, B. D. and H. D. Butler (1985). 'Corporate governance and the Board of Directors: Performance effects of changes in board composition', *Journal of Law, Economics and Organization*, **1**, pp. 101–124.
Berle, A. A. and G. C. Means (1932). *The Modern Corporation and Private Property*. Macmillan, New York.
Bradshaw, P., V. Murray and J. Wolpin (April 1982). 'Do non-profit boards make a difference? An exploration of the relationship between board structure, process and effectiveness'. Unpublished paper, Faculty of Administrative Studies, York University, Ontario.
Bryman, A. (1992). *Charisma and Leadership in Organisations*. Sage Publications, London.
Burt, R. (1980). 'Cooptive corporate actor networks: A reconsideration of interlocking directorates involving American manufacturing', *Administrative Science Quarterly*, **25**, pp. 557–582.
Burt, R. (1983). *Corporate Profits and Cooptation*. Academic Press, New York.
Cadbury, Sir Adrian (1990). *The Company Chairman*. Director Books, London.
Cadbury Report (July 1992). 'Draft Report'. Issued by the Committee on The Financial Aspects of Corporate Governance. Moorgate, London.
Charkham, J. P. (1986). *Effective Boards*. Chartac, London.
Clawson, D., A. Neustadtl and D. Scott (1992). *Money Talks: Corporate Pace and Political Influence*. Basic Books, New York.
Cochran, P. L., R. A. Wood and T. B. Jones (1985). 'The composition of Boards of Directors and the incidence of golden parachutes', *Academy of Management Journal*, **28**, pp. 664–671.
D'Aveni, R. A. (1990). 'Top managerial prestige and organizational bankruptcy', *Organization Science*, **1**(2) pp. 121–142.
D'Aveni, R. A. and I. F. Kesner (1991). 'Top managerial prestige, power and tender offers: A study of elite social networks and target firm cooperation during takeovers', Unpublished paper. Amos Tuck School, Dartmouth College, Hanover, NH.
Davis, G. F. (1991). 'Agents without principles? The spread of the poison pill through the intercorporate network', *Administrative Science Quarterly*, **36**, pp. 583–613.
Davis, G. F. (March 1992). 'The interlock network as a self-reproducing social structure', Unpublished paper. Kellogg Graduate School of Management, Northwestern University.
Davis, G. F. and W. W. Powell (1992). 'Organization—environment relations'. In M. Dunnette and L. M. Hough (eds.), *Handbook of Industrial and Organization Psychology*, 2nd edn., Consulting Psychologists Press, Palo Alto, CA, pp. 315–375.
Donaldson, G. and J. Lorsch (1983). *Decision Making at the Top: The Shaping of Strategic Direction*. Basic Books, New York.
Dooley, P. (1969). 'The interlocking directorate', *American Economic Review*, **59**, pp. 314–323.
Eisenhardt, K. M. and L. J. Bourgeois (1988). 'Politics of strategic decision making in high velocity environments: Toward a midrange theory', *Academy of Management Journal*, **31**(4) pp. 737–770.
Eisenhardt, K. M. (1989). 'Making fast strategic decisions in high velocity environments', *Academy of Management Journal*, **33**(3), pp. 543–576.
Eisenhardt, K. M. and C. B. Schoonhoven (1990). 'Organizational growth: Linking founding team, strategy, environment and growth and US semi-

conductor ventures, 1978–88', *Administrative Science Quarterly*, **35**, pp. 504–529.

Fama, E. F. and M. C. Jensen (1983). 'Separation of ownership and control', *Journal of Law and Economics*, **26**, pp. 327–349.

Fennell, M. L. and J. A. Alexander (Summer 1989). 'Governing boards and profound organizational change in hospitals', *Medical Care Review*, **46**(2) pp. 157–187.

Field, G. W. and J. Higley (1980). *Elitism*. Routledge, London.

Finkelstein, S. and D. Hambrick (1990). 'Top management—team tenure and organizational outcomes: The moderating work of managerial discretion', *Administrative Science Quarterly*, **35**, pp. 484–503.

Flatt, S. (1992). 'A longitudinal study in organizational innovativeness: How top team demography influences organizational innovation', PhD Dissertation. University of California, Berkeley.

Fligstein, N. (1990). *The Transformation of Corporate Control*. Harvard University Press, Cambridge, MA.

Gabarro, J. J. (1987). *The Dynamics of Taking Charge*. Harvard Business School Press, Boston, MA.

Galaskiewicz, J. (1985). *Social Organization of an Urban Grants Economy*. Academic Press, Orlando, FL.

Gersick, C. J. G. (1988). 'Time and transition in work teams: Towards a new model of group development', *Academy of Management Journal* **31**(1), pp. 9–41.

Giddens, A. (1974). 'Elites in the British class structure'. In P. Stanworth and A. Giddens (eds.), *Elites and Power in British Society*. Cambridge University Press, Cambridge, pp. 3–22.

Glasberg, D. S. and M. Schwartz (1983). 'Ownership and control of corporations', *Annual Review of Sociology*, **9**, pp. 311–332.

Goodstein, J. and W. Boeker. (1991). 'Turbulence at the top: A new perspective on governance structure changes and strategic change', *Academy of Management Journal*, **34**(2), pp. 306–330.

Granovetter, M. (1985). 'Economic action and social structure: The problem of embeddedness', *American Journal of Sociology*, **91**, pp. 481–510.

Hambrick, D. C. and P. A. Mason (1984). 'Upper echelons: The organization as a reflection of its top managers', *Academy of Management Review*, **9**(2), pp. 193–206.

Hambrick, D. C. and R. A. D'Aveni (September 1991). 'Top team deterioration as part of the downward spiral of large corporate bankruptcies', unpublished paper. Columbia Business School.

Hamilton, G. G. and N. W. Biggart (1988). 'Market, culture and authority; A comparative analysis of management and organization', *American Journal of Sociology*, **94**, pp. 552–594.

Hermalin, B. E. and M. S. Weisbach (1991). 'The effects of board composition and direct incentives on firm performance', *Financial Management*, **20**(4) pp. 101–112.

Herman, E. S. (1981). *Corporate Control, Corporate Power*. Cambridge University Press, New York.

Hirsch, P. M. (1982). 'Network data versus personal accounts: The normative culture of interlocking directorates', unpublished paper. Graduate School of Business, University of Chicago.

House, R. J., W. D. Spangler and J. Woycke (1991). 'Personality and charisma in the US Presidency: A psychological theory of leader effectiveness', *Administrative Science Quarterly*, **36**, pp. 364–396.

Jackson, S. E. (1992). 'Consequences of group composition for the interpersonal dynamics of strategic issue processing'. In P. Shrivastava, A. Huff and J. Dutton (eds.), *Advances in Strategic Management*, Vol.8, JAI Press, Greenwich, CT. pp. 345–382.

Jensen, M. C. and W. H. Meckling (1976). 'Theory of the firm: Managerial behavior, agency costs and ownership structure', *Journal of Financial Economics*, **3**, pp. 305–360.

Johnson, G. (1987). *Strategic Change and the Management Process*. Basil Blackwell, Oxford.

Kahl, J. (1957). *The American Class Structure*. Rinehart, New York.

Keck, S. L. (1991). 'Top executive team structure: Does it matter anyway?', unpublished paper, School of Business, Texas A & M University.

Keck, S. L. and M. Tushman (1991). 'Environmental and organizational context and executive team characteristics', unpublished paper. School of Business, Texas A & M University.

Kesner, I. F. and R. B. Johnson (1990). 'An investigation of the relationship between board composition and stockholder suit', *Strategic Management Journal*, **11**, pp. 327–336.

Kimberly, J. R. and E. J. Zajac (1988). 'The dynamics of CEO/board relations'. In D. C. Hambrick (ed.), *The Executive Effect: Concepts and Methods for Studying Top Managers*. JAI Press, Greenwich, CT.

Korn/Ferry International (1992). *Boards of Directors Study UK 1992*. Korn Ferry, London.

Kosnik, R. D. (1987). 'Greenmail: A study of board performance in corporate governance', *Administrative Science Quarterly*, **32**, pp. 163–185.

Lawrence, B. S. (April 1991). 'The black box of organizational demography', unpublished paper. Anderson Graduate School of Management, UCLA.

Loose, P. and J. Yelland (1987). *The Company Director: His Functions, Powers and Duties*. Jordan & Sons, Bristol.

Lorsch, J. W. and E. MacIver (1989). *Pawns and Potentates: The Reality of America's Corporate Boards*. Harvard Business School Press, Boston, MA.

Mace, M. (1971). *Directors: Myth and Reality*. Harvard University Press, Cambridge, MA.

Mechanic, D. (1964). 'Sources of power of lower participants in complex organizations', *Administrative Science Quarterly*, **7**(3) pp. 349–364.

Meindle, R. R. (1990). 'On leadership: An alternative to the conventional wisdom'. In B. Staw and

L. Cummings (eds.), *Research in Organizational Behavior*, Vol. 12, pp. 159–203.

Michel, J. G. and D. C. Hambrick (1992). 'Diversification posture and top management team characteristics', *Academy of Management Journal*, **35**(1), pp. 9–37.

Mintz, B. and M. Schwartz (1985). *The Power Structure of American Business*. Chicago University Press, Chicago, IL.

Mizruchi, M. S. (1983). 'Who controls whom? An examination of the relations between management and board directors in large American corporations', *Academy of Management Review*, **8**, pp. 426–435.

Mizruchi, M. S. (1984). 'Review of Johannes M. Pennings, Interlocking Directorates', *Administrative Science Quarterly*, **29**, pp. 142–145.

Mizruchi, M. S. (1992). *The Structure of Corporate Political Action: Interfirm Relations and their Consequences*. Harvard University Press, Boston, MA.

Mizruchi, M. S. and M. Schwartz (eds.) (1987). *Intercorporate Relations: The Structural Analysis of Business*. Cambridge University Press, New York.

Murray, V., P. Bradshaw, and J. Wolpin (1992). 'Power in and around non-profit boards', unpublished paper. Faculty of Administrative Studies, York University, Ontario.

Norburn, D. (1986). 'GoGo's, YoYo's and Dodo's: Company directors and industry performance', *Strategic Management Journal*, **7**, pp. 101–117.

Norburn, D. (1989). 'The chief executive: A breed apart:', *Strategic Management Journal*, **10**, pp. 1–15.

Norburn, D. and S. Birley (1988). 'The top management team and corporate performance', *Strategic Management Journal*, **9**, pp. 225–237.

O'Reilly, C. A. III, R. C. Snyder and J. N. Boothe (1993). 'Effects of executive team demography on organizational change'. In G. Huber and W. Glick (eds), *Organizational Change and Redesign: Ideas and Insights for Improving Performance*. Oxford University Press, New York, pp. 147–175.

Pahl, R. E. and J. T. Winkler (1974). 'The economic elite: Theory and practice'. In P. J. Stanworth and A. Giddens (eds.), *Elites and Power in British Society*. Cambridge University Press, Cambridge.

Palmer, D. (1983). 'Broken ties: Interlocking directorates and intercorporate coordination', *Administrative Science Quarterly*, **28**, pp. 40–55.

Palmer, D., P. D. Jennings, and X. Zhou (1989). 'Growth strategies and institutional prescriptions: Adoption of the multi-divisional form by large US corporations, 1963–1968'. Paper presented to the American Sociological Association, Annual Meeting 1989.

Pearce, J. A. and S. A. Zahra (1991). 'The relative power of CEO's and boards of directors: Association with corporate performance', *Strategic Management Journal*, **12** (2) pp. 135–153.

Pettigrew, A. M. (1973). *The Politics of Organisational Decision Making*. Tavistock, London.

Pettigrew, A. M. (1985a). *The Awakening Giant: Continuity and Change in ICI*. Basil Blackwell, Oxford.

Pettigrew, A. M. (1985b). 'Contextualist research: A natural way to link theory and practice'. In E. E. Lawler (ed.), *Doing Research That is Useful in Theory and Practice*. Jossey-Bass, San Francisco, CA, pp. 222–248.

Pettigrew, A. M. (1990). 'Longitudinal field research on change: Theory and practice', *Organizational Science*, **1** (3), pp. 267–292.

Pettigrew, A. M. (Winter, 1992). 'The character and significance of strategy process research', *Strategic Management Journal*, **13** (this issue).

Pettigrew, M. A. (July 1992). 'Boards of Directors: A review of recent research', Working Paper, Centre for Corporate Strategy and Change, University of Warwick.

Pettigrew, A. M. and R. Whipp (1991). *Managing Change for Competitive Success*. Basil Blackwell, Oxford.

Pfeffer, J. (1972). 'Size and composition of corporate Boards of Directors: The organization and its environment', *Administrative Science Quarterly*, **17**, pp. 218–228.

Pfeffer J. (1983). 'Organizational Demography'. In B. Staw and L. Cummings (eds.), *Research in Organizational Behavior*, Vol. 5. JAI Press, Greenwich, CT, pp. 299–357.

Pfeffer, J. and G. Salancik (1978). *The External Control of Organizations: A Resource Dependence Perspective*. Harper and Row, New York.

Priem, R. L. (1990). 'Top management team group factors, consensus, and firm performance', *Strategic Management Journal*, **11**(6) pp. 469–478.

Rechner, P. L. and D. R. Dalton (1991). 'CEO duality and organizational performance: A longitudinal analysis', *Strategic Management Journal*, **12**, pp. 155–165.

Scott, J. (1991). 'Networks of corporate power: A comparative assessment', *Annual Review of Sociology*, **17**, pp. 181–203.

Singh, H. and F. Harianto (1989). 'Management–board relationships, takeover risk, and the adoption of golden parachutes', *Academy of Management Journal*, **32**, pp. 7–24.

Smith, C., J. Child and M. Rowlinson (1991). *Reshaping Work: The Cadbury Experience*. University of Cambridge Press, Cambridge.

Sonquist, J. A. and T. Koenig (1975). 'Interlocking directorates in the top USA corporations: A graph theory approach', *The Insurgent Sociologist*, **5**, pp. 196–229.

Stewart, R. (1991). 'Chairmen and chief executives: An exploration of their relationship', *Journal of Management Studies*, **28**(5) pp. 511–527.

Stinchcombe, A. L. (1990). 'Weak structural data', a review of intercorporate relations'. In M. S. Mizruchi and M. Schwartz (eds.), *Contemporary Sociology*, **19**, pp. 380–382.

Stogdill, R. M. (1974). *Handbook of Leadership: A Survey and Research*. Free Press, New York.

Stokman, F. N., J. P. Scott and R. Ziegler (eds.) (1985). *Networks of Corporate Power*. Polity Press, Cambridge.

Thomas, A. B. (1988). 'Does leadership make a difference to organizational performance?' *Adminis-*

trative Science Quarterly, **33**, pp. 388–400.

Tricker, R. I (1978). *The Independent Director: A Study of the Non-Executive Director and of the Audit Committee*. Tolley, Croydon.

Useem, M. (1984). *The Inner Circle*. Oxford University Press, New York.

Useem, M. (1991). 'Organizational and managerial factors in the shaping of corporate social and political action'. In *Research in Corporate Social Performance and Policy*, Vol. 12. JAI Press, Greenwich, CT, pp. 63–92.

Vancil, R. F. (1987). *Passing the Baton: Managing the Process of CEO Succession*. Harvard Business School Press, Boston, MA.

Whitt, J. A. (1982). *Urban Elites and Mass Transportation*. Princeton University Press, Princeton, NJ.

Wiersema, M. F. and K. A. Bantel (1992). 'Top management team demography and corporate strategy change', *Academy of Management Journal*, **35**(1) pp. 91–121.

Wilson, C. S. and T. Lupton (1959). 'The bank rate tribunal: The social background and connections of top decision makers', *Manchester School of Social and Economic Studies*, **27**, pp. 30–51.

Zajac, E. J. (1988). 'Interlocking directorates as an interorganizational strategy: A test of critical assumptions'. *Academy of Management Journal*, **31**, pp. 428–438.

Zajac, E. J. (1990). 'CEO selection, succession, compensation and firm performance: A theoretical synthesis and empirical analysis', *Strategic Management Journal*, **11**, pp. 217–230.

Zajac, E. J. (1992). 'Interlocking directorates research and the study of boards of directors', unpublished paper. Kellogg School of Management, Northwestern University, Evanston, IL.

Zeitlin, M. (1974). 'Corporate ownership and control: The large corporation and the capitalist class', *American Journal of Sociology*, **79**, pp. 1073–1119.

The Visionary View

TOP MANAGEMENT TEAMS AND ORGANIZATIONAL RENEWAL

DAVID K. HURST
Federal Industries Metals Group, Toronto, Ontario, Canada

JAMES C. RUSH and RODERICK E. WHITE
School of Business Administration, University of Western Ontario, London, Ontario, Canada

Increasingly the makeup of the top management group is believed to affect the development, identification and exploitation of strategic opportunities. This paper explains a creative management model, which goes beyond conventional strategic management, and identifies the behaviors of top managers needed for the ongoing renewal of their business. It is proposed these behaviors cluster and can be aligned with different and distinct cognitive styles or types. The implication is that top management groups should be composed of a mix of types. This paper posits a mix of Jungian types, Intuitives, Feelers, Thinkers and Sensors. This diversity can yield great strength if the differences can be focused and unified. Propositions and suggestions for further empirical research are developed.

The strategic management (SM) framework which has evolved over the past 40 years and has come to dominate North American thinking about the principal functions of senior managers has, more recently, been the subject of a good deal of criticism, both from practitioners (Peters and Waterman, 1983) and theoreticians (Weick, 1979; Pascale, 1984). It seems that while the conventional SM process allows managers to maintain, direct and improve existing activities, it is less able to promote and accommodate the radical ideas and innovative behaviors needed to renew established businesses. Indeed it may be counter-productive in this regard.

With its emphasis on problem-solving, the SM framework implicitly stresses the role of the senior, synoptic, singular executive: one individual, or group with an established understanding of how the business functions. Within this group there exists a shared 'cause map' (Weick, 1979) or a 'dominant logic' (Prahalad and Bettis, 1986): a structure of knowledge about their business, which for them defines 'rationality'. Facts which can be plotted onto this map of the business are accepted; data which cannot be assigned coordinates are not perceived, are ignored if they are perceived or are treated as an aberration.

For the top management group, behaviors consistent with rational thought are implied. Individuals predisposed to plan, act and evaluate would fit; others, with different behavioral predispositions, would not. Intuition, insight and feelings are suppressed because they do not fit within the accepted SM process. Individuals openly exhibiting these types of behaviors cannot be accommodated within the conventional SM framework and are often excluded from the process, even though their contributions may be valuable. SM fits the people within its rational-analytic procedures, rather than expanding the process to fit the people, and their different abilities, predispositions and preferences.

For these reasons dissatisfaction with the SM framework has increased, resulting in a renewed focus on the top management group, the dominant coalition (Cyert and March, 1963), as it impacts firm strategy and organizational performance. As Hambrick (1987: 88) explains, 'This view contends that performance of an organization is ultimately a reflection of its top managers.' Implicitly this view holds that when it comes to understanding strategy and performance, the people are equally as important, and perhaps more important, than the process. But neither is this view entirely

0143–2095/89/050087–19$09.50
© 1989 by John Wiley & Sons, Ltd.

satisfactory, for it ignores the processes needed by any large organization to make decisions and take concerted action. Even more importantly, it lacks a sense for the role and function of the executive group.

The composition, or form of the top management group needs to be related to its function. Barnard (1938: 215) contends 'Executive work is not that *of* the organization, but the specialized work of *maintaining* the organization in operation.' When narrowly interpreted, this view can be construed as supporting the limited plan–act–evaluate functions for the executive implicit in the SM model. However, in any changing, competitive environment, long-term maintenance/existence of the business requires the ongoing (re)creation of the business and the logic by which it is managed. This renewal, too, is a critical executive function.

Large organizations require a process for taking concerted actions. The broad-based adoption of SM technology suggests it has fulfilled a need in this regard. We must be careful not to discard, out of hand, even a partially useful process. The SM model is powerful because it prescribes a process, as well as a function (or functions) for the top management group within that process. However, the process and prescribed functions are limited and do not take advantage of the full range of human cognitive abilities. The SM framework is not so much incorrect as it is incomplete. A broader perspective on the top management process, an enhanced model, taking more complete advantage of the human potential, could help bridge the gap between the appropriate function of the executive and the makeup of the top management group.

BEYOND STRATEGIC MANAGEMENT

Stepping back and viewing the question from a philosophical perspective, the SM framework's principal shortcoming is its base in a naive realism. It tacitly assumes that reality is a given which exists 'out there' and is accessible through our senses. These sensations, these supposed objective perceptions or facts, can then be subjected to rational thought. Although the need for action is recognized, it is regarded largely as the servant of thought. Facts evaluated by a rational analytic thinking process are regarded as more important than insight, feelings and even empirical experience! The classic SM framework emphasizes the use of conscious, analytic thought processes to the exclusion of any other; even though non-rational or, to use Barnard's word, 'non-logical' processes and their importance have long been recognized (Barnard, 1938; McKenney and Keen, 1974; Mintzberg, 1976).

In a recent article, Hurst (1986) suggested that the emphasis of the SM framework on logic and rationality precludes it from being helpful in the innovative, creative processes which allow organizations to enact fundamental change, to renew themselves. Logic and rationality depend upon normative structures based in the past, and methodologies such as SM which appeal to norms of rationality—measurability, efficiency, consistency—perpetuate the past. In short, because SM is based on a logic developed from past experiences, it is an appropriate methodology for defending an established business, but is less able to prospect. It cannot deal well with novelty and ambiguity; it cannot bring into being those new activities which lie outside the structure of the managers' current understanding of their existing business, but which may well be required as part of tomorrow's business.

A classic example of a flawed logic based upon past experiences is illustrated by the actions of Sewell Avery, CEO of Montgomery Ward following World War II. Avery convinced himself, based upon a study of economic history and his own experiences after World War I, that economic depressions followed wars. Based on this logic, Montgomery Ward, in the years following 1945, did not expand, and even deferred basic maintenance expenditures in order to preserve cash for the anticipated depression. Meanwhile Robert Wood at Sears correctly perceived the 'tremendous foundation of purchasing power that had been held back by the war'. Sears expanded aggressively to become the dominant U.S. department store chain. Avery was forced to depart Wards in 1955 (Worthy, 1984: 219).

The Avery story provides a simple, yet dramatic, example of a flawed logic retrospectively derived from past experiences. The complex of logics and their relationships underlying a sophisticated SM approach in any large organization are many, subtle and difficult to surface. However, business redefinition requires a shift in the logic that is imbedded in any well-developed

SM process. Conventional SM incorporates no means to unlearn what has been learnt, although there have been developments in this direction (DeGeus, 1988). To deal conceptually with this shortcoming, Hurst (1986) has extended the SM framework to encompass what he calls the creative management model.

The creative management model

The creative management (CM) model is built on the philosophical assumption that the real world which surrounds the organization is a dynamic construct enacted by the members of the organization over time. This view is shared by Weick (1979: 228), as he explains, 'the environment is viewed as an output rather than an input. On the basis of enactments and interpretations people construct a belated picture of some environment that could have produced these actions.' Organizational realities, like personal realities, consist of complex interactions of the objective, tangible ('out there') and the subjective cognitive ('in here') elements.

Implicit in the CM model is the assertion that organizations capable of creating tomorrow's businesses while maintaining today's will require a diverse group of senior managers, able to perceive the world differently, yet able to participate in a process that transcends these different views to enact a complex organizational reality. In the CM framework the emphasis is on top management teams which can envision, or recognize and frame, new opportunities, as well as solve or exploit them (Bower, 1982). By embracing recognition, opportunity-framing and problem-solving, the CM model subsumes strategic management and provides additional insights into the composition, leadership and processes of top management teams.

As illustrated in Figure 1, the CM process is conceived of as passing through four levels or modes of cognition. When (subjective) time is considered, the model incorporates seven recursive and not necessarily completely sequential stages whereby an original idea is transformed from an intuitive insight, a vision, into action— eventually to become a remembered 'reality'. Tracking the progress of an idea from its original conception to its final realization helps to explain the model. The classic SM model deals explicitly with only Stages 3 through 5, the 'plan–act–evaluate' stages. Because it does not consider the cognitive levels of intuition and feeling, the SM framework is unable to supply insight into the nature of recognition by organizations. How do organizations come to fundamentally new approaches to the way they go about their business? How do they learn? By ignoring the other stages in the process and overemphasizing the linear, in what is in fact a recursive process, the SM paradigm misses key aspects of the creative learning process.

The CM model makes it clear that strategic thinking (Stage 3) does not take place without antecedents. It is based heavily upon earlier expectations and past experiences (Stages 4 through 7), modified by what happens in Stages 1 and 2. In addition, rationality depends on logic structures developed after action. People, and especially organizations, truly understand (Stage 5) only after they act (Stage 4), not before. Anything else is speculation. The model makes it clear that radical innovation (Stage 1) represents a break with the thought structures, the logic of the past. Initially, an innovation will not be based on rationality and logic because the supporting conceptual structures are not yet in place. Conversely, highly structured thought, as well as tradition, can interfere with, and inhibit, insight and innovation.

Thus, in the CM model a strategy is initially a *post-hoc* rationalization of a successful activity. As Weick (1979: 188) explains:

> The only thing that can be selected and preserved is something that is already there. This simple reality keeps getting lost amidst the preoccupation of people in organizations with planning, forecasting, anticipating and predicting. . . . Organizations formulate strategy *after* they implement it, not before. . . . The more common (and misleading) way to look at this sequence in organizations is to say that first comes strategy and then comes implementation. That commonplace recipe ignores the fact that meaning is always imposed after elapsed actions are available for review.

As the activity becomes standardized, feedback from Stage 5 to Stage 3 occurs. Successful behaviors are interpreted into a causal model which drives the organization's routines and corrects deviations from course.

By making explicit the dimension of time the CM model allows the renewal function to be

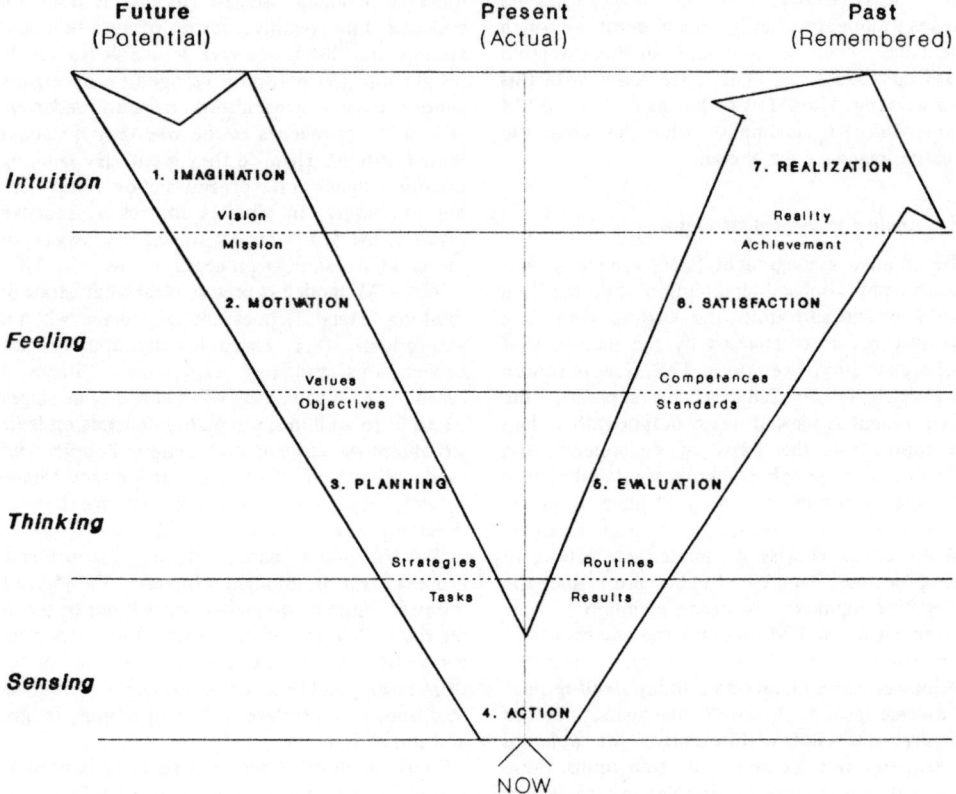

Figure 1. The creative management model

seen as a learning process. The time dimension in Figure 1 is not the objective time of physics but subjective time, views of the future and memories of the past as seen from the perpetual 'now' in which all human cognitive systems function (Jaques, 1982). With subjective time the creative process can be seen to be a learning process whereby successful innovations within an organization, new logics for doing business, are institutionalized and made routine. Not all organizations, and more particularly not all top management groups, are necessarily equally adept at, and receptive to, the development of new logics. These biases may be reflected in the organization's pattern of actions, its strategy.

There is more to the CM model than the capacity for prospective or retrospective thought. The model, as shown in Figure 1, contends that different modes of cognition are dominant at different levels in the process. These different modes are believed to have an underlying relationship with subjective time orientation; sensing may be associated more with the present, intuition more with the future (Mann, Siegler and Osmond, 1971) and one might also suspect with the remembered past (in contrast to the experience of the present). But, more fundamentally, these different modes are believed to represent distinct cognitive preferences.

Cognitive modes

The different levels in the CM model are related to and emphasize different modes of cognition corresponding to the four fundamental psychological functions outlined by Jung (1960). These

Table. 1. Level in the CMM and Cognitive Model

CM Level	Function	
	Information Gathering	Information Evaluation
I	INTUITION	
II		FEELING
III		THINKING
IV	SENSATION	

processes are arranged by CM level and function in Table 1. Jung contends that while all individuals have the capacity for, and make use of, all four modes, each has a dominant function. The Myers Briggs Type Indicator (MBTI) (Myers, 1962) has been used extensively as a measure of an individual's preference on each of these four functions.

The two information gathering modes are *Sensation* (S) and *Intuition* (N). *Sensation* mediates the perception of physical stimuli via the five senses. Through *Sensation* an individual becomes conscious that something exists physically. *Intuition*, on the other hand, mediates perception via what is thought to be an unconscious patterning process—the individual goes beyond the differentiations yielded by the *Sensation* process to see whole relationships and patterns, either in the world of physical phenomena (Extrovert preference), or in the world of ideas (Introvert preference).[1] By allowing the detection of gaps between perceived parts this mode gives individuals the ability to see unrealized potential within the stream of events which surround them. *Sensation* and *Intuition* then are opposite but complementary mental processes used to gather information about the world.

The two information evaluation modes are *Thinking* (T) and *Feeling* (F). Each mode appeals to a different type of evaluative process. *Thinking* links ideas impersonally using logic and notions of cause and effect. *Feeling*, on the other hand, bases evaluation on personal and group values. As Jung makes clear, *Thinking* and *Feeling* are complementary functions for the *evaluation* of information, just as *Sensing* and *Intuition* are complementary processes used in the *gathering* of information. Each process within a pair is in tension with the other, but it can be a creative tension. Subjective time is the dimension which mediates the tension. It is these functions or layers which creative management must transcend.

The levels in the CM process are layered to reflect the renewal function of the executive as it relates to Jung's cognitive functions. Sensing deals with physical stimuli, action and reaction, in the here and now. Behaviors based simply on sensation can be thought of as reflexive; a stimulus evokes an instinctive or reflex response. Actions, other than reflex responses, have input from the higher levels. For example, the thinking–planning level will, based upon accepted logics, delineate tasks to guide action. The results of actions taken also feed back into the thinking/evaluation activity. Sensing and thinking are adjacent layers in the model because, prescriptively, prospective thinking precedes, and retrospective analysis, or sensemaking, follows action.

At the intuitive level a vision or insight into a new way of doing business does not by itself result in action. Because it is outside the established logic of the business, it cannot be evaluated by the thinking process. Therefore its worth, whether positive or negative, cannot be logically derived and must be based upon personal or group values. A positive feeling must be created for the idea if it is to overcome the established logic, result in action and thus change the understanding of the business. Accordingly, the feeling mode is positioned between the intuition and thinking layers in the model.

The layering in the CM model is based upon Jung's conception of the 'psychological functions' for several reasons. This conception may be related to basic human physiology. As Taggart and Robey (1981: 189) point out, 'Jung's theory of personality identifies two dimensions of human information processing that seem directly related to right and left brain activity.' Typically, *Sensing* and *Thinking* are left hemisphere related and *Intuition* and *Feeling* right hemisphere related. This duality and Jung's conception may have deep and perhaps related roots in human information processing, psychology and philosophy. Although there are other cognitive typologies (Hampden-Turner, 1982; Gardener, 1985) on which a model of creative management could be built, in our

---
[1] Jung described Extroversion and Introversion as orientations in attitudes of personality. This distinction can be helpful in a detailed understanding of the CMM and management teams, but will not be developed in this paper.

estimation none has as strong a conceptual and philosophical base for this application. However, in the last analysis this model will be judged by its utility; the meaningful implications it has for the practice of management.

Top managers' behaviours and cognitive preference

The conceptual linkages between the creative management process, cognitive mode and behaviors are sketched in Table 2. Although the empirical relationships require further validation, the table is adapted from existing empirical evidence (Myers, 1962; Keirsey and Bates, 1978; Macdaid, McCaulley and Kainz, 1986). There are other possible arrangement of type (Mitroff and Kilmann, 1975; Keirsey and Bates, 1978). However they tend to be finer-grained, employing more, mixed preferences than the four utilized in Table 2. Given our current understanding, the arrangement in Table 2 seems to depict the most natural flow through the stages of the creative management process.

The cognitive preferences, or types, outlined above cover the spectrum of ways in which information is gathered and evaluated by individuals. In Table 2 each type has been associated with particular cluster of behaviors and positioned within the layers of the CM model. The implication is that to effectively handle a creative process a management group needs these different

Table 2. Relationship between cognitive preference and behaviors

Level in CM process	Cognitive preference	Concerned with	Handle these with	Tends to be	Examples of behaviors
I	Intuition	Possibilities and patterns, ideas	Metaphors and symbols	Ingenious and integrative	Sees what others do not. Espouses new ways of working at things. Proposes new ideas. Disregards practical details. Describes with metaphors and symbols. Creates organizational stories and myths.
II	Feeling	People and values	Force of personality	Enthusiastic and insightful	Inspires peers and subordinates. Responds to a challenge. Sponsors new ideas. Shares information, power and resources. Brings people together. Rewards with recognition and praise. Promulgates organizational stories and myths.
III	Thinking	Cause and effect things	Regulations and language	Reliable and orderly	Matches goals to resources to results (i.e. plans). Organizes people; coordinates. Balances novel with routine. Rewards when outcome exceeds plan.
IV	Sensation	Activities, events	Spontaneity and action	Adaptable and practical	Matches skills to tasks. Attention to practical details. Makes things work. Describes what has occurred in concrete terms. Results are their own reward.

Source: Adapted from Myers (1962) and Keirsey and Bates (1978).

behaviors, and accordingly should be composed of individuals with the different cognitive preferences. Although individuals may be able to exhibit a variety of behaviors it is unlikely they will be equally able at each set of behaviors, or indifferent amongst them. They will have a preference.

Of course, cognitive preference is not the only factor to consider in forming a top management team. The model does not indicate the sources of the raw material for cognition, what information is gathered (and evaluated). However, it is reasonable to expect that, within limits, variety in output (actions) is related to variety of input (information). Much of the information available to a top management group will be directly related to the personal background and experience of team members. Simon (1988: 16) contends that 'expertness is the prerequisite to creativity'. He suggests that experts have 50,000 'chunks' of knowledge in their area of expertise which it takes at least 10 years of experience to acquire. But not every expert (with 50,000 chunks of knowledge in a given area) can necessarily use that knowledge creatively.

Indeed, as Koestler (1976) reports, often the insight occurs after the idea generators have disassociated themselves from the specifics of the puzzle they are attempting to solve. James Watson, whose insight uncovered the double-helix structure of DNA, recounts his need to remove himself from data derived from months of chemical and X-ray experiments, while Francis Crick, his co-researcher, felt a need to remain immersed in the data. (Sensation-Thinking preference versus Intuition-Thinking preference?)

The next few days saw Francis becoming increasingly agitated by my failure to stick close to the molecular models.... Almost every afternoon, knowing that I was on the tennis court, he would fretfully twist his head away from his work to see the polynucleotide backbone unattended.... Francis' grumbles did not disturb me, however, because further refining of our latest backbone without a solution to the bases would not represent a real step forward (Watson, 1969: 114).

None of this is to diminish the importance of expertise acquired through diligence and hard work, but rather to suggest other factors are also at work. We would argue that individual cognitive preference merits consideration. The involvement of different cognitive preferences at different stages in the process and linking the stages together over time has not received the attention it deserves, either in theory or in practice.

Creative management: a need for integration

The argument has been made above that an effective CM process requires different behaviors, and therefore cognitive styles consistent with the roles implicit in the different layers of the CM model. With such differentiation in cognitive orientations comes a need for integration (Lawrence and Lorsch, 1969)—a way of allowing for, or facilitating, the exchanges necessary to bring about coherent action. The most efficient means of achieving the required integration depends on the type of interdependence (Thompson, 1967; Galbraith, 1973). As illustrated in Table 3, the CM process presents different types of interdependences between its different levels.

Table 3. Integrating cognitive types and levels within the creative management process

Level	Cognitive type	Concern	Integrative mechanism	Type of interdependence
I	Intuitive	Patterns and possibilities, ideas	Individual's perceptive abilities	Independent
II	Feeler	People	Informal, face-to-face	Reciprocal
III	Thinker	Cause and effect, plans	Task forces	Reciprocal/sequential
IV	Sensor	Activities, events	Policies, procedures, rules, hierarchy	Sequential

In explaining the interdependences it is helpful to make the simplifying assumption of a different individual at each level. Even though radically new ideas may be stimulated by certain antecedent conditions, they seem to be the independent creation of a single mind (with intuitive preferences and abilities) (Koestler, 1976). Generating new insights is not thought to be a group activity. Once discerned the exchange between the intuitive, idea generator, and the feeler would appear to be reciprocal. If the feeler is to inspire and energize the organization, the feeler and idea generator must talk face-to-face. (They can, of course, be one and the same person.) The feeler must appreciate the idea sufficiently well to move it forward. This requires the feeler to listen to, and question, the idea generator. Also it is likely that articulating the idea causes the idea generator to better define his 'vision'.

Because the idea cannot be evaluated logically the feeler must not only communicate it to the thinker, but also create a sense of energy and excitement about the idea. The thinker can then prepare for implementation. This relationship is also a reciprocal type of interdependence, but may tend towards the sequential as the link between idea generator and feeler may need to be richer interpersonally than the link between feeler and thinker. Given the nature of the task, and their concern for people, feelers are likely to use task forces to accomplish the necessary integration.

The link between thinkers and sensors can be more sequential. Once the thinker has 'planned' for implementation the sensor's role (doing) can be communicated by policy, procedures, rules and specification of tasks (hierarchy). However, to the extent the new idea requires new tasks which are in conflict with established and accepted routines it will be important for the sensor to also have enthusiasm for the initiative.

Such sequencing of interdependent activities may represent a normative ideal; it is not necessarily descriptive of practice. For example, feelers may bypass thinkers, interacting directly with sensors, 'bootlegging' the initial implementation of the creative idea. At the thinking level plans may be developed only after early implementation, not before. Of course, this is more likely to happen when the thinkers in the top management group are wedded to their established plans based upon existing logics and are unwilling to experiment with novel approaches.

This sequence also recognizes that the dominant coalition may not be a group in the social-psychological sense, where all members have frequent face-to-face interactions. Rather, it may be a series of interchanges over (objective) time between individuals, each with a predisposition for certain behaviors. These interchanges are the result of complex stimuli, and detailed consideration of them is beyond the scope of this paper. However, evidence from Belbin's (1981) work with groups of managers in a business simulation suggests that effective groups had members (Belbin called them Chairman and Teamworker) concerned with transcending individual differences and facilitating the process. In our framework such individuals would be oriented towards integrating the levels of the CM process amongst people and organizational units, and over time.

Power and influence in the creative management process

The CM model has significant implications for the study and practice of the processes through which power and influence are exercised within organizations. In the SM model the communication channels and relationships considered important in the exercise of power are those of the formal organization hierarchy. This is consonant with the framework's underlying philosophy—if reality exists objectively and is accessible to rational instruments, then where else can the many partial views be integrated except in the synoptic mind of the CEO/strategist? For only he or she has the panoramic view of reality by virtue of a superior position at the apex of the organization. Information flows up, directives down. In contrast the CM model stresses rich and fluid communication channels and relationships making up the 'neural' network, a cognitive framework within which the organization will scan, describe and develop its version of 'reality'.

How then should an organization in search of renewal proceed? The interaction patterns required for renewal assume a broad distribution of influence within the management team, and that all cognitive types are represented. No single cognitive mode dominates the ongoing negotiation process. In support of this view Friedlander (1983: 200) states that sustained 'power imbalances diminish [the benefits of] heterogeneity and contact and thereby diminish system learning'.

This does not necessarily mean power should, or will, be uniformly and statically distributed. Rather, power must shift according to the 'authority of the situation' (Follett, 1941). At the outset, when the issue is highly ambiguous, the intuitive mode is required and those individuals with significant capacity in this area should assume more influence, regardless of their hierarchical level within the formal organization. As the renewal process moves to the feeling dimension the motivation of the team becomes critical. Individuals capable of evoking and expressing shared values should now have more influence. The intuitives, while still involved, would exhibit less influence. Subsequently as the task shifts to planning and action, the process requires that thinkers and sensors become predominant. Thus, in an ideal process, each cognitive type asumes influence as determined by the needs of the evolving renewal process. The relationships between the individual in the (temporarily) dominant role and the rest of the team has been described by Greenleaf (1977) as *primus inter pares*, first amongst equals. Like strands in a tapestry, now in the front, now in the back, individuals on the team together weave a cognitive fabric, the pattern of which will express their version of a renewed organizational reality.

What happens when a cognitive type is not available on the team? Theoretically, a cognitive (and therefore behavioral) void exists. There is no-one with the cognitive preference needed to influence the renewal process in the desired way at a particular stage. If, however, there exists within the group an awareness of the need for different types of cognition and behavior, as well as some capacity to perform the role, then it is possible that one or more members of the team may spontaneously assume the 'vacant' role. In this process of self-organization the renewal process proceeds by evoking the needed but less preferred cognitive processes from members of the management team. Organizational adaptation and individual learning are combined.

Implications for top management groups

The CM model generates a number of insights into the composition of, and processes within, top management teams. From a *prescriptive* point of view, the CM model suggests that an 'ideal' top management group would be made up of individuals capable of functioning in each of the four cognitive modes. Since individuals seem to have stable cognitive preferences (Myers and McCaulley, 1985), an 'ideal' team needs several different 'types' of individuals to assume the variety of roles required. The general implication is that in addition to the *Sensing* and *Thinking* modes implied by the SM model, *Intuition* and *Feeling* modes are required by the CM model. All four modes need to be represented within the effective top management group and utilized in the management process.

From a *descriptive* point of view, cognitive composition might be expected to evolve as an organization matures. One would expect founders of organizations to be predominantly intuitive in their gathering of information, and to evaluate information using the feeling mode. As organizations mature, intuition and feeling would be expected to give way to sensation and thinking. Although it need not necessarily be the case, the latter style can easily drive out the former. This occurs most dramatically when founders leave (or are forced out) and replaced by 'professional managers', those trained in the SM methodology. More generally, differences in composition within the top management group can be expected to change as an organization develops, and these differences are expected to yield different patterns of behavior. However, the actions of an organization are not directly impacted by the cognitive preferences of its top managers. It is the behaviors of this group and the integration of these behaviors into a pattern of organizational actions which impacts strategy and performance.

BUSINESS STRATEGY AND THE CREATIVE MANAGEMENT MODEL

The CM model is basically an adaptive process and, as such, relates best to strategy concepts, which share this perspective. For example, Miles and Snow (1978: 21) recognized that 'The strategic-choice approach essentially argues that the effectiveness of organizational adaptation hinges on *the dominant coalition's perceptions* of environmental conditions and the decisions it makes concerning how the organization will cope with these conditions' (emphasis added). Based upon their empirical observations, Miles and Snow (1978: 14) identified four patterns of behavior which they reduced to four strategic archetypes, 'representing alternative ways of moving through the adaptive cycle'. These are defender, prospector, analyzer and reactor. Unfortunately, Miles and Snow do not link these types to their underlying concern with the perceptual abilities of the dominant coalition. And while they recognize prospectors as more innovative and willing to experiment with new ideas than their other strategy types, they do not provide much insight into how perceptions impact this process. Furthermore, there is little sense for how established business logics are changed, how unconventional ideas are incorporated into established business strategies. They do not directly address the question of renewal.

In our view, truly *prospecting* organizations have dominant coalitions which search for new ways of doing business and continually use visions of possible futures, ideas about new and different ways of doing business, to feed forward into present behavior and actions. By contrast, in *preserving* organizations past norms and traditions feed back to dominate present behavior. As shown in Figure 2, when viewed in this way, the CM model can be used to distinguish between organizations with a preference for either prospecting or preserving strategies.

The management groups in both prospecting

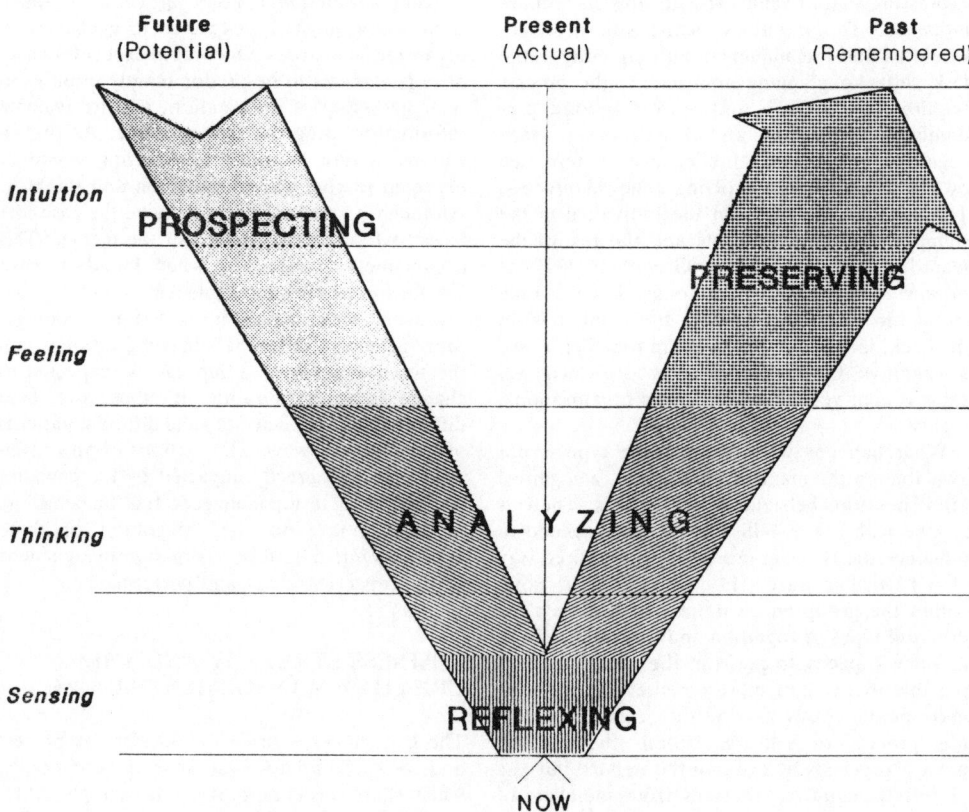

Figure 2. Strategy and the creative management model

and preserving organizations are oriented towards the intuition and feeling levels of the CM model. Preserving managements are able, with their intuitive ability, to perceive patterns in past decisions, actions and events; and by way of their feeling level they extract and express meaning from their firm's past. They have a strong sense of history and tradition; 'what we have been'. Their orientation is towards the past. Prospective managements use the same cognitive abilities (intuition and feeling) but focus them on the future; 'what we might become'. Although both types of organization must function in the perpetual 'now', they do so with different (subjective) time orientations; the managements of prospecting organizations are oriented towards the potential of what might be, the future; in preserving organizations the orientation is towards the remembrance of what has been, the realized vision, the past.

Prospecting organizations can be expected to be radical innovators, willing to experiment with new ideas that do not fit within the accepted logic for the business. In preserving organization realized vision and tradition guide action, resulting in an adherence to past strategies; even incremental adjustments may be difficult because intentions and results are evaluated against values (at the feeling level) not standards derived from a logic (at the thinking level). Both of these strategies, because vision and values drive behaviors, often lack the coherence to their actions provided by the thinking-planning level. Furthermore, these organizations are not highly responsive to direct environmental stimuli.

Within the context of the CM model, the dominant coalition of an *analyzing* organization can be seen as more oriented towards the present than either their preserving or prospecting counterparts. It also functions more at the thinking and sensing levels; less so at the intuition and feeling levels. As a consequence the management of an analyzing organization is less accepting of radical, unproven ideas than the pure prospecting organization, but also less bound by tradition than the preserving organization. Accordingly, the analyzing organization is less likely to be first with a radical innovation, although it may follow an initiative of a prospecting firm once it can be rationalized. It is not just the (subjective) time orientation of the management of an analyzing organization that prevents it from pursuing radical innovations. This inability is also bound up in the interrelated issue of their preferred or dominant cognitive functions, thinking and sensing. The management of an analyzing organization functions more at the thinking and sensing levels, and therefore needs to develop a plausible logic before action. However, the actions they do take are well planned and coherent extension of the established logic.

The remaining strategy orientation outlined in Figure 2 is the reflexing organization. Reflexing organizations (and their managers) exist only in here and now. They have no view of their firm's future, nor sense for its past. Their behaviors are guided by instinctive or reflex responses to given stimuli. They do not attempt to understand their behaviors and actions, either before or after these actions occur. They function solely at the sensation level. Such organizations are highly responsive to a given set of environmental stimuli, but should the environment and the appropriate response pattern change these organizations are unable to adapt, to learn new behaviors.

Given the strategy types identified within the CM model—prospecting, analyzing, reflexing and preserving—what are the corresponding organizational attributes? Consistent with Miles and Snow's original observation about the importance of the dominant coalition's perceptions, the CM model links perception and cognitive preferences suggesting that the composition of the top management teams and their mix of cognitive and time orientations is key to understanding this conception of organization strategy.

Prescriptively it would appear organizations able to renew themselves need some of the attributes of each strategy orientation. The ideal management team needs both prospecting and preserving abilities; these combine a basis in its past with the ability to create its future. This is the problem of renewal: preserving the core of the business while allowing for the ongoing redefinition of that core. Like Janus, the Roman god of the threshold, truly adaptive organizations and their management teams simultaneously look forward, and create their future; and back, and appreciate their past. However, they also strive to understand their actions, and anticipate outcomes while being responsive to environmental stimuli. Even though a balance amongst all strategy orientations might be desirable, it seems likely that most organizations, like most individuals, will have a distinct preference.

Strategy and the composition of top management

The composition and interactions of the top management group affect behaviors which are ultimately reflected in the decisions and actions of the organization. Therefore, differences in composition of the management group should be manifested in patterns of action, that is in strategies (Mintzberg, 1978). The behaviors of the dominant coalition derived from the CM model can be related to the different cognitive types. Accordingly, relationships between the makeup of a top management group and the strategic types of Preserving, Analyzing, Reflexing and Prospecting can be hypothesized (see Table 4). The assertions made are largely descriptive. Prescriptive statements require a link to behaviors, patterns of action and performance.

ON CAUSALITY

To this point the discussion has been largely conceptual, linking cognitive styles, behaviors, team composition and decisions and actions. However, it is recognized that other factors, like personal background and skills, influence managerial behaviors; as do organizational context factors, such as hierarchy, norms, rules, and decision-making style.

Empirical evidence

A complete review of the empirical work related to the CM model and top management team composition is beyond the scope of this paper. However, this section will examine some of the existing work, much of which indirectly supports aspects of the CM framework.

Much research has focused on the relationship between background characteristics of managers and firm performance. After an extensive review of this literature Hambrick and Mason (1984: 203) observed: 'It is doubtful that this research stream can progress far without greater attention to relevant literature in related fields, especially psychology and social psychology.' This article attempts to progress from a psychological base while forging the link to decisions and patterns of action (i.e. strategy) for the enterprise. For the sake of simplicity and brevity, the discussion of empirical support for the model will focus on key relationships.

Team composition ⇒ decisions/actions/ performance

Miles and Snow (1978) observed patterns in action, strategies, consistent with the CM process. Moreover, their strategy typology has been found to be reasonably descriptive of observed strategic attributes (Hambrick, 1983a). However, their observations about the composition of the dominant coalition are limited to functional backgrounds. For Defenders they note that the dominant coalition was typically composed of the

Table 4. Hypothesized relationship between cognitive composition of the dominant coalition and business strategy

Dominant coalition's		
Cognitive composition	Time orientation	Strategy orientation
Mostly Intuitives with some Feelers	Future	Prospecting
Mostly Thinkers with some Sensors	Near Term Future and Past	Analyzing
Mostly Sensors	Now	Reflexing
Mostly Feelers with some Intuitives	Past	Preserving
Mix of Intuitives, Feelers, Thinkers and Sensors	Future⇔Past	Renewing

general manager, the controller, and the heads of production and sales. They go on to state, 'the Prospector's dominant coalition centers around the marketing and research and development functions. Moreover, the Prospector's dominant coalition is also larger, more diverse and more transitory than the Defender's'. Their rationale is based upon the fit between managerial skills and the technical task requirements of the strategy. Although relationships have been observed between functional background and cognitive preference (McKenny and Keen, 1974; Macdaid, McCaulley and Kainz, 1986) no link was made by Miles and Snow to underlying psychological or cognitive attributes of the top management group.

Individual differences within top management teams such as age (Child, 1974), functional track record, education (Kimberly and Evanisko, 1981) and job tenure (Carlson, 1972) have been studied. These variables are usually recognized as proxy for some underlying psychological dimension (e.g. cognitive style, time orientation, tolerance for ambiguity), and used because they are more easily measured. In reviewing the literature on the relationship between background characteristics of top managers and organizational actions and performance, Hambrick and Mason (1984) developed a list of propositions based on demonstrated associations. However, this approach has several problems. First and foremost the propositions lack a consistent conceptual view of the top management group and its role in moving the organization forward. Second, the variables are not clearly related to broader theories of personality, or behavior. Third, despite the observation that the group, and group heterogeneity, are significant factors, most of the work in this area seems to view the group as uniform. Most work employs either an average measure for attributes of the top management group, or selects one executive, usually the general manager, as singularly important.

A major empirical study associating underlying psychological variables and team performance was done by Belbin (1981). He administered a battery of psychological tests to executives taking part in a management training course. During the course, managers participated in business simulations. Team composition was varied and performance was measured. Evidence from this research suggests that:

1. The effectiveness of a team will be promoted by the extent to which members correctly recognize and adjust themselves to the relative strengths within the team, both in expertise and ability to engage in specific team-roles.
2. Personal qualities fit members for some team-roles while limiting the likelihood that they will succeed in others (Belbin, 1981: 132–133).

Belbin's work, although illuminating and highly descriptive, was not done in managerial settings. Neither was it a test, nor development of a theory of management team effectiveness.

Some work on team composition and effectiveness using Jungian types has been conducted. Blaylock (1983), employing a production simulation with business students, formed 17 groups, four of mixed or complementary types and 13 of compatible or relatively uniform types. Three of the four mixed groups finished in the top five, a significant relationship.

The assertion that heterogeneous groups are more effective than homogeneous groups is not new. Filley, House and Kerr (1976), surveyed the literature on group dynamics and concluded that novel problems are best handled by a heterogeneous group and routine problems most efficiently dealt with by a homogeneous group. A concurring note was stated by Ziller (1972). Reviewing studies from further afield, he too found that performance is enhanced in groups with heterogeneity in membership. Rather than differentiate on problem types, he suggested that short-term groups ought to have homogeneous membership while long-standing groups have heterogeneous membership. He concluded that heterogeneity on a wide variety of variables, including race, age, ability and personality and training in group dynamics, improved productivity.

Indeed, the outstanding question pertains not so much to the situational conditions favoring heterogeneity but rather to the appropriate dimensions for the heterogeneity, given the issues being addressed. Addressing this question requires a conceptual perspective. The perspective of the CM model links the executive function of business renewal to cognitive preferences to managerial behaviors and organizational action.

Cognitive modes ⇒ behaviors

The empirical link between the group composition based upon differences or similarities in cognitive preferences and outcomes from group activity is sparse. Evidence associating individual behaviors and cognitive preference is more prevalent.

Several studies have indicated a link between MBTI (Myers-Briggs Type Indicator) and behavioral patterns. Mitroff and Kilmann (1975), Mitroff, Barabba and Kilmann (1978), and Hellriegel and Slocum (1980) have researched how different types view ideal organizations and their heroes. Most of these support the relationships posited by Myers (1962). They found that Sensing–Thinking managers concentrated on specific, factual details, preferring situations in which there is certainty, specificity and control. Their heroes used others to get things done; they were problem-solvers. Intuitive–Thinking managers focused on broad, global issues, general concepts and ill-defined macro-level goals. Their heroes were broad conceptualizers and problem-framers. Sensing–Feeling managers were more concerned with specific people issues, not tasks. Their heroes created personal, warm climates and made organizations like 'home'. Finally Intuitive–Feeling managers focused on broad global themes serving mankind. Their heroes were able to envision new goals and create organizations with a personal sense.

Reporting on the validity of MBTI, Carlyn (1977) states that Intuitives are more likely to participate in imagined events and engage in possibilities while Sensors prefer a command of reality. Although validity studies have been done relating MBTI scores to other personality measures, very little evidence is available linking MBTI directly to managerial behaviors. To the extent that profession and position correlate to behaviors, the data presented in Table 5 tend to inferentially support the relationships posited in Table 3.

As a group, management consultants and high-level executives have a predominant thinking preference for evaluating information; as one would expect, consultants prefer to gather their information more broadly and look for whole relationships (intuition preference). Practicing managers, be they high-level executives, supervisors, accountants or small business managers, have a stronger preference for grounding their information gathering in the immediate representations of the world with which they must deal (sensation preference). Moreover, the proportions of cognitive types do appear to differ by level in the hierarchy. Roach (1986) distinguishes between supervisors–managers–executives and reports that 'over half the executives were Intuition–Thinking' while for supervisors Sensation–Thinking was the largest category. Sensation–Feeling declined dramatically in relation to increasing organizational level.

While intuitive preference appears to increase modestly with level in hierarchy, it varies more dramatically among professions. As shown in

Table 5. Cognitive style by profession and managerial position

	Information gathering		Information evaluation		
	Intuition	Sensing	Thinking	Feeling	n
Managerial					
Management consultants	58%	42%	92%	8%	71
High-level executives	43%	57%	90%	10%	136
Supervisors and managers	42%	58%	64%	36%	3678
Accountants	38%	62%	59%	41%	427
Small-business managers	14%	86%	81%	19%	150
Other professions					
Artists	91%	9%	30%	70%	114
Architects	82%	18%	56%	44%	124
Steelworkers	14%	86%	74%	26%	105
Teachers (grades 1–12)	26%	74%	31%	69%	281

Source: Adapted from Macdaid, McCaulley and Kainz (1986).

Table 5, professions requiring a high degree of creativity (artists and architects) have a strong intuition preference. Architects, however, deal with a technical subject and tend towards the thinking preference for evaluating the content of their intuitive insights. Artists, unconstrained by many technical requirements, evaluate their insights based upon feelings. Teachers and steelworkers, by way of further example, whose professions require them to deal with and respond to direct stimuli, have a stronger sensation preference. Dealing with children, most teachers (grades 1 through 12) evaluate stimuli using feeling; while steelworkers working with a process technology prefer thinking.

While these data are provocative, they do not directly address the question of whether or not cognitive preferences are associated with the behaviors expected at the different levels of the CM model. These questions need to be addressed by empirical research.

TOWARDS RESEARCH

Empirical work from other areas tends to support the general relationships implied by the CM model for the composition of top management groups. However, many linkages in the framework need empirical testing. Our global proposition is that the composition of the top management group will affect firm strategy and performance. More specifically, it is proposed that the task variety implied by the CM model requires cognitive style differences within the top management group. However, diversity alone does not ensure effectiveness. The organization must transcend this diversity. We suspect the patterns of interaction amongst the contributors to strategic actions, who interacts with whom and how they interact, will be a critical aspect of this transcendence.

Although conceptually appealing and with some empirical support, major questions remain to be resolved as the empirical study of top management groups proceeds. These include:

1. What is meant by top management teams? Is the team the management committee? Is membership determined by hierarchical position? Are they the sociometrically determined contributors to major decisions? Does membership vary by decision? Can a parsimonious classification of top management teams be determined?
2. Are effective top management teams composed of individuals exhibiting behavior required by the CM model? Are these behaviors distributed among team members as would be predicted on the basis of their cognitive style, or are they distributed on some other basis? Are the integrative/facilitative behaviors exhibited by those with other substantive contributions to the CM process or do they require specific individuals with different cognitive styles or personalities? Do behavioral patterns account for differences in firm performance or is it just sufficient to see the total set exhibited by the group?

Addressing these issues will require a variety of approaches and research methodologies.

Approaches to researching top management teams

There are two broad ways to approach answering the questions raised above. One is to take the theory to practice, the other is to bring practice to theory.

Theory to practice

This approach calls for the explicit statement of testable hypotheses, tight experimental designs and valid measuring tools. Because of the complexity of the phenomenon under study it is advisable first to conduct tests of these hypotheses under highly controlled conditions. We believe that well-developed behavioral simulations[2] provide many of the controls necessary, but recreate real life sufficiently well to be used as vehicles for such tests.

The following propositions could be tested through these simulations:

1. Individuals with certain cognitive styles exhibit specified behavior, or clusters of behaviors.
2. Exhibited behaviors cluster to reflect contributions to the *levels* of the CM process.

---
[2] Simulations developed by the Center for Creative Leadership, Greensboro, NC, and by the Management Simulations Project group, New York University, are examples.

3. Certain patterns of interaction are better able to transcend these differences than others.
4. The behaviors and interaction patterns result in the expected patterns in action.

A simple research design would involve assigning individuals to top management teams (TMTs) on the basis of their MBTI types to create both homogeneous and heterogeneous groups. All groups then participate in a behavioral simulation. Following the simulation, participants are asked to complete a behavioral checklist (who did what) and asked to indicate who played what role. Linkages in the logic can be tested. Additional studies can test the effectiveness of different interventions prior to the simulation.

Practice to theory

Generalizability is limited with the designs mentioned above. Simulations, no matter how well developed, cannot completely replicate real life. They may unduly force individuals into roles and behavior they would not otherwise exhibit, and they may impose norms on group behavior that do not reflect the real-life behavior of top management teams. Concurrent with highly controlled theory-to-practice designs, real-life top management teams should be observed.

Initially this research should be descriptive. It is hoped that intensive clinical studies of a sample of top management teams would provide the basis for a parsimonious classification of teams. The stability of team membership, who contributes to key decisions and actions, could be examined both over time and over situations. Behaviors exhibited by individuals in different roles can be observed. With a taxonomy of teams and a more detailed behavioral checklist developed, larger-scale research could be conducted to test hypotheses emanating from the theoretical framework. Structured interviews and data collection could be conducted with members of a variety of top management teams. Administered instruments would include measures of cognitive preferences and other behavioral predispositions, checklists of behavior to be completed on self and other top management team members. Performance of the teams could be measured, and effectiveness accounted for, on the basis of individual background and behavioral differences.

Although little has been said in this paper about patterns of interaction among team members, it is clear that performance cannot be thought of strictly as a function of team composition. The case studies and survey research would also be useful for observing, documenting and understanding patterns of interaction. For example, do heterogeneous teams which operate with low status and power differentials outperform those that operate on the basis of hierarchical positions? Does job context suppress or extinguish intrinsic cognitive preferences?

Both types of research should proceed concurrently. Much can be learned from one that is useful to the other. Through studies of managers in simulated settings, reliable measures of behavior could be developed. The validity of these measures could than be assessed in the field. Other intervening variables discovered in the field studies can be manipulated experimentally or statistically in subsequent laboratory studies.

TOWARDS PRACTICE

The ideas of teamwork at the top, cognitive style and innovation are not new to practicing managers (Rowan, 1979; Sherman, 1984; Moore, 1987). Furthermore, Jungian concepts and MBTI types are to a limited extent already being used to help managers better understand their organizations (Mitroff and Kilmann, 1975; Mason and Mitroff, 1981; Moore, 1987). The CM model synthesizes many of these ideas as they relate to the executive function of business renewal. It infers roles, behaviors and differences in cognitive type for the top management group.

The conceptual insights can still be of use to practitioners even though as yet unsupported by detailed direct evidence. The CM model provides managers with an understanding that can make them more aware of their own behaviors and tolerant of others, especially when they appreciate the individual differences in cognitive preference which underlie those behaviors, and that such behaviors may play an important role in the CM process. In other words, it can be hoped that a conceptual understanding will result in a behavioral awareness and modification.

If those responsible for the overall direction of the enterprise were aware of the behavioral requirements of its members as posited by the

CM model they could use that understanding in several ways. First, an examination of the members of the TMT may reveal that they are inclined to exhibit the required behaviors, but feel, because of organizational factors, they cannot do so. A further examination of the cultural norms, power relationships and the reward systems might reveal that those behaviors were discouraged or even punished. It might be a relatively easy step to legitimize those previously suppressed behaviors.

Often a change of context can help. The 'outward-bound' experience for managers, by providing a dramatic shift in context and in some respects tasks, presents an opportunity for latent preferences, suppressed in the normal organization context, to surface. It is well accepted that children learn through play. However, playful experiences for managers need not always occur outside the normal organizational context. It is now being suggested that certain organizational activities be conducted in a playful manner in order to facilitate institutional learning (Rutenburg, 1986; De Geus, 1988).

A second, and possibly a more controversial, use would be to employ the CM model for selection to, and development of, the TMT. With an understanding of the model those responsible for these activities might attend to, document and evaluate the behaviors of potential or current members of the TMT in terms of cognitive type. These behaviors, framed within the CM model, could be assessed and used as one criterion for selection. Development activities might also be suggested for some members who could most likely exhibit certain required behaviors. As a cautionary note we do not believe that use of the MBTI as a cognitive indicator is warranted at this time. The test was not developed, nor has sufficient evidence of reliability and predictive validity been shown, for use in selection or promotion decisions. However, we do feel that Jung's conception of cognitive types does provide a useful way for managers to appreciate observable, individual behaviors and their contribution to the process of organizational renewal.

Throughout these brief suggestions for practice, the emphasis has been on behavior. Managers attempting to employ the CM model should adopt a similar perspective. It is the insights into the behaviors of the TMT provided by the model that have the greatest utility.

SUMMARY/CONCLUSIONS

This paper attempts to build a model of the behavioral requirements for the top management team from two perspectives. First, from the perspective of the individual, it is posited that the behaviors relevant to the renewal function of the executive which need to be exhibited by top managers are at least partly a function of their cognitive preferences. It is argued that the Jungian/Myers Briggs typology is consistent with the model of renewal based upon the creative management (CM) model and an established framework for understanding and predicting these behaviors. Second, it has been asserted that organizations will evolve a pattern of actions, a strategy reflecting the cognitive composition of the top management team. As the cognitive preferences of the top management group vary so too will strategy.

It is suggested that research follow both a theory-to-practice and practice-to-theory approach, simultaneously developing theory and testing specific hypotheses about team composition and patterns of interaction.

This paper makes a case for a management process that utilizes the full range of human potential. The need for a CM model to replace the conventional strategic management framework has been argued on the basis of the latter's inability to utilize the full range of cognitive functions and accordingly its failure to promote new and innovative strategies. The CM model, however, has implications for the dominant coalition. Since theory and evidence suggest individuals have superior or dominant functions a mixture of cognitive types is implied. The CM process suggests that top management groups not only include the *Thinkers* and *Sensors* needed by the SM process but also embace the *Intuitives* and *Feelers* needed to generate and infuse unconventional insights and new ideas. But difference without synthesis is anarchy. The organization and its members must also have the ability to achieve unity from diversity, the ability to transcend.

ACKNOWLEDGEMENTS

We would like to acknowledge the support of the Plan for Excellence, School of Business

Administration, The University of Western Ontario and the assistance of Yasminka Kresic and Ramon Baltazar and three anonymous *Strategic Management Journal* reviewers in the preparation of this paper.

REFERENCES

Barnard, C. I. *The Functions of the Executive*, Harvard University Press, Cambridge, MA, 1938.

Belbin, R. M. *Management Teams: Why They Succeed or Fail*, Heinemann, London, 1981.

Blaylock, B. K. 'Teamwork in a simulated production environment', *Research in Psychological Type*, **6**, 1983, pp. 58–67.

Bower, J. L. 'Solving the problems of business planning', *Journal of Business Strategy*, **2**(3), Winter 1982, pp. 32–44.

Carlson, R. O. *School Superintendents: Careers and Performance*. Merrill, Columbia, OH, 1972.

Carlyn, M. 'An assessment of the Myers–Briggs type indicator', *Journal of Personality Assessment*, **41**, 1977, pp. 461–473.

Child, J. 'Managerial and organizational factors associated with company performance', *Journal of Management Studies*, **11**, 1974, pp. 13–27.

Cyert, R. M. and J. G. March. *A Behavioral Theory of the Firm*, Prentice-Hall, Englewood Cliffs, NJ, 1963.

De Geus, A. P. 'Planning as learning', *Harvard Business Review*, March–April 1988, pp. 62–69.

Filley, A. C., R J. House and S. Kerr. *Managerial Process and Organizational Behavior*, Scott Foresman, Glenview, IL, 1976.

Follett, M. P. *Dynamic Administration: the collected papers of Mary Parker Follett*, edited by Metcalf, H. and L. Urwick, Harper & Bros, New York, 1941.

Friedlander, F. 'Patterns of individual and organizational learning'. In Srivesta, S. and Associates, *The Executive Mind*, Jossey-Bass, San Francisco, CA, 1983.

Galbraith, J. *Designing Complex Organizations*, Addison-Wesley Publishing Co., Reading, MA, 1973.

Gardener, H. *The Minds New Science: A History of the Cognitive Revolution*, Basic Books, New York, 1985.

Greenleaf, R. K. *Servant Leadership*. Paulish Press, New York, 1977.

Hambrick, D. C. 'High profit strategies in mature capital goods industries: a contingency approach', *Academy of Management Journal*, **26**(4), 1983a, pp. 687–707.

Hambrick, D. C. 'Some tests of the effectiveness and functional attributes of Miles and Snow's strategic types', *Academy of Management Journal*, **26**(1), 1983b, pp. 5–26.

Hambrick, D. C. 'The top management team: key to strategic success', *California Management Review*, Fall 1987, pp. 88–108.

Hambrick, D. C. and P. A. Mason. 'Upper echelons: the organization as a reflection of its top managers', *Academy of Management Review*, **9**(2), 1984, pp. 193–206.

Hampden-Turner, C. *Maps of the Mind*, Macmillan, New York, 1981.

Hellriegel, D. and J. W. Slocum. 'Preferred organizational designs and problem solving styles: interesting companions', *Human Systems Management*, No. 1, 1980, pp. 151–158.

Hurst, D. K. 'Why strategic management is bankrupt', *Organizational Dynamics*, Autumn 1986, pp. 5–27.

Jaques, E. *The Form of Time*, Crane Russak, New York, 1982.

Jung, C. G. 'The structure and dynamics of the psyche'. In *Collected Works*, vol. 8, Princeton University Press, Princeton, NJ, 1960.

Keirsey, D. W. and M. Bates. *Please Understand Me*, Prometheus Nemesis Books, Del Mar, CA, 1978.

Kimberly, J. R. and M. J. Evanisko. 'Organizational innovation: the influence of individual, organizational and contextual factors on hospital adoption of technological and administrative innovations', *Academy of Management Journal*, **24**, 1981, pp. 689–713.

Koestler, A. *The Act of Creation*, Hutchinson, London, 1976.

Lawrence, P. R. and J. W. Lorsch. *Organization and Environment*, R. D. Irwin, Homewood, IL, 1969.

Macdaid, G. P., M. H. McCaulley and R. I. Kainz. *Atlas of Type Tables*, Center for Applications of Psychological Types, Gainesville, FL, 1986.

Mann, H., M. Siegler and H. Osmond. 'The psychotypology of time'. In Yaker, H., H. Osmond and F. Cheek (eds), *The Future of Time: Man's Temporal Environment*, Doubleday, Garden City, NY, 1971, pp. 142–178.

Mason, R. O. and I. I. Mitroff. *Challenging Strategic Planning Assumptions*, John Wiley & Sons, New York, 1981.

McKenny, J. L. and P. G. W. Keen. 'How managers' minds work', *Harvard Business Review*, May–June 1974, pp. 79–90.

Miles, R. E. and C. C. Snow. *Organizational Strategy, Structure and Process*. McGraw-Hill, New York, 1978.

Mintzberg, H. 'Planning on the left side and managing on the right', *Harvard Business Review*, July –August 1976, pp. 49–58.

Mintzberg, H. 'Patterns in strategy formation'. *Management Science*, **24**, 1978, pp. 934–948.

Mitroff, I. I. and R. H. Kilmann. 'Stories managers tell: a new tool for organizational problem solving', *Management Review*, **64**(7), 1975, pp. 18–28.

Mitroff, I., V. Barabba and R. Kilmann. 'The application of behavioral and philosophical technologies to strategic planning: a case study of a large federal agency', *Management Science*, **24**, 1977, pp. 44–58.

Moore, T. 'Personality tests are back'. *Fortune*, 30 March 1987, pp. 74–82.

Myers, I. B. *Introduction to Type*, Consulting Psychologists Press, Palo Alto, CA, 1982.

Myers, I. B. and M. H. McCaulley. *Manual: A Guide to the Development and Use of the Myers–Briggs Type Indicator*. Consulting Psychologists Press, Palo Alto, CA, 1985.

Pascale, R. T. 'Perspectives on strategy: the real story behind Honda's success', *California Management Review*, Spring 1984, pp. 47–72.

Peters, T. J. and R. H. Waterman. Beyond the rational model, *The McKinsey Quarterly*, Spring 1983, pp. 19–30.

Prahalad, C. K. and R. A. Bettis. 'The dominant logic: a new linkage between diversity and performance', *Strategic Management Journal*, 7, 1986, pp. 485–501.

Roach, B. 'Organizational decision-makers: different types for different levels', *Journal of Psychological Type*, 12, 1986, pp. 16–24.

Rowan, R. 'Those business hunches are more than blind faith', *Fortune*, 23 April 1979, pp. 110–114.

Rutenberg, D. 'Playful Plans'. Working paper, Queens University, 1986.

Sherman, S. P. 'Eight big masters of innovation', *Fortune*, 15 October 1984, pp. 66–78.

Simon, H. A. 'Understanding creativity and creative management'. In Kuhn, R. L. (ed.), *Handbook for Creative and Innovative Managers*, McGraw-Hill, New York, 1988.

Taggart, W. and D. Robey. 'Minds and managers: on the dual nature of human information processing and management', *Academy of Management Review*, 6(2), 1981, pp. 187–195.

Thompson, J. D. *Organizations in Action*, McGraw-Hill, New York, 1967.

Watson, J. D. *The Double Helix*, Mentor Books, New York, 1969.

Weick, K. E. *The Social Psychology of Organizing*, Addison-Wesley Publishing Co., Reading, MA, 1979.

Worthy, J. C. *Shaping An American Institution: Robert E. Wood and Sears, Roebuck*, University of Illinois Press, Chicago, IL, 1984.

Ziller, R. C. 'Homogeneity and heterogeneity of group membership. In McClintoch, C. G. (ed.), *Experimental Social Psychology*, Holt, Rinehart and Winston, New York, 1972.

Patterns of Strategy Development

Strategy-Making in Three Modes

Henry Mintzberg

How do organizations make important decisions and link them together to form strategies? So far, we have little systematic evidence about this important process, known in business as *strategy-making* and in government as *policy-making*. The literature of management and public administration is, however, replete with general views on the subject. These fall into three distinct groupings or "modes." In the *entrepreneurial* mode, found in the writings of some of the classical economists and of many contemporary management writers, one strong leader takes bold, risky actions on behalf of his organization. Conversely, in the *adaptive* mode, described by a number of students of business and governmental decision-making, the organization adapts in small, disjointed steps to a difficult environment. Finally, the proponents of management science and policy science describe the *planning* mode, in which formal analysis is used to plan explicit, integrated strategies for the future.

I shall begin by describing each mode as its proponents do, in simple terms and distinct from the other two. Considered in this way, each may appear to be a naive reflection of the complex reality of strategy-making. But taken as a set of three, as I shall do in subsequent sections, to be combined and alternated by managers acting under different conditions, these modes constitute a realistic and useful description of the strategy-making process. To illustrate this point, I shall cite studies of the strategy-making behaviors of a number of very different kinds of organizations—hotels, hospitals, car dealerships, modeling agencies, airports, radio stations, and so on. Finally, I shall discuss some important implications for strategic planning.

The Entrepreneurial Mode

The entrepreneur was first discussed by early economists as that individual who founded enterprises. His roles were essentially those of innovation, of dealing with uncertainty, and of brokerage. The entrepreneur found capital which he brought together with marketing opportunity to form, in the words of Joseph Schumpeter, the well known Harvard economist, "new combinations."

In a recent book called *The Organization Makers*, Orvis Collins and David Moore present a fascinating picture of those independent entrepreneures, based on a study of 150 of them. The authors trace the lives of these men from childhood, through formal and informal education, to the steps they took to create their enterprises. Data from psychological tests reinforce their analysis. What emerges are pictures of tough, pragmatic men driven from early childhood by a powerful need for achievement and independence. At some point in his life, each entrepreneur faced disruption ("role deterioration"), and it was here that he set out on his own:

> What sets them apart is that during this time of role deterioration they interwove their dilemmas into the projection of a business. In moments of crisis, they did not seek a situation of security. They went on into deeper insecurity...[1]

A number of management writers view the entrepreneurial mode of strategy-making not only in terms of creating new firms but in terms of the running of ongoing enterprises. Typical of these is Peter Drucker, who writes in a recent article:

> Central to business enterprise is... the entrepreneurial act, an act of economic risk-taking. And business enterprise is an entrepreneurial institution... Entrepreneurship is thus central to function, work and performance of the executive in business.[2]

What are the chief characteristics of the entrepreneurial mode of strategy-making as described by economists and management writers? We can delineate four:

1. In the entrepreneurial mode, strategy-making is dominated by the active search for new opportunities. —The entrepreneurial organization focuses on opportunities; problems are secondary. Drucker writes: "Entrepreneurship requires that the few available good people be deployed on opportunities rather than frittered away on 'solving problems'."[3] Furthermore, the orientation is always active rather than passive. Robert McNamara, when he was Secretary of Defense, stressed the active role for the government administrator:

> I think that the role of public manager is very similar to the role of a private manager; in each case he has the option of following one of two major alternative courses of action. He can either act as a judge or a leader. In the former case, he sits and waits until subordinates bring to him problems for solution, or alternatives for choice. In the latter case, he immerses himself in the operations of the business or the governmental activity...

Henry Mintzberg *is Associate Professor of Management Policy at McGill University and is currently a Visiting Associate Professor at Carnegie-Mellon University. He has published numerous articles and a book on management.*

> I have always believed in and endeavored to follow the active leadership role as opposed to the passive judicial role.[4]

2. In the entrepreneurial organization, power is centralized in the hands of the chief executive. — Collins and Moore write of the founder-entrepreneur: "The entrepreneurial personality... is characterized by an unwillingness to 'submit' to authority, an inability to work with it, and a consequent need to escape from it."[5] In the entrepreneurial mode, power rests with one man capable of committing the organization to bold courses of action. He rules by fiat, relying on personal power and sometimes on charisma. Consider this description of an Egyptian firm:

> The great majority of Egyptian-owned private establishments... are organized closer to the pattern of the Abboud enterprises. Here the manager is a dominant individual who extends his personal control over all phases of the business. There is no charted plan of organization, no formalized procedure for selection and development of managerial personnel, no publicized system of wage and salary classifications.
>
> ...authority is associated exclusively with an individual...
>
> Abboud is the kind of person most people have in mind when they discuss the successful Egyptian entrepreneur.[6]

But while there may be "no charted plan of organization," typically one finds instead that strategy is guided by the entrepreneur's own vision of direction for his organization—his personalized plan of attack. Drucker writes:

> Every one of the great business builders we know of—from the Medici and the founders of the Bank of England down to IBM's Thomas Watson in our days—had a definite idea, indeed a clear 'theory of the business' which informed his actions and decisions.[7]

3. Strategy-making in the entrepreneurial mode is characterized by dramatic leaps forward in the face of uncertainty. —Strategy moves forward in the entrepreneurial organization by the taking of large, bold decisions. The chief executive seeks out and thrives in conditions of uncertainty, where his organization can make dramatic gains. The entrepreneurial mode is probably most alive in the popular business magazines such as *Fortune* and *Forbes* which each month devote a number of articles to the bold actions of manager-entrepreneurs. The theme that runs through these articles is what has been referred to as the "bold stroke," the courageous move that succeeds against all the odds and all the advice.

4. Growth is the dominant goal of the entrepreneurial organization.—According to psychologist David McClelland, the entrepreneur is motivated above all by his need for achievement. Since his organization's goals are simply the extension of his own, we can conclude that the dominant goal of the organization operating in the entrepreneurial mode is growth, the most tangible manifestation of achievement. *Fortune* magazine came to this conclusion in a 1956 article about the Young Presidents' Organization entitled "The Entrepreneurial Ego":

> Most of the young presidents have the urge to build rather than manipulate. 'Expansion is a sort of disease with us,' says one president. 'Let's face it,' says another. 'We're empire builders. The tremendous compulsion and obsession is not to make money, but to build an empire.' The opportunity to keep on pushing ahead is, indeed, the principal advantage offered by the entrepreneurial life.[8]

In summary, we can conclude that the organization operating in the entrepreneurial mode suggests by its actions that the environment is malleable, a force to be confronted and controlled.

The Adaptive Mode

The view of strategy-making as an adaptive process has gained considerable popularity since the publication of two complimentary books in 1963. Charles Lindblom and David Braybrooke wrote *A Strategy of Decision* about policy-making in the public sector, while Richard Cyert and James March published *A Behavioral Theory of the Firm* based on empirical studies of decision-making.

Lindblom first called this approach "the science of 'muddling through'," later "disjointed incrementalism."[9] The term "adaptive" is chosen here for its simplicity. As described by Lindblom, the adaptive policy-maker accepts as given a powerful status quo and the lack of clear objectives. His decisions are basically remedial in nature, and he proceeds in small steps, never moving too far from the given status quo. In this way, the policy-maker comes to terms with his complex environment.

Cyert and March's strategy-maker, although working in the business firm, operates in much the same fashion. Again, his world is complex and he must find the means to cope with it. Cyert and March suggest that he does so in a number of ways. He consciously seeks to avoid uncertainty, sometimes solving pressing problems instead of developing long-run strategies, other times "negotiating" with the environment (for example, establishing cartels). Furthermore, because the organization is controlled by a coalition of disparate interests, the strategy-maker must make his decisions so as to reduce conflicts. He does this by attending to conflicting goals sequentially, ignoring the inconsistencies:

> Just as the political organization is likely to resolve conflicting pressures to 'go left' and 'go right' by first doing one and then the other, the business firm is likely to resolve conflicting pressures to 'smooth production' and 'satisfy customers' by first doing one and then the other.[10]

Four major characteristics distinguish the adaptive mode of strategy-making:

1. Clear goals do not exist in the adaptive organization; strategy-making reflects a division of power among members of a complex coalition.—The adaptive organization is caught in a a complex web of political forces. Unions, managers, owners, lobby groups, government agencies, and so on, each with their own needs, seek to influence decisions. There is no one central source of power, no one simple goal. The goal system of the organization is characterized by bargaining among these groups, with each winning some issues and losing others. Hence, the organization attends to a whole array of goals sequentially, ignoring the inconsistencies among them. The organization cannot make decisions to "maximize" any one goal such as profit or growth; rather it must seek solutions to its problems that are good enough, that satisfy the constraints.

2. In the adaptive mode, the strategy-making process is characterized by the "reactive" solution to existing problems rather than the "proactive" search for new opportunities.—The adaptive organization works in a difficult environment that imposes many problems and crises. Little time remains to search out opportunities. And even if there were time, the lack of clear goals in the organization would preclude a proactive approach:

> ... if [the strategy-makers] cannot decide with any precision the state of affairs they want to achieve, they can at least specify the state of affairs from which they want to escape. They deal more confidently with what is wrong than with what in the future may or may not be right.[11]

Furthermore, the adaptive organization seeks conditions of certainty wherever possible, otherwise it seeks to reduce existing uncertainties. It establishes cartels to ensure markets, negotiates long-term purchasing arrangements to stabilize sources of supply, and so on.

3. *The adaptive organization makes its decisions in incremental, serial steps.*—Because its environment is complex, the adaptive organization finds that feedback is a crucial ingredient in strategy-making. It cannot take large decisions for fear of venturing too far into the unknown. The strategy-maker focuses first on what is familiar, considering the convenient alternatives and the ones that differ only slightly from the status quo. Hence, the organization moves forward in incremental steps, laid end to end in serial fashion so that feedback can be received and the course adjusted as it moves along. As Lindblom notes, "... policy-making is typically a never-ending process of successive steps in which continual nibbling is a substitute for a good bite."[12]

4. *Disjointed decisions are characteristic of the adaptive organization.*—Decisions cannot be easily interrelated in the adaptive mode. The demands on the organization are diverse, and no manager has the mental capacity to reconcile all of them. Sometimes it is simply easier and less expensive to make decisions in disjointed fashion so that each is treated independently and little attention is paid to problems of coordination. Strategy-making is fragmented, but at least the strategy-maker remains flexible, free to adapt to the needs of the moment.

Lindblom provides us with an apt summary of the adaptive mode:

> Man has had to be devilishly inventive to cope with the staggering difficulties he faces. His analytical methods cannot be restricted to tidy scholarly procedures. The piecemealing, remedial incrementalist or satisficer may not look like an heroic figure. He is nevertheless a shrewd, resourceful problem-solver who is wrestling bravely with a universe that he is wise enough to know is too big for him.[13]

The Planning Mode

In a recent book, Russell Ackoff isolates the three chief characteristics of the planning mode:

> 1. Planning is something we do in advance of taking action; that is, it is *anticipatory decision-making*....
>
> 2. Planning is required when the future state that we desire involves a set of interdependent decisions; that is, a *system of decisions*....
>
> 3. Planning is a process that is directed toward producing one or more future states which are desired and which are not expected to occur unless something is done.[14]

Formal planning demands rationality in the economist's sense of the term—the systematic attainment of goals stated in precise, quantitative terms. The key actor in the process is the analyst, who uses his scientific techniques to develop formal, comprehensive plans.

The literature of planning is vast, and is growing rapidly. Much of the early writing concerned "operational planning"—the projecting of various budgets based on the given strategies of the organization. More recently, attention has turned to the planning of organizational strategies themselves, the more significant and long-range concerns of senior managers. Two techniques have received particular attention—strategic planning in business and planning-programming-budgeting system (PPBS) in government.

George Steiner has written what up to this point is the definitive book on business planning, entitled *Top Management Planning*. The general prescriptive flavor of the planning literature is found throughout this book. For example, "Plans can and should be to the fullest possible extent objective, factual, logical, and realistic in establishing objectives and devising means to attain them."[15] Steiner outlines a stepwise procedure for business planning which begins with three studies: (1) fundamental organizational socioeconomic purpose, (2) values of top management, and (3) evaluation of external and internal opportunities and problems, and company strengths and weaknesses. Strategic plans are then devised, and these lead to the formulation of medium-range programs and short-range plans. In Steiner's opinion, comprehensive planning is important because it simulates the future, applies the systems approach, prevents piecemeal decision-making, provides a common decision-making framework throughout the company, and so on.

In PPBS, the focus is on the budget rather than the general plan (although a budget is, of course, one type of plan). The steps in the process are, by now, well known—the determination of overall governmental goals and objectives, the generation of program proposals to achieve these, the evaluation of these proposals in terms of costs and benefits, the choice of a group of proposals that will satisfy the objectives while not overextending the resources, and the translation of these into five-year and one-year budgets for implementation.

We can delineate three essential features of the planning mode:

1. *In the planning mode, the analyst plays a major role in strategy-making.*—The analyst or planner works alongside the manager, and assumes major responsibility for much of the strategy-making process. His role is to apply the techniques of management science and policy analysis to the design of long-range strategies. A U.S. Senator notes the reasons for this:

> I am convinced that we never will get the kind of policy planning we need if we expect the top-level officers to participate actively in the planning process. They simply do not have the time, and in any event they rarely have the outlook or the talents of the good planner. They cannot explore issues deeply and systematically. They cannot argue the advantages and disadvantages at length in the kind of give-and-take essential if one is to reach a solid understanding with others on points of agreement and disagreement.[16]

2. *The planning mode focuses on systematic analysis, particularly in the assessment of the costs and benefits of competing proposals.*— Formal planning involves both the active search for new opportunities and the solution of existing problems. The process is always systematic and structured. As one business planner wrote recently:

> No doubt much of top-level management is unscientific. But by applying a systematic, structured approach to these problems, we have a better basis for analyzing them. We may identify more specifically the challenges and needs in the situation and see how they are interrelated.[17]

Formal planning follows a stepwise procedure in which particular attention is paid to the cost-benefit evaluation of proposals, where the planning methodology is best developed. The planner tests proposals for feasibility, determines their efficiency (or economic value), and relates them to each other. The planner deals best with conditions known to the management scientist as "risk"—where the uncertainty can be expressed in statistical terms. Conditions of certainty require no planning; those of pure uncertainty cannot be subjected to analysis.

3. *The planning mode is characterized above all by the integration of decisions and strategies.*— Ackoff notes that "the principal complexity in planning derives from the interrelatedness of decisions rather than from the decisions themselves."[18] But this interrelatedness is the key element in planning. An organization plans in the belief that decisions made together in one systematic process will be less likely to conflict and more likely to complement each other than if they were made independently. For example, planning can ensure that the decision to acquire a new firm complements (or at least does not conflict with) the decision to expand the product line of an existing division. Thus, strategic planning is a process whereby an organization's strategy is designed essentially at one point in time in a comprehensive process (all major decisions made are interrelated). Because of this, planning forces the organization to think of global strategies and to develop an explicit sense of strategic direction.

To conclude, the planning mode is oriented to systematic, comprehensive analysis and is used in the belief that formal analysis can provide an understanding of the environment sufficient to influence it.

The upper part of Table I presents in summary form the characteristics of the three modes of strategy-making, while Figure 1 depicts these three modes in graphic form. The first figure shows the taking of bold steps consistent with the entrepreneur's general vision of direction. In the second figure, we see a purely adaptive organization taking incremental steps in reaction

TABLE I.—Characteristics and Conditions of the Three Modes

Characteristic	Entrepre-neurial Mode	Adaptive Mode	Planning Mode
Motive for Decisions	Proactive	Reactive	Proactive & Reactive
Goals of Organization	Growth	Indeterminate	Efficiency & Growth
Evaluation of Proposals	Judgemental	Judgemental	Analytical
Choices made by	Entrepreneur	Bargaining	Management
Decision Horizon	Long Term	Short Term	Long Term
Preferred Environment	Uncertainty	Certainty	Risk
Decision Linkages	Loosely Coupled	Disjointed	Integrated
Flexibility of Mode	Flexible	Adaptive	Constrained
Size of Moves	Bold Decisions	Incremental Steps	Global Strategies
Vision of Direction	General	None	Specific
Condition for Use			
Source of Power	Entrepreneur	Divided	Management
Objectives of Organization	Operational	Non-Operational	Operational
Organizational Environment	Yielding	Complex, Dynamic	Predictable, Stable
Status of Organization	Young, Small or Strong Leadership	Established	Large

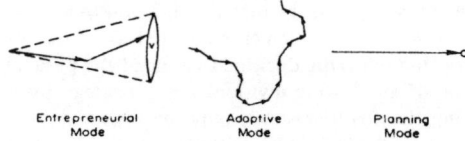

Figure 1.— Paths of the Three Modes

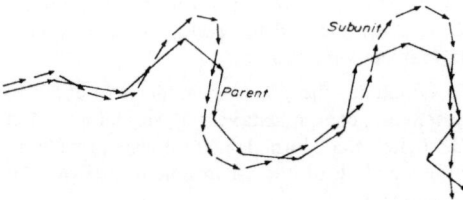

Figure 2.—Muddling Through Times Two

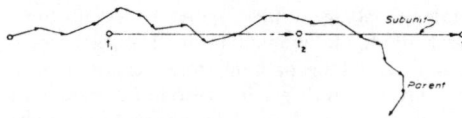

Figure 3.—Planning in an Adaptive Environment

to environmental forces, while the third figure indicates a precise plan with a specific, unalterable path to one clear end point.

The Determination of Mode

What conditions drive an organization to favor one mode of strategy-making over the others? We may delineate a number of characteristics of the organization itself, such as its size and the nature of its leadership, and features of its environment, such as competition and stability. These are discussed below and are summarized in the lower portion of Table I.

The *entrepreneurial* mode requires that strategy-making authority rest with one powerful individual. The environment must be yielding, the organization oriented toward growth, the strategy able to shift boldly at the whim of the entrepreneur. Clearly, these conditions are most typical of organizations that are small and/or young. Their sunk costs are low and they have little to lose by acting boldly. Young organizations in particular have set few precedents for themselves and have made few commitments. The way is open for them to bunch a number of key decisions at an early stage and take them in entrepreneurial fashion. This behavior may also be characteristic of the organization in trouble—it has little to lose by acting boldly, indeed this may be its only hope. In a study of the Montreal radio industry, one student concluded that the less successful stations were predisposed to adopt an entrepreneurial approach in order to catch up and displace the leader (whose behavior was primarily adaptive).

To satisfy the condition of centralized power, the organization must be either a business firm (often with the owner as chief executive), or an institutional or governmental body with a powerful leader who has a strong mandate. The entrepreneurial mode is often found with charismatic leadership. Charles de Gaulle could have been characterized as an entrepreneur at the head of government.

Use of the *adaptive* mode suggests that the organization faces a complex, rapidly changing environment and a divided coalition of influencer forces. Goals cannot be agreed upon unless they are in "motherhood" form and non-operational (they cannot be quantified). Here we have a clear description of the large established organization with great sunk costs and many controlling groups holding each other in check. This is typical of most universities, of many large hospitals, of a surprising number of large corporations, and of many governments, especially those in minority positions or composed of coalitions of divergent groups. Indeed, the American system of government has been expressly designed to create conditions of divided power, and it is, therefore, not surprising that Charles Lindblom, the chief proponent of the adaptive approach, is a student of the U.S. public policy-making process.

In order to rely on the *planning* mode, an organization must be large enough to afford the costs of formal analysis, it must have goals that are operational, and it must face an environment that is reasonably predictable and stable. (This last point inevitably raises the comment that planning is most necessary when the environment is difficult to understand. This may be true, but the costs of analyzing a complex environment may be prohibitive and the results may be discouraging. As one Latin American chief executive commented: "Planning is great. But how can you plan—let alone plan long-term—if you don't know what kind of government you'll have next year?"[19])

The above conditions suggest that formal comprehensive planning will generally be found in business firms of reasonable size that do not face severe and unpredictable competition and in government agencies that have clear, apolitical mandates. NASA of the 1960s is a prime example of extended use of the planning mode in government. Its goal was precise and operational, its funding predictable, its mission essentially apolitical in execution. The communist form of government with its five year plan is another good example. The power system is hierarchical, goals can be made operational, the home environment can be controlled and made more or less stable and predictable (at least as long as the crops are good).

Mixing the Modes

What is the relationship between our three abstractions and strategy-making reality? Clearly, few organizations can rely on a pure mode. More likely, an organization will find some combination of the three that reflects its own needs. Management students at McGill University have examined a number of business and public organizations according to these three modes, and they have uncovered a variety of ways in which organizations mix these modes. I shall discuss four combinations below, citing examples from these studies to illustrate each.

Combination 1: mixing the pure modes.—As we have seen, the literature tends to delineate three modes which are quite distinct in their characteristics. This trichotomy provides a convenient starting point for analysis; however, we cannot preclude the existence of other modes that mix their characteristics. Indeed, studies have revealed various combinations of the modes. We have, for example, found a number of adaptive entrepreneurs. One owned a car dealership. Reluctant to delegate authority but unable to achieve further growth without doing so, he was content to hold power absolutely, like the entrepreneur, but to avoid risk and move in incremental steps, like the adaptive strategymaker.

We can find the two other combinations of the pure modes as well. In entrepreneurial planning, the organization takes bold, decisive steps in terms of a systematic plan for growth, while in adaptive planning the organization reaches a specific goal through a flexible path. Herbert Simon describes an example of adaptive planning found in nature:

We watch an ant make his laborious way across a wind- and wave-molded beach. He moves ahead, angles to the right to ease his climb up a steep dunelet, detours around a pebble, stops for a moment to exchange information with a compatriot. Thus he makes his weaving, halting way back to his home.... [His path] has an underlying sense of direction, of aiming toward a goal.... He has a general sense of where home lies, but he cannot foresee all the obstacles between. He must adapt his course repeatedly to the difficulties he encounters...[20]

Combination 2: mixing modes by function.— Within single organizations, we have found different modes in different functional areas. One group of students carefully studied all departments of a large downtown hotel, and found evidence of all three modes. Where operations were largely routinized and predictable, as in housekeeping and the front office, the planning mode was used. In marketing, where there was room for imagination and bolder action, the hotel tended to act in an entrepreneurial fashion, while in the personnel department, which faced a complicated labor market, the mode was clearly adaptive.

Another group studied a modeling agency and found that in the area of fashion it was forced (as were all its competitors) to adapt to the dictates of the hautes couturieres of Paris, while it was free to be entrepreneurial or to plan in the areas of marketing and operations. Clearly, different parts of an organization can employ those modes which best fit their particular situations.

Combination 3: mixing modes between parent and subunit. —Neil Withers, a member of a group studying the Montreal International Airport (which comes under the purview of the Canadian Department of Transport), became interested in the relationship between a parent organization and its subunit (a division, a subsidiary, an agency, and so on). The question he addressed was: If the parent uses a particular mode, what limitations does that impose on the subunit (assuming, of course, that there is not enough decentralization to allow the subunit to operate independently)? Withers considers all nine possible combinations in which each could use one of the three modes, and he draws some interesting conclusions.

Figure 2 shows the use of the adaptive mode by both parent and subunit—a situation Withers refers to as "muddling through times two." In this case, the subunit merely follows the path of the parent, adapting to its incremental moves, and following a slightly more varied and lagged path. Withers concludes that the adaptive mode is, in fact, always an acceptable one for the subunit, no matter what the mode of the parent.

Withers believes "entrepreneurial duets"—whereby both parent and subunit employ the entrepreneurial mode—to be "the worst possible combination." The subunit is subjected not only to its own bold moves but to the unexpected bold moves of the parent. The disruption may prove intolerable. One is led to conclude that no centralized organization is big enough for two entrepreneurs. Sooner or later one must make a bold, unexpected move that interferes with the other. (In contrast, another group described a decentralized social work agency where strategy-making was largely in the hands of the social workers. They were all entrepreneurs, acting independently to initiate original programs and seeking approval from the main office whose behavior was described as adaptive.)

Finally, Withers considers the conditions under which the subunit can plan. Figure 3 shows a situation where the subunit plans while the parent organization adapts. The subunit at time t_1 anticipates the trend of the parent's strategy and plans accordingly.

Up to time t_2, no difficulties are incurred, and the subunit continues to extrapolate. But soon the parent's direction begins to change, and the subunit finds itself in conflict with the parent. According to Withers, "The use of planning in this uncertainty may not yield sufficiently improved results over [adapting] to justify the cost of planning and the long-term commitment of resources." Withers concludes that subunit planning will work only if the parent plans and if the two planning centers are properly coordinated.

Combination 4: mixing modes by stage of development. —A number of writers have described the growth of organizations in terms of three or four basic stages—generally corresponding to a life cycle beginning with youth and ending with maturity. It appears that we can characterize the various stages by the mode of strategy-making employed.

Generally, the young organization is entrepreneurial—it has few committed resources, it stands to lose little and to gain much by taking bold steps, leadership tends to be charismatic, and there is much spirit associated with its mission. This is the period of expansion and growth. But each new strategic decision commits additional resources, and gradually the organization locks itself into specific strategies, bureaucratic structures, and demanding pressure groups. The adaptive mode sets in. For example, one group of students studied a Montreal hospital which began in a most entrepreneurial fashion, with dramatic innovations in design and operation. Some time later, when the hospital was established, the provincial government took over increasing control of its budgets and by the time of the study these students felt that the adaptive mode was most descriptive of this organization's strategy-making behavior.

The adaptive mode may signal the final stage of maturity, or the conditions may be such that an organization can attempt to regenerate itself through a new period of entrepreneurship. In fact, it appears that the way to turn around a large, adaptive organization requiring major change is to bring in an entrepreneurial leader. Only by consolidating power in the hands of one strong newcomer will it be possible to override the established factions and the entrenched attitudes.

Some organizations appear to develop cyclical patterns in which periods of entrepreneurship are alternated with periods of adaptiveness. They make a set of bold changes in order to grow, then settle down to a period of stability in which the changes are consolidated, later embark on a new period of growth, and so on. Perhaps in some cases these follow economic cycles—an entrepreneurial mode in an expanding economy, an adaptive mode during recession.

Some time ago, I interviewed the president of a hotel chain who traced his firm's strategy through to the third distinct cycle of change and consolidation. The first stage of growth, as a real estate firm, involved the purchase of a number of older downtown hotels as property investments. Later, realizing the potential of investments, the firm entered a period of consolidation in which the properties were developed into an efficient hotel chain. Having reached this point after some years, a second wave of entrepreneurial growth began. First the firm became public in order to obtain expansion capital and then it entered into a major expansion program involving primarily the construction of a chain of modern motor hotels. Toward the end of the program, the firm found that its financial resources were overextended, partly due to higher expansion costs than anticipated. Again growth was halted while the firm consolidated its new units, concentrating on making them efficient, and waiting until its financial reserves were sufficient to begin to grow again. About three years later, at the time of the interview, cycle three has just begun, this time with the emphasis on the construction of larger downtown hotels.

Such an approach to strategy-making may, in fact, be a sensible one. It proceeds on the assumption that it is better to keep the modes distinct, concentrating fully on one mode at a time rather than mixing them and having to reconcile the different styles of strategy-making.

Other organizations, as they mature, tend to use the planning mode—the development of new strategies by controlled, orderly change. As these organizations grow large, they commit more and more of their staff resources to planning. Indeed, this is the thesis of John Kenneth Galbraith who claims, in *The New Industrial State,* that large business firms are controlled by the planners (the "technostructure") who use their techniques to enable the firms in turn to control their markets.

Our studies have not covered these large firms, but analyses of the strategy-making behaviors of a diverse array of smaller organizations—airlines, brokerage firms, universities, race tracks, cultural centers—suggest that virtually all start in the entrepreneurial mode, most later shift to an adaptive mode, and some move on to planning or back to entrepreneurship in their maturity.

Implications for Strategic Planning

What can we conclude from this description of strategy-making? One point merits special emphases. *Planning is not a panacea for the problems of strategy-making.* As obvious as this seems, there is little recognition of it in planning books or by planners. Instead, one finds a focus on abstract, simple models of the planning process that take no cognizance of the other two modes of strategy-making. Little wonder then that one finds so much frustration among formal planners. Rather than seeking panaceas, we should recognize that the mode used must fit the situation. An unpredictable environment suggests use of the adaptive mode just as the presence of a powerful leader may enable the organization to best achieve its goals through the entrepreneurial mode.

Some situations require no planning, others only limited planning. Often the planning mode can be used only when mixed with the others. Most important, planners must recognize the need for the manager to remain partially in the adaptive mode at all times. Crises and unexpected events are an important part of every strategy-maker's reality. Conventional planning requires operational goals which managers cannot always provide (the coalition may simply not agree on anything specific). Furthermore, it must be recognized that good planning is expensive, it often requires unrealistic stability in the environment, and, above all, it is the least flexible of the strategy-making modes. All this is not to conclude that planning is useless; rather, it suggests that the planner must become more realistic about the limitations of his science.

Often there is a need to redesign the formal planning process. Adaptive planning would differ from conventional planning in a number of important respects. The plans would be flexible so that the manager could adjust as the future unfolded itself. He would be able to time his moves accordingly—to begin construction on the new plant when interest rates fall, to reorganize the structure after certain executives retire. The plans would also provide for different options—alternate locations for a new plant depending on impending state legislation, different possible acquisition strategies depending on the success of recent acquisitions, and so on. In other words, like the path of the ant described earlier, strategic plans would specify end points and perhaps alternate routes, but they would also leave the manager with the flexibility necessary to react to his dynamic environment.

In addition, the planner could draw up a series of contingency plans to help the manager deal with any one of a number of possible events that could have a sudden, devastating effect on the organization. He could also be prepared to "plan in the real-time," that is, to apply his analytical techniques quickly for the manager who faces an unforeseen crisis. By preparing in this way, planners can more closely adapt themselves to the realities of strategy-making.

REFERENCES

1. O. Collins and D.G. Moore, *The Organization Makers* (New York: Appleton, Century, Crofts, 1970), p. 134.

2. P.F. Drucker, "Entrepreneurship in the Business Enterprise," *Journal of Business Policy* (1:1, 1970), p. 10.

3. *Ibid.*, p. 10.

4. Quoted in C.J. Hitch, *Decision-making for Defense* (Berkeley: University of California Press, 1967).

5. Collins and Moore, *op. cit.*, p. 45.

6. F. Harbison and C.A. Myers, *Management in the Industrial World* (New York: McGraw-Hill, 1959), pp. 40-41.

7. Drucker, *op. cit.*, p. 5.

8. S. Klaw, "The Entrepreneurial Ego," *Fortune* (August 1956), p. 143.

9. See C. E. Lindblom, "The Science of 'Muddling Through'" *Public Administration Review* (19, 1959), pp. 79-88; C. E. Lindblom and David Braybrooke, *A Strategy of Decision* (New York: Free Press, 1963); C. E. Lindblom, *The Intelligence of Democracy* (New York: Free Press, 1965); and C. E. Lindblom, *The Policy-making Process* (Englewood Cliffs, N.J.: Prentice-Hall, 1968).

10. R. M. Cyert and J. G. March, *A Behavioral Theory of the Firm* (Englewood Cliffs, N.J.: Prentice-Hall, 1963), p. 118.

11. Lindblom, *op. cit.*, (1968), p. 25.

12. *Ibid.*, p. 25.

13. Lindblom, *op. cit.*, (1968), p. 27.

14. R. L. Ackoff, *A Concept of Corporate Planning* (New York: Wiley Interscience, 1970), pp. 2-5.

15. G. A. Steiner, *Top Management Planning* (New York: Macmillan, 1969), p. 20.

16. Quoted in R. N. Anthony, *Planning and Control Systems: A Framework for Analysis* (Boston: Harvard Graduate School of Business Administration, 1965), p. 46-47.

17. M. F. Cantley, "A Long-range Planning Case Study," *OR Quarterly* (20, 1969), pp. 7-20.

18. R. L. Ackoff, *op. cit.*, p. 3.

19. Quoted by H. Stieglitz, *The Chief Executive and His Job* (New York: National Industrial Conference Board, Personnel Policy Study Number 214, 1969), pp. 46-47.

20. H. A. Simon, *The Sciences of the Artificial* (Cambridge, Mass.: MIT Press, 1969), pp. 23-24.

Of Strategies, Deliberate and Emergent

HENRY MINTZBERG
Faculty of Management, McGill University, Montreal, Quebec, Canada

JAMES A. WATERS
Faculty of Administrative Studies, York University, Toronto, Ontario, Canada

Summary

Deliberate and emergent strategies may be conceived as two ends of a continuum along which real-world strategies lie. This paper seeks to develop this notion, and some basic issues related to strategic choice, by elaborating along this continuum various types of strategies uncovered in research. These include strategies labelled planned, entrepreneurial, ideological, umbrella, process, unconnected, consensus and imposed.

How do strategies form in organizations? Research into the question is necessarily shaped by the underlying conception of the term. Since strategy has almost inevitably been conceived in terms of what the leaders of an organization 'plan' to do in the future, strategy formation has, not surprisingly, tended to be treated as an analytic process for establishing long-range goals and action plans for an organization; that is, as one of formulation followed by implementation. As important as this emphasis may be, we would argue that it is seriously limited, that the process needs to be viewed from a wider perspective so that the variety of ways in which strategies actually take shape can be considered.

For over 10 years now, we have been researching the process of strategy formation based on the definition of strategy as 'a pattern in a stream of decisions' (Mintzberg, 1972, 1978; Mintzberg and Waters, 1982, 1984; Mintzberg *et al.*, 1986, Mintzberg and McHugh, 1985; Brunet, Mintzberg and Waters, 1986). This definition was developed to 'operationalize' the concept of strategy, namely to provide a tangible basis on which to conduct research into how it forms in organizations. Streams of behaviour could be isolated and strategies identified as patterns or consistencies in such streams. The origins of these strategies could then be investigated, with particular attention paid to exploring the relationship between leadership plans and intentions and what the organizations actually did. Using the label strategy for both of these phenomena—one called *intended*, the other *realized*—encouraged that exploration. (Indeed, by this same logic, and because of practical necessity, we have been drawn into studying strategies as patterns in streams of actions, not decisions, since the latter represent intentions, too. A paper explaining this shift more fully is available from the authors.)

Comparing intended strategy with realized strategy, as shown in Figure 1, has allowed us to distinguish *deliberate* strategies—realized as intended—from *emergent* strategies— patterns or consistencies realized despite, or in the absence of, intentions. These two concepts, and especially their interplay, have become the central themes in our research, which has involved 11 intensive studies (as well as a larger number of smaller ones),

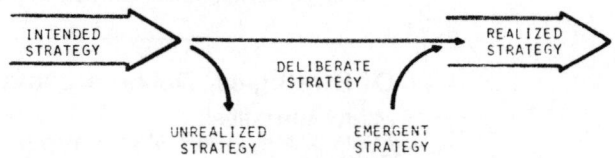

Figure 1. Types of strategies

including a food retailer, a manufacturer of women's undergarments, a magazine, a newspaper, an airline, an automobile firm, a mining company, a university, an architectural firm, a public film agency and a government fighting a foreign war.

This paper sets out to explore the complexity and variety of strategy formation processes by refining and elaborating the concepts of deliberate and emergent strategy. We begin by specifying more precisely what pure deliberate and pure emergent strategies might mean in the context of organization, describing the conditions under which each can be said to exist. What does it mean for an 'organization'—a collection of people joined together to pursue some mission in common—to act deliberately? What does it mean for a strategy to emerge in an organization, not guided by intentions? We then identify various types of strategies that have appeared in our empirical studies, each embodying differing degrees of what might be called deliberateness or emergentness. The paper concludes with a discussion of the implications of this perspective on strategy formation for research and practice.

PURE DELIBERATE AND PURE EMERGENT STRATEGIES

For a strategy to be perfectly deliberate—that is, for the realized strategy (pattern in actions) to form exactly as intended—at least three conditions would seem to have to be satisfied. First, there must have existed precise intentions in the organization, articulated in a relatively concrete level of detail, so that there can be no doubt about what was desired before any actions were taken. Secondly, because organization means collective action, to dispel any possible doubt about whether or not the intentions were organizational, they must have been common to virtually all the actors: either shared as their own or else accepted from leaders, probably in response to some sort of controls. Thirdly, these collective intentions must have been realized exactly as intended, which means that no external force (market, technological, political, etc.) could have interfered with them. The environment, in other words, must have been either perfectly predictable, totally benign, or else under the full control of the organization. These three conditions constitute a tall order, so that we are unlikely to find any perfectly deliberate strategies in organizations. Nevertheless, some strategies do come rather close, in some dimensions if not all.

For a strategy to be perfectly emergent, there must be order—consistency in action over time—in the absence of intention about it. (No consistency means no strategy or at least unrealized strategy—intentions not met.) It is difficult to imagine action in the *total* absence of intention—in some pocket of the organization if not from the leadership itself—such that we would expect the purely emergent strategy to be as rare as the purely deliberate one. But again, our research suggests that some patterns come rather close, as when an environment directly imposes a pattern of action on an organization.

Thus, we would expect to find tendencies in the directions of deliberate and emergent strategies rather than perfect forms of either. In effect, these two form the poles of a continuum along which we would expect real-world strategies to fall. Such strategies would combine various states of the dimensions we have discussed above: leadership intentions would be more or less precise, concrete and explicit, and more or less shared, as would intentions existing elsewhere in the organization; central control over organizational actions would be more or less firm and more or less pervasive; and the environment would be more or less benign, more or less controllable and more or less predictable.

Below we introduce a variety of types of strategies that fall along this continuum, beginning with those closest to the deliberate pole and ending with those most reflective of the characteristics of emergent strategy. We present these types, not as any firm or exhaustive typology (although one may eventually emerge), but simply to explore this continuum of emergentness of strategy and to try to gain some insights into the notions of intention, choice and pattern formation in the collective context we call organization.

THE PLANNED STRATEGY

———————————▶

Planning suggests clear and articulated intentions, backed up by formal controls to ensure their pursuit, in an environment that is acquiescent. In other words, here (and only here) does the classic distinction between 'formulation' and 'implementation' hold up.

In this first type, called *planned strategy*, leaders at the centre of authority formulate their intentions as precisely as possible and then strive for their implementation—their translation into collective action—with a minimum of distortion, 'surprise-free'. To ensure this, the leaders must first articulate their intentions in the form of a plan, to minimize confusion, and then elaborate this plan in as much detail as possible, in the form of budgets, schedules and so on, to pre-empt discretion that might impede its realization. Those outside the planning process may act, but to the extent possible they are not allowed to decide. Programmes that guide their behaviour are built into the plan, and formal controls are instituted to ensure pursuit of the plan and the programmes.

But the plan is of no use if it cannot be applied as formulated in the environment surrounding the organization so the planned strategy is found in an environment that is, if not benign or controllable, then at least rather predictable. Some organizations, as Galbraith (1967) describes the 'new industrial states', are powerful enough to impose their plans on their environments. Others are able to predict their environments with enough accuracy to pursue rather deliberate, planned strategies. We suspect, however, that many planned strategies are found in organizations that simply extrapolate established patterns in environments that they assume will remain stable. In fact, we have argued elsewhere (Mintzberg and Waters, 1982) that strategies appear not to be *conceived* in planning processes so much as elaborated from existing visions or copied from standard industry recipes (see Grinyer and Spender, 1979); planning thus becomes programming, and the planned strategy finds its origins in one of the other types of strategies described below.

Although few strategies can be planned to the degree described above, some do come rather close, particularly in organizations that must commit large quantities of resources to particular missions and so cannot tolerate unstable environments. They may spend years considering their actions, but once they decide to act, they commit themselves firmly. In effect, they deliberate so that their strategies can be rather deliberate. Thus, we studied a mining company that had to engage in a most detailed form of planning to exploit a new ore body in an extremely remote part of Quebec. Likewise, we found a very strong planning orientation in our study of Air Canada, necessary to co-ordinate the purchase of new, expensive jet aircraft with a relatively fixed route structure. Our study of the United States government's escalation of military activity in Vietnam also revealed a rather planned strategy. Once Lyndon Johnson announced his decision to escalate in 1965, the military planners took over and articulated the intentions in detail (or pulled out existing contingency plans), and pursued the strategy vigorously until 1968 when it became clear that the environment was less controllable than it had seemed (Mintzberg, 1978).

(Note the distinction here between unrealized strategy—that is, intentions not successfully realized—and realized strategy that is unsuccessful in its consequences. The intention to escalate was realized, in fact from Johnson's point of view, *over*-realized; it just did not achieve its objective. In contrast, John F. Kennedy's earlier intention to provide advisers to the Vietnam army was not realized to the extent that those advisers became combatants. It should be noted, however, that the degree of deliberateness is not a measure of the potential success of a strategy. In our research, we have come across rather emergent strategies as well as rather deliberate ones that have been highly successful (see the discussion of the experimental film strategy later in the text for an example of the former) and others of both types that have been dramatic failures.)

THE ENTREPRENEURIAL STRATEGY

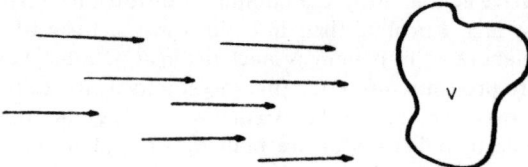

In this second type of strategy, we relax the condition of precise, articulated intentions. Here, one individual in personal control of an organization is able to impose his or her vision of direction on it. Because such strategies are rather common in entrepreneurial firms, tightly controlled by their owners, they can be called *entrepreneurial strategies*.

In this case, the force for pattern or consistency in action is individual vision, the central actor's *concept* of his or her organization's place in its world. This is coupled with an ability to impose that vision on the organization through his or her personal control of its actions (e.g. through giving direct orders to its operating personnel). Of course, the environment must again be co-operative. But entrepreneurial strategies most commonly appear in young and/or small organizations (where personal control is feasible), which are able to find relatively safe niches in their environments. Indeed, the selection of such niches is an integral part of the vision. These strategies can, however, sometimes be found in larger organizations as well, particularly under conditions of crisis where all the actors are willing to follow the direction of a single leader who has vision and will.

Is the entrepreneurial strategy deliberate? Intentions do exist. But they derive from one individual who need not articulate or elaborate them. Indeed, for reasons discussed below, he or she is typically unlikely to want to do so. Thus, the intentions are both more difficult to identify and less specific than those of the planned strategy. Moreover, there is less overt acceptance of these intentions on the part of other actors in the organization. Nevertheless, so long as those actors respond to the personal will of the leader, the strategy would appear to be rather deliberate.

In two important respects, however, that strategy can have emergent characteristics as well. First, as indicated in the previous diagram, vision provides only a general sense of direction. Within it, there is room for adaptation: the details of the vision can emerge *en route*. Secondly, because the leader's vision is personal, it can also be changed completely. To put this another way, since here the formulator is the implementor, step by step, that person can react quickly to feedback on past actions or to new opportunities or threats in the environment. He or she can thus reformulate vision, as shown in the figure below.

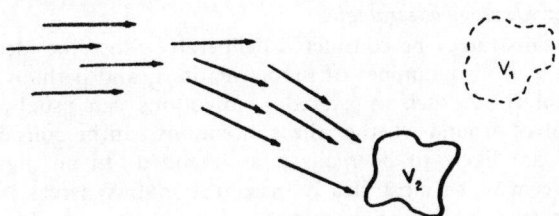

It is this adaptability that distinguishes the entrepreneurial strategy from the planned one. Visions contained in single brains would appear to be more flexible, assuming the individual's willingness to learn,[1] than plans articulated through hierarchies, which are comprised of many brains. Adaptation (and emergentness) of planned strategies are discouraged by the articulation of intentions and by the separation between formulation and implementation. Psychologists have shown that the articulation of a strategy locks it into place, impeding willingness to change it (e.g. Kiesler, 1971). The separation of implementation from formulation gives rise to a whole system of commitments and procedures, in the form of plans, programmes and controls elaborated down a hierarchy. Instead of one individual being able to change his or her mind, the whole system must be redesigned. Thus, despite the claims of flexible planning, the fact is that organizations plan not to be flexible but to realize specific intentions. It is the entrepreneurial strategy that provides flexibility, at the expense of the specificity and articulation of intentions.

Entrepreneurial strategies have appeared in our research, not surprisingly, in two companies that were controlled personally by their aggressive owners—one the food retail chain, the other the manufacturer of women's undergarments. Here, typically, when important aspects of the environment changed, strong new visions emerged rather quickly, followed by long periods of deliberate pursuit of these visions. But as both organizations grew and became more formalized, the visions became the basis for planning (programming), and thereafter decisive changes were less in evidence. This led us to suspect that planned strategies often follow entrepreneurial ones, based on the vision of leaders, sometimes ones who have departed the organization (see Mintzberg and Waters, 1982, 1984).

---

[1] An interesting situation arises when the vision is beyond even the control of the individual himself, so that he or she pursues a pattern of action due to inner, subconscious forces (as, say, when the leader chooses to produce only unconventional products, perhaps because of a phobia about being ordinary). Such 'subconscious' strategies would probably be more difficult to change than those based on more conscious visions.

THE IDEOLOGICAL STRATEGY

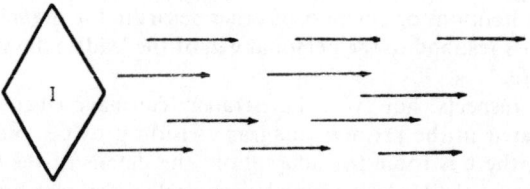

Vision can be collective as well as individual. When the members of an organization share a vision and identify so strongly with it that they pursue it as an ideology, then they are bound to exhibit patterns in their behaviour, so that clear realized strategies can be identified. These may be called *ideological strategies*.

Can an ideological strategy be considered deliberate? Since the ideology is likely to be somewhat overt (e.g. in programmes of indoctrination), and perhaps even articulated (in rough, inspirational form, such as a credo), intentions can usually be identified. The question thus revolves around whether these intentions can be considered organizational and whether they are likely to be realized as intended. In an important sense, these intentions would seem to be most clearly organizational. Whereas the intentions of the planned and entrepreneurial strategies emanate from one centre and are accepted passively by everyone else, those of the ideological strategy are positively embraced by the members of the organization.

As for their realization, because the intentions exist as a rough vision, they can presumably be adapted or changed. But collective vision is far more immutable than individual vision. All who share it must agree to change their 'collective mind'. Moreover, ideology is rooted in the past, in traditions and precedents (often the institutionalization of the vision of a departed, charismatic leader: one person's vision has become everyone's ideology). People, therefore, resist changing it. The object is to interpret 'the word', not to defy it. Finally, the environment is unlikely to impose change: the purpose of ideology, after all, is to change the environment or else to insulate the organization from it. For all these reasons, therefore, ideological strategy would normally be highly deliberate, perhaps more so than any type of strategy except the planned one.

We have not as yet studied any organization dominated by an ideology. But such strategies do seem to occur in certain organizations described in the literature, notably in certain Israeli kibbutzim, 'distinctive colleges', and some charitable institutions (see Clark, 1970, 1972; Sills, 1957; also Mintzberg, 1983: Chapters 11 and 21).

THE UMBRELLA STRATEGY

Now we begin to relax the condition of tight control (whether bureaucratic, personal or ideological) over the mass of actors in the organization and, in some cases, the condition of tight control over the environment as well. Leaders who have only partial control over other actors in an organization may design what can be called *umbrella strategies*. They set general guidelines for behaviour—define the boundaries—and then let other actors manoeuvre within them. In effect, these leaders establish kinds of umbrellas under which organizational actions are expected to fall—for example that all products should be designed for the high-priced end of the market (no matter what those products might be).

When an environment is complex, and perhaps somewhat uncontrollable and unpredictable as well, a variety of actors in the organization must be able to respond to it. In other words, the patterns in organizational actions cannot be set deliberately in one central place, although the boundaries may be established there to constrain them. From the perspective of the leadership (if not, perhaps, the individual actors), therefore, strategies are allowed to emerge, at least within these boundaries. In fact, we can label the umbrella strategy not only deliberate and emergent (intended at the centre in its broad outlines but not in its specific details), but also 'deliberately emergent' (in the sense that the central leadership intentionally creates the conditions under which strategies can emerge).

Like the entrepreneurial strategy, the umbrella one represents a certain vision emanating from the central leadership. But here those who have the vision do not control its realization; instead they must convince others to pursue it. The umbrella at least puts limits on the actions of others and ideally provides a sense of direction as well. Sometimes the umbrella takes the form of a more specific target, as in a NASA that concentrated its efforts during the 1960s on putting a man on the moon. In the light of this specific target, all kinds of strategies emerged, as various technical problems were solved by thousands of different specialists.

The architectural firm in our research provides a good example of umbrella strategy. The partners made it clear what kinds of buildings they wished to design: unique, excellent and highly visible ones that would 'celebrate the spirit of the community'. Under that umbrella, anything went—performing arts centres, office buildings, hotels, etc. The firm occasionally filled in gaps with smaller projects of a more mundane nature, but it never committed itself to a major undertaking that strayed from those central criteria (Mintzberg *et al.*, 1986).[2]

We have so far described the umbrella strategy as one among a number of types that are possible. But, in some sense, virtually all real-world strategies have umbrella characteristics. That is to say, in no organization can the central leadership totally pre-empt the discretion of others (as was assumed in the planned and entrepreneurial strategies) and, by the same token, in none does a central leadership defer totally to others (unless it has ceased to lead). Almost all strategy making behaviour involves, therefore, to some degree at least, a central leadership with some sort of intentions trying to direct, guide, cajole or nudge others with ideas of their own. When the leadership is able to direct, we move towards the realm of the planned or entrepreneurial strategies; when it can hardly nudge, we move toward the realm of the more emergent strategies. But in the broad range between these two can always be found strategies with umbrella characteristics.

In its pursuit of an umbrella strategy—which means, in essence, defining general direction subject to varied interpretation—the central leadership must monitor the behaviour of other actors to assess whether or not the boundaries are being respected. In

---

[2] Of course, to the extent that other architects in the firm embraced these criteria, instead of merely accepting them as the intentions of the central leadership, the strategy could have been labelled ideological.

essence, like us, it searches for patterns in streams of actions. When actors are found to stray outside the boundaries (whether inadvertently or intentionally), the central leadership has three choices: to stop them, ignore them (perhaps for a time, to see what will happen), or adjust to them. In other words, when an arm pokes outside the umbrella, you either pull it in, leave it there (although it might get wet), or move the umbrella over to cover it.

In this last case, the leadership exercises the option of altering its own vision in response to the behaviour of others. Indeed, this would appear to be the place where much effective strategic learning takes place—through leadership response to the initiatives of others. The leadership that is never willing to alter its vision in such a way forgoes important opportunities and tends to lose touch with its environment (although, of course, the one too willing to do so may be unable to sustain any central direction). The umbrella strategy thus requires a light touch, maintaining a subtle balance between proaction and reaction.

THE PROCESS STRATEGY

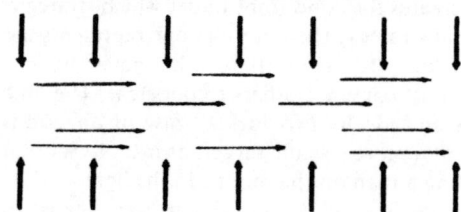

Similar to the umbrella strategy is what can be called the *process strategy*. Again, the leadership functions in an organization in which other actors must have considerable discretion to determine outcomes, because of an environment that is complex and perhaps also unpredictable and uncontrollable. But instead of trying to control strategy content at a general level, through boundaries or targets, the leadership instead needs to exercise influence indirectly. Specifically, it controls the *process* of strategy making while leaving the *content* of strategy to other actors. Again, the resulting behaviour would be deliberate in one respect and emergent in others: the central leadership designs the system that allows others the flexibility to evolve patterns within it.

The leadership may, for example, control the staffing of the organization, thereby determining who gets to make strategy if not what that strategy will be (all the while knowing that control of the former constitutes considerable influence over the latter). Or it may design the structure of the organization to determine the working context of those who get to make strategy. Thus, it was claimed recently that '75 per cent of the (Hewlett Packard) plan is devoted to the new product portfolio generation *process*'.[3]

Divisionalized organizations of a conglomerate nature commonly use process strategies: the central headquarters creates the basic structure, establishes the control systems and appoints the division managers, who are then expected to develop strategies for their own businesses (typically planned ones for reasons outlined by Mintzberg, 1979:384–392); note that techniques such as those introduced by the Boston Consulting Group to manage the

---

[3] Statement by Thomas Peters at the Strategic Management Society Conference 'Exploring the Strategy-making Process', Montreal, 8 October, 1982; emphasis added.

business portfolios of divisionalized companies, by involving headquarters in the business strategies to some extent, bring their strategies back into the realm of umbrella ones.

THE UNCONNECTED STRATEGIES

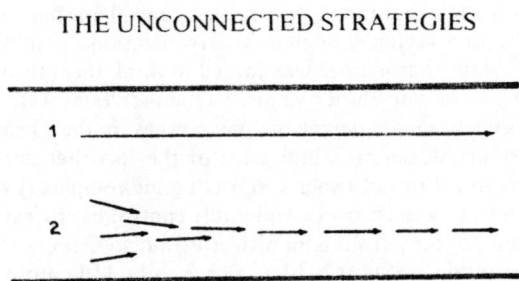

The *unconnected strategy* is perhaps the most straightforward one of all. One part of the organization with considerable discretion—a subunit, sometimes even a single individual—because it is only loosely coupled to the rest, is able to realize its own pattern in its stream of actions. Our clearest example of this appeared in the study of the National Film Board of Canada, a producer of primarily short films, where the central leadership seldom dictated the content of films. From the 1940s to the mid-1960s, the Film Board produced, among many others, a thin but steady stream of experimental films; after that, their number increased significantly. In fact, with one exception, every single film up to 1960 was made by one person, Norman McLaren, the Board's most celebrated film-maker. McLaren, in other words, pursued his own personal strategy—'did his own thing', as the saying goes—for decades, quite independently of the activities of other film-makers.

How deliberate or emergent are these unconnected strategies? Since they come neither from a central leadership nor from intentions in the organization at large, they would seem to be relatively emergent from the perspective of the entire organization. But from the perspective of the unit or individual involved, clearly they can be deliberate or emergent, depending on the prior existence of intentions.

Identifying intentions is a tricky business in any context. Who can be sure that what was articulated was truly intended. Moreover, in the collective context, there is the problem of determining whose intentions really matter, and of dealing with conflicting intentions. These problems may be absent in the context of the individual, but they are replaced by others. For example, the individual pursuing a personal strategy is unlikely to have to articulate his or her intentions before actions are taken, and that can influence the very existence of intentions. Consider the experimental film strategy of Norman McLaren. Was it deliberate? For McLaren himself, it could conceivably have been. That is, he may have developed a general intention to make a stream of experimental films, at least after his initial successes. But why should he have done so? Surely McLaren did not say to himself in 1943: 'I shall make experimental films for the next 30 years'. More likely, he just decided on one film at a time, in effect being deliberate about individual films (although these too may have emerged) but not about the pattern in the sequence of them.

The fact that a Norman McLaren has no need to articulate his intentions (unlike, at least in some cases, a leader in charge of other people) means that no one can ever be sure what he intended (or, more exactly, what he would have claimed he intended). To take another example, used in a previous paper to illustrate the definition of realized strategy (Mintzberg,

1978: 935), Picasso's blue period can be called a personal blue strategy, since there was consistency in his use of colour across a sequence of his paintings. But did Picasso 'decide' to paint blue for a given period of his life, or did he simply feel like using that blue each time he painted during these years?

The fact that neither a McLaren nor a Picasso had to explain their intentions to anyone (McLaren at least not beyond saying enough in his organizational context to get funding for a single film at a time) meant that neither was forced to think them through. This probably allowed those intentions to remain rather vague, to themselves as well as to others around them, and so probably encouraged a degree of emergentness in their behaviours.

The example of Norman McLaren is indicative of the fact that unconnected strategies tend to proliferate in organizations of experts, reflecting the complexity of the environments that they face and the resulting need for considerable control by the experts over their own work, providing freedom not only from administrators but sometimes from their own peers as well. Thus, many hospitals and universities appear to be little more than collections of personal strategies, with hardly any discernible central vision or umbrella, let alone plan, linking them together. Each expert pursues his or her own strategies—method of patient care, subject of research, style of teaching. On the other hand, in organizations that do pursue central, rather deliberate strategies, even planned ones, unconnected strategies can sometimes be found in remote enclaves, either tolerated by the system or lost within it.

As indicated in the previous diagram, unconnected strategies may be deliberate or emergent for the actors involved (although always emergent from the perspective of the organization at large). Also, although they are shown within an umbrella strategy, clearly they can fall outside of these, too. Indeed, some unconnected strategies directly contradict umbrella ones (or even more centrally imposed planned or entrepreneurial ones), in effect developing on a clandestine basis. Allison (1971), for example, describes how President Kennedy's directive to defuse the missile bases in Turkey during the Cuban Missile Crisis was deliberately ignored by the military leaders. We show such clandestine strategies in the figure below as a sequence of arrows breaking out of an umbrella strategy. These arrows signify that even though the strategy is likely to be deliberate from the point of view of its proponents, it cannot be articulated as such: they cannot reveal their intentions. To minimize their risk of exposure, they seek to realize intentions subtly, action by action, as if the strategy was emergent. Of course, that increases the chances that the intentions will get deflected along the way. If they do not, there is still the risk that the leadership will realize what is happening—will recognize the pattern in the stream of actions—and stop the strategy. The leadership can, however, play the game too, waiting to see what happens, knowing it too can learn from clandestine behaviour. If the strategy should prove successful, it can always be accepted and broadened—internalized in the system as a (henceforth) deliberate strategy. Our suspicion is that much strategic adaptation results from unconnected strategies (whether or not clandestine) that succeed and so pervade the organization.

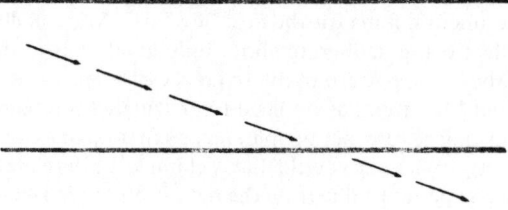

THE CONSENSUS STRATEGY

In no strategy so far discussed have we totally dropped the condition of prior intention. The next type is rather more clearly emergent. Here many different actors naturally converge on the same theme, or pattern, so that it becomes pervasive in the organization, without the need for any central direction or control. We call it the *consensus strategy*. Unlike the ideological strategy, in which a consensus forms around a system of beliefs (thus reflecting intentions widely accepted in the organization), the consensus strategy grows out of the mutual adjustment among different actors, as they learn from each other and from their various responses to the environment and thereby find a common, and probably unexpected, pattern that works for them.

In other words, the convergence is not driven by any intentions of a central management, nor even by prior intentions widely shared among the other actors. It just evolves through the results of a host of individual actions. Of course, certain actors may actively promote the consensus, perhaps even negotiate with their colleagues to attain it (as in the congressional form of government). But the point is that it derives more from collective action than from collective intention.

Our clearest example of a consensus strategy formed so fast that it seemed literally spontaneous. In the early 1950s, the National Film Board of Canada made its first film for television and in a matter of months the organization found itself concentrating two-thirds of its efforts in that medium. Despite heated debate and indications of managerial intentions to the contrary, one film-maker set the precedent by making that first film, and many of the others quickly followed suit. (In fact, the strategy lasted about 4 years and then disappeared just as spontaneously as it began.) Such spontaneity presumably reflects a strong drive for consistency (the Film Board having been groping for a new focus of attention for several years). As soon as the right idea comes along, the consensus crystallizes quickly, much as does a supersaturated solution the moment it is disturbed. We have been speculating on possible uses for the term intuition in a collective context; the spontaneous strategy might be a good example of 'organizational intuition'.

When the convergence is on a general theme rather than a specific activity (such as making films for television), the consensus is likely to develop more gradually: individual actions would take time to be understood and to pervade the organization as precedents. An electronics manufacturer may find itself concentrating on high quality products after it had achieved success with a number of such products, or a university may find itself over the years favouring the sciences over the humanitites as its members came to realize that this is where its real strengths lie.

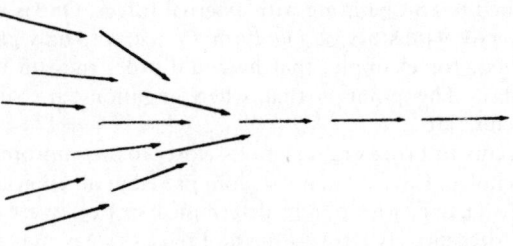

THE IMPOSED STRATEGIES

All the strategies so far discussed have derived in part at least from the will (if not the intentions) of actors within the organization. The environment has been considered, if not benign, then at least acquiescent. But strategies can be *imposed* from outside as well; that is, the environment can directly force the organization into a pattern in its stream of actions, regardless of the presence of central controls. The clearest case of this occurs when an external individual or group with a great deal of influence over the organization imposes a strategy on it. We saw this in our study of the state-owned Air Canada, when the minister who created and controlled the airline in its early years forced it to buy and fly a particular type of aircraft. Here the imposed strategy was clearly deliberate, but not by anyone in the organization. However, given its inability to resist, the organization had to resign itself to the pursuit of the strategy, so that it became, in effect, deliberate.

Sometimes the 'environment' rather than people *per se* impose strategies on organizations, simply by severely restricting the options open to them. Air Canada chose to fly jet aeroplanes and later wide-body aeroplanes. But did it? Could any 'world class' airline have decided otherwise? Again the organization has internalized the imperative so that strategic choice becomes a moot point. To draw from another of our studies, did Lyndon Johnson 'choose' to escalate the United States' involvement in Vietnam in 1965? Kennedy's earlier intended strategy of providing advisers for the South Vietnamese became an emergent strategy of engagement in a hot war, imposed by the environment (namely the actions of the Vietcong; of course, to the extent that the military advisers intended to fight, the strategy might be more accurately described as clandestine). The result was that by the time Johnson faced the decision to escalate, the pressures were almost inescapable. So he 'decided', and the strategy became a planned one.

Many planned strategies in fact seem to have this determined quality to them—pursued by organizations resigned to co-operating with external forces. One is reminded here of the king in the Saint-Exupéry (1946) story of *The Little Prince*, who only gave orders that could be executed. He claimed, for example, that he could order the sun to set, but only at a certain time of the day. The point is that when intentions are sufficiently malleable, everything can seem deliberate.

Reality, however, seems to bring organizations closer to a compromise position between determinism and free choice. Environments seldom pre-empt all choice, just as they seldom offer unlimited choice. That is why purely determined strategies are probably as rare as purely planned ones. Alternatively, just as the umbrella strategy may be the most realistic reflection of leadership intention, so too might the partially imposed strategy be the most realistic reflection of environmental influence. As shown in the figure below, the environment bounds what the organization can do, in this illustration determining under what part of the umbrella the organization can feasibly operate. Earlier we described the umbrella strategy of the architectural firm we studied. During one period in its history, it was repeatedly selected to design performing arts centres, even though it was prepared to work on a wide variety of building types. The environment (namely the clients) made its choices for it and so determined its specific strategy for a time, but only within the strategic umbrella acceptable to it. Just as we argued earlier that virtually all real-world strategies have umbrella characteristics, so too do we add here that virtually all have environmental boundaries.

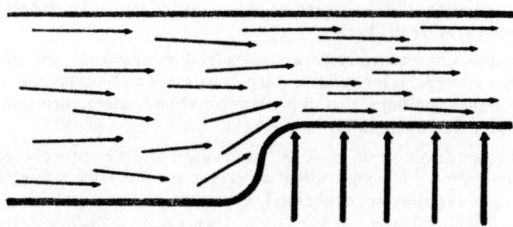

This completes our discussion of various types of strategies. Table 1 summarizes some of their major features.

EMERGING CONCLUSIONS

This paper has been written to open up thinking about strategy formation, to broaden perspectives that may remain framed in the image of it as an *a priori*, analytic process or even as a sharp dichotomy between strategies as either deliberate or emergent. We believe that more research is required on the process of strategy formation to complement the extensive work currently taking place on the content of strategies; indeed, we believe that research on the former can significantly influence the direction taken by research on the latter (and vice versa).

One promising line of research is investigation of the strategy formation process and of the types of strategies realized as a function of the structure and context of organizations. Do the various propositions suggested in this paper, based on our own limited research, in fact hold up in broader samples, for example, that strategies will tend to be more deliberate in tightly coupled, centrally controlled organizations and more emergent in decentralized, loosely coupled ones?

It would also be interesting to know how different types of strategies perform in various contexts and also how these strategies relate to those defined in terms of specific content. Using Porter's (1980) categories, for example, will cost leadership strategies prove more deliberate (specifically, more often planned), differentiation strategies more emergent (perhaps umbrella in nature), or perhaps entrepreneurial? Or using Miles and Snow's (1978) typology, will defenders prove more deliberate in orientation and inclined to use planned strategies, whereas prospectors tend to be more emergent and more prone to rely on umbrella or process, or even unconnected, strategies? It may even be possible that highly deliberate strategy making processes will be found to drive organizations away from

Table 1. Summary description of types of strategies

Strategy	Major features
Planned	Strategies originate in formal plans: precise intentions exist, formulated and articulated by central leadership, backed up by formal controls to ensure surprise-free implementation in benign, controllable or predictable environment; strategies most deliberate
Entrepreneurial	Strategies originate in central vision: intentions exist as personal, unarticulated vision of single leader, and so adaptable to new opportunities; organization under personal control of leader and located in protected niche in environment; strategies relatively deliberate but can emerge
Ideological	Strategies originate in shared beliefs: intentions exist as collective vision of all actors, in inspirational form and relatively immutable, controlled normatively through indoctrination and/or socialization; organization often proactive *vis-à-vis* environment; strategies rather deliberate
Umbrella	Strategies originate in constraints: leadership, in partial control of organizational actions, defines strategic boundaries or targets within which other actors respond to own forces or to complex, perhaps also unpredictable environment; strategies partly deliberate, partly emergent and deliberately emergent
Process	Strategies originate in process: leadership controls process aspects of strategy (hiring, structure, etc.), leaving content aspects to other actors; strategies partly deliberate, partly emergent (and, again, deliberately emergent)
Unconnected	Strategies originate in enclaves: actor(s) loosely coupled to rest of organization produce(s) patterns in own actions in absence of, or in direct contradiction to, central or common intentions; strategies organizationally emergent whether or not deliberate for actor(s)
Consensus	Strategies originate in consensus: through mutual adjustment, actors converge on patterns that become pervasive in absence of central or common intentions; strategies rather emergent
Imposed	Strategies originate in environment: environment dictates patterns in actions either through direct imposition or through implicitly pre-empting or bounding organizational choice; strategies most emergent, although may be internalized by organization and made deliberate

prospecting activities and towards cost leadership strategies whereas emergent ones may encourage the opposite postures.

The interplay of the different types of strategies we have described can be another avenue of inquiry: the nesting of personal strategies within umbrella ones or their departure in clandestine form from centrally imposed umbrellas; the capacity of unconnected strategies to evoke organizational ones of a consensus or even a planned nature as peripheral patterns that succeed pervade the organization; the conversion of entrepreneurial strategies into ideological or planned ones as vision becomes institutionalized one way or another; the possible propensity of imposed strategies to become deliberate as they are internalized within the organization; and so on. An understanding of how these different types of strategies blend into each other and tend to sequence themselves over time in different contexts could reveal a good deal about the strategy formation process.

At a more general level, the whole question of how managers learn from the experiences of their own organizations seems to be fertile ground for research. In our view, the fundamental difference between deliberate and emergent strategy is that whereas the former focuses on direction and control—getting desired things done—the latter opens up this notion of 'strategic learning'. Defining strategy as intended and conceiving it as deliberate, as has traditionally been done, effectively precludes the notion of strategic learning. Once the intentions have been set, attention is riveted on realizing them, not on adapting them.

Messages from the environment tend to get blocked out. Adding the concept of emergent strategy, based on the definition of strategy as realized, opens the process of strategy making up to the notion of learning.

Emergent strategy itself implies learning what works—taking one action at a time in search for that viable pattern or consistency. It is important to remember that emergent strategy means, not chaos, but, in essence, *unintended order*. It is also frequently the means by which deliberate strategies change. As shown in Figure 2, in the feedback loop added to our basic diagram, it is often through the identification of emergent strategies—its patterns never intended—that managers and others in the organization come to change their intentions. This is another way of saying that not a few deliberate strategies are simply emergent ones that have been uncovered and subsequently formalized. Of course, unrealized strategies are also a source of learning, as managers find out which of their intentions do not work, rejected either by their organizations themselves or else by environments that are less than acquiescent.

We wish to emphasize that emergent strategy does not have to mean that management is out of control, only—in some cases at least—that it is open, flexible and responsive, in other words, willing to learn. Such behaviour is especially important when an environment is too unstable or complex to comprehend, or too imposing to defy. Openness to such emergent strategy enables management to act before everything is fully understood—to respond to an evolving reality rather than having to focus on a stable fantasy. For example, distinctive competence cannot always be assessed on paper *a priori*; often, perhaps usually, it has to be discovered empirically, by taking actions that test where strengths and weaknesses really lie. Emergent strategy also enables a management that cannot be close enough to a situation, or to know enough about the varied activities of its organization, to surrender control to those who have the information current and detailed enough to shape realistic strategies. Whereas the more deliberate strategies tend to emphasize central direction and hierarchy, the more emergent ones open the way for collective action and convergent behaviour.

Of course, by the same token, deliberate strategy is hardly dysfunctional either. Managers need to manage too, sometimes to impose intentions on their organizations—to provide a sense of direction. That can be partial, as in the cases of umbrella and process strategies, or it can be rather comprehensive, as in the cases of planned and entrepreneurial strategies. When the necessary information can be brought to a central place and environments can be largely understood and predicted (or at least controlled), then it may be appropriate to suspend strategic learning for a time to pursue intentions with as much determination as possible (see Mintzberg and Waters, 1984).

Our conclusion is that strategy formation walks on two feet, one deliberate, the other emergent. As noted earlier, managing requires a light deft touch—to direct in order to realize intentions while at the same time responding to an unfolding pattern of action. The relative emphasis may shift from time to time but not the requirement to attend to both sides of this phenomenon.

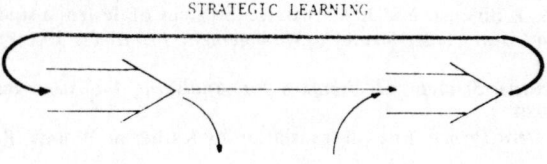

Figure 2

We need to know more about the responding side of this directing/responding dialectic. More specifically, we would like to know more about how managers track the realized strategies of their own organizations. A major component of that elusive concept called 'strategic control' may be in managers doing what we do as researchers: searching for patterns in streams of organizational actions. Pattern recognition is likely to prove a crucial ability of effective managers and crucial to effective organizations may be the facilitation of self-awareness on the part of all its members of the patterns of its own actions and their consequences over time. Strategic choice requires that kind of awareness; a high degree of it is likely to characterize effective managers and effective organizations.

REFERENCES

Allison, G. T. *Essence of Decision: Explaining the Cuban Missile Crisis*, Little, Brown, Boston, 1971.
Brunet, J. P. H. Mintzberg and J. Waters. 'Does planning impede strategic thinking? The strategy of Air Canada 1937–1976,' in Lamb, R (ed.) *Advances in Strategic Management*, Volume 4, Prentice-Hall, Englewood Cliffs, N. J., 1986.
Chandler, A. D. *Strategy and Structure*, MIT Press, Cambridge, 1962.
Clark, B. R. *The Distinctive College*, Aldino, Chicago, 1970.
Clark, B. R. 'The organizational saga in higher education', *Administrative Science Quarterly*, 1972, pp. 178–184.
Galbraith, J. K. *The New Industrial State*, Houghton Mifflin, Boston, 1967.
Grinyer, P. H. and J. C. Spender. *Turnaround: the Fall and Rise of the Newton Chambers Group*, Association Business Press, London, 1979.
Kiesler, C. H. *The Psychology of Commitment: Experiments Linking Behaviour to Belief*, Academic Press, New York, 1971.
Miles, R. and C. Snow. *Organizational Strategy, Structure, and Process*, McGraw-Hill, New York, 1978.
Mintzberg, H. 'Research on strategy-making', *Proceedings of the 32nd Annual Meeting of the Academy of Management*, Minneapolis, 1972.
Mintzberg, H. 'Patterns in strategy formation', *Management Science*, 1978, pp. 934–948.
Mintzberg, H. *The Structuring of Organizations*, Prentice-Hall, Englewood Cliffs, N.J., 1979.
Mintzberg, H. *Power in and Around Organization*, Prentice-Hall, Englewood Cliffs, N.J., 1983.
Mintzberg, H. and A. McHugh. 'Strategy Formation in Adhocracy', *Administrative Science Quarterly*, forthcoming in 1985.
Mintzberg, H., D. Raisinghani and A. Theoret. 'The structure of "unstructured" decision processes', *Administrative Science Quarterly*, 1976, pp. 246–275.
Mintzberg, H. and J. A. Waters. 'Tracking strategy in an entrepreneurial firm', *Academy of Management Journal*, 1982, pp. 465–499.
Mintzberg, H. and J. A. Waters. 'Researching the formation of strategies: the history of Canadian Lady, 1939–1976', in Lamb, R. (ed.) *Competitive Strategic Management*, Prentice-Hall, Englewood Cliffs, N.J., 1984.
Mintzberg, H., S. Otis, J. Shamsie and J. A. Waters. 'Strategy of design: a study of "architects in co-partnership"', Grant, John (ed.) *Strategic Management Frontiers*, JAI Press, Greenwich, CT, 1986.
Porter, M. E. *Competitive Strategy: Techniques for Analyzing Industries and Competitors*, Free Press, New York, 1980.
Saint-Exupery, A. *Le Petit Prince*, English translation by Katherine Woods, Reynal and Hitchcock, New York, 1943.
Sills, D. L. *The Volunteers*, Free Press, New York, 1957.

Three Models of Strategy[1]

ELLEN EARLE CHAFFEE
National Center for Higher Education Management Systems

Three models of strategy that are implicit in the literature are described—linear, adaptive, and interpretive. Their similarity to Boulding's (1956) hierarchical levels of system complexity is noted. The strategy construct is multifaceted, and it has evolved to a level of complexity almost matching that of organizations themselves.

Researchers and practitioners have used the term *strategy* freely—researchers have even measured it—for over two decades. Those who refer to strategy generally believe that they are all working with the same mental model. No controversy surrounds the question of its existence; no debate has arisen regarding the nature of its anchoring concept.

Yet virtually everyone writing on strategy agrees that no consensus on its definition exists (Bourgeois, 1980; Gluck, Kaufman, & Walleck, 1982; Glueck, 1980; Hatten, 1979; Hofer & Schendel, 1978; Lenz, 1980b; Rumelt, 1979; Spender, 1979; Steiner, 1979). Hambrick (1983) suggested that this lack of consistency is due to two factors. First, he pointed out, strategy is multidimensional. Second, strategy must be situational and, accordingly, it will vary by industry.

The literature affirms Hambrick's assessment that strategy is not only multidimensional and situational but that such characteristics are likely to make any consensus on definition difficult. Strategy also suffers from another, more fundamental problem; that is, the term strategy has been referring to three distinguishable mental models, rather than the single model that most discussions assume. Beyond reflecting various authors' semantic preferences, the multiple definitions reflect three distinct, and in some ways conflicting, views on strategy. This paper seeks to analyze the ways strategy has been defined and operationalized in previous treatises and studies. It highlights those aspects of strategy on which authors in the field appear to agree and suggests three strategy models that are implicit in the literature.

Strategy: Areas of Agreement

A basic premise of thinking about strategy concerns the inseparability of organization and environment (Biggadike, 1981; Lenz, 1980a). The organization uses strategy to deal with changing environments. Because change brings novel combinations of circumstances to the organization, the substance of strategy remains unstructured, unprogrammed, nonroutine, and nonrepetitive (Mason & Mitroff, 1981; Mazzolini, 1981; Miles & Cameron, 1982; Narayanan & Fahey, 1982; Van Cauwenbergh & Cool, 1982). Not only are strategic decisions related to the environment and nonroutine, but they also are considered to be important enough to affect the overall welfare of the organization (Hambrick, 1980).

Theorists who segment the strategy construct implicitly agree that the study of strategy includes both the actions taken, or the content of strategy, and the processes by which actions are decided and implemented. They agree that intended, emergent, and realized strategies may differ from one another. Moreover, they agree that firms may have both corporate strategy ("What businesses shall we be in?") and business strategy ("How shall we compete in each business?"). Finally, they concur that the making of strategy involves conceptual as well as analytical exercises. Some authors stress the analytical dimension more than others, but most affirm that the heart of strategy

---

[1] The research reported here was supported by a contract (#400-83-0009) from the National Institute of Education. An abbreviated version was presented at the annual meeting of the Academy of Management, Boston, 1984, and appears in the *Proceedings* of the meeting. The author is grateful to Jane Dutton for several excellent suggestions.

making is the conceptual work done by leaders of the organization.

Beyond these general factors, agreement breaks down. Yet the differences in point of view are rarely analyzed. Only the existence of multiple definitions of strategy is noted and, as in Mintzberg (1973), definitions are sometimes grouped by type. Analysis reveals that the strategy definitions in the literature cluster into three distinct groups.

Three Models of Strategy

The name assigned to each model of strategy represents its primary focus. Although these descriptions represent a collective version of similar views, each model also includes many variations of its central theme. Moreover, as will be shown later, the three models are not independent. However, for present purposes, the three models will be treated according to their independent descriptions in the literature.

Model I: Linear Strategy

The first model to be widely adopted is linear and focuses on planning. The term linear was chosen because it connotes the methodical, directed, sequential action involved in planning. This model is inherent in Chandler's definition of strategy.

> Strategy is the determination of the basic long-term goals of an enterprise, and the adoption of courses of action and the allocation of resources necessary for carrying out these goals (1962, p. 13).

According to the linear view, strategy consists of integrated decisions, actions, or plans that will set and achieve viable organizational goals. Both goals and the means of achieving them are results of strategic decision. To reach these goals, organizations vary their links with the environment by changing their products or markets or by performing other entrepreneurial actions. Terms associated with the linear model include strategic planning, strategy formulation, and strategy implementation.

The linear model portrays top managers as having considerable capacity to change the organization. The environment is, implicitly, a necessary nuisance "out there" that is composed mainly of competitors. Top managers go through a prototypical rational decision making process. They identify their goals, generate alternative methods of achieving them, weigh the likelihood that alternative methods will succeed, and then decide which ones to implement. In the course of this process, managers capitalize on those future trends and events that are favorable and avoid or counteract those that are not. Because this model was developed primarily for profit-seeking businesses, two of its important measures of results are profit and productivity.

Several assumptions that underlie the linear model are not made explicit in most discussions, but they nonetheless follow from the authors' tendency to emphasize planning and forecasting. For example:

> Conceptually, the process [of strategic planning] is simple: managers at every level of a hierarchy must ultimately agree on a detailed, integrated plan of action for the coming year; they [start] with the delineation of corporate objectives and [conclude] with the preparation of a one- or two-year profit plan (Lorange & Vancil, 1976, p. 75).

If a sequential planning process is to succeed, the organization needs to be tightly coupled, so that all decisions made at the top can be implemented throughout the organization. This tight coupling assumption enables intentions to become actions. A second assumption arises from the time-consuming and forward-looking nature of planning. In other words, though decisions made today are based on beliefs about future conditions, they may not be implemented until months, even years, from now. In order to believe that making such decisions is not a waste of time, one must assume either that the environment is relatively predictable or else that the organization is well-insulated from the environment. Also, most authors explicitly assume that organizations have goals and that accomplishing goals is the most important outcome of strategy.

Major characteristics of the linear model and the names of several authors whose definitions of strategy are consistent with this model are listed in Table 1. Note that though the authors' definitions of strategy constitute grounds for classifying them in the model, nearly all authors extend their discussions of strategy into areas that are relevant to more than one model.

As the dates in these citations suggest, interest in the linear model waned in the mid-1970s. Ansoff and Hayes (1976) suggested that the em-

Table 1
Summary of Linear Strategy

Variable	Linear Strategy
Sample definition	"... determination of the basic long-term *goals* of an enterprise, and the adoption of courses of *action* and the allocation of *resources* necessary for carrying out these goals" (Chandler, 1962, p. 13, italics added).
Nature of strategy	Decisions, actions, plans Integrated
Focus for strategy	Means, ends
Aim of strategy	Goal achievement
Strategic behaviors	Change markets, products
Associated terms	Strategic planning, strategy formulation and implementation
Associated measures	Formal planning, new products, configuration of products or businesses, market segmentation and focus, market share, merger/acquisition, product diversity
Associated authors[a]	Chandler, 1962 Cannon, 1968 Learned, Christensen, Andrews, & Guth, 1969 Gilmore, 1970 Andrews, 1971 Child, 1972 Drucker, 1974 Paine & Naumes, 1974 Glueck, 1976 Lorange & Vancil, 1976 Steiner & Miner, 1977

[a] Classified by their *definitions* of strategy. Classification is not intended to imply that authors omit discussion of topics relevant to other models.

phasis moved away from the linear model as the strategic problem came to be seen as much more complex. Not only does it involve several dimensions of the managerial problem and the process, but also technical, economic, informational, psychological, and political variables as well. The model that arose next is labeled here the adaptive model of strategy.

Model II: Adaptive Strategy

Hofer's definition typifies the adaptive model of strategy, characterizing it as

> concerned with the development of a viable match between the opportunities and risks present in the external environment and the organization's capabilities and resources for exploiting these opportunities (1973, p. 3).

The organization is expected continually to assess external and internal conditions. Assessment then leads to adjustments in the organization or in its relevant environment that will create "satisfactory alignments of environmental opportunities and risks, on the one hand, and organizational capabilities and resources, on the other" (Miles & Cameron, 1982, p. 14).

The adaptive model differs from the linear model in several ways. First, monitoring the environment and making changes are simultaneous and continuous functions in the adaptive model. The time lag for planning that is implicit in the linear model is not present. For example, Miles and Snow (1978) portray strategic adaptation as recurring and overlapping cycles with three phases: the entrepreneurial phase (choice of domain), the engineering phase (choice of technology), and the administrative phase (rationalizing structure and process, and identifying areas for future innovation).

Second, the adaptive model does not deal as emphatically as the linear model with decisions about goals. Instead, it tends to focus the manager's attention on means, and the "goal" is represented by coalignment of the organization with its environment. Third, the adaptive model's definition of strategic behaviors goes beyond that of the linear model to incorporate not only major changes in products and markets, but also subtle changes in style, marketing, quality, and other nuances (Hofer, 1976a; Shirley, 1982).

A fourth difference follows from the relative unimportance of advance planning in the adaptive model. Thus, as might be expected, strategy is less centralized in top management, more multifaceted, and generally less integrated than in the linear model. However, top managers in the adaptive model still assume overall responsibility for guiding strategy development.

Finally, in the adaptive model the environment is considered to be a complex organizational life support system, consisting of trends, events, competitors, and stakeholders. The boundary between the organization and its environment is highly permeable, and the environment is a major focus of attention in determining organizational action. Whether taken proactively or reactively, action is responsive to the nature and magnitude of perceived or anticipated environmental pressures.

In sum, the adaptive model relies heavily on an evolutionary biological model of organizations. The analogy is made explicit in the following passage:

> As a descriptive tool, strategy is the analog of the biologist's method of "explaining" the structure and the behavior of organisms by pointing out the functionality of each attribute in a total system (or strategy) designed to cope with or inhabit a particular niche. The normative use of strategy has no counterpart in biology (as yet!), but might be thought of as the problem of designing a living creature... to exist within some environment... (Rumelt, 1979, pp. 197-198).

As interest in strategy as adaptation increased so, too, did attention to the processes by which strategy arises and is carried out. Beginning with Mintzberg's (1973) modes of strategy making, a number of discussions have been presented to deal with the social, political, and interactive components of strategy (Fahey, 1981; Ginter & White, 1982; Greenwood & Thomas, 1981; Guth, 1976; Hofer, 1976b; E. Murray, 1978; J. Murray, 1978-79; Narayanan & Fahey, 1982; Tabatoni & Jarniou, 1976). Each of the authors dealt with organizational processes in the adaptive strategy model.

Adaptive strategy rests on several assumptions. The organization and its environment are assumed to be more open to each other than is implied in the linear model. The environment is more dynamic and less susceptible to prediction in the adaptive model. It consists of competitors, trends, and—of increasing importance—stake-holders. Rather than assuming that the organization must *deal with* the environment, the adaptive model assumes that the organization must *change with* the environment.

The adaptive model attempts to take more variables and more propensity for change into account than does the linear model. Table 2 lists terms that reflect this complexity, along with those authors whose strategy definitions fit the adaptive model. It also outlines the characteristics of the model. A number of authors using the adaptive model suggest that it can successfully handle greater complexity and more variables than the linear model. However, opinion is mounting that the situation is complex in other ways.

Table 2
Summary of Adaptive Strategy

Variable	Adaptive Strategy
Sample definition	"...concerned with the development of a viable match between the opportunities and risks present in the external environment and the organization's capabilities and resources for exploiting those opportunities" (Hofer, 1973, p. 3).
Nature of strategy	Achieving a "match" Multifaceted
Focus for strategy	Means
Aim of strategy	Coalignment with the environment
Strategic behaviors	Change style, marketing, quality
Associated terms	Strategic management, strategic choice, strategic predisposition, strategic design, strategic fit, strategic thrust, niche
Associated measures	Price, distribution policy, marketing expenditure and intensity, product differentiation, authority changes, proactiveness, risk taking, multiplexity, integration, futurity, adaptiveness, uniqueness
Associated authors[a]	Hofer, 1973 Guth, 1976 Hofer & Schendel, 1978 Litschert & Bonham, 1978 Miles, Snow, Meyer, & Coleman, 1978 Miller & Friesen, 1978 Mintzberg, 1978 Dill, 1979 Steiner, 1979 Rumelt, 1979 Hambrick, 1980 Bourgeois, 1980 Snow & Hambrick, 1980 Quinn, 1980 Jemison, 1981 Kotler & Murphy, 1981 Green & Jones, 1981 Hayman, 1981 Jauch & Osborn, 1981 Gluck et al., 1982 Chakravarthy, 1982 Hatten, 1982 Shirley, 1982 Camillus, 1982 Miles & Cameron, 1982 Galbraith & Schendel, 1983

[a]Classified by their *definitions* of strategy. Classification is not intended to imply that authors omit discussion of topics relevant to other models.

To meet this need, a third model of strategy is emerging.

Model III: Interpretive Strategy

Development of interpretive strategy parallels recent interest in corporate culture and symbolic management outside the strategy literature (Dandridge, Mitroff, & Joyce, 1980; Deal & Kennedy, 1982; Feldman & March, 1981; Meyer & Rowan, 1977; Peters, 1978 Peters & Waterman, 1982; Pfeffer, 1981; Smircich & Morgan, 1982; Weick & Daft, 1983). The parameters of the emerging interpretive model of strategy are still unclear. However, a recurring theme suggests that the model is based on a social contract, rather than an organismic or biological view of the organization (Keeley, 1980) that fits well with the adaptive model. The social contract view portrays the organization as a collection of cooperative agreements entered into by individuals with free will. The organization's existence relies on its ability to attract enough individuals to cooperate in mutually beneficial exchange.

The interpretive model of strategy further assumes that reality is socially constructed (Berger & Luckmann, 1966). That is, reality is not something objective or external to the perceiver that can be apprehended correctly or incorrectly. Rather, reality is defined through a process of social interchange in which perceptions are affirmed, modified, or replaced according to their apparent congruence with the perceptions of others.

Strategy in the interpretive model might be defined as orienting metaphors or frames of reference that allow the organization and its environment to be understood by organizational stakeholders. On this basis, stakeholders are motivated to believe and to act in ways that are expected to produce favorable results for the organization. "Metaphors" is plural in this definition because the maintenance of social ties in the organization precludes enforcing agreement on a single interpretation (Weick & Daft, 1983).

Pettigrew (1977) provided an early example of the interpretive model by defining strategy as the emerging product of the partial resolution of environmental and intraorganizational dilemmas. Although his emphasis on the political and processual nature of strategy might be considered compatible with the adaptive model, he offered several innovative contributions. Among them are: (1) his interest in the management of meaning and symbol construction as central components of strategy and (2) his emphasis on legitimacy, rather than profit, productivity, or other typical goals of strategy.

Van Cauwenbergh and Cool (1982) defined strategy broadly as calculated behavior in nonprogrammed situations. They went on to posit middle management's central position in the strategy formulation process, as well as to point out that managing the organizational culture is a powerful tool in the hands of top management. The authors concluded by suggesting that their views differed from the traditional strategy literature in three ways: (1) organizational reality is incoherent in nature, not coherent; (2) strategy is an organization-wide activity, not just a top management concern; and (3) motivation, not information, is the critical factor in achieving adequate strategic behavior. Congruent with these authors' interest in organizational culture, Dirsmith and Covaleski dealt with what they called strategic norms, or

> institutional level action postures ... that serve to guide acceptable behavior. [S]trategic norms involve the establishment of maps of reality or images held of organizations and environments (1983, p. 137).

The new themes in these writings suggest a strategy model that depends heavily on symbols and norms. Hatten (1979) saw this change as moving from the goal orientation of the linear model to a focus on desired relationships, such as those involving sources of inputs or customers. He envisaged a new theory of strategy that was oriented toward managerial perceptions, conflict and consensus, as well as the importance of language. The relatively few entries in Table 3 indicate that the model is too new to have become well-developed.

Rather than emphasizing *changing with* the environment, as is true of the adaptive model, interpretive strategy mimics linear strategy in its emphasis on *dealing with* the environment. There is, however, an important difference. The linear strategist deals with the environment by means of organizational actions that are intended to

Table 3
Summary of Interpretive Strategy

Variable	Interpretive Strategy
Sample definition	Orienting metaphors constructed for the purpose of conceptualizing and guiding individual attitudes of organizational participants
Nature of strategy	Metaphor Interpretive
Focus for strategy	Participants and potential participants in the organization
Aim of strategy	Legitimacy
Strategic behaviors	Develop symbols, improve interactions and relationships
Associated terms	Strategic norms
Associated measures	Measures must be derived from context, may require qualitative assessment
Associated authors[a]	Pettigrew, 1977 Van Cauwenbergh & Cool, 1982 Dirsmith & Covaleski, 1983 Chaffee, 1984

[a] Classified by their *definitions* of strategy. Classification is not intended to imply that authors omit discussion of topics relevant to other models.

affect relations instrumentally, but the interpretive strategist deals with the environment through symbolic actions and communication.

Interpretive strategy, like adaptive strategy, assumes that the organization and its environment constitute an open system. But in interpretive strategy the organization's leaders shape the attitudes of participants and potential participants toward the organization and its outputs; they do not make physical changes in the outputs. This attitude change seeks to increase credibility for the organization or its output. In this regard, interpretive strategy overlaps with the adaptive model. For example, when an adaptive strategist focuses on marketing to enhance product credibility, the strategist's behavior could be classified as interpretive. Because strategy is multifaceted, however, examining marketing in combination with other strategic moves permits surer classification into either the adaptive or interpretive model.

A final noteworthy distinction between the adaptive and interpretive models relates to the ways in which each conceptualizes complexity. Adaptive strategy arose from and attempts to deal with structural complexity, notably conflicting and changing demands for organizational output. Interpretive strategy emphasizes attitudinal and cognitive complexity among diverse stakeholders in the organization.

Each of the three models may be summarized briefly. In linear strategy, leaders of the organization plan how they will deal with competitors to achieve their organization's goals. In adaptive strategy, the organization and its parts change, proactively or reactively, in order to be aligned with consumer preferences. In interpretive strategy, organizational representatives convey meanings that are intended to motivate stakeholders in ways that favor the organization. Each model provides a way of describing a certain aspect of organizational functioning to which the term *strategy* has been applied. By analogy, one would have three descriptions of a single phenomenon if a geologist, a climatologist, and a poet were to model the Grand Canyon.

One value of diverse models, whether they relate to strategy or the Grand Canyon, is that they provide options. In future development of strategy, one might delineate the circumstances under which one model of strategy is more appropriate than the others. However, before such delineation is warranted, the models and their interrelationships require further theoretical attention.

As noted earlier, the three strategy models may not be independent of one another, although so far they have been treated separately in both the literature cited and this discussion. The basis for suggesting that the models are interrelated is that they show some similarity to a well-known hierarchy of systems in which each level incorporates the less complex levels that precede it (Boulding, 1956). If the strategy models were analogous to the systems hierarchy, the relationships among the models would also be hierarchical. The systems hierarchy has certain similarities to the three strategy models. Certain characteristics at each set of system levels match those of one of the strategy models. Furthermore, similarities between each level of systems and one of the strategy models suggest that an organization that functions at a given level in the systems hierarchy will benefit from using the corresponding model of strategy.

Therefore, relating the strategy models to the systems hierarchy makes three contributions toward elaborating on the strategy construct. First, it suggests a means of ordering and interrelating the disparate, more narrowly focused definitions of strategy in the existing literature. Second, discrepancies between system levels and strategy models suggest areas in which the models could profitably be developed. Third, the analogy provides a bridge for moving from a survey of theoretical literature to its implications for practice.

The Hierarchy of Strategy Models

Boulding (1956) developed a nine-level hierarchical framework that was keyed to all classes of systems, including human systems. At the most basic level were three classes that Pondy and Mitroff (1979) grouped together under the metaphor of a machine. In the highest of the three machine classes, a control mechanism regulates system behavior according to an externally prescribed target or criterion. Information flows between the regulator and the system operator. Linear strategy shows similar properties in that the executive is expected to control the organization according to predetermined goals and to change the goals when circumstances warrant.

The three intermediate classes constitute the biological set, the highest of which is the internal image system. At this level, because the system has differentiated receptors, it is imbued with detailed awareness of its environment. Awareness is organized into an image, but the system is not self-conscious. Other characteristics of the biological set include its having the same internal differentiation as the environment, as well as its having a generating mechanism that produces behavior. Adaptive strategy corresponds to the biological level, in that the model calls for the organization to scan, anticipate, and respond to various elements in its environment.

Boulding's most complex set of system levels is the cultural set. It consists of the symbol processing level, in which the system is a self-conscious user of language, and the multicephalous level, a collection of individuals acting in concert and using elaborate systems of shared meaning. Boulding's third level in the cultural set is transcendental, not fully specified. The cultural set is analogous to interpretive strategy. Weick and Daft (1983) place interpretation at level 6, the highest biological level, but they identify interpretation as a cultural phenomenon. Wherever it is placed, interpretive strategy, like the cultural level of systems, emphasizes the importance of symbol manipulation, shared meaning, and cooperative actions of individuals. Although the emphases are the same, interpretive strategy is not as fully developed as its correspondence to the cultural level might imply.

Each level in Boulding's hierarchy subsumes those that preceded it. If the same were true of the strategy models, then adaptive strategy would incorporate linear strategy, and interpretive strategy would incorporate both adaptive and linear strategies. Although the evolution of the strategy construct proceeded sequentially through the hierarchy, beginning at the machine level and recently reaching the cultural level, the shift from each level to the next abandoned, rather than incorporated, the preceding level(s). Boulding's cultural level is more complex than his biological level precisely because it builds on the base of the machine and biological levels. Interpretive strategy ignores linear and adaptive strategy. Dealing with stakeholder attitudes is not inherently more complex than dealing with consumer preferences, nor is conveying productive interpretations necessarily more complex than achieving coalignment with the environment. No interpretive strategist has evaluated the extent to which linear and adaptive strategy are subsumed in the "higher" model. Moreover, the adaptive strategists have largely ignored the linear model.

Some hints at relating the three models have appeared in the literature. For example, Weick and Daft (1983) suggested that one criterion of effective interpretation is detailed knowledge of the particulars of the environment (adaptive model) so that the phenomenon to be interpreted may be seen in context. Another paper implied that the models constitute a series of stages through which the organization itself moves over time as it becomes more sophisticated and adept at strategic management (Gluck et al., 1982). The authors stated that organizations start with financial and forecast-based planning (linear model), then shift to strategic analysis (adaptive model), and finally achieve strategic management (interpretive model). Cummings (1983) outlined two major themes in the literature: management by information (linear/adaptive) and management by ideology (interpretive). Cummings argued that both themes must be integrated to achieve an instrumental organization that serves the purposes of its participants. But he did not explain in operational terms how integration occurs. In the only empirical study that relates directly to the strategy models, Chaffee (1984) found that organizations recovering from decline used adaptive strategy, but it was their use of interpretive strategy that differentiated them from organizations unable to recover. However, like Cummings and like Gluck and his colleagues, Chaffee did not deal with how or why the two models were integrated in organizational functioning.

It is important to integrate each lower level model with models that represent more complex systems because organizations exhibit properties of all levels of system complexity. Adaptive and interpretive strategies that ignore less complex strategy models ignore the foundations on which they must be built if they are to reflect organizational reality. Furthermore, a comprehensive interpretive strategy probably requires some planning as would fit with a linear strategy and some organizational change as would fit with an adaptive strategy; and a viable adaptive strategy may well require some linear planning. But rather than building toward a sophisticated construct that equals the complexities for which it is intended, strategists have selected three key themes and treated them separately. Each may have value as far as it goes, but none integrates all levels of complexity and options for action that are inherent in an organization.

Finding three models of strategy holds implications for organizations, for managers, and for future development of the strategy construct. Even at this point, without deepening the adaptive and interpretive models to include lower levels of complexity, the analysis specifies three diverse ways of viewing the organizational problem and three classes of potential solutions. The models may be used conceptually to examine an organizational situation and consider alternatives for coping with it. For example, a manager might consider whether predictions about the declining demand for a product are: (a) based on firm evidence that will provide sufficient lead time for a planning task force to convene and generate alternatives to deal with the decline, (b) fundamental shifts in consumer preferences that could be addressed by modifying the product or replacing it with another, or (c) symptomatic of a loss of confidence among the buying public that could be remedied by better marketing to build legitimacy.

Futhermore, strategic decision making may profit from an analysis of a given situation's level of complexity. If an organization or a problem exhibits characteristics that are predominantly mechanistic, a linear strategy is called for. Adaptive strategies can be applied when issues of supply and demand are especially salient. Complex interpretive strategies may be reserved for situations in which modifying the attitudes of organizational stakeholders is the primary key to success.

The full value of strategy cannot be realized in practical terms, however, until theorists expand the construct to reflect the real complexities of organizations. Each successive level of strategy should incorporate those that are less complex. Then researchers can examine the ways this construct behaves in real organizations. Ultimately, the construct may emerge as a unitary merger of the three models, such as an interpretive model that incorporates adaptive and linear strategy. Or it may emerge as a hierarchy of three models: a mechanistic linear model; a biological adaptive model incorporating linear strategy; and a cultural interpretive model, incorporating both linear and adaptive strategy. Theoreticians also may find value in still greater model differentiation. Perhaps this can be done by specifying a hierarchy that contains a model of strategy for each of Boulding's nine levels of system complexity.

Whatever the end products may be—and whether or not they finally relate to Boulding's hierarchy—it is time for strategy theoreticians and researchers to begin putting the pieces together. During the past 20 years, the strategy literature has greatly evolved. Today, in fact, it has almost arrived at the point at which it is capable of reflecting the actual level of complexity at which organizations operate. The way is now open to capitalize, both theoretically and empirically, on the richness of that complexity.

References

Andrews, K. R. *The concept of corporate strategy.* Homewood, IL: Irwin, 1971.

Ansoff, H. I., & Hayes, R. L. Introduction. In H. I. Ansoff, R. P. Declerck, & R. L. Hayes (Eds.), *From strategic planning to strategic management.* New York: Wiley, 1976, 1-12.

Berger, P., & Luckmann, T. *The social construction of reality.* New York: Doubleday, 1966.

Biggadike, E. R. The contributions of marketing to strategic management. *Academy of Management Review,* 1981, 6, 621-632.

Boulding, K. E. General systems theory—The skeleton of science. *Management Science,* 1956, 2, 197-208.

Bourgeois, L. J., III. Strategy and environment: A conceptual integration. *Academy of Management Review,* 1980, 5, 25-39.

Camillus, J. C. Reconciling logical incrementalism and synoptic formalism—An integrated approach to designing strategy planning processes. *Strategic Management Journal,* 1982, 3, 227-283.

Cannon, J. T. *Business strategy and policy.* New York: Harcourt Brace Jovanovich, 1968.

Chaffee, E. E. Successful strategic management in small private colleges. *Journal of Higher Education,* 1984, 55, 212-241.

Chakravarthy, B. S. Adaptation: A promising metaphor for strategic management. *Academy of Management Review,* 1982, 7, 35-44.

Chandler, A. D., Jr. *Strategy and structure.* Cambridge, MA: MIT Press, 1962.

Child, J. Organizational structure, environment, and performance: The role of strategic choice. *Sociology,* 1972, 6, 1-22.

Cummings, L. L. The logics of management. *Academy of Management Review,* 1983, 8, 532-538.

Dandridge, T. C., Mitroff, I., & Joyce, W. F. Organizational symbolism: A topic to expand organizational analysis. *Academy of Management Review,* 1980, 5, 77-82.

Deal, T. E., & Kennedy, A. A. *Corporate cultures: The rites and rituals of corporate life.* Reading, MA: Addison-Wesley, 1982.

Dill, W. R. Commentary. In D. E. Schendel & C. W. Hofer (Eds.), *Strategic management: A new view of business policy and planning.* Boston: Little, Brown, 1979, 47-51.

Dirsmith, M. W., & Covaleski, M. A. Strategy, external communication and environment context. *Strategic Management Journal,* 1983, 4, 137-151.

Drucker, P. F. *Management: Tasks, responsibilities, practices.* New York: Harper & Row, 1974.

Fahey, L. On strategic management decision processes. *Strategic Management Journal,* 1981, 2, 43-60.

Feldman, M., & March, J. G. Information in organizations as signal and symbol. *Administrative Science Quarterly,* 1981, 26, 171-186.

Galbraith, C., & Schendel, D. An empirical analysis of strategy types. *Strategic Management Journal,* 1983, 4, 153-173.

Gilmore, F. F. Formulating strategy in smaller companies. *Harvard Business Review,* 1970, 49(5), 71-81.

Ginter, P. M., & White, D. D. A social learning approach to strategic management: Toward a theoretical foundation. *Academy of Management Review,* 1982, 7, 253-261.

Gluck, F., Kaufman, S., & Walleck, A. S. The four phases of strategic management. *Journal of Business Strategy,* 1982, 2(3), 9-21.

Glueck, W. F. *Business policy: Strategy formation and management action.* New York: McGraw-Hill, 1976.

Glueck, W. F. *Strategic management and business policy.* New York: McGraw-Hill, 1980.

Green, J., & Jones, T. Strategic development as a means of organizational change: Four case histories. *Long Range Planning,* 1981, 14(3), 58-67.

Greenwood, P., & Thomas, H. A review of analytical models in strategic planning. *Omega,* 1981, 9(4), 397-417.

Guth, W. D. Toward a social system theory of corporate strategy. *Journal of Business,* 1976, 49, 374-388.

Hambrick, D. C. Operationalizing the concept of business-level strategy in research. *Academy of Management Review,* 1980, 5, 567-575.

Hambrick, D. C. Some tests of the effectiveness and functional attributes of Miles and Snow's strategic types. *Academy of Management Journal,* 1983, 26, 5-25.

Hatten, K. J. Quantitative research methods in strategic management. In D. E. Schendel & C. W. Hofer (Eds.), *Strategic management: A new view of business policy and planning.* Boston: Little, Brown, 1979, 448-467.

Hatten, M. L. Strategic management in not-for-profit organizations. *Strategic Management Journal,* 1982, 3, 89-104.

Hayman, J. Relationship of strategic planning and future methodologies. Paper presented at the 1981 Annual Convention of the AERA, Los Angeles, 1981.

Hofer, C. W. Some preliminary research on patterns of strategic behavior. *Academy of Management Proceedings,* 1973, 46-59.

Hofer, C. W. *Conceptual scheme for formulating a total business strategy.* Boston: HBS Case Services, 1976a.

Hofer, C. W. Research on strategic planning: A survey of past studies and suggestions for future efforts. *Journal of Economics and Business,* 1976b, 28, 261-286.

Hofer, C. W., & Schendel, D. *Strategy formulation: Analytical concepts.* St. Paul, MN: West, 1978.

Jauch, L. R., & Osborn, R. N. Toward an integrated theory of strategy. *Academy of Management Review,* 1981, 6, 491-498.

Jemison, D. B. The contributions of administrative behavior to strategic management. *Academy of Management Review,* 1981, 6, 633-642.

Keeley, M. Organizational analogy: A comparison of organismic and social contract models. *Administrative Science Quarterly,* 1980, 25, 337-362.

Kotler, P., & Murphy, P. E. Strategic planning for higher education. *Journal of Higher Education,* 1981, 52, 470-489.

Learned, E. P., Christensen, C. R., Andrews, K. R., & Guth, W. R. *Business policy*. Homewood, IL: Irwin, 1969.

Lenz, R. T. Strategic capability: A concept and framework for analysis. *Academy of Management Review*, 1980a, 5, 225-234.

Lenz, R. T. Environment, strategy, organization structure and performance: Patterns in one industry. *Strategic Management Journal*, 1980b, 1, 209-226.

Litschert, R. J., & Bonham, T. W. Conceptual models of strategy formulation. *Academy of Management Review*, 1978, 3, 211-219.

Lorange, P., & Vancil, R. F. How to design a strategic planning system. *Harvard Business Review*, 1976, 54(5), 75-81.

Mason, R. O., & Mitroff, I. I. *Challenging strategic planning assumptions*. New York: 1981.

Mazzolini, R. How strategic decisions are made. *Long Range Planning*, 1981, 14(3), 85-96.

Meyer, J. W., & Rowan, B. Institutionalized organizations: Formal structure as myth and ceremony. *American Journal of Sociology*, 1977, 83, 340-363.

Miles, R. E., & Snow, C. C. *Organizational strategy, structure, and process*. New York: McGraw-Hill, 1978.

Miles, R. E., Snow, C. C., Meyer, A. D., & Coleman, H. J., Jr. Organizational strategy, structure, and process. *Academy of Management Review*, 1978, 3, 546-563.

Miles, R. H., & Cameron, K. S. *Coffin nails and corporate strategies*. Englewood Cliffs, NJ: Prentice-Hall, 1982.

Miller, D., & Friesen, P. Archetypes of strategy formulation. *Management Science*, 1978, 24, 253-280.

Mintzberg, H. Strategy-making in three modes. *California Management Review*, 1973, 16(2), 44-53.

Mintzberg, H. Patterns in strategy formation. *Management Science*, 1978, 24, 934-948.

Murray, E. A. Strategic change as a negotiated outcome. *Management Science*, 1978, 24, 960-972.

Murray, J. A. Toward a contingency model of strategic decision. *International Studies of Management and Organization*. 1978-79, 8, 7-34.

Narayanan, V. K., & Fahey, L. The micro-politics of strategy formulation. *Academy of Management Review*, 1982, 7, 25-34.

Paine, F. T., & Naumes, W. *Strategy and policy formation: An integrative approach*. Philadelphia: Saunders, 1974.

Peters, T. J. Symbols, patterns, and settings: An optimistic case for getting things done. *Organizational Dynamics*, 1978, 7(2), 3-23.

Peters, T. J., & Waterman, R. H., Jr. *In search of excellence: Lessons from America's best-run companies*. New York: Harper & Row, 1982.

Pettigrew, A. M. Strategy formulation as a political process. *International Studies of Management and Organization*, 1977, 7, 78-87.

Pfeffer, J. Management as symbolic action: The creation and maintenance of organizational paradigms. In L. L. Cummings & B. M. Staw (Eds.), *Research in organizational behavior*. Greenwood, CT: JAI Press, 1981, 1-52.

Pondy, L. R., & Mitroff, I. I. Beyond open system models of organization. In B. M. Staw (Ed.), *Research in organizational behavior*. Greenwood, CT: JAI Press, 1979, 3-39.

Quinn, J. B. *Strategies for change: Logical incrementalism*. Homewood, IL: Irwin, 1980.

Rumelt, R. P. Evaluation of strategy: Theory and models. In D. E. Schendel & C. W. Hofer (Eds.), *Strategic management: A new view of business policy and planning*. Boston: Little, Brown, 1979, 196-212.

Shirley, R. C. Limiting the scope of strategy: A decision based approach. *Academy of Management Review*, 1982, 7, 262-268.

Smircich, L., & Morgan, G. Leadership: The management of meaning. *Journal of Applied Behavioral Science*, 1982, 18(3), 257-273.

Snow, C. C., & Hambrick, D. C. Measuring organizational strategies: Some theoretical and methodological problems. *Academy of Management Review*, 1980, 5, 527-538.

Spender, J. C. Commentary. In D. E. Schendel & C. W. Hofer (Eds.), *Strategic management: A new view of business policy and planning*. Boston: Little, Brown, 1979, 383-404.

Steiner, G. A. *Strategic planning*. New York: Free Press, 1979.

Steiner, G. A., & Miner, J. B. *Management policy and strategy*. New York: Macmillan, 1977.

Tabatoni, P., & Jarniou, P. The dynamics of norms in strategic management. In H. I. Ansoff, R. P. Declerck, & R. L. Hayes (Eds.), *From strategic planning to strategic management*. London: Wiley, 1976, 29-36.

Van Cauwenbergh, A., & Cool, K. Strategic management in a new framework. *Strategic Management Journal*, 1982, 3, 245-265.

Weick, K. E., & Daft, R. L. The effectiveness of interpretation systems. In K. S. Cameron & D. A. Whetten (Eds.), *Organizational effectiveness: A comparison of multiple models*. New York: Academic Press, 1983, 71-93.

Ellen Earle Chaffee is Director of the Organizational Studies Division, National Center for Higher Education Management Systems, Boulder.

Name Index

Abelson, R. 230
Abravanel, H. 230
Ackoff, Russell xvii, 406, 407
Aiken, M. 327, 329, 332
Aineias xiv
Al-Bazzaz, S. 260
Alderfer, C.P. 368
Aldrich, Howard xix, 143–70
Alexander, J.A. 369
Alexander the Great xiv
Allen, J. Knight 76
Allison, G.T. 229, 422
Allrine, F.C. 251
Andersen, Theodore A. 72
Anderson, C.R. xv
Ando, Albert 317
Andrews, Kenneth R. xiv, xv, xvi, xvii, xviii, 15–43
Andrews, P.W.S. 250
Ansoff, H. Igor xiv, xvii, xviii, 45–61, 248
Anthony, Robert N. 69, 70, 74–6 passim
Argenti, J. xvii
Argyris, Chris 250
Aristotle xiv
Arkwright, R. xvi
Arrow, Kenneth 305
Ashby, W. Ross 164
Atkinson, L. 363
Auletta, K. 360
Avery, Sewell 382

Babbage, Charles 310
Bailey, Kenneth D. 151, 158
Banfield, Edward C. 175
Bantel, K.A. 360, 370, 372
Barnard, Chester E. xvi, xxi, 3–14, 251, 311, 312, 314, 382
Barry, B.A. 329
Bartunek, J.M. 229, 230
Bass, M.M. 369
Bates, M. 386
Bauer, M. 374
Baumol, William xv, 320
Baysinger, B.D. 366
Becker, Gary S. 308
Becker, Selwyn 299
Belbin, R.M. 388, 393
Bennis, Warren G. 252, 293

Benson, J. Kenneth 148
Berg, Norman 32, 262
Berger, P. 433
Berle, A.A. 366
Bertin-Mourot, B. 374
Bettis, R.A. 381
Beyer, J.M. 230
Bierstedt, Robert 293
Biggadike, E.R. 429–38
Biggart, Nicole W. 147, 229, 364, 374
Binkhorst, Din 148
Birley, S. 360, 370
Blalock, Hubert M. 301–2, 328
Blau, Peter M. 146, 147, 293, 295, 296, 297, 327
Blaylock, B.K. 393
Boecker, W. 361, 369, 372
Bogdan, R. 230
Boje, D.M. 241
Bonini, C.P. 320
Boothe, J.N. 360
Borch, Fred J. 97
Bougon, Michael 148
Boulding, Kenneth E. 251, 434, 435, 436
Bourgeois, L.J. 372
Bower, J.L. 229, 383
Bowman, E.H. 248
Bradshaw, P. 361, 369
Brandenberg, R.G. 76, 77
Braybrooke, David 405
Brech xvi
Brittain, Jack W. 150, 157, 165
Bronowski, J. xv
Brooke, M.Z. 341
Brown, M. Craig 147
Brown, R.H. 232
Brunet, J.P. 413
Bryman, A. 365
Burns, T. 249, 329, 339, 341
Burt, R. 360, 362
Butler, H.D. 366
Buzzell, Robert D. 95–103

Cafferata, Gail L. 147
Cameron 429, 431
Campbell, Donald T. 156, 157
Cannon 69
Carlson, R.O. 393
Carlyn, M. 394

Carroll, Glenn R. 157
Cavender, J. Morse 76
Caves, Richard E. 338
Chaffee, Ellen E. xxii, 230, 429–38
Chamberlain, Neil W. 163
Chandler, Alfred D. xiv, xvi, xviii, 159, 240, 259, 340, 341, 430
Charkham, J.P. 365
Child, John xxi, 146, 163, 327–48, 360, 393
Christensen, C.R. xiv, xvi
Christenson, C. 263
Church xvi
Churchill, Winston 130
Churchman, West 192
Clark, Burton R. 297, 418
Clark, Terry N. 293
Clarkson, G.P.E. 320
Clawson, D. 360, 361, 363
Cohen, M.D. 227
Cohen, Steven 203
Collins, Orvis 403, 404
Commons, John R. 311
Cool, Karel 429, 433
Cournot, A. xv
Covaleski, M. 433
Crick, Francis 387
Crozier, Michel xxi, 232, 292, 294, 298, 299, 300
Cummings, L.L. 436
Cummings, S. xiii
Cyert, Richard M. xvii, xxi, 248, 292, 295, 309, 313, 320, 321, 335, 337, 339, 381, 405
Czepiel, J.A. 251

Daft, R.L. 237, 433, 435
Dahl, Robert A. 293
Dahlstrom, E. 293
Dalton, D.R. 366
Dalton, Melville 302
Dandridge, T.C. 237
Dantzig 310
Darwin, Charles xiii, 157
D'Aveni, R.A. 360, 361, 370, 372
Davis, G.F. 360, 362, 363, 367, 368
Davis, S.M. 238
Deal, Terrence E. 241, 433
Dearborn, DeWitt C. 313
Debreu 305
de Gaulle, Charles 408
de Geus, Arie P. xix, 133–7, 383, 397
DeGroot, M.H. 320
Delacroix, Jacques 157
Denzin, N.K. 230
Dirsmith, M.W. 433

Dixit xv
Dodder, Richard 158
Dohrenwand, B.S. 229
Donaldson, G. 367, 368
Dooley, P. 362
Doz, Y. xv
Drucker, Peter F. 132, 404
Dubin, Robert 292, 295, 296, 299, 340
Durant 49
Dutton, John M. 302, 320

Eisenhardt, K.M. 372, 374
Eliasson, G. 313
Emerson, R.E. xxi, 292, 293, 295
Emery, F.E. 330
Etzioni, Amitai xxi, 293
Evanisko, M.J. 393
Evered, Roger D. 148

Fahey, L. 429, 432
Fama, E.F. 368
Fayol, Henri xvi, 310
Fedor, D.B. 241
Feigenbaum, E.A. 320
Feldman, M. 433
Fennell, M.L. 369
Ferris, Kenneth R. 147
Field, G.W. 359
Filley, A.C. 393
Finkelstein, S. 360, 370, 372
Flatt, S. 372
Fligstein, N. 364
Foch, F. xiv
Follet xvi
Ford, Gerald 125
Ford, Henry 49
Forsgren xv
Fredrickson, J.W. 230
Freeman, John H. 150, 157, 165
French, John R.P. 293
Friedlander, F. 241, 389
Friedman, Benjamin M. 317
Friedman, Milton 306, 307
Friesen, P. 227, 240
Frontinus xiv
Frost, Peter 148

Gabarro, J.J. 360
Galaskiewicz, J. 360, 361, 363
Galbraith, Jay R. 163, 330, 387
Galbraith, John K. 411, 415
Gardener, H. 385
Garfinkel, Harold 148
Gause xiii

Geertz, Clifford 148
Ghemawat, P. xv
Giddens, A. 359
Gilbreths xvi
Gilmore, Frank 76, 77
Ginter, P.M. 432
Glasberg, D.S. 361, 362
Glaser, Barney G. 148, 230
Gluck, F. 429
Glueck, W.F. 429
Goldner, Fred H. 300, 301
Goodstein, J. 361, 369, 372
Gordon, Gerald 299
Goronzy, Friedhelm 158, 160
Gouldner, Alvin W. 302, 345
Granovetter, M. 361
Greenleaf, R.K. 389
Greenwood, P. 432
Greiner, L.E. 240
Grinyer, P.H. xvii, xx, 227, 238, 240, 241,
    247–67, 415
Guetzkow, H. 313
Guth, W.D. xiv, xvi, 432

Haas, J. Eugene 158, 160
Hackman, J. Richard 147
Hage, J. 327, 329, 330, 332
Hall, Richard H. 158, 160, 327
Hall, Roger I. 147, 148, 151, 159
Hallen xv
Halsey xv
Hambrick, Donald C. 147, 232, 360, 369, 370,
    371, 372, 381, 392, 429
Hamel, G. xv
Hamilton, G.G. 364, 374
Hampden-Turner, C. 385
Hannan, Michael T. 150, 157
Harianto, F. 367
Harsanyi, John C. 293
Harvey, E. 332
Hatten, K.J. 251, 429, 433
Hayes, J.R. 319
Heaney, Donald F. 95–103
Hedberg, B. 227, 249, 252, 254, 255
Hellriegel, D. 394
Hempel, Carl G. 159
Henderson, B.D. xiii, xvi, xviii
Henry, Harold W. 90
Hermalin, B.E. 366
Herman, E.S. 359, 361, 366, 367
Hicks 305
Hickson, David J. xiv, xxi, 146, 151, 158, 160,
    232, 291–304, 331, 333
Higley, J. 359

Hinings, C.R. xxi, 146, 158, 160, 291–304
Hirsch, P.M. 363, 364
Hitch, Charles 174
Hitler, Adolf 130
Hofer, Charles W. 429, 431, 432
Holt, Charles C. 310, 317
Horowitz, David 148
House, R.J. 369, 393
Howe, W. Stewart 133
Huber, G.P. 230
Huff, A.S. xv, 227, 229
Hurst, David K. xxii, 381–99
Hurwicz 305
Husserl, Edmund 148
Hussey, D. 248

Jackson, S.E. 370, 374
Janis, Irving L. 230, 238, 271
Jaques, E. 384
Jarniou 432
Jennings, P.D. 363
Jensen, M.C. 368
Johanson xv
Johnsen, E. 313
Johnson, Gerry xx, 227–43, 230, 232, 360
Johnson, Lyndon B. 416
Johnson, Norman J. 158, 160
Johnson, R.B. 367
Jones, T.B. 367
Jonsson, S. 227, 249, 252, 254, 255
Jorgensen, Dale W. 308
Joyce, W.F. 237, 433
Jung, Carl G. 384, 385, 393, 396, 397

Kahl, J. 360
Kahneman, Daniel 318
Kaiden, Martin R. 91
Kainz, R.I. 386, 393
Kanter, M. 238, 241
Kanter, Rosabeth M. 155
Kantorovich 310
Kaplan, Abraham 146, 293
Kaufman, S. 429
Keck, S.L. 360, 370, 372
Keeley, M. 433
Keen, P.G.W. 382, 393
Keirsey, D.W. 386
Kennedy, Alan A. 241, 433
Kennedy, John F. 416, 422
Kerr, S. 393
Kesner, I.F. 367
Khandwalla, Pradip N. 146, 330, 341
Kilmann, R. 386, 394, 396
Kimberly, John R. 147, 393

Klein, D. 229
Kleisthenes xiv
Knight, Frank H. 248
Koenig, T. 362
Koestler, A. 387, 388
Koopmans 310
Kornai, Janos 320
Kosnik, R.D. 261, 361, 366, 367, 368
Kotter, J.P. 241
Kozmetsky, G. 313
Kronenberg, P.S. 335
Kuhn, Thomas S. xx, 149, 249, 272, 274, 279
Kunreuther, Howard 318
Kuznets, Simon 313

Lammers, Cornelis J. 151
Landau, Martin 199
Landsberger, Henry A. 301
Lawrence, Paul R. xxi, 143, 145, 146, 291, 292, 294, 295, 296, 299, 300, 327, 329, 330, 331, 371, 387
Learned, E.P. xiv, xvi, xvii
Leblebici, Huseyn 147
Lee, C.A. 291–304
Lenz 429
Levine, S. 334
Levitt, Theodore 46
Levy, Ferdinand 309
Lewontin, R.C. 153, 157
Liebenstein, Harvey 320
Likert, Rensis 143
Lindblom, Charles E. xx, 173–82, 227, 248, 405, 406, 409
Lipset, Seymour M. 296
Litchfield, Edward H. 147
Loose, P. 365
Lorsch, Jay W. xxi, 143, 145, 146, 291, 292, 294, 295, 296, 299, 300, 327, 329, 330, 331, 360, 361, 365, 366, 367, 368, 371, 387
Lucas, Robert E. jr 309
Luckmann, T. 433
Luhmann, Niklaus 293
Lupton, T. 360

McCaskey, Michael B. 163
McCaulley, M.H. 386, 389, 393
McClelland, David 405
McColough 220
Macdaid, G.P. 386, 393
Mace, M. 360, 361, 366, 368
McEwen, W.J. 336
McFarland, James 220
McGregor 74
McHugh, A. 413

McIver, E. 360, 361, 365, 366, 367, 368
Machiavelli xiv, xv
Machlup, Fritz 306
McKelvey, Bill xix, 143–70
McKenney, J.L. 382, 393
McKitterick, Jack 97, 167
McLaren, Norman 421, 422
McNamara, Robert 404
McShane, Owen 192
Malinvaud 305
Mann, H. 384
Mann, M. 340
March, James G. xvii, xxi, 146, 148, 166, 227, 248, 259, 291, 292, 293, 294, 295, 301, 313, 320, 321, 335, 337, 339, 381, 405, 433
Marris, Robin 320
Marschak, Jacob 314, 316
Marshall, Alfred 305
Martilla, J.A. 251
Martin, J. 241
Mason, Edward S. 306
Mason, P.A. 369, 371, 393, 396, 429
Mason, R.O. 241
Masterman, M. 249
Mattson xv
Mayr, Ernst 151, 152, 155, 156
Mazzolini 429
Means, G.C. 366
Mechanic, David 295, 359
Meckling, W.H. 368
Meidl, R.R. 369
Metcalfe xv
Meyer, A.D. 230, 241
Meyer, J.W. 230, 433
Meyer, Marshall W. 147
Meyerson, Martin 175
Mezzich, Juan E. 158
Michel, J.G. 370, 372
Miles, Matthew B. 148, 159
Miles, R.E. 238, 389, 390, 392, 425, 429, 431
Miller, D. xiv, 227, 240
Miller, E.J. 332
Miller, Stephen 164
Mintz, B. 360, 362
Mintzberg, Henry xiv, xvii, xix, xxii, 227, 228, 229, 230, 236, 240, 241, 247, 251, 382, 392, 403–12, 413–28, 430, 432
Mitroff, I. 237, 241, 386, 394, 396, 429, 433, 435
Mizruchi, M.S. 360, 361, 362, 363, 366
Modigliani, Franco 310, 317
Moore, David 403, 404
Moore, T. 396
Moore, William L. 147
Morgan, Gareth 148, 433

Morgenstern, Oscar xv, 316
Morris 320
Mueller, Susan 156
Murray, E. 432
Murray, J. 432
Murray, V. 361, 369
Muth, John 310, 317
Myers, I.B. 385, 386, 389, 394, 397

Narayanan 429, 432
Nash xv
Nelson, Richard R. 320
Neustadtl, A. 360
Newell, Alan 319, 323
Newell, William T. jr 90, 91
Newton, Isaac 322
Niv, Amittai 147
Norburn, D. 360, 361, 370
Normann, R. 335
Normann, T. 248, 250, 252, 264
Nystrom, P.C. 252, 254, 255

Oldham, Greg R. 147
Olsen, J.P. 227
O'Reilly, C.A. 360, 370, 371, 372
Osmond, H. 384
Ouchi, William G. 143, 238
Owen, R. xvi

Pahl, R.E. 360, 361
Paine, F.T. xv
Palmer, D. 360, 362, 363
Papandreou, A. 306
Parsons, Talcott 148
Pascale, R.T. 381
Patton, G.R. 254
Paul, W.J. 332
Pearce, J.A. 361, 365, 366
Pennings, J.M. 291–304
Pericles xiv
Perrow, Charles xxi, 151, 154, 291, 293, 294, 299, 301, 331
Perry, Newman S. jr 155
Peters, Thomas J. 238, 241, 381, 433
Pettigrew, Andrew M. xxi, xxii, 227, 229, 238, 241, 349–58, 359–78, 433
Pfeffer, Jeffrey 147, 157, 230, 232, 236, 360, 361, 362, 366, 371, 433
Phelps-Brown, E.H. 309
Philip of Macedon xiv
Pianka, Eric R. 153
Pondy, L.R. 227, 229, 435
Porter, Michael E. xv, xvi, 157, 425
Powell, W.W. 361, 362, 363, 365

Power, D.J. 230
Powers, M.E. 241
Prahalad, C.K. xv, 381
Price, J.L. 336
Pugh, Derek S. xiv, 146, 158, 160, 295, 327, 332, 334, 336, 338

Quinn, James B. xx, 211–25, 227, 231, 238, 239

Radner, Roy 316
Raisinghani, 227
Raven, Bertram 293
Rawlings, Gen. 216, 217
Reagan, Ronald 166
Rechner, P.L. 366
Remmers, H.L. 341
Rhenman, E. 238, 257
Rice, A.K. 332
Richardson, S.A. 229
Ritzer, George 149
Roach, B. 394
Roberts, David R. 309
Robertson, K.B. 332
Robey, D. 385
Roos, Leslie L. 147
Rosenbaum, James E. 147
Ross, Jerry 147
Rowan, B. 230, 433
Rowan, R. 396
Rowland, K.M. 241
Rowlinson, M. 360
Rumelt, Richard P. xv, 30, 31, 260, 429
Rush, James C. xxii, 381–99
Rutenberg, D. 397

Sadler, P.J. 329
Salancik, Gerald R. 147, 157, 232, 360, 361, 362
Samuelson, P.A. 305
Sathe, V. 230, 241
Schatzman, L. 230
Schein, E.H. 230, 241
Schelling xv
Schendel, Dan xviii, 253, 429
Scheonherr, Richard A. 146
Schneck, R.E. 291–304
Schneider, S. xv
Schoeffler, Sidney 95–103
Schon, D.A. 250
Schoonhoven, C.B. 374
Schrank, R. 230
Schultz, Henry 305, 308
Schutz, Alfred 148, 250
Schwab, Joseph J. 159
Schwartz, M. 360, 361, 362, 363

Scott, Bruce 29, 30
Scott, D. 360
Scott, J.P. 360, 361, 362, 364
Scott, W. Richard 151, 159, 296
Selznick, P. xvi
Senge, P.M. xv
Shapiro, C. xv
Sheldon, Alan xvi, xx, 230, 269–88
Sherman, S.P. 396
Shetty, Y.K. 155
Shirley 431
Shrivastava, P. xv
Shubik, M. 249
Siegler, M. 384
Sills, D.L. 418
Silverman, D. 340
Simon, Herbert A. xxi, 148, 199, 248, 250, 259, 292, 294, 301, 305–25, 387
Singh, H. 367
Sloan, Alfred P. 49, 214, 250
Slocum, J.W. 394
Smircich, Linda xv, 148, 238, 433
Smith, Adam xvi
Smith, C. 360
Sneath, Peter H.A. 151
Snow, C.C. 238, 389, 390, 392, 425, 431
Snyder, R.C. 360
Sokal, Robert R. 151
Solomon, Herbert 158
Sonquist, J.A. 362
Sorge, Richard 130
Spangler, W.D. 369
Spender, J.C. xvi, xx, 227, 238, 240, 241, 247–67, 415, 429
Stalin, Josef 130
Stalker, G.M. 249, 329
Starbuck, W.H. 252, 254, 255, 320
Steiner, George A. xiv, xvii, 63–93, 248, 406
Stern, Robert N. 147
Steuart, J. xvi
Stewart, Robert F. 76, 91, 361, 366
Stigler, George J. 315
Stinchcombe, A.L. 329, 361, 363, 364
Stogdill, R.M. 369
Stokman, F.N. 360, 362, 364
Strauss, Anselm L. 148, 230
Strauss, George 301
Stubbart, C. xv
Stymme, Bengt 302
Susman Gerald I. 148

Tabatoni 432
Taggart, W. 385
Tannenbaum, Arnold S. 292, 293

Taylor, Frederick W. xvi, 310
Taylor, J.S. 230
Theil, Henri 317
Theoret 227
Thomas, A.B. 369
Thomas, H. 432
Thomas, J.H. 252
Thompson, James D. 143, 145, 154, 160, 248, 292, 296, 299, 301, 334, 335, 336, 339, 387
Towne xvi
Trice, H.M. 230
Tricker, R.I. 365
Trist, E.L. 330, 332
Trow, Donald 313
Turner, B. 230
Tushman, Michael 360, 370
Tversky, Amos 318
Tyndall, G. 313

Ulrich, David O. 160, 165
Useem, M. 360, 361, 362, 364

Vahlne xv
Van Cauwenbergh 429
Vancil, R.F. 360
Van de Ven, Andrew H. 159
Van Doorn, Jacques A.A. 293
Van Maanen, John 148
Vickers, G. 251
von Clausewitz, Karl xiv
von Neumann, John xv, 316

Wack, Pierre xix, 121–32
Walleck, A.S. 429
Walters, Alan A. 309
Walton, Richard E. 302
Warriner, Charles K. 151
Wasmuth, W.J. 334
Waterman, Robert H. 238, 241, 381, 433
Waters, James A. xxii, 229, 413–28
Watson, James 387
Watt. James xvi
Weber, Max 292, 332
Webster, F.E. 251
Weick, Karl E. xv, 148, 156, 157, 164, 165, 227, 230, 336, 381, 383, 433
Weisbach, M.S. 366
Whaley, Barton 130
Whipp, R. 360, 369, 374
White, D.D. 432
White, Harrison 301
White, P.E. 334
White, Roderick E. xxii, 381–87
Whitt, J.A. 360

Wiersema, M.F. 360, 370, 372
Wildavsky, Aaron xx, 183–209
Wilkins, A.L. 230, 237, 238
Williamson, Oliver E. 320
Wilson, C.S. 360
Winkler, J.T. 360, 361
Winter, Sidney G. 320
Withers, Neil 410
Wohlstetter, Roberta 130–1
Wolpin, J. 361, 369
Wood, R.A. 367
Wood, Robert 382
Woodward, Joan 299, 327, 331, 334, 340
Woycke, J. 369

Wrigley, Leonard 30
Wrong, Dennis H. 291, 293

Yasai-Rardekani, M. 260
Yelland, J. 365

Zahra, S.A. 361, 365, 366
Zajac, E.J. 361, 362, 363, 364
Zald, Mayer N. 297
Zeitlin, M. 361
Zhou, X. 363
Ziegler, R. 360
Ziller, R.C. 393
Zucker, Lynn G. 157